LEX MERCATORIA:
ESSAYS ON
INTERNATIONAL COMMERCIAL LAW
IN HONOUR OF
FRANCIS REYNOLDS

Professor Francis Reynolds QC, DCL, FBA

LEX MERCATORIA:
Essays on International Commercial Law in Honour of Francis Reynolds

Edited by

FRANCIS D. ROSE
Professor of Commercial Law
University of Bristol

2000

LLP Professional Publishing
(a trading division of the
Informa Publishing Group Ltd)
69–77 Paul Street
London EC2A 4LQ
Great Britain

EAST ASIA
LLP Asia
Sixth Floor, Hollywood Centre
233 Hollywood Road
Hong Kong

British Library Cataloguing in Publication Data

A catalogue record
for this book is available
from the British Library

ISBN 1–85978–543–3

Whilst every effort has been made to ensure that the
information contained in this book is correct neither the
editor nor LLP Professional Publishing can accept any
responsibility for any errors or omissions or for any
consequences resulting therefrom.

Typeset in 10/12 Times New Roman
by Mendip Communications Ltd,
Frome, Somerset
Printed in Great Britain by
MPG Books,
Bodmin, Cornwall

Forewords

Some years ago I chanced to mention the Eldon Law Scholarship to Lord Denning, the doyen of Eldon scholars, and he asked me who was now the chairman of the committee awarding the scholarship. "Francis Reynolds", I replied. "Oh yes", he said approvingly. "He's the best they've got there now". He meant of course that Francis was the outstanding Oxford law tutor of his time. Coming from a man who had profound respect for the tutorial giants of his own generation, this was no mean tribute.

It was a tribute richly earned. For a number of years I had the privilege of serving with, and under, Francis as a member of the Eldon committee, and such was the reputation of the Worcester Law Faculty under his leadership that a constant stream of Worcester candidates presented themselves for election, some successfully, some not. Francis was, as one would expect, the soul of propriety, never allowing a trace of favouritism to cloud his judgement of the candidates' respective merits. But one could not fail to be struck by the extraordinary interest Francis took in his pupils, his gift for engaging them in serious (but not solemn) discussion, his acute assessment of their strengths and weaknesses, his pleasure in their achievements, above all, his affection and respect for them as people. In an age when academic merit tends to be judged by the weight of scholarly publications and research output, the old-fashioned tutorial virtues tend to be undervalued; Francis embodied the Oxford tutorial system at its best and strongest. It is one of the happy perversities of life that an inspired tutor can do so much more good than an uninspired tutor can do harm.

Francis Reynolds' reputation would not, however, stand where it does, and this volume would never have seen the light of day, had his exceptional gifts been bestowed only on the small circle of those fortunate enough to be his pupils. Through his scholarly writings, pre-eminently his editing of successive editions of *Bowstead* and of the L.Q.R., he was able to educate, guide and stimulate a much wider audience, judicial, governmental, professional and academic. In his work could be seen all the scholarly values traditionally associated with his Wykehamist *alma mater*: a scholarship exact, thorough, open-minded and highly intelligent, not pedantic or arid; probing, questioning and critical, not vituperative or wantonly iconoclastic; thoughtful and wise.

This book is a monument to a brilliant career, now reaching the end of what one hopes is only its first phase. It is good to see some of Francis' pupils among the distinguished contributors. It is, in truth, not only a *Festschrift* but a *Liber Amicorum*.

Tom Bingham

I am greatly honoured to be invited to contribute a Foreword to this book of essays written in honour of Francis Reynolds, in recognition of his great service to the law during his distinguished career.

I first came across Francis when, as an undergraduate at Worcester College, Oxford, he entered for an essay prize (I believe that it was the Winter Williams Prize). The two examiners appointed to judge the entries were Hazel Fox and myself, both of us young law tutors at Oxford, only marginally older than Francis himself. We of course awarded one of the prizes to Francis. His promise was manifest even then, but little did I guess how often our paths would cross in our subsequent careers.

Francis was elected as Fellow and Tutor in Law at Worcester, which became for him a much-loved institution to which he has belonged for the whole of his legal career, he and his charming and talented wife Susan setting up home in a beautiful house belonging to the college and adjacent to it. Such was his devotion to Worcester that his many friends became concerned that, under the prevailing rules which required that a person appointed to a professorship should move to the college to which the chair was attached, he might not obtain the promotion which his talents obviously deserved because of his reluctance to leave Worcester. Fortunately, however, the rules were relaxed and he was duly appointed to a professorship in law which permitted him to remain at Worcester. This arrangement was for the mutual benefit of Francis and his college, because Francis was, and indeed still is, an excellent law teacher, as his numerous and very loyal pupils will gladly testify. It was through distinguished former pupils at Worcester (notably Brian Davenport and Stephen Tomlinson) that he forged a connection with my old Chambers at 7 King's Bench Walk in the Temple, of which he later became a member.

Francis is a common lawyer in the classical mould, his principal interest lying in the law of obligations, and especially in the law of contract and commercial law. He has made a notable contribution in his role as one of the editors of *Chitty on Contracts*, providing the chapter on agency, and as one of the editors of the splendid modern edition of *Benjamin's Sale of Goods*. But his magnum opus is undoubtedly the fruit of his collaboration with Brian Davenport in the transformation of *Bowstead on Agency* from a long outdated practitioner's manual in the old style into a first class treatise, based on profound scholarship. This was, in truth, the creation of an important new book on a difficult subject of great practical relevance, which has been of immense benefit not only to innumerable practitioners but also to academic lawyers. It was followed by other editions prepared by Francis alone.

Francis' interest in commercial law led to his appointment as Editor of *Lloyd's Maritime and Commercial Law Quarterly*. He transformed the *Quarterly* into a journal which became highly regarded both by practical men in the City of London and by commercial lawyers—judges, barristers and solicitors—who quickly appreciated its value and came to consult it as a matter of course. Such was his success with this journal that he was a natural candidate for the editorship of the *Law Quarterly Review* when the position became vacant. All his many admirers rejoiced when he was appointed, and he has not failed to live up to their high expectations. I have had the honour of serving him as a member of the Editorial Board. The *Review*, which can still claim to be the premier law review of the common law world, has flourished under his dedicated and highly competent leadership, with contributions not only from this country but also from abroad, perhaps especially from Australia, New Zealand and Singapore, where his connections have been very strong. We open each new issue in the confident expectation that we will find inside case notes and articles of great interest.

Outside his central work of teaching, writing and editing, he has devoted much of his time to public service. May I mention in particular two of these activities, with which I am familiar. First, he was elected a Bencher of my own Inn, the Inner Temple. He has taken a great interest in the work of the Inn, paying particular regard to the Inn's students. He frequently travels up to London from Oxford especially to attend meetings and functions at the Inn, and his advice is regarded as most valuable by his fellow Benchers. He has taken an active part in promoting the Pegasus Scholarship Scheme, looking after the highly talented Israeli Scholars who have read for the B.C.L. degree at Oxford, with conspicuous success. Secondly, he was elected a Fellow of the British Academy, and in due course he succeeded Gareth Jones as Chairman of the Section concerned with Law. He has discharged the duties of that office with his customary diligence and skill.

Francis is a distinguished scholar, but he is also a great public servant who, with modesty and untiring energy, has devoted his considerable talents to the benefit of not only his pupils and his college but also the law itself. The legal profession, and indeed lawyers and scholars all over the common law world, are deeply in his debt. This book of essays is a tribute of gratitude to him for what he has done for us all.

Robert Goff

A view from the Antipodes

This is written in January 2000 at Te Rangiita, Lake Taupo, in the middle of the North Island of New Zealand. As it is doubtful whether the *Law Quarterly Review* or *Bowstead and Reynolds on Agency* enjoys any considerable readership in Patagonia or Antarctica, I can claim to be *prima facie* Francis Reynolds' most distant admirer and friend—risking a quibbling refutation from some lawyer resident in the South Island (I treat the mainland and the rest of New Zealand as an entity), the Falklands or Tierra del Fuego. It is my good fortune that distance has disappeared quite often over the years, especially more recently when we have fraternised at the Inner Temple, Oxford and Singapore, as well as during his visits to New Zealand. Although quintessentially an Oxford scholar and teacher (I avoid "don" after reading in Lord Annan's recent book that the expression is properly more restrictive than would be appropriate for Francis Reynolds), he has provided much highly valued service as visiting professor or conference contributor in other parts of the world, particularly Singapore and Australasia.

The Commonwealth connection is also strongly reflected in the *Law Quarterly Review* under his editorship. Any editor of that journal is necessarily distinguished, but it is in no way disrespectful of the others to say that the previous legendary names have been Pollock and Goodhart, with Megarry commonly linked with the era of the latter. But no periodical can survive on legends (*cf. Punch*); and, when Reynolds took over, the L.Q.R. was beginning to acquire something of a dated look, symbolised by its then familiar buff cover. His selection as editor, after experience as general editor of *Lloyd's Maritime and Commercial Law Quarterly*, was not only logical but an inspired choice. While the quality of his own legal writing—and, no doubt, teaching, though I cannot speak of his teaching from personal experience—well merited a chair at Oxford, it is as a transforming editor of the L.Q.R. that I believe he will go down in legal history.

The transformation was contemporaneously marked by the now even more familiar and distinctive maroon, port or tan glossy cover—my advisers differ as to how the colour should be described. It would be an exaggeration to say that the contents answer the second description of maroon in *Chambers Dictionary*, "a detonating firework". But they have become more diverse, and because of their very diversity more lively. In no degree is the journal a vehicle for one person's ideas, or even one person's influence. Rather it has become a forum in which a wide range of contributions, many of them from the Commonwealth, jostle for space. Once the prevailing tone of the L.Q.R. was magisterial. Now, perhaps, its character is better described as challengingly controversial. The times seem to require this change of emphasis.

Francis Reynolds, himself the most modest of men, might be less than enthusiastic about the current publisher's blurb, "... the leading scholarly journal in its field in the English language" etc. It used to be said that good wine needs no bush, but the L.Q.R. has gone the way of many wine labels. Fortunately, though, this is not a false trade description. Nowadays there is a plethora of academic legal writing, swollen by law school appointments criteria. A first-class piece may appear anywhere. It is probably fair to say, however, that for consistency of quality the *Law Quarterly Review* still reigns supreme in the English-speaking world. Most of the credit belongs to Francis Reynolds.

So many of my friends are now achieving the recognition of Festchrifts that I am beginning to fear suggestions of lion-hunting rather than true amity. But the honorand of this Festchrift will need no reassurance on the point. Nor, having regard to the variety and standard of the contributions, can readers fail to recognise that this volume is a timely and apt tribute to the work of a major figure in the development of academic law in the English language.

Robin Cooke

Francis Reynolds' links with Worcester College, Oxford stretch over 47 years, as scholar/student (1953–57), assistant law tutor under the redoubtable Alan Brown (1958–71), and, since 1971, as senior law fellow.

Of the four undersigned, only one (Simon Brown) had the great good fortune to be taught by Francis; two (Peter Gibson and Anthony May) read Greats; Iain Glidewell had left Worcester before Francis arrived. All of us, however, were equally intent upon subscribing our names to this Foreword and thus paying tribute to Francis as the presiding genius of the Worcester law faculty for so many years. That the faculty stands today in such universally high esteem, that Worcester lawyers are so welcomed in the best City firms, barristers' chambers and Academe, are in large measure the result of Francis' assiduous cultivation of excellence down the years. It is his reputation which has attracted such a dazzling array of law fellows. It is the rigour and enthusiasm of his teaching, and his fastidious good sense and humour, which have produced so many generations of successful law graduates. The college has indeed been fortunate that he never succumbed to the temptation to move elsewhere.

For many years now there has been an annual dinner in college for past and present Worcester lawyers. It is invariably well-attended. Although organised by the undergraduates, it is Francis who secures the guest speaker (generally a senior Law Lord) and Francis whom most old members have come to see. The admiration and affection felt for him by all is palpable.

It is not only as a great teacher of students that Francis excels. All practitioners turn to and rely on his writings in the leading text books which he edits, which are quoted as the authoritative statements they are recognised to be. Under his distinguished editorship, the *Law Quarterly Review* has not merely maintained but enhanced its high standard. As judges we fear the L.Q.R.'s criticism of our judgments every bit as keenly as any disapproval from their Lordships' House. And we know that it is Francis' views on any commercial law topic which the Law Commission is most concerned to ascertain before it dares to go public with its recommendations for law reform.

Each one of us counts and values him as a friend. Each of us delights in the renown he has brought to Worcester. We seize this opportunity to do him honour.

Iain Glidewell
Simon Brown
Peter Gibson
Anthony May

Preface

This year marks the retirement of Francis Reynolds as Fellow and Tutor in Law at Worcester College and as Professor of Law in the University of Oxford. A particular feature of his career is his almost unbroken location at Worcester for nearly half a century. The Forewords to this book reveal his unceasing efforts there to build one of the leading schools for the study of law at Oxford. However, he has not confined his energies to Worcester but has also played a leading role in university administration and teaching. In this he has combined both the traditional and the new. So, not only has he helped keep the flag of Roman Law flying in the face of increasing demands imposed by the expansion of contemporary law but in particular was responsible, with Guenter Treitel, for introducing the course on the law of international trade which, though few may realise now, has been the blueprint for countless imitators and has altered not only the study but, in consequence, the practical development of the subject.

Francis' academic activities are many, significant and international. In addition to his teaching at Oxford, he has taught at Chicago, U.C.L. and Malta; and, in particular, his summers have often been occupied by stints in Singapore, Australia and New Zealand. Throughout all this he has maintained a steady stream of influential articles and notes as well as being a significant contributor to three leading commercial law practitioner books, namely *Chitty*, *Benjamin* and of course *Bowstead*. It is in the nature of writing for such works that contributors' names are often hidden behind the title by which the book is known and therefore especially welcome that the latest, retitled, edition of *Bowstead and Reynolds on Agency* should at last formally recognise Francis' established pre-eminence in the field.

The best of the practitioner books tend to be written by leading academics. But they would not be successful if they did not relate to the demands of busy practitioners. It is a distinctive feature of Francis' career that he has been assiduous in recognising and making the connection between academe and practice, and in cultivating judges and leading practitioners. Thus, as editor of *Lloyd's Maritime and Commercial Law Quarterly* and the *Law Quarterly*

Review, he has not only been careful to encourage writing on matters of practical interest but has consistently attracted contributions from judges and practitioners so that their comments reach a wider audience.

Similarly, Francis has played an active part in the deliberations of the Law Commission, in particular when his former pupil and co-editor of *Bowstead*, Brian Davenport, was a Law Commissioner. Change in the law needs to be informed by consciousness of practical consequences against a clear and precise understanding of its theoretical background.

For someone with Francis' reputation for precision, the title of this collection of essays may suggest that this Festschrift begins with a misnomer. For it is not concerned with the ancient body of law known as the *lex mercatoria*. Nor is it directed to current aspirations to develop a uniform, internationally harmonised world commercial law. Its main focus is, in a broad sense, the area in which Francis has been most active, English commercial law in an international context. It would be impossible to cover the whole area in a comprehensive way. But each essay relates to areas in which Francis has been interested.

Brian Davenport bases his essay, on the classification of contract terms, on Francis' first article on the English law of contract, much of which is derived from international trade cases. Brian Coote continues by examining how the ordinary law of contract has had to be reconciled with the doctrine of deviation, developed within the law of carriage of goods by sea. There follow two essays, by Lord Hobhouse and Hugo Tiberg, on the law of agency, with which Francis' name has become so closely linked. Nicholas Gaskell, Malcolm Clarke, Lindsey East and Stephen Tomlinson return to the maritime theme, which has influenced so much of Francis' work, from his pioneering course of lectures on carriage of goods by sea to many of his published articles and notes. The other elements of his international trade teaching and writing are reflected in Jan Hellner's and Peter Ellinger's essays on the international sale of goods and bankers' commercial credits respectively.

When John Morris, *the* authority on the conflict of laws, retired from teaching, Francis succeeded to the readership vacancy created and embraced the teaching of that subject. It is therefore appropriate that there should be several essays in that area, contributed by Gerhard Dannemann, Adrian Briggs, Roy Goode and Tony Guest. In recent years a particular dimension of international influence on English law has been the assimilation of European developments, a theme explored by Richard Whish and Paul Craig. Finally, Guenter Treitel returns to the law of carriage of goods by sea and the general law of contract, and considers the impact of recent statutory intervention.

A common theme of these essays is that, no matter how far domestic law is concerned with and influenced by international matters, it develops within its own environment. This is not something peculiar to English law. It is the underlying environment of the modern *lex mercatoria*.

Francis Reynolds has inevitably collected the principal honours of the leading academic lawyer. He is a Queen's Counsel (*honoris causa*), a Doctor of Civil Law, a Fellow of the British Academy and an Honorary Bencher of the Inner Temple. His is a distinguished career, to which this collection of essays endeavours to pay tribute.

Francis Rose

Contents

List of Contributors

Editor
Francis Rose
  Professor of Commercial Law, University of Bristol

Forewords
Rt Hon. Lord Bingham of Cornhill
  Lord Chief Justice of England and Wales
Rt Hon. Lord Goff of Chieveley
  Formerly Senior Lord of Appeal in Ordinary
Rt Hon. Lord Cooke of Thorndon
  Lord of Appeal
Rt Hon. Sir Iain Glidewell, Rt Hon. Sir Simon Brown, Rt Hon. Sir Peter Gibson
  and Rt Hon. Sir Anthony May
  Former and current Lords Justices of Appeal

Essayists
Adrian Briggs
  Fellow of St Edmund Hall, Oxford; Barrister, Blackstone Chambers
Malcolm Clarke
  *Professor of Commercial Contract Law, Fellow of St John's College,
    Cambridge*
Brian Coote
  C.B.E., Emeritus Professor of Law, University of Auckland
Paul Craig
  Professor of English Law, Fellow of St John's College, Oxford
Gerhard Dannemann
  *Erich Brost University Lecturer in German Civil and Commercial Law,
    Fellow of Worcester College, Oxford*

Brian Davenport
Q.C.
Lindsay East
Solicitor, Partner, Richards Butler, London
Peter Ellinger
Emeritus Professor of Law, National University of Singapore
Nicholas Gaskell
Professor of Maritime and Commercial Law, former Director of the Institute of Maritime Law, University of Southampton
Sir Roy Goode
C.B.E., Q.C., F.B.A., Professor of Law Emeritus, University of Oxford
Anthony Guest
C.B.E., Q.C., F.B.A., Emeritus Professor of English Law, King's College London
Jan Hellner
Emeritus Professor of Law, University of Stockholm
Rt Hon. Lord Hobhouse of Woodborough
Lord of Appeal in Ordinary
Hugo Tiberg
Professor of Law, University of Stockholm
Sir Stephen Tomlinson
Judge of the High Court of Justice
Sir Guenter Treitel
Q.C., D.C.L., F.B.A., former Vinerian Professor of English Law, University of Oxford
Richard Whish
Professor of Law, King's College London

Table of Cases

Table of European and U.S. Cases

Table of UK Legislation

Table of Overseas Legislation

Table of Conventions

xliii

Chapter 1

Some Thoughts on the Classification of Contract Terms

Brian Davenport

The first published paper by Francis Reynolds was, I believe, "Warranty, Condition and Fundamental Breach."[1] I can still well remember sitting with its author in the lounge (or, rather, the passage by the front door) of a small hotel in Seville reading through the proofs in galley. Its author showed one of his most appealing (though maddening) characteristics: a strong disbelief in his own intellectual abilities. Every paragraph, every sentence, every word was anxiously conned for its accuracy in law. The passers-by in the torrid heat no doubt thought that the two Englishmen were displaying one of their national attributes, an increasing tendency towards madness as the temperature rose. What they were actually seeing was a most formidable mind at work and a rather ordinary mind (mine) running along behind it.

It was much the same with the Bar examination. After the last examination Francis leaned over the bar of the nearest pub explaining that the examiners must fail him because he had left so much out. Nothing would console him. Even the expected (by his friends) award of the top of the first class did little to console: the examiners were wrong. I have long said that his decision not to practise in the law robbed the Bar of what would surely have been one of its foremost brains. It has also robbed the country of a great judge at the highest level. But the world of learning retained one of the brightest stars in its academic firmament. What follows would surely fail his high standard. It is certainly a massive oversimplification of what is a complicated story but I console myself with the thought that sometimes oversimplification can bring out the essence of the subject. At least the subject is in the centre of the first published thoughts of

---

[1] (1963) 79 L.Q.R. 534. This article is full of interest even today. Much of it is concerned with the now obsolete study of the anomalies of the then current doctrine of the fundamental breach—or was it breach of a fundamental term? But much of it contains valuable comments on the condition and warranty in contracts.

Francis Reynolds and, as one of the first of a long line of his students, one can do no better.

It is difficult to state the modern classification of contract terms because the law on this has not settled the list conclusively, and perhaps never will. However, one can oversimplify for present purposes and say that, in principle, there are at least six different classes of contract term recognised today and that which class any particular term is in depends, unless a statute classifies the term, on the intention of the parties.[2] To take the matter further, it may be helpful to look briefly at history and see some of the principal matters to emerge.

Although today it is possible, with a reasonable degree of certainty, to draw up a list of the various types of contract term and ascribe any particular term to its proper class, this was not so until the end of the nineteenth century. Particular problems arose from the use of "warranty". As *Benjamin's Sale of Goods*[3] so gently understates, "The evolution of the law of warranty is complex." Anson said that he had found six different meanings in the cases.[4] According to classical theory, a warranty was a promise that was collateral to the main purpose of the contract. But this could be easier to state than to apply. For example, in marine insurance law (largely created by Lord Mansfield and codified in the Marine Insurance Act 1906), a "warranty" is given the definition of what in any other contract would today probably be described as a promissory condition subsequent. Section 33 of the Act states,

> "(1) A warranty ... means a promissory warranty, that is to say, a warranty by which the assured undertakes that some particular thing shall or shall not be done, or that some condition shall be fulfilled, or whereby he affirms or negatives the state of facts.
> ...
>   (3) A warranty, as above defined, is a condition which must be exactly complied with, whether it be material to the risk or not. If it be not so complied with, then, ... the insurer is discharged from liability as from the date of the breach ..."

That this indeed still is the meaning of "warranty" in a contract of marine insurance was the basis of the decision of the House of Lords in *Bank of Nova Scotia* v. *Hellenic Mutual War Risks Association (Bermuda) Ltd. (The Good*

---

[2] A classical statement of this proposition is to be found in the judgment of Tindal, C.J. in *Glaholm* v. *Hays* (1841) 2 Man. & G. 257. But it is sometimes a difficult question. Thus, for example, in *Schuler (L.) A.G.* v. *Wickman Machine Tool Sales Ltd.* [1974] A.C. 235 the House of Lords decided that a term described as a "condition" in a contract did not give a right to terminate the contract forthwith: to construe it as a warranty was, in its context, clearly what the parties must have intended (but see the powerful dissenting speech of Lord Wiberforce at p. 260). On the other hand, in *Total Gas Marketing Ltd.* v. *Arco British Ltd.* [1998] 2 Lloyd's Rep. 209 the House of Lords held that a term in a contract described as a "condition precedent" had its normal meaning in law: any other conclusion left its construction uncertain in effect and was for this reason unacceptable.

[3] 5th edn. (1997), § 10–015.

[4] Anson, *Principles of the Law of Contract*, 5th edn. (1888), 309n.

Luck).[5] On the other hand, whereas in contracts for the sale of goods by description it was a condition that the goods would correspond with the description, there were implied warranties that where a buyer who wanted goods for a particular purpose relied on the seller's skill or judgement, the goods would be reasonably fit for such purpose and that where goods were bought by description from a seller who dealt in goods of that description, they would be of merchantable quality.[6] But breach of either of these warranties carried much the same consequences as breach of a condition. Other words used included "representation" and "undertakings".[7]

When, in the late 1880s, Judge Chalmers[8] started his work on codifying the law of sale of goods, which ended in the Sale of Goods Act 1893, the uncertainties of the classification of contract terms, especially the warranty, presented him with a problem. His intention was to state the law exactly as it had been decided by the courts,[9] but, in order to produce a coherent code, he had to classify contract terms, especially the implied terms as to quality. After some initial uncertainty (in early versions of the Bill he used the words "terms" and "undertakings"), he selected the words "condition" and "warranty". In the 1889 draft of the Bill he followed the decisions of the courts described above and by clause 56(1) he gave breach of his implied warranty of fitness for the purpose and of merchantable quality the remedy of rejection of the goods. In the final draft (which became the Sale of Goods Act 1893) he made these implied warranties into implied conditions (section 14(1) and (2), now the Sale of Goods Act 1979, section 14(3) and 14(2)). In section 11(1)(b) of the Act (now the Sale of Goods Act 1979, section 11(3)) it was provided that:

> "whether a stipulation in a contract of sale is a condition, the breach of which may give rise to the right to treat the contract as repudiated, or a warranty, the breach of which may give rise to a claim for damages but not a right to reject the goods and treat the contract as repudiated, depends in each case on the construction of the contract."

And in section 62 (now the Sale of Goods Act 1979, section 61) he defined a warranty in classical terms:

> "'Warranty' ... means an agreement with references to goods which are the subject

---

[5] [1991] 1 W.L.R. 1279.

[6] There were various ways in which these terms were expressed but the terminology of the Sale of Goods Act has been used here for the sake of simplicity.

[7] An exposition of the condition and warranty on the eve of the Sale of Goods Act 1893 is to be found in the judgment of Bowen, L.J. in *Bentsen* v. *Taylor, Son, Co. (No. 2)* [1893] Q.B. 274. For a classical definition of "condition", see the judgment of Fletcher-Moulton, L.J. in *Wallis, Son & Wells* v. *Pratt & Haynes* [1910] 2 K.B. 1003, 1012, approved by the House of Lords [1912] A.C. 394.

[8] Later Sir MacKenzie Chalmers.

[9] See the Memorandum to the Sale of Goods Bill 1889 cited in the Introduction to Chalmers, *The Sale of Goods* (London, 1890) and the long title to the Sale of Goods Act 1893, which is "An Act for codifying the Law relating to the Sale of Goods".

matter of a contract of sale, but collateral to the main purpose of such contract, the breach of which gives rise to a claim for damages, but not a right to reject the goods and treat the contract as repudiated."

"Condition" was left undefined.[10]

He classified as an implied condition the promise as to title (section 12(1)) but left as implied warranties those as to freedom from encumbrances and quiet possession (section 12(2)), as they had been defined in the very few cases. Looking at the matter through today's eyes, it might perhaps be more in line with the reasonable expectation of the parties if these had become innominate terms but, of course, in Chalmers's time the courts had not made the jump of declaring such terms to be universal. The terms had to be either a "condition" or a "warranty".

The terms thus classified were terms that defined the rights on breach that they carried as from the moment the contract was made. It became generally accepted that all contract terms not defined by the parties were either a "condition" or a "warranty".[11]

The six different types of contract term which are usually recognised today are as follows.

The warranty. According to classic theory a warranty is collateral to the main purpose of the contract; no breach of a warranty by one party, however serious the consequences, ever entitles the other to bring the contract to an end.[12] Another theory is that, where a breach of warranty (or a congeries of breaches) is so serious as to frustrate the contract, it will entitle the innocent party to bring it to an end. On this theory, however, the warranty would be no different from the innominate term and it should be renamed. There are many arguments for and against the separation of the warranty and the innominate term but for present purposes it is sufficient to note that there may only be five classes of terms.

The innominate term. A breach of an innominate term only entitles the innocent party to bring the contract to an end if the breach is so serious as to frustrate the contract. It is commonly thought to have been invented by Diplock,

---

[10] It is a characteristic of one of Chalmers's drafting techniques to define only one of a binary set. For example, he defines specific goods but not unascertained goods. This is probably a product of codifying rather than starting afresh.

[11] At least this was clear from the lectures delivered at Oxford in 1957 by Mr Fifoot on the law of contracts.

[12] This may explain why in section 35 of the Sale of Goods Act 1893 (and 1979) it is provided that the buyer is deemed to have accepted defective goods which have been delivered to him if he does any act which is inconsistent with the seller's title to them. Chalmers considered that, until this happened, the seller retained title to the defective goods. Compare that thinking to today's, under which title passes to the buyer and then revests in the seller when the buyer rejects them (*Tradax Export Ltd.* v. *European Grain & Shipping Ltd.* [1983] 2 Lloyd's Rep. 100 and *R. V. Ward Ltd.* v. *Bagnall* [1967] 1 Q.B. 534). For this idea the author is indebted to Francis Reynolds.

L.J. in *Hongkong Fir Shipping Co. Ltd.* v. *Kawasaki Kisen Kaisha*[13] and to give the innocent party the right to bring the contract to an end on a serious breach by the other. As will be shown below, neither thought is analytically correct.

The condition. Any breach of a condition by one party, however slight, entitles the other to bring the contract to an end. The contract only comes to an end if the innocent party accepts the breach as a repudiation: "an unaccepted repudiation is a thing writ in water and of no value to anybody".[14] According to strict legal analysts, it is wrong to link "condition" with "breach of contract". To them, if the obligation to continue performance is *conditional* upon the occurrence or non-occurrence (as the case may be) of the event specified in the term, that term is a "condition" of the contract, whether or not either party is in breach. Although that analysis is linguistically, logically and historically sound, in English law today the word "condition" is generally used only for a term which can be broken by one of the parties.

The condition precedent or subsequent. These terms are sometimes misunderstood but are not uncommon in commercial contracts. A condition precedent or subsequent may be non-promissory or promissory. In the case of a non-promissory term, neither party makes any promise that the event will or will not happen, e.g. "if Norway becomes a member of the European Community all further liability under this contract shall cease". Such a term would be a non-promissory condition subsequent: the liability of the parties to continue performance is conditional on Norway's not becoming a member of the European Community, but neither promises that it will not do so. When Norway does join, the parties are relieved from further liability. A promissory condition precedent or subsequent is what it says: one party promises that the event will or will not (as the case may be) occur, e.g. a provision in a sale contract that "neither party shall be under any liability until shipping space has been obtained, which space the seller promises to obtain". Such a term would be a condition precedent: until the shipping space has been obtained neither party has to do anything towards fulfilment of the sale, but the seller will be in breach of contract if he does not obtain shipping space. The occurrence or non-occurrence (as the case may be) of a condition precedent brings the contract to an end (save for existing liabilities) immediately it occurs, although breach of a promissory condition may be waived by the innocent party.

Sometimes it is said that, until the happening of a condition precedent, neither party is bound. This is to adopt an incorrect approach. Neither party is free to walk away from the contract until the event either has not or cannot occur (within a frustrating time).

The home-made term. Few books on contract law mention these types of term. Many business contracts contain terms specially drafted to give effect to

---

[13] [1964] 2 Q.B. 26.
[14] *Howard* v. *Pickford Tools Ltd.* [1951] 1 K.B. 417, 421, *per* Asquith, L.J.

the wishes of the particular parties. For example, in many commodity contracts the buyer's right to reject the goods for non-conformity is restricted. Another common example is a quasi-condition subsequent; the happening of the event gives one (or both) of the parties the right to terminate the contract upon the happening or non-happening of some specified event, e.g. the almost universally found "cancelling clause" in a charterparty (a contract for the use of the services of a ship and her crew for a specified voyage or period of time): "if the vessel does not arrive at the loading port by [x] o'clock on [y date], the charterer may cancel this contract". Some sale contracts contain a specially drafted hybrid warranty/condition, e.g. in many shipbuilding contracts a term that "the ship shall on her trials reach a speed over the measured mile of [x] knots; for each 1/10th of a knot less than [x], the price shall be reduced by [$y], unless she is unable to attain [x−1] knots, in which event the owner may cancel this contract".

A term whereby the innocent party may terminate the contract on breach of a condition unless the breach is so slight that termination would be unreasonable. This new term was created by the Sale and Supply of Goods Act 1994, section 4 and inserted into the Sale of Goods Act 1979 as section 15A. Whether it will be accepted by the courts for general use remains to be seen.[15]

Modern contract law can be seen starting to emerge from the mists of assumpsit in the mid-eighteenth century. Its father was Lord Mansfield, Lord Chief Justice of the King's Bench from 1756 to 1788. His decision in *Boone v. Eyre*[16] has been cited on innumerable occasions since and may be taken as the beginning of the story (although a vestige of its reasoning can be found in *Constable* v. *Cloberie*[17]). The facts were revolting by today's standards but this should not be allowed to obscure the reasoning. The plaintiff agreed that he would convey to the defendant an estate in Jamaica and the stock of slaves on it, in return for which the defendant promised to pay him £500 and £160 per annum for the remainder of the plaintiff's life. The defendant failed to pay the annual sum and, when sued, pleaded by way of defence that the plaintiff had not got a good title to all the slaves in the conveyance. The defence failed. Every part of Lord Mansfield's (wonderfully) short judgment is pregnant with significance for the development of the law:

> "The distinction is very clear; where mutual covenants [promises] go to the whole consideration on both sides, they are mutual conditions, the one precedent to the other. But where they go only to a part, where a breach may be paid for in damages, there the defendant has a remedy on his covenant, and shall not plead it as a condition precedent. If this plea were to be allowed, any one slave not being the property of the plaintiff would bar the action."

---

[15] For details, see *infra*, p. 12.
[16] (1779) 1 Hy. Bl. 273n.
[17] (1625) Palm. 397.

Using modern terminology, a term was only a condition if its non-performance went to the whole consideration. A partial failure to perform did not relieve the other party of his obligations, although he could still obtain damages for the breach.

Lord Mansfield's test was applied in a series of cases during the Napoleonic wars. Almost all concern a charterparty. For example, in *Davidson* v. *Gwynne*[18] the question was whether breach of an undertaking by the shipowner that the ship would sail with the next convoy amounted to breach of a condition, so as to disentitle him from claiming freight. No, said Lord Ellenborough, C.J., not unless the breach went to the "whole root and consideration" of the contract.[19] In *Havelock* v. *Geddes*[20] the question was whether breach of an undertaking in a charterparty that the vessel would be seaworthy on tendering to load entitled the charterer to terminate the contract. Of the charterer's contention, Lord Ellenborough, C.J. said:[21]

> "if this were a condition precedent, the neglect of putting in a single nail for a single moment after the ship ought to have been [seaworthy] would be a breach of the condition, and a defence to the whole of the plaintiff's demand . . . Had the plaintiff's neglect here precluded the defendants from making any use of the vessel, it would have gone to the whole consideration . . ."

The question whether a breach was sufficiently serious to terminate the contract appears most clearly in the many cases where performance was merely delayed. In *Mount* v. *Larkins*,[22] for example, a ship was chartered to proceed from London to Singapore, there load a cargo and return thence to Europe. She left London in September 1823, delayed *en route* in Van Dieman's land (Australia), and did not arrive at Singapore until March 1825. This delay, it was held, went to the root of the contract and the charterer was not liable for refusing to load the cargo. In *Clipsham* v. *Vertue*[23] the shipowner claimed damages from the charterers for their failing to load the agreed cargo at Nantes. The charterers sought to justify their refusal to load by alleging that, because of the owner's breach of contract by not sailing direct to Nantes, the vessel arrived there "a long and unreasonable time late". The result of the case and the reasoning of the court are summed up in the headnote to the report. After setting out the charterers' contentions, it baldly states: "Held bad, for not showing that the

---

[18] (1810) 12 East 381.
[19] *Ibid.*, 389.
[20] (1809) 10 East 555.
[21] *Ibid.*, 563–564.
[22] (1831) 8 Bing. 108.
[23] (1843) 5 Q.B. 1249.

delay frustrated the object of the voyage."[24] It is in order to avoid this uncertainty that modern charterparties invariably contain a "cancelling clause".[25]

Thirteen years later, in *Tarrabochia* v. *Hickie*,[26] the question was whether unseaworthiness in a vessel was such a breach of a charterparty by the shipowner as would entitle the charterer not to perform. The defendant chartered the plaintiff's vessel to proceed from Fiume to Cardiff to load a cargo for carriage to various Mediterranean ports. The plaintiff promised that at the beginning of the voyage the vessel would be "tight, staunch and strong" and that she would proceed with all convenient speed. Both promises were broken and, when the ship arrived in Cardiff later than expected and not seaworthy, the charterer refused to load her. In answer to the shipowner's claim for damages, he alleged that each of the breaches had "frustrated the contract". However, the jury found against him on these allegations. The court held that he had not shown breach of a condition precedent so as to entitle him not to perform.

This line of authorities led directly to the modern doctrine of frustration. In *Jackson* v. *Union Marine Insurance Co. Ltd.*[27] a vessel was chartered to proceed with all due despatch from Liverpool to Newport in South Wales, where she was to load a cargo of rails for San Francisco, "dangers and accidents of the seas excepted". The vessel sailed from Liverpool on 2nd January 1872, ran on the rocks in Caernarvon Bay on 3rd January, was towed off on 15th February and would have completed her repairs by the end of August. Meanwhile, on 16th February the charterers chartered another ship to carry the rails to San Francisco. The jury found that the delay was "so long as to put an end in a commercial sense to the commercial speculation entered into" by the parties. However, the exception of "perils and accidents of the seas" meant that the delayed arrival was not a breach of contract by the shipowner. Were the charterers nevertheless relieved of their obligation to load the ship?

The judgment of the majority of the Court of the Exchequer Chamber was delivered by Bramwell, B. He viewed the decision of the jury as being "that a voyage undertaken after the ship had been repaired would have been a different voyage . . . , a voyage for which at the time of the charter the plaintiff had not in intention engaged the ship"[28] (in substance the same test as that propounded by Viscount Radcliffe in *Davis Contractors Co. Ltd.* v. *Fareham U.D.C.*[29] and

---

[24] The judgments do not use the word "frustrated". Perhaps it was used in argument but thought too colloquial for inclusion in a judgment. This may be the first use of "frustrated" in something like its present context (it had been used in argument in *Davidson* v. *Gwynne*, *supra*, n.18, but in a rather different context).

[25] See *supra*, p. 6.

[26] (1856) 1 H. & N. 183.

[27] (1874) 10 C.P. 125.

[28] *Ibid.*, 141.

[29] [1956] A.C. 696, 728–729.

thereafter generally used). The court held that, although there had been no breach of contract, the delay discharged both parties from further liability. In his judgment Bramwell, B. did not use the word "frustrated", but he referred to his own judgment in *Tarrabochia* v. *Hickie*,[30] to the earlier condition precedent cases and to *Taylor* v. *Caldwell*.[31] (*Taylor* is another source of the doctrine of frustration but is one in which performance of the contract would have been wholly impossible. It was thus particularly relevant to the famous Coronation cases, e.g. *Krell* v. *Henry*,[32] but because in most frustration cases performance would have been possible, although so different as to amount to performance of a different contract, *Jackson* should probably be regarded as the *fons et origo* of the modern principle of frustration rather than *Taylor*.) In short, both parties were immediately relieved from further obligations under the contract when an event occurred which made further performance so different as to frustrate their common intentions when entering into the contract, i.e. it went to root of the contract, although the event was not due to a breach of contract by either.

The only significant development in the present context which occurred between the Sale of Goods Act 1893 and *The Hongkong Fir*[33] was that the condition ceased to be a promissory condition precedent (as Chalmers probably regarded it) and became, as today, a term breach of which only ends the contract if accepted by the other party as a repudiation.[34] The dichotomy of condition and warranty was generally regarded as exhaustive.

In *Hongkong Fir Shipping Co. Ltd.* v. *Kawasaki Kisen Kaisha*[35] the defendants chartered the plaintiffs' vessel *Hongkong Fir* for two years. The charterparty contained a promise by the plaintiffs that, when the charter period started, the vessel would be "in every way fitted for ordinary cargo service". This term was broken in that the chief engineer was an alcoholic and the engine room was under-crewed. As a result, the vessel repeatedly broke down on her first voyage (the chief engineer had to be locked in his cabin during the passage across the Pacific) and it was clear that she would take several months to repair. The charterers terminated the contract, claiming that the seaworthiness obligation in the charterparty was a condition of the contract that had been broken. The shipowners asserted that the term was a warranty and that the breach gave the charterers no right to terminate the contract.

---

[30] *Supra*, n.26.
[31] (1863) 3 B. & S. 826.
[32] [1903] 2 K.B. 740.
[33] *Infra*, n.35.
[34] Apart from the invention of the breach of a fundamental term of the contract and its demise in *Photo Production Ltd.* v. *Securicor Transport Ltd.* [1980] A.C. 827 (but not before the Unfair Contract Act 1977, which rendered it largely unnecessary).
[35] [1962] 2 Q.B. 26.

The Court of Appeal (particularly Upjohn and Diplock, L.JJ.) went back to the reasoning in *Havelock* v. *Geddes*[36] and directly followed that in *Tarrabochia* v. *Hickie*.[37] The analysis of Diplock, L.J. deserves particular study. He pointed out that there are many terms in a contract that may or may not give rise to "an event which will deprive the party not in fault of substantially the whole benefit which it was intended that he should obtain from the contract".[38] These terms could not be classified in advance as a condition or a warranty. If the event were of that character but not caused by a breach, the contract was frustrated and the Law Reform (Frustrated Contracts) Act 1943 would apply. If the same event were a breach of contract, the innocent party could accept it as a repudiation and bring the contract to an end. The test for frustration and the right to terminate for breach of an innominate term was the same (as the nineteenth century cases showed and had been foreshadowed by Devlin, J. in *Universal Cargo Carriers Corporation* v. *Citati*[39]). The obligation to provide a seaworthy vessel was one that could be broken in a trivial or in a catastrophic manner. Following the reasoning in *Havelock* v. *Geddes*, a breach of the term would only give the other party the right to terminate the contract if the breach went to the root and whole consideration, i.e. it was such as to frustrate the contract. The delays, past and prospective, were insufficient to frustrate and the (undeserving) shipowners won the case.[40]

Since *The Hongkong Fir*, the innominate term has become an accepted legal concept. It was praised by the House of Lords in *Reardon Smith Line* v. *Hansa-Tangen*,[41] although the House pointed out in *Bunge Corporation* v. *Tradax Export S.A.*[42] that the courts should not fear to hold that a term was a condition if it was clear that this was what the parties intended.[43] On the other

---

[36] *Supra*, n.20.

[37] *Supra*, n.26.

[38] [1962] 2 Q.B. 26, 69.

[39] [1957] 2 Q.B. 401. In his farseeing judgment (though wrong in its conclusion) Devlin, J. relied heavily on R. G. McElroy (edited by Glanville Williams), *Impossibility of Performance* (Cambridge, 1941), which was a truly pioneering work.

[40] Whether it is a just result that the same event ends the contract, whether due to no-one's fault (when it would now end automatically, following *Jackson* v. *Union Marine*) or because of a breach by one of the parties, may be open to question but the quest for analytical accuracy led Diplock, L.J. to this conclusion. Perhaps this is what caused Lord Diplock to be a worthwhile judge in the Court of Appeal (where he was bound by authority) but a lesser judge in the House of Lords (where he was not so bound).

[41] [1971] 1 W.L.R. 979.

[42] [1981] 1 W.L.R. 811.

[43] The House was there dealing with a term concerned with the giving of notice in a "string" contract. In *Bremer Handelsgesellschaft mbH* v. *Vanden Avenne-izegem p.v.B.* [1978] 2 Lloyd's Rep. 109 the House held that a not dissimilar provision in a similar type of contract was an innominate term. This merely makes the point (always denied by judges in court) that the answer to some cases depends on who is sitting to hear the case.

hand, it is suggested, there is no need to cling to a classification derived from the time when all terms had to be either a condition or a warranty, using those words as having the meaning given by the Sale of Goods Act 1893.

Section 14(3) of the Sale of Goods Act 1893 (section 14(2) of the 1979 Act) implies into every contract of sale by description a condition that the goods will be of merchantable[44] quality. This is a term that can be broken in ways which are trifling or which are catastrophic. Classifying it as a condition raises the very problem raised in the last sentence of Lord Mansfield's judgment in *Boone* v. *Eyre*, by Lord Ellenborough in *Havelock* v. *Geddes* and by the Court of Appeal in *The Hongkong Fir*. A trifling breach will be a repudiation and give the buyer as much right to reject the goods as the most serious breach, however easy it may be to repair or replace it. The first (unwritten) rule of law is that most courts most of the time wish to reach a just result if they can.[45] Where a buyer seeks to justify rejection (often because the market has fallen) by relying on a trifling defect, a court will, by one means or another, try to find in the seller's favour. When this is done by a court of record, there is a real risk of the buyer's rights in later cases being harmed.[46]

A Scottish case made the point well (the Sale of Goods Act applies in Scotland). In *Millars of Falkirk Ltd.* v. *Turpie*[47] Mr Turpie, a solicitor, took delivery of a new car on a Saturday from the plaintiff sellers. On Monday morning he saw some oil on his garage floor and took the car back to the sellers. They returned the car next day but on Wednesday Mr Turpie again saw some oil on his garage floor. This time he took the car back to the sellers and rejected it. He justified his rejection on the grounds that the sellers had been in breach of the implied condition of merchantability but they challenged his entitlement to do so. It was found that the defect was a weeping gland in the power-assisted steering system, which would have cost at most £25 to repair, would have been discovered in a routine servicing long before it would have had any effect and would have caused no danger even if all the oil had leaked out. The Inner House of the Court of Session (equivalent to the Court of Appeal in England) unanimously held that there had been no breach of contract: despite the leak, which obviously had to be repaired, the car was of merchantable quality. Mr Turpie got no damages, so he would not even have been able to recover the cost of the repairs or a day's car hire. In short, the implied condition results in a state of rejectability or nothing.

---

[44] Altered by the Sale and Supply of Goods Act 1994, section 1 to "satisfactory" but without altering its meaning.

[45] The next (unwritten) rule is that it is impossible to overflatter any judge, though all judges will strenuously deny it. The technique is never to let them know.

[46] See, e.g., the decisions of the Court of Appeal in *Cehave N.V.* v. *Bremer Handelsgesellschaft mbH (The Hansa Nord)* [1976] Q.B. 44, which was the subject of one of the most savage case notes ever written: J. A. Weir [1976] C.L.J. 33.

[47] 1976 S.L.T. (Notes) 66.

All commercial lawyers are familiar with the buyer who wants to get out of an unprofitable contract because of some trifling defect (the writer was once asked if a new supertanker could be rejected, *inter alia*, because of a crack in the captain's lavatory seat). In 1986 the Law Commission was working on reforms to the law relating to the sale and supply of goods. In 1987 it recommended[48] that, among other changes to the Sale of Goods Act, a new section should be added. In 1994 Parliament gave effect to this recommendation when it enacted, by the Sale and Supply of Goods Act 1994, section 4, that,

> "(1) Where in a contract of sale—
> (a) the buyer would, apart from this subsection, have the right to reject goods by reason of a breach on the part of the seller of a term implied by section 13, 14 or 15 [of the Sale of Goods Act], but
> (b) the breach is so slight that it would be unreasonable for him to reject them
> then, if the buyer does not act as a consumer, the breach is not to be treated as a breach of condition but may be treated as a breach of warranty."

There is, therefore, a new classification of the term relating to the quality of goods in contracts for the sale and supply of goods where the buyer does not act as a consumer.[49] The classification of terms is (except in the case of statutory terms) for the parties to stipulate; if they do not do so, it is for the court to decide what they intended. There is no reason why the courts should not hold that the test laid down in the Act of 1994 was intended to apply to any particular term of a contract. So to hold would lead to the result that in many situations the parties would probably prefer. It is perhaps something nearer what they would have wanted than the ordinary condition of the contract or the near-opposite test adumbrated by *The Hongkong Fir*, *viz*. the buyer might only terminate if the breach was so serious as to frustrate the contract. The former would result in every breach giving rise to the right to terminate, the latter to almost all breaches giving no such right. The new term results in almost all breaches giving the right. It thus completes the cycle of classification of contract terms.

It is no coincidence that the adviser to the Law Commission on its work on the sale of goods was Francis Reynolds. Every week for more than a year he came up to London, where his contribution to the work of the Commission was invaluable. These trips led, *inter alia*, to the above change in the law relating to the sale of goods. If the courts decide to take up the above suggestion of applying section 4 to a wider use than the Act requires, another of Francis Reynolds's sensible ideas for reform forecast in 1963 will have become the law.[50]

---

[48] *Sale and Supply of Goods*: Law Com. No. 160 (1987).

[49] As the Law Commission's report made clear, the term was retained as a strict condition for consumer contracts for reasons of policy.

[50] I am very grateful to Professor Michael Bridge for reading this through and making many helpful suggestions. The errors are, however, mine.

Chapter 2

Deviation and the Ordinary Law

*Brian Coote**

Francis Reynolds has been a wonderful friend to the Auckland Law School, its staff and its students, and our good wishes for his retirement are warmly felt.

I first met him at a function at Oxford in 1970, at a time when he was soon to make his first visit to Auckland and I was engaged in writing a piece for the *Cambridge Law Journal* on exception clauses and discharge for breach, in response to *Harbutts' "Plasticine"*.[1] As I recall it, he brought the conversation round to the chapter on Deviation in *Exception Clauses*,[2] and asked (in the nicest possible way) to know how I could possibly justify disposing of the *U.S. Shipping Board*[3] case in a mere footnote.[4]

The chapter to which he referred was one part of a lengthy attack on the doctrine of fundamental breach, then (1964) in the ascendant. It began with the assertion that deviation and quasi-deviation belonged to a single genus and were confined to bailment. It argued that, so far as *Hain* v. *Tate & Lyle*[5] had ascribed the incidents of deviation to discharge for breach, it was inconsistent with the more recent House of Lords decision in *Heyman* v. *Darwins Ltd.*[6] It suggested that, where there was a contract, the non-application of exception and limitation clauses could be attributed to their having no reference to the altered risks incurred through a deviation. But, since not all bailments were contracts and the non-application of exculpatory clauses was not the only incident to be accounted for, the wider explanation offered was that deviation and quasi-deviation were what happened when a bailee stepped outside any limitations

---

* I am much indebted to Francis Dawson for the discussions we have had about dependent and independent covenants
[1] *Harbutt's "Plasticine" Ltd.* v. *Wayne Tank & Pump Co. Ltd.* [1990] 1 Q.B. 477
[2] Brian Coote, *Exception Clauses* (London, 1964) (hereafter *"Exception Clauses"*) Chap. 6.
[3] *U.S. Shipping Board* v. *Bunge & Born* (1924) 134 L.T. 303.
[4] *Exception Clauses*, 82.
[5] *Hain Steamship Co. Ltd.* v. *Tate & Lyle Ltd.* (1936) 41 Com. Cas. 350.
[6] [1942] A.C. 356. See also *Exception Clauses*, Chap. 5, esp. pp. 75–76.

14 Lex Mercatoria

attaching to his rights of possession. By so doing, he became a mere detainer, and lost the benefits of the bailment relationship. Neither of those explanations required or depended in any way upon a discharge for breach.

The point Francis Reynolds was making was that the *U.S. Shipping Board* case, in which the House of Lords took it for granted that deviation was a breach which literally terminated a contract of carriage and, for that reason, prevented reliance on its demurrage provisions, was directly contrary to the thesis of the chapter. I might have replied (had I not been too over-awed to do so!) that the chapter had gone on to say that "it would no doubt be unrealistic to expect any such rethinking of the law to take place", in which case "deviation must be expected to remain an anomalous type of breach".[7] Still, I took the admonition to heart and in the finished article[8] was careful to emphasise, not so much that cases like *U.S. Shipping Board* and *Hain* v. *Tate & Lyle* were wrong, but that, being inconsistent with the ordinary law of discharge for breach, they had to be regarded as "*sui generis*". As it happened, that description was taken up by *Cheshire and Fifoot* in their next two editions[9] and (who knows?) it may have been from there that it found its way into the speech of Lord Wilberforce in *Photo Production* v. *Securicor*.[10] If so, it shows what consequences may flow from even the most casual encounter of the Reynolds kind!

Of course, since *Exception Clauses* and the article were written, the House of Lords in *Photo Production* has come down on the side of the *Heyman* v. *Darwins* version of discharge for breach. It has rejected any notion of a substantive doctrine of fundamental breach so that, for the most part, the effect of an exception clause now depends on its interpretation. Even the rights-to-possession theory has gained some support and can now be found in the leading text book on bailment.[11] It might be asked, therefore, what there could be left to say on the subject. Upon re-reading Professor Reynolds' splendid 1990 Butterworth Lecture,[12] I confess to having wondered that myself. On reflection though, there do seem to be a few problems remaining.

The main incidents of deviation by a carrier by water before *Photo Production* were that his obligation to follow the contract route had the status of

---

[7] *Exception Clauses*, 95–96.
[8] "The Effect of Discharge for Breach on Exception Clauses" [1970] C.L.J. 221, 238.
[9] See their *The Law of Contract*, 8th edn. (London, 1972), 140; 9th edn. (1976), 165.
[10] *Photo Production Ltd.* v. *Securicor Transport Ltd.* [1980] A.C. 827.
[11] N. E. Palmer, *Bailment*, 2nd edn. (Sydney, 1991), 1539, and esp. 835, 990, 1270, 1271. See also C. D. Mills, "The future of deviation in the law of the carriage of goods" [1983] L.M.C.L.Q. 587, 588 and Christopher Cashmore, "The Legal Nature of the Doctrine of Deviation" [1989] J.B.L. 492. Contrast Charles Debattista, "Fundamental Breach and Deviation in the Carriage of Goods by Sea" [1989] J.B.L. 22, 32, who sees it as merely a matter of history.
[12] F. M. B. Reynolds, "The Implementation of Private Law Conventions in English Law", in *Butterworth Lectures 1990–1991* (London, 1992) 29–53 (hereafter "Butterworth Lecture").

a promissory condition[13] and that, on a deliberate and unjustified departure from his route,[14] he lost the protection of any contractual limitation and exception clauses, as well as of the common law exceptions.[15] He became strictly liable for any loss of or damage to his cargo which he could not show would have happened anyway.[16] This result followed whether the loss or damage had occurred during, after,[17] or even before the deviation.[18] In the same way, he also lost the protection of other provisions of the contract inserted for his benefit such as demurrage and freight clauses.[19] On the other hand, these disadvantages were prevented or reversed should the goods owner elect to waive the deviation.[20] Many of these incidents, *mutatis mutandis*, followed quasi-deviations in other types of bailment.[21]

What has concerned commentators since *Photo Production* has been how far these various incidents have been altered or abolished as a result of that decision. Did the abolition of the doctrine of fundamental breach mean the demise of deviation and quasi-deviation as well? What are the implications of the preference shown for the *Heyman* v. *Darwins* version of discharge for breach? What should happen, nowadays, if the contract is discharged for breach in mid-voyage? Anyway, ought the obligation to follow the contract route still to be characterised as a promissory condition? And how should cargoes carried on deck in breach of contract now be treated?

THE DOCTRINE OF FUNDAMENTAL BREACH

Fundamental breach and breach of a fundamental term were conceived of by their proponents as two aspects of a single, unified principle, of which the various streams of authority thought to support it were simply examples.[22] It might be tempting, therefore, to conclude that, when the fundamental breach

---

[13] E.g. *Hain* v. *Tate & Lyle* (1936) 41 Com. Cas. 350, 354.

[14] E.g. *Kish* v. *Taylor* [1912] A.C. 604, 617. At common law, deviation is justified to save life or the vessel itself: *The Teutonia* (1872) L.R. 4 P.C. 171. Under Article IV, rule 4 of the Hague rules, deviations to save life or property or which are otherwise "reasonable" are permitted.

[15] *James Morrison* v. *Shaw Saville and Albion Co.* [1916] 2 K.B. 783.

[16] *Davis* v. *Garrett* (1830) 6 Bing. 716; 130 E.R. 1456.

[17] *Joseph Thorley Ltd.* v. *Orchis Steamship Co. Ltd.* [1907] 1 K.B. 660.

[18] *International Guano En Superphosphaatwerken* v. *Robert MacAndrew & Co.* [1902] 2 K.B. 360.

[19] *Hain* v. *Tate & Lyle* (1936) Com. Cas. 350.

[20] *Ibid.*

[21] Quasi-deviation is dealt with in more detail in the text, *infra*, pp. 27–31.

[22] E.g. *Smeaton Hanscombe & Co. Ltd.* v. *Sassoon I Setty & Co. (No. 1)* [1953] 1 W.L.R. 1468, 1470, per Devlin, J. its real originator.

doctrine received its *quietus* in *Photo Production*,[23] deviation, as one of its manifestations, necessarily died too. But by the same reasoning, a similar fate would in that case also have befallen such other purported manifestations as "congeries of defects" and the condition as to title in sale of goods, "difference in kind", total failure of consideration, and the warranty of seaworthiness. That has not so far been suggested, for the very good reason that the respective streams of authority were not manifestations of a single principle at all but quite disparate, each having its separate origins, incidents and justifications.[24]

What the House of Lords actually held in *Photo Production*, effectively for the second time,[25] was that there was no substantive doctrine of fundamental breach at common law which overrode contractual terms clearly expressed to apply in the events which had occurred.[26] Whether those terms applied depended on their proper interpretation.[27] As already mentioned, their Lordships also preferred the version of discharge for breach expressed in *Heyman* v. *Darwins* to that in *Hain* v. *Tate & Lyle,* so far as the latter presupposed a literal termination of the contract from the commencement of the deviation, unless the breach were waived.[28]

That being so, it can no longer be maintained that the special incidents of deviation can be explained by reference to discharge for breach as it is now understood. Accordingly, if the incidents which resulted *exclusively* from earlier concepts of discharge for breach are to remain, it has to be on grounds of authority rather than of principle. Lord Wilberforce was careful to say in *Photo Production*[29] that the body of authority on deviation might be "*sui generis* with special rules derived from historical and commercial reasons". However, deviation was not in issue in that case and, moreover, his reservation was only tentative.

As we shall see, there are good reasons for arguing that several of the special features of deviation have survived. But it would be a pity if those which depend solely on discredited perceptions of discharge for breach were to be amongst them. In *The Antares*,[30] Lloyd, L.J. has expressed the view that deviation ought now to be assimilated into the ordinary law of contract. If by that he meant that, where relevant, the ordinary law of discharge for breach should now be applied,

---

[23] [1980] A.C. 827.

[24] I tried to demonstrate this in *Exception Clauses*, esp Chaps. 3–8.

[25] The first time was in *Suisse Atlantique Société d'Armement S.A.* v. *Rotterdamsche Kolen Centrale* [1967] 1 A.C. 361.

[26] *Photo Production* [1980] A.C. 827, 842, 847.

[27] *Ibid.*, 842–843.

[28] *Ibid.*, 844, 845, 450.

[29] *Ibid.*, 845.

[30] *Kenya Railways* v. *Antares Co. Pte Ltd. (The Antares) (Nos. 1 and 2)* [1982] 1 Lloyd's Rep. 424, 420.

it is easy to agree with him. Whether the assimilation should be taken to have gone beyond that is largely the subject of this essay.

DISCHARGE FOR BREACH

The position prior to termination

If the ordinary rules governing discharge for breach do now apply to deviation and quasi-deviation, several consequences are clear enough. Thus, with a few exceptions, contracts of carriage and bailment remain in full force and effect, despite the commencement of a deviation. They continue to do so unless and until the injured party has elected a "termination" and has notified the carrier or bailee accordingly. If no such election is communicated and the goods are delivered and accepted, the carrier or bailee is able to rely on the terms of the contract, such as those governing freight and demurrage. Should the goods have been damaged, liability turns in the first instance on whether it is covered by any exception or limitation clauses.[31] However, liability may also in part depend on whether, since *Photo Production*, it is to be confined to loss or damage actually proved to have been caused by the deviation, or whether the deviating party remains liable, as before, for loss or damage which he cannot show affirmatively would have occurred even if there had been no deviation. It will be necessary to return to that question.[32]

In the meantime, an area of continuing uncertainty is the law to be applied when a cargo owner, having become aware of a deviation, notifies his election to discharge the contract while the voyage is still in progress. That raises several problems, not least of which is whether the obligation to pursue the ordinary route should any longer properly be characterised as a condition, any breach of which gives a right to terminate even after a voyage has begun. That apart, and assuming a termination, what regime should govern the relations of the parties for the rest of the voyage? And, if the goods should finally be delivered, should the carrier be entitled to his freight or (if not) to payment on any other basis?

Discharge for breach in mid-voyage

It is now well established that when a contract is discharged for breach it does not for that reason cease to exist, either *ab initio* or *in futuro*.[33] What happens, according to the House of Lords in *L.E.P. Air Services Ltd.* v. *Rollowswin*

---

[31] All of these incidents follow from the adoption of the *Heyman* v. *Darwins* model of discharge for breach in the *Photo Production* case.

[32] See *infra*, pp. 27–31.

[33] Again, this follows from the *Heyman* v. *Darwins* model.

Investments Ltd.[34] is that, upon discharge, neither party is obliged or entitled to perform it further. The contract itself governs anything that happened before the discharge and remains in being for the purpose of settling the rights and liabilities of the parties which accrued to that point. It follows that, in the case of a ship in mid-voyage, the contract cannot govern events occurring after it has been discharged unless some sort of new arrangement comes into existence. That rather inconvenient consequence was just as apparent under the law as it was before *Photo Production*.

To fill the gap, one resort was for the courts to hold that, upon a discharge for deviation, the carrier became subject from the commencement of the deviation (or even from the start of the voyage) to the "insurer's" liability of a common carrier at common law. This carried the benefit of the common law exceptions of the acts of God and of the Queen's enemies, and inherent vice in the goods carried, but not the benefit of any of the terms of the contract.[35] As a solution, it was of relatively little value to the carrier because of the onus on him at common law of showing that the loss or damage would have occurred anyway,[36] a burden extremely difficult (though perhaps not altogether impossible[37]) to meet except in the case of inherent vice.

Nor, as a solution, is it without its difficulties conceptually. Thus, it assumes that a carrier's repudiation is directed solely to his contract of carriage and has no reference to his status at common law. Moreover, the notion that a common carrier can operate as such without a contract, express or implied, is itself not easy to envisage. So it is perhaps not surprising that in *Hain* v. *Tate & Lyle*[38] the House of Lords should have left open the possibility that upon a discharge for breach an implied contract might replace the original one. Their Lordships also appear to have favoured the view that, if the cargo were delivered, the carrier would be entitled to a quantum meruit. This, too, seems a little strange since, if there were an implied contract, it might have been expected to give rise (in the

---

[34] [1973] A.C. 331, esp. 345–346, 350. There is a much earlier statement to similar effect by Lord Sumner in *Hirji Mulji* v. *Cheong Yue Steamship Co. Ltd.* [1926] A.C. 497, 509–510

[35] All these consequences would have followed from Pickford, J.'s having held, in *Internationale Guano* [1909] 2 K.B. 360, 365, that the defendants had to be treated after the deviation as common carriers who could not rely on the terms of the contract. See also *F. Kanematsu & Co. Ltd.* v. *The Ship Shelzada* (1957) 96 C.L.R. 477; Baughen, *Shipping Law* (London, 1988) 89; Tan, *The Law in Singapore on Carriage of Goods by Sea,* 2nd edn. (Singapore, 1994) 123; Davies and Dickey, *Shipping Law,* 2nd edn. (Sydney, 1995) 274; Wilson, *Carriage of Goods by Sea,* 3rd edn. (London, 1998) 23; Debattista [1989] J.B.L. 22, 24.

[36] E.g. *Morrison* v. *Shaw Saville* [1916] 2 K.B. 783.

[37] *Cf. Paterson Steamships Ltd.* v. *Robin Hood Mills Ltd. (The Thordoc)* (1937) 58 L.L. L.R. 33, P.C.

[38] (1936) 41 Com. Cas. 350, 358, 367, 368, 370. *Cf. Joseph Thorley Ltd.* v. *Orchis Steamship Co. Ltd.* [1907] 1 K.B. 660, 667.

words of Lord Diplock[39]) to "primary obligations of which the contract is the source", including therefore payment of the contract freight. As Lord Wright emphasised in the *Hain* case,[40] contract freight had always, historically, been regarded as payable on delivery of the cargo, despite any intermediate deviation. As we shall see shortly, this history of the claim for freight may have an even wider significance.

CONDITION OR INNOMINATE TERM?

The change proposed

The problem of what to do after a termination in mid-voyage stemmed, ultimately, from what seems to have been an assumption by the Court of Appeal in the 1907 case of *Thorley* v. *Orchis*[41] and those which followed it, including *Hain* v. *Tate & Lyle* itself, that the incidents of deviation were to be explained by reference to discharge for breach. In consequence, the undertaking to follow the contract route had to be accorded the status of a condition, any breach of which would give a right to terminate, as was done, effectively, by Lord Atkin and Lord Wright in the *Hain* case.[42] It is that characterisation which, in turn, makes it still possible to discharge the contract for deviation halfway through a voyage.

Deviation has often been said to be a breach of a particularly serious kind or of a particularly important undertaking.[43] That might once have been true for reasons of insurance, but cover for deviation has long since been available.[44] In practice, the seriousness of departures from a contract route (as distinct from their potential legal consequences) can vary widely, much as is the case with unseaworthiness. For its part, the warranty of seaworthiness has, since the *Hong Kong Fir* case,[45] been classed not as a condition but as an innominate term,

---

[39] *Photo Production* v. *Securicor* [1980] A.C. 827, 850. The passage reads: "The bringing to an end of all primary obligations under the contract may also leave the parties in a relationship, typically that of bailor and bailee, in which they owe to one another by operation of law fresh primary obligations of which the contract is the source ..."

[40] (1936) 41 Com. Cas. 350, 368.

[41] [1907] 1 K.B. 660. We return to this question in the text, *infra*, after fn. 73.

[42] (1936) 41 Com. Cas. 350, 354, 362 363.

[43] E.g. *Hain* v. *Tate & Lyle* (1936) 41 Com. Cas. 350, 354, 363, 371; *Thorley* v. *Orchis* [1907] 1 K.B. 660, 669; *Cunard Steamship Co.* v. *Buerger* [1926] A.C. 1, 8; *Rio Tinto Co. Ltd.* v. *The Seed Shipping Co. Ltd.* (1926) 24 L.L. L.R. 316, 320; Palmer, *supra*, fn. 11, at 578, 989, 1535; Cashmore [1989] J.B.L. 492, 496.

[44] See e.g. T. E. Scrutton, K.C. in *Thorley* v. *Orchis* [1907] 1 K.B. 660, 663; *Hain* v. *Tate & Lyle* (1936) 41 Com. Cas. 350, 355; *State Trading Corporation of India Ltd.* v. *Golodetz Ltd.* (*The Sara D*) [1989] 2 Lloyd's Rep. 277, 288.

[45] *Hong Kong Fir Shipping Co. Ltd.* v. *Kawasaki Kisen Kaisha Ltd.* [1962] 2 Q.B. 26.

somewhere between a condition and a warranty. Simon Baughen[46] has suggested that deviation ought similarly to be reclassified. Since the main justification for treating the obligation not to deviate as a condition (i.e., that the incidents of deviation were the result of discharge for breach) has gone, that suggestion can now more readily be considered on its merits. More than that, it is believed that a change of that kind can be supported by reference to the earlier law and especially to the history of the claim for freight.

The claim for freight

An appropriate starting point is *Cole* v. *Shallet*,[47] decided in the Court of Common Pleas late in the seventeenth century. To a claim for freight by the master of a ship, the defendant merchant pleaded "divers deviations by which the goods were spoiled". There was also a claim for demurrage to which the defendant pleaded the neglect of the mariners. On both claims, judgment was given for the master on the ground that "the covenants are mutual and reciprocal, whereupon each hath his action against the other and cannot plead the breach of one covenant in bar of the other". The obligation to pay freight was thus treated by the Court as falling within the first of the types of covenant subsequently identified by Lord Mansfield in *Kingston* v. *Preston*.[48] Those of the first kind, he said, were:

> "Such as are called mutual and independent, where either party may recover damages from the other, for the injury he may have received by a breach of the covenants in his favour, and where it is no excuse for the defendant to allege a breach of the covenants on the part of the plaintiff."

Lord Mansfield contrasted that type of covenant with those which, in his words, were:

> "conditions and dependent, in which the performance of one depends on the prior performance of another and therefore, till this prior covenant is performed, the other party is not liable to an action on his covenant."[49]

What distinguished these two kinds of covenant from each other was that, again in the words of Lord Mansfield, this time in *Boone* v. *Eyre*:[50]

> "where mutual covenants go to the whole of the consideration on both sides they are mutual conditions; but where the covenants go only as to a part, and where recompense can be had in damages, it is a different thing."

---

[46] "Does Deviation Still Matter?" [1991] L.M.C.L.Q. 70, 84. Francis Reynolds, in his Butterworth Lecture, *supra,* fn. 12, at 46, also leaves open the possibility.
[47] (1693) 3 Lev. 41; 83 E.R. 567.
[48] (1773) 2 Doug. 689, 99 E.R. 436. For a detailed discussion of this subject, see S. J. Stoljar, "Dependent and Independent Promises" (1957) 2 Sydney L.R. 217.
[49] (1773) 2 Doug. 689, 690–691.
[50] (1779) 1 Hy. Bl. 273n; 126 E.R. 160.

An argument based on a dependent covenant type of analysis was addressed to the court in the later case of *Bornmann* v. *Tooke*,[51] where again a captain who had deviated was suing for his freight. For the defendant it was claimed that the obligation to sail on the first favourable wind by the direct route was a condition precedent to freight becoming due. Lord Ellenborough would have none of this and held for the plaintiff, leaving the defendant to his cross action. On the condition precedent point, his comment was:[52]

> "To hold that any short delay in setting sail or trifling departure from the direct course of the voyage would entirely destroy the plaintiff's right to be remunerated for transporting the cargo would indeed be going *inter apices facti*."

An elaboration of Lord Ellenborough's reasoning appeared at the beginning of his judgment in *Davidson* v. *Gwynn*[53] two years later:

> "The sailing with the first convoy is not a condition precedent: the object of the contract was the performance of the voyage, and here it has been performed. The principle laid down in *Boone* v. *Eyre* has been recognized in all the subsequent cases, that unless the non-performance alleged in breach of the contract goes to the whole root and consideration of it, the covenant broken is not to be considered as a condition precedent, but as a distinct covenant, for the breach of which the party injured may be compensated in damages."

The perception that a claim for remuneration was not to be reduced, and that the injured party was to be left to his cross action, was not confined to contracts of carriage but extended to other contracts of service. In some contexts this proved to be too inconvenient and in 1806 the Court of King's Bench in *Basten* v. *Butter*[54] allowed what was, in effect, a kind of set-off in a claim for work and materials. That change was made easier by the claim having been for a quantum meruit, but there was a suggestion that the same result might also apply to a claim for a fixed price. By the middle of the nineteenth century, Parke, B. was able to say, in *Mondel* v. *Steel*,[55] that this new practice had since been generally followed. As a justification for the original rule as it had existed before *Basten* v. *Butter*, he referred to cases where:

> "the law appears to have construed the contract as not importing that the performance of every portion of the work should be a condition precedent to the payment of the stipulated price, otherwise the least deviation would have deprived the plaintiff of the whole price."[56]

However, having said that the new practice was so convenient that it was generally followed, he went on to make the point that it had not been applied in

---

[51] (1808) 1 Camp. 377; 170 E.R. 991.
[52] (1808) 1 Camp. 377, 378–379.
[53] (1810) 12 East. 381, 389; 104 E.R. 149.
[54] (1806) 7 East. 479; 103 E.R. 185.
[55] (1841) 8 M. & W. 870; 151 E.R. 1288.
[56] (1841) 8 M. & W. 870, 870–871.

all cases. Amongst the exceptions, he mentioned actions for freight, citing *Shiels* v. *Davies*.[57] Freight is still an exception, as was reaffirmed by the House of Lords as recently as 1977 in *Aries Tanker Corp.* v. *Total Transport Ltd.*[58] In other words, the promise to pay freight remains to this day an independent covenant of the seventeenth century kind.

That raises the question whether, in *Cole* v. *Shallet* and *Bornmann* v. *Tooke*, it was solely because the contract had been executed that the obligation to pay freight was treated as an independent covenant and, hence, as not being conditional on the absence of a deviation. Lord Ellenborough referred to *Boone* v. *Eyre*, in which, according to one report,[59] Ashhurst, J. pointed to a difference between executed and executory contracts. It might be argued, therefore, that the obligation to follow the contract route could still be a condition precedent in any context other than a claim for freight. One test for that would be to look to the way in which the courts treated claims for loss or damage suffered after the commencement of a deviation or quasi-deviation. And here it has to be significant that it was not until a hundred years after *Bornmann* v. *Tooke* that a claim of that kind was held to turn on its being a condition precedent that the contract route be followed. Moreover, Lord Ellenborough himself made the point in a third case, *Havelock* v. *Geddes*,[60] that whether undertakings, generally, were conditions precedent could vary, depending on the stage performance had reached.

These early cases amply explain at least the origins of the practice which, according to Lord Wright in *Hain* v. *Tate & Lyle*,[61] had persisted until that time of paying the contract freight for goods delivered, despite an intermediate deviation. They also suggest the need for a reconsideration of *Thorley* v. *Orchis*,[62] not only because it appears to have altered the status of the obligation to follow the contract route but also because it led to the notion that, despite all previous practice, deviation fell outside the ordinary rules governing the payment of freight.

Thorley v. *Orchis* reconsidered

The *Thorley* case was one where, after a ship had deviated on its way to its port of destination, goods which were being unloaded were damaged through the negligence of stevedores employed by the shipowners. The bill of lading

---

[57] (1814) 4 Camp. 119; 171 E.R. 39 (claim for freight following damage due to bad stowage).

[58] [1977] 1 W.L.R. 185.

[59] (1779) 2 Black, W. 1312, 1314n; 96 E.R. 767. See also Stoljar (1957) 2 Sydney L.R. 217, 244, and *Graves* v. *Legg* (1854) 9 Ex. 709, 716–717; 156 E.R. 304.

[60] (1809) 10 East. 555, 564; 103 E.R. 886.

[61] (1936) 41 Com. Cas. 350, 368.

[62] [1907] 1 K.B. 660.

exceptions were expressed to cover such negligence. For the defendant shipowners, T. E. Scrutton, K.C.[63] argued on the analogy of the warranty of seaworthiness that, though the obligation not to deviate was a condition precedent while the contract was executory, once it had been executed by the goods being carried to their destination, it turned into what he called "a warranty in the stricter sense" (what came to be called a warranty *ex post facto*), sounding only in damages.

While Scrutton's arguments reflected developments to the law of discharge for breach which had taken place during the nineteenth century, there is a sense in which he might be said to have sold the pass by, in effect, conceding that the obligation not to deviate was a condition precedent. In hindsight, we now know that the warranty of seaworthiness, which he took as his analogy, is itself not a condition. He may have been influenced to some extent by the comment of Lord Esher, M.R. in *Leduc* v. *Ward*[64] that the obligation was "a most important part of the contract". More immediately, there was a suggestion in the 1900 decision of the Court of Appeal in *Balian and Sons* v. *Joly, Victoria and Co. Ltd.*[65] that "the whole bill of lading [might be] gone", though the report in the *Times Law Reports* is so brief that the reasoning in that case might more probably have been based on bailment or the interpretation of the contract than on discharge for breach. Scrutton could well have been right, though, to characterise as obiter the suggestion that the bill of lading had gone. By contrast, counsel for the goods owners, J. A. Hamilton, K.C., based his argument[66] squarely on the decision in that case and was able to persuade the court that it was both conclusive and binding. Delivering the leading judgment, Collins, M.R. said of it:[67]

> "The principle underlying those judgments seems to be that the undertaking not to deviate has the effect of a condition, or a warranty in the sense in which the word is used in speaking of the warranty of seaworthiness, and, if that condition is not complied with, the failure to comply with it displaces the contract. It goes to the root of the contract, and its performance is a condition precedent to the right of the shipowner to put the contract in suit."

That last sentence is expressed very much in the language of a dependent covenant analysis and carries the inference that deviation is a breach which goes to the whole consideration for the contract. It also, consistently with that sort of analysis, postulates a consequent release of the goods owner from the contract

---

[63] *Ibid.*, 662. His argument was analogous, for example, to the division in the Sale of Goods Act 1893 between conditions and warranties.

[64] (1888) 20 Q.B.D. 475, 481.

[65] (1900) 6 T.L.R. 345.

[66] [1907] 1 K.B. 660, 663–664.

[67] *Ibid.*, 667.

without the need for him to give any notification to the other side. That such notification was unnecessary was apparently the received view at the time.[68]

A logical consequence of this approach is that the right to the contract freight would have been lost. Yet the long-standing practice of paying freight on delivery must still have been in the minds of the judges though, clearly, not the reasons for it. Significantly, in *Balian* v. *Joly*,[69] Lord Esher, M.R. had allowed that both the right to freight and the lien for freight might remain. For his part, in *Thorley* v. *Orchis*[70] Collins, M.R. went on to say:

> "It may be, no doubt, that, although that condition is broken, the circumstances are such as to give rise to an implied obligation on the part of the cargo owner to pay the shipowner the freight, and, it may be, to perform other stipulations which may be implied under the circumstances from the fact of the carriage of the cargo to its destination; but that is quite consistent with the effect of the deviation being to displace the special contract expressed in the bill of lading."

Fletcher Moulton, L.J. also spoke in terms of a claim as a common carrier for the agreed freight.[71] He thought that was "the most favourable position the shipowner could claim" but added "I do not say that in all circumstances he would be entitled as of right to be treated even as favourably as this". The full implications of the supposed disappearance of the contract were finally accepted by the House of Lords in *Hain* v. *Tate & Lyle*,[72] where, as we have seen,[73] it was said that entitlement, if any, was not to the agreed freight but to a quantum meruit.

For present purposes, the significance of all this lies not so much in the claim for freight, as such, as in the light shed on the changing perceptions of deviation. We seen that for a very long time the obligation to follow the contract route was not treated as having in all circumstances the status of a condition precedent. It has to be asked, therefore, why there should have been such a reversal of that view at the beginning of the twentieth century. If deviation did not always go to the whole consideration before then, why should it have been supposed that it did so thereafter? Almost certainly, the explanation lies in a misunderstanding, particularly in *Thorley* v. *Orchis*, of the reasons for the well-established and very serious effects of deviation, especially on exception and limitation clauses. The fact that those effects are automatic, from the commencement of the deviation, without the need for any intervention by the

---

[68] It was reasoned that the innocent party was released, not because the contract had ceased to exist, but because a condition precedent to the wrongdoer's being able to sue had failed. See C. B. Morison, *Rescission of Contracts* (London, 1916), 69; Francis Dawson, "Metaphors and Anticipatory Breach of Contract" [1981] C.L.J. 83, 87–89.

[69] (1900) 6 T.L.R. 345.

[70] [1907] 1 K.B. 660, 667.

[71] *Ibid.*, 669.

[72] (1936) 41 Com. Cas. 350.

[73] Text, *supra*, at fn. 38.

goods owner, makes it impossible, nowadays, to accept a discharge for breach explanation. What made it credible at the time was a then still-current perception of discharge for breach as turning on dependency, without the need for any act of "acceptance of repudiation". There is no evidence in the reports that, in *Thorley* and the subsequent cases, serious regard was paid to the prior question whether the obligation not to deviate really did go to the whole consideration. Rather, the impression left is that it was classified as a condition precedent more because of the established consequences of deviation than by reference to the intention of the parties.[74]

If we now accept that discharge for breach cannot properly explain all the incidents of deviation, it is submitted that we ought also to be free once more to conclude, as was once the case, that deviation does not automatically go to the whole consideration. And, if that is accepted, the way should be open to a recharacterisation of the obligation to follow the contract route such as that suggested by Mr Baughen and left open by Professor Reynolds. It might be tempting to suppose that a change of that kind would be unlikely to occur, but unexpected things have happened in this field before and could happen again.

INTERPRETATION AND CONSTRUCTION

If the incidents of deviation solely attributable to discharge for breach are eliminated, that still leaves the forms of strict liability which existed before *Thorley* v. *Orchis*. In particular, under the law as it then was, exception and limitation clauses ceased to apply as from the start of the deviation unless the deviator could show that the loss or damage would have happened anyway.[75] The same applied to the common law exceptions.[76] In neither case was any contract between the parties necessarily brought to an end.[77]

So long as discharge for breach were thought to be the explanation for the incidents of deviation, it would have seemed plausible to infer that, if the cargo owner did elect to continue the voyage after a deviation, the carrier would be protected by his exceptions in respect of events occurring before as well as after the election.[78] But it is one thing to waive a right to terminate a contract for

---

[74] See especially [1907] 1 K.B. 660, 666–667. Though Collins, M.R. purported to base his judgment on *Balian* v. *Joly* (1900) 6 T.L.R. 345, there was no attempt made in that case to classify the undertaking to follow the contract route.

[75] *Davis* v. *Garrett* (1830) 6 Bing. 716.

[76] *Parker* v. *James* (1814) 4 Camp. 112; 171 E.R. 37.

[77] This follows from the then continuing existence of the right to the contract freight. *Cf. The Good Luck* [1992] 1 A.C. 233, 263; *Reliance Car Facilities Ltd.* v. *Roding Motors* [1952] 2 Q.B. 851.

[78] E.g. *Hain* v. *Tate & Lyle* (1936) 41 Com. Cas. 350, 363, *per* Lord Wright, 372, *per* Lord Maugham.

breach of condition. It is quite another to waive causes of action which, because they arose while the exception clauses did not apply, have accrued since the deviation began. That would ordinarily need fresh consideration.[79] Likewise, unless it could be shown that the hazards of the voyage experienced since the election would have been encountered anyway,[80] there would need to be a variation before the exception clauses could apply to them.

In bailments where a contract exists, a sufficient explanation for the non-application of exception and limitation clauses can be found in their interpretation or construction. Thus, if goods are required[81] to be carried along a particular route or on a particular vessel,[82] on a passenger express rather than a freight train,[83] or be stored in a particular place,[84] or in, say, a cold store rather than an unrefrigerated one,[85] it can be inferred that the exception and limitation clauses were intended to apply only to loss or damage suffered within those parameters.[86] Arguably, that was all that was meant originally by the "four corners" rule,[87] which, unless it were confined in some such way could, as Professor Reynolds has pointed out,[88] prevent reliance on exception clauses wherever there was any "bad" departure from an agreed performance. An alternative approach to interpretation is to enquire whether the exculpatory clauses were intended to apply only to the *risks* that would be encountered on the contract voyage, at the contracted site, or on the contracted conveyance, and so on.[89]

However, while the interpretation approach can explain the automatic non-application of exculpatory clauses as from the very start of the deviation, it

[79] E.g. *Atlantic Shipping Co.* v. *Dreyfus* [1922] 2 A.C. 250, 261–262, *per* Lord Sumner.

[80] E.g., because the vessel would have been in the same place at the same time had it strictly followed the contract route.

[81] *Sleat* v. *Fagg* (1822) 5 B. & A. 342; 106 E.R. 1113.

[82] *Cf. Tobin* v. *Murison* (1845) 5 Moore 110, 129; 13 E.R. 431.

[83] *Gunyon* v. *South Eastern and Chatham Railway Companies' Managing Committee* [1915] 2 K.B. 370.

[84] *Harris* v. *Great Western Railway* (1876) 1 Q.B.D. 515, 534; *Lilley* v. *Doubleday* (1881) 7 Q.B.D. 510; *Roberts* v. *McDougall* (1887) 3 T.L.R. 666.

[85] *Cf. Tor Line A.B.* v. *Alltrans Group of Canada Ltd.* [1984] 1 W.L.R. 48 (height of deck less than specified).

[86] See also *The Cap Palos* [1921] P. 458, 470–471; *Neilson* v. *London and North Western Railway Co.* [1992] 1 K.B. 19, C.A. 197, 204; [1922] 2 A.C. 263, H.L., 273.

[87] *Gibaud* v. *Great Eastern Railway Co.* [1921] 2 K.B. 426; *Alderslade* v. *Hendon Laundry Ltd.* [1945] K.B. 189. I reviewed this line of authority in some detail in *Exception Clauses*, Chap. 7.

[88] Butterworth Lecture, *supra*, fn. 12, at 33.

[89] E.g. *Scaramanga & Co.* v. *Stamp* (1880) 5 C.P.D. 295, 299, *per* Cockburn, C.J.; *A/S Rendal* v. *Arcos Ltd.* (1937) 43 Com. Cas. 1, 15, *per* Lord Wright; *Suisse Atlantique* [1967] 1 A.C. 361, 412, *per* Lord Hodson. Interpretation and construction can, of course, have the result that some of the incidents associated with deviation in bailment contracts can apply to deviations by carriers of passengers.

cannot explain the "insurer's" liability, which descends on bailees who deviate, even where there is no contract. Nor does it explain why the deviater should carry the special burden of showing that any loss or damage happening after the start of the deviation would have occurred anyway.

In *Exception Clauses*,[90] I suggested that a good many of the incidents of deviation could be explained by reference to a "principle" which Lord Wright expounded in *A. S. Rendall* v. *Arcos Ltd.*[91] in these terms:

> "The essence of the principle is that damage has been sustained under conditions involving danger other than and therefore different from the conditions which would have operated if the contract had been fulfilled; for the consequences of such conditions the defendant is held liable. The principle thus applies whenever the breach of contract has the consequence of exposing the subject-matter to conditions of risk different from those which would have operated if the contract had not been broken. ... The defendant must show (if he can) that there must have been the same damage if the contract had not been broken ... the mere fact that the risk is changed will be enough to shift the onus on to the defendant."

That dictum now seems to me to be more a description than a principle, in which case it is hardly surprising that it should reflect so many of the features of deviation and quasi-deviation. What it does not do, though, is identify the kinds of breach which attract the so-called principle. Negligence[92] and unseaworthiness[93] increase or alter the risks of an adventure but they are not deviations. Nor is delay, by itself.[94] And the dictum takes no account of non-contractual bailments. It was mainly for those reasons that in *Exception Clauses*[95] I looked for an explanation within bailment itself.

BAILMENT

Whatever else it might be, a contract for the carriage of goods is a bailment of those goods, as the Privy Council confirmed not long ago in *The Pioneer Container.*[96] It will therefore exhibit the features of a bailment except to the extent those features have been added to or modified by custom or the agreement of the parties.

The modern law of deviation in contracts of carriage by sea is commonly thought to have had its beginning in 1830 in *Davis* v. *Garrett*,[97] though, as we

---

[90] *Exception Clauses*, 87–88.
[91] (1937) 43 Com. Cas. 1, 15.
[92] *Smackman* v. *General Steam Navigation Co. Ltd.* (1908) 13 Com. Cas. 196.
[93] *The Europa* [1908] P. 84; *Kish* v. *Taylor* [1912] A.C. 604.
[94] *The British Monarch* [1949] A.C. 196. Delay may, of course, be caused by a deviation: *Mallet* v. *Great Eastern Railway Co. Ltd.* [1899] 1 Q.B. 309.
[95] *Exception Clauses*, 84–95.
[96] [1994] 2 A.C. 324.
[97] (1830) 6 Bing. 716.

have seen, the term "deviation" itself was used much earlier.[98] And deviation had also for a long time been a ground for vacating a contract of insurance.[99] This last fact has been thought by some commentators and judges to be the explanation for the very serious effects of deviation on contracts of carriage.[100] It is doubtless on the same premise that it has also been suggested that quasi-deviation in other kinds of bailment is a later development, derived by analogy from deviation properly so-called.[101] That may well have been true of incidents solely attributable to the discharge for breach approach adopted in *Thorley* v. *Orchis*.[102] But the essential characteristic of deviation and quasi-deviation, namely the strict liability of a bailee who commits a breach of a particular sort of obligation, can be traced back to Roman law and was well established in English law long before 1830 and *Davis* v. *Garrett*.

In his classic account of bailment in *Coggs* v. *Bernard*,[103] Holt, C.J. referred to several breaches of the quasi-deviation type. Under the heading of "*Commodatum* or lending gratis", he instanced the case of a bailee who had been lent a horse to go westwards, or for a month. If the bailee should go northwards, or keep the horse above a month, and an accident should happen to the horse on the northern journey, or after the expiry of the month, the bailee would be chargeable:

> "because he has made use of the horse contrary to the trust he was lent to him under, and it may be that if the horse had been used no otherwise than he was lent, that accident would not have befallen him."[104]

That can be compared with *commodatum* in Roman times, under which, if goods were borrowed for a specific use and were used in some other way, the borrower was liable for any loss or damage regardless of fault. In the same way, under Roman law the use of goods loaned gratuitously for safe custody (*depositum*) also imported absolute liability.[105] Where Holt, C.J. may have differed slightly was in the seeming inference from his dictum that liability would be avoided if the accident would have befallen the horse anyway.

---

[98] *Supra*, pp. 20–21.

[99] E.g. *Green* v. *Young* (1702) 2 Salk. 444; 91 E.R. 358; *Lavabre* v. *Wilson* (1779) 1 Doug. 284, 291; 99 E.R. 185.

[100] E.g. *Hain* v. *Tate & Lyle* (1936) 41 Com. Cas. 350, 354, *per* Lord Atkin, 363, *per* Lord Wright; *The Sara D* (1989) 2 Lloyd's Rep. 277, 287, *per* Lloyd, L.J.; Simon Baughen, "Does Deviation Still Matter?" [1991] L.M.C.L.Q. 70, 71, 83; Tan, *supra* fn. 35, at 121; Wilson, *supra* fn. 35, at 22; Mills [1983] L.M.C.L.Q. 587, 587.

[101] Mills, *ibid.*, 587. *Cf.* Palmer, *supra* fn. 11, at 835; *Van Dorne* v. *North American Van Lines (Canada) Ltd.* [1979] 2 W.W.R. 385, 385–386.

[102] [1907] 1 K.B. 660.

[103] (1703) 2 Ld. Raym. 909; 92 E.R. 107. He based himself largely on Bracton, who in turn had drawn on Roman law.

[104] (1703) 2 Ld. Raym. 909, 915.

[105] R. W. Leage, *Roman Private Law*, 3rd edn. by A. M. Prichard (London, 1961), 325; J. A. C. Thomas, *The Institutes of Justinian* (Oxford, 1975) 204, 205.

Later in his judgment, under the heading of *vadium* or pawn, Holt, C.J. indicated that if the pawnee were to use the goods for his own purposes he would do so "at his peril". Similar rules, he said, would apply to goods found.[106] He also referred to common carriers, though in this case, without any reference to the special consequences of breaches of the deviation kind. Perhaps this was because, at a period before the use of exception clauses became widespread, he was able to say that the carrier was "bound to answer for the goods at all events ... [other than] acts of God and of the enemies of the King".[107]

In his *Essay on the Law of Bailments*,[108] Jones said that a borrower would be absolutely liable who went to a different destination from the one specified or who left the ordinary road and chose to go instead through thickets where robbers lurked. A hirer would also be liable for loss by robbery if he travelled by an unusual road.[109] So too, he said, all bailees were responsible for losses by casualty or violence who refused after lawful demand to return bailed goods.[110] There was a similar liability for use different from that agreed and for unauthorised use of goods deposited or pawned.[111] Significantly, Jones allowed two exceptions to the absolute liability of a defaulting borrower: that the same accident would have befallen the bailed goods in any event and that the loss or damage had been due to the bailor's default.[112] While it is true that none of these accounts of the law of bailment refers to an effect on exception clauses, that is hardly surprising, given the periods at which they were written or to which they referred.

Examples of quasi-deviation in English law prior to *Davis* v. *Garrett* are not confined to Holt, C.J.'s account or to the early textbooks. Thus, in 1615, in *Isaack* v. *Clark*,[113] it was said that:

> "If a man delivers to another a horse to ride to York, if he rides him on to Carlisle an action [in trespass] well lyeth, the reason is, because he by his wrongful act hath now destroyed the privity of the first bailment by doing contrary to it."

The effect on a warehouseman of keeping bailed goods other than on specified premises was in issue in the 1818 case of *Sidaways* v. *Todd*,[114] as was carriage in

---

[106] (1703) 2 Ld. Raym. 909, 917.

[107] *Ibid.*, 917–918.

[108] (London, 1781) 68, 69.

[109] *Ibid.*, 88.

[110] *Ibid.*, 70, 721.

[111] *Ibid.*, 121.

[112] *Ibid.*, 70.

[113] (1615) 2 Bulst. 306, 309; 80 E.R. 1143. *Cf. Bringloe* v. *Morrice* (1676) 1 Mod. Rep. 210; 86 E.R. 834.

[114] (1818) 2 Stark. 400, 402; 171 E.R. 685.

other than the stipulated form of conveyance in *Garnett* v. *Willan and Jones*[115] in 1821 and in *Sleat* v. *Fagg*[116] the following year. In *Davis* v. *Garrett*[117] itself, a case involving the carriage by sea of a cargo of lime which had been destroyed in the course of a deviation, the argument for the plaintiffs included the following:[118]

> "The exception of perils of the sea and navigation, &c. applies only to perils incurred in the direct and usual course; and of perils encountered out of that course the Defendant must take on himself the responsibility. So, upon policies of insurance, if a loss happen during a deviation it is not a loss within the meaning of the policy, and the underwriter is exonerated. So if a party direct a horse to be led by a given road, and the conductor chooses to proceed by a different track, he will be responsible for any injury the horse may sustain."

The main argument for the defence was that it could not be averred with certainty that the deviation was even the remote cause of the loss. The barge carrying the lime, it was said, might, and probably would, have encountered the same storm if she had proceeded in a direct course. Tindall, C.J.'s response to that argument was that, if it were to prevail, deviation would never, or only under very peculiar circumstances, entitle the plaintiff to recover. One example he gave was of a parcel forwarded by the wrong conveyance, in which case, he said, the defendant would undoubtedly be liable.[119] He then continued:[120]

> "But we think the real answer to the objection is, that no wrong-doer can be allowed to apportion or qualify his own wrong; and that as a loss has actually happened whilst his wrongful act was in operation and force, and which is attributable to his wrongful act, he cannot set up as an answer to the action the bare possibility of a loss if his wrongful act had never been done. It might admit of a different construction if he could shew, not only that the same loss might have happened, but that it must have happened if the act complained of had not been done; but there is no evidence to that extent in the present case."

The fact that the argument of counsel for the plaintiff included a reference to contracts of insurance may help to explain why the special incidents of deviation have been thought to derive from the effects such breaches had on marine policies. But Tindall, C.J. did not himself mention any such reason. Indeed, his dictum has been taken to suggest that, initially, deviation might even have been simply the matter of a special onus of proof.[121] As to that, it needs to be remembered that the Chief Justice was responding to a particular line of argument. But he had also had drawn to his attention, and himself had referred

---

[115] (1821) 5 B. & Ald. 53; 106 E.R. 1113.
[116] (1822) 5 B. & Ald. 342.
[117] (1830) 6 Bing. 716.
[118] *Ibid.*, 719.
[119] *Ibid.*, 723.
[120] *Ibid.*, 724.
[121] F. M. B. Reynolds, Butterworth Lecture, *supra* fn. 12, at 30–32. Though see *Harris* v. *Great Western Railway Co.* (1876) 1 Q.B.D. 515, 534, *per* Blackburn, J.

to, established instances of quasi-deviation in bailment. That being so, it seems, with respect, not unlikely that in referring to the question of onus he was simply applying what he supposed was the explanation for an already existing incident of bailment.

Perhaps the most famous statement of quasi-deviation in bailment as the law stood at the end of the nineteenth century was that of Grove, J. in *Lilley* v. *Doubleday*,[122] a case where goods had been kept at a place other than the one contracted for. He said this:

> "The defendant was entrusted with the goods for a particular purpose and to keep them in a particular place. He took them to another, and must be responsible for what took place there. The only exception I see to this general rule is where the destruction of the goods must take place as inevitably at one place as at the other. If a bailee elects to deal with the property entrusted to him in a way not authorised by the bailor, he takes upon himself the risks of so doing, except where the risk is independent of his acts and inherent in the property itself."

That statement makes no reference to exception and limitation clauses, but it seems from the report that there were no such clauses in the contract.

Whether or not deviation and quasi-deviation originated in bailment will no doubt continue to be a matter of argument. What is indisputable is that the carriage of goods does still involve bailments. Breaches of the deviation type in bailment had incidents which were established and defined long before the Court of Appeal attributed them to discharge for breach in *Thorley* v. *Orchis*.[123] Hopefully, *Photo Production*[124] has eliminated the incidents which followed uniquely from that misattribution. But it would be a strange result if that case had also, by a side wind, put paid entirely to deviation and quasi-deviation as such.

A TEST FOR DEVIATORY BREACHES

Assuming quasi-deviation remains part of the law of bailment and that the parties have no clearly expressed agreement to the contrary, a bailee who commits a deviatory breach will continue, as before, to be strictly liable for loss of or damage to the bailed goods which he is unable to show would have been suffered anyway. However, the fact that these consequences are so special makes it the more important that deviations and quasi-deviations be distinguishable from other breaches of contract since they might otherwise invite a revival of the fundamental breach doctrine, a concern which Professor Reynolds has articulated.[125]

---

[122] (1881) 7 Q.B.D. 510, 511.
[123] [1907] 1 K.B. 660.
[124] *Photo Production* v. *Securicor* [1980] A.C. 827.
[125] Butterworth Lecture, *supra* fn. 12, at 47.

In *Exception Clauses*,[126] I suggested that, if the examples given by Holt, C.J. and the early text writers were brought together, the picture that emerged was of breaches by a bailee which involved:

    (a) retention of bailed goods after the bailee's authority to do so has expired;

    (b) the presence of bailed goods in a place or on a conveyance other than that authorised;

    (c) the use of bailed goods for a purpose, in a manner, to an extent, or by a person, other than the one authorised.

Very few, if any, later cases of deviation and quasi-deviation fall outside this pattern nor, it is believed, are the categories arbitrary. Hence my suggestion,[127] adverted to at the beginning of this essay, that deviation is what happens when a bailee exceeds limitations placed upon his rights to possession. When that happens, he loses those rights, and the protection of the bailment relationship, and becomes a mere detainer.[128] That does not by itself mean that any contract between the parties has been discharged for breach,[129] but it does mean that the immediate right to possession has reverted to the bailor.[130] Put another way, a bailee's rights to possession are conditional upon limitations placed upon them even though the contract itself may not be so conditioned. Accordingly, what is distinctive about deviations is not that they are, necessarily, "bad" breaches, either morally or in terms of the scale of the loss or damage which may result. Rather, they are breaches of a particular type of obligation.

If that is so, it goes a long way to explaining why deviation and quasi-deviation have always, to some degree, involved the presence of goods in the wrong place at the wrong time (location, location!) contrary to an express or implied requirement by the bailor. That, in turn provides a test for distinguishing deviation from other kinds of breach, though there may sometimes be an overlap. One example would be delay, which might be treated as a deviation where it resulted effectively, in a different voyage.[131] Another could be unseaworthiness if, say, a frozen cargo were stowed, in breach of contract, on

---

[126] *Exception Clauses*, 91.

[127] *Ibid.*, 91–93.

[128] *Cf. Hain Steamship Co. Ltd. v. Tate & Lyle Ltd.* (1934) 39 Com. Cas. 259, 284–285, *per* Greer, L.J.; *London and North Western Railway Co. Ltd. v. Neilson* [1922] 2 A.C. 263, 269, *per* Lord Buckmaster.

[129] *Reliance Car Facilities Ltd. v. Roding Motors* [1952] 2 Q.B. 85; *J. Evans & Son (Portsmouth) Ltd. v. Andrea Mezario Ltd.* [1996] 1 W.L.R. 1078, 1084, *per* Roskill, L.J.

[130] *Cf. Gordon v. Harper* (1796) 7 T.R. 9, 12; 101 E.R. 828; *Bryant v. Wardell* (1848) 2 Ex. 479; 154 E.R. 580; *R. v. Poyer* (1851) 2 Den. 233; 169 E.R. 487; *Fenn v. Bittleston* (1851) 7 Ex. 152, 159–160; 155 E.R. 895.

[131] *Brandt v. Liverpool Brazil and River Plate Steam Navigation Co.* [1924] 1 K.B. 575, 601.

an unrefrigerated vessel. That would be a quasi-deviation but the vessel, itself, would also be unfit to receive the cargo.

DECK CARGO

On the "wrong place–wrong time" test, the carriage of cargo on deck contrary to an undertaking not to do so is a classic quasi-deviation. Yet whether it is, or should be, so characterised has become a matter of controversy.[132]

Of course, if a ship goes down and its whole cargo is lost, it may not matter very much to an owner of goods where they were stowed. Short of that, it seems obvious enough that stowage on deck substantially alters and increases the risks of loss or damage. As one writer has said, it is potentially a far more serious departure than a mere geographical deviation.[133] Tetley[134] makes the point that, in the case of containers on deck, it may even affect the stability of the vessel. Short of that, goods on deck are rather more likely to be washed overboard, to shift in a storm, and to suffer water damage than would be the case if they were stowed below deck. So, Lord Wright's test of altered risks is met whether it is founded on interpretation or exists as a separate principle.[135] As Hirst, J. said of a package limitation clause in *The Chanda*,[136] a case involving wrongful stowage on deck:

> "it can hardly have been intended to protect the shipowner who, as a result of the breach, exposed the cargo in question to such palpable risk of damage. Otherwise the main purpose of the shipowners' obligation to stow below deck would be seriously undermined."

At the least, the parties would need to use very clear words if their intentions were different.

Perhaps not surprisingly, unauthorised deck cargo is accorded special treatment in the Hamburg Rules.[137] In relation to the earlier Hague Rules, such unauthorised carriage would anyway have been classed as a deviation because

---

[132] Those against include F. M. B. Reynolds, Butterworth Lecture, *supra* fn. 12, at 47–50; B. J. Davenport (1989) 105 L.Q.R. 521; Yates (ed.), *Contracts for the Carriage of Goods by Land Sea and Air* (London, 1993) 1–392. See also *Tasman Express* v. *Case, The Canterbury Express* (1992) 111 F.L.R. 108, 111 (N.S.W.C.A.). On the other hand, according to Tetley, *Marine Cargo Claims*, 3rd edn. (Montreal, 1988), 656–657 the courts of the world have usually held that unauthorised deck cargo is not covered by the exceptions in the Hague Rules or in the contract of carriage.

[133] Baughen [1991] L.M.C.L.Q. 70, 93.

[134] Tetley, *supra* fn. 132, at 656.

[135] Text, *supra*, at fn. 90.

[136] [1989] 2 Lloyd's Rep. 494, 505. And see *J. Evans & Son (Portsmouth) Ltd.* v. *Andrea Mezario Ltd.* [1976] 1 W.L.R. 1078, 1084, *per* Roskill, L.J., to similar effect.

[137] Article 9, under which carriage on deck contrary to agreement would fall outside the protection of the Rules.

of the decision of the House of Lords to that effect in *Royal Exchange Shipping Co. Ltd.* v. *Dixon*[138] and on that basis would, after *Stag Line Ltd.* v. *Foscolo Mango & Co. Ltd.*,[139] have fallen outside the Rules in cases where the unauthorised carriage was unreasonable.[140] The Hague-Visby Rules do not expressly purport to alter that characterisation but the definition of goods in Article 1(c) excludes cargo stated in the contract to be carried on deck. That exclusion was reversed by the Carriage of Goods by Sea Act 1971, section 1(7). Like other forms of deviation, unauthorised deck carriage is, under those Rules, subject to the time bar in Article III, rule 6[141] though, according to one New Zealand judge, not to the package limitation.[142]

There appear to be two main arguments why wrongful deck carriage should not be classed as a deviation. One is linked to *Photo Production* and the demise of fundamental breach. The other is based on appeals to policy and convenience. The leading judicial expression of the former view is that of Lloyd, L.J. in *The Antares,*[143] where machinery had wrongfully been stored on deck and had been seriously damaged. It was argued for the cargo owner that at common law stowage in that manner was a fundamental breach which displaced the exception clauses in the bill of lading, including in this case the time bar in Article III, rule 6 of the Hague-Visby Rules. Neither Steyn, J. at first instance[144] nor the Court of Appeal had much difficulty in holding that since, under the Carriage of Goods by Sea Act 1971, the Hague-Visby Rules had the force of statute law and the time limit was expressed to apply "in any event" to "all liability whatsoever", the carrier was entitled to be protected by it. On that basis, the exact characterisation of wrongful carriage on deck was hardly relevant. To some extent, therefore, what was said about deviation as a fundamental breach might be regarded as unnecessary to the decision.

Referring to the argument based on fundamental breach, Lloyd, L.J. commented:[145]

"The doctrine of fundamental breach on which [counsel] relies, that is to say the doctrine that a breach of contract may be so fundamental as to displace exception clauses altogether, no longer exists."

He cited *Suisse Atlantique* and *Photo Production* and then went on to refer to a

---

[138] (1887) 12 App. Cas. 11.

[139] [1932] A.C. 328.

[140] *The Chanda* [1989] 2 Lloyd's Rep. 494; *Svenska Traktor Aktiebolaget* v. *Maritime Agencies (Southampton) Ltd.* [1953] 2 Lloyd's Rep. 124, 129–130; *St. Simeon Navigation Inc.* v. *A. Couturier & Fils Ltee* (1974) 44 D.L.R. (3d) 478, 480 (S.C.C.).

[141] *The Antares* [1987] 1 Lloyd's Rep. 424.

[142] *Nelson Pine Industries Ltd.* v. *Seatrans New Zealand Ltd. (The Pembroke)* [1995] 2 Lloyd's Rep. 290 (N.Z.H.C.).

[143] [1987] 1 Lloyd's Rep. 424.

[144] [1986] 2 Lloyd's Rep. 633.

[145] [1987] 1 Lloyd's Rep. 424, 429.

submission that the deviation cases might have survived the demise of fundamental breach and with them, by analogy, the rules relating to carriage on deck. He referred to Lord Wilberforce's contrasting dicta in *Suisse Atlantique*[146] and *Photo Production*[147] and concluded:[148]

> "Whatever may be the position with regard to deviation cases strictly so-called, (I would myself favour the view that they should now be assimilated into the ordinary law of contract) I can see no reason for regarding the unauthorised loading of deck cargo as a special case. The sole question therefore is whether on its true construction art III r 6 applies."

If Lloyd, L.J. could see no reason for regarding unauthorised loading of deck cargo as a special case, it may be that the matter had not been fully canvassed before him. There is nothing in the published reports of *The Antares*, at first instance or in the Court of Appeal, to indicate that the specifically bailment aspects of deviation and quasi-deviation were drawn to the attention of the Court or were considered by the judges. Nor was anything said about those aspects by their Lordships sitting in the *Photo Production* case.

The policy considerations against treating wrongful deck carriage as a quasi-deviation were canvassed by Mr B. J. Davenport in a note[149] on the decisions of Hirst, J. in *The Chanda*[150] and the *Captain Gregos No. 1*.[151] Those cases, and the note itself, are concerned mainly with the application of the Hague and Hague-Visby Rules respectively but they both also address wider issues. In the note, reference is made to the conclusion of Hirst, J. in *The Chanda* that an exceptions clause in that case did not apply because it was intended to do so only if the goods were stowed under deck. The note continues:[152]

> "the supposed intention of the parties does seem to lead to somewhat perverse results. Thus, they must evidently have intended that the shipowners could have limited their liability if the [article carried] had been stowed under deck but so inadequately lashed down that it broke loose in a storm and had to be written off. Likewise, they presumably intended that the shipowners could limit their liability if the ship was so badly maintained that she sank, carrying the [article carried] to the ocean floor. The extent which the almost geographical basis underlying *Lilley* v. *Doubleday*[153] and *Gibaud*[154] is sound today requires detailed analysis. Although any contract must be carefully construed in order to decide how far the parties intended it to apply in unexpected circumstances, the supposed intention of the parties must be derived

---

[146] [1967] 1 A.C. 361, 424.
[147] [1980] A.C. 827, 845.
[148] [1987] 1 Lloyd's Rep. 424, 430.
[149] "Limits on the Hague Rules" (1989) 105 L.Q.R. 521.
[150] [1989] 2 Lloyd's Rep. 494.
[151] [1989] 2 Lloyd's Rep. 633.
[152] (1989) 105 L.Q.R. 521, 522.
[153] (1881) 7 Q.B.D. 510.
[154] *Gibaud* v. *Great Eastern Ry.* [1921] 2 K.B. 426.

from more than a mixture of legal concepts of uncertain status and a healthy dislike of any clause limiting the damages recoverable for a gross breach of contract to an almost nominal sum."

The learned writer returns to these seeming inconsistencies at the end of his note. Nor is he alone in not wanting unauthorised deck carriage treated as a type of deviation. In his Butterworth Lecture,[155] Professor Reynolds describes such carriage as "simply another example of a very bad breach" and he goes on to observe:

"Quite apart from the general difficulties of deviation, wrongful deck stowage has attained a significance beyond what is appropriate. Other breaches as to stowage, and other breaches in general (such as furnishing an unseaworthy ship) may be just as serious."

I am not competent to assess the practical implications of what Mr Davenport and Professor Reynolds are saying. All I can do is suggest, very tentatively, that those who come to make decisions in this area have regard to such considerations as the following:

- wrongful deck carriage is a classic form of quasi-deviation;
- it seems to be generally agreed that the risks of carriage on deck differ from those of carriage below deck and are in a number of respects greater;
- quasi-deviation has a very long history in a wide range of bailment relationships;
- the common law system of decision by analogy would mean that judicial abolition of quasi-deviation in one kind of bailment would have a similar effect in others;
- quasi-deviation is not merely another form of bad breach. Rather, it is the breach of a particular kind of obligation in bailments;
- if the relationship of quasi-deviation to rights of possession is accepted, it can the more readily be distinguished from other kinds of breach;
- neither explicitly, nor by inference, did the decision of the House of Lords in *Photo Production* necessarily involve any reversal of the law of bailment as it existed before *Thorley* v. *Orchis*.

CONCLUSION

By ascribing the effects of deviation to discharge for breach in *Thorley* v. *Orchis*, the Court of Appeal opened the way to a series of distortions the removal of which, fortunately, has now been made possible by the House of

---

[155] *Supra*, fn. 12, at 50.

Lords in the *Photo Production* case. But it does not follow that deviation and quasi-deviation have thereby ceased to have special effects. Some of these may turn on the interpretation of exception and limitation clauses. Others, though, are very long-established incidents of a continuing law of bailment, the relevance of which may not yet have been fully appreciated.[156]

---

[156] Since this essay was written Professor M. Dockray has published "Deviation: Doctrine all at Sea?" [2000] L.M.C.L.Q. 76, an interesting and valuable contextual study of some of the leading cases.

Chapter 3

Agency and the Criminal Law[1]

Rt Hon. Lord Hobhouse of Woodborough

It is a privilege to be permitted to contribute to this volume in honour of Francis Reynolds and in recognition of his outstanding contributions to the understanding and development of English law and in particular to the law of agency. His published work provides invaluable insights into the rationale of the concept of agency as used in the law of contract, partnership and property and in the law of torts. In the common law there is a coherent scheme of attributing civil responsibility to a principal for the acts and omissions of his agent or of a person whom the law treats as his agent. The basic concept is that of authorisation. In the law of contract extensions have to be made to cover ostensible authority and agency by estoppel. In the law of tort the principle of vicarious liability and "course of employment" provide similar extensions. Thus, responsibility arises either from actual authorisation, express or implied, by the principal or from conduct of the principal not amounting to actual specific authorisation which the law treats as carrying the same consequential responsibility for the acts of the agent.

In the criminal law, although liability arising from agency exists, its existence is often not recognised and it appears to be the conventional view to deny that it exists. Under these circumstances it is perhaps not surprising that there is no adequate analysis of the concept or the rationale upon which it is based. The reason for this state of affairs is primarily historical but history is an inadequate justification. It leads to unsatisfactory anomalies and to the failure, on occasions, of both academics and judges to provide answers to questions which should be capable of satisfactory analysis and resolution. The need for further discussion of the questions raised is demonstrated by a recent article by

---

[1] This is a subject which the author has already visited in a judicial capacity in the course of judgments in the Court of Appeal: *R.* v. *Stewart and Schofield* [1995] 1 Cr.App.R. 441 and *Credit Lyonnais* v. *E.C.G.D.* [1998] 1 Lloyd's Rep. 19. The former was strongly criticised by Sir John Smith, Q.C. in notes at [1995] Crim.L.Rev. 296 and 420.

Professor Sir John Smith, Q.C. in the *Law Quarterly Review*[2] and the speeches of the House of Lords in *R.* v. *Powell, R.* v. *English*.[3] What is most striking about these highly authoritative contributions is the absence of reference to some of the leading authorities and the lack of a fully coherent analysis.

In this essay I will first say something about the basic structure of criminal law and the principle of *accessory* liability. Most of what I will have to say under this head will be relatively elementary (and inevitably simplified) and has been often covered in textbooks and elsewhere.[4] It is necessary to do this because it is the thesis of Sir John Smith that the liability of anyone other than the person who actually performs the criminal act can only be an accessory liability. The accessory principle, sometimes called complicity,[5] is not an agency principle.

Responsibility in the criminal law differs from responsibility in the civil law in that in the criminal law responsibility must (apart from immaterial statutory exceptions) be based upon both a criminal act (*actus reus*) and a state of mind (*mens rea*) of the person to be held criminally responsible. It is important to note that the *actus reus* is an objective concept: it is an act having a certain *objective* characteristic. The state of mind of the performer of that act is only relevant to his *mens rea* and is, of course, subjective. The *actus reus* of rape is the act of sexual intercourse without the woman's consent (objective); the *mens rea* is the knowledge that she is not consenting or not caring whether she is or not (subjective). An offence against the Offences Against the Person Act 1861, section 18 requires causing another grievous bodily harm (objective) with the intent to cause such harm (subjective). At any criminal trial, whether or not a defendant can be convicted of a crime—and, if so, what crime—will depend upon each of the two requisites being proved.

Where more than one person is involved in some criminal activity it is obvious that those persons may not all have played the same role nor may they have all had the same state of mind. It is possible for more than one person actually to perform the physical criminal act charged. Where two burglars both enter the building together as trespassers they both perform the actual criminal act. In a gang of pickpockets only one will perform the actual act of stealing. This essay is concerned with the criminal liability of a person who does not

---

[2] "Criminal Liability of Accessories: Law and Law Reform" (1997) 113 L.Q.R. 453 (hereafter "the article"). The article drew on views already expressed by Sir John Smith in Smith & Hogan, *Criminal Law*, notes in the *Criminal Law Review* and an article "Putting Joint Enterprise in its Place", *Archbold News*, 1st June 1995. See also now Sir John Smith, "Joint Enterprise and Secondary Liability" (1999) 50 N.I.L.Q. 153.

[3] [1999] A.C. 1.

[4] including at 113 L.Q.R. 453 *et seq.* And see the Law Commission Consultation Paper No. 131: *Assisting and Encouraging Crime* (1993).

[5] K. J. Smith, *A Modern Treatise on the Law of Criminal Complicity* (1991); R. J. Buxton, "Complicity in the Criminal Code" (1969) 85 L.Q.R. 252.

himself perform the criminal act. I will call him "D", being the defendant whose criminal liability is in question. The person who actually performs the criminal act I will call "A", the actor. He may or may not also be before the court. (For the purposes of the discussion, I will assume that there is only one actor: what I say will be equally applicable if there is more than one actor.)

Historically, the criminal law has had no difficulty where the criminal act is performed by a person who has a wholly innocent state of mind. The actor lacking the requisite *mens rea* can be treated as a mere instrument of another (D) who caused him so to act and has the requisite *mens rea*. The other person (D) is treated as the person responsible for the criminal act and, since he had the *mens rea*, he is guilty of the crime which corresponds to that act and that state of mind. D's liability is not, and cannot be, an accessory liability: D is therefore, in the terminology of the criminal law, described as the principal, that is to say, as the "principal in the first degree", even though he did not physically perform the criminal act. A clear statement of this principle was recorded by Keyling, C.J. in 1665:[6]

> "if A giveth poison to B to give unto C; and B not knowing it to be poison but believing it to be a good medicine giveth it to C, who dieth of it. In this case A who is absent is principal; or else a man should be murdered and there would be no principal. For B, who knew nothing of the poison, is in no fault, though he gave it to C. So if A puts a sword into the hand of a madman, and bids him kill B with it: and then A goeth away, and the madman kills B with the sword as A commanded him, this is murder in A though absent, and he is principal. For it is no crime in the madman who did the fact, by reason of his madness."

The maxim *qui facit per alium facit per se* is sometimes used in this connection. It is an agency principle. It is often referred to as the principle of the "innocent agent", so raising the implication that it cannot be used when the agent is not wholly innocent.

The view that (with the possible exception of the "innocent agent") denies the existence of any agency principle derives from the history of the English law of criminal procedure. The person who committed the crime was the person who actually performed the relevant criminal act. He was, and still is, confusingly termed the "principal". The physical act plus the state of mind of the person who actually performed it determined what crime had been committed. For felonies the role of any one else was described as secondary or accessory. Thus a person who was present when the act was committed was a "principal in the second degree". A person not present might be an accessory "before" or "after the fact".

---

[6] Kel. J. 52. Similar statements of the law, expressed in more modern language are to be found in modern textbooks, e.g. *Archbold, Criminal Pleading, Evidence and Practice*, 1999 edn., para. 18–7: "the inciter though absent when the act constituting the crime is committed is liable for the act of his agent and is a principal." See also *Attorney-General's Reference No.1 of 1999* [1999] 3 W.L.R. 769.

By statute,[7] these categories were extended to cover aiders and abettors, which effectively removed for this purpose the distinction between felonies and misdemeanours. But, still, a conviction based on aiding and abetting depended upon proving the commission by another of the crime which the defendant was alleged to have assisted or encouraged. The accessory principle has been summarised in these words:[8]

> "A simple but important point is sometimes overlooked, namely that when the law relating to principals and accessories as such is under consideration there is only one crime although there may be more than one person criminally liable in respect of it."

This structure, parts but not all of which have been amended or abolished with the abolition of the distinction between felonies and misdemeanours, founds upon the supposition that there is only one crime that is committed, the crime actually committed by the principal in the first degree. The guilt of anyone else derives from some complicity in the commission of that crime. He is an accessory to the crime of the principal. The accessory principle is indiscriminate. It precludes any distinction between the guilt of the accessory and that of the principal. This can work both ways. The accessory is typically convicted of a crime that he has not committed. But, if the case against D is solely based upon an allegation of being an accessory to the crime of another, the accessory principle can likewise result in D's conviction being restricted to a lesser crime inadequate to reflect his true degree of guilt.

This central feature of the accessory principle creates a number of anomalies. The accessory may have no actual knowledge of any particular crime which may or may not be committed provided that he foresees that a crime or crimes of that type may be committed.[9] It may be a matter of complete indifference to him. The act which makes him complicit need only be some antecedent act of assistance or encouragement. No further conduct on his part need be involved. Yet the accessory principle treats him exactly the same as if he was present at the scene of the crime, knew all about it and was as guilty as the person who did actually commit the crime. Thus the accessory may be charged with the commission of that crime and convicted as if he had committed it. What is more, where the crime is one for which the punishment is fixed by law—for murder, formerly death, now life imprisonment—he must be sentenced to that punishment. This is a complete fiction, objectionable and capable of considerable injustice. Further it amounts to a lottery what if any crime or crimes the aider may be convicted of. A man who sells a gun to a criminal may thereafter be convicted of any of a number of foreseeable crimes, a murder, manslaughter, woundings with or without intent, a whole string of bank robberies, or of nothing at all depending purely upon the chance of what, if any, of the

---

[7] The Accessories and Abettors Act 1861.
[8] J. W. C. Turner, *Russell on Crime*, 12th edn. (1964) 128.
[9] *R. v. Maxwell* [1978] 1 W.L.R. 1350.

foreseeable uses the criminal may happen to have put the gun to. Normally there will be a causal relationship between the act of assistance or encouragement and the actual commission of the crime by the person who commits it but this is not necessarily so.[10]

Likewise at the level of the accessory's state of mind, there are similar anomalies. As already observed, the accessory need have no particular knowledge; he merely has to contemplate the possibility that his own act may assist or encourage the commission of some class of criminal activity. This leads to the anomaly that the accessory can be convicted of a crime of specific intent without having that intent. In *R. v. Powell*[11] in the Court of Appeal, Lord Taylor, C.J. had referred to this as an anomaly which might be thought unacceptable and this submission was adopted by counsel for the appellants in the House of Lords.[12] Lord Hutton responded:[13]

> "My Lords, I recognise that as a matter of logic there is force in the argument advanced on behalf of the appellants and that, on one view it is anomalous that, if foreseeability of death or really serious harm is not sufficient to constitute *mens rea* for murder in the party who actually carries out the killing, it is sufficient to constitute *mens rea* in a secondary party. But the rules of the common law are not based solely on logic but relate to practical concerns and, in relation to crimes committed in the course of joint enterprises, to the need for effective protection of the public against criminals operating in gangs."

If the accessory liability were to be recognised for what it is, not the commission of the principal crime but the criminal act of assisting or encouraging such a crime, this and other anomalies would disappear. D would be convicted of a crime which he has committed not one that he has not and his *mens rea* would be appropriate to that crime. The existing state of the law of accessories, the fiction it depends on and the anomalies it creates have been criticised both by Professor Spencer in a powerful essay[14] and by the Law Commission in the Consultation Paper already referred to.[15] Yet it forms the corner-stone of Sir John Smith's defence of its retention and his analysis of all secondary liability in terms of aiding and abetting.[16] In its present form it remains a surviving example of constructive crime similar to the former doctrines of "felony murder" and "constructive presence" at the scene of the crime. Indeed, Sir John Smith reinforces his exposition of the law in terms of aiding and abetting by adding a

---

[10] Sir John Smith cites the case of *R. v. Gianetto* [1997] 1 Cr.App.R. 1, where it was said that it was enough for D to be convicted of murder that he simply said "Oh goody" when told by A that he was going to kill his wife.

[11] [1996] 1 Cr.App.R. 14, 22.

[12] [1999] A.C. 1, 23 *et seq.*

[13] *Ibid.*

[14] J. R. Spencer, "Trying to Help Another Person to Commit a Crime", in Peter Smith (ed.), *Criminal Law: Essays in Honour of J. C. Smith* (1987) 148.

[15] Law Com. No. 131.

[16] 113 L.Q.R. 453.

further artificiality, "parasitic accessory liability".[17] Such terminology puts one on enquiry whether the analysis has not taken a wrong turning.

Those who knowingly or recklessly assist in the commission of crime should undoubtedly be liable to prosecution and the imposition of criminal sanctions. Inchoate offences are recognised in the criminal law. It is a criminal offence to conspire with another to commit a crime and it does not matter whether that crime has actually been committed. The criminal offence and the criminal act is the two or more persons conspiring together. Similarly it is a freestanding criminal offence to solicit or incite another to commit a crime. Here again it does not matter whether the solicitation or incitement was successful. The defendant's criminal act was to solicit or incite. In substance aiding and abetting have the same character. The act which makes the defendant criminally liable is his voluntary act of assistance or encouragement. This reality has been recognised in other legal systems based on the common law. Professor Spencer comments on this.[18]

It is now settled that the state of mind required of an aider or abettor is that of contemplating the commission of a crime—being aware of the risk of the commission of a crime—knowing that a crime may be committed: various phrases of equivalent meaning are used. Two points arise from this.

The first is that the accessory is not and does not need to be concerned with the state of mind of the actor A. If D sells A a gun contemplating that A may kill someone with it, that necessarily includes the appreciation that he may do so intentionally. If he contemplates that he may do someone serious harm, again he must appreciate that that act may be intentional. The appreciation of the performance of the act carries with it the appreciation that the act may be intentional.[19] The consequence of this for those engaging in legal analysis or reasoning is that they may not need, and therefore fail, to distinguish between the act and the state of mind of A. The essential element is the foresight of the risk of the performance of the criminal *act*. Once D has foreseen that *act*, he becomes an accessory to whatever crime the performance of that act happens to constitute, which in some cases will depend upon what intent A had at the material time.

It is possible to suggest circumstances which might at first sight be thought to be inconsistent with this proposition. Suppose that D gives A and his friends permission to use D's land for a clay pigeon shoot notwithstanding that it adjoins a public footpath. On these facts D has assisted in the carrying on of a

---

[17] *Ibid.*, 455.

[18] *Supra*, n. 14.

[19] See the formulation of Lord Lane, C.J. in *R. v. Slack* [1989] Q.B. 775, 781; and similarly but less clearly Lord Scarman and Lowry, C.J. in *R. v. Maxwell* [1978] 1 W.L.R. 1350, 1363. See now also *R. v. Uddin* [1999] Q.B. 431 and *R. v. Nelson*, 26th February 1999, unreported.

dangerous but otherwise innocent activity. D foresees the possible consequences of that dangerous activity, including the unlawful killing or wounding of a walker on the path. He does not foresee some collateral act not arising from the dangerous activity such as A taking the opportunity gratuitously to kill one of his companions. The difference is that in the former case the act was foreseeable as a possible consequence of the act of assistance and in the latter it was not. To put it another way, he encouraged and assisted the dangerous activity but not the wholly collateral conduct of A.

The second point is that the foresight test used for complicity will almost invariably give in practice the same answer as the contemplation test used for the scope of a joint criminal venture. Both involve asking what risk of possible conduct by A did D contemplate.[20] This can lead to the confusion that joint enterprise and accessory liability are the same thing. It is a feature of both the judicial and some of the academic writing that terminology is used elastically and distinctions not necessary for the decision of a given case are not made. There is nothing surprising about this but it does tend to obscure the true nature of the principle being used.[21]

To summarise, the key characteristic of criminal liability as based upon complicity or aiding and abetting is that it is dependent upon the *actus reus* and the *mens rea* of the actor, A (the principal in the first degree). The criminal liability of the accessory, D, is determined by treating him as complicit not only in the act done by A but also in whatever may happen to be A's state of mind at the time of performing that act. It is this attribution of not only A's act but also his state of mind to D which is, or should be, at the root of any discussion of the distinction between complicity and agency in criminal law. On an agency basis, the *act* of A is attributed to D and the crime thus committed by D is determined by D's own state of mind. In the great majority of the cases coming before the criminal courts this distinction will be unimportant: the intent of all those concerned is the same. But in a minority of cases this is not so and the distinction is relevant to the decision of the case. But whether this is so or not the distinction remains important to the analysis and the correct identification of the principle being used.

The aspect of the criminal law where the distinction is necessarily relevant is what is known as "joint enterprise" or "joint venture". This is an essentially simple and convenient doctrine:

---

[20] *R. v. Rook* [1993] 1 W.L.R. 1005, a case which includes a useful reiteration of the foresight test, referring to "the principal's acts", but elsewhere contains a confusion between accessory liability and that based on joint venture. Withdrawal is relevant to liability based on joint venture but is not relevant nor does it provide any defence to one who has earlier assisted A or encouraged him.

[21] Similar confusions can arise through the failure to distinguish between inciting and aiding and abetting.

"It is a principle of law that if several persons act together in pursuance of a common intent, every act in furtherance of such intent by each of them is, in law, done by all."[22]

This is a partnership (i.e. agency) concept. It arises from the pursuit of a common purpose. It attributes the *act* of one participant to all the participants. It does not involve any attribution of intent. It derives from a proper application of the principles of agency and involves no artificiality. The criminality of the individual defendant is determined by the act which he has expressly or implicitly authorised and his own state of mind.

The extent of the joint venture is the starting point for the application of this doctrine. The defendant is only liable for acts which fall within the scope of the joint venture. This has been encapsulated in a formulation by Geoffrey Lane, Q.C.[23] adopted by the Court of Appeal in *R. v. Anderson and Morris*:[24]

"where two persons embark on a joint enterprise, each is liable for the acts done in pursuance of that joint enterprise, and that includes liability for unusual consequences if they arise from the execution of the agreed joint enterprise but ... if one of the adventurers goes beyond what had been tacitly agreed as part of the common enterprise, his co-adventurer is not liable for the consequence of that unauthorised act."

This again is an agency formulation which then is applied to responsibility for the *act*. It is important to note that it is not a complicity principle. But it is always necessary to establish the element of express or implicit authorisation. If the act was not authorised, there is no attribution and no criminal liability of the defendant for it: if that act is what the prosecution relies on, the defendant must be acquitted. This is an application of the agency principle. What was the extent of the joint venture and what was implicitly authorised by participation in it is a question of fact and can give rise to difficulties of resolution. It was to aid this resolution that the Lane formulation has been adopted. It is often difficult to decide whether a killing by A fell within the scope of the joint venture in which D joined; the answer is to see whether the *act* of A which had this consequence was done in pursuance of the joint enterprise and was implicitly agreed to by D although, maybe, in no way desired by him. One of the problems always liable to arise in any branch of the law of agency is the extent of the authority actually or impliedly given by the principal to the agent. The presence of such a problem in the criminal law confirms and does not contradict the fact that the principle involved is one of agency. In assessing the scope of the implicit authorisation in homicide cases one of the facts to which the courts attach importance is whether D knew that A was carrying the weapon used by A to kill.[25]

Once it has been established what was the scope of the joint venture and that

---

[22] *R. v. Macklin* (1838) 2 Lewin 225; 168 E.R. 1136.
[23] Later Lord Lane, C.J.; [1966] 2 Q.B. 110.
[24] [1962] 2 Q.B. 110, 118. Followed and applied in (among many other cases) *R. v. Lovesey and Peterson* [1970] 1 Q.B. 352 and *R. v. English* [1999] A.C. 1.
[25] E.g., *R. v. English* [1999] A.C. 1.

the act of A was within it, the next question is for what crime each of the participants in the joint venture is liable to be convicted. It must be said at the outset that in any such situation D is virtually certain in some way to have assisted or encouraged A and therefore to be liable to be convicted as an aider or abettor of A's crime. Under the existing law D's complicity is proved and D can be convicted of A's crime regardless of the fact that D did not have A's state of mind.[26] This is what normally happens in criminal trials. No further enquiry is undertaken: no distinctions are made. But if the state of mind of D is criminally more serious than that of A, the question arises whether D should be convicted of the crime corresponding to his own state of mind or should only be convicted of the lesser crime corresponding to A's state of mind. This forces the law to choose whether to recognise the agency principle or to deny its existence in the criminal law of England and convict only upon the complicity principle as an accessory. In his article and elsewhere, Sir John Smith denies the existence of the agency principle and states that D can only be convicted of the lesser offence. The agency principle has already been accepted by the criminal law in respect of the "innocent agent". The rejection of the agency principle in relation to joint enterprise therefore involves making a distinction between an agent who is wholly innocent and one who has even a minor degree of criminal responsibility for his act. But this is not the law.

The factual context in which accuracy of analysis is required is where the actual crime committed depends upon the intention with which the criminal act was done, i.e. the *mens rea* of A. Most of the reported cases concern a homicide committed by one of a number of persons in the course of carrying out some other crime such as robbery. Potentially lethal weapons may or may not be being carried. The criminal liability of the person striking the lethal blow depends upon his own intention at the time he did it. But on what does the criminal liability of each of the other participants in the robbery depend? Having determined that the act was within the scope of the joint venture, the question of D's *mens rea* has to be addressed. The principled and non-fictional approach is to look at the state of mind of D. The correctness of this approach was clearly stated in the 1994 edition of *Archbold*:[27]

> "A person who is a party to a joint enterprise, the pursuance of which results in causing another's death, may be criminally liable for that death either on the basis that he is guilty of murder or on the basis that he is guilty of manslaughter. It is fundamental to a conviction of either offence that the accused must have been a party to the act which caused death. The application of the law concerning joint enterprise in cases of homicide in practice raises two problems: (i) whether in the circumstances the accused was a party to the act which caused death; (ii) if he was, whether his state of mind was such as to make him guilty of murder or of manslaughter."

This statement of the law, based upon a clear line of Court of Appeal authority,

---

[26] *R.* v. *Powell, ibid.*
[27] Para. 19–23. *R.* v. *Richards and Stober* (1992) 96 Cr.App.R. 258 also referred to.

was expressly approved by the Court of Appeal in *R. v. Stewart and Schofield*.[28] It is convenient to start with two cases where convictions based on aiding and abetting, the accessory principle, were conceded to be unsustainable on that basis but were upheld applying the agency principle.

The first of these cases strikingly illustrates the application of the agency principle. *R. v. Cogan and Leak*[29] is as an example of an "innocent agent" but its significance goes beyond that. At the trial Cogan was charged with raping Leak's wife and Leak was charged with aiding and abetting him. The jury returned verdicts of guilty against both defendants. On appeal, Cogan's appeal was quashed on the basis that he may have believed that the woman was consenting to intercourse: he lacked *mens rea*. But Leak knew that she was not consenting and had compelled her to submit; his intention was to punish her by making her have intercourse with Cogan against her will and it was at his instigation that Cogan did so. Leak's conviction was upheld. It could not be upheld on the basis of aiding and abetting Cogan for Cogan had committed no crime. Leak was liable as a principal not an accessory.

Lawton, L.J. delivering the judgment of the Court of Appeal said:[30]

> "Her ravishment had come about because Leak had wanted it to happen and had taken action to see that it did by persuading Cogan to use his body as the instrument for the necessary physical act. In the language of the law, the act of sexual intercourse without the wife's consent was the *actus reus*: It had been procured by Leak, who had the appropriate *mens rea*, namely, his intention that Cogan should have intercourse with her without her consent. In our judgment it is irrelevant that the man whom Leak had procured to do the physical act himself did not intend to have sexual intercourse with the wife without her consent. Leak was using him as a means to procure a criminal purpose."

Leak was responsible for the act of Cogan and himself had the state of mind requisite to the crime of rape. The Court of Appeal upheld Leak's conviction as a conviction for rape.

If one changes the facts a bit and supposes that the victim was not the wife of Leak but his 14 year old daughter, Cogan would have committed offences— indecent assault and unlawful sexual intercourse. Although not guilty of rape, he would not be wholly innocent. Would Leak still be liable to be found guilty of rape or only of one of the lesser offences for which Cogan could also be convicted? The school of thought which treats all those other than the principal in the first degree as accessories would answer this question by saying: Only the lesser offences. They would quote *Hawkins' Pleas of the Crown*:[31]

---

[28] This approval led to what surely must be the unique situation of the editors of the textbook in their subsequent edition removing the judicially approved passage and introducing statements of the law inconsistent with it.

[29] [1976] Q.B. 217.

[30] *Ibid.*, 223.

[31] 8th edn. (1824), vol. 2, c.29, para. 15, as quoted by Lord Lane, C.J. in *R. v. Howe* [1986] Q.B. 626, 642.

"I take it to be an uncontroverted rule that [the offence of the accessory can never rise higher than that of the principal]."

But this begs the question: is Leak no more than an accessory? If Leak was liable for rape as a principal, what has cancelled that liability? No satisfactory answer can be given to this question. The *actus reus* for which he is responsible and his *mens rea* remain the same as before. To deny his liability on the ground that Cogan was also, but differently, liable lacks both logic and realism. Yet the Court of Appeal in *R.* v. *Richards*[32] held that a defendant who had employed two men to attack and inflict serious harm on her husband was only guilty of a section 20 offence because the two men, although they had in fact caused serious injury to her husband, had not when it came to the point actually intended to do so. Her liability was reduced because of the reduced *mens rea* of the two men.

The correctness of the decision in *Richards* was considered by the Court of Appeal and the House of Lords in *R.* v. *Howe*.[33] The main point in the case was whether duress was a defence to murder. But there was the further point whether D, the instigator of a homicide, could be liable for murder if A, the actual killer (or killers), had killed without intending to do so or even cause serious injury. The Court of Appeal expressed their disagreement with *Richards* and the House of Lords unanimously overruled *Richards*. The headnote summarises the conclusion of the House of Lords:

> "In circumstances where a defendant had procured or incited another to commit murder but that person was convicted of manslaughter, the defendant could be convicted of the murder of the victim."

Lord Mackay of Clashfern approved the statement of Lord Lane:[34]

> "Counsel before us posed the situation where [D] hands a gun to [A] informing him that it is loaded with blank ammunition and telling him to go and scare X by discharging it. The ammunition is in fact live as [D] knows, and X is killed. [A] is convicted only of manslaughter, as he might be on those facts. It would seem absurd that [D] should thereby escape conviction for murder."

Lord Mackay added:[35]

> "It seems to me that the reasoning of Lord Lane, C.J. is entirely correct and I would affirm his view that, where a person has been killed and that result is the result intended by another participant, the mere fact that the actual killer may be convicted only of the reduced charge of manslaughter for some reason special to himself does not in any way result in some compulsory reduction for the other participant."

R v. *Cogan* was approved.[36]

---

[32] [1974] Q.B. 776.
[33] [1986] Q.B. 626; affd [1987] A.C. 417.
[34] *Ibid.*, 458. See also the argument of counsel *ibid.*, 421.
[35] *Ibid.*
[36] *Ibid.*, 426.

The case of *Cogan* in conjunction with *Howe* is therefore clear authority for the existence of the agency principle in English criminal law, that its application is not confined to the wholly innocent agent, that it is distinct and independent of the accessory principle and can be relied on when the application of the accessory principle would produce a different result.

The second case I would refer to is *Chan Wing-Siu* v. *R.*[37] where the judgment of the Privy Council was delivered by Sir Robin Cooke.[38] Three men gained entry to a flat armed with knives intending to rob the two occupants. It resulted in one of the occupants being killed and the other seriously wounded. They were all convicted of murder. Owing to the terms in which the judge had directed the jury it was conceded that the convictions could not be upheld on the basis of aiding and abetting. The accessory principle, therefore, could not be relied upon. However that was not the end of the case. Sir Robin said:[39]

> "The case must depend rather on the wider principle whereby a secondary party is criminally liable for *acts* by the primary offender of a type which the former foresees but does not necessarily intend. That there is such a principle is not in doubt. It turns on contemplation or, putting the same idea in other words, *authorisation*, which may be express but is more usually implied. It meets the case of a crime foreseen as a possible incident of the common unlawful enterprise. The criminal culpability lies in participating in the venture with that foresight."

The language is less clear than that in *Howe*—Sir Robin uses the phrase "secondary" party—but it has the same import. The use of the words *acts* and *authorisation* confirm that it is an agency principle that he is referring to. The principle is distinct from and independent of the accessory principle although the language of foresight is (as observed earlier) the same.

The law as stated in *Howe* and the citation from the 1994 edition of *Archbold* is entirely in line with a number of decisions of the Court of Appeal. They are discussed in *Stewart and Schofield*.

In *R.* v. *Smith (W)*,[40] Slade, J. delivering the judgment of the Court of Appeal approved, saying it was legally unassailable, a summing up in these terms:

> "Several persons at the death of a man may be guilty of different degrees of crime—one of murder, others of manslaughter. Only he who intended that unlawful and grievous bodily harm should be done is guilty of murder. He who intended that the victim should be unlawfully hit and hurt would be guilty of manslaughter if death results."

This direction and its approval was expressly adopted and followed by Lord

---

[37] [1985] A.C. 168.
[38] Now Lord Cooke of Thorndon.
[39] [1985] A.C. 168, 175 (emphasis added).
[40] [1963] 1 W.L.R. 1200, 1206.

Parker, C.J. giving the judgment of the Court of Appeal *R.* v. *Betty*.[41] In *R.* v. *Reid*,[42] Lawton, L.J. delivering the judgment of the Court of Appeal, said:

> "When two or more men go out together in joint possession of offensive weapons such as revolvers and knives and the circumstances are such as to justify an inference that the very least that they intend to do with them is to cause fear in another, there is, in our judgment, always a likelihood that, in the excitement and tensions of the occasion, one of them will use his weapon in a way which will cause death or serious injury. If such injury was not intended by the others they must be acquitted of murder; but having started out on an enterprise which envisages some degree of violence, albeit nothing more than causing fright, they will be guilty of manslaughter."

In *Hui Chi-ming* v. *R.*,[43] the Privy Council implicitly approved a summing-up which adopted the same formulations as in *Reid*. If the act causing death was within the scope of the joint venture, a given defendant can be guilty of no more than manslaughter because he did not intend that serious harm should result from the act. These citations are all strongly confirmatory of the existence in criminal law of the agency principle making one defendant responsible for the act of another. The only criticism that can be made of some of these statements of the law is that they fail to make reference to the possibility that a conviction of D for the more serious crime committed by A may on occasions be capable of being upheld on the fictional basis derived from the accessory principle.

Sir John Smith has been consistent in his disapproval of this line of authority and any recognition of the agency principle: he rejects the authority of *Smith (W.)*, *Betty, Reid* and *Stewart and Schofield*. He contends that all such cases must be decided by recourse to the accessory principle alone and that the phrase common or joint enterprise is no more than a reflection of this: it has no separate existence. The Law Commission Consultation Paper does treat joint enterprise as a separate basis of criminal responsibility not dependent on aiding and abetting. In the course of the Paper the Commission refer to and cite among other cases *Cogan* and *Howe*. They suggest that the law of aiding and abetting should be reformed to remove the anomalies: they do not contemplate altering the law of joint enterprise. This has led Sir John Smith to say in his article[44] that he found the Paper "frankly baffling" and the suggestion that the doctrine of joint enterprise was something different from the law of aiding and abetting was a "notion which was news to me".

The views of Sir John Smith on such a subject, particularly when expressed so emphatically, must be carefully taken into account. However it is fair to examine upon what they are based. The article makes it clear that they are based upon the procedural history of the criminal law and a concept, confessedly of his own formulation, of "parasitic accessory liability". The artificiality that this

---

[41] (1963) 48 Cr.App.R. 6, 9.
[42] (1975) 62 Cr.App.R. 109, 112.
[43] [1992] A.C. 34, 46.
[44] 113 L.Q.R., 453, 461–462.

involves is self evident. It fails to reflect the authorities to which I have referred. No reasoned objection is raised to the agency principle. Indeed, the article cites authorities which affirm the criminal responsibility of one joint adventurer for the *act* of another.[45] He glosses the authorities he cites to support the proposition that the "secondary" party must foresee not only the act of the "principal" but also his state of mind at the critical time. The authorities do not justify the gloss which he places upon them although it is essential that he do so to support the full extent of his thesis. The authorities which recognise that there may be different criminal liabilities for the same act arising from the different states of mind of the particular joint adventurers are inconsistent with the gloss and are not addressed.

The article seeks to support the views expressed by discussing situations which would arise from the acceptance of the Law Commission's proposals to turn aiding and abetting into an inchoate offence:

> "D, the dominating leader of a gang, sends out his minion P to explode a bomb without warning in a shopping centre. The bomb kills twenty people. P is liable to conviction on twenty counts of murder. D, the "mastermind", is liable for the single offence of encouraging murder."[46]

> "D sends out P to cause grievous bodily harm to V, say to knee-cap him. P does exactly as instructed. V dies of the injury. P is guilty of murder and liable to a mandatory sentence of life imprisonment. Under the proposed law, D would be guilty only of assisting or encouraging an offence of causing grievous bodily harm with intent contrary to s.18 of the 1861 Act."[47]

These passages disclose a fundamental failure to recognise the existence of the principle of agency as part of the criminal law and are contrary to the decided cases. They illustrate again the anomalous consequences which can flow from analysing all cases of joint enterprise exclusively in terms of the accessory principle.

Sir John's article also cites[48] *Chan Wing-Siu* as an example of the application of the law of aiding and abetting as an essential mechanism for the conviction of joint adventurers of murder when one of them, it is not known which, kill in the course of that joint venture. This disregards the fact that Sir Robin Cooke based his decision not on aiding and abetting but on "the wider principle" which makes use of agency concepts[49] and the fact that the decided cases on the agency principle and the law of joint enterprise demonstrate that the conviction of all three adventurers for murder in such situations is possible.

One can also detect a belief that to make one person criminally liable for the physical act of another offends common sense and that the agency principle

---

[45] E.g., *Johns* v. *R.* (1980) 143 C.L.R. 108, *per* Street, C.J.
[46] 113 L.Q.R. 460.
[47] *Ibid.*
[48] *Ibid.*, 460–461.
[49] [1985] A.C. 168, 175.

involves artificiality.[50] Even if this were so, it would be as nothing compared with the anomalies and artificialities of the accessory principle as it is used in the criminal law. But the agency principle in truth involves no artificiality. Agency is a commonplace relationship within the everyday experience of the ordinary juryman. It is to be found in every other branch of the law. What would be objectionable and anomalous is if the criminal law were to fail to recognise the relationship and give effect to the responsibilities to which it gives rise.[51]

Sir John's article was published at a time between the decisions of the Court of Appeal and the House of Lords in *Powell and English*.[52] The leading speech in the House of Lords was that of Lord Hutton. The certified question was expressed in terms which raised only an aspect of the accessory principle and assumed that the accessory foresaw that the primary party might kill "with intent to do so". The question asked was: "must the secondary party have had that intention himself?" As I have pointed out earlier in this essay, the assumption is realistic and suffices for the majority of cases. But it does not address the question upon which I have been focusing. The debate therefore was concerned with the contrast between a reckless state of mind and a specific intention. The speeches were directed to this question and the application of the foresight test in relation to accessories. As I have observed, this is not one of aspects where there is an important practical difference between the agency and accessory principles; the foresight of the act will normally include the foresight of the possible consequences and that the act may be deliberate. Counsel's arguments as reported did refer to the anomalies which arise from the criminal law concerning accessories but it would not have advanced the appellants' cases to have argued for the existence and application of the agency principle. It is therefore understandable that the opportunity was not taken to consider the agency principle.[53]

However, two comments can be made upon the speeches. The first is that there is a marked contrast between that of Lord Steyn and those of the other members of the House. Lord Steyn clearly endorses Sir John Smith's analysis of that branch of the criminal law. He bases his speech upon and adopts the article and other published writings of Sir John Smith to the same effect. He formulates foresight in terms which embrace foresight of both the act and the state of mind

---

[50] The decision in *Cogan* v. *Leak* has been objected to on this ground. But the objection is based upon the view that rape ought to be treated as a personal crime incapable of being committed by anyone other than the man who penetrates the woman This is not an objection to the agency principle as such and, indeed, is equally a criticism which can be made of the application of the accessory principle to rape. The criticism is irrelevant to the validity of the principle of agency as is illustrated by *Howe*.

[51] The agency principle has been recognised and is used in relation to statutory offences giving rise to criminal sanctions.

[52] [1999] A.C. 1.

[53] It is tempting to speculate upon what might have been said in the full speech prepared by Lord Mustill had he delivered it.

of the "principal". He nevertheless expressed his full agreement with the speech of Lord Hutton, which is based upon foresight of the act. This is an important distinction which affects both the accessory principle and the agency principle. To require D to have specifically foreseen the actual state of mind of A at the time A committed the relevant act would be contrary to a number of earlier decisions of unquestioned authority. The element of uncertainty already existed because the view expressed by Lord Steyn was already to be found in the published writings of Sir John Smith. The speech of Lord Hutton, save for two passages[54] where he is clearly using the terminology of the certified question, proceeds on a basis which, in accordance with the authorities which he cites, concentrates upon the act of A not his state of mind. This is clear from his discussion of the "knee-capping" cases from Northern Ireland[55] and from his citation[56] of *R. v. Smith (W)*,[57] a case which formulates the relevant test in terms of the act. Whilst *Powell* itself may not have set this point to rest, two subsequent decisions of the Court of Appeal, *R. v. Uddin*[58] and *R. v. Nelson*[59] have done so, expressly endorsing the view that it is the act rather than the state of mind of the actual killer which has to be foreseen.[60]

The second comment that I would make is that the speeches recognise some of the anomalies to which the existing law of accessory liability give rise but they do not provide any answer to them beyond expediency.[61] Lord Mustill was more troubled. Having referred to *Anderson and Morris*[62] and the requirement that the act of A must have been within the scope of the joint venture as contemplated by D, he continued:[63]

> "Intellectually there are problems with the concept of joint venture, but they do not detract from its general practical worth, which has proved itself over many years. In one particular situation there is, however, a problem which this time-honoured solution cannot solve. Namely, where [D] foresees that [A] may go too far; sincerely wishes that he will not, and makes this plain to [A]; and yet goes ahead, either because he hopes for the best, or because [A] is an overbearing character, or for some other reason. Many would say, and I agree, that the conduct is culpable, although usually at

---

[54] *Ibid.*, 18B and 27E.

[55] *Ibid.*, 28–30.

[56] *Ibid.*, 18.

[57] [1963] 1 W.L.R. 1200.

[58] [1999] Q.B. 431.

[59] 26th February 1999, unreported; pet. diss. (H.L.). The certified question in the case was "whether it is sufficient to found a conviction for murder, where the primary party cannot be identified, for a secondary party to have foreseen that a lethal weapon would be used by anyone of a group or whether there must be foresight by the secondary party of the primary party's intent."

[60] But see also *Charles* v. *The State* [2000] 1 W.L.R. 384 (Trinidad and Tobago P.C.), 394 to the opposite effect.

[61] See the earlier reference to Lord Hutton in [1999] A.C. 1, 25.

[62] [1999] A.C. 2 Q.B. 110.

[63] [1999] A.C. 1, 11.

a lower level than the culpability of the principal who actually does the deed. Yet, try as I may, I cannot accommodate this culpability within a concept of joint enterprise. How can a jury be directed at the same time that [D] is guilty only if he was a party to an express or tacit agreement to do the act in question, and that he is guilty if he not only disagreed with it, but made his disagreement perfectly clear to [A]? Are not the two assertions incompatible?"

Lord Mustill then went on to consider and adopt the approach of Sir Robin Cooke in *Chan Wing-Siu*. As Sir Robin implicitly recognises, there comes a time when D, having appreciated the character of the venture in which he is about to take part and what conduct of the other participants may be involved, has to decide whether himself to participate in the venture. If he does decide to participate, he becomes responsible for the acts of the others done as part of that venture. There is nothing objectionable or fictitious about this conclusion. The problem of duress in this connection was the subject of *R. v. Howe*, as discussed above. But *Howe* also provides the answer to Lord Mustill's other difficulties. Once the agency principle is recognised, the concept of partnership provides a coherent and intellectually satisfactory analysis of the law of joint venture. Furthermore, it provides a route whereby the conviction of D can correspond to his actual guilt. If he truly was not a party to A's state of mind, he will only be convicted of the crime which corresponds to his own state of mind. On Lord Mustill's example, it might be possible for D to be convicted of manslaughter rather than murder, as *Howe* and other authorities show. However, if D joined in a joint venture contemplating killing or the infliction of serious injury, it will be difficult for D to dispute that he had the *mens rea* for murder.[64] The intellectually satisfying, and correct, analysis of the law of joint enterprise for which Lord Mustill was searching was to hand.

But, as the Law Commission has pointed out, this does not remove the anomalies of the present state of the English criminal law of accessory liability and the fiction upon which it is based. The injustices which Lord Mustill and others such as Professor Spencer have observed will remain so long as the procedural law of complicity enables defendants to be indiscriminately convicted of crimes which they have not committed and of which they are not in truth guilty. The procedural history of the criminal law, no matter how firmly entrenched in peoples' minds, should not be treated as a justification for its perpetuation.

Further, it is time that the existence of the principle of agency was properly recognised in the textbooks and other writings on the criminal law as it is in the key authorities. The law of agency is part of the criminal law. There are problems of ascertaining the extent of the authorisation conferred in the criminal law just as in other branches of the law: actual or implied, express or

---

[64] *R. v. Reid* (1975) 62 Cr.App.R. 109.

implicit. The criminal law has[65] and can find answers to the questions raised in the same way as other branches of the law. The principle of agency is not confined to the case of the "innocent agent" nor is it justifiable that it should be so confined.[66] The concept of agency, not complicity, is the true basis of the doctrine of joint enterprise and when used it provides the satisfactory analysis and just results. The continuing denial of its existence is doing no service to the criminal law.

---

[65] E.g., *R.* v. *Anderson and Morris* [1966] 2 Q.B. 110. See also the treatment of the agency principle and delegation in relation to statutory offences. An interesting example of the partial adoption of the distinctions made in this essay can be found in the Homicide Act 1957, section 2 (diminished responsibility).

[66] *R.* v. *Howe* [1987] A.C. 417.

Chapter 4

Power and Authority in the Law of Agency

Hugo Tiberg

There is nothing more central in the law of agency than the rules relating to the agent's powers to bind his principal, and one might expect that this would be an area in which the legal systems of the world would long since have reached a common accord. Yet we find that the attitudes are sharply distinguished between an Anglo-Saxon attitude—which for the purpose of this very general exposition will be referred to as English except as otherwise stated—and one which with considerable simplification I shall call Continental,[1] and we note that the differences are such as hitherto to have defied any attempts to be overbridged by an accepted international Convention.

In a volume in honour of Francis Reynolds it seems appropriate to try to bring some clarity into the differences. I venture to do this by exposing mainly the codified Nordic law of agency as, perhaps, one particularly clear-cut exponent of the Continental principles and to confront it with the common law system of England as it can be understood from Francis Reynolds's own work.[2]

> "What an Attorney does and concludes according to Power of Attorney, that shall be equally valid as if his Principal did or concluded it himself. If the Attorney goes further than has been entrusted to him, then he shall himself rectify all damage—and the Principal shall be exempt."

Through this provision in the Swedish Code of 1734,[3] the legislator made it

---

[1] I have in mind primarily the German, Swiss and Nordic legal systems, where the distinctions to the Anglo-American approach are much pronounced, while the *"mandat"* in French law bears more affinity to the English system. No attempt will be made to describe the French law of agency, although occasional references will be made in the footnotes to the presentation in Malaurie & Aynés, *Les Contrats Commerciaux*, 11 edn. (Paris, 1997) (hereinafter *"Malaurie & Aynés"*).

[2] I shall use throughout that broad presentation appearing in *Bowstead and Reynolds' Law of Agency*, to which I shall refer in its 16th edn. (London, 1996) (hereinafter *"Bowstead & Reynolds"*).

[3] Swedish Code of 1734, Book on Commerce, Chap. 18 on Delegates and Attorneys, section 2 (author's translation).

clear that a principal was bound by acts undertaken through an agent only to the extent that the agent was in fact authorised to act for him. The "Power of Attorney" mentioned in the section was an expression of this authorisation and required neither a document to be shown to the person with whom the agent would contract nor indeed any writing at all.[4] Consequently, the "power" in this sense was needed also when the agent was to appear in his own name and thus the principal would be undisclosed.[5]

Clearly the Code presupposed that the principal's "entrusting" a particular task to the agent gave the latter power to act and bind the principal irrespective of what was clarified to the third party, while on the other hand the agent's power ended with the "entrusting", that is with what the agent had been given the right to contract. The assumption, in other words, was that the power and the mandate would match ("mandate powers").

Thus, if the agent exceeded his mandate powers, the principal was not bound: he was to be "exempt"[6] as the Code had it. Instead the agent was the one to be liable to the third party and to "rectify all damage". This applied whether the agent had been acting in his own name or in that of the principal.

This was the general view of agency in Europe until the middle of the nineteenth century. Through Laband's[7] and Lenel's[8] studies the agent's or other middleman's power was divorced from his mandate, so that the two became separate institutions. The new ideas were introduced into the Swiss Civil Code of 1881 and the German Civil Code of 1896, and the same principles were developed in the Nordic countries by Trygger, Lassen and Stang and eventually found their way into the Agency chapter of the Contract Act 1915, which is still in effect in all the Nordic countries.

The basic idea in all these systems is that the capacity of the agent to bind his principal (Sw. "*fullmakt*", Germ. "*Vollmacht*", lit. "full power") derives independently of authorisation from a message to the contracting third party. This may be conceived in different ways, but the most straightforward explanation, which also explains the ease with which the rules fit into the framework of contract law, is to see the power as a superstructure to the general law of contract, where the agent's message to the third party is an outflow of the principal's own contractual dealings. In other words: instead of dealing directly with the third party, the principal clarifies to the latter that it is from the agent's mouth that the contractually binding expressions will issue. This explanation is

---

[4] Hasselrot, *Om sysslomän* (Stockholm, 1903), 1273 with further references.

[5] *Ibid.*, 1271–1272.

[6] The delightful old Swedish term "*saklös*" (literally "matterless") suggests that no case or action may be raised against him.

[7] Laband, *Die Stellvertretung bei dem Absluß von Rechtsgeschäften nach dem allg. deutsch. Handelsgesetzbuch, Zeitschrift für Handelsrecht* vol. 10 (1866), 183 ff.

[8] Lenel, "Stellvertretung and Vollmacht" (1866) 10 *Ihering Jahrbücher*, 183 ff.

appropriate both to the *written power of attorney*,[9] which is invoked in relation to the third party,[10] and to other recognised situations where a token of some kind is given or conceived to be given by the principal to the third party that the agent is empowered to speak or act for him.

In the Nordic Contract Act recognised such transfers of power other than the written power of attorney include the *powers of positon*,[11] which is the deliberate placing of a person in a position which by custom or by law endows the possessor with particular functions, such as a shop attendant or a shipmaster, the *third party notice authorisation*,[12] where an express message to the third party gives a tangible ground for the power, and the practically rare *public notice authorisation*,[13] where a public announcement is stated to put third parties in general upon notice of the agent's powers. Case law has further developed the recognition of *tolerance powers* consisting of a third party reliance engendered by the principal's repeated fulfilment of an agent's contracts, and there also exist various provisions and practices which endow middlemen of several kinds with *special powers*, for example, because they have been entrusted with the principal's goods or with his contract forms or, in shipping, bill of lading forms. While in many situations the principal's conferring of authority upon an agent may seem somewhat esoteric and is not always fully apparent to the principal himself, the situations described are largely type situations where the trade's need to rely upon the agent's capacity has been taken to outweigh the occasional unwitting principal's interest in remaining unbound because he never really intended to confer an agency power or one of the asserted scope.

In all these situations, where the principal is taken to have given a token to the third party that "this is the person who shall speak for me", the "*Vollmacht*" is said to be *independent* in the sense that it comes from the principal independently of the mission that has been entrusted to the agent. The "*Vollmacht*" is manifested in the token, and by that token the principal is bound, even if he did not in the individual case intend to pass such powers or if, while he did authorise the agent to contract, he also gave him special limitations such as a price limit for the purchase of particular goods. The power of the agent finds an end only where the trust of the third party becomes objectively unjustified so that there is no good faith on his part worth defending, such as the purchase for a named principal of a junk car at a preposterous price; we say that, where a token

---

[9] Nordic Contract Act 2:13 and 2:16. The writing requires no particular form.

[10] Actual exhibition of the document is not taken to be indispensable, provided it is available, Tiberg and Dotevall, *Mellanmansrätt*, 9th edn. (Stockholm, 1997) (hereinafter "*Mellanmansrätt*"), 46–47.

[11] "*Ställningsfullmakt*", Nordic Contract Act 2:10 second paragraph. The term "powers of position" has been introduced by Professor Kurt Grönfors.

[12] Nordic Contract Act 2:13.

[13] Nordic Contract Act 2:14.

of authority is given, the scope of that authority is limited by the third party's good faith.

There remains, however, the particular type of the "*mandate agency*" (or "uncertified agency")[14] where a message or token from the principal is lacking so that the third party relies only on the assurance of the agent himself. This situation has sometimes been pressed into the scenario of a message to the third party, the explanation being that, by purporting to a contract for a principal as far as actually empowered, the middleman passes a correct message to that effect to the third party. More realistically, I submit, the power granted the middleman in this situation is a practical application of the principle of the "mandate powers" of the old law, that is, a power derived from actual authorisation, acceptable to the principal because it is limited to what he had actually permitted and acceptable to the third party because he, in turn, can look to the agent as guarantor for performance of the contract or compensation if no contract arises.[15] The correctness of this approach is borne out by the rules of *ratification* of the agent's contact, where ratification to the agent is considered sufficient to restore the agent's power of binding the principal to the limit of his internal authorisation.

Whether the middleman is acting on the strength of a message given to the third party or on the agent's own assurance of authority, the tie to the general law of contracts renders it essential that a bond to the third party should arise only where the middleman purported to act on behalf of a principal—whether named or unnamed in the contract[16]—and such a principal existed at the time of contracting.[17] Contracts made by an agent in his own name—in the Nordic countries and Germany called commission contracts[18]—bind only the agent himself, as will be explained later.[19]

The development on the Continent including the Nordic countries, from an earlier principle based on the mandate power to a modern one based on a

---

[14] "*Uppdragsfullmakt*". Nordic Contracts Act 2:18. "Uncertified agency" is the term introduced by the present author in Swedish Law (Stockholm, 1994); but "mandate agency" translates the Swedish and seems more clarifying for purposes of this presentation.

[15] So it surely appears to most men of the trade. But strictly the agent does not usually guarantee fulfilment; for if the principal should be insolvent or unable to fulfil, the agent is not liable. See further *Mellanmansrätt*, 74–75.

[16] A typical example might be a chartering agent signing a charterparty "as agent only".

[17] An agent contracting for an unnamed principal cannot be suffered subsequently to invent a purported principal and then perhaps hide behind that person's insolvency or inability to perform the contract: *Mellanmansrätt*, 90 with the Supreme Court case N.J.A. 1941 A 61.

[18] Not to be confused with "commissionaire" under French law, see *infra*, fn.24.

[19] See *infra*, pp. 66–67.

message to the third party, did not occur in the common law systems England and the U.S.A., nor did it occur in France.[20] The principles of agency are still based on the "authority" given by the principal to the agent through a message given to the latter. A contract within the agent's authority binds the principal, while one outside the authority leaves the principal unbound, generally speaking whether the contract was made in the name of the principal or that of the agent himself. With the necessity, for the functioning of trade and business, of supplementing these principles by others permitting third parties to rely upon representations of persons acting as agents though they might lack actual authority, the structure of the common law has however been left in a state of confusion, which even the clarity of a Reynolds is at pains to unravel with a transparency wholly apparent to an outsider—if even to an insider.

It appears that the entrusting of authority to the agent which is the core of authority in English law is regarded in Continental and Nordic law as mainly a right for the agent, and thus a defence to any claim by the principal for damages for excess of authority. In addition, however, entrusting authority to the agent in Continental law does at least confer the power actually entrusted, and this is the gist of that "mandate agency" which as an exceptional form of authority enables the agent lacking a third party "*Vollmacht*" to bind the principal by his contracts. Thus, the dependent or "mandate" power which is the exception in Nordic and Continental law is "actual authority" and the rule in English law, while the independent powers that are the rule in Continental law are the exceptions ("apparent authority") in England.

It may however be noted that the "mandate agency" which is the conceptual exception in Continental law seems to be quite common in practice. Not only will agents often present themselves without further evidence as acting for this or the other principal, but they will even, especially if they are substantial middlemen in shipping, contract "as agent" without individualising their principal. The contracting third party then looks to the agent as guarantor of the performance promised through the agent.[21] Conversely, it is said in English law that "apparent authority is becoming the common form in practice and is resorted to increasingly".[22]

Against that background, it may be asked whether the opposite starting points of the two systems must necessarily cause the incompatibility which we sense

---

[20] The French law has many affinities to English law. There also, the agent's power is based on his actual authorisation (*Malaurie & Aynés*, No. 571, pp. 329–330), and there also, it has been felt necessary to supplement this power by apparent authority ("*mandat apparant*", *Malaurie & Aynés*, Nos. 576–583).

[21] Improperly so, as pointed out *supra*, in fn. 15, because the agent—unless he contracts "del credere"—guarantees only his authority and not the solvency of the purported principal: *Mellanmansrätt*, 78.

[22] *Bowstead & Reynolds*, 105 and *passim*.

in their refusal to range themselves into a common international system and in the very divergent presentations that we meet in legal literature. Indeed some important incompatibilities seem hard to ignore.

First of all, since as a point of departure in English law "authority" is based on representations to the agent and not on what the third party may have learned or gathered, there is no reason to distinguish from ordinary agency those contracts which the middleman has made for the principal in is own name. The sharp cleavage of the Continental systems between dealings in another's name ("*Vollmacht*") and dealings in one's own name (commission, German and Nordic "*Kommission*")[23] does not exist in England. An English "agent" may appear as such, explaining that he represents some particular principal, in which case the latter is described as "disclosed". He may also clarify that he represents someone without disclosing the name or identity of that person, in which case the principal is described as "unnamed" or "semi-disclosed".[24] But, even if our middleman acts or contracts wholly in his own name—as a "commissioner" in the Continental sense—he remains the same kind of agent under English law, though his principal is "undisclosed". In all these cases the principal is bound by the agent's contract provided the agent had "authority", though in somewhat different manners, as will be seen later.

Secondly, through the "internal" vantage point, the scope of "authority" loses clarity compared to the Continental "*Vollmacht*". Indeed the very use of the term "authority" in legal parlance seems to deplete the word of its usual pregnancy—for do we not think of the authority with which a person speaks as being a power or strength flowing from his position or his personal posture supported by that position?[25]—while under the law it is limited to an inner relation to a principal. If nothing is apparent to the third party of the basis of the agent's authority, the width of that notion has shrunk into a mere instrument of registration that the agent may in fact possess the requisite power. To describe an ability to bind we need other and more general notions such as power or capacity.

Legally, also, there lies a limitation in the English approach that "authority" must issue from the internal relationship. The power which in the Continental systems flows from the message to the third party can draw upon the principles of contract law, while that which under English law may flow from the mandate

---

[23] The term should be distinguished from the corresponding "*commission*" in French, see following footnote.

[24] In French law, a middleman presenting himself in this manner is regarded as a "*commissionaire*", while one appearing in his own name does not seem to qualify as an agent at all; see *Malaurie & Aynés*, No. 538, pp. 297–298.

[25] "Authority", says the *Oxford Dictionary*, is basically the power or right to enforce obedience.

needs its own definition. In Continental law the power follows from contractual rules as soon as the principal's third party message gives the agent the status to speak with the principal's mouth; in English law the direct effect of authorisation requires its own definition, while "apparent authority" becomes a discretionary extension necessitated by considerations of trade and commerce.[26] This has made for a compound system, where over-lapping legal constructions are often used to justify similar results.

"Implied" authority generally refers to what may be implied between a principal and his agent, and this may concern both the existence of the agency itself[27] and the scope of authority of an established agent;[28] a large part of the latter is "incidental authority", suggesting the kind of authority that necessarily or naturally follows from a particular type of agency. But authority may also arise from the principal's assurance to a third party and is then apparent authority—usually explained as a result of estoppel—and there can be no reason why such assurance should not arise by implication rather than express words, so that, notionally, implied authority might also refer to the external relationship. Authority may also arise from a usual state of things, and such "usual authority" may be classified as actual implied authority, apparent authority based on estoppel or otherwise, and possibly also as an indepedent form of authority recognised in the American Restatement of Agency as "inherent agency power" but considered to be doubtful in England.[29] In addition there is case law about various type situations such as receipt of payment, and managerial and professional agents, where particular rules can be distinguished.

These somewhat incongruous categories have developed in case law and lack the systematical simplicity of the independent "powers" of the Nordic and Continental systems. While the latter may be divided into a few straightforward categories, mainly third party notification, powers of position and tolerance powers, the English law uses a comprehensive battery of alternative and partly overlapping methods, where similar results may be reached by different avenues. The common purpose of satisfying a commercial need has undoubt-

---

[26] "Power" does not, like "authority" or "*Vollmacht*" in Continental law, suggest any other than a registered power; Reuschlein & Gregory, *Handbook on the Law of Agency & Partnership* (St. Paul, Minn, 1979) (hereinafter "*Reuschlein*"), 32: "The agent bound the principal; therefore he had the power to bind him. When we speak of authority, we assume power and we are addressing ourselves to the oughtness and lawfulness of the power."

[27] *Bowstead & Reynolds* article 3, 28.

[28] *Ibid.*, article 27, 117.

[29] *Ibid.*, 107–109.

edly allowed the creation of resembling effects in the different systems,[30] but the means of reaching these results are much more cumbersome for the common law lawyer. One reason for the maze of theory surrounding the practical categories needed for actual business may lie in the unsystematical development of any case law system compared with one where distinctive types of agency can be consciously chiselled out by a legislator. But in the present area particularly, the absence of a direct tie to the ordinary contract law and consequent need to resort to other and varying legal principles has probably complicated the issue. But there are other difficulties.

The division between two kinds of bases of authority—one real and one seeming—appears to invite confusion even on the central question of the effect of a written "power of attorney". Such a document, the delivery of which is described as the archetype method of conferring actual authority, must according to statute be executed under seal in order to empower the agent to certain acts.[31] If the authority conferred by the "power" is actual authority, it might be expected that the function of the document would not be tied to its exhibition to the third party contractor but to the internal "authorisation" of the agent; so that the faith evoked in the third party would be immaterial and might be established by other tokens (e.g. estoppel) even for a "power" not created by deed. However, it seems obvious that the purpose of a document of this kind must be to be shown to the third party, and there is said to be a duty for the third party of examining the power of attorney as a prerequisite for relying on it.[32]

Similarly, ratifications ought to be classified according to their addressee. Logically, a ratification to the agent should restore his actual authority, while a ratification to the third party might amount to a confirmation of the contract but should otherwise be a case of apparent authority. However, ratification of an *ultra vires* contract is said to be directed to the third party contractor.[33]

The actual authority arising under English law from the principal's entrusting a task to the agent is naturally wed to the notion of identity between agent and principal: "*qui facit per alium, facit per se*". Consequently the agent's authority is limited by the principal's power. This has the consequence, *inter alia*, that, if

---

[30] "Resembling effects" may be exemplified by Lord Keith of Kinkel's speech in *Armagas Ltd.* v. *Mundogas S.A.* (*The Ocean Frost*) [1986] A.C. 717; [1986] 2 Lloyd's Rep. 110, where (at 777 and 112 respectively) the recognition of ostensible general authority through principal's honouring of transactions corresponds to "tolerance powers" and (at 778 and 113) the recognition (in *Berryere* v. *Fireman's Fund Insurance Co.* (1965) 51 D.L.R. 2d 603) of an implied authority arising from the principal's having supplied the agent with cover note forms corresponds to the special powers arising in Continental law from such acts.

[31] Such a power of attorney is needed particularly for acts which themselves need to be executed by deed, for example the conveyance of real property. See further *Bowstead & Reynolds*, 111.

[32] *Ibid.*, 305.

[33] *Ibid.*, article 13ff. with comments.

the principal dies or becomes incapacitated, the agent's power ceases immediately. On the Continent, on the other hand, there is no principle necessarily limiting the effect of the passing of authority, which instead is a matter of expedience. In some systems, such as the Nordic one, the grant of power as a rule survives the principal's death. Recently, English law has also reacted to the need for an enduring authority, and legislation has been passed permitting such extension, but only by means of power of attorney.[34]

The policy reasons for apparent authority or other authority based on the third party's reliance come to an end where the agent no longer invokes the authority of a principal but acts in his own name, and to a lesser extent where he invokes but does not name a particular principal whom he pretends to represent. Where the principal is "undisclosed" and in some degree where he is "unnamed", there is no longer any third party reliance on the existence of a principal to protect. Yet English law still holds the principal bound by the agent's contracts on the same basis of actual authority as in disclosure situations.

Here again the English rule is the Continental and Nordic exception; for the latter systems do give the agent a power to bind the undisclosed principal in special situations. This may be because undisclosed principals are viewed with disfavour, at least in particular situations in which they can easily abuse their position to the detriment of trusting third parties. Or more generally, it is felt that, the principal being the real transactor who gets the substantial profit from the contract, he should not escape responsibility for the fulfilment of that which earns him that profit.

The English law rules that the principal is bound by the agent's contract in his own name is an anomaly from a general contractual point of view and contrary to the requirement of privity of contract.[35] But the rule is firmly established and an integral part of both the English and the American world of agency. The rule is considered to fulfil a practical purpose, and justice is thought to require that the person who stands behind the contract should also be responsible for its fulfilment.

The principal's boundness under either the English rule or the Nordic/ Continental exception is, however, not unqualified. The English law satisfies both the behind-the-contract reasoning and the third party's need for protection of appearances by allowing the third party to raise alternative claims—against the agent because of reliance and against the principal because of the actual authority which he has granted the agent.

The difference of this approach to the Continental one is felt already where the principal is unnamed and thus unidentifiable to the third party. In this

---

[34] Enduring Powers of Attorney Act 1985.
[35] This is well recognised both in English and American law: see *Bowstead & Reynolds*, 313; *Reuschlein*, 158–159.

situation it might be said that, while the third party did or could take the existence of the principal into account, he never relied on this unknown person's solvency. Still, the Nordic and Continental law classifies this as a case of "*Vollmacht*", where the unknown principal becomes responsible for the fulfilment while the agent escapes such responsibility and, always provided there was a principal in existence at the time of contracting,[36] can excuse himself by the insolvency of that person. English law reaches the same result not because a principal was indicated to the third party but because the principal had given actual authority to be bound, and there is not in the absence of special customs a general possibility of claiming against the agent instead.[37] American law on the other hand allows a claim against the agent, who is presumed to be responsible as if he were a principal in certain situations such as the intended principal's bankruptcy.[38]

The differences really come out starkly where the principal is not only unnamed, but undisclosed. The Anglo-Saxon starting-point that the agent's power flows out of the principal's authorisation still makes it possible to bind the principal alternatively with the agent, as we have seen.[39] This differs from the Nordic solution in the exceptional situations where the principal can be held, in that the principal's and agent's liability is then joint and several rather than alternative.

From a Nordic standpoint, the third party's right under English law to sue or claim from the principal appears like an unearned windfall. Having once contracted with a party appearing in his own name and having relied on that person and his solvency, the third party should not need another debtor in addition. Such is the theory both in Scandinavian and German law;[40] and in Sweden, at least, this applies also in situations where an agent is well known to represent others but appears as a matter of form in his own name ("typified commission").[41] The principal, on the other hand, is not a stranger to the agent's contract, and in Nordic law he is considered to acquire contractual rights directly from the third party;[42] the German law is the same, except that it requires the agent's "cession" (*Abtretung*) of the acquired rights.[43]

The Continental, and particularly the Nordic, solution may be described as a superstructure on the principles of disclosed agency. The principal wants to act

[36] On this requirement, see the Swedish decision N.J.A. 1941 A 61.
[37] *Bowstead & Reynolds*, 451, citing *The Santa Carina* [1977] 1 Lloyd's Rep. 478.
[38] *Reuschlein*, § 23; *Restatement of Agency*, § 321.
[39] While the principal's and agent's liability is alternative, they may possibly be sued simultaneously; *Bowstead & Reynolds*, 349 ff; *Reuschlein*, 159.
[40] Commission Agency Act, section 57; German Commercial Code, section 392.
[41] Swedish Supreme Court N.J.A. 1975, 152; *Mellanmansrätt*, 88–89.
[42] Nordic Commission Agency Act, section 57; *Mellanmansrätt*, 103. In this connection, the term "commission" is proper in French law also, but the agent becomes personally responsible for fulfilment: see *Malaurie & Aynés*, No. 538.
[43] German Commercial Code sections 391 and 392.

through an agent and gives the latter the faculty of acquiring rights on his, the principal's, behalf. The agent acquires those rights directly for the principal, and with reservation for the agent's lien for commission and reimbursement claims, the principal takes over those rights and can assert them in various critical situations, including the agent's bankruptcy.[44] But binding the principal directly is out of the agent's power, because that would give the third party the windfall of unforeseen rights and an unforeseen additional debtor.

The result in Nordic and German law is that the third party contracts a debt to the principal and a right against the agent. In Nordic law title (i.e. mainly creditor protection) to goods sold or bought by agency passes with the handing over to the buyer, i.e. from principal to third party and vice versa, directly and without ever lodging with the agent, who possesses the goods on the principal's behalf.[45]

This raises problems in the agent's bankruptcy. Suppose a purchase agent has bought goods on credit for his principal and goes bankrupt while the goods are in his possession. Under the principle of direct passage of title, the principal can separate the goods from the bankruptcy estate, against covering the agent's counterclaims, which include the debt of the unpaid purchase money undertaken by the agent through the purchase. While the estate may thus claim or deduct cover for the debt it has contracted for the principal, the law's rejection of a direct claim reduces the corresponding debt to the third party to a dividend in the bankruptcy, so that the estate is enriched at the third party's expense. This is criticised by some, who would permit a direct claim in some of these situations,[46] but it is consistent with the agent's appearance as ostensible principal upon whose person and solvency the third party relied on contracting.[47]

In some situations it may, however, appear unjust that the principal, who reaps the fruits of the contract, should be allowed to escape obligations to the third party. Such considerations have been provided for, particularly where the middleman has been an undercapitalised daughter company inserted between the principal and the third party,[48] and when an agent has been a "man of straw" used in avoidance of mandatory legislation or otherwise for illegal or disloyal

[44] Further Commission Agency Act, section 57; *Mellanmansrätt*, 103.

[45] A proposal by the Commission Agency Committee in Sweden's Official Investigations (SOU) 1988:63 that the third party seller should retain his seller securities to individualised goods in the possession of a bankrupt purchase agent's possession did not result in any amendment of the law: see *ibid.*, 141–142.

[46] Hult, *Om Kommissionärsavtalet* I (Stockholm, 1936), 30 ff.

[47] For those who can read Swedish, reference is made to my presentation in *Mellanmansrätt*, 103–104.

[48] From case law, the Supreme Court of Sweden in N.J.A. 1975, 45, 63. For Swedish writings, reference is made particularly to Grönfors, *Ställningsfullmakt och bulvanskap* (Stockholm, 1961), 311–312; Håstad, *Studier i sakrätt* (Lund, 1980), 9 ff; and to the Committee Inquiry S.O.U. 1983:46 Bulvanlag, 33 and *passim*.

purposes.[49] In such situations case law has allowed the contractual liability to penetrate to the principal, although the agent has remained jointly and severally liable.[50]

The recognition of such right of "penetration" of a third party claim against the principal is not the effect of any power on the part of the agent to bind the principal but has been adopted in special situations to protect a third party who might otherwise suffer loss as a result of the construction of the rules. This is far removed from the English and American recognition of a general power to bind, which historically may have been an anomaly but which in today's law of agency is very much a consequence and an integral part of the "authority" which is regarded as the real and final basis for binding the principal. No special reasons need to be adduced to justify the third party's rights against the principal. The mere entrusting with authority suffices. Notably, also, as shown above, the liability of the principal and agent is alternative, while in the Nordic countries in the corresponding situation it is joint and several.

The fundamental differences thus existing between Anglo-Saxon and Continental law concerning the agent's power of binding his undisclosed principal have been sought to be bridged in the UNIDROIT Convention on Agency in the International Sale of Goods 1983. The Convention has met limited response and does not seem likely ever to come into force, but it was an interesting attempt to find a common platform between the approach based on the principal's authorisation of the agent and that based on third party reliance.

The Convention covers both the really undisclosed principal, whose existence the third party neither knew of or ought to have known of, and such "typified commission", where a commercial agent known to be such ostensibly acts in his own name.

The Convention was designed to satisfy Anglo-Saxon interests by permitting a direct third party claim against the principal in situations when the third party really needed it, i.e. where the agent did not or could not fulfil the contract, generally because of insolvency or bankruptcy, and also by limiting the principal's direct claims against the third party to the same kinds of situations.

In accordance with Anglo-Saxon law, also, the Convention eschews the Continental combination of placing the contractual duties on the agent while granting the rights to the principal; instead both the principal and the third party are given the election to skip the middleman. In the Convention, however, this right of election arises only where the middeman fails to fulfil his engagements, whether that depends on insolvency or some other reason. The election is exercised by notice to the counterparty, who thereafter is not permitted to raise a

---

[49] *Mellanmansrätt*, 107–109.
[50] *Ibid.*, 110 and the Supreme Court decision of N.J.A. 1932 A 392.

claim against the middleman. This technique avoids the complications in Continental law of the claims between the various parties not being mutual.

Through the Convention's solution the principal becomes guarantor for fulfilment of the contract even though the third party did not know of his engagement. But this guarantee gives no significant increase to the principal's exposure compared to Nordic law, where today he must be prepared to cover a bankrupt agent's credit debts to the third party. Where the Convention is significantly different from Nordic law is in moving the insolvency risk from the third party to the agent's general creditors and bankruptcy estate.

The Convention also defines the dividing line between disclosed and undisclosed situations in a manner which should be both generally clarifying and reasonably comprehensible from an Anglo-Saxon point of view. Under it, the principal is bound directly under disclosed agency ("*Vollmacht*") rules whenever in the eyes of the third party he has seemed or ought to have seemed to be a middleman, whereas his engagement is reduced to that of a guarantor in the above sense when he was totally undisclosed or could only be glimpsed behind a typified agent.

The rules do not permit the direct creation of contractual rights in favour of an undisclosed principal whom the contractor would not have accepted at the time of contracting.

The Convention has not adopted the Anglo-Saxon idea of an "authorisation" giving the agent the power of creating rights against a concealed principal. Mere "authority" in the English sense cannot give a third party an additional contractor beside the acting one. It is not a binding power sprung from the principal's authorisation but the parties' need for protection that justifies the Convention's direct claim between the ultimate parties to the contract. But the Continental method of subjecting a third party to direct claims from the contractor's unknown principal is equally rejected. Again it is not the agent's principal-created power that justifies the Convention's direct acquisition of rights but the third party's need of protection when the person with whom he contracted turns out to be an insolvent middleman.

So the Convention aims at realities and avoids trying to derive contracting power or authority from theoretical constructions. Whether its compromise is optimal or even suitable for the realities of present international commerce may be uncertain. The rejection of the Convention from both sides may be due to common resistance to novelty but may perhaps partly be explained by different commercial structures having developed on the basis of the two basically different legal systems. In any case it feels like a gain that the cards have been put on the table, and there will certainly have to be new attempts made along a similar pragmatic approach in our ever more integrated world of commerce.

Chapter 5

Pollution, Limitation and Carriage in
The Aegean Sea

Nicholas Gaskell

1 INTRODUCTION

The Aegean Sea was a Greek registered O.B.O. (57,801 g.r.t.) which went aground at La Coruña in Spain on 3rd December 1992, after a voyage from the U.K. with a cargo of 80,000 tonnes of crude oil. The casualty itself caused enormous pollution and gave rise to many compensation claims. The *Aegean Sea* casualty has raised important questions of maritime legal principle in different legal systems. One part of the litigation has now been decided in the English High Court: see *Aegean Sea Traders Corporation* v. *Repsol Petroleo S.A. and Another (The Aegean Sea)*.[1]

The Aegean Sea is a good example of a major casualty which has raised a host of interesting legal questions, often interlocking, which can be litigated owing to the large amounts at stake and the conclusions of which will be a source of reference. The judgment of Thomas, J. in the High Court deals with so many legal points that it could almost be an answer to an ambitious academic examination problem. Discussion of decisions in particular cases can sometimes consider only part of the larger legal picture. The aim of this essay is to consider those legal issues which have arisen in the High Court, but also those which arise in the wider context of such a casualty. Three main areas of law will be discussed, namely, the law relating to international maritime pollution compensation, international limitation of liability and the carriage of goods by sea.[2] The law of carriage of goods by sea is one of many where Francis Reynolds' knowledge and expertise have been highly influential and where this writer, at least, treads with some apprehension.

---

[1] [1998] 2 Lloyd's Rep. 39. It is understood that there will be no appeal.
[2] The casualty has no doubt given rise to many other legal issues, but these three illustrate quite well the broad range of maritime law issues and the many different concepts which maritime law brings to commercial law generally.

The English litigation concerning *The Aegean Sea* is essentially concerned with the contractual fallout of the casualty. There are salvage proceedings under the L.O.F. 1990 as well as cargo claims. But the recent High Court decision concerned claims by the shipowner[3] (Aegean Sea Traders Corporation) to recover the amounts for which pollution related claims have been brought against it, together with the value of the vessel, bunkers and freight (in total about U.S.$65 million). Those claims were made against the voyage charterer, R.O.I.L. (hereafter the charterer) and the intended receiver of the cargo (Repsol).

The claims against the charterer were made under the Asbatankvoy charter, on the basis (i) that the nomination of La Coruña was a breach of the express safe port warranty in the charter and, in the alternative, (ii) that the shipowner is entitled to an implied indemnity for complying with the charterer's voyage orders. These claims are the subject of a reference to arbitration. However, the threat of such claims prompted the charterer to seek to limit its liability in England. The limitation issues will be discussed in Part 3 below.

The claim against Repsol was made on the basis that Repsol became subject to liabilities under a bill of lading by virtue of the Carriage of Goods by Sea Act 1992, section 3, in that it allegedly became a "lawful holder" of the bill. As the bill did not itself contain any express provisions about the port of destination, the carrier had then to argue that there were implied terms in the bill that (i) Repsol had the right to nominate the port of discharge under the bill and (ii) that any nomination made would be of a safe port. In addition, the carrier claimed an implied indemnity (similar to that put forward in the case against the charterer) on the basis of compliance with Repsol's orders. An additional ground for the claim against Repsol was on the basis that it had assumed independent obligations under a letter of indemnity (L.O.I.) issued to the carrier to enable it to deliver cargo without production of the bill of lading. The carriage issues will be discussed in Part 4 below.

However, before considering the issues in the English High Court, there will be a discussion of the pollution claims which have prompted the attempt by the shipowner to pass on liabilities to the charterer and Repsol. Those claims are being litigated in Spain.

---

[3] The expression "shipowner" will be used in the context of the charterparty claim. Where that shipowner is claiming against the receiver under the bill, the expression "carrier" will be used.

2 THE POLLUTION LITIGATION

a. Background

The Aegean Sea pollution-related compensation claims amount to £92 million.[4] Those claims are governed by the International Convention on Civil Liability for Oil Pollution Damage ("C.L.C.") 1969 and International Convention on the Establishment of an International Fund for Compensation for Oil Pollution Damage ("the Fund Convention") 1971 and are subject to proceedings in the Spanish courts. Considerable controversy has already arisen at the international level about the handling of those claims, which will almost certainly be subject to a limit of liability under the 1971 Fund Convention of 60 million SDR.[5] A Spanish criminal court has held that both the master and pilot were criminally negligent and, in the same proceedings, has found them jointly liable for the civil consequences of the grounding. In addition, the shipowner, the Spanish state, the P. & I. Club and the International Oil Pollution Compensation Fund ("I.O.P.C.") Fund were also held directly liable.[6]

It appears that some aspects of the Spanish judgments are in conflict with the policy and provisions of the international Conventions (in particular the finding of separate liability of the master) and there have been considerable discussions at the I.O.P.C. Fund Executive Committee about how far the judgment is enforceable against the 1971 Fund, in so far as it appears to be contrary to the 1971 Convention. As the 1971 Fund Convention gives jurisdiction and competence to national courts, the I.O.P.C. Fund may not be able to resist a claim for execution, even if the judgment appears to have been decided contrary to the Convention. Nevertheless, the 1971 Fund Assembly has the final say about the level of payments where the claims exceed Fund limits, as it may have to pro rate claims for limitation purposes.

There is a clear tension here between private law mechanisms of compensation adopted in an international Convention, which has also set up a body, the Fund, which is accorded separate legal personality in international law under Article 2(2) of the 1971 Fund Convention. In retrospect, it might have been better to have established a separate court or tribunal (such as the Tribunal on the Law of the Sea, established by the U.N. Convention on the Law of the Sea 1982) with full competence, in place of national courts. In the climate of 1969 and 1971, after the *Torrey Canyon* grounding in 1967, this may not have been acceptable and recent attempts to reopen the issue have not been successful.

---

[4] See the Note by the Director of the 1971 I.O.P.C. Fund: 71/Fund/Exc.59/2, 23rd October 1998.

[5] In 2000 sterling values, this equates to about £50 million, but there are disputes about the correct method of transposing the limits into pesetas, with some claimants wanting a conversion to be made on the basis of gold francs.

[6] The decision has been upheld on appeal: see 71Fund/Exc.61/3, 16th April 1999.

b. Defences and compromises

The compensation regime of the C.L.C. and Fund Convention, taken together, is generally favourable to claimants, as it provides for strict liability for pollution damage and compulsory insurance with direct action against the insurer.[7] Claimants and their lawyers may not be familiar with its special provisions, however, and this has caused problems in other cases, especially in relation to time bars. There is generally a three year time bar from the date of the damage (with an upper limit of six years from the date of the incident causing the damage). This may be shorter than national time bars for tort or delictual claims. In the claims which have arisen out of the *Haven* casualty in Italy in 1981 a number of claimants issued proceedings against the *shipowner* under the C.L.C. within the appropriate time limit, but failed to appreciate that under Article 6(1) of the Fund Convention 1971 separate proceedings had to be brought against the *Fund* or that notification had to be given to it under Article 7(6) to enable it to intervene in the C.L.C. proceedings.[8] In that case the I.O.P.C. Fund Assembly took the view that the time bars should be operated strictly.[9] In this sense the Fund, which is financed through levying contributions on oil importers in State parties, is almost operating like an insurance company in resisting claims. Its position is different in that it is not protecting shareholders, but the oil importers in all the member states who would have to contribute. States such as Japan, which has been the largest contributor to the system (as it is the largest oil importer) have been particularly keen to ensure that claims fall strictly within the Convention.[10] Discussions at the I.O.P.C. Fund Executive Committee have been sensitive, because the overwhelming purpose of the Fund

---

[7] Over 100 claims have been made against the 1971 Fund since its inception and most have been settled.

[8] This is one consequence of the fact that the oil pollution liability regime is split between two Conventions, largely a historical accident. The Convention on Liability and Compensation for Damage in Connection with the Carriage of Hazardous and Noxious Substances by Sea 1996 (the HNS Convention) provides a single instrument for dealing with pollution from substances other than oil. Article 37 of the HNS Convention 1996 provides an almost identical formula to that of the C.L.C. and Fund Convention, but the provisions are all contained in one article. Although enacted in the Merchant Shipping and Maritime Security Act 1997, Sched. 3, this Convention is not yet in force. The I.O.P.C. Fund does now produce a very helpful *Claims Manual* which is made available to claimants and which does warn about time bars.

[9] See e.g. *I.O.P.C. Funds Annual Report 1998*, 43 *et seq.*

[10] Thus, the 1971 Fund Convention levy in 1997 was £64 million to cover claims arising. The sum was in the main contributed to by a relatively small number of states. Japanese importers contributed 22.83% of funds, Italy 11.96%, Republic of Korea 9.39%, Netherlands 8.54%, France 7.99% and the U.K. 6.2% (*I.O.P.C. Funds Annual Report* 1997). In 1998, the Japanese contribution dropped to 15% and Italy became the largest contributor with 22%. This was because Japan, with states such as the U.K., is now a major contributor to the successor Fund established by the 1992 Fund Convention (*I.O.P.C. Funds Annual Report* 1998).

system, set up by states, is to *pay* claims of pollution victims. States which vote on the admissibility of claims in the Executive Committee are always conscious that their citizens may soon be faced with a major casualty. So the natural desire to be cautious in settling claims is tempered by the knowledge that an insistence on a restrictive interpretation of the Convention may later result in national victims being uncompensated. In this sense, discussions at the I.O.P.C. Fund are very political, although properly based in legal analysis. There is always an acute awareness of precedent, in that a state which takes a hard line on, e.g. time bars, may find the same arguments used against it later.

In the *Aegean Sea* discussions, the precedent of the *Haven* has been to the fore.[11] It appears that some of the Spanish claimants had not taken the necessary formal steps to stop the Fund's time bar expiring, as they may (erroneously) have believed that it was enough simply to submit compensation claims in the criminal proceedings. The Spanish Government has obtained legal opinions to the effect that the time limits have not expired under Spanish criminal procedure law, while the Fund has obtained the opinion of a former Spanish Supreme Court judge that the time bar operated.[12] What is significant here is that ultimately this matter will be settled by the Spanish courts, even if all the states party to the Convention (apart from Spain) consider that this interpretation is contrary to international law (i.e. a "true" interpretation of the Convention).[13] But it is also important to note that the settlement of this sort of large and sensitive claim (where there has admittedly been great loss to local communities and fisheries) will inevitably involve a great deal of political horse-trading in the margins of the I.O.P.C. Fund Executive Committee and Assembly. In the *Haven* incident, the Fund (and the shipowner's P. & I. Club) agreed to compromise the disputed claims as part of an overall settlement[14] in much the same way that other large commercial claims are settled, albeit that in this case Governments were heavily involved. No doubt the Spanish claimants who would be affected by the time bar will try to persuade their Government to negotiate a similar settlement.

[11] See N. Gaskell, "Developments in International Maritime Law" (1998) 28 *Environmental Policy and Law*, 165–170.

[12] *I.O.P.C. Funds Annual Report* 1998, 53.

[13] Contrast the position in the *Sea Prince* case, where the opinion of the Fund's lawyers was that Korean law would not treat certain claims as time barred: see the Draft Record of Decisions of the 61st Session of the Executive Committee (71Fund/Exc.61/wp.1, 29th April 1999), 10. It is significant that the "notification" required by Article 7(6) has to be made "in accordance with the formalities required by the law of the court seised". It is where such procedural issues are left to national law that a lack of uniformity may occur.

[14] *I.O.P.C. Funds Annual Report* 1998, 49, Draft Record of Decisions of the 61st Session of the Executive Committee (71Fund/Exc.61/wp.1, 29th April 1999).

c. Limitation of pollution liability

A further source of dispute in the operation of the C.L.C. and Fund Convention systems has been the existence of limits of liability in both Conventions. The concept is familiar to maritime lawyers.[15] In the *Haven* incident, a 109,977 g.r.t. Cypriot tanker exploded while at anchor in Genoa in 1991. Initial claims were for £294 million, including a £100 million claim by the Italian Government for clean-up operations. Italy also lodged a claim for £340 million for environmental damage. The latter sum was rejected by an Italian court and a sum of £15.4 million allowed, but the court held that some £74 million worth of clean-up claims were admissible. The shipowner agreed to pay its proportion of the claims up to its C.L.C. limit of 14 million SDR (about £12 million), but the main issue became whether the Fund's liability was to be quantified according to its Convention limits of 60 million SDR (about £52 million) or whether this liability was to be measured in gold francs, which, according to the Italian courts, produced a limit of £296 million. One main outstanding claim was that by the Italian Government. As indicated, there had been disputes about the method by which the limitation of liability of the I.O.P.C. Fund should be calculated, i.e. whether such claims should be converted into lire on the basis of the market value of gold francs. The ruling by the Italian courts on conversion had been contrary to the views of the I.O.P.C. and would have greatly increased the liabilities of the Fund above the normal limits calculated on the basis of the 60 million SDR figure. As already noted, the claimants' position was compromised to some extent because a number of claims had not been made within the time period laid down in the Fund Convention 1971. In the light of the uncertainty, the Fund had proposed a global compromise settlement. Although the Italian Government had been unable to accept this compromise in 1995, it was able to announce agreement to the overall package in 1998. As part of the settlement, the shipowner's P. & I. Club agreed to make an *ex gratia* payment. The settlement is significant as it reinforces the determination of the Fund to protect its limits, although it recognises some flexibility in settlements.

One problem with the limits of liability under the C.L.C. 1969 and Fund Convention 1971 in major casualties is that they are regularly being exceeded by claims. This presents a real barrier to the early settlement of those claims, as it is not clear at the start whether they will eventually need to be prorated. In a number of cases, such as that concerning the grounding in the Shetland Islands of the 44,989 g.r.t. Liberian tanker *Braer* in January 1993, the Executive Committee has had to authorise only limited payments out of the fund on a provisional basis to those with clearly proven and admissible claims. This naturally causes great anxiety and anger amongst claimants and puts great pressure on states at Executive Committee meetings. In *The Aegean Sea*, claims

---

[15] See e.g. N. Gaskell, "New Limits for Passengers and Others in the United Kingdom" [1998] L.M.C.L.O. 312.

which have been established as admissible have been paid on a 40 per cent basis, in case the overall claims exceed the Fund's limits (as seems likely), but the Spanish state has criticised the handling of the claims on the basis that the payments are unreasonably low. Fortunately, the 1992 Protocols to the C.L.C. and Fund entered into force on 30th May 1996 and future claimants will have considerably higher limits with which to contend,[16] but *The Aegean Sea* pollution litigation is one of a series of cases (such as the *Braer*) which still have to be decided under the old regime.

d. **Damages available**

An additional factor of interest in the C.L.C. and Fund cases concerns the type of compensation or damages payable. An enormous amount of experience has been built up within the Fund about the admissibility of claims falling within the definition of "pollution damage" under the Conventions[17] and much of the practice is recorded in the Annual Reports of the Fund.

There has been no reported decision on the interpretation of the Convention provisions until recently. In *Landcatch Ltd.* v. *I.O.P.C. Fund*,[18] a case arising out of the *Braer* sinking in 1993, the Court of Session in Scotland had to deal with the question whether Landcatch's claim against the Fund was admissible as being a category of pollution damage under the 1971 Fund Convention, i.e. whether there was "damage caused by contamination". In *Landcatch*, the claimants reared salmon from eggs to smolt in freshwater conditions so that they could be sold for growing to maturity in seawater conditions. The facilities were developed principally to supply the Shetland salmon farms, which were themselves subject to contamination from the sinking of the *Braer*. The problem was that the facilities were situated some 500 km from the site of the casualty and no direct loss was caused to the claimants. The court found that there was not the level of proximity required at common law to justify such

---

[16] In total the aggregate of liability under the C.L.C. 1992 and Fund Convention 1992 is currently 135 million SDR (about £115 million). Claims from the *Erika* sinking in France (December 1999) may even exceed this limit and have resulted in moves for a 50% increase.

[17] Under C.L.C. 1969, Article 1(6), " 'Pollution damage' means loss or damage caused outside the ship carrying oil by contamination resulting from the escape or discharge of oil from the ship, wherever such escape or discharge may occur and includes the cost of preventive measures and further loss or damage caused by preventive measures". The C.L.C. 1992 has refined that concept to deal with economic loss claims and provides: "Pollution damage" means: (a) loss or damage caused outside the ship by contamination resulting from the escape or discharge of oil from the ship, wherever such escape or discharge may occur, provided that compensation for impairment of the environment other than loss of profit from such impairment shall be limited to costs of reasonable measures of reinstatement actually undertaken or to be undertaken; (b) the costs of preventive measures and further loss or damage caused by preventive measures".

[18] [1998] 2 Lloyd's Rep. 552; affd [1999] S.C.L.R. 709 (Ct.Sn.(I.H.)).

economic loss claims where the claimant had itself suffered no loss to its proprietary or possessory interests. The court therefore followed established precedents which rejected economic loss claims resulting solely from the fact that a contract with a third party was rendered less profitable. It specifically rejected an argument that the claimant's business activities were "bound with" the Shetland salmon fishing industry and were "closely integrated" with it, so as to create the necessary degree of proximity between the claimants and the loss suffered by the fish farmers. The claimant was no more than a potential supplier to the farmers. This finding is an important one in the general law of tort, upholding the courts' concerns not to expose defendants to indeterminate liability and to require that there be a distinction made between the principal or direct victims and those who were secondary or too remote.

However, the practice of the I.O.P.C. Fund has consistently been to make payments to economic loss claimants in certain defined circumstances, e.g. where the claimant's business is closely related to the activities of the sea or coastline, e.g., tourist hotels or fishermen. In this sense, the Fund is achieving the aims of the Goverments which established it—namely to pay claims, not to resist them. It is a victims', not a defendants', Convention. There is little doubt that the practice of the Fund goes beyond the legal principles on economic loss in many states (including Scotland, England and Wales). It was therefore of great significance how the Scottish courts viewed this practice, as, once again, there is the possibility of there being differences in interpretation not only between courts in different member states, but also between such courts and the Fund itself. The Fund, the shipowner and its P. & I. Club specifically admitted in the proceedings that economic loss claims were admissible under the C.L.C. and Fund Convention, but argued that not all claims were admissible. It is highly significant that at first instance and on appeal, the courts took the view that their task was to interpret the legislation as it had been enacted in the U.K., whether or not that was compatible with the aims of the Convention. It was only if the provisions were ambiguous that resort could be had to the wider policy considerations underlying the Conventions. Even though "loss" as expressed in the Convention was apt to include claims of pure economic loss, in the context of the U.K. legislation, that did not entail that every claim for pure economic loss was admissible, particularly where, as here, the claim was of a secondary or relational type. The court did not accept the defenders' contention that claims should be distinguished by reference to the geographical location of the fishermen's home port. "Loss" as included in "damage" for the purposes of section 1(1) of the Merchant Shipping (Oil Pollution) Act 1971[19] did not cover secondary or relational claims. At first instance, the court found that, despite the admissions by the defendants on economic loss, there was nothing in the

---

[19] Which enacted the C.L.C. and Fund Convention in U.K. law. See now the consolidating Merchant Shipping Act 1995.

legislation "to suggest that the limitations upon the recoverability of economic loss in the general law are to be displaced".[20] This approach was upheld on appeal. While such an approach is consistent with existing authorities on the interpretation of conventions it is a very narrow and rather parochial view. It is arguable that the court should recognise that the I.O.P.C. Fund has in effect been developing principles of international law.[21] In any event, the court found that there was nothing in the travaux préparatoires of the Conventions which supported the claimant's arguments.

The dismissal of *Landcatch's* claim is clearly correct in law, although it seems unlikely that courts in other states would take such a restrictive view of recovery under the Conventions. Fortunately, the 1992 Protocols to the C.L.C. and Fund entered into force on 30th May 1996 and future claimants will have considerably higher limits with which to contend,[22] but *The Aegean Sea* pollution litigation is one of a series of cases (such as *Landcatch*) which still have to be decided under the old regime. It is likely that the disputes about compensation, limitation of liability, time bars and execution of judgments in *The Aegean Sea* may run on for years. In addition, the Fund itself is considering recourse actions against the shipowner and the Spanish authorities which employed the pilot.

e. Oil pollution regime

This brief excursion into marine pollution compensation law has tried to show that the international community has adopted some very special legal provisions and administrative mechanisms to deal with a particular problem facing it. The solutions and methods chosen represent a modern attempt to achieve international uniformity and provide some extremely useful models on which to build liability systems. Indeed, the central principles of the C.L.C. and Fund systems (e.g. strict liability, channelling, compulsory insurance and direct

---

[20] [1998] 2 Lloyd's Rep. 552, 567.

[21] The narrow approach of the court may therefore call into question the existing practice of the Fund, at least where U.K. claims are concerned. It is now perfectly normal to pay for the economic losses of hoteliers and fishermen, even where no property of theirs is damaged. On ordinary economic loss principles in England and Wales (and seemingly also in Scotland) these claims would probably fail. Yet they are the sort of claims that the C.L.C. and Fund Convention were designed to cover.

[22] Despite some sympathy for the *Landcatch* claimant, it should also be recalled that the operation of the principle of limitation of liability means that any increase in the category of claims may mean that the totality of existing claimants may suffer in that their claims will be prorated and reduced. Even though the limits of liability operating today under the C.L.C. and Fund Convention 1992 are much greater than those which would apply in *Landcatch* or *The Aegean Sea*, a more "sympathetic" approach taken to the remote victims may mean that the direct victims (e.g., those paying for clean-up and reinstatement) will suffer as the overall fund has been diminished.

action against the insurer) are being used as examples in other maritime contexts at the International Maritime Organisation, e.g. in recent discussions on bunker liability, passenger claims and wreck removal. No system is perfect, but the writer's opinion is that this is a system which is rooted in the learning of practical maritime lawyers[23] and which works in practice. Claims of victims of pollution *are* paid and often within a remarkably short time. The major problems have really been caused by the operation of limits of liability whose levels have not kept pace with inflation or the risks posed in modern transport. To some extent, these defects will be remedied by the increasing adoption of the C.L.C. 1992 and Fund Convention 1992.[24]

3 LIMITATION OF LIABILITY ISSUES

Assuming that there were going to be considerable liabilities on the shipowner, the latter sought recourse from the charterer, R.O.I.L., and the intended receiver, Repsol. The claims against Repsol will be dealt with in Part 4 below. It was in relation to the claims against the charterer that the latter sought to limit its liability. There were two main limitation issues: (i) whether the charterer was entitled to limit under the Convention on Limitation of Liability for Maritime Claims 1976 (L.L.M.C. 1976); and (ii) if the charterer was entitled to limit, whether the various claims fell within L.L.M.C. Article 2 or were excepted under Article 3. In fact, the charterer lost on the first issue, but the conclusions on the second issue, albeit *obiter*, will still be of general relevance, even though Thomas, J., rather modestly, stated that he would give his views "briefly" on the second issue.

a. Limitation of the charterer's liability to the shipowner

The original privilege of limitation was granted to shipowners, not charterers. But the whole history of limitation of liability displays a natural tendency for claimants to try to avoid the statutory limits, e.g. by finding someone to sue who is not a shipowner, or by framing the claim in such a way that the claim does not fall within the precise wording of the appropriate Convention or national

---

[23] It started life in the Comité Maritime International (C.M.I.) a private organisation, now over 100 years old, which is composed of lawyers and members of the shipping and commercial communities.

[24] The decline in the number of states party to the original 1971 Fund Convention has given rise to other, extremely difficult, problems about how to wind up the 1971 Fund. The international community has had to adopt some novel devices to overcome the problems, e.g. where a state ceases to be party to the 1971 Fund Convention, on acceding to the 1992 Fund Convention, but whose industries remain liable for claims still outstanding. In theory the state would also cease to have voting rights at the Executive

statute. Once the loopholes become apparent, there is a natural tendency for the legislature to try to close the gaps in order to preserve the original rationale for limitation.[25] Thus, demise charterers were granted the right to limit under the Merchant Shipping Act 1894 by the Merchant Shipping Act 1906, section 71, presumably because they were thought to deserve the same protection as shipowners when sued by third party claimants. The 1957 Limitation Convention went further, in Article 6(2), by extending the limitation provisions to the "charterer, manager and operator" of the ship "as they apply to an owner himself". In other words, if the shipowner would be entitled to limit liable, e.g. to cargo owners, then a time charterer should also be entitled to limit (e.g. where it was the contracting carrier).

When the 1957 Limitation Convention was enacted into U.K. law by the Merchant Shipping (Liability of Shipowners and Others) Act 1958, the Convention wording was unfortunately altered so as to omit the reference to "as they apply to an owner himself". This redrafting of Convention provisions was an unfortunate feature of legislative drafting in the U.K. which has afflicted many maritime conventions and still causes problems today.[26] At one time judges may have taken the wording literally, but a more enlightened view prevails today, and they are more prepared to look to the international origins of the Convention and to consult the travaux préparatoires. Thomas, J. was prepared to conclude that, despite the wording of the 1958 Act, the terms of the 1957 Convention made it difficult to see how it can have been intended for charterers to limit for claims made against them by shipowners. In particular, the concept of a single fund pointed to the total liabilities of the shipowners and charterers being treated as one, although there was nothing in the travaux préparatoires to point clearly one way or the other. The phrase "as they apply to an owner himself", although omitted in the U.K. statute, also indicated that the protection envisaged for the charterer was against liabilities of the kind to be expected by a shipowner when sued by third parties.

L.L.M.C. 1976 made a number of changes to limitation law, but there was

---

Committee in respect of such a claim. In fact, an ad hoc arrangement has been agreed whereby account is taken of the opinions of former members of the 1971 Fund regime and this was used recently to approve an interpretation in the *Sea Prince* case that certain claims were not time barred: see Draft Record of Decision of the 61st Session of the Executive Committee (71Fund/Exc.61/wp.1, 29th April 1999), 10.

[25] See generally, M. Mustill, "Ships are different — or are they" [1993] L.M.C.L.Q. 490.

[26] E.g. in the way the oil pollution compensation conventions have been incorporated in U.K. law in the Merchant Shipping Act 1995. See also N. Gaskell, "The Interpretation of Maritime Conventions at Common Law", in J. P. Gardner (ed.), *United Kingdom Law in the 1990s* (British Institute of International and Comparative Law, London, 1990), 218–240.

nothing in Thomas, J.'s view to indicate that there was an intention to change the position of the charterer, and the travaux préparatoires were again silent. Thomas, J. found that the policy considerations were balanced, e.g. in that it might be unfair for a shipowner to be able to limit against a charterer but not vice versa, although charterers were able to protect themselves by the terms of the charterparty. In the absence of a clear guide in the words of the 1976 Convention, which approach should be adopted? Salvors were treated separately in L.L.M.C. 1976 in order to deal with the unfortunate consequences of *The Tojo Maru*.[27] The fact that the words "as they apply to an owner himself" did not appear in L.L.M.C. 1976 was held to be irrelevant as the same means were achieved by different drafting techniques in L.L.M.C. 1976. More significant was Article 9, which provided for aggregation of all claims against the shipowner (including those persons categorised as shipowner in Article 1[28]). If there was one fund for all claims against shipowners and charterers, how would that work when the charterer itself brought a claim against the shipowner in its capacity as operator of the ship? The conclusion was that the shipowner's claim against the charterer was not subject to limitation under L.L.M.C. 1976.

This is perhaps the most important and controversial part of the decision in the case and will have significant implications for charterers and their insurers. In the light of the huge sums at stake in the case, especially for the pollution claims, it appears that there is now a rather large gap in the protection available to maritime traders under L.L.M.C. 1976. The limitation rules will always throw up seemingly arbitrary distinctions about circumstances where there is a right to limit,[29] given that there is no general right to limit liability for claims arising on land.[30] In a literal sense R.O.I.L. was a "charterer" and therefore within the category of persons named in Article 1(2) as entitled to limit. It might have been thought that allowing the charterer to limit under L.L.M.C. 1976 was workable in the circumstances such as *The Aegean Sea*, as the charterer would simply be another claimant against the limitation fund,[31] even if it was at the same time also a defendant against claims made against it (e.g. if it had been a contracting carrier). Of course, this would mean that the other third party claimants would suffer as the limitation fund itself would be reduced by the charterer's claim. The logic of the decision is that even a ship manager would not be entitled to limit liability if the shipowner sued it for damage caused to the

---

[27] [1972] A.C. 242.

[28] Article 1(2) provides that the term "shipowner" shall mean the owner, charterer, manager or operator of a seagoing ship.

[29] See e.g. *The Tojo Maru* [1972] A.C. 242.

[30] Thus a shipowner can limit liability under L.L.M.C. 1976 for damage to cargo occurring on board ship, caused by crew negligence, but not to cargo which has been unloaded into the shipowner's warehouse and damaged negligently by his shoreside personnel.

[31] As aggregated under Article 9.

ship itself, e.g. where the manager sent the ship to sea in an unseaworthy state. If a third party claimant sued the manager (e.g. because it had assets and the shipowner was a one-ship company whose ship had sunk) it would now seem that the manager would be able to limit in respect of that claim, but would not have protection against any claim by the shipowner. It could be said that the manager and charterer are in a different position when sued by the shipowner, rather than directly by third party claimants, as they can control their liability to the shipowner through contract. This is correct, but there are other circumstances where there is a right to limit even though contractual provisions might have achieved the same effect. Thus, a shipowner can limit liability for damage to a tug, even though the towage contract might have exempted the liability of the shipowner.[32] It seems rather perverse that the shipowner could limit liability for claims made by the charterer against it, e.g. where there was damage to the charterer's cargo or, more seriously, where the charterer was made directly liable under some local law for pollution damage, but that the reverse protection would not apply. Similarly, if the crew were negligent, they would be entitled to limit liability to third parties under L.L.M.C. 1976, Article 1(4) but would it now follow that if sued by shipowner they could not limit? It may be that this category of claim would be subject to limitation of liability even under *The Aegean Sea*, as the crew's liability arises because they act in the same way as the owner itself.

Only a passing mention[33] was made in the judgment of Article 2(2), which provides that "claims set out in paragraph 1[34] shall be subject to limitation of liability even if brought by way of recourse or for indemnity under a contract or otherwise ...". This provision would naturally cover the position where Ship B causes a collision with Ship C, personal injury claims are made against Ship C and the latter claims from Ship B (by way of recourse) its proportion of damage.[35] The claim by the shipowner against R.O.I.L. could certainly be categorised as a "recourse" claim. If the casualty had been caused by the negligent navigation of another ship, the shipowner of *The Aegean Sea* would have been strictly liable for the pollution damage under the C.L.C., but would have had a recourse claim against the other ship and there is no doubt that this claim would have been subject to limitation under L.L.M.C. 1976, so it is arguably unfortunate if two different categories of recourse claim would be decided differently. The reasoning in the judgment would suggest that Article 2 was irrelevant to the immediate question, which was whether the charterer

---

[32] In practice, most towage contracts contain clauses which exempt the liability of the tug-owner, but in the absence of such clauses there would be a right to limit.

[33] [1998] 2 Lloyd's Rep. 39, 47.

[34] Whether the particular claims in *The Aegean Sea* fell within Article 2(1) will be dealt with in Part 3h below, but Thomas, J. found that the pollution claims made against the shipowner did generally fall within Article 2.

[35] See the Merchant Shipping Act 1995, s.189.

could fall within the category of person entitled to limit under Article 1, but the learned judge was prepared to look at other articles of the L.L.M.C. 1976 for guidance and it might have been thought that Article 2(2) was at least consistent with R.O.I.L.'s case.

Thomas, J. considered that L.L.M.C. 1976, Article 9 also supported his conclusions. That article deals with the constitution of the limitation fund. The provision is complicated and there would certainly be complications if the charterer was allowed to limit against the shipowner. But it is notorious that there are many complications in the working of limitation funds, especially where there are multiple claims, and there is nothing inconsistent with allowing a person who sets up the fund to be both a claimant and a defendant in respect of it. Under Article 5(8) of the C.L.C. 1969 (and 1992) a shipowner can prove against the fund set up by it to cover its own expenses which it has incurred to clean up the pollution it caused. Admittedly, this is an express provision (to which there is no equivalent in L.L.M.C. 1976) and the policy considerations are different in the C.L.C. (as there is intended to be a deliberate encouragement of owners to become involved in clean-up). Nevertheless, it is difficult to believe that it would be impossible to find a workable procedural solution to the operation of the limitation fund if R.O.I.L.'s claims had succeeded.

Thomas, J.'s view was that the overall policy of L.L.M.C. 1976 was not to favour R.O.I.L.'s position. The arguments are evenly balanced but, standing back a little, the possible consequences of the decision could give rise to some concern. The international community has produced a finely balanced regime for the compensation of pollution incidents, in which limitation of liability is central. One reason for this was that the insurance market said that it needed the certainty of limits in order to be able to cover the potentially massive liabilties. Of course, the C.L.C. is designed to protect claimants and, largely, does so and the system of channelling of liability only to the registered shipowner means that there should be no need for double insurance.[36] It is therefore a little ironic that one consequence of the decision in *The Aegean Sea* is that charterers may well need to take out extra insurance cover for their potential pollution

---

[36] Article 3(4) of the C.L.C. 1969 and 1992 effectively provide that only the registered shipowner can be sued (and only under the Convention, not in negligence) and that others cannot be sued. The C.L.C. 1969, Article 3(4) prevents direct claims by pollution victims against servants or agents of the shipowner. (It is for this reason that a direct suit against the master is almost certainly contrary to the C.L.C. 1969; see Part 2(a) above.) The C.L.C. 1992, Article 3(4) extends this protection, *inter alia*, to charterers, managers and operators.

liabilities if sued by shipowners.[37] Yet their liability insurers may well be the same, in the sense that they may be members of the International Group of P. & I. Clubs who have always been anxious to avoid double insurance, in order to make full use of the capacity of the market to provide the largest possible amount to claimants. It has already been noted that it might be considered unfortunate if the law treated differently recourse claims made against another shipowner from those against the charterer, although this may simply be accepted as an inevitable consequence of the arbitrary dividing lines drawn by limitation provisions. It is unclear whether the international maritime community, e.g. at the International Maritime Organisation, would regard the decision in *The Aegean Sea* as revealing yet another lacuna in the protection offered through limitation of liability which might need at some time to be filled. Given the difficulty in agreeing a Protocol to the L.L.M.C. in 1996,[38] which is not yet in force, there is no reasonable prospect of any change in limitation rules for many years. Overall, as a matter of policy, the question is whether the regime of limitation of liability is improved or undermined by the decision on this point. The history of limitation of liability shows that the ingenuity of lawyers and courts have always created gaps. These stimulate litigation on narrow technical points and can cause uncertainty and imbalances in protection. A recent example of a sensible and practical approach to interpretation is *M.S.C. Mediterranean Shipping Co. S.A.* v. *Polish Ocean Lines (The Tychy)*,[39] where the Court of Appeal decided that a "slot charterer" was a charterer for the purposes of the Supreme Court Act 1981 (and Arrest Convention 1952). This decision avoided making technical distinctions between different kinds of charterers. There is no reason why the same reasoning could not apply to a slot charterer for the purposes of L.L.M.C. 1976. By comparison, it could be said that, in an entirely different context, the decision in *The Aegean Sea* creates unnecessary distinctions between types of claim and complicates what should ideally be a clear overall picture of liabilities and their limitation. Experience shows that litigation is only encouraged where in the same adventure there are some persons who are, and some who are not, subject to limitation of liability. If one of the aims of a system

---

[37] As noted in the previous footnote, charterers are not *expressly* protected by the channelling provisions of the C.L.C. 1969, although in many states the expression "servants or agents" might cover them. So it would, theoretically, have been possible for R.O.I.L. to have been sued directly by the pollution victims for negligence. Under the C.L.C. 1992, charterers such as R.O.I.L. could have no direct liability. Of course, if the shipowner is entitled to limit to third parties, then its recourse claim will also be so limited and thus the charterer will gain indirect protection through the shipowner's limits.

[38] See Gaskell, "New Limits for Passengers and Others in the United Kingdom" [1998] L.M.C.L.Q. 312.

[39] [1999] 2 Lloyd's Rep. 11. *Cf.* B. J. Davenport (2000) 116 L.Q.R. 36.

of limitation of liability is to encourage settlement between parties who have access to insurance, the conclusion of *The Aegean Sea* on this issue may not be entirely welcome.

The reasoning of Thomas, J. on this, as on all other points in the case, is careful, considered and undoubtedly has persuasive force—irrespective of its status as a binding precedent. If it is correct, charterers (and managers) will almost certainly need to be advised in future to seek to obtain protection through the terms of the charterparty. There could either be straight exclusion of liability, e.g. for pollution consequences of port nominations, or provisions which by contract give the charterer the same protection against the shipowner as if there was a right to limit under L.L.M.C. 1976. There can, however, be no guarantee that such clauses would always be effective and enforceable in all parts of the world, so more consideration will need to be given to charterers' (and managers') insurance cover and its extent. As the particular claim in *The Aegean Sea* was a recourse action, the charterer would not have to pay more than the shipowner itself paid (which will probably be limited under the C.L.C. 1969); but, if the shipowner were deprived of the right to limit,[40] then the charterer would have to indemnify the shipowner without limit and would therefore need high insurance cover. It may be that some charterers already need such cover in some parts of the world, but *The Aegean Sea* demonstrates that it may be more necessary than had been thought.

b. Claims subject to limitation under L.L.M.C. 1976, Article 2

In view of the fact that Thomas, J. held that the charterer, R.O.I.L., was not entitled to limit at all under L.L.M.C. 1976, it was not strictly necessary to go on to consider whether the specific claims in the case fell within L.L.M.C. 1976, Article 2. Thomas, J. nevertheless expressed his views on the claims and these are of some interest. The claims fell into two broad categories, (i) the direct claims for the loss of the ship, freight and bunkers, and (ii) the recourse or indemnity claims for sums which the shipowners paid for salvage and pollution to third parties. As a starting point it was accepted that the court had to look at the nature of the claim rather than its legal categorisation, as Article 2(1) talks of "claims, whatever the basis of liability may be". This is obviously sensible, given the fact that L.L.M.C. 1976 has to be applied in widely differing legal systems.

---

[40] E.g. because of the existence of "actual fault or privity" under the C.L.C. 1969, or intention and recklessness under the C.L.C. 1992.

i. Direct Losses

R.O.I.L. contended that the loss of the ship itself fell within L.L.M.C. 1976, Article 2(1)(a).[41] Thomas, J. held that the expression "loss of property … occurring … in direct connection with the operation of the ship" did not in its ordinary meaning cover the actual loss of the ship itself. There is an attraction to this finding, in that it is the operation of the ship itself which will normally cause the loss of other property. However, these words were really designed to draw a distinction between land-related activities, which do not give rise to a right to limit, and ship related activities, which do.[42] The particular language was adapted from Article 1(1)(b) of the 1957 Limitation Convention in order to reverse the effect of *The Tojo Maru*,[43] where the House of Lords had held that a salvor not operating on board the salvage vessel was unable to limit. The wording in L.L.M.C. 1976, which mainly achieves this reversal, is "occurring … in direct connection with … salvage operations". So the ship can be "property" in the first part of the paragraph, where salvors are concerned. While the language of the paragraph does more easily fit the interpretation of Thomas, J., it is also capable of the alternative meaning which would have allowed R.O.I.L. to limit.

If the freight for the voyage had not been earned, the shipowner had a claim for damages, on the assumption that an incorrect port order was given. Thomas, J. held that there could be no right to limit for this claim as it was covered by the same principle governing the loss of the ship. However, R.O.I.L. also based the claim on the enigmatic Article 2(1)(c).[44] The expression "infringement of rights other than contractual rights" is not entirely clear, but Thomas, J. considered that the shipowner's claim was a claim for freight lost under a contract and was for an infringement of contractual rights. He also rejected the suggestion by R.O.I.L. that a claim for an indemnity was not for an infringement of contractual rights. Given that the claim was for damages, or for an indemnity, under the charterparty the decision was clearly right on this point.

The ship's bunkers were also lost in the stranding. Thomas, J. rejected a rather technical argument by the shipowner that the bunkers were only lost when they were later taken into possession of Repsol at the refinery for disposal.

---

[41] "Claims in respect of loss of life or personal injury or loss of or damage to property (including damage to harbour works, basins and waterways and aids to navigation), occurring on board or in direct connection with the operation of the ship or with salvage operations, and consequential loss resulting therefrom".

[42] It is noticeable that Article 1(1)(b) of the 1957 Limitation Convention made this connection rather clearer by its emphasis on, e.g. acts which occur in "the navigation or the management of the ship".

[43] [1972] A.C. 242.

[44] "Claims in respect of other loss resulting from infringement of rights other than contractual rights, occurring in direct connection with the operation of the ship or salvage operations".

He accepted that, if the consequence of the orders from R.O.I.L. to sail to La Coruña were that the bunkers were lost, then this a "loss of property ... occurring ... in direct connection with the operation of the ship". The giving of orders was clearly part of the operation of the ship and was not confined to orders actually given on board the ship. Charterer's orders would, of course, be given from the charterer's place of business. In the same way a misrepresentation about a ship's capacity or equipment would occur in direct connection with the operation of the ship,[45] as would an operational decision taken by the ship's managers ashore.[46] The decision, rejecting a narrow interpretation of L.L.M.C. 1976, Article 2(1)(a) on this point, is again clearly correct.

ii *Recourse and indemnity claims*

Pollution claims
Potentially the largest claim of the shipowner was the recourse claim in respect of sums paid or payable to the pollution claimants.[47] Thomas, J. held that these were clearly claims arising in direct connection with the operation of the ship within Article 2(1)(a).[48] They either arose in respect of "loss of or damage to property" (i.e. the property damaged by oil) or were "consequential loss resulting therefrom". Not all pollution claims do cause loss or damage to property. Damage to ships in marinas, quay walls, power station outlets, fishing nets and aquaculture would be the usual examples. It is stretching language a little to extend the concept of property here to sand or rocks on beaches, but there is no reason why they could not also be considered as property. In any event, the huge costs of clean up operations and the economic losses, such as loss of fishing, would be "consequential loss". The fact that the claims were based on strict liability was irrelevant as the claims are covered "whatever the basis of liability" in Article 2(1). Moreover, the pollution claims could also be fitted into other sub-paragraphs of Article 2(1): e.g. Article 2(1)(c) (loss of fishing profits were an "infringement of rights other than contractual rights, occurring in direct connection with the operation of the ship"); Article 2(1)(d) (removal of the ship); Article 2(1)(e) (oil cargo removal). Thomas, J. also considered that the bunker removal fell within sub-paragraphs (d) and (e),[49]

---

[45] See *Caspian Basin* v. *Bouygues (No. 4)* [1997] 2 Lloyd's Rep. 507; [1998] 2 Lloyd's Rep. 461. Whether a shipowner should be entitled to limit liability for fraud is another issue, but that would depend upon whether the intentional act of the shipowner was committed "with the intent to cause such loss, or recklessly and with knowledge: that such loss would probably result" within L.L.M.C. 1976, Article 4.

[46] *Cf. The Marion* [1984] A.C. 563.

[47] See Part 2(a), above.

[48] See *supra*, Part 2(a)(i).

[49] These cover "(d) claims in respect of the raising, removal, destruction or the rendering harmless of a ship which is sunk, wrecked, stranded or abandoned, including anything that is or has been on board such ship; (e) claims in respect of the removal, destruction or the rendering harmless of the cargo of the ship".

although strictly bunkers would not normally be considered as part of the "cargo" within (e). They would, however, be something "that is or has been on board" the ship.

Thomas, J. rejected a submission by R.O.I.L. that some clean-up claims could also fall within sub-paragraph (f).[50] He considered that the claims were by the shipowner and, as the shipowner was liable, the claims did not fall within the sub-paragraph. At first sight this seems obvious, but this conclusion depends upon the correct categorisation of the recourse claim. The victim or helper who tries to minimise loss has a direct claim against the shipowner under the C.L.C. and, when that claim is sought to be passed down to the charterer in this case, it is difficult to see why it is still not a claim within the sub-paragraph.[51] Claims for cargo removal under sub-paragraph (e) are also made by a victim or helper against the shipowner, but do not seem to lose that categorisation merely because a recourse action is sought. This issue arose more directly in relation to the salvage claims.[52]

Article 3 of L.L.M.C. 1976 excepts from limitation of liability "claims for oil pollution damage within the meaning of the International Convention on Civil Liability for Oil Pollution Damage dated 29th November 1969 or of any amendment or Protocol thereto which is in force". The intention here was clear, i.e. to exclude claims for limitation under L.L.M.C. 1976 which were subject to limitation of liability under the separate regime of the C.L.C. The limits under the latter stand alone and are much higher, so a shipowner could not claim to limit to the pollution victim on the basis of the lower L.L.M.C. 1976 limits. L.L.M.C. 1976 was originally enacted in the Merchant Shipping Act 1979 and Schedule 4, Part II, paragraph 4(2) of that Act states that the "claims excluded from the Convention by paragraph (b) of Article 3 are claims in respect of any liability incurred under section 1 of the Merchant Shipping (Oil Pollution) Act 1971".[53] There is immediately apparent a potential difference between the C.L.C. Article 3 exception and the U.K. exception intended to give effect to it. Whereas the former could be said to cover any claim for oil pollution *damage* within the meaning of the C.L.C., the U.K. statute requires there to be a *liability* under the statute. This C.L.C. wording could mean that liability does not have to be incurred *under* the C.L.C., but merely that liability for the sort of damage

---

[50] "Claims of a person other than the person liable in respect of measures taken in order to avert or minimise loss for which the person liable may limit his liability in accordance with this Convention, and further loss caused by such measures".

[51] See also "Salvage Claims" (following section).

[52] *Ibid.*

[53] The corresponding provision in the consolidating Merchant Shipping Act 1995 is Sched. 7 Part II, para. 4(2), which refers to "section 153 of this Act". Section 153 is the consolidated section 1 of the Merchant Shipping (Oil Pollution) Act 1971.

described by the C.L.C. has been incurred.[54] The U.K. statute is much more specific as it refers to liability under it, e.g. where there has been pollution within U.K. waters. R.O.I.L. therefore argued that, as the liability in Spain was not covered by the U.K. statute, then the exception in L.L.M.C. 1976, Article 3 could not apply and therefore it was entitled to limit for the pollution claims under L.L.M.C. 1976. As it had already been held that the claims fell within L.L.M.C. 1976, Article 2, it should therefore be entitled to limit. Thomas, J. accepted this argument on the meaning of the statute. In principle this seems to be correct, for the purpose of the exclusion in Article 3 is really to protect the direct C.L.C. claimant and there is no reason why a recourse defendant, such as R.O.I.L., should not have the benefit of the ordinary L.L.M.C. 1976 limits.[55] The wider interpretation of Article 3 would also mean that a defendant shipowner (e.g. a tanker owner) who was held liable for pollution damage in a state not party to the C.L.C. (but party to L.L.M.C. 1976) would not be entitled to limit liability at all for the pollution damage: there would be no limit under the C.L.C. (as it was not applicable in that state) nor would there be limitation of liability under L.L.M.C. 1976. In this sense Article 3 has to be interpreted as if "within the meaning of" means "brought under". That is an eminently sensible conclusion by the judge. It also followed that any liability of the shipowner to C.R.I.S.T.A.L.[56] was not excepted either and R.O.I.L. would have been entitled to limit in respect of this recourse claim as well.

Salvage Claims

The final category of recourse claims concerned the claim by the shipowner to be indemnified against salvage claims made against it by salvors. There were two questions again here. First, did the recourse claim fall within Article 2? Secondly, if they did, were they excepted from limitation of liability on the basis that under L.L.M.C. 1976, Article 3 the rules of the Convention shall also not apply to "claims for salvage and for contribution in general average"?

Thomas, J. held that, for the reasons given in relation to the claim for the loss

---

[54] E.g., in a State not party to the C.L.C. but which applies national law: see E. Selvig, "The 1976 Limitation Convention and Oil Pollution Damage" [1979] L.M.C.L.Q. 21. In fact, in *The Aegean Sea* there would be a liability under the C.L.C. as Spain is a party to it.

[55] The argument would be even stronger where the recourse defendant was another shipowner, e.g. a colliding container ship, which could legitimately expect to limit according to the normal limitation rules applicable to that ship, i.e. L.L.M.C. 1976.

[56] C.R.I.S.T.A.L. was the voluntary agreement which in some circumstances gave pollution victims higher protection than that available under the 1971 Fund. It was originally intended as a stop-gap arrangement before the Fund Convention 1971 entered into force, but it continued in existence until 1997, when the 1992 Fund was fully in

of the ship,[57] a claim in relation to the salvage of the ship was not one for which the charterers could limit. However, that part of the salvage claim which was in respect of the cargo could be limited by the charterer as it was consequential on the loss of the cargo, which itself was "property" within Article 2(1)(a). Moreover, the Article 3 exception was only designed to apply to the direct claim against the shipowner *for* salvage. It followed that a shipowner would be entitled to limit for claims by cargo for its proportion of general average or any salvage claim made by it. In other words, an ordinary cargo owner's recourse action would not be categorised as salvage or general average for the purposes of L.L.M.C. 1976.[58] Thomas, J. refused to look at "the original basis of the claim being made", but was concerned with "the claim being made against the party seeking limitation, not the original claim or its original or factual legal basis".[59] The result was that the recourse claim for salvage by the shipowner in *The Aegean Sea* would have been subject to limitation of liability.

This is an important and correct conclusion. It means that the original direct claim against the shipowner loses its characterisation as "salvage" once it becomes part of a recourse action. In the latter, it is merely a form of consequential loss for limitation purposes. Presumably, if the recourse action had been brought against a colliding shipowner, the latter could have limited as the claim would have been loss consequential on the loss of the ship. The decision may affect other categories of recourse claim in the context of limitation of liability. Thus, where claims are made against one ship (e.g., for general average, personal injury, wreck raising, or pollution damage), they will be subject to the appropriate limit for such claims against that ship. When that ship includes any payments made to such primary claimants in its recourse action against another ship, e.g., as a result of a collision, the question arises whether the claims should continue to be categorised in the same way (e.g., as salvage, personal injury, wreck raising etc.) or whether they then form a different type of claim (e.g., a consequential loss resulting from damage to the first ship). It has been held in Australia, under the 1957 Limitation Convention, that a wreck claim (which is usually not subject to limitation of liability) should continue to be categorised as a wreck claim even when part of a recourse

---

force. In cases such as *The Aegean Sea* there were extremely complicated arrangements where the Fund and C.R.I.S.T.A.L. would both operate. The existence of such voluntary schemes as C.R.I.S.T.A.L. (and its C.L.C. equivalent, T.O.V.A.L.O.P.) is an interesting sidelight itself into how industries can voluntarily co-operate with Governments and assist convention regimes.

[57] See *supra*, Part 2(b)(i).
[58] And see *The Breydon Merchant* [1992] 1 Lloyd's Rep. 373.
[59] [1998] 2 Lloyd's Rep. 39, 55.

action.[60] It is submitted that this approach is incorrect and is inconsistent with both *The Aegean Sea* and earlier English case law.[61]

4 CARRIER-RECEIVER CLAIMS UNDER THE BILLS

a. Introduction

The Aegean Sea gave rise to a number of extremely interesting and difficult questions concerning the potential liability of the intended cargo receiver, Repsol. The relevant facts are set out in Part 4(h) below.

The first issue was whether Repsol had been in breach of any obligations under the bill of lading or had assumed any under a letter of indemnity (L.O.I.). This depended upon whether there was an obligation under the bill (as opposed to the charterparty) in respect of the nomination of a safe port. Secondly, on the assumption that there was a responsibility, e.g. of the shipper, it would then become necessary to consider whether any such liabilities passed to Repsol.

Most of the issues concerning Repsol's liability, i.e. on the second issue, depended upon the interpretation of the Carriage of Goods by Sea Act 1992 (C.O.G.S.A. 1992). It will be recalled that this Act was enacted on the recomendation of the Law Commissions[62] to replace the Bills of Lading Act 1855[63] and entered into force on 16th September 1992. In general, the aim of C.O.G.S.A. 1992 is to deal with the right of a person to sue the carrier under the contract of carriage. There is no problem normally with the right of a shipper to sue where it has made a contract with the carrier, e.g. as evidenced by a bill of lading. C.O.G.S.A. 1992 deals with the question of how far a transferee of such a bill should also have rights and liabilities under the contract of carriage.

The shipowner's claim was that Repsol became the lawful holder of the bills of lading and by demanding delivery of the cargo, or by taking delivery of a

---

[60] See *The Tiruna* [1987] 2 Lloyd's Rep. 666 (Qld S.C.).

[61] See e.g. *The Arabert* [1961] 1 Lloyd's Rep. 363 and S. Gault (general ed.), *Marsden: Collisions At Sea*, 12th edn. (1997), 540, n.12.

[62] Law Commission, *Rights of Suit in Respect of Carriage of Goods by Sea: Law Com. No. 196* (H.C. 250, 1991) (hereafter Law Com. No. 196).

[63] See generally on C.O.G.S.A. 1992: J. Beatson and J. Cooper, "Rights of Suit in Respect of Carriage of Goods by Sea" [1991] L.M.C.L.Q. 196; J. Cooper, "Carriage of Goods by Sea Act 1992" [1992] *Current Law Statutes Annotated*; B. Davenport, "Reform to Bill of Lading Law—Some Implications for Banks" [1992] J.I.B.F.L. 305; R. Bradgate & F. White, "The Carriage of Goods by Sea Act 1992" (1993) 56 M.L.R. 188; F. Reynolds, "The Carriage of Goods by Sea Act 1992", *B.M.L.A. Annual Report 1992*. See also N. Gaskell, "Bills of Lading", in D. Yates (Gen. Ed.) *Contracts for the Carriage of Goods* (1993–1999) (hereafter *Contracts for the Carriage of Goods*) paras 1.6.5.6 *et seq.* for comments on the 1992 Act and *The Aegean Sea*.

small part of it, became subject to the liabilities under the bill. It also argued that the bill contained implied terms giving the other party the right to nominate the port of discharge and that any port so nominated would be safe (and an implied indemnity). As La Coruña was nominated by Repsol (as the other party to the bill of lading or on that party's behalf), Repsol became liable for the consequences of the stranding in the allegedly unsafe port.

In fact, Thomas, J. dealt with the issues under C.O.G.S.A. 1992 before considering whether there was any underlying liability which could be passed on to Repsol.[64] For convenience, the same order will be used here.

b. Holder of the bill

In *The Aegean Sea* the first question which arose on C.O.G.S.A. 1992 was whether a cargo receiver became a "holder" of a bill for the purposes of the Act. The shipowner (the carrier under the bill of lading) sought to claim an indemnity for the enormous pollution claims, essentially on the basis that the receiver had nominated an unsafe port.[65] As there was a short haul voyage, it was contemplated that the vessel would reach the disport before the bill and the voyage charter provided that the shipowner was to release cargo without production of bills of lading, but in exchange for a letter of indemnity.[66] On 20th November 1992, the charterer sold the oil cargo covered by the bill to its parent company Repsol (an oil refiner). The ship grounded on 3rd December 1992. The bill had been drawn to the order of the charterer's supplier, who in turn endorsed it to Repsol on 17th December 1992. The bill and invoice were sent to the charterer, who in turn forwarded the bill to Repsol. The endorsement was made in error, as it was clear that it should have named the charterer, and so the bill was returned to the supplier, who later re-endorsed the originals of the bill to the charterer.

The carrier argued that C.O.G.S.A. 1992, section 5(2)(b)[67] required Repsol, if it were to become the holder, to have possession as a result of completion of any endorsement or by delivery. The carrier accepted that a person could not

---

[64] The order in which the issues were decided raises the question of which could strictly be termed *obiter* and which part of the *ratio*. If the implied terms issued had been treated first, then all the conclusions on C.O.G.S.A. 1992 (Part 4a–e of this essay) would have been *obiter*. See further *infra*, Part 5.

[65] See *infra*, Part 4(f) for discussion of the safe port issues.

[66] See *infra*, Part 4(e)(i).

[67] This provides: "5(2) References in this Act to the holder of a bill of lading are references to any of the following persons, that is to say— ... (b) a person with possession of the bill as a result of the completion, by delivery of the bill, of an indorsement of the bill or, in the case of a bearer bill, of any other transfer of the bill". The sub-section continues "... and a person shall be regarded for the purposes of this Act as having become the lawful holder of a bill of lading wherever he has become the holder of the bill in good faith".

possess a bill of lading under section 5(2)(b) unless that person knew that he had it, but argued that no more was required. In effect, the terms of section 5(2)(b) were satisfied once the supplier put the bill in the post endorsed to Repsol, and the latter received it: it did not matter that Repsol did not want to accept it on its own behalf, or as endorsed to it, or that it had been endorsed to it in error. Thomas, J. rightly rejected this argument, on the basis that Repsol did not become a "holder" under section 5(2)(b) merely because it obtained the bill in consequence of someone endorsing it and sending it to Repsol. The section required Repsol to have possession as a result of the completion of an endorsement by delivery and it was necessary for Repsol to have received the bill into its possession and to have accepted the delivery before it became the holder. Moreover, the bill had never been delivered by the supplier to Repsol, as it had been sent directly to the charterer as principal, rather than as agent for Repsol. It followed that Repsol never obtained possession of the bill as a result of completion by delivery of the bill by endorsement. The requirement that there should be a consensual element, on the part of the endorsee or transferee, to the question of possession as a result of the completion by delivery of an endorsement was reinforced by the judge's conclusion that "good faith" in section 5(2) should be interpreted narrowly.[68]

Thomas, J. noted that the endorsement required did not have to be an endorsement that was intended to pass property, as that would be to re-introduce the very link between the passing of property and rights under the bill which the 1992 Act sought to remove.

c. Lawful holder of the bill

A second question in *The Aegean Sea* on C.O.G.S.A. 1992 was whether the cargo receiver became a "lawful" holder of the bill. The carrier contended that as Repsol obtained the bill honestly, that was sufficient to make it a lawful holder. As already noted,[69] it was held that Repsol was not a holder at all, but Thomas, J. agreed, probably *obiter*, that a broad meaning should not be attributed to "good faith" in C.O.G.S.A. 1992, despite the absence of any limiting definition. In the commercial context of bills of lading, it was necessary for the expression to be "clear, capable of unambiguous application and consistent with the usage in other contexts and countries".[70] He held that the expression "connotes honest conduct and not a broader concept of good faith such as 'the observance of reasonable commercial standards of fair dealing in the conclusion and performance of the transaction concerned' ".[71] It followed that, as Repsol had acquired the bill in honest circumstances, it would have been

---

[68] See [1998] 2 Lloyd's Rep. 39, 60, and *infra*, Part 4(c).
[69] See *supra*, Part 4(b).
[70] [1998] 2 Lloyd's Rep. 39, 60.
[71] *Ibid.*

a lawful "good faith" holder (had it not been for the finding that it never became a holder at all).

d. Rights of receiver under section 2(1)

A consequential point concerned the effect of any rights obtained by Repsol under section 2(1), if it had become a lawful holder.[72] The carrier argued that in such circumstances the supplier would not have been entitled to re-indorse the bill to the charterer without a previous re-indorsement by Repsol to the supplier. It might be thought that the right to indorse or re-indorse the bill arose from the general principles of negotiability, rather than from the operation of the 1992 Act (which regulates rights and liabilities under the contract of carriage), but the existence of the argument reinforced the judge's view that Repsol could not have been a holder in the first place, merely by the receipt of the bill in error.

e. Actions incurring liability of receiver

Assuming that Repsol was a lawful holder of the bill (which Thomas, J. found that it was not), had it taken any of the actions specified in C.O.G.S.A. 1992, section 3,[73] which would pass liabilities to it? In particular, had Repsol (i) made a *demand* within section 3(1)(a) or (c), or (ii) *taken delivery* of some of the oil within section 3(1)(a) or (c)?

i. Demanding delivery

As to issue (i), whether Repsol had made a "demand", it was assumed that it had issued orders on 19th November 1992 for the vessel to discharge in La Coruña and on 26th November it had issued a letter of indemnity (L.O.I.) in its own name (not on behalf of charterers, whose L.O.I. would have been unacceptable

---

[72] This provides "2(1) Subject to the following provisions of this section a person who becomes—(a) the lawful holder of a bill of lading ... shall (by virtue of becoming the holder of the bill ...) have transferred to and vested in him all rights of suit under the contract of carriage as if he had been a party to that contract".

[73] This provides "3(1) Where subsection (1) of section 2 of this Act operates in relation to any document to which this Act applies and the person in whom rights are vested by virtue of that subsection

  (a) takes or demands delivery from the carrier of any of the goods to which the document relates;

  (b) makes a claim under the contract of carriage against the carrier in respect of any of those goods; or

  (c) is a person who, at a time before those rights were vested in him, took or demanded delivery from the carrier of any of those goods;

that person shall (by virtue of taking or demanding delivery or making the claim or, in a case falling within paragraph (c) above, of having the rights vested in him) become subject to the same liabilities under that contract as if he had been a party to that contract."

to the carrier). The L.O.I. was in respect of liabilities which the carrier might incur for delivery of the cargo without production of the bill,[74] but also contained a promise later to produce duly endorsed bills which vested property in Repsol. The carrier argued, in effect, that the L.O.I. was a demand for delivery within section 3(1)(c) made on 26th November, before the rights under section 2 became vested in it.[75] It was held (arguably *obiter*) that the L.O.I. was not a demand for delivery. It did not oblige Repsol to take delivery, but was merely an undertaking to provide an indemnity for certain claims if delivery was in fact taken. Moreover, the carrier remained obliged to deliver to the lawful holder and was not bound to deliver under the L.O.I.

However, it should be noted that the Law Commissions clearly contemplated that, "where a person takes or demands delivery before he has any contractual rights (as where he takes delivery pursuant to an L.O.I.) he becomes liable under the statute when he subsequently has the rights conferred on him".[76] On the facts of *The Aegean Sea* it seems that Repsol did not take delivery pursuant to the L.O.I., but in accordance with the demands of the civil government.[77] In any event, it was also held that Repsol did not become liable to the carrier independently under the terms of the L.O.I. itself,[78] in particular because the L.O.I. was only intended to operate if Repsol took delivery under the bill.

ii. Taking delivery

As to issue (ii), whether Repsol had taken delivery of any oil, some 5,427 tons of oil cargo (about 7 per cent of the total) had been salved from the vessel and was received into Repsol's refinery pursuant to orders from the local civil government dealing with the pollution incident. The carrier argued that Repsol had therefore taken delivery of part of the cargo within either section 3(1)(a) or (c) (depending on when it became the lawful holder) and that it was irrelevant that the vessel had not reached its contractual destination, or that delivery had not been taken under the bill. Thomas, J. rejected these arguments, holding that the receipt of oil under compulsion from the civil government, after transportation by the salvors by road, was not a taking of delivery within section 3. A taking of delivery within section 3 required "delivery under the bill of lading of the cargo to which the bill of lading relates from the carrier itself (or from someone who holds them for the carrier such as a warehouseman or a person to whom the carrier has entrusted them for delivery) after discharge at the port of destination. It would also include some other form of delivery from the carrier where there had been a consensual variation of the contract; for

---

[74] See generally, *Contracts for the Carriage of Goods*, para. 1.6.15.2.9.

[75] For another case on "demand", see *Borealis A.B.* v. *Stargas Ltd. and Others (The Berge Sisar)* [1999] Q.B. 863; [1998] 2 Lloyd's Rep. 475; *infra*, Part 4(e)(iii).

[76] Law Com. No. 196, p. 51.

[77] See *infra*, Part 4(e)(ii).

[78] [1998] 2 Lloyd's Rep. 39, 63–64.

example, if the vessel did not complete her voyage and an agreement was made to take the cargo at that stage, in many cases delivery would be taken under the contract contained in the bill of lading as varied. There was no element of consensual variation in this case".[79] Further, the intention of the Act was to impose liabilities on a lawful holder who voluntarily made a claim or took delivery and not in consequence of the involuntary act of being compelled by the civil government where the recipient was the only person with the facilities to receive it. When the oil was received at the refinery between 11th–15th December, it remained the property of the charterer and was held for its account. Repsol did not receive the bill of lading until after 22nd December and so the claim under section 3(1)(a) could not succeed in any event.

iii. Liability of intermediate lawful holder

A further question arose as to whether an intermediate lawful holder of a bill of lading (Repsol) would be discharged from liabilities under the bill where it subsequently transferred the bill (to the charterer) but after having made a demand for delivery. C.O.G.S.A. 1992, section 2(5)[80] only deals expressly with the loss of rights of the intermediate holder after transfer of the bill and does not provide for a person who comes under liabilities to cease to have those liabilities if he ceases to be the lawful holder. It was held, *obiter*, that if a person is the lawful holder, at the time he makes the demand for delivery within section 3,[81] then the conditions in section 3 are satisfied as he is at that time the person in whom "rights are vested" under section 2 and liabilities are therefore imposed on him under section 3 and they remain with him. This conclusion seems correct in principle, but the question might then arise as to whether any subsequent transferee of the bill might also incur liabilities. The section 3 liabilities only attach to a person making a demand or taking delivery who has the rights vested by virtue of section 2. In a situation such as that in *The Aegean Sea*, the transferee (the charterer) might only become the lawful holder after the exhaustion of the bill and would have to fit itself within section 2(2)[82] by

---

[79] *Ibid.*, 62.

[80] This provides "2(5) Where rights are transferred by virtue of the operation of subsection (1) above in relation to any document, the transfer for which that subsection provides shall extinguish any entitlement to those rights which derives—(a) where that document is a bill of lading, from a person's having been an original party to the contract of carriage ...".

[81] See *infra*, Part 4(e)(i).

[82] This provides "2(2) Where, when a person becomes the lawful holder of a bill of lading, possession of the bill no longer gives a right (as against the carrier) to possession of the goods to which the bill relates, that person shall not have any rights transferred to him by virtue of subsection (1) above unless he becomes the holder of the bill—(a) by virtue of a transaction effected in pursuance of any contractual or other arrangements made before the time when such a right to possession ceased to attach to possession of the bill ...".

showing that it became the holder pursuant to a transaction made before the bill became spent. In these circumstances, it seems theoretically possible that more than one person might incur concurrent liabilities.

Subsequent to the decision in *The Aegean Sea* the Court of Appeal decided *Borealis A.B.* v. *Stargas Ltd. and Others (The Berge Sisar).*[83] In that case, a shipowner made a claim for damage to the ship against the charterer (Stargas), the shipper named in the bills (S.A.) and a bill of lading holder (Borealis). Borealis, the intended receiver, requested delivery of the cargo on 5th November 1993 but, after taking samples, thereafter rejected it. It was accepted that this was a "demand" within section 3(1)(c). On 11th November Borealis had sold the cargo to Dow for delivery at another port. On 12th November, Borealis requested delivery into Dow's terminal at the other port. In fact, Borealis did not receive the bills until 19th January 1994, when they were forwarded to Dow. Although Borealis did not have possession of the bills, the question arose whether it was liable on the bills for the period of 24 hours on 19th January. It seemed that it fell within section 2(2) as it later became the holder of the bills under a prior contractual arrangement. It also seemed that under section 2(5) Borealis (as an intermediate holder) lost all rights of suit when the bills were transferred to Dow, but the question arose whether that liability ceased when the bills were then endorsed to Dow. The majority in the Court of Appeal (Millett and Shiemann, L.JJ.) held that the bill of lading holder who had taken one of the steps in section 3(1) and then afterwards endorsed the bill and transferred the goods to a third party was then discharged from liabilities under the Act. Until the holder took actual delivery of the goods (and their position was thus irreversible) it could withdraw the claim or demand and endorse the bill to a third party. The majority considered that there was no good reason why the liability should be additional to instead of in substitution for the previous holder of the bill or why it should be liable simply because it had made a claim which was withdrawn. Neill, L.J. dissented, following the provisional views of Thomas, J. in *The Aegean Sea*, that liabilities once incurred remained with the holder.

Borealis' demand for the delivery of the cargo in the first port was not irrevocable in the sense that the delivery of the bulk was declined, although it is difficult to see why, if it once became liable under the provisions of the Act, it should be allowed later to renounce that liability for some reason (e.g. that it did not want to take delivery of the cargo). The same conclusion would apply, *a fortiori*, in relation to the situation on 19th January. One of the objects of the Act must have been to enable the parties to say with some precision who was liable and that inevitably will involve some mechanical (if not arbitrary) allocation of responsibilities. There is a considerable difference between the position of some intermediate holder who has not triggered the liability provisions of the

---

[83] [1999] Q.B. 863; [1998] 2 Lloyd's Rep. 475.

Act (*cf. Smurthwaite* v. *Wilkins*[84] where an intermediate holder was not liable for freight) and that of a holder who has become liable, even if for a short time. It is submitted, with respect, that the decision of Neill, L.J. is to be preferred. The decision of the majority could cause great uncertainty, e.g. where a holder is dithering about whether to withdraw the claim and it is clear that the Act does contemplate concurrent liabilities in some circumstances, e.g. of the holder and the shipper.[85]

Francis Reynolds himself has recently commented on the decision in *The Berge Sisar*.[86] His view was that the end result of the majority decision may seem fair, but that "it is obviously rather undignified that such a carefully drafted modern Act, far longer and more elaborate than its three section predecessor, should require to be salvaged by a case of 1862 on an Act of 1855".[87] He also questioned whether the majority view was correct and doubted whether there was in fact a "demand" at all. The present writer is therefore somewhat comforted in his own doubts about the decision. Leave to appeal to the House of Lords has been granted.

f. Implied Terms

i. *Nomination of port*
In *The Aegean Sea* the charterparty entitled the charterer to nominate a European port and the bill provided for delivery "at the port of SPAIN", although it was contemplated by all parties that delivery would be made at La Coruña. Under the charter, the bill should have incorporated the charterparty, but in fact merely incorporated the U.K. Carriage of Goods by Sea Act 1971 (and therefore the Hague-Visby Rules). In other circumstances the carrier may have sought to dispute the authority under which the bill had been issued, as it was not in the form provided under the charter, but in this case presumably ratified the authority of the issuer of the bill as the carrier sought to rely upon it. Owing to the form of the bill actually issued, it could not be said, however, that the endorsee of the bill could have acquired any express rights to nominate the port. In fact, the telex instruction to sail to La Coruña was issued by Repsol in its own name, although its evidence was that this was an error and that it should have been signed on behalf of the charterer (which was a subsidiary company of Repsol). The carrier sought to argue that it was an implied term of the bill that the other party to it was entitled to nominate the discharging port or berth in Spain and that there was also, therefore, an implied term as to the safety of the

---

[84] (1862) 11 C.B. (N.S.) 842.
[85] And see *Effort Shipping Co. Ltd.* v. *Linden Management S.A. (The Giannis NK)* [1998] A.C. 605; [1998] 1 Lloyd's Rep. 337.
[86] "The Carriage of Goods by Sea Act 1992 put to the test" [1999] L.M.C.L.Q. 161.
[87] *Ibid.*, 163.

port, so that it could claim as damages from Repsol the cost of the pollution claims.

There were inherent difficulties in formulating any implied term in the bill and, in particular, in defining who was the "other party". On the facts of the case, it could not have been the "receiver" as Repsol would never have become lawful holders of the bill by the time that the nomination had to be made. Moreover, a *prospective* holder (other than the shipper or the person to whom rights passed under C.O.G.S.A. 1992, s. 2) could not be the "other party". There would also be difficulties in identifying the appropriate person where there were string sales of the oil cargo, as f.o.b. shippers and intermediate holders would have little interest in nomination. Even if there had been c.i.f. sales it would still have been necessary to say which seller in the string had the right to nominate and to determine if that nomination could be changed, or would bind subsequent parties in the chain without notice.

As the bill constituted a separate contract of carriage, it must have provided for delivery to a specific place. Given the nature of the oil trade, and the fact that there was a short haul voyage, Thomas, J. concluded that it must have been contemplated by the parties to the separate contract contained in the bill that there was a charterparty in existence and the f.o.b. sellers must have appreciated that the charterer would be the last in a string of f.o.b. sellers and the first c.i.f. or ex ship, seller. It was the person in that position who would be the party interested in giving instructions as to the discharging port. It would therefore be understood that the right to give discharge instructions had been reserved to the charterer and that no-one else in the chain would have any interest in nominating a port before the vessel arrived, especially in the case of the ultimate receiver, who would have had no rights under the bill at the time that nomination was required. On this basis, Thomas, J. correctly (it is submitted) held that there was no necessity to imply a term. Additional factors against implying a term were the fact that the charterparty itself dealt expressly with the safe port requirement (so the shipowner did not need a remedy against the receiver) and that a very heavy contractual burden would be imposed on those becoming subject to the bill if a term were to be implied (for which insurance cover would be needed). If a charterparty bill had been issued, the safe port warranty could then have been incorporated in the bill expressly by reference, and it would then have been necessary to consider whether the charterer's obligations could, by the ordinary rules of incorporation, pass on to the bill of lading holder.[88] The existence of this possible route of liability against an indorsee shows again how risky it is for merchants to accept charterparty bills with general incorporation clauses.

---

[88] If the charterparty obligation was stated to arise on behalf of the "charterer", then this would probably not impose an obligation on an indorsee of an incorporated bill. See generally *Contracts for the Carriage of Goods*, para. 1.6.18.1.26.

ii. Safe port

It followed that if there was no implied right of Repsol to nominate, it could not also be implied that there was also a duty to nominate a safe port, but there was a discussion on the basis that there had been an implied term as to nomination. This involved an interesting diversion into a vexed question of charterparty law, namely whether it would be appropriate to imply a term of safety into a voyage (rather than a time) charter where that charter was silent on the point. It is an open question whether a term should be implied in a voyage charter where there is a range of unnamed ports (e.g. "East Coast U.S.A.")[89] and no express safety term. Thomas, J. was not convinced on the authorities that a term could be implied—given that express safety clauses were commonly inserted into many voyage charters. Although sympathetic to the wide view expressed in *Voyage Charters*[90] that there would be an obligation to nominate a safe port, Thomas, J. stated that "I do not think that one can conclude in *general* that a term as to safety will *always* be implied into voyage charterparties where there is an unspecified range of ports. The issue as to whether a term should be implied as to safety and the extent of the obligation may turn on the specific terms of the charter".[91] This must be the correct approach, although it does seem to favour implication as a natural starting point (if not presumption) which may be answered by the charterer pointing to the express terms as showing that the shipowner accepted the risks of a particular port.

Thomas, J. was prepared to accept the wider view in *Voyage Charters* for the purposes of argument in the context of the bill of lading and assumed that there had been an implied term in the bill as to nomination. He nevertheless took the view, in any event, that, even if it was correct that a term would be implied into *voyage charters*, it did not follow that one should be implied into the *bill of lading*, although there might be a term that the port or berth nominated was one at which it was *possible* for the vessel to discharge the cargo. Unlike the charterer, the bill of lading holder was not normally involved in direct negotiations with the shipowner and would be unlikely to have the equivalent of charterer's liability insurance. It follows that any safe port warranty in a bill of lading would have to be express.

iii. Indemnity

The carrier also claimed an implied indemnity on the independent basis that, if there was a right to nominate, then there was a tacit offer to indemnify against the consequences of obeying an order (by analogy with the charterers' orders

---

[89] Where there is a range of named ports it may be difficult to say that the charterer has promised the safety of a port that the shipowner is well able to check from its own knowledge: and see *The A.P.J. Priti* [1987] 2 Lloyd's Rcp. 37.

[90] J. Cooke (ed.), *Voyage Charters* (1993), 76: *cf.* the more cautious view in *Scrutton on Charterparties*, 20th edn. (1996), Article 69.

[91] [1998] 2 Lloyd's Rep. 39, 68 (emphasis added).

cases dealing with employment and indemnity clauses).[92] It was again held that there was no need to incorporate a term which was so onerous and uncertain in scope into a bill of lading, as opposed to a charter.[93]

iv. *"Shipper" defence under Hague-Visby Rules, Article IV rule 3*

A final argument by Repsol was that, if there had been any implied terms, any liability which it had would depend upon its being negligent, on the basis that under the Hague-Visby Rules, Article IV rule 3,[94] the shipper would only be responsible for its own fault and that Repsol could not have any higher liability under C.O.G.S.A. 1992, section 3. This would have been important as any implied obligation as to the safety of La Coruña would in effect have been strict. Thomas, J. considered that he was bound by Court of Appeal authority[95] to hold that the word "act" in Article IV rule 3 includes the act of shipment, as a positive act irrespective of whether there was also fault in it. By analogy, the shipowner argued that an act of nomination was also a positive act which removed any negligence defence in Article IV rule 3. However, he clearly had doubts about this conclusion,[96] reached in the context of a case on Article IV rule 6, and expressly left the nomination point open.

The point of more general importance was the inter-relationship between the Hague-Visby Rules use of the expression "shipper" and C.O.G.S.A. 1992, section 3, where any liabilities of a receiver are those "as if he had been a party" to the contract of carriage. The provision does not say "as if he had been a shipper", because that would have had the effect of altering the holder's status as consignee or endorsee.[97] Article IV rule 3, Article III and Article IV rule 6 of the Hague-Visby Rules all make reference to the rights or obligations of a "shipper". Thomas, J. held that "shipper" in Article IV rule 3 (and Article III

---

[92] See e.g. *Triad Shipping Co.* v. *Stellar Chartering & Brokerage Inc. (The Island Archon)* [1994] 2 Lloyd's Rep. 227.

[93] *Cf. Naviera Mogor S.A.* v. *Société Metallurgique de Normandie (The Nogar Marin)* [1988] 1 Lloyd's Rep. 412.

[94] Article IV rule 3 provides that "The shipper shall not be responsible for loss or damage sustained by the carrier or the ship arising or resulting from any cause without the act, fault or neglect of the shipper, his agents or his servants". Article III rule 5 provides that "The shipper shall be deemed to have guaranteed to the carrier the accuracy at the time of shipment of the marks, number, quantity and weight, as furnished by him, and the shipper shall indemnify the carrier against all loss, damages and expenses arising or resulting from inaccuracies in such particulars. The right of the carrier to such indemnity shall in no way limit his responsibility and liability under the contract of carriage to any person other than the shipper".

[95] *Effort Shipping Co. Ltd.* v. *Linden Management S.A. (The Giannis NK)* [1996] 1 Lloyd's Rep. 577 (C.A.): [1998] A.C. 605 (H.L.).

[96] At [1998] 2 Lloyd's Rep. 39, 70, where he cited some doubts of Lord Lloyd of Berwick in the House of Lords in *The Giannis NK* [1998] A.C. 605, 615; [1998] 1 Lloyd's Rep. 337, 343.

[97] *Contracts for the Carriage of Goods*, para. 1.6.5.1.31.

rule 5) of the Hague-Visby Rules means only the (actual) shipper and not the person on whom liabilities are imposed by C.O.G.S.A. 1992.[98] It follows that any protection given to the shipper in Article IV rule 3 would not also apply to qualify other obligations arising under the bill when it was transferred to another holder.

5 CONCLUSION

For shipowners, the decision of the High Court in *The Aegean Sea* is a mixed blessing, but on the whole advantageous. Claims against charterers for damage to the ship or consequential losses will not be subject to limitation of liability. By contrast, it may not be so easy to make claims for liabilities against cargo receivers.

For charterers (and their liability insurers) the decision on the limitation of liability point may be of great concern. Charterers do have a solution in that they can try to insist on terms in the charterparty to restrict their liabilities, either generally or by reference to L.L.M.C. 1976 (which could be incorporated contractually and made expressly to apply to the charterparty situation).

For cargo receivers and issuers of L.O.I., the case will provide some relief in that it restricts the circumstances in which they may incur liabilities under the Carriage of Goods by Sea Act 1992.

It is arguable that a large part of the judgment is strictly *obiter* in that, once Thomas, J. found that the charterer was not entitled to limit, the conclusions on L.L.M.C. 1976, Article 2 were not necessary. Similarly, once it was found that Repsol was not a holder of the bill, it was equally unnecessary to decide other points on the application of C.O.G.S.A. 1992. However, the case was fully argued and a full reasoned judgment was delivered on nearly all of the points under discussion. In those circumstances, it is rather artificial to isolate the first conclusions on limitation and liability under the bill, and to say that all the rest was obiter. It can be said that the decision is of considerable importance to the maritime community, but it is doubtful if the master and pilot of the *Aegean Sea* can have appreciated how much legal debate their actions would cause.

---

[98] [1998] 2 Lloyd's Rep. 39, 69.

Chapter 6

The Carrier's Duty of Seaworthiness under the Hague Rules

Malcolm Clarke

1 THE SCHEME OF THE RULES

The liability of a carrier for loss or damage to goods or delay in their delivery (L.D.D.), which has been caused by the unseaworthiness of the carrier's ship, is an issue that arises both under charterparties and under the Hague or Hague-Visby Rules (the Rules). It is with liability under the Rules that this paper is concerned.

a. An overriding obligation: Article III rule 1

The way the issue of seaworthiness arises in a dispute governed by the Rules is determined by the legal burden of proof. After a review of the English authorities, Lloyd, J. in *The Hellenic Dolphin*[1] described it as follows:

First, the claimant cargo-owner:

> "can raise a *prima facie* case against the shipowner by showing that cargo which had been shipped in good order and condition was damaged on arrival. The shipowner can meet that *prima facie* case by relying on an exception, for example, perils at sea. The position in that respect is exactly the same whether the Hague Rules are incorporated or not."

Second, the claimant:

> "can then seek to displace the exception by proving that the vessel was unseaworthy

---

[1] [1978] 2 Lloyd's Rep. 336, 339; quoted with approval by Phillips, J. in *The Theodegmon* [1990] 1 Lloyd's Rep. 52, 54. U.S.A. in this sense: *The Sabine Howaldt* [1971] 2 Lloyd's Rep. 78 (2 Cir); *Austracan* v. *Neptune Orient* (1985) 612 F.Supp. 578 (S.D.N.Y.); *Quaker Oats* v. *Torvanger* (1984) 734 F.2d 238 (5 Cir); *E.A.C. Timberlane* v. *Pisces* (1984) 745 F.2d 715 (5 Cir); *Pacific Employers Ins. Co.* v. *m/v Gloria* (1985) 767 F.2d 229 (5 Cir); *The Tuxpan* (1991) 765 F.Supp. 1150, 1174 (S.D.N.Y.); *The Jalavihar* (1997) 118 F.2d 328, 331 (5 Cir).

at commencement of the voyage and that the unseaworthiness was the cause of the loss ... But if at the end of the day, having heard all the evidence and drawn all the proper inferences, the court is left on the razor's edge, the cargo-owner fails on unseaworthiness and the shipowners are left with their defence of perils of the sea."

Third,

"If, on the other hand, the court comes down in favour of the cargo-owners on unseaworthiness, the shipowners can still escape by proving that the relevant unseaworthiness was not due to any want of due diligence on their part or on the part of their servants or agents".

The Rules were originally drafted for voluntary adoption by carriers in their bills of lading. However, almost none of them did so, and the Rules were used as the basis of a binding (and far from complete) international convention, signed at Brussels in 1924.[2] The scheme of the Rules was one that assumed a framework and substratum of common law[3] which, subsequently, English courts were not slow to read in with scant regard for uniformity of application between contracting states. As late as 1959, Lord Somervell said of Article III rule 1, that it "is an overriding obligation. If it is not fulfilled and the non-fulfilment causes the damage, the immunities of Article IV cannot be relied on."[4] This is still how the common law sees the obligation under the Rules to provide a seaworthy ship; but it was equally how the common law saw the obligation of seaworthiness before the Rules had been conceived.[5] Breach of an obligation, whether of seaworthiness at common law or of due diligence under the Rules, is overriding in its effect only after a defence has been established by the carrier. The breach overrides, i.e. destroys the defence.

A significant feature of English common law is that, to establish a defence, generally the carrier does not have to prove that he was not negligent. In England at least, that perspective has been carried over to the Rules. In some civil law countries that is not the view at all. Indeed, there has been nothing like unanimity within the wider world of common law. The most widespread view[6] is indeed the English perspective; but there is another view that it is a condition precedent to any defence, notably one based on one of the exceptions to liability

---

[2] Sturley, *The Legislative History of the Carriage of Goods by Sea Act* (Littleton, 1990), vol. 1, pp. 8 ff.

[3] See to this effect e.g. *Minister of Food* v. *Reardon Smith Line Ltd.* [1951] 2 Lloyd's Rep. 265, 271–272, *per* McNair, J. *Idem* in Canada: *The Farrandoc* [1967] 2 Lloyd's Rep. 276, 284, *per* Noel, J. (Exch. Ct.). But *cf. The Bunga Seroja* [1999] 1 Lloyd's Rep. 512, 518 (H.C.A.).

[4] *Maxine Footwear Co. Ltd.* v. *Can. Govt. Merchant Marine* [1959] A.C. 589, 602–603 (P.C.). See also *The Fiona* [1994] 2 Lloyd's Rep. 506, 519, *per* Hirst, L.J. (CA).

[5] E.g. Lord Sumner in *Matheos (Owners)* v. *Louis Dreyfus & Co.* [1925] A.C. 654, 666, with reference to *The Northumbria* [1906] P. 292.

[6] J. F. Wilson, *Carriage of Goods by Sea*, 3rd edn. (1998), 190.

set out in Article IV rule 2 of the Rules, that the carrier first establishes that he has exercised reasonable care, reasonable care to make the ship seaworthy or reasonable care of cargo, as the case may be.

The "condition precedent" is prominent in Canada, where Tetley, for example, maintains that "due diligence to make the vessel seaworthy in respect to the loss must be proven by the carrier *before* he may exculpate himself under art.4(2)".[7] He gets collateral support in the theory of *présomption de responsabilité*—a tendency of French courts to read into every exception to liability under the Rules the absence of fault,[8] to be proved, of course, by the carrier. Some Canadian courts do indeed take the same (conditional) view;[9] however, others do not. In *The Farrandoc*,[10] for example, the court applied the English view of the Rules: "it is for the cargo-owner to establish the damage to its goods, and in the event the shipowner establishes that he is entitled to an immunity provided for in the bill of lading, it should then become incumbent upon the cargo-owner to establish affirmatively (a) that the ship was unseaworthy and (b) that that unseaworthiness caused the damage . . ."

Moreover, with one reservation, most courts in the U.S.A. also take a view like that in England.[11] The reservation is that some courts state that the carrier may meet a *prima facie* case against him not only by establishing that the L.D.D. was caused by one of the excepted causes listed in Article IV rule 2 (i.e. the English position) but, alternatively, by proof (not of any specific exception

---

[7] W. Tetley, *Marine Cargo Claims*, 3rd edn. (Montreal, 1988) (hereafter "Tetley") 372 (emphasis added).

[8] E.g. *Oceanic, Rouen 11.6.1948*, DMF 1950.65; *Pacific Express, Rouen 22.7.1950*, DMF 1950.547. R. Rodière, *Traité Général de Droit Maritime* (Paris, 1967–1970), paras 752 and 754.

[9] E.g. *Toronto Elevators Ltd.* v. *Colonial Steamships Ltd.* [1950] Ex. C.R. 371, 375, *per* Angers, J.

[10] [1967] 2 Lloyd's Rep. 276, 284, *per* Noel, J. (Exch. Ct.). He continued with what seems to be a reference to "unless the shipowner has already proven unseaworthiness in order to establish that he falls within the conditions of the exception he is claiming". See also *Goodfellow Lumber Sales Ltd.* v. *Verreault* [1971] 1 Lloyd's Rep. 185, 188, *per* Ritchie, J. (Can. S.C.), with a reference to the speech of Lord Wright in *Smith Hogg & Co.* v. *Black Sea & Baltic Inc. Co.* [1940] A.C. 997, which belongs to the English school. *Idem* in the U.S.A.: *The Eurybates* 1981 A.M.C. 2350, 2355 (E.D. La.). France: *Ville d'Anvers, Rouen 30.6.1972*, DMF 1972.722.

[11] *Isbrandtsen Co.* v. *Federal Ins. Co.* (1952) 113 F.Supp. 357 (S.D.N.Y.); *aff'd* (1953) 205 F.2d 679 (2 Cir.), cert. denied (1953) 346 U.S. 866; *The Black Heron* 1964 A.M.C. 42 (2 Cir.); *The Irish Spruce* [1976] 1 Lloyd's Rep. 63, 72 *per* Goettel, J. (S.D.N.Y.); *The Lindenbank*, 1979 A.M.C. 283, 290–291 (S.D.N.Y.); *The Frank Phipps* 1983 A.M.C. 1288, 1295 (E.D. La); (1990) 903 F.2d 675 (9 Cir.); *The Tasman Star* (1995) 69 F.3d 418 (11 Cir.). Note, however, that the conditional view has been taken by some courts in cases decided not under the Rules but under the U.S. Harter Act: e.g. *The Ultramar* (1987) 685 F.Supp. 887, 897 (S.D.N.Y.); also *The Hans Leonhardt* (1989) 719

but simply) that he exercised due diligence to make the ship seaworthy.[12] However, the alternative is less of an alternative than at first it appears. Schoenbaum, surely, is correct in his argument[13] that it is not enough for the carrier to show due diligence in general: that would excuse him when the cause of L.D.D. was unknown. On the contrary, the carrier must show due diligence against a specific danger which, in effect, converts the carrier's response into a particular defence under Article IV rule 2 such as perils of the sea (rule (c)). That being so, the U.S. position is very much the same as the English position—not least because, as is explained next,[14] the issue of due diligence, which in England usually arises indirectly via another exception, can also arise via Article IV rule 2(p) as is seen more commonly in France and the U.S.A.

b. The place of Article IV rule 1

The English view, with its assumptions about the impact of English common law on the Rules, is not obvious at all from the Rules themselves. Whereas the common lawyer understands Article IV rule 1 as a statement of the second phase in the legal burden of proof,[15] French lawyers, for example, have been puzzled by its significance. Rodière, a leading French commentator of his day, said that Article IV rule 1 was perplexing to the dogmatic Latin mind but was just a typical English compromise, which French lawyers had to put up with.

To French lawyers Article IV rule 1 appears to stand alone but alongside the cluster of exceptions to liability in Article IV rule 2, as just another such exception.[16] To the English lawyer the idea of unseaworthiness as a defence, as

---

F.Supp. 479, 504 (E.D. La.), with reference to *The Vallescura* (1934) 70 F.2d 13; 293 U.S. 303, decided before the Rules came into force in the U.S.A. Under the Harter Act, Cardozo, J. in the Supreme Court stated that due diligence to make the ship seaworthy is a "condition" of exoneration, apparently whether want of due diligence is a cause of L.D.D. or not: *The Isis* (1933) 290 U.S. 333, 343.

[12] E.g. *The Tuxpan* (1991) 765 F.Supp. 1150, 1173 (S.D.N.Y.). *Idem* when the facts concern not the condition of the ship (Article III rule 1) but care of cargo (Article III rule 2): e.g., *The Cruz del Sur* (1985) 748 F.2d 563, 566 (11 Cir.); *The Gloria* (1985) 767 F.2d 229, 239 (5 Cir.); *The Gilda* (1986) 790 F.2d 1209, 1213 (5 Cir.). Schoenbaum, *Admiralty and Maritime Law*, 2nd edn. (St Paul, 1994), 569.

[13] *Ibid.*, 567, n. 16.

[14] *Infra*, Part 1(b)–(c).

[15] *Supra*, Part 1(a).

[16] R. Rodière, *Traité Général de Droit Maritime* (Paris, 1967–1970), paras. 618 and 754. *Idem*: De Juglart Sem. Jur. 56-II-9135; Prodromides DMF 1963.706; Lamy, *Transports* (1998), vol. 2, para. 506. *Coral Acropora, Paris 1.2.1977*, DMF 1977.650, 660; *Arno, Cass. com. 27.6.1995*, DMF 1996.302 note Régnier. A contention of that kind was rejected in England in *Leesh River Tea Co.* v. *B.I.S.N. Co. Ltd.* [1967] 2 Q.B. 250 (C.A.).

an exception to liability, is simply bizarre. But, if the English lawyer were to look at the Rule not in the context of common law but in isolation, the French view of the Rule might seem less bizarre. In the original 1924 version of the Rules and the Carriage of Goods by Sea Act of that year,[17] Article III is headed "Responsibilities and Liabilities"; and Article IV is headed "Rights and Immunities". First in the list of "Rights and Immunities" is Article IV rule 1. Moreover, like Article IV rule 2, which includes well known exceptions such as perils of the sea and acts of God, Article IV rule 1 begins with the words "Neither the carrier nor the ship shall be liable for loss or damage". It then refers to what is apparently an event which, like those listed in Article IV rule 2, excuses the carrier. In the case of Article IV rule 1 that event is unseaworthiness.

Moreover, it is entirely consistent with the French view that the obligation of due diligence to make the ship seaworthy is in Article III rule 1, which is headed "Responsibilities and Liabilities". If asked to relate that to Article IV rule 1, the French lawyer would have little hesitation: the former is an exception to the latter. The carrier is excused by unseaworthiness, unless it was caused by his failure to exercise the requisite diligence. So, it is not for the carrier to prove compliance with Article III rule 1 (the common law view) but for the claimant to show that it has been broken. Nothing strange about that: there are many other exclusions of that kind, not least Article IV rule 2(b), whereby the liability of the carrier is excepted "unless caused by the actual fault of the carrier".[18]

Be that as it may, that is not the predominant common law view. According to the common law before the Rules, when the carrier had established a defence, it was for the claimant to negate the defence by proving breach of an overriding obligation, such as seaworthiness.[19] The natural tendency would be for the common lawyer to see the Rules *mutatis mutandis* in the same way. The simplest adaptation of the common law to the Rules would have been to say that, when the carrier had established a defence, it was for the claimant to negate the defence by proof of breach of the (overriding) obligation to exercise due diligence to make the ship seaworthy. However, for the claimant that would have made a hard burden of proof even harder.[20] To prove, for example, failure in some dry dock procedure in a distant part of the world at some time in the past would be too much. So, according to the actual adaptation of the common law

---

[17] *Cf.* the corresponding text of the Carriage of Goods by Sea Act 1971

[18] See also the Institute Time Clauses Hulls, cl. 7. *Cf.* cases under the similar wording of the Fire statute, 46 U.S. Code sec. 182, such as *The Eurypylus* 1982 A.M.C. 1710 (2 Cir.).

[19] Alternatively the claimant might defeat the carrier's defence by establishing lack of care of cargo. In the Rules care of cargo is required by Article III rule 2.

[20] It should be recalled that in England, although less so in other common law jurisdictions, it is relatively easy for the carrier to raise a defence such as peril of the seas: see Clarke [1998] U.L.R. 351, 335–356.

scheme to the Rules, the claimant, who must establish breach of an overriding obligation of some kind, gets some help from Article IV rule 1. The scheme, phase 2 of the legal burden of proof, is that, if the claimant has established that L.D.D. has resulted, not from lack of due diligence, but from the unseaworthiness of the ship at the beginning of the voyage, "the burden of proving the exercise of due diligence shall be on the carrier". Clearly, proving unseaworthiness is less difficult than proving the lack of due diligence, if any, that led to it. By establishing unseaworthiness, the claimant makes a lesser but sufficient case of want of due diligence—sufficient for the onus to be passed back to the carrier to prove that in fact due diligence, as required by Article III rule 1 has been exercised.

c. The place of Article IV rule 2(p): latent defects

In the Rules the cause of clarity is not promoted by the possibility that seaworthiness, in the narrow sense of the condition of the ship,[21] may arise not only under Article IV rule 1 in the way described[22] but also in connection with one of the excepted perils, Article IV rule 2(p). According to this rule the carrier is not responsible for L.D.D. "arising or resulting from ... Latent defects not discoverable by due diligence". Insofar as the defect in question is in the ship,[23] to the English lawyer that seems to be something "already covered by [Article IV] Rule 1"[24] and, by implication, largely superfluous. The exception in Article IV rule 2(p) is pleaded much more often in France[25] and in the U.S.A. Indeed, in the U.S.A. the legal burden of proof is sometimes stated (differently from that in England) to take in both possibilities.[26] In England very few judgments have addressed the exception directly. However, in *The Antigoni*[27] it was discussed by Staughton, L.J.:

> "The shipowners relied at the trial on two defences under article IV of the Hague-Visby Rules. The first was in rule 1, that the casualty (or rather the unseaworthiness of the vessel) was not caused by want of due diligence on their part

---

[21] On this distinction, see *infra*, Part 2(b).

[22] *Supra*, Part 1(b).

[23] It might lie in other equipment for which the carrier is responsible.

[24] *Scrutton on Charterparties and Bill of Lading*, 20th edn. (1996) 445. That is true only in the literal sense that liability in respect of defective ships is dealt with in Article IV rule 1: the onus of proof is patently different as the defect must be proved not by the claimant but by the carrier; e.g. *De Carvalho* v. *Kent Line* (1951) 32 M.P.R. 282, 295, *per* Winter, J. (Nfdld S.C.).

[25] Clarke, *Aspects of the Hague Rules* (The Hague, 1976) 136 ff. Lamy, *Transports* (1998), vol. 2, paras 506–8.

[26] *Supra*, Part 1(b).

[27] [1991] 1 Lloyd's Rep. 209, 222 (C.A.); applied in *The Fjord Wind* [1999] 1 Lloyd's Rep. 307, 319, by Moore-Bick, J. See also *ibid*., 327. Another notable exception is *The Amstelslot* [1963] 2 Lloyd's Rep. 223 (H.L.), *infra*, Part 4(b).

to make the ship seaworthy; the second, under rule 2(p), that the casualty was caused by a latent defect not discoverable by due diligence. In either case the burden of proof lay on the shipowners—under rule 1, because the rule says so, and under rule 2 by virtue of the common law principle that he who seeks to rely upon an exception in his contract must bring himself within it.

However, the two defences were alternatives. The shipowners could succeed if they established either one of them, and did not need to establish both. Mr Crookenden on their behalf complains that the Judge misunderstood the law, and imposed a duty on them to establish both defences. Mr Anthony Diamond, Q.C. has immense experience of the Hague-Visby Rules. But it is possible for even the most experienced to err; and the relationship between Article IV rule 1 and rule 2(p) is not wholly apparent at first sight."

The view of *Scrutton*[28] is that, as "due diligence must be exercised not only by the shipowner himself but also by his servants or agents, the protection given by the rule in relation to the physical condition of the ship protects, in effect, only against latent defect".

Staughton, L.J. stressed that it was indeed, in effect, that that was so and observed that, although the carrier does not have to "establish a latent defect if he seeks to rely on Article IV rule 1", nonetheless "he will find it much easier to establish due diligence if he can point to the likelihood of a latent defect, and much more difficult if he can suggest none, or only one which is wholly implausible".[29]

Further, the judge approved[30] the view of *Scrutton* that, as Article IV rule 2(p) covers "defects which would not have been discovered by the exercise of due diligence even though the shipowner could not show that he had in fact exercised such diligence",[31] the carrier gets an immunity additional to that provided in Article IV rule 1.

2 UNSEAWORTHINESS

As the common law context for which the Rules were intended had its own definition, no necessity was seen for a definition of unseaworthiness in the Rules. The assumption was that the common law meaning applied. Moreover,

---

[28] *Scrutton on Charterparties*, 19th edn. (1984) 446 (20th edn. (1996), 441) in a comment written on Article IV rule 1 and quoted by Staughton, L.J. in *The Antigoni* [1991] 1 Lloyd's Rep. 209, 213.

[29] *Ibid.*, 213. See also: *The Subro Valour* [1995] 1 Lloyd's Rep. 509, 516–517, *per* Clarke, J.; and *The Lydia Flag* [1998] 2 Lloyd's Rep. 652, a case under Institute Time Clauses Hulls, cl. 11, in which the defendant insurer found it impossible to prove that the insured owner had lacked due diligence without also being able to establish the nature of the defect.

[30] [1991] 1 Lloyd's Rep. 209, 213 with reference to *Scrutton*, 19th edn. 450.

[31] 20th edn. 445. That view had the support of Branson, J. in *Corporacion Argentina de Productores de Carnes* v. *Royal Mail Lines Ltd.* (1939) 64 Ll.L.Rep. 188, 192.

although the onus of proof is different, the meaning of notions such as unseaworthiness is generally understood[32] to be the same as that in an insurance policy.[33] According to the common law, the "ship must have that degree of fitness which an ordinary careful owner would require his vessel to have at the commencement of her voyage having regard to all the probable circumstances of it".[34] The question to ask is whether "a prudent owner would have required that it should be made good *before* sending his ship to sea, had he known of it?"[35] The standard beforehand has been stressed because at common law "it is well established that a ship is not unseaworthy because of a defect, at the beginning of the voyage, which can easily in the ordinary course of management be rectified on the voyage".[36] This is commonly illustrated by the open porthole[37] or leaking tap[38]—as long as it is one that will be sealed in good time.[39] Nor, on the one hand, is a ship unseaworthy because it is exposed to an ephemeral risk of an event such as fire which, if it occurred, would make the ship unseaworthy.[40] However, on the other hand, if electrical wiring or its insulation were in such a poor condition at the commencement of the voyage that an electrical fire could well be started, and did so, the ship would be

---

[32] E.g. White [1995] L.M.C.L.Q. 221, 222. This appears to have also been the view of *Arnould's Law of Marine Insurance and Average*, 16th edn. (1981) (hereafter "*Arnould*") vol. 2; see e.g. para. 735. *Quaere* whether the limitation cases on "actual fault and privity" are, as suggested by White [1995] L.M.C.L.Q. 221, 232 relevant here; see *contra*, e.g. *The Hyundai Explorer* (1996) 93 F.3d 641 (6 Cir.); Tabrisky (1997) 28 J.M.L.C. 359.

[33] See *Arnould*, paras 730 ff. As regards unseaworthiness in charterparties, see Liang [2000] J.B.L.

[34] *McFadden* v. *Blue Star Line* [1905] 1 K.B. 697, 706, *per* Channell, J., applied to the Rules by e.g. Scrutton, L.J. in *F. C. Bradley & Sons Ltd.* v. *Federal S.N. Co.* (1926) 24 Ll.L.Rep. 446, 454 (C.A.); and, more recently, by Moore-Bick, J. in *The Fjord Wind* [1999] 1 Lloyd's Rep. 307, 315. U.S.A.: *The Southwark* (1903) 191 U.S. 1; generally see *Benedict on Admiralty* vol. 2A (ed. Sturley) (hereafter "*Benedict*"), ch. VII.

[35] *McFadden* v. *Blue Star Line* [1905] 1 K.B. 697, 706 (emphasis added).

[36] *Bradley* v. *Federal S.N. Co.* (1926) 24 Ll.L.Rep. 446, 455.

[37] *Steel* v. *State Line S.S. Co.* (1877) 3 App. Cas. 72.

[38] *Virginia Co.* v. *Norfolk Shipping Co.* (1912) 17 Com. Cas. 277, 278, *per* Lord Sumner.

[39] *The Apostolis* [1996] 1 Lloyd's Rep. 475, 483, *per* Tuckey, J.; decision reversed on other grounds [1997] 2 Lloyd's Rep. 241 (C.A.). In *The Indiana* (1901) 181 U.S. 218 the ship was unseaworthy because the officers and crew were unaware that a porthole near the water line was open and then the sea entered and damaged cargo.

[40] A ship "will not be unseaworthy simply because she or her cargo will be endangered if an act or activity occurs on board her which it is not necessary to perform while she is in that conditon and which reasonable care requires shall not be performed while she is in that condition": *The Apostolis* [1997] 2 Lloyd's Rep. 241, 257, *per* Phillips, L.J. See also *ibid.*, 245, *per* Leggatt, L.J.

regarded as unseaworthy.[41] In all cases the prudence required is an international rather than local standard.[42]

a. Relative unseaworthiness

The requirement of seaworthiness is not absolute: ships are not required to be fit to carry any cargo anywhere at any time. The requirement is relative.[43] What is required of a particular carrier in a particular case depends on at least four points.

The requirement of seaworthiness depends, first, on the cargo. A ship which has pumps in the hold but not pumps that can cope with the cargo, such as a cargo of wet sugar, is unseaworthy.[44] A ship contracted to carry cattle, which had not been properly cleaned after its last voyage so that the cattle on the next voyage caught disease, was unseaworthy for the later voyage.[45]

The requirement depends, secondly, on the voyage. Clearly, more can be expected of a ship that is to cross the oceans than one that is to follow the coast.[46] Moreover, a ship that departs from A to B without enough fuel to reach B is unseaworthy for the voyage to B.[47] Less obviously, a ship which, having come from A, departs on a voyage from B to D via C with goods for D and which, because it has come from A, is not allowed into C without fumigation which damages the goods, is unseaworthy as regards those goods on that voyage.[48] The decision would have been the same in that case if, because of their provenance, the goods could not have been discharged at D. In a later decision,[49] Staughton, J. said:

---

[41] *The Subro Valour* [1995] 1 Lloyd's Rep. 509, 516, *per* Clarke, J.; *Scrutton*, 19th edn., 84

[42] In *The Kapitan Sakharov* (20th February 1998) Unreported (Adm. Ct) Clarke, J. rejected the argument that the standard should be that of the (Russian) flag state, rather than an international standard. *Cf. Arnould*, para. 731.

[43] *Steel* v. *State Line S.S. Co.* (1877) 3 App. Cas. 72, 77, *per* Lord Cairns. Australia: *The Bunga Seroja* [1999] 1 Lloyd's Rep. 512, 517 (H.C.A.); Belgium; *H.B. Antwerp 2.1.1996* (1996) 31 E.T.L. 667. Germany: Herber, *Seehandelsrecht* (1999), para. 28.2; Prüssmann and Rabe, *Seehandelsrecht* (1992), para. 559 Bl. U.S.A.: *The Southwark* (1903) 191 U.S. 1.

[44] *Stanton* v. *Richardson* (1875) 45 L.J.Q.B. 78 (H.L.).

[45] *Tattersall* v. *National S.S. Co.* (1884) 12 Q.B.D. 297.

[46] *Charles Brown & Co. Ltd.* v. *Nitrate Producers S.S. Co. Ltd.* (1937) 58 Ll.L.Rep. 188, 190, *per* Porter, J.

[47] *The Vortigern* [1899] P. 140.

[48] *Ciampa* v. *B.I.S.N. Co. Ltd.* [1915] 2 K.B. 774 (lemons from Naples to London via Marseille on a ship from Mombassa). *Cf. The Derby* [1984] 1 Lloyd's Rep. 635; *affd* [1985] 2 Lloyd's Rep. 325 (C.A.), in which a time charterer ordered the chartered ship to a port where she was "blacked".

[49] *The Good Friend* [1984] 2 Lloyd's Rep. 586, 592.

"Seaworthiness at common law in my opinion included, under the heading of what is sometimes called cargoworthiness, an undertaking that the ship shall be reasonably fit to receive and carry the cargo and deliver it at the specified destination. If the ship's condition is such that she is not reasonably fit for those tasks, the undertaking has been broken, even if the cargo suffers no physical damage."

Damages are recoverable for delay (and loss of market) as well as damages for damage to goods, if caused by unseaworthiness in breach of Article III rule 1. In contrast, "there is no case in which a ship has been held to be unseaworthy merely because she has to lighten in order to get into port. So also if she has to lighten in order to get through the canal."[50] As long as the goods can be delivered on time and in appropriate condition at the agreed destination, albeit at extra cost, the ship is seaworthy.

The requirement depends, thirdly, on the time of year. Clearly, a voyage across the North Atlantic in June requires rather different measures from one across the North Atlantic in January.[51] An obvious difference is that, for a winter voyage, pipes must be protected from low temperatures.[52]

Finally, the requirement of seaworthiness depends on the state of knowledge at the time. It would not be enough for the carrier to say "at the time this ship was built she was seaworthy in the state of knowledge then existing, and I am not going to alter her in view of later discoveries".[53] "The standard of seaworthiness must rise with the improved knowledge of shipbuilding and navigation."[54]

b. Kinds of unseaworthiness

Seaworthiness in one sense, a strict and narrow sense, concerns the ship's defences against nature. Nature includes not only the wind and the waves but also rocks and shoals. Clearly, a ship that leaks more than a little is unseaworthy. However, a ship is more than a refuge; it is a construction with a positive role. A ship that cannot make way because it lacks fuel[55] or the right kind of fuel,[56] or cannot go the right way because of defects in navigation

---

[50] *The Acquacharm* [1982] 1 Lloyd's Rep. 7, 9, *per* Lord Denning, M.R. (C.A.) concerning the (considerable) cost of lightening a ship to get through the Panama Canal.

[51] *Charles Brown* v. *Nitrate Producers* (1937) 58 Ll.L.Rep. 188, 190, *per* Porter, J.

[52] *Brussels 13.10.1967* (1968) 3 E.T.L. 373.

[53] *F. C. Bradley & Sons Ltd.* v. *Federal S.N. Co.* (1926) 24 Ll.L.Rep. 446, 454, *per* Scrutton, L.J. (C.A.).

[54] *Burges* v. *Wickham* (1863) 3 B. & S. 669, 693, *per* Blackburn, J.

[55] *The Vortigern* [1899] P. 140; *The Susquehanna* [1975] 1 Lloyd's Rep. 216 (S.D.N.Y.).

[56] *The Makedonia* [1962] 1 Lloyd's Rep. 316; *The Evje (No. 2)* [1976] 2 Lloyd's Rep. 714. *Idem* proper ballasting: *The Canada Mail* (1974) 377 F.Supp. 657, 660 (W.D. Wash).

equipment[57] is not fit for the role of navigation and, for that reason, unseaworthy.

Seaworthiness both at common law and under the Rules is also understood in a second sense, a broader sense, that includes cargoworthiness, i.e. the fitness of the ship as a temporary mobile store for the cargo in question. That role requires that the cargo areas, including containers provided by the carrier,[58] be sufficiently clean, dry, secure and free from contamination[59] and likely to remain so throughout the voyage. Moreover, the ship that was detained en route for fumigation, because she lacked the right documents such as a "bill of health", was not seaworthy when she set out.[60] The same is true of a ship susceptible to arrest.[61] However, the more specific contention that, "if two parcels of cargo are so stowed that one can injure the other during the course of the voyage, the ship is unseaworthy" has been rejected.[62]

Other kinds of defect straddle the line between unseaworthiness in the narrow sense and uncargoworthiness. Clearly such is the case of a defect that allows seawater into the hold in such quantity that it not only damages cargo but endangers the ship. That is also the case of some shortcomings in the competence of members of the crew. Most obviously, the master must be sufficiently conversant with the handling characteristics of the ship[63] and with

---

[57] *The Irish Spruce* [1976] 1 Lloyd's Rep. 63 (S.D.N.Y.). Evidently the ship must have up to date charts: e.g. *The Janet Quinn* (1971) F.Supp. 1329 (S.D.N.Y.). However, courts have not always insisted that a vessel have radar: e.g. *The Jalavihar* (1997) 118 F.2d 328 (5 Cir.); *Tetley*, 384. Concerning whether the ship must take on a pilot, see *Arnould*, para. 741.

[58] *The Sealand Voyager* (1992) 27 E.T.L. 361, 370 (3 Cir.). *Cf. The Skanderborg* (1995) 897 F.Supp. 659 (D. Puerto Rico).

[59] Including smells associated with previous cargo, such as fishmeal, which might adversely affect the next cargo, such as coffee beans: *BGH 9.4.1990*, TranspR. 1990, 333.

[60] *Levy* v. *Costerton* (1816) 4 Camp. 389, accepted as correct but distinguished by Hobhouse, J. in *The Derby* [1984] 1 Lloyd's Rep. 635, 640. *Cf. Rankin* v. *Potter* (1865) L.R. 1 Q.B. 162, 166, *per* Erle, C.J., that the ship there was not unseaworthy because it lacked "a document which relates merely to a compliance with the requisitions of the statute in the port of loading; . . . it does not at all bear upon the risk of the voyage after the ship is out of the port, or upon the admissibility of the ship at her port of discharge".

[61] Unless the carrier has the resources to obtain her release or can post a bond such as that provided by a P. & I. Club: *The Faith* (1965) 252 F.Supp. 54, 58 (N.D. Ohio).

[62] By Swinfen Eady, L.J. in *The Thorsa* [1916] P. 257, 261 (C.A.) with reference to the possible contamination of chocolate by cheese; cited with approval by Phillips, L.J. in *The Apostolis* [1997] 2 Lloyd's Rep. 241, 257 (C.A.). But *cf. The Anthony II* [1966] 2 Lloyd's Rep. 437 (S.D.N.Y.). *Cf.* also, Germany, Prüssmann and Rabe, *Seehandelsrecht* (1992), para. 559 C3.

[63] *Standard Oil* v. *Clan Line* [1924] A.C. 100.

the needs of the particular cargo.[64] Engineers must be competent to run the particular machinery.[65] Moreover, competence depends not only on skill and knowledge[66] but also on personality and character. Such matters become more important as the ship's complement diminishes but the technical skills required of its members increase.

> "In considering efficiency, the matters to be considered, in my view, are not limited to a disabling want of skill and a disabling want of knowledge. A man may be well qualified and hold the highest grade in certificates of competency and yet have a disabling lack of will and inclination to use his skill and knowledge so that they are well nigh useless to him. Such a man may be unable efficiently to use the skill and knowledge which he has through drunken habits or through ill-health."[67]

c. Unseaworthy when?

When the state of the ship arises under Article IV rule 2(p), the status of the latent defect as something which excuses the carrier indicates clearly that it must have caused the L.D.D. and, therefore, that it must have existed at the time of the loss or damage[68] or, if the claimant's case is based on delay, shortly before the delay began.

When the state of the ship arises under Article IV rule 1, the concern is with unseaworthiness "caused by want of due diligence" on the part of the carrier.

---

[64] E.g. concerning the temperature and stowage of bananas: *The Heinz Horn* [1970] 1 Lloyd's Rep. 191 (5 Cir.); the sensitivity of coffeebeans: *BGH 9.4.1990*, TranspR. 1990.333.

[65] *The Makedonia* [1962] 1 Lloyd's Rep. 316; *The Eurybates* 1981 A.M.C. 2350 (E.D. La.). See also *Hongkong Fir Shipping Co.* v. *Kawasaki Kisen Kaisha* [1962] 2 Q.B. 26 (C.A.), in which Salmon, J. found (at 34) as a fact, accepted on appeal, that "the machinery was in a reasonably good condition at Liverpool but, by reason of its age, it needed to be maintained by an experienced, competent, careful and adequate engine room staff". See also *Cerro Sales* v. *Atlantic Marine* 1976 A.M.C. 375 (S.D.N.Y.): the crew's inability to handle an emergency fire situation rendered the ship unseaworthy.

[66] E.g. *Standard Oil* v. *Clan Line* [1924] A.C. 100.

[67] *The Makedonia* [1962] 1 Lloyd's Rep. 316, 335, *per* Hewson, J. See also *Standard Oil Co.* v. *Clan Line* [1924] A.C. 100, 121, *per* Lord Atkinson; and in Canada: *The Farrandoc* [1967] 2 Lloyd's Rep. 232, *affd ibid.*, 276 (Exch. Ct.). The ill health, notably of the master, may be temporary but nonetheless render the ship unseaworthy at the time: *Arnould*, para. 739. *Cf. Re Intercontinental Properties Management S.A.* 1977 A.M.C. 1841 (E.D. Va.): a ship is not rendered unseaworthy merely because one ordinary seaman "goes berserk", even though he sinks the ship. For a study of the human aspects of seaworthiness, see White [1995] L.M.C.L.Q. 221.

[68] In France, where this exception is often pleaded, courts have taken this view: *Oceanic*, Douai, 23.4.1953, DMF 1953.451; *Zit*, Aix 9.6.1959, DMF 1959.534; *General Dufour*, Aix 6.1.1960, DMF 1961.25. *Idem*: Rodière (*supra*, n. 16), para. 756; and D. J. Markianos, *Die Übernahme der Haager Regeln in die nationale Gesetze über die Verfrachtung* (Hamburg, 1960) 132. However, in one of the rare cases of Article IV rule 2(p) in England, the court applied the common law reference to the beginning of the voyage: *The Amstelslot* [1963] 2 Lloyd's Rep. 223, 234, *per* Lord Devlin (H.L.).

According to Article III rule 1 that diligence must be exercised "before and at the beginning of the voyage" in question. "At" suggests a particular time, and fuels the assumption that on this point the rule is the same as that of the common law, that the seaworthiness that the diligence seeks to achieve should be tested at the beginning of the voyage.[69] Indeed, such is the strength of the assumption that Salmon, L.J., said that any other view would "be a very strained and, indeed, altogether impossible meaning" to put upon Article IV rule 1.[70] As a matter of interpretation, that may be so. However, in Germany, the wisdom of the view has been questioned. In 1977 the Bundesgerichthof referred (only) to German writers on the subject and concluded that to require the claimant to establish unseaworthiness at the beginning of the voyage rather than later might be to impose too onerous a burden of proof on the claimant.[71] Moreover, more recently a prominent German writer has pointed out[72] that the beginning of the voyage was originally chosen as the critical time on the supposition that, once the ship had left, the state of the ship was outside the control of the carrier; and that today better communications and the practice of round trips makes that view more doubtful.

d. Proof of unseaworthiness

Proof by the claimant that someone else's ship was unseaworthy at a specific time in the not too recent past might be very difficult indeed, if the court were not willing to draw certain inferences. In cases of so-called "functional breakdown",[73] some part of the ship fails suddenly at sea and the source of the defect may or may not be susceptible to age assessment by inspecting rust or the rings on a tree. If, however, the breakdown occurs soon after the ship has commenced the voyage, courts are prepared to assume that the defect was sufficiently developed at the commencement of the voyage for the ship to have been unseaworthy at that time.[74] That does not, of course, necessarily mean that the carrier failed in due diligence, for the defect may not have been discoverable; but nonetheless it will be presumed to have been unseaworthy

---

[69] *The Makedonia* [1962] 1 Lloyd's Rep. 316, 338, *per* Hewson, J. See also *The Amstelslot* [1963] 2 Lloyd's Rep. 223; in Canada: *Western Canadian S.S. Co.* v. *Canadian Commercial Corp.* [1960] S.C.R. 632; *De Carvalho* v. *Kent Line* (1950) 26 M.P.R. 77, 87, *per* Dunfield, J. (Nfdl S.C.). and in the U.S.A.: *The S.S. Anghyra* (1957) 157 F.Supp. 737, 750 (E.D. Va.).

[70] *Leesh River Tea Co.* v. *B.I.S.N. Co. Ltd.* [1967] 2 Q.B. 250, 275 (C.A.).

[71] *BGH 23.2.1978* (1978) 13 E.T.L. 452, 355. *Idem*: Prüssmann and Rabe, *Seehandelsrecht* (1992) para. 559 D6. But *cf.* Herber, *Seehandelsrecht* (1999), para. 28.2.

[72] Herber, *ibid.*

[73] E.g. *de Carvalho* v. *Kent Line* (1951) 32 M.P.R. 282, 305, *per* Dunfield, J. (Nfdl S.C.).

[74] *Lindsay* v. *Klein* [1911] A.C. 194, 197, *per* Lord Loreburn, L.C.

then in the absence of proof that the defect might have developed later because, for example, the ship subsequently met unusually severe weather.

In one case a leak which became apparent after three days of sailing in normal weather was taken to have begun at least three days earlier.[75] In another case steering gear which broke down after three days of fair weather was presumed to have been defective when the ship commenced the voyage.[76] Decisions on this basis have been reached in the U.S.A. although the interval was longer. When "a vessel founders and sinks in weather and sea conditions which are normal and expectable, there is a presumption that the vessel was unseaworthy", even after six days at sea, "unless the foundering and sinking can be otherwise explained".[77] So it was also when a rudder fell off in an "expectable" wind of Force 7 on the Beaufort scale some two weeks after leaving port.[78]

When there is unseaworthiness other than "functional breakdown", its origin in point of time must be proved in some other way. Clearly that can sometimes be inferred from the age of the defect; for example, metallurgists can put an age on corrosion.[79] The sheer volume of seawater in the ship may indicate how long the ship has been leaking.[80] Otherwise proof may be difficult except in two kinds of case: when the unseaworthiness lies in a defect in design;[81] or, unless it is lost during the voyage, in lack of essential equipment.

e. Causation

To succeed against the carrier the claimant must prove that the L.D.D. was one "arising or resulting from unseaworthiness": Article IV rule 1. Although the judges sometimes refer to it as the "real", "effective" or "dominant" cause, what is required is not the causal connection between ordinary breach of contract and damage but merely the "but for" connection sometimes referred to as

---

[75] *The City of Alberni* [1947] 2 D.L.R. 647, 651. See also *The Perama* (1968) 388 F.2d 434 (2 Cir.). *Benedict*, para. 63.

[76] *The Assunzione* [1956] 2 Lloyd's Rep. 468. See also *The Friso* [1980] 1 Lloyd's Rep. 469; and *The Fjord Wind* [1999] 1 Lloyd's Rep. 307, 319, *per* Moore-Bick, J. *Arnould*, para. 734.

[77] *Transpacific Lines Inc.* v. *Marianas Maritime Corp.* 1979 A.M.C. 1467, 1475 (Pacific Islands).

[78] *The Columbia* 1976 A.M.C. 931 (S.D.N.Y.).

[79] E.g. *The Bryntawe* (1928) 32 Ll.L.Rep. 155, 157, *per* Judge Chetwynd Leech; *Cranfield Bros. Ltd.* v. *Tatem S.N. Co. Ltd.* (1939) 64 Ll.L.Rep. 264, 267, *per* Hilbery, J.

[80] *R. Silcock & Sons Ltd.* v. *Maritime Lighterage Co. Ltd.* (1937) 57 Ll.L.Rep. 78, 80, *per* Slesser, L.J. (C.A.).

[81] *Angliss* v. *P.&O. S.N. Co. Ltd.* [1927] 2 K.B. 456.

"causation in fact". That is what seems to have been in the mind of Lord Wright, with whom other members of the House of Lords agreed, when he said that:[82]

> "the shipowner will be liable for any loss in which those other causes covered by exceptions co-operate, if unseaworthiness is a cause, or if it is preferred, a real, or effective or actual cause. The law is, I think, correctly stated by the late Judge Carver in Carriage of Goods by Sea, s. 17 ... The words of the section are: 'And further the shipowner remains responsible for loss or damage to the goods, however caused, if the ship was not in a seaworthy condition when she commenced her voyage and if the loss could not have arisen but for that unseaworthiness.'"

For example, in the case before Lord Wright, the ship went over when bunkering because of the combined effect of poor seamanship on the part of the master at the time (excused under Article IV rule 2(a)) and the instability of the ship because she had been overloaded (unseaworthiness) at her port of departure. The House held that the unseaworthiness caused the loss.

Support for the "but for" view can also be found in a statement by Neill, J. in *The Tolmidis*.[83] However, in the same judgment he quoted a slightly later opinion of Lord Wright, that causation "is to be understood as the man in the street, and not as either the scientist or the metaphysician, would understand it. Cause here means what a business or seafaring man would take to be the cause without too microscopic analysis but on a broad view."[84] Neill, J. went on to say that he: "must also look at 'the whole complex of circumstances'" (adopting again the words of Lord Wright a few years later) and should approach the issue "in a broad common-sense way".[85] This kind of approach is more like the broad and flexible line taken by some courts in the U.S.A. In *The Irish Spruce*,[86] for example, the ship lacked data required for effective navigation.

> "The question is whether compliance with the duty to maintain a seaworthy ship might have prevented the intervening cause, viz., the error in navigation ... This is, of course, a question of fact. We must determine whether the direct or intervening cause 'is a significant part of the risk involved in the defendant's conduct, or is so reasonably connected with it that responsibility should not be terminated', or, more simply, whether the intervening cause is foreseeable."

---

[82] *Smith Hogg & Co.* v. *Black Sea & Baltic Ins. Co.* [1940] A.C. 997, 1004–1005 A different but *obiter* view was expressed in *The Apostolis* [1996] 1 Lloyd's Rep. 475, 483, *per* Tuckey, J.; reversed on other grounds [1997] 2 Lloyd's Rep. 241 (C.A.).

[83] [1983] 1 Lloyd's Rep. 530, 540.

[84] *Yorkshire Dale Steamship Co.* v. *Minister of War Transport* [1942] A.C. 691, 706.

[85] [1983] 1 Lloyd's Rep. 530, 540, with reference to *Monarch Steamship Co.* v. *Karlshamns* [1949] A.C. 196, 228.

[86] [1976] 1 Lloyd's Rep. 63, 73 (S.D.N.Y.), with reference to Prosser, *Torts*, 4th edn. (1971), 272.

3 DUE DILIGENCE

a. Meaning

At one time the obligation of due diligence was considered "indistinguishable from an obligation to exercise reasonable care". That was the view expressed in *The Muncaster Castle*[87] by Willmer, L.J. in the Court of Appeal. This remains the general view except on one point, on which that decision was reversed by the House of Lords: the range of persons for whose negligence the carrier is liable. The House took the view[88] that the obligation is a "non-delegable duty"[89] somewhere between an obligation of reasonable care and an obligation, a more onerous obligation, to see that care is taken.[90] The House approved the view, expressed in the U.S.A. in *The Colima*,[91] that the law requires diligence on the part of all agents that the carrier may employ and to whom the carrier may have committed the work of fitting the vessel for sea. Lord Merriman said: "what is required is due diligence in the work itself", and "this is the personal responsibility of the shipowner".[92]

In *The Muncaster Castle*,[93] the carrier was liable for the carelessness of a competent independent contractor brought in to check storm valves: the contractor's employee did not replace inspection covers properly. The House indicated, as was held in *The Colima*,[94] that the carrier would also be liable for the negligence of a stevedore properly appointed to load or unload goods. The House distinguished *Angliss*,[95] a decision of Wright, J., that a carrier was not liable for the carelessness of a shipbuilder. The House approved it,[96] however, on the basis that "whether a ship is built for, bought by, or chartered to the carrier, he should not be held liable for bad workmanship for which he had no responsibility before the ship came into his possession". The carelessness of the builder in such a case occurs before the ship has come within the carrier's sphere of risk, so the builder is not the agent of the carrier in question.[97] "The

---

[87] [1960] 1 Q.B. 536, 581. See also e.g. *The Amstelslot* [1963] 2 Lloyd's Rep. 223, 235, *per* Lord Devlin (H.L.); and *The Danica Brown* [1995] 2 Lloyd's Rep. 264, 266 *per* Waller, J. U.S.A. in this sense: *Benedict*, ch. VIII. *Cf.* Germany, where a more restricted view of contractors for whom the carrier is responsible has been taken: Prüssmann and Rabe, *Seehandelsrecht* (1992), para. 559 D4.
[88] [1961] A.C. 807. Applied in Canada in e.g. *The Thor* [1965] 2 Ex. C.R. 469.
[89] Also in this sense: *The Perama* (1968) 388 F.2d 434, 439 (2 Cir.); *The Euryplus* (1983) 574 F.Supp. 418, 428 (S.D.N.Y.); *Benedict*, para. 84.
[90] Jolowicz [1960] C.L.J. 17; [1961] C.L.J. 164.
[91] (1897) 82 Fed. 665, 678, *per* Justice Brown.
[92] [1961] A.C. 807, 850.
[93] [1961] A.C. 807. See also *The Nicholas H* [1996] A.C. 211.
[94] (1897) 82 F. 665 (S.D.N.Y.).
[95] *W. Angliss & Co. (Australia) Pty., Ltd.* v. *P.&O. S.N. Co. Ltd.* [1927] 2 K.B. 456.
[96] [1961] A.C. 807, 860.
[97] See Lord Merriman, *ibid.*, 862, and Lord Radcliffe, *ibid.*, 867.

carrier's responsibility for the work itself does not begin until the ship comes into his orbit, and it begins then as a responsibility to make sure by careful and skilled inspection that what he is taking into his service is in fit condition for the purpose and, if there is anything lacking that is fairly discoverable, to put it right."[98]

b. Due diligence: timing

The implication is that the carrier's duty of due diligence begins when the ship first enters the carrier's sphere of risk—when he buys it or has it built. In any particular case, however, the focus is likely to be on a particular voyage, and the investigation of the carrier's diligence is likely to centre mainly on events in the period running up to that voyage. The period, however, "means from *at least* the beginning of the loading until the vessel starts on her voyage. The word 'before' cannot . . . be read as meaning 'at the commencement of the loading'. If this had been intended it would have been said."[99] This is obvious enough. However, clearly the enquiry commonly goes much further back than that. The duty is a mounting and virtually continuous duty which comes to a crescendo at the time of loading and departure, having begun perhaps imperceptibly at the time the ship was acquired. In practice, attention focuses not only on the final preparations for the voyage in issue but also on the ship's most recent surveys; and on the carrier's system for the inspection, ascertainment and repair of damage[100] not only at the time of departure but also when she was last at sea.[101] Moreover, while the master and crew are keeping an eye on the ship, the carrier's management team should be monitoring the performance of the master and crew.[102]

[98] *Ibid.*, *per* Lord Radcliffe.

[99] *Maxine Footwear Co. Ltd.* v. *Can. Govt. Merchant Marine* [1959] A.C. 589, 603, *per* Lord Somervell (P.C.) (emphasis added). He also said (*ibid.*): "The question when precisely the period begins does not arise in this case, hence the insertion above of the words 'at least'." He also stressed (at 604) that it was "unnecessary to consider the earlier cases as to 'stages' under the common law". However, he continued: "When the warranty was absolute it seems at any rate intelligible to restrict it to certain points of time. It would be surprising if a duty to exercise due diligence ceased as soon as loading began, only to reappear later shortly before the beginning of the voyage." That the common law of stages does not apply to the Rules: *The Canada Mail* (1974) 377 F.Supp. 657 (W.D. Wash).

[100] See e.g. *The Toledo* [1995] 1 Lloyd's Rep. 40.

[101] E.g. *The Makedonia* [1962] 1 Lloyd's Rep. 316, 338, *per* Hewson, J.; and *The Kriti Rex* [1996] 2 Lloyd's Rep. 171, 185, *per* Moore-Bick, J.

[102] See e.g. a leading limitation case: *The Marion* [1984] 1 A.C. 563, 575, *per* Lord Brandon. Carriers must now comply with the International Safety Management Code: see White [1995] L.M.C.L.Q. 221, 236. For a general view of the Code, see Lord Donaldson [1998] L.M.C.L.Q. 526; Huybrechts (1996) 34 E.T.L. 17, and Hodges [2000] I.J.I.L. 39.

From one point of view the duty never ends: as we have seen, what is done (or not done) during one voyage is performance (or non-performance) of the duty owed for the next voyage. As regards the particular voyage, however, the duration of the duty ends, according to Article III rule 1, "at the beginning of the voyage". When exactly does that beginning end? It has been held in the U.S.A. that a ship, which loaded at six different points in the landlocked Puget Sound, did not complete loading and begin the voyage until the sixth and last departure.[103] Generally, however, the voyage begins as soon as the ship casts off, and has begun even though she is still in the dock.[104] Any negligence after that, which allows the sea to enter, is characterised as something else, such as peril of the seas (excused by Article IV rule 2(c) or error in navigation and management (in that example excused by Article IV rule 2(a)).

> "Even though the failure to stop the flow of water upon reaching the top of the tank be an error in management for which the shipowner would not be responsible had it occurred after the commencement of the voyage, the same error may be a lack of due diligence on the part of the shipowner to make the vessel seaworthy when such conduct occurs before the beginning of a voyage."[105]

c. Due diligence: proof

i. Personnel selection

If the case concerns errors by the officers or crew, for the carrier to produce certificates of competence is essential but not enough. Their efficiency depends not only on technical competence but also on personal characteristics.[106] The carrier must show that he sought to assess character when appointing the person and has to some extent monitored their behaviour since. In *The Makedonia*,[107] a five minute interview for a chief engineer was not enough. However, in *The Hongkong Fir* case,[108] an interview for such a person in the early hours of the morning on a London railway station did not attract adverse comment.

ii. Surveys

If the case against the carrier concerns the state of the ship, the carrier tends to produce certificates of surveys carried out by classification societies. These too

---

[103] *The Canada Mail* (1974) 377 F.Supp. 657 (W.D. Wash).
[104] E.g. *The Del Sud* (1959) 270 F.2d 345 (5 Cir., 1959). *Tetley*, 377.
[105] *The Canada Mail* (1974) 377 F.Supp. 657, 661, *per curiam*.
[106] *Supra*, Part 2(b).
[107] [1962] 1 Lloyd's Rep. 316.
[108] *Hongkong Fir Shipping Co.* v. *Kawasaki Kisen Kaisha* [1962] 2 Q.B. 26 (C.A.).

are necessary but not alone enough.[109] A certificate is only likely to be conclusive in cases of defective design which, at the time of the survey, had not been condemned as such. If the carrier can produce a classification certificate which, in terms or in effect, states that at the time of the survey the design of the ship is sound, then the carrier has shown due diligence in that regard.[110] In other cases, the probatory value of surveys depends on what exactly was the subject of the survey and on how much time has elapsed since it was made.[111] Moreover, if the surveyor has recommended certain measures, those measures must have been carried out.[112] In any case, in view of the decision in *The Muncaster Castle*,[113] surveys do not assist the carrier's case unless the judge of fact is willing to assume that the surveyor carried out the work properly. However, usually the surveyor is a recognised classification society and, in the absence of evidence to suggest otherwise, the tendency is for judges to make this assumption.[114]

In particular, for the survey to be a telling testimony of due diligence on the part of the carrier, it must have covered the part of the ship later found to have been defective and have been as thorough as could reasonably have been expected.[115] This is also what the carrier has to establish to make out a defence under Article IV rule 2(p), that latent defects not discoverable by due diligence: what is discoverable depends on where and how the carrier's surveyor can be expected to look and, thus, specifically, on what tests should have been carried out.

---

[109] *Cranfield Bros. Ltd.* v. *Tatem S.N. Co. Ltd.* (1939) 64 Ll.L.Rep. 264, 267, *per* Hilbery, J.; *The Assunzione* [1956] 2 Lloyd's Rep. 468, 487, *per* Willmer, J. Belgium: *Rb Antwerp 15.1.1986* (1986) 21 E.T.L. 402. Germany: *BGH 29.10.1979* (1984) 19 E.T.L. 192. U.S.A.: *The Hugo Oldendorff*, 1982 A.M.C. 2505, 2515 (S.D.N.Y.); *The Euryplus* (1983) 574 F.Supp. 418, 428 (S.D.N.Y.). For a review of early decisions in the U.S.A., see Villareal (1971) 2 J.M.L.C. 763.

[110] *Waddle* v. *Wallsend Shipping Co. Ltd.* [1952] 2 Lloyd's Rep. 105, 130, *per* Devlin, J. See also *Thomson* v. *Micks, Lambert & Co.* (1933) 47 Ll.L.Rep. 5.

[111] *Cranfield Bros. Ltd.* v. *Tatem S.N. Co. Ltd.* (1939) 64 Ll.L.Rep. 264, 267, *per* Hilbery, J. *Cf. Arno, Cass.* com. *27.6.1995*, DMF 1996.302 note Regnier, in which the French court, often the scourge of the carrier, accepted certificates in combination with evidence of smooth operation since the surveys, and without insisting that the certificates be specifically related to the cause of the trouble.

[112] *Cranfield Bros. Ltd.* v. *Tatem S.N. Co. Ltd.* (1939) 64 Ll.L.Rep. 264, 267, *per* Hilbery, J.: *The Assunzione* [1956] 2 Lloyd's Rep. 468, 486, *per* Willmer, J. U.S.A.: *The Don Jose Figueras* 1973 A.M.C. 2241 (W.D. Wash); *The Susquehanna* [1975] 1 Lloyd's Rep. 216 (S.D.N.Y.).

[113] [1961] A.C. 807.

[114] E.g. *Charles Brown & Co. Ltd.* v. *Nitrate Producers S.S. Co. Ltd.* (1937) 58 Ll.L.Rep. 188, 191, *per* Porter, J.

[115] *The Assunzione* [1956] 2 Lloyd's Rep. 468, 487, *per* Willmer, J. *The Euryplus* (1983) 574 F.Supp. 418 (S.D.N.Y.). *Ragnhild Brovig, Paris 26.10.1970*, DMF 1971.395; *Gogofrio, Rennes 13.6.1985*, DMF 1986.625.

In *Brown*,[116] Porter, J. said that latent defect:

"does not mean latent to the eye. It means latent to the senses, that is, it may be hammer-tested, or there may be any other test. The only question is whether by 'latent' it means that you have to use every possible method to discover whether it exists, or whether you must use reasonable methods. I cannot myself believe that in every case it is obligatory upon a ship's officer on the commencement of a voyage to go and tap every rivet to find if it has a defect or not. If that were so, ships would be held up in port for a very long time while the rivets were being tapped and eyes used to determine whether a defect existed or not. I think it means such an examination as a reasonably careful man skilled in that matter would make."

Today the leading case on the point in England is *The Amstelslot*.[117] In a dissenting judgment, approved on appeal,[118] Diplock, L.J. developed the question posed previously by Porter, J. in *Brown*. The question, he said, "can be further dissected into two questions, namely, (1) did the defendants make the kind of examination which a reasonably careful man skilled in the matter would make, and (2) did they carry out such examination with reasonable skill, care and competence?" The second depended on the judge's view of the evidence presented, whereas the first question gave rise to more general considerations. On appeal in *The Amstelslot*, Lord Reid said that there must be "some compromise or balance in deciding what steps to take".[119] In Diplock, L.J.'s judgment, "the nature of the examination which a reasonably prudent man, skilled in the behaviour of reduction gears, would make involves striking a balance between the likelihood of there being a fatigue crack detectable by way of the methods suggested by the plaintiffs and the delay, expense and possible risk involved by the use of such methods".[120] Such considerations of expense and inconvenience are like some of those, in a tort action, which determine whether the defendant has fulfilled his duty of care.[121] Indeed, courts in the U.S.A. have recognised in carriage cases under the Rules that the "standard of reasonable prudence under the circumstances is familiar from tort law".[122]

First, the court considers the likelihood that the danger (leading to unseaworthiness and associated L.D.D.) will occur. The more likely the danger the more that can be expected of the carrier to forestall it. An obvious example is

---

[116] *Charles Brown & Co. Ltd.* v. *Nitrate Producers S.S. Co. Ltd.* (1937) 58 Ll.L.Rep. 188, 191.

[117] [1962] 2 Lloyd's Rep. 336; *rvsd* [1963] 2 Lloyd's Rep. 223 (H.L.).

[118] [1962] 2 Lloyd's Rep. 336, 345.

[119] [1963] 2 Lloyd's Rep. 223, 230–231, applied in *The Fjord Wind* [1999] 1 Lloyd's Rep. 307, 320, by Moore-Bick, J.

[120] [1962] 2 Lloyd's Rep. 336, 346–347.

[121] This "heuristic stratagem" by judges and others has been observed in other contexts, such as the interpretation of "loss prevention" conditions in insurance policies: Clarke, *Policies and Perceptions of Insurance* (1997), 139 ff.

[122] *The Hellenic Glory* [1979] 1 Lloyd's Rep. 424, 430, *per* Broderick, D.J. (S.D.N.Y.).

that posed by heavy seas: the more likely it is that such conditions will be met on the voyage, the more that must be done to safeguard the ship and the cargo.[123] Hatch covers, for example, should be the subject of at least a visual check before each voyage.[124] Sensitive cargo may require special care.[125] Another example is the likelihood of particular defects in the particular ship; this depends mainly on her history and age.[126] The standard of diligence required of the carrier is "not what he might do in another vessel but in this vessel under the particular circumstances here present".[127]

Second, the court considers the seriousness of the consequences if the relevant L.D.D. were to occur. "'Due diligence' requires a carefulness of inspection and repair proportionate to the danger."[128] For example, it has been held in France that valves which enable the master to flood the holds in case of fire must be checked every time the holds are emptied.[129]

Third, if the first two considerations suggest that something should be done, the next question is: what? The court seeks evidence of general practice. However, that means "not merely what ship owners usually do, but what a reasonably prudent one would do".[130] In particular, as regards the state of the ship, the court considers the standards set by the classification societies. These show when a ship must undergo surveys and what must be done. If the carrier has satisfied the standards and requirements of the societies, although courts state and restate that the onus of proving due diligence is on the carrier and that class certificates are not conclusive,[131] courts then tend to require the claimant to suggest what else the carrier could and should reasonably have done.[132] In one case, for example, the evidence was that there was no test then known "which would reveal the notch brittle quality of a steel, and at that time the dangers of

---

[123] *The Assunzione* [1956] 2 Lloyd's Rep. 468, 487, *per* Willmer, J. Again, such is the propensity of rats for food, the carrier must check for rats every time he takes on foodstuffs: *Mintaka 'N', T.C. Rouen 9.3.1962*, DMF 1963.407.

[124] *BGH 29.10.1979* (1984) 19 E.T.L. 192, 199.

[125] E.g. bananas as regards inspection of the refrigeration equipment: *The Calanca* (1972) 342 F.Supp. 447 (S.D.N.Y.); coffee beans as regards traces of previous cargo: *BGH 9.4.1990*, TranspR. 1990.333.

[126] *Charles Brown & Co. Ltd.* v. *Nitrate Producers S.S. Co. Ltd.* (1937) 58 Ll.L.Rep. 188, 192, *per* Porter, J. *The American Trader* (1973) 354 F.Supp. 389 (S.D.N.Y.).

[127] *The Hugo Oldendorff*, 1982 A.M.C. 2505, 2512 (S.D.N.Y.).

[128] *The Hellenic Glory* [1979] 1 Lloyd's Rep. 424, 430, *per* Broderick, D.J. (S.D.N.Y.), quoting from *The Millie R. Rohannon* (1894) 64 Fed. 883, 884 (S.D.N.Y.).

[129] *Citta di Siracusa, T.C. Marseille 11.6.1963*, DMF 1964.438. See also *Oceanic, Cass. com. 23.7.1951*, DMF 1951.533. Villareal (1971) 2 J.M.L.C. 763, 768.

[130] *The Hugo Oldendorff* 1982 A.M.C. 2505, 2512 (S.D.N.Y.).

[131] E.g. *ibid.*, 2515.

[132] E.g. *ibid.* A similar pattern of enquiry can be seen when a court assesses the conduct of a road carrier under the C.M.R.: e.g. *J.J. Silber Ltd.* v. *Islander Trucking Ltd.* [1985] 2 Lloyd's Rep. 243, 249, *per* Mustill, J.; *BGH 8.10.1998*, TranspR. 1999.59, 61. *Arno, Cass. com. 27.6.1995*, DMF 1996.302 note Régnier.

such steel were just being uncovered". Liability, said the court, "cannot be imposed for failure to safeguard against hazard not then generally known in the shipbuilding industry and for failure to conduct non-existent tests".[133] If there was nothing that could have been done about it, a carrier cannot be impugned for doing nothing.

Finally, if, indeed, the claimant is able to suggest something that the carrier should have done, the court considers how burdensome that would have been for the carrier. In particular, the court considers how much it would have cost. The greater the expense the harder for the claimant to sustain the argument that the carrier should have done it. For example, in *The Australia Star*,[134] Bucknill, J. held that the removal of insulation from a refrigerated hold before every voyage to check against the possibility of leaks from adjacent tanks was impracticable on grounds of expense. In contrast, French courts have been typically more demanding of carriers, requiring, for example, "l'examen le plus total qui puisse être".[135] Moreover, "the cure is sometimes worse than the disease" and the court will not ignore any risks to the ship. For example, in *The Yamatogawa*,[136] Hobhouse, J. said: "Dismantling any piece of gearing, particularly one as large as this and in an engine room as cramped as this one was, involves an element of risk which should not be undertaken unless there is some adequate reason for doing do."

d. Causation

A defence under Article IV rule 2(p) succeeds only if the L.D.D. was one "arising or resulting from" latent defect, i.e. a defect not discoverable by due diligence. When the defence fails because the defect was not latent, it is because the defect was a defect "discoverable by due diligence". In the second case failure of due diligence was at least a "but for" cause of what occurred; and to a degree at least the L.D.D. was not "arising or resulting from" latent defect but from the lack of due diligence. However, it cannot be assumed that a defect, if discovered by the exercise of due diligence, could also have been rectified. That possibility gives rise to a third case in which, if the carrier has failed to exercise due diligence, the carrier's failure is not a cause. He is liable nonetheless, however, because, although the L.D.D. was caused by the defect, the defect was not a latent defect, i.e. a defect "not discoverable by due diligence". The exonerating event specified by Article IV rule 2(p) has not occurred.

A defence centred on a paragraph of Article IV rule 2, other than paragraph (p), succeeds unless, subject to proof by the carrier that he has exercised the due

---

[133] *Peter Paul, Inc.* v. *Rederi A/B Pulp* (1958) 258 F.2d 901, 905 (2 Cir.).
[134] (1940) 67 Ll.L.Rep. 110, 118. See also *Charles Brown & Co. Ltd.* v. *Nitrate Producers S.S. Co. Ltd.* (1937) 58 Ll.L.Rep. 188, 191, *per* Porter, J., quoted above.
[135] *The Anson P.K. Safford, Paris 20.10.1952*, Gaz. Pal. 1953.I.10.
[136] [1990] 2 Lloyd's Rep. 39, 50.

diligence required by Article III rule 1, the claimant has shown that the L.D.D. was one not only "arising or resulting from unseaworthiness" but also, the court concludes that it was "*caused* by want of due diligence on the part of the carrier to make the ship seaworthy", and so on.[137] In contrast with the position under Article IV rule 2(p), if the court concludes that the carrier failed to exercise the diligence required but that his failure was not a cause of the unseaworthiness, the result may be that the carrier is excused nonetheless.[138]

If a defence centred on a paragraph of Article IV rule 2, other than paragraph (p), fails for want of due diligence, that failure must have been at least a "but for" cause of the unseaworthiness, which in turn must have been a "but for" cause of the L.D.D.[139] For example, if the carrier proves (defence under Article IV rule 2(a)) that a crewman made an error in management involving a pipe outlet, but the claimant can show that the man probably would not have made the mistake if the outlet had been properly marked (unseaworthiness), the carrier loses that defence unless (unlikely) the carrier can show that the state of the pipe was not caused by a failure of due diligence.[140] However, it also follows from the requirement of causation that the carrier is not required to prove that he exercised due diligence in all respects but only in those which, if it had not been exercised, would have caused the unseaworthiness in question.[141] For example, in *The Captayannis 'S'*,[142] the L.D.D. was caused by the navigational error of a competent master and, even though some members of the crew were incompetent, the carrier was excused under Article IV rule 2(a).

4 CONCLUSION

The Rules are showing their age and it is an age past, an age of common law concepts for export. The difficulty that non common lawyers have had in understanding what seemed only too obvious to some of the English judges in the first 30 years of the Rules underlines a point that is now widely accepted: that uniform law should not be drafted in the idiom of any one legal system or family of legal systems.[143] Moreover, some people think that the Rules are too

---

[137] Emphasis added.

[138] E.g. *The Yamatogawa* [1990] 2 Lloyd's Rep 39, 48, *per* Hobhouse, J.; and *The Fjord Wind* [1999] 1 Lloyd's Rep. 307, 327, *per* Moore-Bick, J.

[139] *Supra*, Part 2(e).

[140] *The Coastal Rambler* (1986) 404 F.2d 151 (9 Cir.). Holland: The decision of the Supreme Court (Hoge Raad) in *The Quo Vadis, 11.6.1993*, 1994–1995. U.L.R. 355, appears to be to the same effect. *Cf. The Columbia Brewer* 1973 A.M.C. 676 (E.D. La.).

[141] *The Erwin Schroder* [1970] Ex. C.R. 426. U.S.A.: *The Heinz Horn* [1970] 1 Lloyd's Rep. 191, 198 (5 Cir.), with reference to *Benedict on Admiralty* (ed. Knauth), para. 96.

[142] (1969) 306 F.Supp. 866 (D. Oregon).

[143] See further Clarke [1999] L.M.C.L.Q. 36, 53 ff. and references cited.

kind to carriers. As we have seen, the assumption has been questioned in Germany that the carrier should benefit from a partial release of responsibility when the ship sets sail and becomes, according to tradition, beyond his control.[144] Moreover, whereas sea carriers are required only to exercise due diligence to make their ships seaworthy, carriers by road and by air face a stricter level of responsibility for the defects in their lorries and aircraft respectively.[145] If there is to be any real progress in the development of uniform law for multimodal or intermodal transport, there will have to be not only neutrality of language but evenness of responsibility and regulation. Currently the carrier by sea is decidedly offshore.

---

[144] Herber, *supra* n. 72.
[145] Clarke 1988 U.L.R. 351, 357 and references cited.

Chapter 7

The Duty of Care in a Marine Context—
Is There Someone to Blame?

Lindsay East

As a solicitor who has spent his entire career in the marine field I have watched with interest the growth of the concept, imported I believe from America, that if a loss is suffered then someone must be liable for it. In the shipping arena this principle has been vigorously put forward. As in a number of other areas, what drives the claim is a search for a deep pocket, i.e. someone who can in fact pay for the loss which the plaintiff has suffered.

The general concept of whether or not a duty of care is owed, so that a plaintiff may succeed in a claim in tort against a defendant, has been the subject of much judicial comment over the last 15 years. A look at the law reports gives the impression that there is little else other than claims of this nature against a wide array of defendants. The purpose of this essay is to focus on the liability owed by regulatory authorities in the shipping field, primarily that of the classification society. Nevertheless I cannot help referring to a perhaps somewhat bizarre case that I was involved with a couple of years ago which resulted from the dispute over the shipping of calves and sheep to the continent. The case in fact dealt with breach of a statutory duty.

I was approached by clients who were involved in the shipment of these animals to France. They had chartered a vessel and were seeking to export their cargo from various ports along the south coast. Two, at least, of the ports refused to allow the vessel to dock and load the animals as the harbour authority were concerned that there would be considerable disruption from animal rights' activists and others. Under the Harbours Docks and Piers Clauses Act 1847, a harbour authority is under a duty to make the port available to any person who wishes to use it on payment of the appropriate fee. We took the view that it would be possible to sue the harbour authority for breach of that duty and the question arose that, if a breach of duty was established, was it then possible to make that breach sound in damages. I am glad to say that the case was settled, on terms that were acceptable to our clients, particularly since there was a subsequent case on the very point, *K.A. & S.B.M. Feakins Ltd.* v. *Dover Harbour Board*[1] which decided that in such circumstances no claim for damages could be in fact be made!

To return, however, to the main thrust of this essay. My main aim is to consider the recent decision of the House of Lords in *Marc Rich & Co. A.G.* v. *Bishop Rock Marine Co. Ltd. (The Nicholas H).*[2] In order to do this I would like to make some general comments about the role and liability of the classification society and about the development of the doctrine of duty of care.

It is perhaps important to bear in mind that, although we are looking at decisions which are a matter of law, commercial pressures cannot be disregarded. As I have already mentioned, one of the main contemporary concerns is that the aggrieved plaintiff thinks that they are entitled to recover their loss from somebody, and therefore an appropriate target is sought. I believe that our courts are becoming as guilty as the U.S. courts in trying to achieve what they consider to be the correct commercial or moral result, which may not be the proper result as a matter of law. For example, in 1995 the House of Lords decided *White* v. *Jones*,[3] a case which led to the House of Lords being split three judges to two as to whether or not, in the circumstances of that case, a duty of care was owed to the plaintiff. Lord Mustill, one of those in the minority, said: "The first assumption [made by the plaintiffs], which comes to this, is that there must be something wrong with the law if the plaintiffs do not succeed."[4] In other words, there is a natural feeling that, if someone has suffered loss and in general terms, someone else could be said to be "responsible" for that loss, then that someone should be made liable. In my view this rather happy general principle is not (or should not be) part of English law and is a relevant consideration when one comes on to consider the classification society as defendant.

1 INTRODUCTION

This essay is dealing with the liability of, for example, a classification society in tort. I do not propose to consider the liability of classification societies in contract, since this would involve a detailed examination of the various terms and conditions that the classification societies have developed over the years with the general intent of trying to make themselves immune from suit if at all possible.[5] Accordingly the essay will primarily be dealing with the question whether or not a third party may seek redress against the classification society.

[1] (1998) 10 Admin. L.R. 665.
[2] [1996] A.C. 211.
[3] [1995] 2 A.C. 207.
[4] *Ibid.*, 277.
[5] See the comments by Phillips, J. in *The Morning Watch* [1990] 1 Lloyd's Rep. 547.

I would nevertheless like to refer to an American case, *The Sundancer*[6] for some of the comments made there. This was a case where a shipowner sought to sue his own classification society in contract. The action failed, both before the district judge and before the Court of Appeals. The decision of the American courts was that the classification society defendant in that case, the American Bureau of Shipping, could successfully rely on the immunity that it was given under the law of the flag of the vessel, the law of the Bahamas, which immunity applied to the issuing of the SOLAS and loadline certificates. The immunity was held not to extend to cover A.B.S. for its issuing of the ordinary classification certificate, a document which is needed for purely private purposes. Accordingly, the owners sought to say that A.B.S. should be liable for the consequences of all the defects in the vessel that were not found by the classification surveyor, who was alleged to be negligent. The vessel was a luxury cruise ship which hit an underwater rock off the coast of British Columbia and sank. Claims were substantial and the owners sought damages for U.S.$264,000,000 from A.B.S. The U.S. Court of Appeals said that:

> "it reflects our view that a ship owner is not entitled to rely on a classification certificate as a guarantee to the owner that the vessel is soundly constructed."[7]

They went on to say:[8]

> "probably most significantly, the ship owner, not A.B.S., is ultimately responsible for and in control of the activities on board the ship. In the case of '*Sundancer*', for example, Sundance had full responsibility for the conversion, repairs and mainten-ance of the vessel. This ongoing responsibility for the vessel is supplemented by the maritime law requirement that the ship owner has a non-delegable duty to furnish a seaworthy vessel."

They drew a rather entertaining analogy when they said:[9]

> "We agree with the District Court that the Sundance's posture in this law suit is somewhat similar to one who causes a vehicle accident and then sues the Motor Vehicle Bureau for damages to his car because it issued him a driver's licence that falsely represented his fitness to drive ... put simply, the purpose of the classification certificate is not to guarantee safety, but merely to permit Sundance to take advantage of the insurance rates available to a classed vessel."

That last comment is one with which a number of people in the industry might disagree. Although, from a commercial point of view, it is clearly correct that an owner will be unable to obtain insurance, or indeed any other form of cover, unless the vessel is in class, I think that owners would expect a classification society at least to guarantee that all the items covered by the survey are in good working order. The difficulty is, as all practitioners are aware, that an inspection

---

[6] [1994] 1 Lloyd's Rep. 183; also reported at (1993) 7 F.3d 1077.
[7] [1994] 1 Lloyd's Rep. 183, 211.
[8] *Ibid.*, 212.
[9] *Ibid.*

of a vessel by a class surveyor is relatively superficial on an annual survey and, indeed, even on a special survey it is not possible for the surveyor to provide an absolute guarantee that the vessel is in perfect condition. It is probably this that the Court of Appeals meant.

Whilst still talking commercially, it is worth referring to the strains and stresses to which a classification society is put by owners of vessels. These strains can be evident in various ways. The obvious way is when an owner is seeking to sell a vessel to a buyer and is aware that there maybe some problem with the vessel. The buyer, who will have inspected the vessel, may also be aware of the problems and will be seeking to get the classification society to place a recommendation on the class records, so as to allow him either not to go ahead with the purchase or, more likely, to negotiate a reduction in the price. The seller will be seeking to maintain the status quo.

There have been a succession of cases in English law in relation to recommendations, or lack of them, in sale and purchase disputes and recently *The Niobe*[10] has made its way to the House of Lords to give, it is hoped, a final decision on the vexed question of the knowledge of the owners in relation to defects in the vessel, which would have led to the imposition of the recommendation.

The difficulty with this sort of situation is that the buyers may in fact be right. It is not just a case, necessarily, that buyers are seeking to chip away, say, US$200,000 from the price; they may actually have genuine concerns as to the state of the vessel, and as to the problems which they may face if they are obliged to go through with the purchase.

I was involved in a case which illustrates this point, where I was representing a classification society. The vessel concerned was a large one and was obliged to put into a port, during the course of a loaded voyage, because she had suffered a collapse of a number of frames in holds 3 and 5. The class surveyor was called in and recommended temporary repairs so that the vessel could proceed to her discharge port and discharge the cargo. However, the vessel was then ordered to return to have further permanent repairs carried out.

The vessel duly did this and the further repairs were carried out. During all this time there had been considerable correspondence between the owners of the vessel and her buyers. The vessel had in fact been sold prior to the voyage, with completion and delivery after the voyage, and the buyers had concerns about the condition of the vessel which they had already expressed in messages to the owners and the brokers. The problems that were then found in holds 3 and 5 led the buyers to become very much more concerned and they spent a considerable time trying to insist that the classification society carried out an immediate detailed survey. The classification society thus found themselves in a very difficult position.

---

10 [1995] 1 Lloyd's Rep. 579.

The contract is between the classification society and the owners. The owners pointed out that the vessel was up to date with all her surveys and that all repairs recommended by the surveyor in the port of refuge had been carried out. Accordingly they refused, literally, to allow the classification society to carry out any further detailed survey. The buyers went so far as to attend a meeting with the classification society and explained their fears. They demanded that the society intervene and inspect the vessel. The classification society were then put under equally strong pressure from the owners, who said that, under the terms of the contract between them and the classification society, the society had no right to make a further inspection.

To cut a long story short, the vessel was sold and, unfortunately, turned out to be in a very poor condition. The buyers then pursued a claim against the society, in tort, for the not inconsiderable sum of U.S.$9,000,000. The reason that the claim was being brought, in tort, against the classification society was that the sellers were a one ship company and had no assets. Accordingly, the classification society was the obvious next target. At this point I would like to mention an argument that was ventilated in *The Sundancer*. The argument was that the classification society does not get a great deal of money for its work. This point was also referred to in *The Nicholas H*. I am, myself, not convinced by this argument but the U.S. Court of Appeals seemed to place some reliance on this. They said:[11]

> "the great disparity between the fee charged (U.S.$85,000) by A.B.S. for its services and the damages sought by Sundance (U.S.$264,000,000) is strong evidence that such a result [i.e. the liability of the Society to the owner] was not intended by the parties. We can only conclude that the small fees charged could not have been intended to cover the risk of such liability; the ship classification industry could not continue to exist under such terms."

The court referred to another U.S. case, *Vitol Trading S.A. Inc. v. S.G.S. Control Services Inc.*,[12] decided in 1989, which had quoted the Restatement (Second) of Contracts, which stated:[13]

> "The fact that price [charged] is relatively small suggests that it was not intended to cover the risk of such liability."

As I will mention, this point is discussed in some detail in *The Nicholas H* and two of their lordships came to opposite views as to whether it was a useful question of not. Personally I am not persuaded. I think we have all had instances of advice being given both by lawyers, accountants or bankers, the advice being modest and any fee charged being equally modest. Nevertheless the result of acting on that advice may be catastrophic, and I have never heard it said, in connection with a claim against a solicitor, that the fact that he charged a modest

---

[11] [1994] 1 Lloyd's Rep. 183, 211.
[12] (1989) 874 F.2d 76, 81–82.
[13] Section 351 cmt f.

fee meant that he is not liable for all the consequences of the advice, however far reaching! Indeed I do not think that this is a defence which would ever even be likely to be argued. In the field of accountancy, advice allegedly given in informal circumstances recently led to a firm of accountants being successfully sued for a sum in the region of £65,000,000: see *A.D.T* v *B.D.O. Binder Hamlyn.*[14]

One other area which concerns the classification society is fraud. Classification societies are bodies that exist in competition with each other. In some ways an analogy can perhaps be drawn between classification societies and Examination Boards in England and Wales. It is generally thought, insofar as examination boards are concerned, that certain boards are easier than others and some schools, therefore, will select these boards in order to get better results. So far as classification societies are concerned, the leading societies are all members of one group called the International Association of Classification Societies but, inevitably, they are in competition one with another and there are commercial pressures being brought to bear at all times by owners to achieve the result that they want. We are all aware, I think, in the industry, of cases where economic pressure has been brought to bear by owners with unfortunate results. I was involved in a case of this nature myself where we were certain that a leading classification society had produced forged documentation—forged in the sense that, although the documentation had been signed by a relevant officer of the society, the information contained in it was inaccurate to the certain knowledge of the surveyor who signed the certificate. The vessel subsequently became a constructive total loss and we were advising the clients in relation to their claim againt the society. For reasons which were unrelated to the case, the matter did not proceed. That case was in the 1980s, that is to say before the decision of Phillips, J. in *The Morning Watch.*[15]

2 DUTY OF CARE

In this essay one can do no more than mention a few general principles and some examples taken from case law in relation to the development of the general principle of duty of care. Books have been written about the existence and extent of the concept of and imposition of a duty of care and it is difficult to make any general definition. It may be worth restating the general principle that it is not for every careless act that persons may be held responsible in law, nor even for every careless act that causes damage. They will only be liable in negligence if they are under a legal duty to take care. The issue has been further complicated, in English law, by a distinction being drawn between a careless act

[14] [1996] B.C.C. 808.
[15] [1990] 1 Lloyd's Rep. 547.

that causes physical damage or loss and a careless act that causes only economic loss. This essay deals only with economic loss.

The English law on duty of care first came to prominence with the case that every student is taught at university, *Donoghue* v. *Stevenson*.[16] This case found its way to the House of Lords, where the leading speech was given by Lord Atkin. He said, *inter alia*:[17]

> "The rule that you are to love your neighbour becomes, in law, you must not injure your neighbour; and the lawyer's question 'Who is my neighbour?' receives a restricted reply. You must take reasonable care to avoid acts or omissions which you can reasonably foresee would be likely to injure your neighbour. Who, then, in law is my neighbour? The answer seems to be—persons who are so closely and directly affected by my act that I ought reasonably to have them in contemplation as being so affected when I am directing my mind to the acts or omissions which recorded the question."

This case involved physical damage in the sense that the plaintiff, a young lady, had become ill. The "neighbour principle" nevertheless continued to be used and developed by the courts. Perhaps the high point of this principle was the case of *The Home Office* v. *Dorset Yacht Co. Ltd.*,[18] where Lord Reid suggested that the time had come to regard the "neighbour principle" of *Donoghue* v *Stevenson* as applicable in all cases where there was no justification or valid explanation for its exclusion. This suggestion was taken up by the House of Lords in a subsequent case, *Anns* v. *Merton London Borough Council*[19] in particular in the speech of Lord Wilberforce, who said that the matter should be approached in two stages:[20]

> "First, one must ask whether there was a sufficient relationship of proximity or neighbourhood between plaintiff and defendant such that in the defendant's reasonable contemplation carelessness on his part might cause damage to the plaintiff. If so a prima facie duty of care arises. Then, the second stage, it is necessary to consider whether there were any considerations which ought to negative, or to reduce or limit that duty."

This was the first reference to the proximity principle, which now is one of the accepted tests. The concept was taken up with enthusiasm and indeed led to a rather extraordinary consequence. This was that within ten or twelve years the case was overruled, and is no longer regarded as good law. The reason for this appeared to be that the courts were getting so enthusiastic that the situation was getting out of control. In *Junior Books Ltd.* v. *Veitchi Ltd.*[21] the House of Lords relied on the statement of Lord Wilberforce, in *Anns* to deal with the loss in that

---

[16] [1932] A.C. 562.
[17] *Ibid.*, 580.
[18] [1969] A.C. 1004.
[19] [1978] A.C. 728.
[20] *Ibid.*, 751–752.
[21] [1983] 1 A.C. 520.

case, a claim against a sub-contractor, which, at least on one view was economic in nature, and imposed a liability which appeared to conflcit with hitherto well established principles. Accordingly in 1991 the House of Lords in *Murphy* v. *Brentwood District Council*[22] decided that the extent of the doctrine of duty of care would have to be restricted. It seems that the English courts became concerned with what has been known as the "floodgates" argument. In *Junior Books*,[23] Lord Fraser of Tullybelton referred to a famous dictum from one of America's well known judges, Judge Cardozo, C.J. in *Ultramaras Corporation* v. *Touche*:[24] "The spectre of a liability in an indeterminate amount for an indeterminate time to an indeterminate class." In any event, in *Murphy* the House of Lords held that in the case they were considering, which was a claim against a local authority for negligence in relation to the inspection of the foundations of a house, the damage was economic loss and as such no duty of care arose in the absence of a special relationship.

I would also like to mention the well known case of *Caparo Plc* v. *Dickman*.[25] That case, which involved pure economic loss, is often cited as evidence of the hardening attitude of the courts to the founding of a duty of care. In that case, the plaintiffs, Caparo, alleged that they had been induced to take a controlling interest in a public company, in which they already held a minority interest, by the negligence of that company's auditors in reporting with approval on the company's annual accounts, when these were in fact inaccurate. The issue of whether the auditors owed Caparo a duty of care was tried as a preliminary issue. The Court of Appeal held by two members to one that the auditors did owe a duty of care. The House of Lords held that no such duty of care was owed. The mere fact that the plaintiffs, Caparo, in fact relied on the auditors' report was not good enough. It needed to be shown, *inter alia*, that the auditors knew that their report would be communicated to the plaintiff specifically in connection with a particular transaction.

Caparo also laid down some general principles as to when a duty of care arises which were applied in *The Morning Watch* and in *The Nicholas H*. I will come on to these shortly. One of the interesting points to note here is the fact that this general discussion of the leading decisions on the doctrine of duty of care has already referred to six decisions of the House of Lords made in under 20 years on the same topic, some of them disagreeing with each other. This just shows that the current situation of law in this area is unsatisfactory. There appears to be in this area a surplus of concepts and not every case will deploy all of them. The law of negligence seems to have become inordinately doctrinally complex in the last decade. One of the purposes of this essay is to seek to

---

[22] [1991] 1 A.C. 398.
[23] [1983] 1 A.C. 520.
[24] (1931) 174 N.E. 441, 444.
[25] [1992] A.C. 605.

show that the House of Lords in *The Nicholas H* in fact seems to have taken a rather simplistic approach.

3 *THE MORNING WATCH*[26]

This decision of Phillips, J., in 1990, is regarded as the first authority for the proposition that it is not possible to sue a classification society in tort for negligence. I think it is worthwhile looking at this decision in a little detail because that general proposition, I would suggest, is not correct. In order to consider the decision one has, briefly, to look at the facts.

The case involved a yacht which was inspected by Lloyd's Register in November 1984 and underwent a special survey. This is a more rigorous survey which is carried out every four years. It was found as a fact in the case that Lloyd's Register knew that the special survey was requested with a view to putting the vessel on the market for sale, but no more than that. The sellers told the buyers, correctly, that the vessel had passed its special survey and the vessel was then purchased. An important point is that the interim certificate of class, which indicated that the vessel had passed a special survey, was not shown to the buyer. After the vessel had been purchased, defects were located which, it was subsequently agreed, should have been located by a competent surveyor carrying out a special survey. Accordingly a claim was made against Lloyd's for damages for economic loss suffered as a consequence of relying on mis-statements negligently made.

Having reviewed all the relevant authorities, Phillips, J. opined:[27]

"A duty of care could only arise where:
  (i)   it is reasonably foreseeable to the defendant that the plaintiff is likely to rely on his statement;
  (ii) there is the necessary proximity between the plaintiff and the defendant;
  (iii) it is just and reasonable in all the circumstances to impose a duty of care on the part of the defendant to the plaintiff."

The judge accepted that Lloyd's Register deliberately maintain a system of classification whereby parties other than the owners were expected to rely on the fact that a vessel was maintained in class as providing an assurance that the vessel was maintained in good condition. Nevertheless he rejected the general proposition that Lloyd's owed a duty of care, so to speak, at large. He said:[28]

"To accept the general proposition that Lloyd's owes a duty of care to those foreseeably liable to suffer economic loss in consequence of reliance on the negligent

---

[26] [1990] 1 Lloyd's Rep. 547.
[27] *Ibid.*, 556.
[28] *Ibid.*, 560.

classification of a vessel would be to make a substantial further advance in the law of negligence."

Accordingly the judge went on to consider each of the three areas that he had set out as needing to be satisfied.

a. Foreseeability and reliance

As he had already said, Lloyd's Register knew that third parties do rely on their classification documentation. Accordingly the judge found that, although in November 1984 Lloyd's did not have the plaintiff in contemplation as a potential purchaser, they had been expressly informed that the owner wished to put her through a special survey prior to putting the vessel on the market. In those circumstances the judge found that it was reasonably foreseeable by Lloyd's that a purchaser would be influenced by or rely on the results of a special survey. Accordingly the first element was satisfied.

b. Proximity

The judge said that foreseeability that lack of care might result in harm is good enough when the harm foreseen is physical damage. This is a reference back to *Donoghue* v. *Stevenson*. He went on to point out, however, that this does not of itself give rise to a duty of care where the damage is limited to economic loss. There must be a sufficient degree of proximity (see *Murphy*).

This is an easy test to state but not, apparently, an easy one to decide. The judge, again, ran through a number of cases on the topic and came to the conclusion that no universal test can be applied. On the contrary, he said, it was made clear in the authorities that there is no universal test. Helpful comments had been made, such as the following by Lord Keith of Kinkel:[29]

> "the question of whether a duty of care should be imposed, is a question of *intensely* pragmatic character, well suited for gradual development but *requiring* most careful analysis".

Faced with such comments, Phillips, J. tried to develop a general test.

(a) Where the defendant voluntarily assumes responsibility to the plaintiff and the plaintiff relies on that assumption of responsibility, sufficient proximity will often be created.
(b) But voluntary assumption of responsibility is not an essential element in creating the necessary proximity.
(c) Where the relationship between the plaintiff and the defendant has many, though not all, the incidents of a contract, sufficient proximity may well exist.

[29] *Rowling* v. *Takaro Properties* [1988] A.C. 473, 501 (N.Z. P.C.).

(d) While foreseeability of reliance will not automatically give rise to a
duty of care, foreseeability must, he said, play an important part. The
more obvious it is that A's act or omission will cause harm to B, the
less likely a court will be to hold that the relationship of A and B is
insufficiently proximate to give rise to a duty of care.

Phillips, J. came to the conclusion that there was not sufficient proximity. It
appears that the factors that influenced him were that the purchasers did not pay,
either directly or indirectly, the survey fees of Lloyd's Register. Further, the
survey was not carried out for the sole reason of selling the yacht to this
purchaser. When the survey had been carried out, the plaintiff in the action had
not even been identified and accordingly that plaintiff was not intended to act on
the result of that survey; he was merely one of an indeterminate class of persons
who might do so.

Phillips, J. also considered a number of other ways in which Lloyd's might be
said not to have the necessary proximity. He pointed out, for example, that there
was no statutory scheme to protect purchasers of vessels. The object of Lloyd's
was not primarily directed to the protection of such interests; indeed, their
primary purpose was to enhance the safety of life and property at sea and his
Lordship did not feel that in the circumstances of this case there was any
relationship akin to contract.

It may be worth contrasting this with *Smith* v. *Eric S. Bush*,[30] another case that
went to the House of Lords. In that case the relationship under consideration
was that of a valuer and a purchaser of a house. The valuer was instructed by a
prospective mortgagee, i.e. a bank or building society, who would only lend the
purchaser monies needed to buy the house if the valuation was satisfactory. The
valuation fee was paid by the purchaser directly to the mortgagee. The valuer
knew that the purchaser would be informed if the valuation was satisfactory
and, in that event, was likely to rely upon that fact in proceedings with the
purchase. The House of Lords found, in those circumstances, the relationship of
the valuer and the purchaser was sufficiently proximate to give rise to a duty of
care. Interestingly, the judges who gave reasoned speeches disagreed as to the
reasons for the proximity.

Lord Templeman found that the relationship was akin to contract and that the
valuer had assumed responsibility to the purchaser, two tests that I mentioned
earlier. Lord Griffiths said that he did not think that voluntary assumption of
responsibility was helpful or realistic. He considered that the necessary
proximity.[31]

"arises from the surveyor's knowledge that the overwhelming probability is that the
purchaser will rely upon his valuation ... and the fact that the surveyor only obtains
the work because the purchaser is willing to pay his fee."

[30] [1990] 1 A.C. 831.
[31] *Ibid.*, 865.

Lord Jauncey of Tullichettle did not consider that the relationship was equivalent to contract. He preferred to approach the matter by asking:[32]

> "whether the facts disclose that the appellants in inspecting and reporting must, but for the disclaimers, by reason of the proximate relationship between them, be deemed to have assumed responsibility towards [the purchaser] as well as to the building society who instructed them."

No one mentioned that the valuer's fee was very small in relation to the claim! I thought it worthwhile mentioning this case because I think it does show, on the facts, how different it was from *The Morning Watch*. Thus, although *The Morning Watch* has been taken as authority for the general proposition that a classification society will not be liable in damages to a prospective purchaser, I do not think that it shows that at all. All it shows is that in the circumstances of that case no duty of care arose. It seems to me that, where the facts were more favourable to the plaintiff—for example where the plaintiff purchaser told the classification society that it would be relying on a survey to be carried out and indeed did so rely—that the situation may be rather different.

c. Just and reasonable

All three of the tests have to be satisfied and therefore it was not strictly speaking necessary for Phillips, J. to deal with this. Regrettably, therefore, he decided he would not do so. All he did was to say that the argument by Lloyd's was that, as their certificates contain a general disclaimer of liability, it would not be just and reasonable to impose upon Lloyd's a duty of care in respect of their certificates when relied on by a third party. However, the judge made no comment on this.

He did observe, however, that:[33]

> "insofar as negligence in relation to classification is liable to harm economic interests, I see no general ground for distinguishing between the economic interests of the charterer, the mortgagee and the purchaser. All are foreseeably liable to rely on the class status of the vessel—often to the extent of making the maintenance of class a contractual condition—and all are at risk of being caused economic loss if class surveys are not carried out with proper skill."

This was a point that was more in evidence in *The Nicholas H*.

The Morning Watch was not appealed, and this may well have been because the case had already cost too much to fight, bearing in mind the amount at stake. The case lasted eight days before the Commercial Court, leading counsel were instructed on one side and there were a number of witnesses. The total amount the judge found that he would have awarded as damages was only £30,000. The total costs may have been ten times this. The case received considerable

---

[32] *Ibid.*, 871.
[33] [1990] 1 Lloyd's Rep. 547, 559.

comment, and as I have said, led to a general assumption that a classification society was immune from suit. This assumption did not last for long.

4 *THE NICHOLAS H*

The Morning Watch was decided in February 1990. In July 1992 in the Commercial Court, Hirst, J. gave judgment at first instance in *The Nicholas H*.[34] In this case the classification society was again the defendant, though the plaintiff was not a purchaser, but the owners of the cargo laden aboard the vessel.

The vessel, which had on board a cargo of lead and zinc, anchored off Puerto Rico and reported that she had a crack to her hull. She was surveyed by N.K.K., the Japanese classification society. The surveyor, Mr Ducat, put a recommendation on the classification documentation that the vessel must proceed to the nearest port with repair facilities and make permanent repairs before she could continue on her voyage. This would have been an expensive undertaking and this gives rise to another of the points to which I referred earlier. The ship owners were very keen that these permanent repairs were not done owing to the substantial cost. It is not clear, from the case, whether or not the crack to the hull was caused by a marine peril, and therefore covered by hull insurance or not. It is certainly possible that these were mere corrosion cracks, the repairs of which would be for the owners' own account.

The vessel would have had to have been dry-docked, and possibly the cargo unloaded, which would have cost no doubt many hundreds of thousands of dollars. A week later Mr Ducat surveyed the vessel again, some temporary repairs having been carried out by a travelling gang, flown in from Greece. Mr Ducat reversed his original recommendation and said that the vessel may proceed, the temporary repairs having been done, to her discharge port in Italy. The repairs should then be made permanent. I do not know what discussions took place between the owners and Mr Ducat. It may well be that severe pressure was put upon Mr Ducat to allow the vessel to proceed. Unfortunately, shortly after the vessel sailed, the temporary repairs failed and the vessel sank, luckily without loss of life.

In the ordinary course of events the cargo owners obviously look to the ship owner, suing for a breach of the bill of lading contract. They did so in this case but it appears that they were met with a plea of limitation, the limitation fund being U.S.\$500,000. Apparently the limitation fund could not be breached and, accordingly, the cargo owners were only able to recover the sum of U.S.\$500,000 from the vessel. This left them with a balance of their claim, which was U.S.\$5.5 million, for which they could not recover. Accordingly

---

[34] [1992] 2 Lloyd's Rep. 481.

they cast around for someone else to sue. Perhaps it would be more accurate to say that they cast around for someone else to sue who could actually pay. They alighted on the classification society, which they thought had the necessary funds to meet any judgment.

Cargo interests (or their insurers) then advanced an argument against the classification society based on a breach of a duty of care which they said was owed to them as cargo owners. Sensibly, the issue as to whether or not a duty of care arose was ordered to be tried as a preliminary issue. Hirst, J. found that the cargo owners were indeed owed a duty of care. Thus he was not daunted by the decision of Phillips, J. This caused some surprise and the case went to the Court of Appeal, where Hirst, J. was reversed and the Court of Appeal, unanimously, held that in these circumstances no duty of care arose.[35] Undaunted, the owners then appealed to the House of Lords.[36]

The House of Lords upheld the Court of Appeal, in holding that no duty of care arose, but by four judges to one. Two of their Lordships had shipping experience and those two, Lord Steyn and Lord Lloyd of Berwick, fundamentally disagreed. Lord Steyn gave the judgment of the majority, holding that no duty of care existed. Lord Lloyd argued passionately that this was a case where a duty of care should have been imposed. I think it interesting, therefore, to look at these two judgments in some detail and see if any principle can be established, and indeed try and express a view as to which of the approaches is the most satisfactory.

The judgment of the majority, given by Lord Steyn, is largely devoid of any great analysis of legal issues. There is of course reference to case law, but not perhaps the very detailed analysis that one would have expected. This is probably because, as I think was the case in *White* v. *Jones*,[37] basically Lord Steyn thought that this was a case where the just result was that there should be no duty of care and therefore decided to achieve that result on the facts. In *White* v. *Jones* the majority of the House of Lords obviously thought that the right result was that the plaintiff should succeed against the defendant and therefore, again, were happy to find that a duty of care existed.

White v. *Jones* involved a solicitor who had been asked by a testator to draw up a will in favour of two daughters. Negligently the solicitor forgot to do so, the testator died and the two daughters were uanble to receive the inheritance they should have received. It was claimed that they were owed a duty of care by the solicitor. The House of Lords split 3:2 in favour of holding that there was a duty of care. Lord Goff of Chieveley, in my view at least, seems to have proceeded on the view that there ought to be a remedy and therefore he was determined to find one. The two dissenting judges, Lord Keith of Kinkel and Lord Mustill,

---

[35] [1994] 1 W.L.R. 1071; [1994] 1 Lloyd's Rep. 492.
[36] [1996] A.C. 211.
[37] [1995] 2 A.C. 207.

seemed to me to be appalled by the prospect of tailoring the law to meet the desired result and indeed said so. As Lord Keith said:[38]

> "I am unable to reconcile the allowance of the plaintiff's claim with principle, or to accept that to do so would represent an appropriate advance on the incremental basis from decided cases."

I think this case, and indeed *The Nicholas H*, show that the courts at the moment, in cases such as this, seem to be looking at the result they wish to achieve first, and then adapting the facts and the law to achieve that result.

In any event Lord Steyn, like many other people, started with *Donoghue* v. *Stevenson* in commenting that, if one looks at all the cases that had been cited to the House, right up to *White* v. *Jones*:

> "None of the cases cited provided any realistic analogy to be used as a springboard for a decision one way or the other in this case. The present case can only be decided on the basis of an intense and particular focus of all its distinctive features, and then applying established legal principles to it."[39]

However, Lord Steyn did cite, with approval, the comment made by Saville L.J. in the Court of Appeal, which effectively repeated the three tests set out by Phillips, J. in *The Morning Watch*. What Saville, L.J. said was:[40]

> "whatever the nature of the harm sustained by the plaintiff, it is necessary to consider the matter not only by enquiring about foreseeability [i.e. test one] but also by considering the nature of the relationship between the parties; [i.e. test two proximity] and to be satisfied that in all the circumstances it is fair, just and reasonable to impose a duty of care [i.e. test three]."

Interestingly Saville, L.J. had attempted to weld all these three tests together. He went on to say:

> "Again in most cases of the direct infliction of physical loss or injury through carelessness, it is self-evident that a civilised system of law should hold that a duty of care has been broken, whereas the infliction of financial harm [i.e. economic loss] may well pose a more difficult problem. Thus, the three so-called requirements for a duty of care are not to be treated as wholly separate and distinct requirements but rather as convenient and helpful approaches to the pragmatic question of whether a duty should be imposed in any given case. In the end whether the law does impose a duty in any particular circumstances depends upon those circumstances ..."

That seems to be giving carte blanche to the courts to decide really whatever they like in relation to a duty of care so long as they can provide what they consider to be a satisfactory analysis of the position. What Lord Steyn then did, really rather shortly, was to run through what he considered to be the material

---

[38] *Ibid.*, 251.
[39] *The Nicholas H* [1996] A.C. 211, 236.
[40] [1994] 1 W.L.R. 1071, 1077; [1994] 1 Lloyd's Rep. 492, 496; cited at [1996] A.C. 211, 235.

factors in this case and then come to the conclusion that they did not point towards the imposition of a duty of care.

Counsel for the cargo owners had said that it was clearly foreseeable that the carelessness of the surveyor in conducting the survey of the damaged vessel, or in the making of recommendations, was likely to expose the cargo actually on board the vessel to the danger of physical damage. The surveyor was brought in because there was concern for the safety of the vessel on the intended voyage. Lord Steyn pointed out, however, that exactly the same dangers would affect the hull and cargo on that voyage. Counsel for cargo owners went on to point out that in the circumstances, particularly in the light of the fact that the cargo was on board when the surveyor carelessly performed his professional services, the element of proximity was satisfied. Lastly, it was said that neither the contract of carriage between the owners of the vessel and the cargo owners nor the contract between the owners and classification society militated against the recognition of the legal duty of care. Given that third parties, such as cargo owners, are known in practice to rely on the recommendations of classification societies, it was submitted that it was fair, just and reasonable to recognise a duty of care in this case.

In order to determine the issues, Lord Steyn said that he was happy to assume that the questions as to foreseeability and proximity (i.e. tests one and two) were satisfied. This was interesting as it seems to me that there was in fact less proximity here than in *The Morning Watch*. The main question which Lord Steyn asked himself was whether it was fair just and reasonable that a duty of care should be imposed. A number of other factors were considered.

a. Did the carelessness of the surveyor cause direct physical loss?

Lord Steyn said that the carelessness did not involve direct infliction of physical damage in the relevant sense, in that you do not drop a lighted cigarette into a cargo hold known to contain a combustible cargo, causing an explosion. If that had happened then he would have thought it would have been a strong case that the classification society was in breach of a duty of care.

b. Did the cargo owners rely on the recommendations of the surveyor?

This was an important point. In the present case there was no contact whatever between the cargo owners and the classification society. As had been pointed out, it was not even suggested that the cargo owners knew that N.K.K. had been brought in to survey the vessel. The cargo owners simply relied on the owners of the vessel to keep it seaworthy and to look after the cargo. The Court of Appeal regarded that feature as sufficient to demonstrate that proximity was absent. Lord Steyn merely said that it was one item that should be considered.

c. The impact of the contract between the ship owners and the cargo owners

There had been considerable discussion in the Court of Appeal about the impact of the bill of lading contract. This aspect of the decision had received wide publicity. Saville, L.J. had pointed out that the owners were bound by their bill of lading contract with the cargo owners and that those contracts contained the Hague Rules. If the proposition advanced by the cargo owners was correct, this would add an identical or virtual identical duty owned by the classification society to that already owed by the ship owners but without any of those balancing factors, introduced by the Hague Rules, which are internationally recognised and accepted.

In other words, basically, the classification society would be more likely to be liable to the cargo owners than were the ship owners. This was felt to be unfair. The judgment of the Court of Appeal on this point has been criticised, particularly by Professor Cane.[41] Nevertheless, Lord Steyn did say that, if a duty of care by classification societies to cargo owners was recognised in this case, it would have a substantial impact on international trade. The argument would be that classification societies would have substantially to increase their liability insurance, there would be a greater increase in claims and ultimately those costs would be paid by owners in any event. Lord Steyn therefore agreed, effectively, with Saville, L.J. and said that the result of the recognition of the duty of care would be to enable cargo owners, or rather their insurers, to disturb the balance created by the Hague Rules. He therefore felt that this was a factor that militated against the imposition of a duty of care.

d. The contract between the classification society and the ship owners

The argument here is that, as there was already a contract between N.K.K. and the ship owner, this was a factor against recognising a duty of care to the cargo interest. Lord Steyn made no comment on this.

e. Position and role of N.K.K.

There was considerable argument about the fact that N.K.K. was an independent and non-profit making entity, established for the sole purpose of

---

[41] "The Liability of Classification Societies" [1994] L.M.C.L.Q. 363.

promoting the collective welfare of, mainly, the safety of lives and ships at sea. Would classification societies be able to carry out their functions as efficiently if they became the ready alternative target of cargo owners, who already have contractual claims against ship owners? Lord Steyn concluded that, if this were to be the case, then classification societies would adopt, to the detriment of their traditional role, a more defensive position.

f. Policy factors

The argument here was that, if a duty of care was recognised, then classification societies would be sued at all times and by all people. Lord Steyn agreed with that. He thought that, if a duty was recognised in this case, there was no reason why it should not extend to other surveys such as annual surveys, docking surveys, special surveys, and so on. As he pointed out, N.K.K. carry out 14,500 surveys per year and thus their potential liability would be very substantial indeed.

Basically what Lord Steyn concluded was that, if classification societies were held to owe a duty of care in circumstances such as this, then it would add an extra layer to cargo claims. Instead of cargo owners suing ship owners, they would also be able to sue classification societies, an extra layer of insurance would become involved, and this was an undesirable situation.

Lord Steyn then aggregated all these factors and decided that arguments advanced on behalf of the cargo owners were clearly outweighed by the cumulative effect of the matters discussed in paragraphs (c), (e) and (f) above, that is to say the outflanking of the bargain between ship owners and cargo owners.

In his summary he said that the recognition of such a duty would be unfair as against the ship owners, who would ultimately have to bear the costs of holding classification societies liable, such a consequence being at variance with the bargain between ship owners and cargo owners based on an internationally agreed contractual structure. It would also be unfair and unjust towards classification societies, notably because they act for the collective welfare and, unlike ship owners, they would not have the benefit of any limitation or other defences. Insofar as the cargo owners are concerned, they currently have the protection of the Hague Rules, which enable them to sue ship owners subject to defences under those rules and the tonnage limitation provisions. Under the existing system any shortfall is readily insurable. This is perhaps an interesting point. Lord Steyn realised that basically what was at stake here was which insurer should ultimately bear the responsibility. Although there was, as I have said, a shortfall of U.S.$5.5 million, the cargo owners themselves, ordinarily at least, would already have been paid by their cargo insurers.

Accordingly and without reference to much authority, Lord Steyn decided that no duty of care was owed, and three other members of the House agreed with him without comment. However Lord Lloyd did not. Basically he agreed with the judgment of Hirst, J. He again accepted that there were three tests and the first test, reliance, was easy as it had been accepted.

Insofar as proximity is concerned, Lord Lloyd felt there was very close proximity (Lord Steyn had also accepted that there was sufficient proximity). An interesting point that Lord Lloyd made was that it seemed to him self evident that Mr Ducat, the surveyor, owed a duty of care towards the members of the crew. He knew that their lives would be at risk if he allowed the ship to sail in an unseaworthy condition. He went on to say that he thought the relationship between Mr Ducat and the cargo was even closer. He used, by way of support for this argument, what he referred to as a universal rule of maritime law that ship and cargo were taking part in a joint venture. Thus, when the master called in Mr Ducat, and thereafter incurred expenditure for the common safety, he was acting as much in the interest and on behalf of the cargo as the ship.

Lord Lloyd referred to the principal of general average, where of course both cargo and ship contribute to expenses incurred to preserve the common adventure. He therefore thought it almost impossible to say that, while Mr Ducat owed a duty of care to the ship, he owed no duty of care to the cargo. He thought that the fact that the cargo owners were unaware that Mr Ducat had been called in had been quite beside the point.

Like Lord Steyn, therefore, he came on to consider the question of fair, just and reasonable. First, he dealt with the question of the fact that there was already a contract between the ship owner and the cargo owner which contained the Hague Rules. He made an interesting point, which was not dealt with by Lord Steyn, which was that the cargo might as well have been carried under the terms of a charter party, the bill of lading being a mere receipt. He then went on to say that, as the Hague Rules do not apply to charter parties, the argument advanced on this point fell away. With respect, I think he displayed insufficient understanding of the general situation. Whilst Lord Lloyd said that he was aware that the Hague Rules were incorporated into voyage charter parties, this was only by agreement. That is true; but in my experience, if a ship owner carries a cargo under a charter party and does not incorporate the Hague Rules, he will, apart from anything else, avoid his P. & I. cover.

Lord Lloyd went on to say that, even if all the carriage of goods by sea were subject to the Hague Rules, he would have difficulty in seeing why the balance of rights and liabilities between ship owners and cargo would be upset by holding the defendants liable for the consequence of Mr Ducat's negligence. This seems to me somewhat to miss the point. That point is that, whether or not one should not seek to bring in another head of claim against a third party, when there is already a natural route for the claim, that is to say against the ship owner.

I think that point was made when he analysed cases in which a third party had been held liable in tort. He pointed out that, on the analogy of cases such as

Midland Silicones Ltd. v. *Scruttons Ltd.*,[42] a repairer of a vessel could easily be held to owe a duty of care to the cargo on board a ship. If a repairer negligently fails to secure an inspection cover, and a week later sea water enters the hold, damages the cargo and the vessel sinks, should the ship repairer escape liability because the "primary" responsibility to make the ship seaworthy is on the ship owners?

Lord Lloyd pointed out that counsel for N.K.K. ultimately conceded that ship repairers should owe a duty of care to the cargo on board. Accordingly, Lord Lloyd said, he could see no reason why a surveyor in these circumstances should not be in exactly the same position. What would happen if in the case he had just mentioned the surveyor had negligently told the ship repairer that four bolts were sufficient to repair the cover instead of the usual six. How could it be fair, just and reasonable that the surveyor should not be liable if the repairer is? He therefore concluded that the existence of the contract between the owners and the cargo was irrelevant.

Finally, he made some general comments about the other points to which I have already referred that affected the decision of Lord Steyn. Lord Lloyd said that the House of Lords had been told that there had never yet been a successful claim against a classification society in tort. He regarded this as irrelevant, and I think he was right to do so. As he pointed out, the same argument was raised by salvors in *The Tojo Maru*[43] that they were not liable for damage caused by the negligence of their employees, one reason being that no such claim had ever been successful. In that case, in which my firm acted for the salvors, the argument was disregarded.

Lord Lloyd quoted *The Tojo Maru* again to deal with the point that it would be unfair to hold the classification society liable for an unlimited amount in tort in contrast to ship owners, who have a limitation fund available. He pointed out that the defendant salvors in *The Tojo Maru* were also not entitled to limit; although the House of Lords held that they had some sympathy with them, they still found against them. Ultimately, interestingly, the limitation provisions were extended to cover salvors. However, it was not even suggested, said Lord Lloyd, in *The Tojo Maru* that the inability of salvors to limit was a ground for holding them immune from the consequences of their negligence. Again I think he is right about this. Lord Lloyd was then rather amusing about the suggestion that, as a classification society was charitable and non-profit making, then somehow this militated against a duty of care. He pointed out that the remedies in law of tort are not discretionary:[44]

---

[42] [1962] A.C. 446.
[43] [1972] A.C. 242.
[44] *The Nicholas H* [1996] A.C. 211, 228.

"Hospitals are also charitable non-profit making organisations. But they are subject to the same *common* duty of care under the Occupier's Liability Acts 1957 and 1984 as are betting shops or brothels."

Again, it had been said in *The Tojo Maru* that, if salvors were held liable, they may be discouraged from their beneficial activities and therefore there was a public policy point. That point was rejected in *The Tojo Maru* and again Lord Lloyd thought it should be rejected here.

He went on to say that N.K.K. should be able to afford the cost of insurance: it was the third largest classification society and would have a substantial net income. Lord Lloyd pointed out that A.B.S. had a net profit income of U.S.$11 million in 1990 and operating revenue of U.S.$122 million. N.K.K. had apparently put in evidence saying that they would be unlikely to survive if they were held liable for claims such as the present. Lord Lloyd said that he did not believe that point, and I agree with him.

The attitude of N.K.K. is probably influenced to a large extent by the marketplace in which they normally operate. Traditionally they insured Japanese vessels; and Japanese ship owners do not, as a matter of policy, ever sue their classification society. Thus, N.K.K. would be very unused to dealing with such claims. Had they been used to a more robust environment, they would be unlikely to have made such a comment. Having said that, however, I think Lord Lloyd did not really give sufficient consideration to the damages that are often demanded in cases such as this.

This case involved U.S.$5.5 million; the case with which I have been involved and which I mentioned earlier involves U.S.$9 million; and *The Sundancer* involved U.S.$266 million. It does not take a genius to work out that, if classification societies were regularly sued for these amounts and if any of those suits were successful, then the costs of their insurance would rapidly become astronomic. It is fair to say that, if their insurance cover were ever avoided, then serious problems may arise. That is not to say that this should be a decisive factor but it is something that should be recognised.

Lord Lloyd in fact dealt with this by saying that the question of the availability of insurance was irrelevant and that courts should not reach conclusions as to the existence of a duty of care purely on the availability of insurance. I think, as a matter of law, that this is probably correct; but, if one is prepared to take a commercial view on the result of a case, then it is something that should be borne in mind. Lord Lloyd thought that the cost of such insurance would not be passed on to owners, whereas Lord Steyn thought that it would be. I think that it is likely to be passed on in the way of increased fees.

Finally, Lord Lloyd in this section of his speech made a rather interesting observation with which I am not sure everyone would agree. He said:[45]

---

[45] *Ibid.*, 229.

> "more generally, I suspect, a decision in favour of the cargo owners would be welcomed by members of the shipping community at large, who are increasingly concerned by the proliferation of substandard classification societies."

This raises a more general point, on which I have not yet touched, as to the general ability of and/or confidence in classification societies. Obviously any classification society is only as good as its surveyor on the spot. I have already referred to the commercial pressures and, possibly, financial pressures that are put on surveyors that I think makes it more likely that they may produce an incompetent and/or misleading certificate. On the other hand it is well known that a number of classification societies do not have the high standards of some of the traditional classification societies and this matter has now been addressed, at least by insurers, who are beginning to insist, certainly in the P. & I. field, that a vessel must be classed by a classification society which is a member of the I.A.C.S. The aim of this organisation was to exclude those societies which have shown themselves clearly either incompetent or to be inclined to agree with any comments made to them by owners.

Lord Lloyd concluded by referring to what he called the "Retreat from Anns" culminating in *Murphy*. He saw no difficulty, however, in side stepping those cases. He came back to saying that basically this was a claim where cargo had suffered physical damage to their property and that damage was caused by the negligence of Mr Ducat. He took the view that the concept of proximity, and the requirement that it should be fair, just and reasonable to impose a duty of care in the particular circumstances of the case, had been developed as a means of containing liability for pure economic loss under the principle stated in *Donoghue* v. *Stevenson*. He took the view that there were no difficulties in this case:[46]

> "where the facts cry out for the imposition of a duty of care between the parties as they do here, it would require an exceptional case to refuse to impose a duty of care on the grounds that it would not be fair just and reasonable. Otherwise there is a risk that the law of negligence would disintegrate into a series of isolated decisions without any coherent principles at all, and the retreat from *Anns* will turn into a rout."

It is clear that there is very little common ground between the judgment of Lord Lloyd and that of Lord Steyn. However, Lord Lloyd was in the minority; so, however attractive we may find his judgment, it does not represent the law.

5 CONCLUSIONS

In my view the judgment of the House of Lords in *The Nicholas H* has only put paid to any prospect of a claim being made successfully against a classification

---

[46] *Ibid.*, 230.

society by a cargo owner on those particular facts. Bearing in mind the very broad approach adopted by Lord Steyn, it is not inconceivable that on a different series of facts the principle may yet revisit the courts. Where, for example, cargo interests are consulted by the classification society, and perhaps decide not to tranship the cargo on the advice of the classification surveyor, the decision could be different.

Is it also fair to assume that other parties in similar circumstances to cargo owners, such as charterers, would be unlikely to succeed in any claim? My view is that it will depend on what Lord Steyn called the "basis of an intense and particular focus".[47] What the case shows, I believe, along with *White* v. *Jones*, is that the House of Lords have moved towards a more pragmatic approach. *White* v. *Jones* was an interesting case in that a decision by three to two is always unsatisfactory, particularly where, as there, one of the dissenting judges, Lord Mustill, was one of the more powerful members of the court. Accordingly there can be no absolute certainty, when classification societies are considered as a useful defendant, as to what the answer will be.

I hope I have shown, when discussing *The Morning Watch*, that that case, on its own, certainly is not authority for the proposition that a purchaser of a vessel will be unable to sue the classification society. The facts of *The Morning Watch* were unhelpful to that particular plaintiff and I can see a situation where the facts could be very much more helpful and where there will be a clear risk that the classification society may be held liable. I do not think that any of the elements in Lord Steyn's speech in *The Nicholas H* militate against a purchaser's succeeding in a claim.

In the case in which I myself was involved, where I was acting for a classification society, I think that there is undoubtedly a risk that the society could have been held liable. In *The Morning Watch* Phillips, J. concluded that there was not sufficient proximity. One of the conclusions was that the relevant survey was not carried out for the sole reason as selling the yacht to the particular purchaser who became the plaintiff. The judge concluded that the plaintiff was not intending to act on the result of the survey; he was merely one of the indeterminate class of persons who might do so. In the case in which I was involved, obviously, the society was very much involved in the sale of the vessel to the particular purchaser who became the plaintiff. They were receiving detailed arguments from both sides and being asked both to intervene and not to intervene. They were very well aware of the problems that the plaintiff might suffer and, indeed, ultimately did suffer. As I have said, the case was settled but we certainly took the view, I think correctly, that our clients stood a substantial risk of losing the case despite the very recent authority of the House of Lords in *The Nicholas H*.

---

[47] *Ibid.*, 236.

6 RECENT DEVELOPMENTS

One purpose of this essay was to seek to show that the decision of the House of Lords in *The Nicholas H*, far from laying down a general rule, in fact allows individual judges to make up their own mind as to whether or not a duty of care should be imposed. There have been two recent cases, with contrasting results, which show how different results can be achieved. Both are decisions of the Court of Appeal. The first is *Reeman v. Department of Transport*.[48]

This case involved a fishing vessel which had been sold to Mr and Mrs Reeman in 1989. She carried a certificate issued by the Department of Transport that certified that she complied with the necessary statutory regulations designed to ensure that she was seaworthy. She had been surveyed by Mr Jones, a surveyor employed by the Department of Transport who had made a series of negligent errors when calculating the stability of the vessel. These errors were continued by Mr Jones in subsequent certificates, the last of which was in force when the vessel was sold to Mr and Mrs Reeman. Subsequently the Department of Trade carried out stability tests and found that the vessel did not meet with the minimum requirements and the vessel was thus unable to trade. Mr and Mrs Reeman began an action against the Department of Trade for breach of a duty of care and the case was decided at first instance by Judge Robert Taylor, who concluded that a duty of care had arisen. He applied the standard three tests. He concluded that there was a virtual certainty that the certificate would be communicated to prospective purchasers such as the plaintiff; there was an extreme likelihood that such prospective purchasers would rely on that certificate in deciding whether to purchase, and there was an overwhelming probability that they would do so without independent verification. He held that all these facts were known actually or inferentially to the Department of Transport and established the requisite degree of proximity between the plaintiffs and the Department of Transport.

The judge then adopted what I would call the bleeding heart test, which is something of a theme of this essay He concluded that the plaintiffs did not appear to have a remedy against anyone other than the Department of Transport and, applying the criteria of fairness, justice and reasonableness, it was possible to set out an acceptable control mechanism which substantially avoided the mischief in question; this would be to confine the duty to persons who actually purchased the relevant vessel during the currency of the certificate; here there was no question of the plaintiffs being in any way responsible for the condition, safety or stability of the vessel prior to their purchase of it; and it would be fair, just and reasonable to hold that the duty of care existed towards the plaintiffs.

[48] [1997] 2 Lloyd's Rep. 648.

He therefore found in favour of the plaintiffs. He felt quite able to do this despite having considered both *The Morning Watch* and *The Nicholas H.*

The Department of Transport appealed and the Court of Appeal allowed the appeal. They gave detailed reasons but what they are saying, in my view, is that they did not feel that it was just and reasonable to impose a duty of care and therefore decline to do so. A number of points were raised. These included the fact that, if there was insufficient proximity of relationship to give rise to a duty of care in respect of death or injury to the skipper or crew of a certificated vessel in respect of economic loss directly caused to the owners of the vessel at the time of the certification, it was hard to accept that such proximity existed between the Department of Transport and those who might rely on the existence of a certificate in relation to commercial transactions that involved the risk of economic loss.

They also referred to the fact that the statutory framework was one designed to promote safety at sea and that the way of achieving this was to impose duties as to seaworthiness on the owners of the vessels and then to provide for the Department of Transport to check and certify that those duties have been complied with. The court did not accept that in the case of fishing vessel certificates a subsidiary purpose which the certificate was issued was to inform those who might in the future consider entering into commercial transactions such as purchase in relation to the certified vessels. The Court of Appeal also held that, as the builders of fishing vessels were not liable to subsequent purchasers in relation to the costs of remedying defects attributable to lack of care in construction, there was no obvious reason why the Department of Transport's duty to regulate the seaworthiness of British vessels should impose a greater duty of care than that borne by those who built the vessels.

They also pointed out that it would be open to a party entering into a commercial transaction in relation to a certificated vessel to take steps such as surveying the vessel or stipulating for contractual warranties that would provide protection against the risk that the certificate did not reflect the true condition of the vessel. This seems a strange conclusion for the Court of Appeal to come to, since Mr and Mrs Reeman had indeed retained a surveyor to check the vessel, who had also failed to spot the problem with stability. The surveyor had been a defendant to the action but had gone into liquidation. The point as to contractual warranties is also unrealistic, since in most cases the seller of the vessel is a one ship company that will have no assets.

In any event all these points, and others, enabled the Court of Appeal to decide that the judge had come to the wrong conclusion and that it was not fair, just and reasonable to impose a duty of care on the Department of Transport. They concluded that a body such as the Department of Transport, when performing its regulatory functions under the Merchant Shipping Acts, performed a similar role to that of classification societies, i.e. they existed for the purpose of further safety at sea rather than for the protection of commercial interest.

My own reading of this case is that it supports the argument that I have been putting forward, which is that the House of Lords in *The Nicholas H* effectively gave power to the courts to come to whatever conclusion they found to be fair in the circumstances, tailoring their findings of fact to the conclusion that they thought should be achieved. It is interesting that the first instance judge did not find any difficulty in coming to the conclusion that a duty of care existed and the Court of Appeal had no difficulty in concluding that it did not.

The other case which I would like to mention is *Perrett* v. *Collins*.[49] This was a case decided by a different division of the Court of Appeal and involved a light aircraft built by a Mr Collins. Mr Collins put in a different gearbox from the gearbox supplied with the kit. He should also have changed the propeller, if he was to change the gearbox, but did not. In order for the aircraft to be allowed to fly, it needed a Certificate of Airworthiness, which was provided by the Popular Flying Association, whose inspector, Mr Usherwood, inspected the aircraft at various stages of construction and knew and approved of the change of the gearbox. Mr Usherwood signed a document, which was the permit to fly, which stated:

> "I hereby declare that the aircraft has been overhauled and prepared to my entire satisfaction, and that it is in an approved condition."

Mr Collins then took the aircraft on a test flight with Mr Perrett as a passenger. The aircraft crashed and Mr Perrett was injured. The plaintiff sued both Mr Collins and Mr Usherwood, and also the P.F.A. His case was that the personal injuries that he suffered when the aircraft crashed were caused by the negligence of one or more of the defendants. The second and third defendants, i.e. Mr Usherwood and the P.F.A., denied that they owed a duty of care to the plaintiff. At first instance Judge Hallgarten, Q.C. held that the second and third defendants did owe the plaintiff a duty of care. Both *The Nicholas H* and *Reeman* v. *The Department of Transport* were considered by the Court of Appeal. The Court of Appeal held that it was foreseeable that, if the second and third defendants granted a certificate of fitness to fly in respect of this aircraft with an inappropriate gearbox, there was likely to be an accident, and they ought reasonably to have had in contemplation a person travelling as a passenger on the test flight in the aircraft as being so affected when they were directing their minds to the acts or omissions which were called into question. They further concluded that the role of Mr Usherwood was not a subsidiary one to that of Mr Collins. Mr Usherwood had an independent and critical role in the granting of a certificate of fitness of flight, without which it could not take off. Mr Usherwood was involved with the inspection of the aircraft throughout and

---

[49] [1998] 2 Lloyd's Rep. 255.

therefore a greater injustice would be done to a person injured in circumstances such as those that arose in this case by not imposing a duty on those responsible for issuing a fitness to fly certificate than would result to the defendants in imposing such a duty. In other words the Court of Appeal decided that it was fair, just and reasonable in the circumstances that a duty of care should be imposed.

Although the facts in this case are somewhat different, it shows in my view that, where a court decides that a duty of care ought to be imposed, they are able to use the ratio of the House of Lords in *The Nicholas H* to achieve exactly that result. Speaking as a practitioner in maritime law, therefore, the decision of *The Nicholas H* has made our lives more difficult, since we now have the problem of deciding whether or not a court is likely to take the view that a duty of care should be imposed or not. This is likely to be an empirical decision made by the court at the time. Although, obviously, we can advise on the law, we also now have to try and decide what any particular court is likely to decide is the "right" decision as the court will be able to come to that decision, whether in favour of imposing a duty of care or not, by using exactly the same legal principles.

Chapter 8

Due Diligence and Delegation

*Sir Stephen Tomlinson**

To a modern generation of commercial lawyer the expression "due diligence" summons up visions of a slide rule (if such still exists) being run over the books of a target company in the context of an impending merger or acquisition. For a previous generation the words are inextricably linked with the obligation imposed upon a carrier of goods by sea before and at the beginning of the voyage to exercise due diligence to make the ship seaworthy. This is the duty imposed by Article III, rule 1(a) of the Hague Rules, as given effect by the Carriage of Goods by Sea Act 1924. Article IV, rule 1 likewise refers to "want of due diligence on the part of the carrier to make the ship seaworthy".[1]

Most shipping lawyers think that they have a pretty good idea what is involved in the exercise of due diligence to make a ship seaworthy, and it is second nature that the duty so cast upon a carrier, whatever its precise ambit and extent, is personal to him, liability for non-performance or non-observance of which cannot be avoided by delegation to another.[2] Before its incorporation into English law by the Carriage of Goods by Sea Act 1924 the expression "to exercise due diligence to make the ship seaworthy" had a long lineage of use in the same context in, at least, the United States Harter Act 1893, the Australia Sea Carriage of Goods Act 1904 and the Canadian Water Carriage of Goods Act 1910. Furthermore, before the Hague Rules were framed there were decisions of English courts in which the language of the Harter Act had fallen to be construed by virtue of its provisions being embodied in bills of lading.[3]

---

* The keen-eyed reader may detect that the author was the unsuccessful advocate in *Dow Europe S.A.* v. *Novoklav Inc.* [1998] 1 Lloyd's Rep. 306, when that case reached the Commercial Court, so his views should no doubt be approached with suitable caution.

[1] See now the equivalent provisions of the Hague-Visby Rules as given the force of law by the Carriage of Goods by Sea Act 1971.

[2] *Riverstone Meat Co. Pty Ltd.* v. *Lancashire Shipping Co. Ltd. (The Muncaster Castle)* [1961] A.C. 807. See also *Bowstead and Reynolds on Agency,* 16th edn. (1996), Article 92(2)(b).

[3] See *The Muncaster Castle* [1961] A.C. 807, 836, *per* Viscount Simonds.

It is only natural that the concept of due diligence should thereafter have been borrowed and adapted for use in other contracts concerning or related to maritime adventures. However, because of its origins, and because of the meaning attributed to it in the precursors to the Hague Rules, as in turn authoritatively adopted into English law by the House of Lords in *The Muncaster Castle*,[4] it has sometimes been thought that the expression "due diligence" has some intrinsic meaning involving non-delegability. Thus, in *Dow Europe S.A.* v. *Novoklav Inc.*[5] Timothy Walker, J. remarked of a due diligence provision appearing in a time charterparty that:

> "The standard construction of a due diligence provision is that the obligation is one of due diligence 'by whomsoever it may be done' even if the obligation is delegated to an independent contractor (see *The Muncaster Castle*) unless this is ousted by clear words restricting the obligation to one of personal want of due diligence."

The learned judge went on to point out that there are well-known examples of forms of charterparty which do achieve this result, i.e. the restriction of the obligation to one of personal due diligence only, for example the Baltime Form considered by McNair, J. in *The Brabant*.[6]

This approach is, it is respectfully suggested, something of an over-simplification. There is nothing in the words "due diligence" themselves which compels the result that the person on whom the obligation is cast is, *ipso facto*, responsible for the acts or omissions of all those of whose services he may make use in discharge of his obligation. The more relevant enquiry however is what is the ambit and extent of the obligation imposed by the words and the answer to this question is, inevitably, to be found in the context in which they appear. It was to this enquiry that the speeches in *The Muncaster Castle*[7] were largely directed. What was determinative in that case was the history of the words "due diligence to *make the ship seaworthy*".[8] Building on an observation of Judge Brown in the District Court for the Southern District of New York in 1897,[9] the House of Lords held that the Hague Rules required due diligence *in the work itself*.[10]

Lord Radcliffe pointed out[11] that there were two ways of looking at the intrinsic nature of the obligation. If the content of the carrier's obligation was that it should, as a legal person, observe the standard of reasonable care that would be required at common law in a matter of this sort, which involves skilled and technical work, and if there was nothing more in the carrier's obligation

---

[4] [1961] A.C. 807.
[5] [1998] 1 Lloyd's Rep. 306.
[6] [1965] 2 Lloyd's Rep. 546.
[7] [1961] A.C. 807.
[8] Emphasis added. See esp. [1961] A.C. 807, 863–864, *per* Lord Radcliffe.
[9] *The Colima* (1897) 82 Fed. Rep. 665.
[10] Emphasis added.
[11] [1961] A.C. 807, 862–863.

than that, then on the facts of the case he would not have regarded the carrier as being in default. It will be remembered that the carrier, in fact also the owner of the vessel, had entrusted her to reputable shipbuilders for annual survey and repair. Due to the negligence of a fitter employed by the ship repairers as the result of which negligence could not have been detected by subsequent visual examination, an inspection cover had thereafter admitted sea water and caused damage to cargo.

The second way of looking at the intrinsic nature of the obligation was however materially different. Lord Radcliffe described it in this way:[12]

> "It is to ask the question, when there has been damage to cargo and that damage is traceable to unseaworthiness of the vessel, whether that unseaworthiness is due to any lack of diligence in those who have been implicated by the carriers in the work of keeping or making the vessel seaworthy. Such persons are then agents whose diligence or lack of it is attributable to the carriers. An enquiry on these lines is not concerned with distinctions between carelessness on the part of officers or servants of the carriers or their supervising agents, on the one hand, and carelessness on the part of their contractors or those contractors' contractors, on the other. The carriers must answer for anything that has been done amiss in the work. It is the work itself that delimits the area of the obligation, just as it is the period 'before or at the beginning of the voyage' that delimits the time at which any obligation imputed to the carriers can be thought to begin."

Lord Radcliffe considered that the natural meaning of the words "due diligence to make the ship seaworthy" as used in the Hague Rules did not accord well with either approach. What was decisive in favour of adoption of the second approach was the uniform meaning attributed to the same words in connection with sea carriage of goods when they had hitherto fallen to be considered by courts both in England and in the United States. Equally cogent perhaps was the notion that the task of making a ship seaworthy, whether by inspection or by repair or by both, is one which a carrier must almost inevitably have done on his behalf by others, be they shipyards, ship repairers, surveyors or even his own employees. In the context of a dispute between cargo owner and carrier it is only natural that the responsibility for seeing that the ship is in a fit and proper condition for the carriage undertaken should devolve upon the carrier, and it would be odd if the cargo owner's rights of recovery from the carrier should depend on particular circumstances in the carrier's situation, for example, whether he had the requisite expertise amongst his own employees or was obliged (or elected) to make use of the services of independent contractors. Thus, concluded Lord Radcliffe as we have seen above, it is the work itself that delimits the area of the obligation, just as it is the period "before and at the beginning of the voyage" that delimits the time at which any obligation imputed to the carrier can be thought to begin.

This last point is particularly relevant to the decision of Wright, J. in *W.*

---

[12] *Ibid.*, 862.

Angliss & Co. (Australia) Pty Ltd. v. *P.&O. Steam Navigation Co.*[13] That case, also a claim under a bill of lading governed by the Hague Rules, concerned the question whether, when a carrier who was also the owner of the ship had contracted for its construction, that carrier is liable for lack of due diligence on the part of the shipbuilders or their workmen in the construction of the vessel. Wright, J. held that such a carrier was not so liable, unless he had failed to engage builders of repute and to adopt all reasonable precautions, for example, requiring the builders to satisfy one of the recognised classification societies and engaging skilled naval architects to advise him and skilled inspectors themselves to supervise the work with the due diligence to be expected of such persons.

The decision in *Angliss* is readily explicable for a number of reasons. The principal amongst those is perhaps what Lord Radcliffe called the "time situation" of the builders.[14] Any causative carelessness in the *Angliss* case took place at a time before the carrier's obligation under the bill of lading contract had attached and in circumstances therefore where the builders and their men could not properly be described as agents for the carrier "before and at the beginning of the voyage to make the ship seaworthy". This analysis however sits uneasily with Wright, J.'s own reasoning, which involved that a carrier (at any rate one who had contracted for the building of the ship) did at the least have an obligation to employ a reputable builder. If the time situation is determinative, whence springs the obligation to employ a reputable shipbuilder? For present purposes however it is perhaps sufficient to note that the decision in *Angliss* tells strongly against any notion that there is a standard construction of a due diligence provision and that the obligation is therefore inevitably one of due diligence "by whomsoever it may be done".

The obligation to make a ship seaworthy is "non-delegable" because reason and authority requires, as between goods owner and carrier, due diligence in the work itself. Once one is concerned with something other than the task of making a ship seaworthy for the purposes of a contract of carriage, neither reason nor authority compels the conclusion that an obligation couched in terms of due diligence is of necessity "non-delegable". Furthermore, recitation of the mantra of "non-delegability" can have the effect of concealing what should be the relevant enquiry—what is the ambit and extent of the obligation imposed by the words in the context in which they have been used?

Dow Europe S.A. v. *Novoklav*[15] was concerned with something other than the obligation of making a ship seaworthy for the purposes of a contract of carriage. It was concerned with the obligation cast upon a time charterer under the Shelltime 4 form of time charter so far as concerns the safety of the place at

[13] [1927] 2 K.B. 456.
[14] See *The Muncaster Castle* [1961] A.C. 807, 867.
[15] [1998] 1 Lloyd's Rep. 306.

which the vessel is ordered to load. The vessel *Acina* was owned by Acina 1 K.S. ("the owners"). She was time charterered to Novoklav Inc. ("Novoklav") on a Shelltime 4 form. Novoklav in turn voyage chartered the vessel to Dow Europe S.A. ("Dow"). Pursuant to those arrangements the vessel loaded at berth B1 at the Algerian port of Arzew a cargo of condensate, a highly volatile hydrocarbon which is produced in conjunction with the exploitation of natural gas. During the loading process there occurred a fire which caused very considerable damage to the vessel. The owners sought to recover from Novoklav their loss, which appears to have been in the region of U.S.$9.5 million. Novoklav in turn sought to recover from Dow an indemnity in respect of any liability they might have to the Owners. The two claims were to be heard at the same time by arbitrators, the same arbitrators having been appointed in each reference so that each tribunal was identically constituted.

The basis of the claim was in each case that the charterer, first Novoklav the time charterer and then in turn Dow the voyage charterer, was in breach of its obligations so far as concerned the safety of the place at which the vessel had been ordered to load. The situation was however complicated by the fact that the two charters, quite apart from the fact that they were contracts of an entirely different type, one being a time charter and the other a voyage charter, were, so far as concerned the obligation of the respective charterers in respect of the safety of places at which the vessel might be ordered to load, not "back to back". At the bottom of the chain Dow as voyage charterer by its charterparty gave an absolute warranty that the vessel would load at a safe berth. The obligation as between owners and Novoklav was governed by clause 4 of the Shelltime 4 form, which provides as follows:

> "Charterers shall use due diligence to ensure that the vessel is only employed between and at safe places (which expression when used in this charter shall include ports, berths, wharves, docks, anchorages, submarine lines, alongside vessels or lighters, and other locations including locations at sea) where she can lie safely afloat.
>
> Notwithstanding anything contained in this or any other clause of this charter, charterers do not warrant the safety of any place to which they order the vessel and shall be under no liability in respect thereof except for loss or damage caused by their failure to exercise due diligence as aforesaid."

The wording of clause 4 of the Shelltime 4 form, in particular the words "charterers shall use due diligence *to ensure* that the vessel is only employed between and at safe places" is redolent of an observation of Lord Radcliffe in *The Muncaster Castle* as to the approach adopted in that case by McNair, J. and the Court of Appeal. There both McNair, J. and the Court of Appeal had concluded that the carriers (in fact also the owners) were not in breach of their obligation to exercise due diligence to make the vessel seaworthy by reason of the negligence of the fitter employed by the reputable ship repairing company to which they had entrusted the vessel for drydocking. Lord Radcliffe remarked[16] of this approach which was espoused by the Respondents to the appeal before the House of Lords:

> "If the Respondents' reading is adopted, the one that has commended itself to McNair J and the Court of Appeal, one must treat the words 'due diligence to make the ship seaworthy' as if they were equivalent to 'due diligence to see that the ship is made seaworthy,' and that is not the same thing."

Due diligence to see that a ship is made seaworthy is surely an obligation as respects seaworthiness which is equivalent to an obligation in respect of safety of loading places which is couched in the terms "charterers shall use due diligence to ensure that the vessel is only employed between and at safe places". This is surely a pointer, albeit perhaps a small one, to a construction of the words in the Shelltime 4 form which does not involve the inevitable imposition upon charterers of liability for the acts or omissions of all those who may be implicated in the task of the selection of loading places and the evaulation of their safety.

One can however begin the debate from first principles. The wording in Article III, rule 1 of the Hague Rules was, in *The Muncaster Castle* and other cases, construed in the light of the contractual relationship in the context of which it appeared, which was the relationship of goods owner and carrier by sea. So too should the wording of clause 4 of the Shelltime 4 form be construed in the light of the fact that it is a clause governing the relationship of owner and time charterer. The clause should at first be approached on the footing that it is likely to seek to impose upon the time charterer an obligation to carry out those enquiries which a reasonably careful and prudent charterer would ordinarily regard as appropriate and to impose an obligation generally to inform himself in the manner in which a reasonably careful and prudent charterer would ordinarily do.

One finds an echo of this approach in *K./S. Penta Shipping A/S* v. *Ethiopian Shipping Lines Corp. (The Saga Cob)*[17] in the judgment of Parker, L.J. in the Court of Appeal. That was a case concerned with the identically worded clause 3 in the Shelltime 3 form, the precursor of clause 4 in the Shelltime 4 form. The charter provided that the vessel was to be employed in the Red Sea, the Gulf of Aden and East Africa. In the course of performing the charter, between January and August 1988, the vessel called about 20 times at the Ethiopian Port of Massawa without any untoward consequences. However, in September of that year whilst at Massawa pursuant to the charterers' directions, the vessel was attacked by Eritrean guerrillas in motor boats using heavy machine guns and rocket grenades. The Master was wounded and the vessel suffered substantial damage. The owners claimed that the charterers were in breach of their due

---

[16] [1961] A.C. 807, 863.
[17] [1992] 2 Lloyd's Rep. 545.

diligence obligation under clause 3 and claimed damages. The judge at first instance in the Commercial Court (His Honour Judge Diamond, Q.C.) held that the charterers were in breach of their obligation, but his conclusion was reversed by the Court of Appeal. Giving the judgment of the court Parker, L.J. said:[18]

> "There is in our judgment at least a strong argument that the test should be expressed thus—'If a reasonably careful charterer would on the facts known have concluded that the port was prospectively unsafe.'"

Admittedly this observation was in the context of political danger, where what has to be assessed is necessarily subjective, rather than physical danger, such as a sandbank or a reef. As to the former, Parker, L.J. in a slightly earlier passage than that quoted above asked rhetorically, if a charterer comes to a reasonable conclusion as to the safety of the port, why should he be said to have failed to exercise due diligence? It is respectfully suggested that this approach is entirely appropriate. In particular, if a time charterer informs himself by reference to the views of users of the port, surely he cannot be said to have failed to exercise due diligence by reason only that the views on which he relied might not themselves, unbeknown to the charterer, have been formed with due care.

Turning to physical safety, one can see that due diligence will require a charterer to take all those steps reasonably open to him to inform himself as to the navigational hazards such as sandbanks or reefs. There are of course publications in which such matters are listed, and a charterer's duty might perhaps extend further to making enquiry of reputable local agents as to the existence of any more recondite features of the port which may not be immediately apparent from published material—not least perhaps so as to ensure that charterers proceed upon the basis of up to date information. It seems unlikely however that Parker, L.J. had in mind that a time charterer would be in breach of a due diligence provision if there was some feature of the port or loading berth selected which rendered it unsafe which feature could not reasonably be ascertained by the sort of enquiries which a reasonably careful charterer could be expected to make. That however is the practical effect of the approach adopted in the *Dow Europe* case.

The issue of Novoklav's liability as time charterer to the owners in that case arose in a curious and indirect way for, three weeks before the date appointed for the hearing of the two claims in arbitration, the owners against Novoklav and Novoklav against Dow, Novoklav settled the owners' claim, essentially on the basis of 100 per cent liability. The arbitration as between Novoklav and Dow however proceeded, it then falling to Dow rather than to Novoklav to argue that Novoklav had in fact been under no liability to the owners.

The arbitrators held that berth B1 at Arzew was unsafe. The unsafety consisted in there being in place no emergency shut-down system to stop the

---

[18] *Ibid.*, 551. The passage cited was in fact unnecessary to the decision.

flow of condensate should an emergency occur. The arbitrators further held that it was the absence of an emergency shut-down system which caused the accident.

The question however remained whether Novoklav was in breach of its due diligence obligation owed to the owners. Timothy Walker, J. set out in his judgment[19] the three paragraphs in the arbitrators' award in which the arbitrators expressed their conclusion on this point. They read as follows:

> "Most commercial people would expect that if a party carried out its contractual obligations through another it will be liable for any damages which might arise as a result of negligence in the way these obligations are carried out. That is indeed what occurred in this case. The charterers under both the voyage and the time charterparty simply ordered the vessel to proceed to Arzew. Novoklav's telexed order of 11th December 1990, mirroring Dow's instructions, was as follows: 'after completion of bunkering proceed Arzew and anchor off port limit'. That was in effect an order to go to such loading place on or after arrival there as the harbour authorities should designate. That indeed is the analysis used by Staughton, J. in the *Erechthion*.[20] In the same case Staughton, J. distinguished the *Isabelle*,[21] which he said 'was dealing with an express clause concerning orders to wait, not an order to proceed to a particular place'. Staughton, J. went on to find that the order given by the harbour authority in the case of the *Erechthion* was to be considered as a charterer's order for the purpose of the implied obligation of indemnity. That was not the case in the *Mediolanum*,[22] where the charterers had in effect given orders for the vessel to bunker at a particular place.
>
> The wording of Clause 4 itself specifically provided that it was a charterer's obligation to use due diligence to ensure that the vessel is only employed at safe places which expression, when used in this charter, should include ports, berths, wharves, docks, anchorages, submarine lines, alongside vessels or lighters and other locations including locations at sea. We are satisfied that the clause clearly identified the charterer's obligation to use due diligence in directing the vessel to a particular berth. In the light of that clear obligation we were unable to accept Dow's contention that having ordered the vessel to Arzew the obligation to exercise due diligence went no further than the choice of that port.
>
> We find, accordingly, that the order given to the vessel to berth at B1 was Novoklav's order. It matters not whether the order was given through Sonotrach or through EPA. Obviously Sonotrach were aware of the system of loading and should have been aware that it was unsafe. The same must be true of EPA. They employed the loading gang and V120 and part of the pipeline is situated in the port area under their ownership or control."

The judge recited,[23] that the port of Arzew is controlled by the Algerian oil company Sonotrach and he further explained[24] that the port authority at Arzew was EPA, which is referred to by the arbitrators as being the entity under the

---

[19] [1998] 1 Lloyd's Rep. 306, 307–308.
[20] [1987] 2 Lloyd's Rep. 180.
[21] [1982] 2 Lloyd's Rep. 81.
[22] [1984] 1 Lloyd's Rep. 136.
[23] [1998] 1 Lloyd's Rep. 306, 307.
[24] *Ibid.*, 308.

ownership or control of which lay the port area and certain relevant loading facilities, i.e. pipelines etc. For present purposes the apparent overlap in control as between Sonotrach and EPA is probably unimportant. One may probably infer that Sonotrach as the Algerian oil company may be the only entity supplying hydrocarbon products at the port of Arzew and it seems likely that they may have been the ultimate sellers of the cargo which was being loaded when the fire occurred.

The learned judge dealt with Dow's appeal essentially on the basis that the arbitrators had found as a matter of fact that Novoklav had delegated to the port authorities at Arzew their obligations under clause 4 of the Shelltime charterparty so far as concerned the safety of the loading place. Since the judge regarded the arbitrators as having gone on to make further findings of fact to the effect that both the port authrities at Arzew and indeed Sonotrach themselves were negligent in that regard, that was an end to the matter. Faced with the finding of delegation, Novoklav could not escape responsibility for the negligence of their agents.

The learned judge was of course obliged to be loyal to the arbitrators' findings of fact. It may however be questioned whether the underlying analysis in terms of agency is sound and whether the result achieved renders it possible for a time charterer in such a situation to have any control over the discharge of his contractual obligations. It would be a strange irony if an obligation which had as its origin the replacement of the absolute warranty of seaworthiness by a less exacting standard ended up, when translated into a different maritime context, imposing upon those to whom it applies an obligation with which in the real world they simply cannot comply. Thus in modern conditions it is probably in many if not most cases simply unreal to think that a time charterer has any control at all over the allocation of the berth at which his time chartered vessel is to load or discharge. In circumstances where nothing untoward is known about the port or its set-up, and where the allocation of berths is the exclusive province of the port authority, should it really be said that a time charterer who directs a vessel to proceed to such berth as the port authorities may designate has, by so doing, delegated to the port authority his obligation to use due diligence to ensure that the designated place is safe?

Both the arbitrators and Timothy Walker, J. referred to a somewhat puzzling trilogy of cases—*Cosmar Compania Naviera S.A.* v. *Total Transport Corp. (The Isabelle)*,[25] *Mediolanum Shipping Co.* v. *Japan Lines Ltd. (The Mediolanum)*[26] and *Newa Line* v. *Erechthion Shipping Co. S.A. (The Erechthion)*.[27] None of these cases was concerned with an alleged delegation of the obligation to use due diligence, although the last was concerned with the owner's implied

[25] [1982] 2 Lloyd's Rep. 81 (Robert Goff, J.) affirmed by the Court of Appeal without additional reasons [1984] 1 Lloyd's Rep. 366.
[26] [1984] 1 Lloyd's Rep. 136 (C.A.).
[27] [1987] 2 Lloyd's Rep. 180 (Staughton, J.).

right to an indemnity in respect of the consequences of compliance with a time charterer's order as to employment of the vessel, in circumstances where a vessel grounded and struck a submerged object within the port to which she had been sent. The interest in the cases lies in the light they shed upon the agency analysis espoused by the arbitrators and by the judge in the *Dow Europe* case.

The Isabelle was a voyage charterparty case where the charterers had an express obligation to order the vessel to a loading berth. The charterers ordered the vessel to load at Bejaia, where the cargo was to be supplied by the Algerian national oil company, Sonotrach. Because the charterparty was a "berth" as opposed to a "port" charterparty, *prima facie* the owners bore the risk of delay by reason of the nominated berth being inaccessible when the vessel arrived at the port. Clause 14 of the charter however provided that, whether or not the specified berth was available and accessible, if the vessel was nevertheless ordered by charterers to wait before proceeding thereto, laytime should commence six hours after Notice of Readiness was received and the vessel was securely moored at the customary anchorage. In the event the vessel had to wait at the anchorage during a period when no berth was available to her because of a combination of congestion and weather conditions. The charterers had simply ordered the vessel to Bejaia. Robert Goff, J. found that the port authority must have ordered the vessel to wait at the anchorage. Were those orders to be attributed to the charterers so that, pursuant to clause 14, laytime started to run after arrival at the anchorage?

The learned judge was prepared to assume that the charterers simply left it to the port authority to nominate a berth, i.e. to identify the berth where the vessel was to load. That was a delegation by the charterers of their obligation to order the vessel to a loading place. However, the judge went on to hold that it did not follow from that that any order that the port authority gave ancillary to identification of the berth was given on behalf of the charterers. When therefore the port authority ordered the vessel to wait, that was not an order given in any agency capacity on behalf of the charterers. The port authority was acting on no instructions from the charterers, who had no control over the port authority in this respect. Robert Goff, J. found it "impossible to infer that the orders of the port authority to wait were the orders of the charterers". The judge pointed out that every port authority exercises control over the ships in the area of the port; and where, as there may have been the case, there was only one loading jetty for tankers and congestion in the port, it is inevitable that the port authority, in the exercise of its own administrative function, will order vessels to wait outside the harbour while other vessels load at the jetty.

This case therefore provides no support for the notion that a time charterer who, in circumstances where he has no option to do otherwise, leaves it to the port authority to designate the precise berth or loading place to which the vessel will proceed, *ipso facto* delegates his obligation to use due diligence to ensure that the berth to which the vessel proceeds shall be safe. That is not to say that a charterer who leaves it to the port authority to allocate the berth absolves himself of all responsibility with regard to the safety of the berth in due course allocated. Far from it. If by the enquiries reasonably to be expected of a prudent and careful charterer he would ascertain that one of the berths (or even the only berth) to which the port authority might send the vessel is unsafe, he would plainly be in breach of his obligation to use due diligence to ensure that the vessel is employed at safe places if he took no steps to ensure that the vessel was not directed to that unsafe berth.

The next case in the trilogy is *The Mediolanum*.[28] Clause 2 of the New York Produce Exchange form of time charter prescribes that the charterers shall provide and pay for all fuel. Clause 8, the employment provision, carries with it the implied right of indemnity as regards the consequences of compliance with charterers' orders as to employment of the vessel. The charterparty in that case further provided that the vessel was to trade in lawful trades between safe ports. Charterers made arrangements for the vessel to take bunkers (fuel oil) at Las Minas in Panama. The pilot, an employee of the refinery, on the instructions of the refinery directed the Master to proceed to a bunkering place other than the one to which he had been directed by the charterers' agents. In proceeding towards this new bunkering place the vessel took the ground on an uncharted coral reef and suffered damage. Two vastly experienced and highly respected maritime arbitrators (the late Cedric Barclay and the late Ralph Kingsley) made what the Court of Appeal plainly regarded as an odd finding to the effect that the refinery was to be treated as the agent of the charterers for the purpose of indicating the bunkering spot or, to put it another way, of selecting the exact place for bunkering at Las Minas. This was apparently a matter of inference from the fact that the charterers had stemmed bunkers at Las Minas. It was to be inferred that they left it to the suppliers, the refinery, to indicate the bunkering spot. The Court of Appeal, in a judgment delivered by Kerr, L.J., regarded this as a very doubtful proposition. The Court of Appeal accepted that, for the purposes of the charterers' obligation under clause 2 to provide the fuel, the refinery was, as between the owners and the charterers, the agent of the charterers quite simply because the refinery was used by the charterers in order to perform one of their obligations under the contract. The Court of Appeal was however doubtful whether the refinery could also properly be described as the charterers' agent for the purpose of indicating or selecting the ultimate place within the port of Las Minas to which the vessel was to proceed for bunkering, which place turned out to be unsafe, particularly when the charterers' agents had previously ordered the vessel to proceed to a different and safe place within the port. Kerr, L.J. added:[29]

"In this context, as it seems to us, the refinery might well be regarded as performing

28 [1984] 1 Lloyd's Rep. 136.
29 *Ibid.*, 140.

similar functions to those of a harbour master or port authority whose acts would not be treated as the acts of the charterers: *cf.* the decision of Robert Goff, J. in *Cosmar Compania Naviera S.A.* v. *Total Transport Corp. (The Isabelle)*."

In the event the Court of Appeal did "with the greatest misgivings" proceed on the assumption that the arbitrators had been entitled to draw the inference which they had. Nonetheless, the court concluded that, even assuming that the refinery had and retained the charterers' authority, as the charterers' agent, to select the exact place for bunkering at Las Minas, still it did not follow that the charterers were liable to the owners for the fact that the vessel grounded as she did. The charterers had ordered the vessel to a safe port and had not warranted the safety of every spot within the port. Even given the assumed agency relationship between charterers and refinery, this raised only a question of vicarious liability of a principal for the acts or omissions of his agent. The assumed agency relationship did not supply what was otherwise absent, anything in the nature of an absolute warranty of safety on the part of the charterers. The reef was uncharted and there was no finding that either the refinery or its servant the pilot had been negligent. The charterers were not liable to the owners.

The significance of this case is, it is suggested, its reaffirmation that, simply because, as a matter of practicality and/or necessity, there are functions within a port such as the allocation of loading, discharging or bunkering places which are routinely carried out by a harbourmaster or port authority, it does not follow that a charterer who leaves it to the port authority to carry out that administrative function (as to which the charterer will ordinarily have no choice in any event) will thereafter be responsible for the acts or omissions of the port authority as if they were his own.

The final case in the trilogy, *The Erechthion*,[30] was again concerned with a time chartered vessel which struck an uncharted submerged obstruction within a port to which she had been ordered, Port Harcourt on the Bonny River in Nigeria. There was no doubt that the charterers had ordered the vessel to discharge at Port Harcourt. Traffic in the river was controlled by the Port Harcourt harbour authority. The harbour authority instructed the vessel to proceed to Dawes Island anchorage, which included an area between buoys 11 and 12 and between buoys 12 and 13 in the river. The pilot advised the Master to proceed to an area about halfway between buoys 11 and 12 at which he should anchor. In proceeding towards the anchorage place thus designated, the vessel struck an uncharted submerged object.

It was accepted that the order to proceed to Port Harcourt, admittedly given on behalf of the charterers, was not itself the cause of the casualty. It was not argued that the advice given by the pilot amounted to orders given on behalf of the charterers. What was however alleged to have been the causative order was

---

[30] [1987] 2 Lloyd's Rep. 180.

the order of the harbour authority to proceed to the Dawes Island anchorage, which, it was said, was an order as to employment of the vessel given by the harbour authority as agent on behalf of the charterers. On that basis, the owners relied upon the implied right of indemnity in respect of the consequences of complying with the charterers' orders as to employment of the vessel which arose under clause 8 of the charterparty, which appears again to have been on the New York Produce Exchange form.

Staughton, J. was referred to both *The Isabelle* and *The Mediolanum* but he preferred an analysis which was not one of agency but which was that the charterers had ordered the vessel to such discharging place as the port authority might nominate. He explained as follows:[31]

> "In theory at any rate, it is the right of the charterer of a time chartered vessel to give all orders as to the vessel's employment—where she shall load, what cargo she shall carry, and where she must discharge it ...
>
> But in practice, at many if not most ports in the world, it is the harbour authority which decides when and where a vessel shall discharge her cargo. Until the harbour authority has allocated a discharging place, the charterer is unable to give any effective orders. Once a discharging place has been allocated by the harbour authority, it would be an idle formality for the charterer to issue confirmation in the shape of an order to the vessel to go there. I suppose that a pedantic charterer might expressly reserve to himself the right to give the order; or an eccentric charterer might even countermand the harbour authority's instruction and tell the master to wait in the roads rather than proceed to the berth allocated. But that again is theory. In practice, so far as the vessel was concerned at this port, it is manifest that the charterers left it to the harbour authority to instruct the vessel where to go in order to discharge the cargo. If the master had refused to comply until those orders had been confirmed by the charterers, I have no doubt that they would have reproached him for wasting time at their expense.
>
> One analysis of the owners' argument is that, so far as they were concerned, the harbour authority was the charterers' agent to give orders. For my part, I prefer the way that it was put in argument by Mr Mocatta in *Stag Line Ltd.* v. *Ellerman and Papayanni Lines Ltd.*[32] as recorded by Morris, J.:
>
>> Mr Mocatta, I think submits further that even though the orders to go to a particular berth were the orders of the military, they were in effect the orders of the charterers because the charterers had ordered their Master to Naples and presumably to go then to the particular berth to which he was directed by the military. Mr Mocatta points to clause 3 of the charterparty and says that it is for the charterers to arrange for unloading ...
>
> Morris, J. did not find it necessary to rule on that argument. I consider it well-founded. Applied to the present case, it means that the charterers' order to go to Port Harcourt meant to go to such discharging place on arrival there as the harbour authority should designate."

The judge accordingly agreed with the arbitrators' conclusion that the order given by the harbour authority to proceed to Dawes Island should be considered

---

[31] *Ibid.*, 183.
[32] (1949) 82 Ll.L.Rep. 826, 835.

as the charterers' order for the purposes of the implied obligation of indemnity. On the facts the judge was unable to infer an unequivocal finding by the arbitrators that the damage to the vessel was proximately caused by the charterers' order to proceed to Dawes Island anchorage, and history does not relate what occurred when the case was remitted to the arbitrators to enable them to reconsider that point. The interest in the case is however not the outcome but the learned judge's analysis of the practice which occurs at many ports where it is the harbour authority which decides when and where a vessel shall load or discharge. In such circumstances the orders of the harbour authority as to the identity of the berth to which the vessel proceeds are treated as orders of the charterers, because the charterers' direction was to go where ordered by the harbour authority. This involves no question of agency or delegation and seems, with respect, a preferable analysis to that attributed by the judge in the *Dow Europe* case to the arbitrators who decided that case, who were themselves evidently under the impression that they had in fact applied Staughton, J.'s analysis.

Where one is concerned with the implied right to an indemnity consequent upon compliance with charterers' orders, one can well understand why an order in the form "go where you are directed" should lead to charterers' liability in the event that compliance with the subsequent direction leads to damage. Rather different considerations surely apply where one is concerned with a contractual régime pursuant to which, before liability can attach, it has to be shown that the charterer is in breach of his obligation and where that obligation is couched not in absolute terms but in terms of due diligence. Against the background described by Staughton, J., can it seriously be suggested that owners and time charterers contemplate, when agreeing to impose upon a charterer a duty as to the safety of loading and discharging places which is couched in terms of due diligence rather than that of absolute obligation, that the charterers shall nonetheless be responsible for a lack of care by an authority into whose hands they have no option but to entrust themselves and over whose actions they have no control? If that is the intended result the obligation might as well be cast in absolute terms. Since it is not, and since both parties to the transaction must be taken to be equally cognisant of modern practice, does not the adoption of the due diligence standard suggest that the time charterers are to be judged by the standards of a reasonably careful charterer?

It is moreover wholly unsatisfactory to analyse a situation in terms of principal and agent if the actors involved have done nothing to bring about such a relationship and almost certainly would not recognise it as such. The law of agency rightly regards as strictly limited the circumstances in which an agency relationship arises by implication or necessity. Although the judge in the *Dow Europe* case regarded himself as bound by what he saw as the arbitrators' finding of fact that Novoklav as time charterers delegated to the port authority their obligation to use due diligence to nominate a safe berth, such a conclusion was in fact implausible on the facts of that case and will be equally implausible in most typical situations, largely for the reasons given by Staughton, J. in *The Erechthion*. There are however perhaps three further considerations. First, a time charterer would only expect to exercise the diligence reasonably to be expected of someone in his position. No-one expects a time charterer to seek the advice of a port authority as to the safety of the berths within its control—still less could an objective answer be expected to such an enquiry. Secondly, a charterer would be likely only knowingly to delegate a function of any substance to an agent over whose activities he had some measure of control. Any delegation to a port authority would be expected to be limited to purely administrative functions which the port authority alone would in any event carry out. Finally, the interests of the charterers and the port authority would not coincide and indeed may be diametrically opposed. The port authority's interest is in keeping vessels moving in and out of the port. Whether the port authority at Arzew could realistically be expected to reveal to a user of the port the feature of berth B1 which was held to render it unsafe may be debatable. Its significance may not have been appreciated. The lack of an emergency shut down system is likely to have been a feature which had been present for many years and to have given rise to no problem hitherto and indeed by its very nature it would give rise to no problem unless and until an emergency occurred.

The real vice of the decision in the *Dow Europe* case lies in the fact that, in all probability, the particular feature of the berth which rendered it unsafe is something which the time charterers could never by their own enquiries have discovered. It is odd that in such circumstances a time charterer should be regarded as having failed to exercise due diligence. One might also ask what is a time charterer subjected to this duty to do? He cannot go to the port and himself inspect every valve—apart from being unreal, such an exercise would in many if not most ports simply not be permitted. Is he to make a contract with the port authority formally constituting it as his agent and requiring it pursuant to its terms to carry out investigations and to disclose to the charterers everything it knows or discovers? The proposition has merely to be stated to be seen to be similarly unreal.

If a contract provides unequivocally that the risk of unsafety is on one party rather than the other, so be it. Surely however a due diligence obligation is not apt to secure this result.

Most charterparties contain an arbitration clause. Since the coming into force of the Arbitration Act 1979, and in particular since the gloss imposed upon that Act by the House of Lords[33] as to the circumstances in which appeals should be permitted to be brought against arbitration awards, the opportunities to debate before the courts interesting areas of shipping law such as this have been strictly limited. Timothy Walker, J. plainly took the view that loyalty to what he

---

[33] See *Pioneer Shipping Ltd. v. BTP Tioxide Ltd. (The Nema)* [1982] A.C. 724.

regarded as the arbitrators' findings of fact precluded the use of the *Dow Europe* case as such an opportunity. It seems unlikely however that that case can be the last word on the subject. It ought to be recognised that, save in a case where conventional principles would allow it, an analysis which regards as the agent of the time charterer an authority which is carrying out purely administrative functions is unreal and unacceptable. A time charterer upon whom is imposed a duty to use due diligence to ensure that the vessel is only employed between and at safe places should be regarded as discharging that obligation by satisfying himself, in the manner in which a similarly placed prudent and reasonable charterer would, that there are not amongst the places to which the vessel might potentially be ordered by the authorities places which are unsafe.

Chapter 9

The Law of Sales and the Law of Contract: Some Remarks on the United Nations Convention on International Sales

Jan Hellner

Francis Reynolds is best known for his work on agency.[1] Personally I have profited much from his mastery of this subject, which is particularly difficult to understand for a Continental lawyer. However, not everyone who contributes to a Festschrift in honour of Francis Reynolds can write on agency, even if I personally have felt a certain inclination to do so. I have therefore chosen to write on a subject that lies on the borderline between the law of sales and the law of international conventions, which both belong to the fields of interest of Francis Reynolds.

THE GENERAL PROBLEM

The U.K. has not ratified the United Nations Convention on Contracts for the International Sale of Goods adopted in Vienna 1980 (C.I.S.G.).[2] All the same, British lawyers will probably sometimes come into contact with C.I.S.G., in connection with contracts in which at least one of the parties has his place of business in a state that has ratified C.I.S.G. If the law of such a state is the proper law of the contract, C.I.S.G. will generally govern international sales of goods.[3]

---

[1] *Bowstead and Reynolds on Agency*, 16th edn. (Sweet & Maxwell, London, 1995).
[2] In spite of the fact the U.K. has not ratified the Convention, there is an English official issue of the text (Cmnd. 8074).
[3] It is possible for a state, by a reservation under Article 95 of the Convention, to declare that it will not be bound by sub-paragraph (1)(b) of Article 1 of the Convention. This provision refers to cases when the rules of private international law lead to the application of the law of a contracting state. The U.S.A. has made such a reservation. In practice this means that the Convention will apply only when both parties have their places of business in contracting states. The Convention will therefore not apply to contracts between parties in the U.K. and the U.S.A.

C.I.S.G. is part of the national law of such a state, and for international sales contracts it replaces the law of domestic sales. The same is true when there is an explicit reference in the contract to a state's law. A reference to German law, or to Swedish law, in an international contract will therefore, unless there are strong indications to the contrary, be taken to be a reference to C.I.S.G. This has apparently been a surprise to some parties to international contracts, but the fact should be well known now.

There are a number of reported decisions on C.I.S.G., and in addition there are an unknown number of unpublished arbitration awards. The literature is already enormous.[4]

Even if it is clear that in principle C.I.S.G. applies to a contract, the relationship between C.I.S.G. and the general law of contracts, and in some cases the law of property or the law of tort, may give rise to problems.

Some Continental states, e.g. Germany, have a structure that leads to particular problems. The German Code contains a general part (Book 1), which contains rules that are common to all private law relations. The law of obligations (Book 2) also has a general part, which covers all obligations, and special parts, of which the chapter on sales (§§ 433–515) is one. It is comparatively rare that within this system there will be any conflict between the more general parts and the law of sales, since it can be assumed that the legislator has constructed his system so as to avoid such conflicts. However, when the law relating to domestic sales is replaced for international sales by an international convention, conflicts will be more common. Even if there is no clear conflict, there will always be cases in which it is possible that the principles of the general parts should supplement the rules of C.I.S.G.

For states that have no comprehensive civil code, the situation is somewhat different. The principles of C.I.S.G. can on the whole more easily be adjusted to those of general contract law as these are less rigid. The problems will generally present themselves in the shape of finding principles that can fill in gaps in C.I.S.G.

In principle, a Convention decides itself to which questions it applies, by delimiting its subject and by the contents of its various provisions. However, both in principle and in practice numerous problems will arise. On what questions will the Convention prevail, and on what subjects can or should national law be applied? Sometimes the creators of an international Convention, who are internationally-minded people, like to have it apply to as many questions as possible. On the other hand, it is also possible that courts of law

---

[4] For cases see "Case-law: Discovery Tools": J. Honnold, *Uniform Law for International Sales*, 3d edn. (Kluwer International, 1999) xxi ff. M. Will publishes regularly surveys of case law under C.I.S.G.: *The First 444 or so Decisions* (Geneva, 1998) covers the period 1988–1997. Although some decisions are noteworthy and helpful for the understanding of C.I.S.G., others are less interesting, particularly those that state simply that a court did not find C.I.S.G. to be applicable to the dispute.

will prefer to apply their own national law of contracts, with whose qualities they are well acquainted, rather than an international Convention with which they are less familiar and of whose qualities they may not be fully convinced.

The questions mentioned now arose already under the Uniform Law on the International Sale of Goods of 1964 (U.L.I.S.). Article 17 of this Convention prescribed simply: "Questions concerning matters governed by the present Law which are not expressly settled therein shall be settled in conformity with the general principles on which the present law is based." Article 2 of the same Convention prescribed that rules of private international law were excluded for the purposes of the application of the Law, subject to any provision to the contrary in the Law. It was apparently assumed that each and every question that arose concerning an international sale could be decided by referring to the general principles of the Law. There are comparatively few cases reported that concern Article 17, but there is one that illustrates the difficulties that Article 17 created. A Netherlands court faced the question, on which debt, when a buyer had several outstanding debts to the same seller, a payment should be considered to have been effected, when the buyer himself had made no indication. The court stated that the principle underlying U.L.I.S. was that the payment should be considered to refer to the oldest outstanding debt.[5] As far as I know, there is no provision of U.L.I.S. on which such an analogy could be based. It can be guessed that the principle applied agrees with Netherlands law.[6]

C.I.S.G. takes a more realistic view on these matters, and the field has become very complex. The principal provision is Article 7 which reads as follows:

> (1) In the interpretation of this Convention, regard is to be had to its international character and to the need to promote uniformity in its application and the observance of good faith in international trade.
> (2) Questions concerning matters governed by this Convention which are not expressly settled in it are to be settled in conformity with the general principles on which it is based or, in the absence of such principles, in conformity with the law applicable by virtue of private international law.

It would be possible to devote much space to investigating the consequences of the requirement of good faith in international trade, which is mentioned in Article 7(1). It could also be debated which are the general principles on which the Convention is based (Article 7(2)). It is somewhat surprising to see how many and how detailed conclusions that have been drawn from these two

---

[5] RB Alkmar 27 May 1982. See P. Schlechtriem & U. Magnus eds., *Internationale Rechtsprechung zu EKG und EAG* (Nomos, Baden-Baden, 1987), 184.

[6] *Cf.* German Civil Code, § 366 which contains a similar provision. The principle applied by the Netherlands court does not agree with Swedish law, which, for cases when the debtor has not made any indication of his choice, lets the creditor decide on which debt payment is effected.

provisions.[7] However, I shall not deal with these issues but with the principle indicated at the end of Article 7(2), i.e. the possibility of applying a national law indicated by private international law.

There are a number of provisions other than Article 7 that must be also taken into account when considering the relationship between C.I.S.G. and general contract law. I shall present them here in connection with the various practical issues.

Sometimes a distinction is made between "external" and "internal" gaps in the Convention.[8] An external gap occurs when a subject does not fall within the sphere of application of the Convention. As an example a set-off between opposed claims by the seller and the buyer may be mentioned. The rules relating to set-offs cannot be considered to be part of the law of sales. An internal gap is found when a subject might well be treated by the Convention but in fact is not. As an example may be mentioned the right to the proceeds of the goods accruing during the period between the formation of the contract and its full completion. Who shall have the proceeds, the seller or the buyer? However, the distinction between external and internal gaps does not seem to have any great practical importance. For both types, the gap is generally filled by the national law indicated by the rules of private international law (Article 7(2)).

VALIDITY OF THE CONTRACT

According to Article 4(a), the Convention is not concerned with the validity of the contract or of any of its provisions or of any usage. It may seem fairly clear that C.I.S.G. does not apply to invalidity based e.g. on fraud, duress or undue influence, whatever the special rules under a national system may be, since C.I.S.G. does not contain any rules that can be said to refer to such grounds for invalidity. But what about misrepresentation and mistakes of various kinds?

Suppose that a buyer might have declared a contract avoided because of the non-conformity of the goods (Article 49(1)(a)), but has lost this right because he has not declared the contract avoided within a reasonable time after he knew or ought to have known about the breach (Article 49(2)(b)(i)). Can he plead that the contract is invalid under the general rules of the law indicated by the principles of private international law? In Austrian law there are rules of "*Irrtumsanfechtung*" for mistakes regarding the quality of goods sold and a debtor's ability to pay his debts.[9] Some Austrian writers have maintained that these rules can be pleaded even if the contract in other respects is governed by

---

[7] See in particular U. Magnus, "*Die allgemeinen Grundsätze im UN-Kaufrecht*" 1995 *Rabels Zeitschrift* 469 ff, with further references.

[8] See in particular P. Schlechtriem, *Internationales UN-Kaufrecht* (Mohr: Tübingen, 1996), note 33.

[9] Austrian General Civil Code, § 871.

C.I.S.G.[10] This opinion has not been accepted by non-Austrian writers.[11] However, it is admitted that the situation is open to doubt.[12]

A similar issue concerns the case in which a party invokes the general principle, found in many legal systems, under which a contract is void if it requires a performance that is objectively impossible.[13] Opinions are divided.[14] In my view, the uniformity and clarity that an international Convention is supposed to further would be curtailed if, besides its special rules, very general principles, whose consequences are extremely uncertain, could be applied. There is a difference between principles that refer to the circumstances in which a contract comes into being, and principles that refer to the contents of the contract. The former, but not the latter, should *in dubio* be considered to lie outside the scope of the Convention.

PROPERTY IN THE GOODS SOLD

According to Article 4(b), the Convention is not concerned with the effect which the contract may have on the property in the goods sold. Property is to be understood, in accordance with what seems now to be the accepted view at least in Continental law, as the relation to third parties. There are considerable differences among national laws on these subjects. As an example the buyer's protection against the creditors of the seller may be mentioned. Under some laws the contract in itself suffices to give the buyer protection against the seller's creditors; under others the buyer must take possession of the goods, or some other act must be performed.[15]

However, there are a number of problems that are connected with the fact that the rights and duties of third parties cannot be quite separated from those of the

---

[10] See e.g. F. Bydlinski, in P. Doralt (ed.), *Das UNCITRAL-Kaufrecht im Vergleich zum österreichischen Recht* (Manz-Verlag: Wien, 1985), 84 ff.; M. Karollus, *UN-Kaufrecht* (Springer-Verlag, Wien, 1991), 41–42.

[11] See U. Huber, "UN-Kaufrecht und Irrtumsanfechtung", 1994, *Zeitschrift für Europäisches Privatrecht* 85 ff.; and R. Herber, in P. Schlechtriem, *Commentary on the UN Convention on the International Sale of Goods* (hereafter "Schlechtriem, Commentary"), note 13 on Article 4.

[12] See P. Schlechtriem, *Internationales UN-Kaufrecht* (Mohr: Tübingen, 1996), note 36, fn. 50.

[13] See, e.g., German Civil Code, § 306.

[14] See on the one hand, e.g., Schlechtriem, *Internationales UN-Kaufrecht*, note 36, who rejects the idea that § 306 could be pleaded when C.I.S.G. is applicable, and, on the other hand, e.g., K. Neumayer & C. Ming, *Convention de Vienne sur les contrats de vente internationale de marchandises* (Cedidac: Lausanne, 1993), 73–74 with numerous further references. These authors argue that, since according to C.I.S.G., Article 4(a) the Convention is not concerned with the validity of the contract, one should not make any difference between various types of invalidity.

[15] *Cf.*, e.g., Schlechtriem, *Internationales UN-Kaufrecht*, note 37.

parties to a sales contract. Suppose that by a clause in a sales contract the seller retains the property of the goods until he has received payment. In a number of legal systems this clause is effective not only against the buyer himself but against third parties on the buyer's side as well. Suppose further that the seller under the domestic law of sales can retake the goods, as soon as the buyer is in arrears with a single instalment payment.[16] This right can be exercised even if the buyer is bankrupt.[17] If the sale is an international sale, the law may be less favourable to the seller, e.g., because the non-payment of a single instalment need not constitute a fundamental breach of contract (as is required under C.I.S.G., Article 4(a)). Can the seller yet claim that he can retake the goods if the buyer is bankrupt, because he would be entitled to do so under the national rules regarding property?[18] In my opinion no. It seems clear that the seller cannot have a better right against the buyer's creditors than he would have had against the buyer himself. If this is correct, the rules of C.I.S.G. may affect even the application of general rules of property. The rules of property must be adjusted to the rules regarding the relation between the parties, even if these rules are found in C.I.S.G.

Another problem relating to the position of third parties arises with regard to "stoppage in transit", which is treated in C.I.S.G., Article 71(2). This provision entitles the seller, under the circumstances set out in Article 71(1), to prevent the handing over of the goods to the buyer even though the buyer holds a document which entitles him to obtain them. The importance of the rule in C.I.S.G. lies primarily in the fact that, if the transporter has refused to hand over the goods to the buyer, the buyer cannot against the seller plead that the seller committed a breach of the sales contract by ordering the transporter not to hand over the goods to the buyer. It is expressly stated that this rule relates only to the rights in the goods as between the buyer and the seller. It might be assumed that the right of stoppage has no effect on the position of the transporter. However, the duties of the transporter are decided by the contract between him and the shipper. This contract is subject to national law, and the maritime laws on this subject might differ.[19] Without going into details it may be stated that there is a possibility that sales law will affect even transporters under transportation law.

---

[16] This is the rule under German Civil Code, § 455. The special legislation on instalment sales, on the other hand, limits the right of retaking.

[17] A similar situation might arise under Swedish law, although in most cases the buyer would have better protection under mandatory rules regarding instalment sales.

[18] *Cf.* on German law U. Huber in Schlechtriem, *Commentary*, note 8 to Article 30.

[19] *Cf.* H. G. Leser in Schlechtriem, *Commentary*, note 34 to Article 71.

This is the case in Swedish law.[20] However, the general position is uncertain. The same seems to be true for other legal systems.[21]

Altogether, the principle that third parties are not affected by the provisions of C.I.S.G. appears to be somewhat less simple than might be imagined from the text of Article 4(b). The problems that arise under a national system of law cannot be entirely avoided by its being replaced by an international convention.

PRODUCT LIABILITY

The relationship between contract law and tort law figures prominently in the law of product liability. Most of the general discussion concerning product liability has centred on liability towards consumers, i.e. non-commercial buyers. This liability is not affected by C.I.S.G., which does not apply to consumer sales (Article 2(a)). However, the remaining field of controversy is large enough. This is not the place to discuss the matter in depth, but something must be said with regard to C.I.S.G., Article 5. This provision states that the Convention does not apply to the liability of the seller for death or personal injury caused by the goods to any person.

It can be deduced from Article 5 *e contrario*—although not with complete certainty—that damage caused to property from goods sold is subject to the Convention. This conclusion seems to be accepted by most writers.[22] Accordingly, if a manufacturer buys raw material for his fabrication and, because of a defect in the material, a machine belonging to the buyer is damaged, the seller of the machine is liable for this damage under the rules relating to the non-conformity of the goods (Article 45(1)(b)). However, suppose that under a national system of law, such damage is subject to tort law

---

[20] The Swedish Maritime Code contains an express provision (Chap. 13. s. 57), referring to the seller's right of stoppage in transit. The provision of the Maritime Code is aimed primarily at the right of stoppage in transit according to the Swedish Sale of Goods Act (s. 61(2)), but it can be assumed that it applies to the corresponding rule in C.I.S.G. as well.

[21] Leser in Schlechtriem, *Commentary*, note 34 to Article 71, states that the buyer has no right against the transporter, unless the seller has transferred his claim to the transporter. Against this opinion it can be held that the transporter may find himself in a very difficult position, if it is uncertain whether the seller had any right that he could transfer. Leser is, however, cautious in so far as he states that the matter is subject to national law.

[22] See R. Herber in Schlechtriem, *Commentary*, note 10 to Article 5 with further references; Schlechtriem, *Internationales UN-Kaufrecht*, notes 40, 159; M. Karollus, *UN-Kaufrecht* (Springer: Wien, 1991), 44.

rather than contract law.[23] Will the rules of C.I.S.G. prevail against this principle? Apparently yes; the only escape seems to be that a conclusion *e contrario* is always open to some doubt.[24] The consequences are important. The seller is liable for all damage, due to non-conformity, subject only to the exemptions mentioned in Article 79, and not only because of negligence or quasi-negligence, as would be the result of applying tort rules. On the other hand, the buyer's claim for damages under C.I.S.G. is subject to a limitation period of two years from the date on which the goods were actually handed over to the buyer (Article 39(2)), a limitation that does not apply to tort claims.

This conclusion gives rise to new questions. Can the buyer elect to base his claim for damages on tort rules rather than on contract rules and in this way escape from the limitation period? German writers seem willing to allow such an election, whereas a French writer has stated that he considers the contractual remedy to be exclusive.[25] Underlying this controversy is the general question whether an aggrieved party has a right to elect between contractual and tort remedies when a damage has been caused by a party with whom he has contractual relations.[26]

Let us now return to the liability for death and personal injuries. Article 5 is firm on the point that a seller is not liable under the Convention. However, there is also the possibility of a recourse action. Suppose that an injured party has successfully claimed damages from a party for a personal injury, and that the injury was caused by defective goods that the latter party has bought from a seller by an international sale. The buyer then turns to the seller with an action, based on the loss that he (the buyer) has suffered by paying damages to the injured party. The seller rejoins that under Article 5 this loss is not covered by C.I.S.G., but should be judged according to domestic law. German writers seem to arrive at the same result, but a German court has applied C.I.S.G.[27]

The aim of C.I.S.G., Article 5 was undoubtedly to provide clarity with regard to an important question, i.e. on product liability for personal injuries. Part of the result, however, has been to complicate some other, perhaps practically less important, questions.

---

[23] Such is the case with Scandinavian law (see for Swedish law the Sale of Goods Act of 1990, s. 67(1). German law seems to make a difference between various kinds of damage and loss.

[24] See Herber, *supra*, n. 22; Schlechtriem, *Internationales UN-Kaufrecht*.

[25] Herber in Schlechtriem, *Commentary*, note 55 to Article 5; Schlechtriem, *Internationales UN-Kaufrecht*, note 40; V. Heuze, *La vente internationale de marchandises* (G.L.N. Joly: Paris, 1992), 216–217.

[26] See regarding this controversial question *Henderson* v. *Merrett Syndicate Ltd.* [1995] 2 A.C. 145, *per* Lord Goff. *Cf.* T. Weir, "Complex Liabilities", *International Encyclopedia of Comparative Law*, vol. XI, ch. 12:47–72.

[27] See Herber in Schlechtriem, *Commentary*, note 7 to Article 5; Schlechtriem, *Internationales UN-Kaufrecht*, note 39. The German decision is Oberlandesgericht Düsseldorf, 8th January 1993, reported 1993 *Recht in Wirtschaft* 325.

SPECIFIC PERFORMANCE

Few provisions of C.I.S.G. have aroused as many controversies as Article 28. This article states that if, in accordance with the provisions of this Convention, one party is entitled to require performance of any obligation by the other party, a court is not bound to enter a judgement for specific performance unless the court would do so under its own law in respect of similar contracts of sale not governed by this Convention.

Both the background and the wording of this provision seem to be clear. The background consists of the well-known principles of specific performance that are found in Anglo-American law. Suppose that a Swedish buyer sues a seller in a U.S. court, claiming specific performance under C.I.S.G., Article 46(1) because the seller has not performed his obligation of delivery of the goods. Suppose further that the court finds that this provision of C.I.S.G. is applicable in principle. The court nevertheless will not enter a judgement for specific performance unless the court would have done so in respect of a contract based on American law. It seems clear that Article 28 relates to what the court should do, nothing else. The impact of this provision is therefore comparatively limited. There is nothing in the wording of the provision that prevents a buyer from claiming performance of the contract extrajudicially according to Article 46(1). Such a claim may, if it does not result in performance by the seller, have an influence on the application of other provisions of C.I.S.G. (e.g. Articles 74–77 on damages).

What has been said now is confirmed by the legislative history of Article 28. For a long time the various drafts of a Convention for international sales contained provisions regarding performance of the contract as a remedy for breach of contract. This remedy was stated to be subject to there being a right to it according to the rules of national law.[28] This was unclear, and it did not satisfy the British delegation at the Diplomatic Conference at the Hague in 1964. They vigorously opposed the idea that a British Court might have to enforce a claim for specific performance based on principles other than those of English law.[29] A new solution was chosen.[30] A general provision was introduced in U.L.I.S.,

---

[28] See the proposal for a Uniform Law for International Sales 1963 (which was the basis of the work at the Diplomatic conference at the Hague 1964), Article 27(1). As a prerequisite for the right to claim specific performance it was mentioned that such a right *"n'est pas interdite par le droit national de la jurisdiction saisie"*. See *Conférence diplomatique sur l'unification du droit en matière de la vente internationale, Actes et documents*, T. 11 (The Hague, 1966) 216.

[29] The same arguments were presented when C.I.S.G. was adopted. See U. Magnus in J. von Staudinger, *Kommentar zum BGB* 13. Bearbeitung. *Wiener Kaufrecht*. Notes 3–5 to Article 28.

[30] The new formulation was introduced by a proposal of the drafting committee: see *Actes et documents* (*supra.*, n. 28) II, p. 379. There were informal deliberations, in which I took part as a member of the Swedish delegation.

Article 16 and also in Article VII of the Convention relating to U.L.I.S. C.I.S.G., Article 28 is substantially similar to the Article in U.L.I.S.

Article 28 is accordingly to be understood literally, i.e. it affects only the courts. Presumably no other courts than those applying Anglo-American principles of common law and equity will be affected.[31] Article 28 refers to what a court would do, not to the validity between the parties.

However, it is not surprising that Article 28 has been invoked for other, more or less respectable purposes as well. One such purpose is to avoid the unfortunate consequences of the fact that Article 79, concerning exemptions, refers only to claims for damages (Article 79(5)).[32] Even if a seller is exempted from liability to pay damages under Article 79, the buyer is apparently yet entitled to claim performance, with the same practical results for the seller as a claim for damages would have. There seems to be general consensus that this consequence cannot be accepted, although it is uncertain what the basis for rejecting it should be. Anyhow, Article 28 is a poor means of correcting this defect of legislative drafting. Its literal meaning should not be strained in order to arrive at satisfactory solutions of problems that have no connection with the reasons underlying this article.

LACK OF CONTROL, FORCE MAJEURE AND FRUSTRATION

One of the most important provisions of C.I.S.G. is Article 79, on exemptions. The two first paragraphs of the article read as follows:

> (1) A party is not liable for a failure to perform any of his obligations if he proves that the failure was due to an impediment beyond his control and that he could not reasonably be expected to have taken the impediment into account at the time of the conclusion of the contract or to have avoided or overcome it or its consequences.
>
> (2) If the party's failure is due to the failure by a third person whom he has engaged to perform the whole or a part of the contract, that party is exempt from liability only if:
>
> (a) he is exempt under the preceding paragraph; and
> (b) the person whom he has engaged would be so exempt if the provisions of that paragraph were applied to him.

A few preliminary remarks may be permitted before going on to the relationship of these rules to general principles of contract law. In view of the

---

[31] There seems to be a remote possibility that e.g. a Swedish court would face a claim for specific performance of a contract for the sale of illegal drugs, and that in such a case article 28 might be applicable. However, even this supposition seems too fanciful.

[32] See B. Gomard & H. Rechnagel, *International Købelov* (København, 1990), 222. *Cf.* U. Huber in Schlechtriem, *Commentary*, notes 20, 33 to Article 28; H. Stoll in Schlechtriem, *Commentary*, notes 55–57 to Article 79 with numerous references.

numerous and very different situations that may be considered, Article 79 is remarkably void of contents. There is in Article 79(2) a detailed rule for cases in which the impediment is due to a third party, but otherwise there is nothing that indicates what kinds of impediments that are contemplated. What about wars, civil uprisings, labour conflicts, illegality, export and import restrictions, currency restrictions, etc.? Even the discussions that preceded the introduction of Article 79 provide little information on this subject. However, the reason why no special events are mentioned or discussed is easily understood; it would in all probability have been impossible to achieve sufficient unity on these issues. Even a few examples might have provoked questions why just these events were mentioned. The only practical way to achieve agreement was to leave most problems unsolved.[33]

However, this leads to the main question treated here, i.e. how far can national principles of contract law be invoked in lieu of Article 79, when the factual situation develops in an unforeseen manner? In so far as the events that are involved refer to the possibility of performing an obligation, there are good reasons for excluding national principles of contract law.[34] C.I.S.G. will then apply exclusively, unless there is a contractual provision that applies, which is extremely common. This is the case with most of the events mentioned here before (wars, civil uprisings, labour conflicts, etc.).

There are, however, in various systems of national law principles that have another structure and are not primarily based on the influence of certain events on the possibility of performance. As an example may be mentioned the German doctrine of *Wegfall der Geschäftsgrundlage* ("failure of the foundation of the contract"), which covers numerous situations other than those contemplated in Article 79. The same seems to be true of the doctrine of frustration in English law. In the well-known case of *Krell* v. *Henry*[35] there was no impediment to performance. The person who had hired windows in order to look at the coronation process had no difficulty in providing the money to pay for the use of the windows, nor was there any difficulty for the owner to provide access to the windows on the day agreed. The trouble was that no one had any interest in using the windows when the procession was cancelled. Similar problems could arise under other legal systems.

It follows from what has just been stated that, in so far as these rules contemplate situations to which Article 79 may be applicable, they should be considered to be replaced by that article. On the other hand, problems relating to situations in which the issue is not whether performance has been affected

[33] See in particular the comparative survey by D. Tallon, in C. M. Bianca & M. J. Bonell (eds.), *Commentary on the International Sales Law* (Milano, 1987), notes 2 and 3 to Article 79.

[34] See references in the preceding note to Schlechtriem, *Commentary*.

[35] [1903] 2 K.B. 740.

should in my opinion be judged according to national law.[36] This is not only a matter of sticking to the wording of Article 79; it depends on the fact that the problems may be factually quite different from what is contemplated in Article 79. *Krell* v. *Henry* has already been mentioned. Moreover, consider the following case: a buyer who has bought raw materials for his production states that his factory has been bombed and, since he will have no production for the next few years, he has no use for the goods bought. He argues that he should be exempt from his obligation under the contract. Although this case might be considered one that according to C.I.S.G., Article 7(2) should be settled according to the general principles of the Convention, I find it impossible to deduce any consequences either from Article 79 or from any other provision of C.I.S.G. for this case. *Ex nihilo nihil*: when there is no guidance to be had anywhere it is useless to look for guidance.[37]

However, we should then return to Article 7(1), which speaks of the need to promote uniformity in the application of the Convention and of the observance of good faith in international trade. Even if a matter does not fall within the formal ambit of the Convention, it is possible to apply principles that take due account of a contract's international character. Disputes concerning international contracts should be decided on grounds that are valid internationally; nationalism based on formal interpretation of statutory provisions or on national case law should be taken into account but not be allowed to prevail against what is reasonable in international trade. This has been true for a long time before the adoption of C.I.S.G., and there are particularly good reasons for applying this principle in the cases now discussed.

CONCLUSIONS

The possible conflicts between C.I.S.G. and national law are of course much more numerous than has been indicated here. However, some conclusions can be drawn.

In the first place, the possibility of conflicts does not depend on C.I.S.G. only but just as much on the national legal system that is involved. There is a greater

---

[36] R. Herber, in Schlechtriem, *Commentary*, note 14 to Article 4, makes no difference between various applications of the doctrine of *Geschäftsgrundlage*. Those who are in favour of letting national rules supplement C.I.S.G. generally, have no reasons for making any distinctions. See e.g. Neumayer & Ming, *Convention de Vienne*, notes 6, 7 to Article 4.

[37] In Swedish law such a situation would probably be judged according to a doctrine of "presupposed conditions", which is not codified but yet universally acknowledged to be valid. Since this doctrine applies to a number of situations that have no connection either with sales or with impossibility of performance, it would be strange to refuse completely to apply it to any contracts of international sales.

risk of conflict if a system contains a number of abstract principles that are applicable also to sales than if the general principles of contract law are based principally on the law of sales. The latter is the case e.g. in Scandinavia.

On the other hand, it is clear that, if there is a gap in C.I.S.G., it is easier to fill it with national law if the law involved contains abstract principles aiming at dealing with all sorts of question, regardless of which particular type of contract is concerned. This circumstance might encourage reliance on the general principles of C.I.S.G. However, as has appeared already, I am personally somewhat sceptical as to the possibilities of squeezing much contents out of the provisions of C.I.S.G., many of which are coloured by the need to find compromises that were acceptable to all states involved.

I have more confidence in the application of the basic idea of Article 7(1), i.e. that solutions should be sought that promote the observance of "good faith in international trade". Such good faith involves taking into account general principles that can be assumed to be known to those who are engaged in international trade. In this way, British law may be relevant because of its well-known importance for international trade, regardless of the fact that the United Kingdom has not ratified C.I.S.G.

Chapter 10

The Doctrine of Strict Compliance: Its Development and Current Construction

Peter Ellinger

1 ITS DEVELOPMENT

The doctrine of strict compliance has governed the law of letters of credit since the beginning of the twentieth century. It is echoed in *Basse and Selve* v. *Bank of Australasia*,[1] which concerned a certificate of quality, and was explained by Bailhache, J. in *English Scottish and Australian Bank* v. *Bank of South Africa*,[2] in what has become one of the classical statements in point:

> "It is elementary to say that a person who ships in reliance on a letter of credit must do so in exact compliance with it terms. It is also elementary to say that a bank is not bound or indeed entitled to honour drafts presented to it under a letter of credit unless those drafts with the accompanying documents are in strict accord with the credit as opened."

The rationale behind this strict, uncompromising, doctrine is the notion that banks are financiers and not traders. They are not—and cannot be expected to be—familiar with the commercial elements of their customers' business activities. Accordingly, banks should not be dragged into disputes respecting the conformity of goods supplied by or to their customers.

This very consideration has led also to the development of the other major principle of the law of letters of credit, which is the autonomy doctrine.[3] Under it, the letter of credit constitutes a transaction separate from and unqualified by the underlying commercial contract financed by it. If the beneficiary has

---

[1] (1904) 90 L.T. 618, following *Re an Arbitration between Reinhold & Co. and Hansloh* (1896) 12 T.L.R. 422.

[2] (1922) 12 Ll.L.R. 21, 24; and see *Belgian Grain and Produce Co. Ltd.* v. *Cox & Co. (France) Ltd.* (1919) 1 Ll.L.R. 256, 257.

[3] Currently spelt out in Articles 3 and 6 of the Uniform Customs and Practice for Documentary Credits (1993 Revision), I.C.C. Brochure 500 ("U.C.P.-500").

complied with the terms of the letter of credit, the issuing bank is bound to pay.[4] The strict compliance doctrine is, in reality, complementary to the autonomy of the credit. "Strict compliance" provides the yardstick for determining whether or not the beneficiary has complied with the terms of the letter of credit. As long as the issuing bank adheres to it when it examines the documents tendered under the letter of credit, it remains within the ambit of its contract with the applicant for the credit. As stated by Viscount Summer in the landmark case of *Equitable Trust Co. of New York* v. *Dawson Partners:*[5]

> "It is both common ground and common sense that in such a [letter of credit] transaction the accepting bank can only claim indemnity if the conditions on which it is authorised to accept are in the matter of the accompanying documents strictly observed. There is no room for documents which are almost the same, or which will do just as well. Business could not proceed securely on any other lines. The bank's branch abroad, which knows nothing officially of the details of the transaction thus financed, cannot take upon itself to decide what will do well enough and what will not. If it does as it is told, it is safe; if it declines to do anything else, it is safe; if it departs from the conditions laid down, it acts at its own risk."

Seen in commercial terms, his Lordship based strict compliance on a narrow premise. It is that, although banks are able to verify that documents tendered to them conform in terms of form with the requirements of the letter of credit, they are incapable of assessing the compliance of documents in functional or commercial terms. Authorities decided during the seventy years following Viscount Sumner's formulation, have reaffirmed the underlying premise and have further entrenched the doctrine.[6] Indeed, even the time honoured rule, to the effect that *de minimis non curat lex*, has at one time been held not to apply to a letter of credit transaction.[7]

Notwithstanding this formal nature of "strict compliance", the doctrine has, thus, stood the test of time. Indeed, its formulations in the leading cases of the

---

[4] The leading English cases in point are *Urquhart Lindsay & Co.* v. *Eastern Bank Ltd.* [1922] 1 K.B. 318; *Hamzeh Malas & Sons* v. *British Imex Industries Ltd.* [1958] 2 Q.B. 127; *United City Merchants (Investments) Ltd.* v. *Royal Bank of Canada (The American Accord)* [1983] A.C. 168.

[5] (1926) 27 Ll.L.R. 49, 52.

[6] See, e.g., *Rayner (J. H.) & Co. Ltd.* v. *Hambro's Bank Ltd.* [1943] 1 K.B. 37; *Bank Melli Iran* v. *Barclays Bank D.C.O.* [1951] 2 Lloyd's Rep. 367; *Kydon Compañia Naviera S.A.* v. *National Westminster Bank Ltd. (The Lena)* [1981] 1 Lloyd's Rep. 68; *Commercial Banking Co. of Sydney* v. *Jalsard* [1973] A.C. 279, 286; *Banque de l'Indochine et de Suez S.A.* v. *J. H. Rayner (Mincing Lane) Ltd.* [1983] 1 Q.B. 711; *Westpac Banking Corporation* v. *S.C.N.B.* [1986] 1 Lloyd's Rep. 311.

[7] *Moralice (London) Ltd.* v. *E. D. & F. Man* [1954] 2 Lloyd's Rep. 526; *Soproma SpA* v. *Marine and Animal By-Products Corporation* [1966] 1 Lloyd's Rep. 367; *Astro Exito Navegacion S.A.* v. *Chase Manhattan Bank (The Messiniaki Tolmi)* [1986] 1 Lloyd's Rep. 455, affd. [1988] 2 Lloyd's Rep. 217.

present decade[8] makes no attempt to depart from it or even to inject new blood into it by skilful restatement. Basically, the doctrine continues to reign supreme.

2 STRICT COMPLIANCE IN PRACTICE

An ardent supporter—inspired by the rhetoric of old and new authorities—may describe strict compliance as a stronghold of the law of letters of credit. Many merchants and bankers, in contrast, have come to look on it as a stranglehold, employed by unscrupulous importers to defeat the rightful claims of exporters and their negotiating banks. A review of current letters of credit practice demonstrates that their misgivings are not the product of baseless disgruntlement.

The stipulation for the furnishing of a letter of credit is a term of the contract of sale or of services, the parties to which are the applicant for the credit and the beneficiary. Usually, the term in question is brief, spelling out the commercial terms and whether the letter of credit is to be "irrevocable" or "irrevocable and confirmed".[9] It is uncommon to stipulate at this stage the documents to be tendered under the letter of credit or even whether or not it is to be a "negotiation credit" sanctioning negotiation by any bank.[10] Detailed provisions covering these issues are, usually, spelt out in the "application form" executed by the applicant when he orders his bank to issue the credit. His instructions are duplicated in the letter of credit issued in the beneficiary's favour. Usually, he is advised of the opening of the credit by a telex, dispatched to him by the issuing bank's local correspondent.

The execution of the application form gives the applicant for the credit the opportunity to call for documents, or to make other provisions, ostensibly aimed at this protection against sharp practices. The stipulation for certificates, such as certificates of origin, of quality and of inspection is an instance in point. So is the call for a transport document, such as a bill of lading, the delivery of which gives its holder—be he the applicant for the credit or his banker—a pledge or other security interest in the goods. Unfortunately, though, the filling in of the application is seen by many importers as an opportunity to include

---

[8] *Seaconsar Far East Ltd.* v. *Bank Markazi Jamhouri Islami Iran* [1993] 1 Lloyd's Rep. 236, 240, rcvd. on other grounds [1994] A.C. 438; *Glencore International A.G.* v. *Bank of China* [1996] 1 Lloyd's Rep. 135, 150; *Kredietbank Antwerp* v. *Midland Bank Plc* [1998] Lloyd's Rep. Bank. 173, 177 *et seq.*, affd. [1999] C.L.C. 1108 (C.A.). For a neat formulation see *Bhojwani* v. *Chung Khiaw Bank* [1990] 3 M.L.J. 260 (Singap. C.A.).

[9] As to the meaning of these terms, see U.C.P.-500, Articles 6, 9. Occasionally, the documentary credit clause may, further, identify the confirming bank or simply require that it be a "first class bank" in the beneficiary's country.

[10] As defined in UCP-500, Article 10(b).

provisions which put obstacles in the ready winding up of the transaction. Basically, the applicant for the credit includes requirements so onerous as to render strict compliance unattainable.[11]

When the beneficiary receives such a letter of credit he faces a Hobson's choice. Undoubtedly, he can, on occasions, insist that the letter of credit furnished to him is not as agreed in the underlying contract and, on this basis, refuse to ship the goods.[12] In a falling or oversupplied market, though, he may thereupon end up with unsaleable goods on his hands. If he decides to accept the credit "as is"—for better or worse—he may be unable to tender a set of fully complying documents. The applicant for the credit may, then, utilise the "discrepancies" in the documents as a lever for demanding a hefty discount or, in some markets, as an excuse for rejecting the documents and the goods[13] with the hope of purchasing the latter at a much lower price when they are sold by the hapless beneficiary, by the negotiating bank, or by the carriers in a public auction.

It would be inaccurate to assert that "strict compliance" is used solely, or even primarily, as a bargaining device by importers. In many cases, importers waive discrepancies in documents provided the commercial object of the underlying transaction is attained by the shipment of the goods and the ensuing tender of the documents.[14] In others, "strict compliance" is a defence raised where the importer discovers that the goods shipped are defective or that the exporter has perpetrated a fraud involving, for instance, the shipment of rubbish or the tender of false or fraudulent documents. In the first type of case, the autonomy doctrine defeats the importer's attempt to use the exporter's breach of the underlying contract as a defence to an action based on the letter of credit.[15] In the second type of case, he often finds the fraud exception too narrow.[16] In consequence, the importer's better course is to rely on a discrepancy—

---

[11] The stipulation for ill conceived documents or the spelling out of exceptionally detailed requirements are amongst the common devices employed. A recent "favourite" is a term calling for the inclusion of the importer's fax and telephone number even in documents other than the invoice, e.g., in the packing list.

[12] See, e.g., *Furst (E.) & Co.* v. *W. E. Fisher Ltd.* [1960] 2 Lloyd's Rep. 340; *Wahbe Tamari & Sons Ltd.* v. *Colprogeca Sociedade Geral de Fibras Produtos Coloniais Lda* [1969] 2 Lloyd's Rep. 18, 21.

[13] And see *Shamsher Jute Mills* v. *Sethia (London) Ltd.* [1987] 1 Lloyd's Rep. 388, in which the tender of non-complying documents under the credit was held to involve also a breach by the seller of the terms of the contract of sale.

[14] And note that UCP-500, Article 14(c) confers on the issuing bank the discretion to consult the beneficiary. However, the bank is not obliged to do so and, under Article 14(b), the determination of whether or not the documents are in order is left to the bank.

[15] For an extreme case, see *Discount Records Ltd.* v. *Barclays Bank Ltd.* [1975] 1 W.L.R. 315.

[16] See *United City Merchants (Investments) Ltd.* v. *Royal Bank of Canada* [1983] A.C. 168; *Benjamin's Sale of Goods*, 5th edn. (1997), §§ 23–122 to 23–129; but note the wider scope of exceptions in the United States, *ibid.*, §§ 23–130 *et seq.*

meaningless as it may be from a commercial point of view—rather than to base his defence (or his objection to payment) on the true contractual grievance.

It is easy to sympathise with the use made by the importer of the discrepant nature of the documents where the case involves a blatant breach of the contract of sale or fraud by the exporter. But, even in cases of this type, the resort to the discrepancies involves an element of fiction. Just as in the case of the misuse of discrepancies by the ruthless importer, whose real object is to obtain a discount or to make an unfair gain, the discrepancies pleaded by a commercially aggrieved or a defrauded importer is not the real commercial motive for his rejection of the goods. The function of the alleged discrepancies is to provide the formal legal basis for the importer's repudiation of the transaction, motivated by the faulty performance or by the deceit to which he has been subjected by the exporter.

The law in point, though, is clear. As long as the bank's checkers discover a valid discrepancy in any one of the documents called for in the credit, the set constitutes a bad tender. The importer and the bank are entitled to raise all the technical defences they identify![17] Unlike Swiss Law,[18] English does not employ a doctrine of good faith to combat the unfair use of discrepancies.[19]

3 PRINCIPLES USED TO AMELIORATE STRICT COMPLIANCE

A rigid application of the doctrine of strict compliance is, obviously, bound to lead to results that would, on many occasions, be regarded as both unfair and unsound by the business world in general. Indeed, such is the trepidation invoked by the doctrine that, in certain trades, there has been a shift from the traditional forms of documentary or commercial letters of credit to standby credits. Although the doctrine of strict compliance applies even to such transactions,[20] it is, quite erroneously, believed that the simple nature of the

---

[17] Decided as early as 1925 in *Guaranty Trust Co. of New York* v. *Van Den Berghs* (1925) 22 Ll.L.R. 447, 455; but note an amelioration in the United States; *Exotic Transfers Far East Buying Office* v. *Exotic Trading U.S.A. Inc.* (1991) 717 F.Supp. 144; and see *Benjamin's Sale of Goods*, 5th edn., § 23–181.

[18] Discussed by Saville, J. in *Mannesman Handel A.G.* v. *Kaunlaran Shipping Corp.* [1993] 1 Lloyd's Rep. 89; and see *Benjamin's Sale of Goods*, 5th edn., § 23–182.

[19] But note that in *Transpetrol Ltd.* v. *Transöl Olieprodukten Nederland B.V.* [1989] 1 Lloyd's Rep. 309, 310–313, Philips, J. achieved a comparable result by treating a nonsensical requirement as ineffective; and see *Benjamin's Sale of Goods*, 5th edn., §§ 23–068, 23–182.

[20] See, e.g. *Kelly* v. *First Westroads Bank* (1988) 840 F.2d 554 (8th Circ.); U.C.P.-500, Article 2, under which standby credits can be made subject to the Code; the ISP98, Article 4.01; *Benjamin's Sale of Goods*, 5th edn., § 23–225.

documents to be tendered[21] under standby credits renders compliance an easy task.

In respect of documentary or commercial credits, the courts and the business world developed five principles that are used to combat strict compliance. The first is that, in construing a letter of credit, the document has to be construed as a whole. Effectively, this means that specific terms of the letter of credit may be read together with, or elucidated, on the basis of other clauses.[22] American courts have achieved similar results by construing the terms of the credit so as to uphold, or even to give business efficacy, to the transaction.[23]

A second principle, also developed by the courts, is to dismiss patent misprints and meaningless deviations as trivialities, to be distinguished from discrepancies. Originally, this principle was proclaimed in the United States.[24] It was applied by Kaplan, J. in the High Court of Hong Kong in *Hing Yip Fat Co. Ltd.* v. *Daiwa Bank Ltd.*,[25] in which the variation between "Cheergoal *Industries* Ltd." and "Cheergoal *Industrial* Ltd." was treated as a mere misprint which did not constitute a discrepancy. The principle has been adopted in Singapore[26] and by the English courts.[27] In commercial terms, this principle gives effect to a view, held for a long time amongst bankers, according to which not "every little discrepancy" is a "discrepancy". Coached in legal phraseology, the doctrine asserts that not every trivial departure in the documents from the wording of the letter of credit is a discrepancy justifying the rejection of the documents. Obviously, *de minimis non curat lex* has now been made applicable to letters of credit!

The third principle is to be found in U.C.P.-500, Article 13(a), the second sentence of which states: "Compliance of the stipulated documents on their face with the terms and conditions of the Credit, shall be determined by international banking practice as reflected in these Articles." It is clear this article militates

---

[21] Usually, a default certificate and a bill of exchange. Experience, though, shows that, even these simple, beneficiary issued, documents are often discrepant.

[22] *Elder Dempster Lines Ltd.* v. *Ionic Shipping Agency Inc.* [1969] 1 Lloyd's Rep. 529, 535–536.

[23] *Venizelos S.A.* v. *Chase Manhattan Bank* (1970) 425 F.2d 461; *Bank of North Carolina* v. *Rock Island Bank* (1978) 570 F.2d 202. English courts, though, will not apply a term into a letter of credit except in the most unusual circumstances: *Cauxell Ltd* v. *Lloyds Bank Plc* [1995] T.L.R. 707.

[24] *Beyene* v. *Irving Trust Co.* (1985) 762 F.2d 4. *Cf. Bank of Montreal* v. *Federal National Bank* (1986) 622 F.Supp. 6; and see *Benjamin's Sale of Goods*, 5th edn., §§ 23–178 *et seq.*

[25] [1991] 2 H.K.L.R. 35.

[26] *United Bank Ltd.* v. *Banque National de Paris* [1992] 2 S.L.R. 64.

[27] *Bankers Trust Co.* v. *State Bank of India* [1991] 1 Lloyd's Rep. 587, affd. [1991] 2 Lloyd's Rep. 443; *Kredietbank Antwerp* v. *Midlands Bank Plc* [1998] Lloyd's Rep. Bank. 173, affd. [1999] C.L.C. 1108 (discussed at length below). Note that Philips, J.'s decision in *Transpetrol Ltd.* v. *Transöl Olieprodukten Nederland B.V.*, *supra* n. 19, is in the same spirit.

against any attempt to treat the compliance of a document as a mere exercise of proof reading, based on a mere comparison of its language with the words of the letter of credit. The issue has to be determined on the basis of "international banking practice". Banking practice, however, is not too readily determinable and tends to vary in its finer details from place to place and even from bank to bank. Expert witnesses from all over the world have found it easy to support irreconcilable positions taken about it. Moreover, the words "as reflected in these Articles"[28] have done little to clarify the meaning of "international banking practice"—a phrase which is, in any event, subject to controversies.

The fourth principle, likewise developed in practice, is stated in Article 13(c). "If a Credit contains conditions without stating the document(s) to be presented in compliance with them, banks will deem such conditions as not stated and will disregard them." Whilst this provision does not combat the utilisation of trivial deviations in the documents, it enables banks to ignore onerous conditions which, usually, seek to introduce into the letter of credit terms of the underlying contract of sale without specifying documents to be tendered in order to establish compliance therewith. In English law a similar result was achieved, even prior to the inclusion of this clause in the Code, by reading the terms of letters of credit together with the provisions of the Code. Thus, in *Forestall Mimosa Ltd.* v. *Oriental Credit Ltd.*[29] the Court of Appeal construed a term, under which the bank's liability arose only if it accepted a draft drawn under the credit, as subject to Article 10(a) of the 1983 Revision of the U.C.P.,[30] under which a bank that opened a letter of credit available by acceptance was bound both to accept and to pay a draft accompanied by conforming documents. The policy involved, though, is not of universal application. The Singapore Court of Appeal, for instance, took a different stand, holding that, notwithstanding Article 13(c), a non documentary condition was effective because the parties were free to agree on any terms acceptable to them.[31]

The last principle which seeks to soften the rigours of strict compliance is based on an American doctrine, under which the bank is treated as waiving discrepancies not stated in the notice rejecting the documents.[32] This principle,

---

[28] A well known question, for instance, is whether the practice as recognised in the U.C.P. takes into account trade practices prevailing in specific places. To date, the issue remains unsettled.

[29] [1986] 1 W.L.R. 631.

[30] Currently Article 9(a) of the U.C.P.-500.

[31] *Kumgai-Zenecon Construction Pte Ltd. (in Liq.)* v. *Arab Bank Plc* [1997] 3 S.L.R. 770, 779–781.

[32] See, e.g., *Bank of America* v. *Whitney-Central National Bank* (1923) 291 F. 929, 937; *Dovenmuehle Inc.* v. *East Bank of Colorado Springs* (1977) 563 F.2d 24; *Pringle-Associated Mortgage Corp.* v. *Southern National Bank* (1978) 571 F.2d 871; *Kerr-McGee Chemical Corp.* v. *Federal Deposit Insurance Corp.* (1989) 872 F.2d 971.

which was consistently rejected by the English courts,[33] was adopted with some modification in Article 16 of the 1983 Revision of the U.C.P. and is currently set out in Articles 13(b) and 14 of the U.C.P.-500. According to Article 14(e), the effect of these provisions is to estop the issuing bank from pleading discrepancies unless they have been stated in a notice of rejecting complying with the procedure laid down in the Code. To be effective, the notice must be given within a reasonable time not exceeding seven business days (Article 13(b)),[34] must be communicated without delay once the bank has reached its decision to reject (Article 14(d)(i)), has to spell out all the discrepancies in respect of which the documents are rejected (Article 13(d)(ii)), and must, further, state that whether the documents are being held at the "presenter's" disposal or are being returned (Article 13(d)(ii)).

Articles 13(b) and 14 seek to combat the highly formal doctrine of strict compliance by laying down an equally formal doctrine governing the rejection of a faulty tender. An issuing bank that fails to follow the precepts of the latter relinquishes the right to rely on the former. It is true that in *Seaconsar Far East Ltd.* v. *Bank Markazi Jomhouri Islami Iran*[35] the Court of Appeal held that a rejection notice can be communicated in a telephone conversation[36] or *inter presentem*. In this way their Lordships have abated the strict, purely formal, construction of the provisions which, earlier on, had been given a predominantly mechanical construction.[37] But the basic requirements of Articles 13(b) and 14 are still ignored by an issuing bank at its own peril.

The state of the law, following the promulgation of the U.C.P.-500 and the general body of case law, was that the doctrine of strict compliance remained sacrosanct. True, the five exceptions just discussed introduced some counter measures. All the same, if the issuing bank was able to identify just one "discrepancy"—other than a mere misprint or patent triviality—it was entitled to reject the documents. Provided it complied with the precepts of the rejection procedure, laid down in Articles 13(b) and 14 of the U.C.P.-500, it could ignore the protests of the negotiating bank and the beneficiary.

---

[33] *Skandinaviska Kreditaktiebolaget* v. *Barclays Bank* (1925) 22 Ll.L.R. 523, 525; *Soproma SpA* v. *Marine and Animal By-Products Corporation* [1966] 1 Lloyd's Rep. 367, 387; *Kydon Compañia Naviera* v. *National Westminster Bank Ltd.* [1981] 1 Lloyd's Rep. 68, 78–80 (failing to give effect to Article 8(e) of the 1974 Revision of the U.C.P.).

[34] Note that Article 16(c) of the 1983 Revision referred to reasonable time without mentioning seven days or any other fixed time.

[35] [1999] 1 Lloyd's Rep. 36; aff'g [1997] 2 Lloyd's Rep. 89.

[36] Which they held to be a "telecommunication" within the meaning of Article 14(d)(i).

[37] See, e.g., *Bankers Trust Co.* v. *State Bank of India, supra*, n. 27, and cases there cited; but *cf. United Bank Ltd.* v. *Bank Nationale de Paris* [1992] 2 S.L.R. 64; and note that in *Amixco Asia (Pte) Ltd.* v. *Bank Bumiputra Malaysia Brhd* [1992] 2 S.L.R. 943 Selvam, J. held that Article 14 applied only to documentary discrepancies.

4 THE *KREDIETBANK ANTWERP* CASE

This, then, was the state of the authorities when the new case of *Kredietbank Antwerp* v. *Midland Bank Plc*[38] came up for decision. Importers based in Jersey ordered 6,000 mt of heavy smelting steel scrap from Swedish exporters. Acting on the instructions of the M Bank in London, who had, in turn been instructed by the importers, the K Bank advised the exporters that an irrevocable but unconfirmed letter of credit had been opened in their favour. The documents to be tendered included, *inter alia*, a "draft survey report" and "a certificate of quality" both to be issued by Griffith Inspectorate at port of loading …".

A set of documents, negotiated in due course by the K Bank was rejected by the M Bank in reliance, *inter alia*, on an alleged discrepancy related to the name, or designation, of the surveying firm that issued the certificate of quality and the draft survey report. Instead of being issued by "Griffith Inspectorate", the two documents tendered were issued on the letterhead of "Daniel C Griffith (Holland) BV" and signed for that company. However, at the foot of each document, as part of the printed notepaper, there was a logo stating "Inspectorate" and underneath it appeared the words: "Member of the Worldwide Inspectorate—dedicated to the elimination of risk".

The K Bank brought an action to enforce the letter of credit; the importers sought to enjoin the M Bank from making payment thereunder on the ground that the documents were discrepant. Under an order made by Mance, J., the two causes were tried jointly.

In the first part of his decision, Diamond, Q.C. (sitting as a judge of the High Court) discussed the general tenets of the strict compliance doctrine. Referring to the view of the expert witnesses, his Honour said:[39]

> "there was considerable discussion before me by the distinguished experts who gave evidence … as to the degree of strictness required; one view being that if too strict a standard be adopted, this can and does result in abuse of the letter of credit procedure, and in a contractual provision for payment by letter of credit becoming an excuse for non-payment, rather than a method of affecting payment; the other view being that a bank should strictly perform its mandate subject to not taking what was called a 'robotic approach to the documents' or seeking a 'mirror image reproduction' between the requirements of the credit and the documents tendered under it."

Judge Diamond, though, did not adopt either of the two yardsticks so populated because he felt bound to follow the traditional test[40] which emphasises the bank's duty to pay only against "documents which comply strictly with the terms of the credit." Judge Diamond[41] further pointed out that

---

[38] [1998] Lloyd's Rep. Bank. 173; affd. [1999] C.L.C. 1108 (C.A.).
[39] [1998] Lloyd's Rep. Bank. 173, 177.
[40] As described by Sir Thomas Bingham, M.R. in *Glencore International A.G.* v. *Bank of China* [1996] 1 Lloyd's Rep. 135, 150.
[41] [1998] 2 Lloyd's Rep. Bank. 173, 177–178.

this test had been restated in recent times by Lloyd, L.J. in *Seaconsar Far East Ltd.* v. *Bank Markazi Jomhouri Islami Iran*,[42] which traced the history of strict compliance and decided that, where a letter of credit stipulated that its number and the buyer's name appear on each document, that requirement had to be observed. It would be inappropriate to ignore the term, or to dismiss it as an irrelevant requirement not calling for strict compliance, merely because its object was unclear or unknown. Judge Diamond[43] noted, at the same time, that—even in the light of Lloyd, L.J.'s reasoning in *Seaconsar*—the doctrine of strict compliance did not require a rigid and meticulous adherence to the precise wording of the letter of credit and that some leeway must and can be allowed. He held that this would be so, specifically, where there was some ambiguity, as in such case it would be essential for a banker to adopt a reasonable approach.

Judge Diamond then referred to the second sentence of Article 13(a) of the U.C.P.-500, under which, it will be recalled, the regularity of documents is to be determined, *inter alia*, with reference to "international standard banking practice" as reflected in the Code. He concluded:[44]

> "While a banker is not ... concerned as to whether the documents ... serve any useful commercial purpose, a banker does have to make decisions as to whether a document... complies with the requirements of the credit. Where those requirements are ambiguous, it is permissible, and indeed ... essential in practice, for the banker to adopt a reasonable interpretation of those requirements. In considering what is a reasonable interpretation a banker is not precluded from having regard to the commercial function of the document... if that function is or should be apparent to a banker examining the documents with reasonable care. It is in this sense that in my view a banker's approach to document verification should be functional rather than literal or rigid."

Applying these principles, his Honour found the documents tendered by the K Bank to be regular. Referring to the principle that a sheer misprint or typographical error does not render a document irregular, he pointed out that, although the certificate and draft survey report were made out by a firm whose name differed from the one spelt out in the credit, the logo and the words printed beneath it showed that they were executed by a firm that was a member of the Griffith Inspectorate Group. He concluded[45] that "a banker examining the documents on their face would have realised that there was an obvious misnomer in the letter of credit, and that what it required was certificates issued by a Griffith company, part of the Inspectorate organisation."

---

[42] [1993] 1 Lloyd's Rep. 236, 239.
[43] [1998] 2 Lloyd's Rep. Bank. 173, 179. His Honour adopted the reasoning of Lord Diplock in *Commercial Banking Co. of Sydney* v. *Jalsard Pty Ltd* [1973] A.C. 279, 286, later on relied upon by Parker. J. in *Banque de L'Indochine et de Suez* v. *J. H. Rayner & Co. (Mincing Lane) Ltd.* [1982] 2 Lloyd's Rep. 476, 482; affd. [1983] 1 Lloyd's Rep. 228.
[44] [1998] 2 Lloyd's Rep. Bank. 173, 179.
[45] *Ibid.*, 184.

His Honour, thus, did not seek to depart from the tenets of strict compliance, as understood traditionally, but read it subject to the principle that obvious misprints or meaningless trivialities are to be ignored. In a sense, he considered the functional significance of the deviation rather than its formal import.

The Court of Appeal affirmed, treating the discrepancy in the two documents as insignificant. However, Evans, L.J., who delivered the Court's judgment, departed in certain regards from Judge Diamond's reasoning on the tenets of the doctrine of strict compliance. To start with, his Lordship reiterated that an issuing bank was concerned only with the form of the documents presented to it and not with the underlying facts. At the same time, his Lordship accepted that mere trivialities or misprints had to be ignored.[46] Evans, L.J. concluded:[47]

> "the requirement of strict compliance is not equivalent to a test of exact literal compliance in all circumstances and as regards all documents. To some extent, therefore, the banker must exercise his own judgment whether the requirement is satisfied by the documents presented to him."

His Lordship added:[48]

> "the requirement of a Report and Certificate of Quality issued by 'Griffith Inspectorate' is amply met by the documents issued by the Dutch company named which declares itself a member of the Inspectorate Group. If there is a literal requirement that the name 'Griffith Inspectorate' shall appear in the documents, then it does so, assuming only that there is a world-wide Inspectorate group and that the company bearing the name Daniele Griffith (Holland) is a member of it. That is an assumption which, as the judge held, an experienced banker can be expected to assume."

CONCLUSION

It is clear that the decision in *Kredietbank Antwerp* militates against any future attempts to apply a "mirror image" test as the yardstick of strict compliance. In this regard, the decision departs from Lloyd, L.J.'s approach in *Seaconsar*. But even in *Kredietbank Antwerp* neither the Court of Appeal nor the trial judge sought to modify the strict compliance doctrine. That fundamental doctrine of the law of letters of credit remains intact but is to be applied in a reasonable as opposed to a literal or robotic manner.

---

[46] Chao Hick Tin's decision in *United Bank Ltd.* v. *Banque Nationale de Paris* [1992] 2 S.L.R. 64 and *Beyene* v. *Irving Trust Co. Ltd.* (1985) 762 F.2d 4 (relied upon by Chao, J.) are cited with approbation.

[47] [1999] C.L.C. 1108, 1112.

[48] *Ibid.*, 1121.

There is, actually, room for the argument that, in one sense, Evans, L.J.'s decision reverts to the spirit of *Equitable Trust Co. of New York* v. *Dawson Partners*,[49] which defined the doctrine of strict compliance.[50] It is true that the House of Lords held that a certificate executed by a single "expert" is a bad tender where the document has to be issued by "experts". Their Lordships, though, took a less rigid stand as regards another deficiency in the certificate considered by them, which was its being countersigned by the "Handels-vereeniging te Batavia" (meaning, literally "the Trade Organisation of Batavia") instead of by the "Chamber of Commerce" as stipulated. Viscount Cave[51] accepted, on this point, the holding of the Court of Appeal, which refused to treat the document as discrepant on this ground.[52] So did, by implication, Lord Carson, who delivered a dissenting speech. Viscount Sumner[53] left the point open and Lords Atkinson and Shaw did not deal with it. It is clear that a decision to the effect that "Chamber of Commerce" had to be spelt out verbatim in the certificate would have defined "strict compliance" as meaning "literal compliance". Such a test would have gone well beyond Viscount Sumner's reasoning, cited at the outset.

Seen in this light, *Equitable Trust* is not a decision calling for literal compliance. In point of fact, it might actually have foreshadowed the two common law exceptions introduced to ameliorate the rigours of strict compliance. These, it will be recalled, are the construction of the credit as a whole and the disregard of sheer trivialities or misprints. It is, thus, arguable that, as early as 1927, the House of Lords favoured a liberal rather than a literal or robotic application of strict compliance. *Kredietbank Antwerp*, accordingly, rests on a sound foundation. Whilst it leaves the doctrine of strict compliance unscathed, it calls for a reasonable approach in its application. It is believed that the decision constitutes a step in the right direction and does much to clear the air.

---

[49] (1926) 27 Ll.L.R. 49.
[50] See passage cited *supra*, p. 188.
[51] (1927) 27 Ll.L.R. 49, 51.
[52] (1926) 25 Ll.L.R. 90 (Bankes and Atkin, L.JJ.; Scrutton, L.J. dissenting).
[53] (1927) 27 Ll.L.R. 49, 54.

Chapter 11

The "Battle of the Forms" and the Conflict of Laws

Gerhard Dannemann

INTRODUCTION

Most readers will know that "battle of the forms" denounces the situation where, during contractual negotiations, both parties keep on referring to their own set of standard terms and then go ahead with the performance without having actually resolved between them which one of these two sets should govern the contract. Scholars have devoted considerable attention to this topic. One gains the impression that the number of learned articles exceeds the number of reported cases where such a "battle" has occurred.[1] This somewhat unhealthy ratio may account for the fact that, to my knowledge, Francis Reynolds has never raised his voice in this lively academic debate.

Yet the reverse ratio between academic writing and jurisprudence emerges when one looks at cases where commercial law and conflicts of law—two areas of law to which Francis Reynolds has devoted much of his work—join up for a "battle of the forms" on questions of conflict of laws.[2] By this, I mean diverging provisions in standard terms which relate to choice of law, choice of jurisdiction (including arbitration clauses) or choice of place of performance.

If legal systems throughout this world could agree on one standard solution for the "battle of the forms", which applied equally to substantive law, choice of

---

[1] The *Index to Legal Periodicals* alone lists 21 articles on the "battle of the forms" which have been published since 1981.

[2] Conspicuous silence as to the conflicts implications of a "battle of the forms" prevails in the literature, be it standard textbooks such as *Dicey & Morris on the Conflict of Laws*, 13th edn. (by L. Collins with Specialist Editors) (1999), Rule 173, 1222, and including the *Fourth Cumulative Supplement* 1997; *Cheshire and North's Private International Law*, 13th edn. by P. M. North and J. J. Fawcett (1999), 560, 563, 587, or G. Kegel, *Internationales Privatrecht*, 7th edn. (1995), 487 *et seq.*; but also in a monograph on standard terms by a leading authority on conflicts law: A. Boggiano, *International Standard Contracts: the Price of Fairness* (1991) 155 *et seq.*

applicable law, and choice of jurisdiction, there would be no problem. But quite the reverse is true. In practice, we can distinguish at least four approaches towards the "battle of the forms". And, even within one legal system, different solutions may be applied for, e.g., substantive law and choice of jurisdiction. I will first outline the different approaches and then discuss particular problems which arise in relation to choice of substantive law, choice of jurisdiction, and choice of place of performance.

MAIN APPROACHES TOWARDS DECIDING THE "BATTLE"

There are four main approaches as to the fate and the content of a contract in the event of a "battle of the forms", namely (a) there is no agreement and thus no contract, (b) there is a contract on the terms of the party which was first to propose its standard terms, (c) there is a contract on the terms of the party which was last to insist on its standard terms, and (d) there is a contract on the individually negotiated terms, and any conflicting standard terms are replaced by the background law, i.e. the rules which apply if parties have made no specific provision in the contract.[3]

a. No contract

The notion that a contract is formed only if the acceptance is the "mirror image" of the offer is widespread. Most legal systems have a rule that a purported acceptance with alterations or modifications constitutes a rejection of the offer, coupled with a counter-offer.[4] When strictly applied to the "battle of the forms", this will normally imply that there is no contract.

---

[3] From the comparative literature, see in particular E. H. Hondius and Ch Mahé, "The Battle of Forms: Towards a Uniform Solution" (1998) 12 J.C.L. 268; A. T. von Mehren, "The Battle of the Forms: A Comparative View" (1990) 38 A.J.C.L. 265. It is interesting to note that the last three approaches were discussed as possible solutions under English law by Lord Denning, M.R. in *Butler Machine Tool Co.* v. *Ex-Cell-O Corp.* [1979] 1 W.L.R. 401 (C.A.), 404–405.

[4] England: *Hyde* v. *Wrench* (1840) 3 Beav. 334; *Brogden* v. *Metropolitan Railway Co.* (1877) 2 App. Cas. 666. Germany: BGB, § 150(2) (if in doubt); France: Com. 17.6.1967, Bull. cass. 1967.III.299; Italy: C.C., Art. 1326(5); Czechia and Slovakia: Občanský zákoník, section 44(2); Netherlands: BW Art. 6:225(1) (but see also below); Vienna Convention on the International Sale of Goods 1980, Art 19(1) (C.I.S.G.); UNIDROIT Principles of International Commercial Contracts, Art. 2.11 (excluding terms which do not materially alter the offer). But see below for the Swiss OR (Code of Obligations), Article 2.

In a case decided by the *Landgericht* Bielefeld in 1988, the defendant was a German buyer who had ordered from the Italian plaintiff and seller clothing under "German conditions".[5] The seller and subsequent plaintiff purported to accept by referring to standard terms of the German textile industry and asked for express confirmation. The buyer did not reply, but took delivery of the goods. The Court, applying the Hague Uniform Law for International Sales, Article 7(2), held that there was no contract. The reference to an entire set of standard terms was a counter-offer, which was never accepted, not even by taking delivery. The plaintiff's only remedy was therefore in the law of restitution.

This is a very rare example of a case where a court has held that there was no contract if parties performed on what they thought to be a contract after an exchange of standard forms.[6] Although there has been some academic support for this type of solution,[7] it is easy to see why courts are so hesitant to rule that the "battle" has prevented the conclusion of a contract. This solution will very frequently ignore the will of both parties who wanted to have a contract regardless of its precise terms.

b. Contract on the standard terms first referred to

The new Dutch Civil Code contains the following interesting rule. If parties refer to different standard terms in offer and acceptance, the second reference is without effect, and the contract is formed on the standard terms of the party which first referred to its standard terms. The second party can prevent this effect only by an express refusal to contract on the first party's terms (Article

---

[5] LG Bielefeld 5.6.1987, *Praxis des Internationalen Zivil- und Verfahrensrechts* (IPRax) 1988, 229. For a critical view, see I. Schwenzer, " 'The Battle of the Forms' und das EAG", IPRax 1988, 212–214.

[6] *Poel* v. *Brunswick-Balke-Colender Co.* (1915) 110 N.E. 619 (N.Y.) is occasionally quoted as an example of a strict application of the "mirror image rule" to a "battle of the forms", i.e. that there is only a contract if the acceptance is the mirror image of the offer (e.g., by H. D. Gabriel, "The Battle of the Forms: A Comparison of the United Nations Convention for the International Sale of Goods and the Uniform Commercial Code", (1994) 49 Bus. Law. 1053, 1058; see also von Mehren (1990) 38 A.J.C.L. 265, 270. It should be mentioned, though, that in *Poel* it was only the buyer who had, in the last communication, referred to standard terms, and had also requested their express acceptance. When the seller did not respond and market prices fell, the buyer walked out of the contract *before* the seller had performed.

[7] E. McKendrick, "The Battle of the Forms and the Law of Restitution" (1988) 8 O.J.L.S. 197.

6:225(3)).[8] Much will, of course, depend on what is understood to be an "express" refusal, and whether a previous express refusal can become ineffective through subsequent conduct. In principle, however, Dutch law clearly saddles the second party with the risk of unresolved differences between standard terms. The U.S. Uniform Commercial Code, s. 2-207(1) and (2) favours the same approach.[9] Gabriel notes that, in recent practice, it will normally be the offeror's terms which prevail in a "battle of the forms" under U.C.C., s. 2-207.[10]

This rule has some advantages. Commercially, it makes sense that there is a contract. It is also ecnomically advantageous that the law will not encourage parties to delay the conclusion of a contract in the attempt to make the last reference to one's terms as under the "last shot rule" discussed below. And it will often be more easy to identify the first reference to standard terms rather than sorting out which party was the last to insist on its own terms.

c. Contract on the standard terms last referred to

The rule that, in a "battle of the forms", it is on the terms of the party which last referred to them that a contract is formed, is prevalent in England today (where it is called the "last shot rule"),[11] and used to be applied in Germany until some twenty-five years ago (where it was called the "theory of the last word").[12]

Three good things can be said about this rule: (a) it appears consistent with the mirror image rule, as the last offer is construed to be ultimately accepted in total by conduct; (b) it is commercially more sound than the rule that there is no

---

[8] See Hondius and Mahé (1998) 12 J.C.L. 268, 269; J. Sperling, "Battle of the forms: een vergelijking tussen Amerikaans en Nederlands recht", *Nederlands Tijdschrift voor Burgerlijk Recht* 1995, 10. As a general rule, though, BW, Article 6:225(1) maintains that an acceptance which deviates from the offer is to be treated as a refusal coupled with a counter-offer. However, an insignificant deviation in the acceptance becomes part of the contract unless the offeror objects without delay (BW, Article 6:225(2). One "battle of the forms" decision by the Hooge Raad (HR 18.3.1994, RvdW 1994, 76) is discussed by Sperling, but was unfortunately not accessible to me.

[9] U.C.C., s. 2-207 is an elaborate provision with three subsections with a somewhat unclear meaning and a disputed relationship. Effectively, however, it is only deviations which do not materially alter the offer which can become part of the contract under subsection (2). Any significant deviations from the offer will therefore only become part of the contract if individually negotiated; but see also below for subsection (3). For comparative literature on this provision see, e.g. von Mehren (1990) 38 A.J.C.L. 265; Gabriel (1994) 49 Bus. Law. 1053; E. Jacobs, "The Battle of the Forms: Standard Term Contracts in Comparative Perspective" (1985) 34 I.C.L.Q. 297.

[10] Gabriel (1994) 49 Bus. Law 1053.

[11] *British Road Services* v. *Arthur V. Crutchley & Co.* [1968] 1 All E.R. 811 (C.A.), 817; *Butler Machine Tool Co.* v. *Ex-Cell-O Corp.* [1979] 1 W.L.R. 401, (C.A.); *O.T.M. Ltd.* v. *Hydranautics* [1981] 2 Lloyd's Rep. 211 (Q.B.: Com.).

[12] RG 27.6.1916, RGZ 88, 377; RG 14.12.1928, RGZ 123, 97.

contract; and (c) it appears to have worked for English law, as is evidenced by the fact that, to my knowledge, there are no more than three reported cases in which the "battle of the forms" was a contested and relevant issue.[13] On the negative side, it has to be mentioned that it may be far from obvious which party was the last to refer to its terms. In two out of these three cases, the last reference to one party's terms was ultimately unsuccessful and declared to be a mere reference to the goods, or alternatively as having come too late.[14] Cynics might conclude that English law has, in fact, clandestinely been applying the "second last shot rule" for the last twenty years. It also encourages parties to delay the conclusion of the contract by keeping on insisting on their own terms in every communication or act of performance.

d. Contract excluding any conflicting standard terms

The fourth and final general approach is that there is a contract between the parties, but that the standard terms referred to during negotiations become part only in so far as they are specifically negotiated or uncontested. Any conflicting standard terms are ineffective and replaced by those rules which would apply to a contract which has made no specific provision for the legal issue which may be in question.

While this approach is often presented as the contemporary challenge to the "classical" rules (namely, the three other above-mentioned approaches),[15] it is probably the oldest rule on the "battle of the forms". It was applied in three French cases decided in 1912, which, interestingly enough, all concerned conflicting (local) jurisdiction clauses in standard terms.[16] The judgments by the Commercial Courts of Cambrai and of Cherbourg are most explicit on this issue. Taken together, they held that (a) if the parties have agreed on the essentials of the contract, the mere fact that conflicting ideas concerning non-essential points were not resolved do not prevent the conclusion of a contract; (b) if one of the terms was on a printed form and the other was

---

[13] See above. "Battle of the forms" was a contested issue in *Muirhead* v. *Industrial Tank Specialities Ltd.* [1986] Q.B. 507, 530. Robert Goff, L.J. (as he then was) held that an action against the third defendant in tort for pure economic loss would have been defeated by a limitation clause in a contract between the third and the second defendant on the ground that the third defendant's terms constituted the "last shot"; however, he held that there was no liability for pure economic loss in the first place (at 530).

[14] *Butler* v. *Ex-Cell-O* [1979] 1 W.L.R. 401, 404, 406, 408; *O.T.M.* v. *Hydranautics* [1981] 2 Lloyd's Rep. 211, 215.

[15] von Mehren (1990) 38 A.J.C.L. 265, 268 *et seq.*, 272; Hondius and Mahé (1998) 12 J.C.L. 268, 269. However, Hondius and Mahé also refer to the French applications of the "knock out rule" in 1912 (see note 16).

[16] Cass. req. 24.6.1912, *Jurisprudence Générale* (Rec. Dalloz) 1913 I 363; Trib. Comm. Cambrai 16.4.1912 and Trib. Comm. Cherbourg 6.9.1912, both Rec. Sirey 1914 II 49 with case note by R. Demogue.

handwritten, the handwritten one was more significant; (c) conflicting terms were to be replaced by the *droit commun*. The approving case note by R. Demogue observes that the rule (a) follows the same idea as Article 2 of the Swiss Code of Obligations.[17] This Code, which had been enacted only months before the first of these French judgments, is probably the only European codification which had the foresight to formulate its general rules on formation of contracts in such a way that they can deal directly with a "battle of the forms".[18]

The Cour de Cassation was shorter in its reasoning than the two commercial courts. It held that, where, after an initial oral agreement, one party had introduced a standard jurisdiction clauses within a written confirmation, a reply with a conflicting standard jurisdiction clause was sufficient to indicate refusal of the first jurisdiction clause.[19] This rule was generally applied to conflicting standard jurisdiction clauses by the Cour de Cassation in 1934, on the ground that the attempted derogation from the *droit commun* did not demonstrate the necessary certain intention of the parties.[20] One could argue that this strict line on choice of forum agreements has found its successor in Article 17 of both the Brussels and the Lugano Conventions.[21] A similar point can be made for the writing requirement for arbitration agreements which are subject to English law.[22] We will examine below whether the same could be true for choice of applicable law under Article 3(1) of the Rome Convention.[23]

There are, however, a number of legal systems which follow the same "knock out" approach for substantive law clauses as well. Two of the French 1912 cases

---

[17] *Ibid.*

[18] OR Article 2: (1) "If parties have agreed on all essential items, it is presumed that a reservation as to non-essential items will not prevent the contract from becoming effective. (2) If no agreement is reached on such reserved non-essential items, the judge will decide these in accordance with the nature of the contract."

[19] Cass. req. 24.6.1912, *Jurisprudence Générale* (Rec. Dalloz) 1913 I 363.

[20] Cass. req. 5.2.1934, Rec. Sirey 1934.1.110; Gaz. Pal. 1934.1.638. Cass. civ.[2] 16.11.1961, Rec. Dalloz 1962 jurisprudence 420–421 (with case note by G. Pochon) confirms this view; in this case of a wine sale, however, both parties had referred to their "terms of sale", and the unfortunate buyer was ruled out with his choice of jurisdiction clause on the ground that he should instead have referred to his "terms of purchase".

[21] Convention on Jurisdiction and Enforcement of Judgments in Civil and Commercial Matters (Brussels, 1968 and Lugano, 1988), enacted in the U.K. by the Civil Jurisdiction and Judgments Act 1982 (as amended).

[22] While it was held in *Zambia Steel & Building Supplies* v. *James Clark & Eaton Ltd.* [1986] 2 Lloyd's Rep. 224 that an arbitration and English choice of law clause contained in a standard form used by the defendant (seller) did meet the requirements of the Arbitration Act 1950, section 32, it appears that the same question has not been decided for a "battle of the forms". Nor is the Arbitration Act 1996, sections 5 and 6 particularly clear on this issue.

[23] Rome Convention on the Law Applicable to Contractual Obligations, enacted in the U.K. by the Contracts (Applicable Law) Act 1990.

concerned also clauses which regulated payment and place of performance.[24] Likewise, the above-mentioned Article 2 of the Swiss Code of Obligations applies to all contractual clauses. In 1935, Raiser discarded the "theory of the last word" as then applied by German courts as "profusely primitive" and sought to replace conflicting provisions in unresolved "battles of the form" by statutory rules or trade usages.[25] It took German courts some forty years to heed this advice.[26] Austrian courts now follow the same approach.[27] In the U.S., the view has gained ground that a "battle of the forms" should be covered by subsection (3) rather than subsections (1) and (2) of U.C.C., s. 2-207, which would also lead to a "knock out" effect.[28] Simultaneously, there has been strong support for the proposition that the entire section be amended to incorporate the "knock out" rule.[29] Moreover, both the UNIDROIT and the European Principles of Contract Law have adopted the approach that in an unresolved "battle of the forms", conflicting provisions in standard terms are without effect.[30] On an international level, it can be said that this "knock out" approach has gained the upper hand, with the exception of the Vienna Sales Convention. Ironically, Article 19 of that Convention mimics rather than solves the problem: different

[24] Trib. Comm. Cambrai 16.4.1912 and Trib. Comm. Cherbourg 6.9.1912, both Rec. Sirey 1914 II 49.

[25] L. Raiser, *Das Recht der Allgemeinen Geschäftsbedingungen*, 224, quoted from the unaltered 1961 reprint of the 1935 original.

[26] BGH 26.9.1973, BGHZ 61, 282: in a case where both parties had (partly) performed the contract, the Federal Court of Justice ruled that parties were estopped from relying on the invalidity of the contract, and held conflicting rules in standard terms to be without effect. OLG Köln 19.3.1980 Betriebs-Berater 1980, 1237 is probably the earliest clear application of the "knock out" rule and concerns a local jurisdiction clause which, although referred to in a "last shot", was held to be inoperative. The Federal Court of Justice completed the change to the new rule five years later: BGH 20.3.1985, NJW 1985, 1838. See B. Markesinis, W. Lorenz and G. Dannemann, *The German Law of Obligations, Vol. I: The Law of Contracts and Restitution*, 61–63, with English translations of OLG Köln 19.3.1980 (case 13) and BGH 20.3.1985 (case 16).

[27] OGH 7.6.1990, IPRax 1991, 419.

[28] See von Mehren (1990) 38 A.J.C.L. 265, 282 *et seq.*

[29] See T. J. McCarthy, Ending the "Battle of the Forms": A Symposium on the Revision of Section 2-207 of the Uniform Commercial Code. An Introduction: The Commercial Irrelevancy of the "Battle of the Forms" (1994), 49 Bus. Law. 1019.

[30] UNIDROIT, Principles of International Commercial Contracts (1994), provide in "Art. 22.2 (battle of the forms)" as follows: "Where both parties use standard terms and reach agreement except on those terms, a contract is concluded on the basis of the agreed terms and of any standard terms which are common in substance unless one party clearly indicates in advance, or later and without undue delay informs the other party, that it does not intend to be bound by such a contract." (See e.g. M. J. Bonell, *An International Restatement of Contract Law: the UNIDROIT Principles of International Commercial Contracts*, 2nd edn. (1997), 124.) Similar, but with some more detail, Principles of European Contract Law, Article 2:209; see Hondius and Mahé (1998) 12 J.C.L. 268, 271.

ideas were presented at the conference, no agreement could be reached, and the High Contracting Parties went ahead without having resolved which of the proposed solutions should be followed.[31]

While this "knock out" approach flies in the face of the mirror image rule, the case can be made that it does the most to turn the intentions of the parties into legal reality, namely that (a) there is a contract, and (b) on all terms on which parties have actually agreed, and (c) not on any particular terms on which parties have not agreed.[32] The main disadvantage of this approach is that, given the frequency of general rejection clauses in standard terms, it may be difficult and time consuming to find out what exactly parties have agreed upon. It also does less to discourage parties from delaying agreement by continuous insistences on their terms than the "first shot" approach.

"BATTLE" BETWEEN CONFLICTS CLAUSES

In an international agreement, the "battle of the forms" can easily involve two legal systems which differ in their solutions for the "battle". Even more confusingly, in one and the same case, the "battle" may involve conflicting choice of law clauses, conflicting choice of jurisdiction clauses, and perhaps even conflicting choice of place of performance clauses.

One such case is *O.T.M. Ltd.* v. *Hydranautics*.[33] In this case, the seller's standard terms contained a Californian choice of law clause, an arbitration clause with the seller's Californian seat as the place of arbitration, and a clause which stipulated delivery f.o.b. at seller's seat. The buyer's standard terms, on

---

[31] C.I.S.G., Article 19 treats any material alteration of an offer as counter-offer, regardless of whether or not the deviations are negotiated explicitly or contained in standard terms. See P. Schlechtriem (ed.), *Commentary on the UN Convention on the International Sale of Goods* (C.I.S.G.), 2nd edn., transl. by G. Thomas (1998), Article 19, para.19–20. Schlechtriem argues that parties which go ahead after an unresolved "battle of the forms" are presumed to have waived Article 19 with the effect that conflicting provisions are replaced by C.I.S.G. rules. This view is shared by J. Honnold, *Uniform Law for International Sales under the 1980 United Nations Convention*, 3rd edn. (1999), Article 19, paras. 170.2–170.4, whereas the "last shot rule" should apply under Article 19 according to E. A. Farnsworth, in: C. M. Bianca and M. J. Bonell, *Commentary on the International Sales Law: the 1980 Vienna Sales Convention* (1987), Article 19, at 3.1. Both solutions have been adopted by different German courts: see Oberlandesgericht München, 11.03.1998, Case 7 U 4427/97, C.I.S.G. online (http://www.jura.uni-freiburg.de/ipr1/cisg/default.htm) case no. 310 ("last shot"), A G Kehl 6.10.1995, NJW-RR 1996, 565 ("knock out").

[32] See also H. Kötz, *Europäisches Vertragsrecht, Band I: Abschluß, Gültigkeit und Inhalt des Vertrags. Die Beteiligung Dritter am Vertrag* (1996) 47–48. Kötz also argues that it would make very little economic sense to force parties to negotiate every last detail where their standard terms disagree; similar Honnold (*supra*, n. 31), para. 165.

[33] *O.T.M. Ltd.* v. *Hydranautics* [1981] 2 Lloyd's Rep. 211 (Q.B. Com.: Parker, J.).

the other hand, contained a clause for arbitration to "be held in the U.K. and conducted in accordance with U.K. law". Apparently, the buyer's counter-offer also stipulated the place of performance to be in the U.K.[34] The following three questions can arise: (a) Has an effective choice of substantive law been made? (b) Has there been an effective choice of jurisdiction (including arbitration)? If one of these questions is answered in the negative, one may need to examine whether (c) there has been an effective choice of place of performance, as this can influence both applicable law and jurisdiction.

a. Choice of applicable substantive law

The validity and effectiveness of a choice of law clause combines substantive contract law with particular conflict of laws aspects.[35] In principle, conflicts law could leave this question entirely to the proper law which allegedly has been chosen, thus treating choice of law provisions the same as any other contractual stipulations. Frequently, however, conflicts rules will contain additional requirements for a choice of law clause to be effective. This implies that not everybody who would succeed in a "battle of the forms" under substantive law rules will at the same time have succeeded with a choice of law clause contained in this party's form.

The Rome Convention contains such a combination of contract and conflict rules for a choice of law. Article 3(1) provides that a choice of law "must be expressed or demonstrated with reasonable certainty by the terms of the contract or the circumstances of the case". On the other hand, Article 3(4) in conjunction with Article 8(1) provide that the existence of a choice of law clause is to be determined by the law which would govern it under the Convention if it existed. The relationship between these two provisions is not entirely clear.[36] *Dicey & Morris* suggests that a choice of law clause is not a question of existence, but a question of interpretation,[37] but that does not hold true for choice of law clauses contained in diverging standard forms: here the very question is if they have become part of the contract.

No particular problems arise if only one of the conflicting standard terms contains a choice of law clause, whereas the other just generally rejects all other clauses. Let us assume that in *O.T.M.* v. *Hydranautics,* the Californian seller's

---

[34] This is not mentioned explicitly in the judgment, but can be taken from Parker, J.'s argument that "the initial simple f.o.b. contract offered, and of which Californian law might well have been the proper law, ... had become a contract the most real connection of which was ... with England."

[35] See, generally, H. Stoll, "Das Statut der Rechtswahlvereinbarung—eine irreführende Konstruktion", in: *Rechtskollisionen. Festschrift für Anton Heini zum 65. Geburtstag"* (ed. by I. Meier and K. Siehr) (1995), 429.

[36] See *Dicey & Morris*, Rule 173, 1222.

[37] *Ibid.*

standard terms had contained no choice of law clause. In this case, there is only one law which could govern the contract by way of party choice, namely the buyer's clause whereby arbitration was to "be held in the U.K. and conducted in accordance with U.K. law". We take it from the judgment that, under English substantive law, this amounts to an effective choice of English law. It is then up to Article 3(1) of the Rome Convention (and not quite without doubt) whether a provision whereby *proceedings* were to be *conducted* in accordance with *U.K. law* should be interpreted as an express or reasonably certain choice whereby *English substantive law* should govern the contract.

But what if both standard forms seek to choose their own substantive law, as happened in *O.T.M.* v. *Hydranautics*, but also in one Austrian[38] and one German case?[39] The Austrian Supreme Court overlooked the conflicts issue and decided this "battle" between standard choice of law clauses on purely contractual arguments by applying the "knock out" rule, which—certainly not by coincidence—is the solution adopted by Austrian substantive law. No harm was done in this case, as the alternatively chosen German law follows the same approach, so that in this case the result—neither choice of law clause being effective—must be right. In the German case—decided at the lowest (i.e., Amtsgericht) level—both Italian and German law lead to the application of the Vienna Sales law, which, however, left to domestic law one of the contested issues, namely the level of interest to be paid on outstanding money. As the Vienna Convention was applicable regardless of any choice of law, it was C.I.S.G., Article 19 which had to sort out the "battle" between two diverging choice of law clauses. The Court held that parties had agreed that the contract was "on", that they had thus derogated from C.I.S.G., Article 19 via C.I.S.G., Article 6(1) and that conflicting standard terms had thus not become part of the contract. To cut a long story short, there was no party choice, and German conflicts law invoked Italian law to determine the rate of interest payable.

O.T.M. v. *Hydranautics* is the most complicated amongst these "battle of choice of law terms" cases. For, whatever interpretation is given to the Californian version of U.C.C., section 2-207, it will not invoke the "last shot" rule. It might either uphold the "first shot" choice of law under its subsections (1) and (2), or knock out both choice of law clauses under subsection (3). Thus, there would be either a valid choice of Californian law, or no choice of law at all under Californian "battle of the forms" rules. English law, on the other hand, would of course uphold the choice made in the "last shot".

It is only by a combination of extraordinary circumstances, possibly poor pleading, but most certainly great argumentative skill that, in *O.T.M.* v. *Hydranautics*, Parker, J. could avoid the most difficult question whether

---

[38] OGH 7.6.1990, IPRax 1991, 419 (Austrian and German choice of law clauses).
[39] AG Kehl 6.10.1995, NJW-RR 1996, 565 (Italian and German choice of law clauses).

Californian, English, or a combination of both rules should decide the "battle of standard choice of law terms". In this case, the U.K. buyer had answered the Californian seller's offer by instructing them to go ahead with the production while they were preparing a formal purchase order "subject to our usual terms and conditions". Although the seller apparently did go ahead as requested, Parker, J. held that this was no acceptance under either English or Californian law.[40] Shortly afterwards, the buyer sent the purchase order with the aforementioned arbitration clause and its reference to "U.K. law". The sellers, after expressing their amazement that they were now facing "*ex post facto* contract terms", negotiated on a number of new items in the purchase order, but not the arbitration clause. Finally, the last of these items was resolved between the parties, and the buyer wrote to the seller asking whether they wished to receive a new purchase order to reflect the negotiations. Parker, J. held that the contract was concluded at that time, and that it included the buyer's arbitration clause under both English and Californian law.[41]

The seller replied to this communication two months later by a "conditional order acceptance", declined to have a fresh purchase order issued, referred to the number and the goods description of its first offer, and, in a standard clause, made its acceptance conditional to the same as the original conditions (i.e., including the Californian choice of law and arbitration clause). Shortly later, the buyer signed a copy of this letter and sent it back to the seller. Parker, J. held that, under English law:[42]

> "[t]here was nothing left to accept. The contract was made and the document was not, and was not intended to be anything more than a mere formality. The reference to the original offer was for identification only as in *Butler Machine Tool* ..."

As to whether this written agreement was significant under Californian law, Parker, J. held:[43]

> "No special provision of Californian law is relied on here, and I reject the suggestion for the same reasons as I reject it in English law."

We therefore end up with the extraordinary case of a written agreement, signed by both parties, including standard terms, being superseded by different standard terms which were never expressly agreed, let alone signed. Given standard commercial practice, I would also be greatly surprised if the buyer's first purchase order had not contained a clause according to which any deviations negotiated between the parties were ineffective unless confirmed in an amended purchase order. At any rate, the position adopted in the judgment relieved Parker, J. from answering what may be the most difficult question,

---

[40] *O.T.M. Ltd.* v. *Hydranautics* [1981] 2 Lloyd's Rep. 211, 214 and 216 respectively.
[41] *Ibid.*
[42] *Ibid.*, 215.
[43] *Ibid.*, 216–217.

namely which law is to decide an unresolved "battle" between two different standard choice of law clauses.

Of course, Parker, J. must be applauded for naming the conflicts issue and for examining the case under both English and Californian law. But what if both laws do disagree, as is very likely in a conflict between U.C.C., section 2-207 and the English "last shot" rule? Invoking the *lex fori* is no longer an option under Articles 3 and 8 of the Rome Convention. There is, in my view, only one solution. Under Article 8, the purportedly chosen law must decide for each choice of law clause whether it has emerged victorious in a "battle of the forms". If neither one of the two clauses passes this test, the normal conflicts rules in Article 4 apply. If both clauses are effective according to their own substantive law, Article 3(1) would, in my view, rule both of them out, as two different choices of law within the same contract cannot be considered "expressed" or "certain". If only one choice of law clause is upheld by its own law, it will still have to pass the hurdle of Article 3(1), as would any other choice of law clause. It has been suggested above that a clause which calls for arbitration in the U.K. to be *conducted* in accordance with U.K. laws, as in *O.T.M.* v. *Hydranautics*, might not pass this second hurdle of an express choice of English substantive law. It can equally be doubted whether a reference in one of two conflicting sets of standard terms, even if it emerges victorious under English "battle of the form" rules, can be considered a "reasonably certain" choice of law for the purposes of the Rome Convention, Article 3(1). The additional requirements which Article 3(1) of the Rome Convention places on a choice of law clause in order to be effective are not easily met in a "battle of the forms". Much will depend on the individual circumstances of the case, though. If in *O.T.M.* v. *Hydranautics*, the court had upheld the Californian choice of law clause by the virtue of the buyer's signature on the seller's document, this would, in my view, have been sufficient as an expressed choice of law for the purpose of the Rome Convention, Article 3(1).

b. Choice of jurisdiction

Choice of jurisdiction issues arise within a "battle of the forms" if these contain one or several clauses which seek to regulate which instance is to settle disputes arising from the contract, be it by choosing a particular local court within a given domestic system, the courts of a particular legal system in an international case, or arbitration proceedings. We may again have two different sets of rules which compete when determining whether or not a choice attempted in conflicting standard forms will be effective, namely (1) the substantive contract rules which apply to the agreement according to the conflict rules of the forum, and (2) particular requirements by the forum law which must be satisfied in order for the forum's jurisdiction to be either derogated or prorogated. As will be shown below, each forum may also have to consider the particular requirements which the potential other forum establishes for an effective choice of jurisdiction.

Even more than for choice of law, the trend appears to be that requirements for an effective choice of jurisdiction are stricter than requirements for the stipulation of a substantive contractual clause. For one, the Brussels Convention (Articles 16, 12 and 15) generally prohibits choice of jurisdiction in a variety of situations. More importantly, Article 17 of the Brussels Convention (which, however, does not apply to arbitration proceedings) provides that a choice must be made in writing, or be confirmed in writing after an oral agreement, or correspond with a form requirement established by custom between the parties, or by an international trade usage. Although in particular the addition of the last option in the 1989 revision has considerably facilitated a choice of jurisdiction in international trade, the Brussels Convention, Article 17 nevertheless adds a form requirement which not every standard terms clause which should apply under the applicable contract law rules will necessarily meet.[44]

For the first option of a written agreement, the E.C.J. requires that both parties have actually signed a contract which contains the jurisdiction clause or makes an express reference to those standard terms which contain the clause.[45] Again, the Californian jurisdiction clause in *O.T.M.* v. *Hydranautics* would have passed this test, but this is exceptional. Most "battle of the form" jurisdiction clauses will fall at this hurdle.

The second option requires that an oral agreement was reached which includes the jurisdiction clause, and that this agreement was then confirmed by one of the parties in writing, without the other party having raised an objection.[46] If, on the other hand, parties have agreed orally on a contract, and it is only the written confirmation which introduces the jurisdiction clause, this is not good enough for Article 17.[47] So jurisdiction under this option is very unlikely to give rise to a "battle of the forms" case.

Under the third option, if parties have established between themselves a custom concerning the form of a jurisdiction agreement, observation of that form is sufficient. This could apply in a "battle of the forms" case if parties already have an established business relationship, although one wonders how

---

[44] See also T. Rauscher, "Gerichtsstandsbeeinflussende AGB im Geltungsbereich des EuGVÜ", *Zeitschrift für Zivilprozeßrecht* (1991), 271.

[45] *Estasis Salotti* v. *Rüwa Polstereimaschinen* (Case C–24/76), [1976] E.C.R. 1831.

[46] *F. Berghoefer GmbH & Co. K.G.* v. *A.S.A. S.A.* (Case C–221/84), [1985] E.C.R. 2699, 16.

[47] *Galeries Segoura S.P.R.L.* v. *Société Rahim Bonakdarian* (Case C–25/76), [1976] E.C.R. 1851; BGH 9.3.1994, NJW 1994, 2699. Similar: Cass. 13.1.1978, *Giustizia Civile* (1978) 1506.

likely it is that they will then enter into a "battle of the forms" on jurisdiction clauses.[48]

The fourth option may be the most promising for establishing jurisdiction in a "battle of the forms" situation. It is sufficient if parties observe a form which is established by international trade practice. This option relates to form requirements, such as an international trade usage to acknowledge oral agreements, or written clauses not signed by the other party, etc.[49] Furthermore, the E.C.J. has recently held that, where particular jurisdiction clauses constitute an international trade usage, consent on such a jurisdiction agreement is presumed if both parties were, or ought to have been, aware of this practice.[50] This would imply that a choice of jurisdiction clause could survive a "battle of the forms" if it corresponded in substance and form to an international trade practice. But the Court held in the same judgment that, in these circumstances, silence or payment of bills could be construed as consent to a standard jurisdiction clause. In a "battle of the forms" situation, however, there will always be some form of objection, be it specific (by a divergent jurisdiction clause) or general. So even this most promising amongst the four options presents an uphill struggle for anyone wishing to rely on a jurisdiction clause in a "battle of the forms".

Many choice of jurisdiction rules outside the Brussels Convention will likewise place requirements of written form (e.g., the Arbitration Act 1996, section 5), or of actual consent, or certain prohibitions on choice of jurisdiction (including arbitration) agreements. Again, some of the stricter requirements will rarely be met in a "battle of the forms" situation.[51] This can frequently lead to the situation where a clause which stipulates e.g. English law and English jurisdiction might pass the hurdles of being "expressed" under the Rome

---

[48] Nevertheless, this amended version of Article 17 could have made a difference in OLG München 28.9.1989, IPRax 1991, 46 (decided under the previous version). In this German-Canadian case, more than a hundred individual contracts had previously been concluded on the seller's terms, which included a German jurisdiction clause; in the case in question, however, the form had not been signed by the buyer and thus failed the writing requirement. See R. Geimer, "Ungeschriebene Anwendungsgrenzen des EuGVÜ: Müssen Berührungspunkte zu mehreren Vertragsstaaten bestehen?", IPRrax 1991, 31. However, this is again not a "battle of the forms" case. Additionally, it can be doubted whether there was the consent which is required under Article 17.

[49] An international trade practice concerning the "battle of the forms" itself is therefore not required. If there is any such practice (which presently can be doubted), it would, in the light of what has been said above, most likely be the "knock out" approach.

[50] *Mainschiffahrts-Genossenschaft* v. *Les Gravières Rhénanes S.A.R.L.* (Case C–106/95) [1997] I E.C.R. 932, at para. 19.

[51] For example, Article II (2) of the New York Convention on the Recognition and Enforcement of Arbitral Awards 1958 requires the arbitration agreement to be either signed by both parties, or to be contained in written communications exchanged by both parties. Again, though, the Californian arbitration clause in *O.T.M. Ltd.* v. *Hydranautics* [1981] 2 Lloyd's Rep. 211 would have met this requirement. *In re Marlene Industries*

Convention, Article 3(1) and being the "last shot" under English law, but be invalid for lack of form as far as choice of jurisdiction is concerned. The unwanted consequence of such discrepancies may well be that the competent court will have to apply a foreign rather than its own substantive law.

Rather than combining general contract law and particular choice of jurisdiction requirements, one could instead leave the existence and validity of a choice of jurisdiction clause entirely to the procedural law of the forum. Some have argued that the Brussels Convention, Article 17 has this effect of superseding contractual rules for choice of jurisdiction clauses.[52] There is, however, one E.C.J. judgment which is difficult to reconcile with this view.[53] Furthermore, one can doubt the wisdom of such a rule, as this will increase the likelihood that only one half of a joint choice of law and jurisdiction clause is valid. For the main difference which this approach would make in practice is that a choice of jurisdiction clause, which would fail on contractual grounds, can nevertheless be effective under procedural rules. For example, in an English-German "battle of the forms", an English choice of law clause might fail under English law because it was not the "last shot". However, the corresponding choice of English jurisdiction could, in principle, succeed on the ground that it conformed with an international trade usage. Rather than having an English court hear an English law case on the offeror's terms, or a German court a German law case under the offeree's terms, we might end up with a German court hearing a case governed by English law, which, it is normally fair to assume, neither one of the parties will initially have wanted.[54] This somewhat unfortunate result is likely to occur whenever the rules for the validity of standard choice of law clauses differ from the rules for the validity of

---

Corp. and Carnac Textiles Inc. (1978) 380 N.E.2d 239, involved two sets of standard terms, one containing an arbitration clause, the other a general rejection clause. The court (at 242) held that the arbitration clause "must be clear and direct, and must not depend upon implication ...", and failed on this ground, but also on the "first shot" approach effectively favoured by U.C.C., s. 2-207(2).

[52] E.g. by H. Schack, *Internationales Zivilverfahrensrecht*, 2nd edn., para. 472. See also Rauscher (*supra*, n. 44), 278–282 and 296–299.

[53] *Iveco Fiat SpA* v. *Van Hool N.V. (Case C–313/85)* [1986] E.C.R. 3337, at para. 7. This case concerned the validity of an orally agreed extension of a written jurisdiction clause with a time limitation. The E.C.J. left it to the applicable domestic law to decide whether such an extension could be agreed orally; if that was the case, the extension was also valid for the purpose of Article 17.

[54] But see OLG Frankfurt 17.10.1995, IPRax 1998, 35, where one party's terms combined a German choice of law with a Turkish choice of jurisdiction clause (although the latter was held not to be intended as exclusive).

jurisdiction clauses,[55] but leads to particularly confusing situations in a "battle of the forms".

Such an outcome is inconvenient, because it is likely to lead to unnecessary costs, delay and complications. Other results of a "battle of standard jurisdiction clauses" may be more serious. The different rules which are applied for solving the "battle" may lead to different courts or tribunals competing for jurisdiction, or even to the situation where no court or tribunal is willing to hear the case.

Again, *O.T.M.* v. *Hydranautics* is a case in point. The plaintiff (buyer), on 29th July 1980, sued the defendant (seller) at the High Court for damages.[56] (This court should, incidentally, have been incompetent under either one of the party's standard terms, as the buyer's terms had sought to stipulate arbitration in the U.K. However, this defence was not raised.[57]) The writ was served on the defendant on 30th July. On 7th August, the defendant commenced proceedings in the Superior Court of California, requesting this court to order the plaintiff to arbitrate their claim in California. Proceedings in California were contested by the plaintiff and, after a temporary injunction against the plaintiff was first issued and then dissolved, the Superior Court of California, on 7th November, concluded its judgment with a request to the English High Court that it should stay further proceedings in this action. The plaintiff, however, entered judgment in default in England on 11th November without notice to the defendant's solicitors, and without informing the High Court of the request by the Californian court. At the end of the day, Parker, J. did not adhere to the Californian request, on the ground that "it had been overtaken by events" due to the fact that the defendant was forced to admit that any decision by the High Court on the effectiveness of the Californian arbitration clause would have to be final.[58] This somewhat unsavoury race between two jurisdictions as to who is first to sue, to serve, to obtain an injunction, a judgment on jurisdiction and finally on the merits of a case is an unfortunate consequence of different standards being applied on the question of the "battle of the forms".

But the reverse case can happen just as easily, i.e. that a choice of jurisdiction clause contained in one standard form threatens to leave a case without a court or tribunal to hear it. No actual case of such a "battle" involving two divergent choice of jurisdiction clauses is known to me. However, there are some cases involving the disputed incorporation of a jurisdiction clause by reference to one set of standard terms where the threat of a case without court to hear it was either raised or imminent.

A recent German-Dutch case decided by the *Oberlandesgericht* Celle

---

[55] BGH 9.3.1994, NJW 1994, 2699: standard terms used by one party, choice of German law valid, choice of German jurisdiction not valid for failure to meet form requirements of Article 17.

[56] *O.T.M. Ltd.* v. *Hydranautics* [1981] 2 Lloyd's Rep. 211, 213.

[57] *Ibid.*, 214.

[58] *Ibid.*, 214.

concerned a bill of lading which contained standard terms on the reverse, including a clause worded: "To be used with Charter-Party". The charterparty, a copy of which was not attached to the bill of lading, contained a Dutch choice of law and jurisdiction clause. The court, without further ado (but wrongly, as I respectfully submit) applied German law to the question whether the Dutch jurisdiction clause had thus become part of the contract, and held that this choice of Dutch jurisdiction met both German substantive contract law and the Brussels Convention, Article 17 form requirements, the latter on the ground that such a clause conformed with international trade practice.[59] More importantly, when the plaintiff raised the possibility that the Dutch courts might equally decline jurisdiction, the court not only failed to examine whether the same clause was valid under Dutch substantive law, but also held—rather daringly, I suggest—that Dutch courts were bound by its decision and were, under the Brussels Convention, Article 17, not entitled to re-examine their own jurisdiction![60] There is a somewhat more complicated English-German case involving a charterparty where the *Landgericht* Düsseldorf declined its jurisdiction in favour of an allegedly stipulated London tribunal, and where that tribunal subsequently also held that it could not hear the case. At the time of the second decision, the case was still on appeal in Germany. The *Oberlandesgericht* Düsseldorf then held that, regardless of whether or not the arbitration clause should cover the litigation according to the applicable English law, the bottom line was that this case would either be heard by the German courts or not at all, so that, whatever the right interpretation of the clause, German courts must be competent to hear the case.[61] But such happy endings cannot be guaranteed. Therefore, in any case involving conflicting or doubtful choices of jurisdiction, a certain amount of investigation into the potential other forum's jurisdiction rules may be required, and perhaps even some form of co-ordination appropriate, as attempted (although with limited success) by the Superior Court of California in *O.T.M* v. *Hydranautics*.

c. Choice of place of performance

Standard clauses which stipulate the place of performance gain particular importance if there is no or no effective choice of either law or jurisdiction. "Battle of the forms" cases where diverging choice of place of performance

---

[59] OLG Celle 1.11.1995, IPRax 1997, 417; see H. Koch, "AGB-Klauseln über Gerichtsstand und Erfüllungsort im europäischen Zivilrechtsverkehr: Größere Gerechtigkeit ohne Parteivereinbarung?", IPRax 1997, 405–407.

[60] OLG Celle 1.11.1995, IPRax 1997, 417, at 418, *verbatim:* "Eine erneute Zuständigkeitsprüfung nach niederländischem Recht ist nicht zulässig."

[61] OLG Düsseldorf 17.11.1995, IPRspr. 1995 Nr. 189 S. 384 = RIW 1996, 239. That "London tribunal" is not further specified in the judgment.

clauses each sought to establish jurisdiction have a long tradition.[62] Nowadays, the same question arises under the Brussels Convention, Article 5(1). Although this is not an exclusive jurisdiction, Article 5(1) nevertheless allows one party to sue the other at the contractually stipulated place of performance. This allows a non-exclusive choice of jurisdiction which, according to the E.C.J., is not subject to the requirements for a choice of jurisdiction in Article 17.[63] This implies that if the applicable substantive law under Articles 3, 4 of the Rome Convention provides that a standard choice of place of performance emerges victorious in a "battle of the forms", this will establish jurisdiction at this place under Article 5(1) Brussels Convention. We can therefore have "last shot" jurisdiction under e.g. English law, or "first shot" jurisdiction under e.g. Dutch law. However, a recent E.C.J. judgment places some limitations on this indirect choice of jurisdiction. If a place of performance is stipulated at which the obligations arising under the contract cannot be actually performed, and with the sole aim of giving jurisdiction, then such a clause must meet the requirements of Article 17.[64] However, such a restriction will only affect contracts where performance is clearly limited to one certain place or region. Most contracts contain an element of performance at more than one place, in particular where goods are sold and transported.

The effect of a chosen place of performance on the applicable law is far less straightforward. Within the Rome Convention, the chosen place of performance can only become relevant as one factor in determining whether a contract is more closely connected to the place of the one or of the other party under Article 4(1) or (5) of the Rome Convention. In particular, this may concern cases where there is no "characteristic performance" under subsections (2) and (5), or where the place of performance is to be used as an indicator that the contract is not most closely connected to the place of the party whose performance is characteristic. However, it does take a particular applicable law in order to find out whether parties have agreed on a place of performance. If the choice of place of performance clause is part of a "battle of the forms", we seem to end up with the legal equivalent of Catch 22: without applicable law, we do

---

[62] The earliest case known to me is OLG Dresden 15.2.1918, Seuff. Archiv 73 Nr. 174 (283). In this peculiar case, two "last shots" were exchanged simultaneously, and the court upheld the choice contained in the terms which the seller had last insisted on before the final, simultaneous exchange of communications. Nowadays, German courts would "knock out" both choice of place of performance clauses.

[63] *Zelger* v. *Salinitri* (Case C-56/79), [1980] E.C.R. 89; BGH 28.3.1996, IPRax 1997, 416, 417 (English-French-German case concerning standard forms in auction catalogues).

[64] *Mainschiffahrts-Genossenschaft* v. *Les Gravières Rhénanes* (Case C–106/95), [1997] I E.C.R. 932. The contract was for the charter of a vessel to be used for the transport of gravel on the Rhine, predominantly between French ports, but which stipulated Würzburg (which is situated on the Main rather than on the Rhine) as the place of performance.

not know whether there is a choice of place of performance, but without knowing whether a place of performance has been chosen we may not know the applicable law. Perhaps one can distinguish as follows.

If both legal systems involved apply the same rule for the "battle of the forms", we should know whether the choice of place of performance is valid, regardless of the applicable law. If it is valid, it may tilt the balance under Article 4(1) or (5); if not, it is irrelevant. On the other hand, if e.g. Dutch law would uphold the Dutch offeror's choice of performance clause as the "first shot", but English law the English offeree's choice of performance clause as the "last shot", these clauses must be entirely irrelevant for determining the applicable law under the Rome Convention, Article 4. There remains the situation where one of the potentially applicable laws would uphold the choice of place of performance: e.g., as the "last shot" under English law, but not the other (e.g., under German "knock out" rules). This might be seen as a slight advantage for the law under which the choice of performance clause is valid, but in my view it would have to be a very rare case indeed where this should be able to tilt the balance between these two laws.

CONCLUSIONS

As concerns the relationship between substantive law and conflicts law aspects of the "battle of the forms", the following observations can be made in conclusion.

First, a strict application of the "mirror image" rule to offers and acceptances which refer to conflicting standard terms seems commercially inappropriate and overly conceptual as a matter of legal doctrine. Ultimately, it must be up to the parties to agree that there is a contract, even if they have not sorted out which of their conflicting standard terms should prevail.

Second, thus discarding the "no contract" approach to the "battle of the forms", one can analyse as follows the effects which the three other principal approaches exert on conflicts of law issues. Both the "first shot" and the "last shot" approach favour a choice of law and of jurisdiction (be it directly, or via a chosen place of performance), whereas the "knock out" approach makes it unlikely that there will be a choice of either law or jurisdiction in an international "battle of the forms". Some might wish to argue that this marks a weakness of the "knock out" approach, as, at the turn of the millennia, the view prevails firmly that it is best left to the parties to agree which law should govern their contract. However, the "knock out" rule does in no way prevent parties from agreeing on applicable law and jurisdiction. It only prevents the construction of a choice where parties have in fact failed to agree. So there seems to be little force behind this argument.

On the other hand, the approach which is chosen does make a considerable difference as concerns the different implications for choice of law and choice of jurisdiction in particular. As shown above, different standards applied to these two issues make it likely that only one half of a joint choice of law and jurisdiction clause is valid, which will often imply that the case will be tried by a court which has to apply a foreign rather than its own substantive law. Under both the "first shot" and the "last shot" rules, this likelihood is far greater than under the "knock out" approach. For under both the "first shot" and "last shot" approach, a choice of law will succeed without any actual agreement being reached between the parties either orally or in writing. If the same victorious standard form contains a choice of jurisdiction, this is unlikely to pass the additional form or other requirements established by rules such as the Brussels Convention, Article 17. On the other hand, under the "knock out" rule, a choice of law will only be upheld if parties have actually agreed to it. An agreement on jurisdiction—be it signed by both parties, or orally agreed and repeated in writing in one set of standard forms—will also normally pass the test of Article 17. On an overall appreciation, the "knock out" rule is most likely to achieve consistent results for standard contract terms, be they simple contract law clauses, choice of place of performance, of law, or of jurisdiction clauses.

Third, as discussed, a "battle of the form" can lead to a choice of jurisdiction being effective in one forum but not in another, or even to two different choices of jurisdiction which are each effective in one forum but not the other. There is the danger of jurisdictions competing for the same case, or even of both jurisdictions declining their competence. It is mostly the fact that the two legal systems involved follow a different approach towards the "battle of the forms" which is to blame for these discrepancies, rather than any individual approach in itself. However, it is nevertheless fair to point out that one of these problems, namely that each forum upholds its own choice of jurisdiction, is unlikely if at least one of them follows the "knock out" approach. More generally, these problems can only occur if a questionable choice of jurisdiction is upheld by one forum. The "knock out" rule generally weeds out questionable choices, whereas both the "first shot" and the "last shot" approach tend to uphold questionable choices of jurisdiction. On overall, from a conflicts view, the "knock out" rule appears to be the preferable approach towards the "battle of the forms".

Chapter 12

Anti-Suit Injunctions in a Complex World

Adrian Briggs

Everyone will know that the conflict of laws, as practised and as taught, has ceased to be recognisable as the subject it was thirty years ago. Even if choice of law is not quite dormant,[1] from a reading of the law reports, international civil litigation seems only infrequently to reach the point where issues of choice of law arise for final decision. It is rules of jurisdiction and of international civil procedure which now dominate the thinking of scholars and the daily practice of the courts. And within this *terra nova*, one of the most vibrant developments has been the use of the final[2] injunction to restrain proceedings pending or threatened in a foreign court. Had English judicial jurisdiction remained a thing of the common law it would have been hard enough for the theory to keep up with the practice. But the arrival of the remedy when the jurisdictional landscape was itself in a period of radical change has made it much harder still. This paper has as its modest aim a general stocktaking, and an attempt to see whether some of the contradictions in the jurisprudence may yield to some gentle reinterpretation. No apology is made for the fact that the impact of the Brussels and Lugano Conventions requires them to take up the lion's share of the space.

An anti-suit injunction is an order addressed to a party ("the respondent"), who will usually also have the character of plaintiff in proceedings in a foreign court. It requires him to discontinue, or not to bring, an action in a foreign court. Obviously he must be or be made subject to the personal jurisdiction of the English court in the first place by being served with process in the injunction

---

[1] Most of the novelty has come in the form of legislative amendment to the law, and not from seminal cases on difficult points.

[2] Such injunctions are also sought and granted in interlocutory form. The special characteristics of this remedy are not the direct concern of this paper, though for the cases which suggest that they are not like other interlocutory injunctions, see *Apple Corps Ltd.* v. *Apple Computer Inc.* [1992] R.P.C. 70; *C.S.R. Ltd.* v. *Cigna Insurance Australia Ltd.* (1997) 189 C.L.R. 345, 395–397.

application, but this may be accomplished by service as of right or by permission of the court,[3] as the need may be. The terminology of "anti-suit injunction" is today used without the raising of eyebrows which once accompanied it: it has been adopted by the House of Lords and by the High Court of Australia and, hallowed by such authority, it will be used here. Less common, but still not rare, is the anti-anti-suit injunction: an order by a court ordering a party subject to *its* personal jurisdiction not to seek an anti-suit injunction from another court; and rare but not unknown is the anti-anti-anti-suit injunction.[4] As a matter of logic, at least, there is no end to it. The speed with which this potent remedy has come to dominate the early jurisdictional skirmishing has undoubtedly been one reason for the unsettling inconsistencies which pervade the jurisprudence. One might have expected that in this area the highest courts in the common law world might have helped to generate a coherent body of principle, not least because there appears to be no common law jurisdiction which has repudiated the anti-suit injunction. But English equity now has to co-exist with the Brussels and Lugano Conventions, and the direct and indirect obligations of these international agreements have trimmed (or should trim) the autonomy of equity in this area. Canadian equity appears to have become submerged in an evolving and embracing theory of jurisdiction and judgment recognition which starts from the peculiar circumstances of Canadian constitutional reality[5]. And Australian equity has chosen to develop by incorporating a striking reluctance to take any step which might be construed as criticism, always invidious, of a foreign law or foreign courts.[6] Given these

---

[3] R.S.C. Order 11, rule 1, as amended by C.P.R. Sched. 1. But there is no head of rule 1(1) which is dedicated to applications for an anti-suit injunction. It is arguable that an interlocutory anti-suit injunction may be applied for by service with permission under R.S.C. Order 11, rule 8A, for it is in some sense at least a form of interim relief.

[4] Such were obtained as part of the pre-history in *Shell (U.K.) Exploration and Production Ltd.* v. *Innes* 1995 S.L.T. 807.

[5] Originating in *Morguard Investments Ltd.* v. *de Savoye* [1990] 3 S.C.R. 1077 (a case on enforcement of judgments) and extended in *Tolofson* v. *Jensen* [1994] 3 S.C.R. 1022 (a case on choice of law in tort) the Supreme Court has begun to develop a restatement of the conflict of laws in which consideration of the appropriateness of a forum plays an increasing part. In the cases mentioned the Supreme Court was dealing with issues arising between Canadian provinces; it remains to be seen whether any modification will be made if these cases are sought to be applied to properly-foreign cases. In this respect, however, the Supreme Court may have to adjudicate disputes which appear as if arranged in concentric circles. In the light of the legal area created for the United Kingdom by the increasing number of European Conventions in this field, it is possible that the English courts will increasingly find that they have to develop a distinction between intra-European and "outer world" issues. An aspect of this possibility is examined in this chapter.

[6] Building on a tendency first observed in *Att.-Gen. (U.K.)* v. *Heinemann Publishers Australia Pty Ltd.* (1988) 165 C.L.R. 30.

political and legal facts, it may even be unhelpful to speak of the common law world as if it constituted a homogenous whole in this area of judicial activity. The result is that the complaint made some years ago, that the theoretical foundations of this remedy have not been properly appreciated,[7] is no longer true; but the attempt to get to grips with it has laid bare much more contradiction than consistency as between the streams of authority.

These contradictions should not be under-estimated. Though they do overlap, some of them can be enumerated. First, there are cases which hold that an injunction should not be sought until an application has first been made to the foreign court, but others which observe that this is the very antithesis of what comity requires. Secondly, there are cases which hold that, where the injunction is applied for by pointing to the jurisdictional rules of an international convention, the grant of an injunction is almost a matter of course, but others which observe that, as the foreign court will itself apply the same jurisdictional rules as the English court, there is no need for the English court to interfere. Thirdly, there are cases in which a choice of court agreement has been treated as entitling the applicant to relief, but others in which an injunction was not seen as the automatic reaction to its breach.[8] Fourthly, there are cases which show special benevolence to a respondent who argues that he can bring his claim only in the foreign court, but others in which such partiality is regarded as irrelevant, and still others where the fact that the relief can be obtained only from the foreign court is regarded as evidence of vexation. And, fifthly, where the language of the law speaks of a right not to be sued, there are cases in which these rights are defined by recourse to rules of choice of law, but others where no notice appears to be taken of such concerns.

Given such difficulties it is tempting to confess defeat and believe that particular judicial instinct, more than legal reasoning, will dominate the result in any individual case. It may be that the early development of the *Mareva* injunction[9] ran along similar lines. Certainly the lack of proper theoretical support for that novel remedy has been to both the despair of Meagher Gummow and Lehane[10] and the puzzlement of Lord Mustill.[11] It is therefore timely to ask whether there is an underlying order to the law on anti-suit injunctions, to examine the way the remedy has developed in England and in certain other common law jurisdictions, and to ask whether English, Canadian

---

[7] *National Mutual Holdings Pty Ltd.* v. *Sentry Corporation* (1989) 87 A.L.R. 539, (Aust. Fed. Ct.), 563, *per* Gummow, J.

[8] Questions of whether such clauses should be construed widely (as in English law) or more restrictively (as in the case of Article 17 of the Conventions) will also arise, but are not pursued here.

[9] Forerunner of today's freezing injunction: C.P.R. Part 25.

[10] *Equity Doctrines and Remedies*, 3rd edn. (1992), 607–608.

[11] *Mercedes Benz A.G.* v. *Leiduck* [1996] 1 A.C. 284, 299–301.

and Australian equities have reached the optimal solution to the issues which arise or ought to arise. Developments in the United States, by contrast, lie outside the scope of the analysis, mainly because the lush greenery of the American legal landscape does not transplant easily, and would tend to swamp any account of the law as found in the more closely related systems of common law.

A GEOGRAPHICAL SURVEY

It is well known that the modern form of the anti-suit injunction has been accepted into the laws of England, Australia, and Canada, and the leading authorities from these jurisdictions will be examined below. It has also been accepted in Scotland,[12] India,[13] Singapore,[14] and Brunei.[15] More to the point, it has not been rejected by any jurisdiction in the common law world. In these three major jurisdictions three broad approaches have emerged. In England and Scotland, *S.N.I. Aérospatiale* v. *Lee Kui Jak*[16] and *Airbus Industrie G.I.E.* v. *Patel*[17] establish that an injunction may not generally be ordered unless England is the natural forum for the litigation. But once that is shown, if the foreign action is oppressive or vexatious, or is otherwise unconscionable, it may be restrained. Predominant, though increasingly reinterpreted,[18] Court of Appeal authority holds that, if there is a choice of court agreement for England, an injunction lies more or less as of right; and there is authority for the view that (sometimes at least) relief must be sought from the foreign court itself. It is a legitimate conclusion that, once the English court is shown to be the natural forum for the dispute, the focus of the enquiry is into the wrongful quality of the respondent's conduct.

In Canada the law has a different initial focus and a different structure. Though in *Amchem Products Ltd.* v. *British Columbia (Workers' Compen-*

---

[12] *Pan American World Airways Inc.* v. *Andrews* 1992 S.L.T. 268 (O.H.); *F.M.C. Corp.* v. *Russell* 1999 S.L.T. 99 (O.H.).

[13] The proceedings in England in *Airbus Industrie G.I.E.* v. *Patel* [1999] 1 A.C. 119 had been preceded by the granting of a final anti-suit injunction by the court at Bangalore.

[14] *Koh Kay Yew* v. *Inn Pacific Holdings Ltd.* [1997] 3 S.L.R. 121 (Sing. C.A.).

[15] *S.N.I. Aérospatiale* v. *Lee Kui Jak* [1987] A.C. 871, which was decided by the Privy Council on appeal from the courts of Brunei.

[16] [1987] A.C. 871 (P.C., on appeal from the courts of Brunei). The Board observed that the relevant laws of England and Brunei were identical.

[17] [1999] 1 A.C. 119.

[18] For a good example of a revisionist reading, see *Credit Suisse First Boston (Europe) Ltd.* v. *M.L.C. (Bermuda) Ltd.* [1999] 1 Lloyd's Rep. 767.

sation Board)[19] the Supreme Court indicated its general agreement with *Aérospatiale*, it took the view that the analysis began with examination of the jurisdiction of the foreign court. If the foreign court had taken jurisdiction on grounds which generally accorded with those of Canadian law and with its doctrine of *forum conveniens*, no injunction would be granted; if by contrast it had asserted a jurisdiction significantly wider, it had paid no heed to comity, and could expect none in return,[20] At that point the Canadian court would be free to give effect to its doctrine of *forum conveniens* and would generally grant an injunction if the natural forum had been and still was in Canada.[21] Though the existence of a legitimate advantage to the respondent from the proceedings in the foreign court might prevent an injunction, an advantage was not legitimate if it accrued only in an inappropriate court.[22] This Canadian interpretation of comity would also require that an application to have the proceedings dismissed or stayed be first made to the foreign court.[23] On a fair reading, the focus of the enquiry is on the jurisdictional rules of the foreign court and their compatibility with the corresponding rules of Canadian law, and only after that on the wrongful behaviour of the respondent.

In Australia, the High Court in *C.S.R.* v. *Cigna Insurance Australia Ltd.*[24] has re-stated Australian equity in terms which are more mechanical and much less receptive to the making of judgments in relation to foreign proceedings. If the relief sought from the foreign court cannot be obtained in its entirety from the Australian court, the foreign action, at least if commenced first, will not be seen as oppressive or vexatious and may not be restrained,[25] and the question whether application first be made to the foreign court is irrelevant.[26] By way of possible[27] exception, if the foreign action was brought after the Australian action and in order to frustrate it, it may be that this is vexatious, and justifies an injunction no matter the availability of distinct relief. It appears that the High Court considered it to be invidious for an Australian court to be asked to pass

---

[19] [1993] 1 S.C.R. 897 (Can. S.C.).

[20] *Ibid.*, 934. Sopinka, J. spoke in general terms of its judgment not being entitled to be recognised. It is not clear whether he was referring to recognition as *res judicata*, or to some more unspecific form of taking notice of the judgment. But the latter would be less controversial.

[21] *Ibid.*, 931.

[22] *Ibid.*, 933.

[23] *Ibid.*, 930–931.

[24] (1997) 189 C.L.R. 345.

[25] *Ibid.*, 395.

[26] *Ibid.*, 396.

[27] Possible, because this was the basis on which the parallel action in the New South Wales courts, commenced within a few days of the American action, was stayed. It was not made clear by the High Court whether a similar view—that the institution of the second action was vexatious—would be taken if the foreign action had been commenced after the local one. And *cf. Henry* v. *Henry* (1996) 185 C.L.R. 571, 591.

any adverse judgment upon the law applied by a foreign court, whether jurisdictional or substantive; and, if an assessment of the wrongfulness of a respondent's conduct would require this to be done, then the court would refrain from making it.

It is not surprising that these leading judgments contain elements which are strikingly similar, and contain statements paying tribute to each other; but it is dangerous and misleading to conclude from this that the ingredients can be mixed and matched to produce a coherent product. Each law has developed what it regards as a complete set of rules to deal with applications for an anti-suit injunction. If each is internally coherent, there is danger in extracting parts of the judgment and transplanting them into a context for which they were not designed. As much as anything else it is the concern of this paper to mark the limits beyond which an English court should not consider itself to be free, or obliged, to make borrowings from the jurisprudence of other common law jurisdictions. With that said, it is time to examine the points of contradiction identified earlier.

MUST THE APPLICANT FIRST SEEK RELIEF FROM THE FOREIGN COURT FIRST?

There is an inveterate concern that the court which is applied to for an anti-suit injunction should pay proper regard to the principles of comity, and some cases have interpreted this as meaning that an anti-suit injunction should not be applied for before the court in which proceedings are pending has itself been applied to for relief. This has been descrived in England as the "usual" practice,[28] and may represent a near-absolute precondition to the granting of relief in Canada.[29] But other judicial voices have gone on record to say that for an English court to entertain (never mind grant) an application for relief after a foreign court has delivered its judgment makes for the very antithesis of comity;[30] and the possible policies of the law are in open conflict.

The reassertion of comity as a guide to the development of the conflict of laws has been noticeable in recent years.[31] In this context it indicates a

---

[28] *Barclays Bank Plc* v. *Homan* [1993] B.C.L.C. 680, 686–687 (Hoffmann, J.); 694, 703 (C.A.); *Deaville* v. *Aeroflot Russian International Airlines* [1997] 2 Lloyd's Rep. 67. But note that in *Homan* Glidewell, L.J. said that prior recourse to the foreign court was *prima facie* appropriate only when the proceedings were not vexatious or oppressive. But, as this is the principal ground on which any injunction will be granted if granted at all, it makes a very substantial inroad into any proposition of law that the foreign court must be applied to first.

[29] *Amchem* [1993] 1 S.C.R. 897, 930–931.

[30] *The Angelic Grace* [1995] 1 Lloyd's Rep. 87, 95 (Leggatt, L.J.).

[31] In England, most significantly in *Airbus Industrie G.I.E.* v. *Patel* [1999] 1 A.C. 119, 133–137, 138–140.

recognition that two principles may be in conflict in a particular case: that a local court which has personal jurisdiction over a defendant is entitled to exercise it, and that a foreign court before which proceedings are brought is entitled to have its adjudicatory sovereignty respected by other tribunals. Traditionally this uneasy relationship was conjured out of sight by the equitable myth that the injunction involves passing no judgment, still less making any order, against the foreign court, with the result that the injunction could be seen as having no impact on the foreign court. But, if this ever was taken seriously, recent cases have brought home the fact that, whether under the scheme of the Brussels Convention or at common law, foreign courts do not appreciate the subtlety of this distinction any more than would (one imagines) an English court.[32] Another means of respecting the rights of the other court therefore needed to be found; and one solution is, so the argument goes, to require that the application for relief first be made to the foreign court.

In principle, such a rule might have some merit. It is undeniable that it acknowledges the interest of the foreign court in the matter. Moreover, the modern concern of the common law to encourage disputes to be resolved in their most appropriate forum points directly to having the jurisdiction of the foreign court argued about before and resolved by a judge of that court. But this last point should not be taken too seriously though, for it will frequently be that the injunction applied for in an English court is not based on the same arguments as would have been made to the foreign court by way of jurisdictional challenge; and any reasoning which suggests that "this" question should first be raised before the foreign court misses the point that they will be different, and perhaps very distinct, questions and arguments which will be put to the two courts. One is not therefore in the first instance directing the argument—as opposed to directing the applicant—to the court in which it most naturally belongs. As example, consider what would happen if this were applied in relation to proceedings brought in the United States. The applicant would be required to appear before the American court to contend that it had no jurisdiction over him, or that if it did the American court was, in its eyes, *forum non conveniens* and should therefore dismiss the claim. If the relief sought is not granted, the application to the English court will seek to impugn the behaviour of the respondent in invoking the jurisdiction of the American court which, *ex hypothesi*, it has, seeking to show that it is vexatious or oppressive for him to do

---

[32] The distinction was denied by the Supreme Court of the United States in *Peck* v. *Jenness* (1849) 48 U.S. 612, 625. For a more recent American view of an English anti-suit injunction, see *Laker Airways Ltd.* v. *Pan American Airways* (1983) 559 F. Supp. 1124, 1128 (affd. (1984) 731 F.2d 909). For a German view, see *Re the Enforcement of an English anti-suit injunction* (Case 3 VA 11/95) [1997] I.L.Pr. 320 (Regional Court of Appeal, Düsseldorf). For an account of the history of the Laker litigation, see L. A. Collins, *Essays in International Litigation and the Conflict of Laws* (1994), 107–117.

so. Precisely the same English argument would be made if the application were made prior to (or in the absence of) the application to the American court. The substance of the arguments is not the same, and the one does not preclude the other.[33]

As a matter of authority, this approach has appeared most noticeably in the Canadian jurisprudence. Sopinka, J. in *Amchem* elevated it to the level of a precondition, at least in those cases where the jurisdictional rules of the foreign court appear to make it reasonable for the application to be made to it.[34] It has appeared in English decisions as well, and has been described as the "usual practice".[35] But it is submitted that it is wrong to see this as the correct interpretation of English law. The better view is that there are two ways at least, of which this is only one (and not the best one), of acknowledging the interest of the foreign court and the inappropriateness of any intervention by the English court.

In *Airbus Industrie*,[36] Lord Goff of Chieveley went out of his way to pay tribute to the work of Sopinka, J. in general, and to the general lines of his judgment in *Amchem* in particular. But he also refrained from endorsing the detail of the approach in *Amchem*.[37] This is wholly understandable, for it is submitted that Lord Goff understood the manner in which comity was to be respected in a wholly different way. The rule he laid down as a general principal was that an English court was justified in granting an injunction if England was the natural forum for the dispute[38] (or perhaps for the claim which was being brought in the foreign court): in such a case the interest of the English court in the matter was objectively superior to that of any other court, and, that being so, the grant of an injunction was a proper exercise of its jurisdiction. But if England were not the natural forum it would be inappropriate for it to act in this way;[39] and it would be nothing to the point whether an application had first been made to the foreign court.

---

[33] It is unclear whether a finding by an American court that it has jurisdiction because it finds itself to be *forum conveniens* will establish an issue estoppel in a later English application for an injunction. No case has so far held this, but the possibility has been brought closer as a result of *The Sennar (No. 2)* [1985] 1 W.L.R. 490 and *Desert Sun Loan Corp.* v. *Hill* [1996] 2 All E.R. 847.

[34] *Amchem* [1993] 1 S.C.R. 897. There can be no legitimate requirement that a forum conveniens application be made to a foreign court whose law does not admit it as a principle.

[35] See *supra*, n. 28.

[36] [1999] 1 A.C. 119, 133, 135, 139.

[37] *Ibid.*, 139F.

[38] *Ibid.*, 138H.

[39] It was not in *Airbus Industries: ibid.*, 140–141. As a result it was irrelevant to ask whether the respondent's conduct might be seen as vexatious or oppressive.

The necessary[40] reconciliation of the two statements of principle is therefore this. It is necessary to place limits upon the exercise by an English court of the jurisdiction which it has, and which reflect and respect the rights of the foreign court to form its own view of its jurisdiction, and of the propriety of its being exercised. But the practical implementation of this principle gives rise to a diversity of possibilities, and to require that recourse first be had to the foreign court, or to demand self-restraint by the English court unless it is the natural forum, are two sufficient, but distinct and not cumulative, ways of giving effect to it. It is submitted that it would therefore be a misreading of *Airbus Industrie* to see it as endorsing the view that application must first be made to the foreign court. As in English law, at least, it is necessary to show that England is the natural forum for the claim, and that it is inequitable, or vexatious or oppressive, or unconscionable, for the party suing in the foreign court to invoke its jurisdiction to allow him to do so, it is pretty obvious that this argument may not be made to the foreign court. Yet, once it is acknowledged that this represents the substance of the right to an injunction, *Amchem* would require that a separate argument must first be made to the foreign court. This is a doubtful use of time and resources, and a potential source of difficulty if it is then contended by the respondent that issue estoppel arises out of the foreign court's determination. Moreover, it makes no sense if the application to the foreign court would be doomed to fail in any event. If, to meet this last point, *Amchem* is modified so that the foreign court must be applied to unless it would not, in this sense, be useful to do so, litigation in the English court will centre upon what a foreign court might have done had these arguments been addressed to it. Whilst this would not be an impossible theoretical position to adopt, it would have all the appearances of having allowed the best to become the enemy of the good. Not only that, but as Leggatt, L.J. pointed out in *The Angelic Grace*,[41] the claims of comity are hardly met if an English court claims the right to sit on appeal from the order not made by the foreign court but to which application had first been made. And if it is sought to answer Leggatt, L.J. with the argument that the position is not so stark because the English court will be applying a different set of rules to the application made to it, this demonstrates the fallacy of the argument that "the" application could (never mind should) first be made to the foreign court.

It is for these reasons that the proposition that application first be made to the foreign court is probably unsound in principle and would be unwelcome in practice, at least as an addition to the present state of English law. Whether the

---

[40] Because Lord Goff, *ibid.*, 139H, did consider his formulation to be "consistent with the approach adopted by the Supreme Court of Canada in the *Amchem Products* case ...".

[41] [1995] 1 Lloyd's Rep. 87, 95.

analysis is any different when the context is that of jurisdiction arising or taken under the Brussels Convention will be examined next.

DO SPECIAL RULES APPLY TO INJUNCTIONS AGAINST PROCEEDINGS IN ANOTHER CONTRACTING STATE?

Perhaps the most contentious aspect of injunctions is that of the limitations placed on the power of the court by the fact that the proceedings to which the injunction refers are taking place in the courts of a contracting state to the Brussels or Lugano Conventions.[42] There have been sharply worded divergences in the Court of Appeal, and it seems difficult to reconcile the decisions, still less the general philosophy underpinning them. Some judges have expressed the view that there is no incompatibility between the granting of an injunction and the fact that the court concerned is in another contracting state, and it has even been suggested that the sooner the English court acts, the better:[43] *Continental Bank N.A.* v. *Aeakos Compania Naviera S.A.*[44] and *The Angelic Grace*[45] exemplify this approach. By contrast, others have interpreted the context of the Convention as the justification for a much greater restraint, on the principal ground that the mutual trust between courts will be impaired or contradicted by the grant of anti-suit injunctions: *Philip Alexander Securities and Futures Ltd.* v. *Bamberger*[46] and *Toepfer International GmbH* v. *Soc. Cargill France*[47] stand for this more cautious tendency. In some of the cases in which an injunction has been ordered, the basis for the relief has been a choice of court[48] agreement for the English courts which has been flouted by the respondent in his attempting to seise of a foreign court; in such cases the Court of Appeal has expressed with some vigour its view that the injunction should be granted and never mind the Convention.[49] This bullish approach has even been taken in cases involving no such jurisdiction agreement,[50] but has not quite

---

[42] A similar question arose in relation to foreign proceedings governed by the Warsaw Convention in *Deaville* v. *Aeroflot Russian International Airlines* [1997] 2 Lloyd's Rep. 67. Brice, Q.C. (sitting as a deputy judge of the High Court) refused to pre-empt the jurisdictional decision of the French court by granting an injunction.

[43] *Continental Bank N.A.* v. *Aeakos Compania Naviera S.A.* [1994] 1 W.L.R. 588; *The Angelic Grace* [1995] 1 Lloyd's Rep. 87, 95, 96–97.

[44] [1994] 1 W.L.R. 588.

[45] [1995] 1 Lloyd's Rep. 87.

[46] [1997] I.L.Pr. 73, affd. *ibid.*, 104.

[47] [1998] 1 Lloyd's Rep. 379, 386.

[48] Or arbitration agreement.

[49] See the cases in note 43, above.

[50] *Turner* v. *Grovit* [1999] 3 All E.R. 616 (C.A.), where the objection was that the Spanish court should have concluded that Article 21 of the Brussels Convention and prior English proceedings deprived it of jurisdiction.

reached the point of holding that an injunction may be awarded whenever the respondent has seised a foreign court with a case which it does not have, or should not be asked to conclude that it has, jurisdiction to hear.[51] What is one to make of this?

In *Airbus Industrie G.I.E.* v. *Patel*,[52] Lord Goff compared and contrasted the systems of jurisdictional law created by common law systems (broad jurisdictional rules, to which *forum conveniens* is an antidote) and by civilian systems (with narrower jurisdictional rules and no room for discretion, and of which family the Conventions may be seen as an intellectual part). He identified the principle of *forum conveniens* as the subtle and civilised implement by which practical justice was produced by and between autocephalous common law jurisdictions,[53] and rigid legislative drafting with mandatory effect as the starting point of the civilian systems. His going on to examine the part played by the anti-suit injunction was, however, less clear. For, although it is undoubtedly an integral part of the common law system, it will generally be unnecessary where the other court itself adopts the principle of *forum conveniens*. Given that, it might make more sense to reserve it to those cases where the foreign court does not (more properly, cannot) give effect to *forum conveniens* in the particular case, even though, or perhaps because, the particular jurisdictional rule was drafted narrowly,[54] and to deduce that it operates most usefully in relation to civilian jurisdictions. But Lord Goff also described the common law jurisdictional world and the civilian jurisdictional world as if they were two discrete hemispheres.[55] The easy conclusion to be derived from this may be that the injunction may operate, but will often be unnecessary, in relation to common law jurisdictions, and is unknown within civilian ones. Where the clash of jurisdictions arises between England and a civilian system, it might be thought to be uncertain which approach should prevail. But where the jurisdiction of the English courts is derived from the Convention it may be that English courts should regard themselves as being essentially civilian, for they are exercising a jurisdiction conceived and drafted in civilian style. Whatever the result his Lordship had in mind, it goes to show the real difficulty in finding a secure basis for the injunction in a legal system which is now hybrid in its underlying jurisdictional structure.

---

[51] Though the logic of *Turner* v. *Grovit*, *supra* n. 50, is that, when the foreign court has no jurisdiction, and the respondent was behaving wrongfully in bringing proceedings which he knew of should have known that the foreign court had no jurisdiction to hear, an injunction may be granted to "enforce" the Convention.

[52] [1999] 1 A.C. 119.

[53] *Ibid.*, 132.

[54] *Cf. Custom Made Commercial Ltd.* v. *Stawa Metallbau GmbH (Case C–228/92)* [1994] I E.C.R. 2913, which makes the point (at 2955–2957) that there is no possibility of using the doctrine of forum non conveniens to permit a court with jurisdiction conferred by the Brussels Convention to decline to proceed to exercise it.

[55] [1999] 1 A.C. 119, 131–133, 141.

It is clear that the judicial divergences reflect the fact that there is more than one policy which needs to be accommodated by the common law and the Conventions. Enforcing an international convention to the greatest extent possible, or a binding agreement on where and how to resolve future differences, is a worthy and proper aim of a legal system, and might suggest that anti-suit injunctions ordered in furtherance of this aim are a proper measure. After all, one substantial objection to an anti-suit injunction may be that it involves an English court running its rule over the jurisdiction of the foreign court and, when this is given a failing mark, granting an English remedy against the deficiency. Indeed, modern Canadian equity is unambiguous on the point: if the foreign court has jurisdictional rules which do not observe comity, they can expect no comity from a Canadian court.[56] There is something inherently unattractive about the prospect of obtaining a remedy by indirectly superimposing English jurisdictional standards on a foreign court's own law. But, where the other court is in a contracting state, an injunction founded on the argument that the foreign court has no jurisdiction is itself founded on the jurisdictional rules of the Convention, and hence on the jurisdictional rules of the foreign court itself. That being so, the potential offence done by the assertion of English judicial power is less than where the remedy is founded on the superiority and difference of English jurisdictional values.

On the other hand, the need to give foreign courts the opportunity which an English court might expect for itself, and the duty to repose trust in the competence of the foreign court to apply its law, especially when its law is the same as English law, all adds up to a good reason why an injunction should *not* be granted. It is not easy to discover whether anti-suit injunctions are frequently ordered by foreign courts in relation to English proceedings, but where this does happen it will not always allow an English court to implement the overriding objective of its civil procedural system,[57] especially that of dealing with the case expeditiously and fairly.[58]

It is well known that the Conventions say nothing specific on whether injunctions in relation to proceedings in another contracting state are to be permitted. But the European Court of Justice has made it clear that, subject to (so far) two non-textual exceptions,[59] one court is not entitled to review, or to

---

[56] *Amchem* [1993] 1 S.C.R. 897, 934.
[57] C.P.R. Part 1.
[58] C.P.R. 1.2(d).
[59] The second ruling in *Overseas Union Insurance Ltd.* v. *New Hampshire Insurance Co.* (*Case C–351/89*) [1991] I E.C.R. 3317 was without prejudice to the case where the court considers that it has exclusive jurisdiction under the Brussels Convention, Article 16. And jurisdictional review of proceedings pending in the first court may be undertaken in order to deal with a case to which the transitional provisions of the Convention apply: *Von Horn* v. *Cinnamond* (*Case C–163/95*) [1997] I E.C.R. 5451 (at 5476–5477).

second guess, the jurisdiction of another court over proceedings pending in that court. In *Overseas Union Insurance Ltd.* v. *New Hampshire Insurance Co.*[60] an English court asked whether it was entitled to conclude that proceedings which had been brought earlier in France had been brought in breach of the rules of the Convention, so that these could be disregarded as an obstacle[61] to the English proceedings. The Court said no: having made the point that the English court was no better placed than the French court to interpret the Convention, it went on to say that, "[m]oreover, the case in which a court in a contracting state may review the jurisdiction of a court in another contracting state are set out exhaustively in Article 28 and the second paragraph of Article 34 of the [Brussels] Convention ... It follows that, apart from those limited exceptions, the Convention does not authorise the jurisdiction of a court to be reviewed by a court in another contracting state".[62] The principle was reaffirmed in *Von Horn* v. *Cinnamond*,[63] where it was accepted that, in order to give effect to Article 54, second paragraph,[64] the transitional provisions of the Convention did require a court to assess whether the jurisdiction exercised by a court of a state which had not yet acceded to the Convention did conform to Title II of the Convention, so that the judgment could be recognised under Title III. But this led to only a very limited further exception and did not call into question the principle made clear in *Overseas Union Insurance*: it was reaffirmed that the rules of the Brussels Convention "are common to both courts and may be interpreted with equal authority by the courts of both Contracting States".[65]

It is a remarkable fact that *Overseas Union Insurance* has not been much cited in judgments in anti-suit injunction cases. One inference is that this is because it would make it very difficult to reconcile *Overseas Union Insurance* with the power to grant anti-suit injunctions in relation to proceedings in another contracting state. But, unless there is a further exception within the text of the Convention, waiting to be discovered, an injunction which has as its basis the submission and conclusion that the first court has misapplied the Convention, and has wrongly concluded, or may wrongly conclude, that it has jurisdiction, cannot be supported. This need not mean that there is no power to make such an order where proceedings are in another contracting state, but that it is impermissible to do so by reasoning that the foreign court has no jurisdiction under the Convention. Bearing this in mind, there may still be a couple of ways to trace a path around *Overseas Union Insurance*.

First, if it can be argued that the English court is not reviewing the jurisdiction of the foreign court, but is ruling on its *own* jurisdiction, albeit that this entails

---

[60] (*Case C–351/89*) [1991] I E.C.R. 3317.
[61] Otherwise presented by reason of the Brussels Convention, Article 21.
[62] Paragraph 24 of the judgment.
[63] (*Case C–163/95*) [1997] I E.C.R. 5451.
[64] San Sebastián Convention, Article 29(1).
[65] *Von Horn* [1997] I E.C.R. 5451, 5477 (para. 25).

the automatic consequence that the foreign court cannot have jurisdiction,[66] it may be possible to stay on the right side of *Overseas Union Insurance*. This would mean that, where the English court found that it had jurisdiction under Article 16, it would be bound and entitled to draw the conclusion, without ever looking at the proceedings in the foreign court, that the foreign court did not have jurisdiction, and could act according to that finding. The obvious question, therefore, is whether an English court is entitled to conclude that it has jurisdiction under Article 17, and to draw the inexorable conclusion that a foreign court, seised before it, did not have jurisdiction. The answer is no. If an English court has Article 17 jurisdiction, this need not mean that the foreign court does not have jurisdiction. To be sure, it would be necessary to examine the proceedings in the foreign court, the formulation of the cause of action and the construction of the jurisdiction clause, and so forth, to decide whether Article 17 serves to deny the jurisdiction of the foreign court over the action raised before it. Moreover, a jurisdiction agreement yields to waiver or submission. It cannot be argued that a court which considers itself to have Article 17 jurisdiction has necessarily concluded that the foreign court cannot possibly have had jurisdiction, and this escape route appears to be closed off by the reasoning in *Overseas Union Insurance*.

Secondly, if the injunction has a different foundation, such as the unconscionable, vexatious or oppressive behaviour of the respondent in seising the first court with jurisdiction *which it does in fact have and which is not being reviewed or questioned by the English court*, the granting of an injunction would appear at first sight not to fall foul of *Overseas Union Insurance*. Though this may involve some very delicate footwork, it may be sound in principle. All contracting states may be assumed to have doctrines of good faith, or abuse of right,[67] and so forth, by which to regulate the assertion or invocation of legal rights—including rights of access to a court—which is undertaken unconscionably. The power to order an anti-suit injunction may be seen to fall within the general family of doctrines which allow the unconscionable exercise of legal rights to be restrained. It is true that civilian systems tend not to extend their doctrines to the exercise of rights in foreign courts or under foreign laws, but this may be regarded as a difference in domestic or procedural laws, nothing more.[68] Moreover, the Court of Justice said, in *Kongress Agentur Hagen GmbH*

---

[66] This may be the reason for the exception made in *Overseas Union Insurance* for cases where a court believes that it has exclusive jurisdiction under Article 16: by ruling on its own jurisdiction it necessarily follows as a consequence—but not from a review of *that* court's own jurisdiction—that the other court has no jurisdiction.

[67] For this, see the French Civil Code, Article 1383, notes 6 11, esp. 10 (ed. Litec 1997–98, 717).

[68] After all, procedural remedies, such as freezing injunctions and order of *saisie* will often have widely differing reaches and effects.

v. *Zeehage B.V.*,[69] that a national court might have recourse to its rules of procedure so long as its doing so did not prejudice the practical effect of the Convention. The scope of this permission has not been tested, but the argument being advanced here may be thought to fall within it. The practical effect of the Convention is not prejudiced if the national court stays on the right side of *Overseas Union Insurance* by eschewing any invitation to review the jurisdiction of the foreign court but by accepting that (Article 16 cases apart) the foreign court does have jurisdiction. On this hypothesis, if the applicant can make his case without pleading that, or asking the court to investigate whether, the foreign court had no jurisdiction, the basis for an injunction may be preserved. It may be that this provides a means by which *Turner* v. *Grovit*[70] could be defended. The Employment Tribunal was sciscd first, proceedings were then commenced in Spain which were designed, as the court found, to frustrate and confound the English action. To the extent that Laws, L.J. analysed the proceedings in the Spanish court and reached his own conclusion that the Spanish court had no jurisdiction[71] the injunction is, it is submitted, insupportable. But, if the reasoning had been confined to examining whether, though the Spanish court had jurisdiction, its invocation by the respondent was nevertheless unconscionable, the principle of *Overseas Union Insurance* would not be infringed by the granting of an injunction. We will have to look at a possible answer to this line of reasoning below.

Legally respectable, and logically sound, as this might be, it is awfully counter-intuitive. The two cases in which the Court of Appeal has been most ready to order an injunction arose where the foreign court showed signs of misapplying the Convention by concluding that it has jurisdiction when in law it should have known that it had none. In *Continental Bank*, proceedings in Greece were restrained on the ground that Article 17 of the Convention gave to the English courts, and denied the Greek courts, jurisdiction over the action brought in Athens. And in *Turner* v. *Grovit* proceedings in Spain were restrained on the ground that Article 21 of the Convention gave to the Employment Tribunal, and denied to the Spanish courts, jurisdiction over the action brought in Spain.[72] These feel at first sight to be the strongest cases for an

---

[69] (*Case C–365/88*) [1990] I E.C.R. 1845 (on the admissibility of new third party claims close to the date of the trial).

[70] [1999] 3 All E.R. 616 (C.A.).

[71] This may well be seen as the reasoning which was used by the Court of Appeal. The reference by Laws, L.J. to Article 21, and the (ab)use of the decision in *Drouot Assurances S.A.* v. *Consolidated Metallurgical Industries* (*Case C–351/96*) [1998] I E.C.R. 3075 to widen the scope of Article 21, was designed to demonstrate that the Spanish court had no jurisdiction.

[72] The difficulties in seeing quite how the claims advanced in Spain could have been brought in the Employment Tribunal (still less that they were the same claim as that brought in the Tribunal) are not pursued here. But they are not minor.

injunction, based as they are on the clear words, and clear violation, of an international convention, rather than on the uncertain and imprecise equitable doctrines of vexation, oppression, and unconscionability. Yet in the light of *Overseas Union Insurance* they appear to be the cases in which such relief may not be given. Is there therefore any other way to distinguish *Overseas Union Insurance* so that it does not apply to prevent the granting of an injunction on the simple basis that the foreign court did not have jurisdiction?

In *Overseas Union Insurance*, proceedings had been commenced in France based on Article 4 of the Convention; proceedings were then begun in England; it was alleged that Article 21 did not impede these as jurisdiction under Article 4 was exercised outside the scope of the article; and in any event the French court had erred in considering itself to have jurisdiction. The Court's rejection of the submission was accompanied by the observation that it was not open 'to the court seised second to assess for itself the jurisdiction of the first court. The underlying reason for this conclusion was that, if the second court asserted jurisdiction, there was a risk of judgments conflicting and being denied recognition[73] and which would, if not checked, frustrate the purpose of the Convention.

It may be thought that this interpretation allows *Overseas Union Insurance* to be confined to cases where the proceedings in the second court are founded on the same underlying claim, so that there is a possibility that two courts will give separate and conflicting judgments. And it may be said that, if an English court orders an injunction, such an order makes no findings about the merits of the respondent's claim, and certainly does not constitute a rejection of them. It would follow, so the argument would proceed, that there was no risk of conflicting judgments, and *Overseas Union Insurance* was accordingly irrelevant. But this is not, ultimately, convincing. True, an anti-suit injunction is not irreconcilable with a judgment on the merits of the claim: they will not constitute proceedings having "the same cause of action" for the purposes of Article 21, as they have different ends in view and may also be based on different facts and rules of law.[74] This was the technical, jurisdictional, reason why Article 21 was not an impediment to the making of the order in *Continental Bank*, and in the light of *The Tatry*[75] it looks correct. It must also follow that the two judgments are not irreconcilable, for the rule in Article 27.3 denying recognition is deliberately narrower than that in Article 21.[76] Even so, non-recognition of the foreign judgment obtained by the respondent in defiance

---

[73] Article 27.3.

[74] *Cf. The Tatry* [1994] I E.C.R. 5439.

[75] [1994] I E.C.R. 5439.

[76] Article 21 applies if there is a *possibility* that irreconcilable judgments might ensue *Gubisch Maschinenfabrik K.G. v. Palumbo (Case 144/86)* [1987] E.C.R. 4861: see esp. paragraph 8 of the judgment. Article 27.3 only applies to judgments in which this possibility has come about.

of an anti-suit injunction and in contempt of the English court will necessarily follow from Article 27.1;[77] and the consequence foreseen and deprecated by the Court in *Overseas Union Insurance* will have materialised. Taking the underlying reasoning in *Overseas Union Insurance* as given, and interpreting the Convention in accordance with it, it is equally wrong for the English court to base an injunction upon a finding of misapplication by the foreign court of the jurisdictional rules of the Convention. It follows that *Overseas Union Insurance* prevents an injunction being ordered on the basis of such an impermissible jurisdictional review of the foreign court's proceedings. The result is, it is submitted, that the strongest cases provide the weakest justification for an anti-suit injunction: though an injunction to restrain wrongful conduct raises issues distinct from the claim on the merits, one to reinforce the jurisdictional rules of the Convention is impermissible.

We must now return to the proposition that, if the injunction is founded on the vexatious or oppressive behaviour of the respondent, and involves no review of the jurisdiction of the foreign court, it may be compatible with the Convention to order an injunction, and test this against the broader principle of *Overseas Union Insurance* (for in such a case the immediate principle of *Overseas Union Insurance* is not directly relevant) as just described. If that decision stands for the general proposition that a court may not deliberately act so as to create *de novo* an impediment to the free circulation of judgments, an injunction to restrain vexation or oppression is just as objectionable, and is equally incompatible with the economy of the Convention. There is nothing in the Convention or in *Overseas Union Insurance* which compels this conclusion. But there may be an analogy to be drawn with Article 16.5. That provision confers exclusive jurisdiction, regardless of domicile, "in proceedings concerned with the enforcement of judgments [upon] the courts of the contracting state in which the judgment has been or is to be enforced". It is sensible that a court in which an enforcement action is pending should have untrammelled jurisdiction to deal with issues arising in that action. It does not take a great leap of imagination to deduce that by parity of reasoning (though absence of text) a court in which an adjudicatory action is pending should have exclusive jurisdiction over issues arising in it, and for precisely the same reasons. To the objection that the Convention does not say so, one answer is that Article 21 goes some way towards showing it; Article 16.5 is entirely consistent with it; and Article 24 constitutes the single specific exception to it.[78] Moreover, the absence of a specific textual basis for the argument may indicate that it would never have occurred to those drafting the Convention that a court in one contracting state

---

[77] *Philip Alexander Securities and Futures Ltd.* v. *Bamberger* [1997] I.L.Pr. 73, affd. *ibid.*, 104, at 115 (Leggatt, L.J.).

[78] Article 24 allows for provisional, including protective, measures to be obtained regardless of whether the court applied to has or could not have jurisdiction to hear the action on the merits.

might have jurisdiction to interfere with proceedings pending in the courts of another.

In the final analysis it is just too hard to accept that there is any tenable basis for the granting of an anti-suit injunction which relates to proceedings[79] in the courts of another contracting state. Any attempt to navigate a course around the jurisprudence of the Court of Justice bristles with difficulty, even if it is not formally impossible. If this is seen as a matter of regret it can really only be on the basis that a foreign court cannot be trusted to take the view which would have commended itself to the English court, or to grant a sufficient remedy to the party who has been wrongly brought before the court. This is surely the very conclusion which the Convention makes inadmissible and impossible to hold.

SHOULD A CHOICE OF COURT AGREEMENT AUTOMATICALLY JUSTIFY AN INJUNCTION?

As a matter of common law, to bring proceedings in a foreign court when it has been contractually agreed that these would be brought, if anywhere, in England is a breach of contract; and there is a general view that summary enforcement of a contract is an appropriate response to its breach.[80] Authority exists for the proposition that the best way to enforce a negative covenant is by injunction;[81] and if a more traditional answer would first ask whether a damages remedy would be sufficient to compensate for loss, it is easy to accept that it would not be.[82] The practice of the Commercial Court, at least, appears to be to grant an injunction to restrain proceedings brought in breach of a jurisdiction clause unless good cause is shown not to;[83] and the restatement of principle in *Airbus Industrie* went out of its way to say nothing about injunctions based on legal rights not to be sued.

Despite the commercial utility of such agreements and enforcements, it is arguable that a more cautious approach should be taken to the grant of an injunction in such cases. The basis of the argument is that a choice of court

---

[79] If the proceedings have not yet been brought, but are merely threatened, many of the objections go away and any objections to an injunction will be few.

[80] *Continental Bank* v. *Aeakos* [1994] 1 W.L.R. 588; *The Angelic Grace* [1995] 1 Lloyd's Rep. 87. See also *A/S D/S Svendborg* v. *Wansa* [1996] 2 Lloyd's Rep. 559; *Petromin S.A.* v. *Secnav Marine Ltd.* [1995] 1 Lloyd's Rep. 603; *Schiffahrtsgesellschaft Detlev von Appen* v. *Vöest Alpine Intertrading GmbH* [1997] 1 Lloyd's Rep. 179; *Akai Pty Ltd.* v. *People's Insurance Co. Ltd.* [1998] 1 Lloyd's Rep. 90, 105. But for a more cautious view, see *Toepfer International GmbH* v. *Soc. Cargill France* [1998] 1 Lloyd's Rep. 379, 386; *Credit Suisse First Boston (Europe) Ltd.* v. *M.L.C. (Bermuda) Ltd.* [1999] 1 Lloyd's Rep. 767.

[81] Originating perhaps in *Doherty* v. *Allman* (1877) 3 App.Cas. 709.

[82] *Continental Bank* v. *Aeakos* [1994] 1 W.L.R. 588, 598.

[83] See the cases in n. 80, above.

agreement is rather different from other terms in a commercial contract, albeit that in many cases it may have been the subject of a specific negotiation and bargain. Recent authority has re-established that a court is not bound to give effect to a choice of court agreement for a foreign court.[84] Several reasons can be given for this, but predominant is the fact that the court has public responsibilities which go beyond the enforcement of the private contractual bargain between the parties, and which include a unique duty to secure the administration of justice: this public responsibility cannot be sacrificed to the private interests of the parties, and especially not where this would jeopardise the interests of those not party or privy to the agreement.[85] Moreover, it is never part of the analysis of cases where there is a choice of court agreement for a foreign court that the question is one which should be answered by the allegedly chosen, or prorogated, court: it is apparently enough to say that the jurisdiction of the English court has been derogated from, and that an English court may therefore construe and, if necessary, enforce the clause.

This last point appears to deal with the argument, sometimes heard, that, where there is a clause which prorogates the jurisdiction of the English court, the English court is best placed to interpret and to enforce it. In *Continental Bank* it was submitted by the respondent that the Greek court should be left to construe the clause and to enforce it in the event that it was found to derogate from the jurisdiction of the Greek courts, but the argument was summarily rejected. The truth is, however, that a choice of court agreement prorogates and derogates, effects which are as significant for the prorogated as for the derogated court, and which cannot be seen as the predominant concern of the prorogated court.[86] If this is so, there is neither reason nor right for a prorogated English court to claim the role of exclusive enforcer of such a contractual term. Nor is it convincing to bolster the argument which found favour in *Continental Bank* by asserting that the contract containing the clause will often be governed by the law of the prorogated court. This is certainly the English point of view, but other laws evidently do not consider the effect of a choice of court agreement as a contractual matter governed by the law of the contract in which it appears.[87] If that had been so in *Continental Bank* it would have been wrong to

---

[84] Most recently in *Bouygues Offshore S.A.* v. *Caspian Shipping Co. (Nos 1, 3, 4, 5)* [1998] 2 Lloyd's Rep. 461; but also in *The El Amria* [1981] 2 Lloyd's Rep. 119 and *Citi-March Ltd.* v. *Neptune Orient Lines Ltd.* [1996] 1 W.L.R. 1367.

[85] *Bouygues Offshore S.A.*, *supra* n. 84 (though not in so many words).

[86] From which it follows from *Overseas Union Insurance* that no court has a superior claim to interpret the Convention and the effect of the clause in relation to it.

[87] This appears to be why choice of court and arbitration agreements were excluded from the Rome Convention on the law applicable to contractual obligations: Contracts (Applicable Law) Act 1990, Sched. 1, Article 1.2(d). For the possibilities as they appear to a French writer, see Gaudemet-Tallon, *Les Conventions de Bruxelles et de Lugano*, 2nd edn. (1996), para. 131.

say that the construction and effect of the clause was easier for an English than for a Greek court.[88]

But the nature of injunctive relief is that the English court, *qua* prorogated court, claims a predominant right to enforce the jurisdiction agreement by injunction. Were it uncontroversial that the bringing of the foreign proceedings amounted to a breach of contract, an injunction might be an uncontroversial measure. But in such a case as well, the foreign court may also be expected to come to the same view; and if it decides, exceptionally, not to, it will be acting as did the Court of Appeal in *The El Amria*[89] and in *Bouygues Offshore S.A.* v. *Caspian Shipping Co. (Nos 1, 3, 4, 5)*[90] and overriding the intended effect of the clause. In either case the matter does not appear to be one in which an English anti-suit injunction is called for. In cases where it is controversial whether the agreement is legally binding, or whether the claim advanced in the foreign court falls within its scope, there is much to be said for the view that the foreign court is best placed to undertake such an evaluation. This view was rejected in *Continental Bank*, but appears to have surfaced as a dominant concern in *Credit Suisse First Boston (Europe) Ltd.* v. *M.L.C. (Bermuda) Ltd.*[91] Rix, J., wholly correctly, it is submitted, took the view that causes of action arising under United States' legislation may not come within the scope of a choice of court agreement, and left it to the American courts to decide the particular jurisdictional issue for themselves.

In this difficult area of the law there is always a danger of letting theory get the better of practice. But, if there is a general lesson to be drawn from these cases, it has to be that the enforcing of jurisdiction clauses by injunction as if there were an automatic right to such relief from the English court is something which calls for reconsideration. To repeat: these are not ordinary contactual terms the enforcement of which is a matter of right at all times and in all places, but terms which may have effects on third parties, and on judges in at least two courts. Seen against this background the summary enforcement procedure in *Continental Bank* and *The Angelic Grace*, but also the recent approach to the Commercial Court, is increasingly questionable.

It is next necessary to look at two specific issues upon which we have touched incidentally. The first is whether it is necessary for an English court to be the

---

[88] There was a question of construction of the clause, and a question of the correct analysis of the action brought under Article 919 of the Greek Civil Code. The latter was undoubtedly a question more easily approached by a Greek court; the former was one which was no easier for an English than for a Greek court to decide (depending on the law by reference to which the Greek court would consider it appropriate to ascertain the scope of the clause). In such a case the balance of convenience may have favoured leaving both questions to the Greek, and not to the English, court. And *cf. Charm Maritime Inc.* v. *Kyriakou* [1987] 1 Lloyd's Rep. 433.

[89] [1981] 2 Lloyd's Rep. 119.

[90] [1998] 2 Lloyd's Rep. 461.

[91] [1999] 1 All E.R. (Comm.) 237.

natural forum before it is appropriate for it to exercise its discretion by ordering an injunction. In *Airbus Industrie*[92] Lord Goff excluded this case from his formulation of a general principle. The reason presumably was that the issues are substantially different when the injunction is sought in support of a legal right not to be sued. But it has been sought to show that, although the issues may be different, the relevant issue is whether the English court is the most appropriate court to act as enforcing court; and the fact that it appears to have been chosen is not a sufficient guarantee that it has a closer connection to the enforcement issue than does the foreign court in which the proceedings have been commenced. For this reason it is submitted that Lord Goff's general requirement that the English court consider itself to be the natural forum for the resolution of the dispute is appropriate also in the case where it is alleged that England is the prorogated court.[93]

Second, how different is the position when the other court is that of a contracting state to the Convention? If it is correct to see the effects of the clause as prorogation and derogation, there is, as has now been said several times, no *a priori* reason to conclude that the prorogated court has a better claim to enforce the agreement than does the derogated court. This will not be because Article 21 means that the second, chosen, court has no jurisdiction: the proceedings in the first court are likely to be on the merits of the dispute, while the claim for an injunction, and especially if this is the only relief sought in the case, has a different end in view. There is no question but that the agreement should be construed and (if enforceable) enforced, but it is not more appropriate for the prorogated than for the derogated court to construe and give effect to the terms of the agreement so far as they are enforceable. And to assert that commercial common sense dictates a different answer fails to pay heed to the commercial common sense of the Convention itself. It does not improve the Convention to amend it by *ad hoc* unilateral endeavour; and, if it is submitted that the Convention does, but should not, make it harder to hold parties to their judgments, the solution is to amend the Convention.

---

[92] [1999] 1 A.C. 119, 138F.

[93] It is almost inevitable that, where the chosen court is not English, it will be impossible to see England as the natural forum for the litigation, and almost impossible for the test in *Airbus Industrie* to result in an injunction.

DO SPECIAL PRINCIPLES APPLY WHERE THE
PLAINTIFF CAN SUE ONLY IN THE FOREIGN COURT?

Almost from the beginning of the renaissance in anti-suit injunction cases there has been a sporadic line of argument and authority[94] which holds that different treatment be given, or different principles applied, in a case where the respondent claims that he is able to advance his claim only in the foreign court. These cases, now known as "single forum" cases, continue to represent an unprincipled exception to the view that all applications for an anti-suit injunction may be accommodated within the principles of *Aérospatiale* and *Airbus Industrie*. The reasoning goes this way: if England has to be shown to be the natural forum for the litigation of the claim, this condition is incapable of being met if the cause of action asserted by the respondent as plaintiff in the foreign court could not be advanced in England, usually because English choice of law principles preclude its being advanced: useful examples might include relief under the (United States) Clayton-Sherman Acts, or under the (Australian) Trade Practices Act 1974.[95] For the English court to order an injunction in such a case would have the effect of summarily determining the litigation in favour of the applicant without regard to the merits; this is an extraordinary step which a court should be reluctant to take. Obviously this argument has something to be said for it, for it is an unremarkable fact that foreign law differs from English law, and it is bold for an English court to prevent a party seeking to determine his rights in accordance with that law. Claims are entitled to be given a hearing[96] and, if they are preposterous or manifestly unfounded, one may expect the foreign court to have its own means of dealing with the potential for abuse. So, even if England is the natural forum, it will be inappropriate for it to act to try to shut out the respondent from all hope of relief. And this perception lies at the heart of *C.S.R. Ltd.* v. *Cigna Insurance Australia Ltd.*:[97] if the relief

---

[94] *British Airways Board* v. *Laker Airways Ltd.* [1985] A.C. 58; *Airbus Industrie G.I.E.* v. *Patel* [1999] 1 A.C. 119. In addition, the formulation of the law of Australia in *C.S.R. Ltd.* v. *Cigna Insurance Australia Ltd.* (1997) 189 C.L.R. 345 tends to the same effect, for if the relief claimed in the foreign court cannot be obtained from the action in Australia an injunction will not be granted: see *ibid.*, 375, and text to notes 24–27, above.

[95] It is possible that these are to be regarded as tort claims and, since the coming into force of the Private International Law (Miscellaneous Provisions) Act 1995, capable in principle of being brought in England. But the fact that the claim under the Clayton-Sherman Acts is for treble damages will presumably separately prevent its being brought in England. The Protection of Trading Interests Act 1980, section 5, prohibits the enforcement of foreign judgments given under such legislation; it must follow that a rule of English public policy, if not the literal text of the 1980 Act, prohibits an action in an English court for the same relief.

[96] *Cf. Spiliada Maritime Corp.* v. *Cansulex Ltd.* [1987] A.C. 460, 483–484.

[97] (1997) 189 C.L.R. 345.

claimed in the foreign court could not be sought from an Australian court, the Australian court has no right to prevent the respondent from making his case.

However, it is submitted that the argument is misguided in principle. Aside from cases of jurisdictional immunity, whether *rationale materiae* or *ratione personae*, it is not correct to characterise cases in which the claim which the respondent wishes to bring may not be brought as such in England as single forum cases. English law, or conflict of laws rules, may allow the respondent to reformulate the facts and matters to advance a different claim: those which gave him his Clayton-Sherman Acts claim as one for conspiracy to injure, or for damages for breach of competition legislation; or those which gave him his Trade Practices Act claim as one for damages for misrepresentation. Against such a background it is hard to capture the sense in which the claim is a single forum one. But the point may be that the respondent will elect not to proceed in England, because he is aware that the facts of his claim will not combine to make a successful cause of action in England. If that is so, it is submitted that the argument should be inadmissible. It has been as plain as can be, ever since *Spiliada Maritime Corp.* v. *Cansulex Ltd.*,[98] that it is not the proper role of the English judge to be partial as between the two parties and to allow a claim to proceed or not according to whether there is advantage to one side or the other. The case in which the respondent will win overseas, but will lose if required to make his claim in England, reflects the argument made when a claimant opposes a stay with the plea that he will obtain higher damages if he is allowed to stay in England. It is an inadmissible plea in that context,[99] and it should be given equally short shrift in this. Looking at it from the other side of the fence, it is not usually thought that the fact that the defendant will be able to advance a successful *defence* in a foreign court is a conclusive reason why permission to serve out under R.S.C. Order 11 should be withheld: "defendant's single forum case" has not yet been written into the lexicon of the law.

Nor is the claimant entitled to obtain permission to serve process out of the jurisdiction unless he satisfies the *Spiliada* and *Seaconsar*[100] criteria: no special allowance is made for a submission that if he is not enabled to sue in England he will effectively lose. Still further, choice of law rules are not disregarded by an English court simply because the effect of their application is that a claim founded in a foreign law will fail when that law is not applied by an English court. The principle of impartial even-handedness is well established in this

---

[98] [1987] A.C. 460, esp. 482–484.

[99] *Ibid.*, 482. There are exceptions to this principle, but they are unsound in principle: *cf. The Herceg Novi* [1998] 4 All E.R. 238. In *Midland Bank Plc* v. *Laker Airways Ltd.* [1986] Q.B. 689 the Court of Appeal ordered an injunction to restrain a claim in the American courts which could not have been brought in England. In *Airbus Industrie* [1999] 1 A.C. 119, 137–138, Lord Goff refrained from commenting upon the rightness of that decision.

[100] *Seaconsar Far East Ltd.* v. *Bank Markazi Jomhouri Islami Iran* [1994] 1 A.C. 438.

area of the law; to permit rules which are essentially impartial to be set aside in this one category of injunction cases where the effect will be to favour the respondent is, surely, unacceptable.

And the English experience is that there are single forum cases in which the relief sought *ought* to be prevented from being obtained. In *Midland Bank Plc* v. *Laker Airways Ltd.*[101] the Court of Appeal considered that the overreaching scope of the Clayton-Sherman Acts was sufficient reason to order an injunction; the fact that the relief was available only in the United States even though the conduct complained of took place in England seemed to be the very proof of its objectionable character. A rule requiring benevolent treatment of a single forum case would have been quite out of place, given the analysis of the facts adopted by the Court.

It is right that there should be caution if the effect of an injunction is that the respondent will simply and summarily lose, especially in a case where there appears to be a good cause of action under a foreign law. But there are cases where this is the right result, and where the applicant should not be put to further inconvenience of defending a vexatious action. We are presupposing that the case is one in which the natural forum for the resolution of the differences between the parties is England and where, if the respondent sues here, he will lose.[102] If we have any confidence in our domestic law and in our choice of law rules, this is a fact unworthy of remark: litigation produces a roughly equal number of winners and losers, and any submission which has the effect of tilting the playing field against one of the parties needs to be very carefully justified; and in this regard it is submitted that *Airbus Industrie* will need to be reconsidered.

THE BASIS FOR AN INJUNCTION: LEGAL OR EQUITABLE RIGHTS NOT TO BE SUED

Strange as it may seem, the grounds upon which an injunction is available as a remedy, as distinct from the question when the court will in its discretion make the order, remain uncertain. Where the injunction is sought to enforce a legal right not to be sued, the legal right must be identified by reference to the system of law under which it is said to arise; and, if the right is identified, the remaining questions relate to the discretion of the judge, but which he will not exercise in any event unless England is the natural forum for the litigation. If there is any remaining difficulty in this area it lies only in the definition of a legal right not to be sued. Contractual agreements to this effect are easy to accept, but there may be other cases where the right is said to arise from a statute, or from (say) the

---

[101] [1986] Q.B. 689.
[102] *Midland Bank Plc* v. *Laker Airways Ltd.* [1986] Q.B. 689.

provisions of the Brussels Convention. No court has quite held that an applicant has a legal right which is enforceable by injunction not to be sued in a court which, on a true construction of the Brussels Convention, has no jurisdiction over him;[103] but, if such a right can arise from an agreement which is validated by Article 17 of the Convention, an argument can be made that where Article 16 (or sections 3 and 4 of Title II)[104] means that the applicant is not liable to be sued in the foreign court, that is equally a legal right entitled to be enforced.

However, where the right giving rise to the remedy is equitable, there are two, and larger, uncertainties. The first is a choice of law question: if a legal, say contractual, right not to be sued must be demonstrated by reference to the law which governs the contact, what law applies to show the existence of an equitable right?[105] Choice of law as it applies to equitable rights is very underdeveloped, but the best view of the current authority is that the *lex fori* applied in a liberal fashion is the answer.[106] The second centres on the relationship between the equitable right not to be sued, and vexatious or oppressive conduct, and unconscionable behaviour by the respondent. It has never been clear, despite the apparent distinction in the terminology, that an equitable right not to be sued is distinct from vexatious or oppressive behaviour; nor that either is distinct from unconscionability. Some textbook authority treats them as separate categories,[107] as do some cases, but the content of the distinction is not clear. It is unlikely that it has any importance unless it comes to be recognised that the existence of an equitable right not to be sued raises a potential question of choice of law to establish the right, whereas unconscionability, vexation and oppression are defined and determined by the *lex fori*. But it will be critically important if this possibility *is* recognised as being correct; and, notwithstanding *Airbus Industrie*, the work remains to be done.

---

[103] The Court of Appeal in *Turner* v. *Grovit* [1999] 3 All E.R. 616 came very close, but based the injunction upon the conclusion that the foreign proceedings were oppressive or vexatious, and not brought in breach of a legal right not to be sued.

[104] That is, the jurisdictional rules for insurance and consumer contracts.

[105] This question was looked at by the writer in [1997] L.M.C.L.Q. 90, and the contents of that article are not repeated here. In *Airbus Industrie* the House of Lords did not directly support the view that there was a choice of law to be made; but, by ensuring that England was required to be the natural forum for the claim, it meant that English equity would apply only when English was the law with which the litigation had its closest and most real connection. This may be seen as a first cousin to a choice of law rule.

[106] See the valuable analysis of all the available material in *Paramasivam* v. *Flynn* (1998) 160 A.L.R. 203, 214–218 (Fed. Ct. Aust., Full Ct.).

[107] Cheshire & North, *Private International Law*, 13th edn. (1999), 361–373 notes the lack of consensus as to the organisation of the case law.

CONCLUSIONS

In a sense there are no conclusions to be drawn. One reason why an anti-suit injunction fits rather uneasily into the various contexts in which it may arise is that these contexts are now just too divergent to be treated uniformly. Had the United Kingdom never signed up to the Brussels and Lugano Conventions, England would have remained a common law jurisdiction, and the anti-suit injunction would have remained as a remedy in which equity alone was concerned to define its proper limits. But the impact of the Brussels and Lugano Conventions is that England is no longer, is no longer always to be thought of as, a common law jurisdiction. If the acceptance of this which may be the key to an understanding of whether the Conventions allow an English court to order an anti-suit injunction in the Convention context. (Outside this, there is still a degree of interference which may be inappropriate to inflict on a foreign court, even if it is held that (to English eyes) there is a contractual right to be protected.) It is the broad submission of this paper that, though there exist respectable arguments which would seek to shield the anti-suit injunction from the effects of the Conventions, these are difficult and will, in the end, be held to be unsustainable. When that day arrives—it will probably dawn first in Luxembourg—another piece of the common law will be discovered to have been surrendered in the cause of greater European ideal, never to be seen again.

Chapter 13

The Role of the *Lex Loci Arbitri* in International Commercial Arbitration

Sir Roy Goode

It is difficult to imagine Francis Reynolds in retirement. His devotion to his students is legendary; and he has a very wide conception of pastoral care. I recall many years ago inviting Francis to take part in a summer school at Queen Mary College for practising lawyers from all over the world. He agreed to give some lectures. But at the end of the day, told that there was a reception for those on the course, he decided that it was incumbent on him (which it certainly was not) to defer his return to Oxford in order to help look after the course participants. That is characteristic of Francis Reynolds, and it is one of the reasons why his class on international trade law, taught with Professor Sir Guenter Treitel, scores top marks on every count every year. A meticulous and wide-ranging scholar, he has made a great contribution, both here and abroad, to learning in a variety of fields: contract, sale of goods, international trade, carriage of goods by sea, and the conflict of laws. He has a remarkable memory for cases but has not allowed this to stultify his critical faculties; and he is respectful of those opinions that may differ from his own, deferring judgement until he has time for reflection. With his retirement Oxford will be losing (though we hope not altogether) a fine scholar and a wonderful colleague.

This modest contribution to the essays in his honour is concerned with the rôle of the *lex loci arbitri* in international commercial arbitration[1] and the extent to which judgments or orders made by a court of that state[2] should influence a foreign court of another state in which the arbitral award is sought to be enforced. Much has been written about the concept of international commercial arbitration as an autonomous, anational institution the procedures of which are not subject to the constraints of national laws. If any excuse is needed for adding yet more to the literature on the subject, it is its relevance to the future development of international co-operation in cross-border dispute resolution.

---

[1] That is, the procedural law of the state where such an arbitration takes place.
[2] Hereafter "the court of origin".

1 INTRODUCTION

The genesis of the autonomy concept

The relationship between courts and private tribunals has not always been as benevolent as it is today. In England the central courts for centuries jealously guarded their domain, watchful of encroachments on their jurisdiction. Even among the courts themselves there were strenuous turf battles as each sought to enlarge its jurisdiction at the expense of others. One unfortunate victim of this rivalry was commercial law, which lost much of its international character as the common law courts gradually usurped the powers of those institutions most responsive to external influences, notably the ecclesiastical courts, the courts of Admiralty and the merchant courts. Similarly, arbitration was for a long time viewed with disfavour, being seen as a private dispute settlement mechanism designed to oust the jurisdiction of the courts and to substitute private adjudication for public decision-making. This hostility to the private process of arbitration was not confined to English courts but was a widespread phenomenon.

However, every action prompts reaction. The stricter the controls, the more vehement the demand for liberation. Ultimately, in England as elsewhere, pressures from the commercial community were not to be denied. Fierce judicial opposition to arbitration gradually gave way to a wary acceptance, but under the closest judicial scrutiny, and it is only in the last half of this century (and in England only in the past two decades) that courts have finally come to terms with the fact that parties to arbitration agreements want privacy, confidentiality and finality in the settlement of their disputes, and view judicial intervention in the arbitral process or in the review of awards as a measure to be taken only in exceptional circumstances. Since the parties had entrusted the determination of their dispute to an arbitral tribunal it was the arbitrators and the parties rather than the courts who should control the procedure, and it was not the courts but the arbitral tribunal which in the first instance should decide such matters as the validity of the contract in dispute and the extent of the tribunal's jurisdiction. Now we have gone further. Not merely have we adopted the principle that the arbitration clause is to be considered separate from the rest of the contract, so that the invalidity of the contract does not deprive the arbitral tribunal of jurisdiction, but our Arbitration Act 1996 provides that the tribunal may even adjudicate on the validity of the agreement to arbitrate.[3]

Though the Arbitration Act does not distinguish domestic from international commercial arbitration, it is the latter which has forced the pace of change. It is now almost universally accepted that disputes involving parties and arbitrators from different countries cannot be constrained by the same rules as govern courts. So in this country, as elsewhere, we now recognise that arbitrators are

---

[3] Section 30(1).

not bound by rules of procedure and evidence applied by courts; that they need not apply the conflict of laws rules of the forum to determine the applicable law and, in the absence of party choice, may apply whatever conflict rules they consider appropriate; and that courts should intervene during the arbitral process, and arbitral awards should be set aside, only in exceptional circumstances.[4] In these developments the UNCITRAL Model Law on International Commercial Arbitration has proved to have a much greater influence than at one time seemed likely, and the Arbitration Act, unlike early versions of the draft Arbitration Bill prepared for the Departmental Advisory Committee on Arbitration, bears the strong impress of the Model Law.[5]

But these relaxations in judicial control in England and elsewhere came too late to stem the pent-up frustrations of certain leading international arbitrators, particularly French scholars, at what was rightly perceived to be an excessive judicial interference with party autonomy, which deprived parties to arbitration the predictability, finality and confidentiality to which they attached so much importance. Hence the movement, developed in particular by leading French scholars[6] and strongly supported by a number of other international authorities,[7] to promote the idea of international arbitration as something variously described as "anational", "stateless", "delocalised" and "detached".[8] By this was meant that in international commercial arbitration the arbitral procedure and any resulting award were autonomous, being unconnected to any national legal system and deriving their force solely from the agreement of the parties. Accordingly an arbitral award not only took effect from the time of its issue but

---

[4] The Arbitration Act recognises three categories of case: want of jurisdiction, serious procedural irregularity and error of law. The right of appeal in a case within one of the first two categories is mandatory; an appeal against an award on the ground of error of law may be freely excluded by agreement and, even where it is not, is subject to fairly stringent additional criteria.

[5] The Arbitration Act was drafted with a degree of clarity and user-friendliness unusual in modern parliamentary drafting. Indeed, this was so widely noted that at a major conference held at King's College London to examine the Act a compliment paid to the draftsman, Mr. Geoffrey Sellers, by one of the speakers attracted thunderous applause from the audience—a reaction surely unprecedented in the annals of Parliamentary drafting!

[6] Notably Professors René David, Berthold Goldman and Philippe Fouchard. However, the idea first appears to have been suggested by a Greek scholar, Professor Fragistas. See F. A. Mann, "Lex Facit Arbitrum", in Pieter Sanders (ed.), *International Arbitration: Liber Amicorum for Martin Domke* (Martinus Nijhoff, The Hague, 1967), 158.

[7] Including in particular Jan Paulsson and Professors Pierre Lalive and Arthur von Mehren.

[8] For an early example see Berthold Goldman, "Les Conflits de Lois dans l'Arbitrage International de Droit Privé" (1963) 109 *Recueils des Cours* 351; and for a recent restatement Phillipe Fouchard, "La portée internationale de l'annulation de la sentence arbitrale dans son pays d'origine" (1997) Rev. Arb. 329.

from then on became the prospective beneficiary of the recognition laws of a putative foreign state of enforcement and was thus unaffected by any subsequent order made by the court of origin setting the award aside. In other words, at the very moment of its birth, produced by the consensual coupling of the parties in the arbitration process, the award took off and disappeared into the firmament, landing only in those places where enforcement was sought.

The rebellion against the constraints imposed by national law on the conduct of arbitration went hand in hand with a sustained assault on the conflict of laws and its central thesis that all disputes had to be determined in accordance with a national legal system which it was the function of the conflict rules to identify. Why, it was asked, should parties to an international contract be locked into a national law that in all probability was designed primarily for domestic transactions? Why should they not be free to have their substantive rights determined by customary commercial law (*lex mercatoria*) or by general principles of law or even by public international law? Why should they not be free to designate as the applicable law an international convention such as the Vienna Convention on Contracts for the International Sale of Goods 1980? Hence the drive for freedom of arbitral procedure from national laws was paralleled by a move towards resurrection in modern form of the medieval *lex mercatoria* as a supposedly free-floating, autonomous body of law which was neutral in character and obviated the need to resort to national legal systems and, in consequence, rules of private international law.

The imagery of an autonomous *lex mercatoria* enforced by anational arbitration procedure leading to a stateless award captured the Gallic imagination. As has so often happened in the history of ideas, it was the proponents of the new spirit of revolution who tended to make the running in arbitration literature, not simply because they expressed their ideas with elegance and force but because they were able to conjure up a picture of transnationality that seemed so much more exciting than the more down to earth approach of traditional scholars. And, as so often in the past, the attention given to these new doctrines has been in inverse proportion to their practical impact. Yet we owe a good deal to the advocates of the *lex mercatoria*, and to others involved in the development and formulation of international principles of contract, commercial law and arbitration procedure, for they have had considerable success in shifting the balance of decisional authority from the courts to the arbitrators and in freeing the hands of arbitral tribunals in international arbitration from constraints which parties and their lawyers undoubtedly found unduly irksome.

2 THE NEW YORK CONVENTION

Before we discuss the opposing concepts of territoriality and party autonomy it is necessary to say a few words about the United Nations Convention on the Enforcement of Foreign Arbitral Awards 1958 (the New York Convention). The purpose of the convention is to facilitate the international enforcement of arbitral awards. The New York Convention has been astonishingly successful, no fewer than 121 states having become parties to it. The two articles with which we are particularly concerned are Articles V and VII.[9]

Article V provides that recognition and enforcement of a foreign arbitral award may be refused, at the request of the party against whom it is invoked, only if that party furnishes to the competent authority where the recognition and enforcement is sought proof of one of the matters listed in the ensuing paragraphs. Among these is the ground mentioned in paragraph (e), namely that the award "has not yet become binding on the parties, or has been set aside or suspended by a competent authority of the country in which, or under the law of which, that order was made". It is clear that Article V is mandatory only in precluding refusal of enforcement on grounds other than those set out in it. Proof of the existence of one of those grounds entitles the courts of a convention state to refuse recognition and enforcement but does not oblige them to do so. Refusal is discretionary.[10]

Under Article VII the provisions of the Convention are not to affect the validity of multilateral or bilateral agreements concerning the recognition and enforcement of arbitral awards entered into by the Contracting States "nor deprive any interested party of any right he may have to avail himself of an arbitral award in the manner and to the extent allowed by the law or the treaties of the country where such an award is sought to be relied on". One of the more remarkable features of the territoriality/party autonomy debate is that the protagonists on both sides invoke the New York Convention to support their position: the territorialists on the ground that numerous provisions of the

---

[9] For the convenience of the reader the full text of Articles V–VII is set out in the Appendix to this paper.

[10] A great deal of ink has been spent on the significance of the word "may" in the English text, as opposed to "shall". It is astonishing how many writers have concluded that the discretion to allow enforcement despite the existence of a ground for refusal in Article V exists because the word "shall" was not used. This can only be ascribed to unfamiliarity with the nuances of the English language. The discretionary effect of Article V would not have been changed one whit if the word "shall" had been used, because it would have to be read not in isolation but in conjunction with "only". Thus, the phrase would have become: "Recognition and enforcement of the award shall be refused … only if …" That means no more than that the courts of an enforcing state shall not/may not/cannot refuse enforcement unless one of the stated grounds for so doing exists. It does not imply that if such a ground does exist the court must enforce the award. That construction would necessitate a phrase such as "shall be refused if and only if".

Convention explicitly recognise the role of the *lex loci arbitri*;[11] the advocates of party autonomy and the statelessness of awards, on the ground that Article VII plainly establishes the right of enforcement states to allow enforcement of a foreign award which complies with their domestic law, despite its annulment by the court of origin, where that annulment is not a ground under the domestic law for refusal of recognition of the award. One thing seems clear, and that is that the New York Convention recognises the important role of the *lex arbitri*; and, while Article VII allows the *lex arbitri* to be bypassed, it certainly provides no warrant for the concept of a stateless award. On the contrary, it is strongly arguable that a stateless award would not be enforceable under the Convention. In the words of a leading authority on the Convention:[12]

> "It is not only the legislative history of the Convention which seems to be contrary to the Convention's applicability to the 'a-national' award. The system and text of the Convention too appear to be against such interpretation. The Convention applies to the enforcement of an award made in another State. Those who advocate the concept of the 'a-national' award, on the other hand, deny that such award is made in a particular country (*'sentence flottante'*, *'sentence apatride'*). How could such award then fit into the Convention's scope?"

3 TERRITORIALITY VERSUS AUTONOMY

The territoriality/party autonomy spectrum

The traditional theory of territoriality is based on the general principle of international law that a state is sovereign within its own borders and that its law and its courts have the exclusive right to determine the legal effect of acts done (and consequently of arbitral awards made) within those borders. The concept

---

[11] See in particular Article II(1) ("differences ... in respect of a defined legal relationship ... concerning a subject matter capable of settlement by arbitration", which is implicitly a reference to the *lex arbitri*); Article II(3) (which requires a court to refer a dispute to arbitration under the arbitration agreement "unless it finds that the said agreement is null and void, inoperative or incapable of being performed"—again matters to be determined under the *lex arbitri*); Article V(1)(a) (enabling the court to refuse recognition if it finds that the arbitration agreement is not valid under the law to which the parties have subjected it or, failing any indication thereon, under the law of the country where the award was made); Article V(i)(d) (composition of the arbitral tribunal not in accordance with the agreement of the parties or, failing such agreement, not in accordance with the law of the country where the arbitration took place); Article V(e) (previously set out); and Article VI (empowering the court of the state of enforcement to adjourn the enforcement proceedings if an application is pending before the competent authority of the country in which, or under the law of which, the award was made).

[12] Albert Jan van den Berg, *The New York Convention of 1958* (Kluwer Law and Taxation Publishers, Deventer, Netherlands, 1981), 37. After 18 years Professor van den Berg's book is still the seminal work on the New York Convention.

of party autonomy is arbitration predicates that the binding authority of an award derives solely from the agreement of the parties, not from national law. However, neither of these two approaches embodies a single, homogenous concept. The scope of the territoriality principle varies according to the degree of respect the courts of a particular state are willing to accord to the decisions of courts of other states of competent jurisdiction. Similarly, there is no single concept of party autonomy. In fact, territoriality and party autonomy do not represent a sharp dichotomy but together occupy a spectrum, along which we can identify at least six possible, and at least four actual, models, arranged in ascending order of delocalisation.

In the first model the law of the enforcing state *requires* its courts, in the absence of specified conditions, to refuse recognition and enforcement of an arbitral award that has been set aside by a court of competent jurisdiction. In other words, such law adopts the substance of Article V(e) of the New York Convention but as a mandatory, not a discretionary, provision. Examples of this model are the Italian Code of Civil Procedure and the Netherlands Private International Law Act. Article 840, limb (5), of the former provides as follows:

> "The Court of Appeal shall refuse recognition or enforcement of the foreign award if in the opposition proceedings the party against whom the award is invoked proves any of the following circumstances:
>
> . . .
>
> (5) the award has not yet become binding on the parties or has been set aside or suspended by a competent authority of the State in which, or under the law of which, it was made."

Article 1076(1)(A)(e) of the Netherlands Private International Law Act is differently formulated but produces the same effect. Under this Article:

> "If no treaty concerning recognition and enforcement is applicable, or if an applicable treaty allows a party to rely on the law of the country in which recognition or enforcement is sought, an arbitral award made in a foreign State may be recognised in the Netherlands and its enforcement may be sought in the Netherlands . . . unless:
>
> . . .
>
> (e) the arbitral award has been set aside by a competent authority of the country in which the award is made."

Thus, under both Italian and Dutch law the setting aside of the arbitral award in or under the law of the place where it was made makes it mandatory to refuse enforcement. These laws provide good examples of the strong form of territoriality.

In the second model it is recognised that within its own territory a state is sovereign and its courts have the exclusive right to adjudicate on the legality of acts done within that territory. What is said, however, is that laws and court decisions made within the state are not entitled to recognition *erga omnes*—which is clearly correct—but that for policy reasons the decision of a foreign court of competent jurisdiction setting aside an award will usually be respected by courts of the state of enforcement, subject to rights of impeachment in cases such as procedural unfairness or the obtaining of a judgment by fraud. States following this model generally adopt provisions in their arbitration laws which follow those of Article V of the New York Convention, with or without modification, and, like Article V, allow a discretion to enforce notwithstanding the order annulling the award. Examples are the English Arbitration Act 1996,[13] the Mexican Commercial Code,[14] the German Code of Civil Procedure,[15] and the Swiss Private International Law Act 1987.[16] The first two track the wording of Article V(1)(e); the German and Swiss legislation simply incorporates the provisions of the New York Convention by reference.

The third model is the same as the first except that under the laws of the enforcing state the grounds for refusal of recognition of a foreign arbitral award are more restricted than those of Article V and in particular do not include the setting aside of the award under the *lex loci arbitri*. The courts of such states are then permitted by Article VII of the New York Convention to recognise the right of the party obtaining the award to benefit from the more generous approach of the domestic law of the state of enforcement and, if the requirements of that law are met, to have the award enforced even though it has been annulled by the court of origin. Nevertheless, though the annulling order is not as such a ground for refusal of recognition, to the extent that it is based on grounds which have a counterpart in the domestic law of the enforcing state the courts of that state may be willing to hold that there is a conclusive, strong or at least *prima facie* presumption that such grounds have been established for the purposes of its domestic law. This approach reflects a traditional principle of the conflict of laws.

In the fourth model the law of the enforcing state, while still recognising the concept of a *lex arbitri*, does not recognise an annulment order in the court of origin either as a ground in itself for refusing recognition of the award or as raising any kind of presumption that such an order establishes facts which would bring the case within an equivalent ground under the law of the enforcing state.

The fifth, and very intense, model is to be found in French legislation and in the jurisprudence of French courts, which have carried the delocalisation principle to the point where an international award—by which is presumably meant an award in an international arbitration—is stateless and derives its force

---

[13] Section 103(2).
[14] Article 1462(1)(e).
[15] Section 1061.
[16] Article 194.

not from the *lex loci arbitri*, or indeed from any other national law, but solely from the will of the parties. This result, which needs a brief historical account, was reached only in stages. First came the decision in the *Götaverken* case,[17] in which the Paris Court of Appeal declined jurisdiction to set aside an I.C.C. award rendered in Paris on the ground that, while the arbitration had taken place in Paris, neither the parties nor the contracts had any connection with France and they had not designated French law—or, indeed, any law—as the procedural law apart from the procedural rules of the I.C.C., and that accordingly the award had no connection with the French legal order and was not a French award. Meanwhile the Swedish courts, asked to recognise the award at a time when the challenge to it was still pending in the French courts, held that the award was binding, not under French law but by the agreement of the parties to be bound, an agreement recognised and enforceable under Swedish law, so that the mere fact that the award was being challenged in France was not a ground for suspending the recognition proceedings in Sweden.

The judgment of the Paris Court of Appeal did not say in terms that arbitral awards in international arbitration were stateless, merely that on the facts there was no connection with the French legal order. But, since courts of a state other than that of the seat of the arbitration are unlikely to take jurisdiction in the absence of agreement by the parties, the effect of the *Götaverken* decision, if it were to be applied universally, is that, unless the parties themselves agree to submit to the procedural law of a particular state, the arbitral proceedings are not reviewable by any court other than the court of a state in which enforcement is sought.

The next stage came in a series of cases[18] in which the Court of Cassation held that the setting aside or suspension of an award by a court did not deprive the party obtaining the award of his right to enforce it in France in the conditions

---

[17] *General National Maritime Transport Co.* v. *Götaverken Arendal A.B.*, Court of Appeal, Paris, Feb. 21 1980, 1980 Rev. Arb. 107, (1981) 6 Y.B. Com. Arb. 221. For an excellent and balanced discussion, see Jan Paulsson, "Arbitration Unbound: Award Detached from the Law of its Country of Origin" (1981) 30 I.C.L.Q. 358; and for a response, William W. Park, "The *Lex Loci Arbitri* and International Commercial Arbitration" (1983) 32 I.C.L.Q. 21.

[18] *Pabalt Tikeret Sirketi* v. *Norsolor*, Cas. le civ., 9th October 1984, 1985 Rev. Arb. 431; *Polish Ocean Line* v. *Jolasry*, Cas. le civ., 10th March 1993, 1993 Rev. Arb. 255; *Hilmarton Ltd.* v. *Omnium de Traitement et de Valorisation (O.T.V.)* Cass. le civ., 23rd March 1994, 1994 Rev. Arb. 327, the last of these involving an extraordinary judicial saga in a number of countries; *Arab Republic of Egypt* v. *Chromalloy Air Services*, C.A. Paris, 14th January 1997, 1997 Rev. Arb. 395.

permitted by French law. These decisions were plainly correct,[19] since, while Article V of the New York Convention gave a discretionary power to the court of enforcement to refuse to recognise an award that had been set aside by the competent authority of the state where it was rendered, Article VII expressly preserved the right of an interested party to rely on the more favourable provisions, if any, of that state's domestic law. The provisions of the French Code of Civil Procedure did not then, and the provisions of the New Code of Civil Procedure do not now, include as a ground for refusing enforcement of a foreign award the fact that it had been set aside by the court of origin. Accordingly up to this point, if criticism was to be made, it was of the restrictive approach of the French legislation rather than that of the French courts. Moreover, it seems that, where the grounds for the foreign annulment are comparable to those contained in the French Code of Civil Procedure, French courts are nevertheless unwilling to recognise that they have any competence to treat the annulment order as raising a strong, or even *prima facie*, presumption that such grounds have been established for the purposes of French domestic law. The effect of the three decisions above mentioned is thus that French courts will enforce an award which is enforceable under French domestic law even if it has been set aside, or suspended under the *lex loci arbitri*.

Unfortunately, in *Hilmarton*[20] the Court of Cassation, not content with relying on the provisions of its domestic law, appears to have gone out of its way to say, in effect, that judgments of the court of origin setting aside an arbitral award were of no significance whatsoever in France, for in an international commercial arbitration the award, though made in a particular state (in that case, Switzerland), was itself international and was thus "not integrated into the legal system of that State". Accordingly a decision of Switzerland's highest court annulling an award was entirely irrelevant to its enforceability in France. This has widely been seen as a regrettable and unnecessary (if surely unintended) affront to a foreign court of the highest standing. One commentator

---

[19] The same cannot necessarily be said of that part of the reasoning of the Federal District Court for the District of Columbia in the American *Chromalloy* case denying *res judicata* effect to the decision of the Cairo Court of Appeal annulling an arbitral award rendered in Egypt. See *Chromalloy Air Services* v. *The Arab Republic of Egypt* (1996) 939 F.Supp. 907, and the critical comment on this aspect of the case by Georgios Petrochilos (1999) 48 I.C.L.Q. 856, and Eric Schwartz, "A Comment on *Chromalloy*— Hilmarton *à l'americaine*" (1997) 14 J. Int. Arb. 125. For a recent review of these developments see Emmanuel Gaillard, "Enforcement of Awards Nullified in the Country of Origin: The French Experience" in Albert Jan van den Berg (ed.), *Improving the Efficiency of Arbitration Agreements and Awards: 40 Years of Application of the New York Convention* (I.C.C.A. Congress Series No. 9, Kluwer, Deventer, Netherlands, 1999) 105.

[20] *Supra*, n. 18.

who is not unsympathetic to the internationalist approach has nevertheless observed:[21]

> "Although consistent with a conception of international arbitration that has a noble and prestigious heritage in France, this presumption, I might timidly venture to ask, is nevertheless just a little bit presumptuous, is it not? For on what authority can a French court decide what does or does not form part of the Swiss legal order? I would have thought that this was a matter for Swiss legislators and courts, and not the French Court of Cassation, to decide."

A similar decision was by the Paris Court of Appeal in *Egypt* v. *Chromalloy Air Services Ltd.*:[22]

> "The award made in Egypt is by definition an international award which, by definition, is not integrated in the legal order of that State so that its existence remains established despite its being annulled and its enforcement in France is not in violation of international public policy."

To this one might add: is it not paradoxical that French law, while declining to recognise the integration of a foreign award into the legal system of the *locus arbitri*, sees no difficulty in empowering French courts to set aside French awards in an international arbitration?

It has been held that French courts will undertake the review of an award challenged before them by the losing party even if the court of origin had already dismissed a challenge on the same grounds.[23] Hence the position now reached in France is, in effect, that Article V of the New York Convention will rarely be applied and can for all practical purposes be regarded as a dead letter.

Finally, we come to the most extreme delocalisation model, adopted by the Belgian legislation, to the effect that no court in Belgium could set aside an award unless at least one of the parties was Belgian. As noted later, that law has been modified to allow the parties the choice whether to retain or to opt out of judicial review in Belgium. If they do, then the resulting award becomes truly stateless.

---

[21]   Eric A. Schwartz (1997) 14 J. Int. Arb. 125, 131. The approach of the English courts has traditionally been rather different. "For the English court to pronounce on the validity of the law of a foreign state within its own territory, so that the validity of that law became the *res* of the *res judicata* in the suit, would be to assert jurisdiction over the internal affairs of that state. That would be a breach of the rules of comity. In my view this court has no jurisdiction to do so": *Buck* v. *Attorney-General* [1965] Ch. 745, 770, *per* Diplock, L.J.

[22]   14th January 1997, I.C.C.A. Y.B.

[23]   *Unichips Finanziaria* v. *Gesnouin (No. 3)*, Court of Appeal, Paris, 1st Chamber, 12th February 1993.

The question to be addressed

It is clear that a judgment of a court at the seat of an arbitration setting aside the arbitral award has no effect in another state except to the extent that the law of that state is willing to give effect to it. In some jurisdictions such a judgment may be treated as grounding a plea of *res judicata*, precluding the party who obtained the award from relitigating the issue of its validity. In others, the judgment does not attract the principle of *res judicata* but will nevertheless be respected in the absence of exceptional circumstances. In yet other jurisdictions, notably France, the annulling judgment will be regarded as of no significance whatever, being rooted in a legal order to which the award is not subject. The question for consideration, then, is not whether the courts of an enforcing state *must* respect the foreign judgment—which plainly is not the case—but rather whether as a matter of policy they *should*. Adoption of the latter course is necessarily inconsistent with the theory of the stateless award. It will be contended: first, that the arguments are overwhelmingly against the concept of the stateless award, not only from the viewpoint of legal theory but also in terms of policy, practicality and the general legislative approach among states: second, that courts asked to enforce an award should, where permitted by their own law, defer to decisions of the court of origin under the *lex loci arbitri* in the absence of special circumstances; and, third, that any legislative barriers to the adoption of such an approach should be removed. I hope to show that, apart from other considerations, the theory of the stateless award is riddled with inconsistencies. In particular, it is founded on party autonomy, yet the parties' choice of their procedural law is ignored; it is motivated by the desire to promote the concept of internationality in cross-border arbitration, yet its effect, at any rate under French law, is totally to ignore international considerations and to rely exclusively on national law; its proponents declare that an award is not integrated into the legal system under which the arbitration takes place, or any legal system, yet they simultaneously insist that the award is integrated into the legal system of the state of enforcement, recognising that there has to be some court somewhere able to protect the parties against gross procedural unfairness or the exercise by arbitrators of a jurisdiction they do not possess.

4 THE CENTRAL ROLE OF THE *LEX LOCI ARBITRI*

No contract without law

One can begin with the simple proposition relating to substantive rights that a contract is not law, and no award can be binding simply by virtue of the parties' agreement to be bound. A contract depends for its force on recognition by law. The point was made by Dr Francis Mann in characteristically trenchant style in a passage from his seminal piece "*Lex Facit Arbitrum*",[24] which has been cited on countless occasions but is worth repeating:

> "No one has ever or anywhere been able to point to any provision or legal principle which would permit individuals to act outside the confines of a system of municipal law; even the idea of the autonomy of the parties exists only by virtue of a given system of municipal law and in different systems may have different characteristics and effects. Similarly, every arbitration is necessarily subject to the law of a given State. No private person has the right or the power to act on any level other than that of municipal law. Every right or power a private person enjoys is inexorably conferred by or derived from a system of municipal law which may conveniently and in accordance with tradition be called the *lex fori*, though it would be more exact (but less familiar) to speak of the *lex arbitri* or, in French, *la loi d'arbitrage*.

The same is true of usage, whether domestic or international.[25] A usage is not law; it is effective only so far as recognised by municipal law as having binding force. Even an international trade usage must be established. The only difference between litigation and international arbitration is that in the former the usage, if not already established by law, will need to be proved to the satisfaction of the judge, and to be accepted by the judge as conforming to the legal prerequisites of a binding usage, if it is to be enforceable, whereas in an international arbitration a tribunal may feel free to infer the existence of usage without the same degree of stringency in requiring evidence or in applying legal criteria, confident in the knowledge that nowadays the judicial review of arbitral awards is severely restricted.

Even the most ardent advocates of party autonomy appear to accept that arbitration must act within some system of law. Their case is that the only relevant system is that of the state of enforcement. But this argument never gets off the ground, for it presupposes that the arbitral process works in a complete legal vacuum unless and until application is made to enforce the award as a foreign award. If that were so, then at the time of its rendering the award would have no legal underpinnings at all. It would undoubtedly be the product of the parties' agreement, under which they assented to be bound, but as stated earlier that assent is no more than an agreement, lacking any legal force unless accepted as binding by the relevant national law; and the only possible law is the *lex loci arbitri*.[26] Moreover, one may ask what, under the autonomy concept, is

---

[24] *International Arbitration: Liber Amicorum for Martin Domke* (Martinus Nijhoff, The Hague, 1967) 157, 160. See to similar effect in a conflict of laws context Horacio A. Grigera Naon, *Choice-of-law Problems in International Commercial Arbitration* (J. C. B. Mohr (Paul Siebeck), Tübingen, 1992), 84–85.

[25] See generally Roy Goode, "Usage and its Reception in Transnational Commercial Law" (1997) 46 I.C.L.Q. 1.

[26] That is true even if the parties were unwisely to select as the curial law the law of a state other than that of the seat of the arbitration. The foreign curial law could be applied at the seat of the arbitration only so far as permitted by the *lex loci arbitri* and subject to its own mandatory provisions.

the status of the arbitral proceedings prior to the award? Do these too rest solely on the will of the parties? Such a contention has only to be stated for its absurdity to become obvious. A great many states around the world have now enacted arbitration status designed to accommodate international arbitration. Are these to count for nothing? Are they simply instruments writ in water? What does it mean to say that the arbitral proceedings are not constrained by national laws when all over the globe we find national laws which do exactly that?

Belgium, in the hope of attracting more international arbitration, introduced what it thought would be a popular provision into its law excluding the power of Belgian courts to entertain an application for annulment of an award only if at least one of the parties to the dispute was Belgian.[27] This ingenious measure back-fired as the arbitration community came to see that its effect was to leave parties who wanted judicial assistance or had good grounds for annulment with nowhere to go.[28] Faced with this criticism[29] Belgium followed the lead of the Swiss Private International Law Act,[30] and changed its law to give the parties the option to exclude judicial review by agreement. So also did Sweden.[31] However, it appears that in Swiss arbitrations most foreign parties, following the advice of leading commentators on the Swiss Private International Law Act, have not availed themselves of that exclusion option.[32] This strongly suggests that most parties do not wish to take themselves wholly outside a legal framework in settling their disputes through arbitration.

Respect for party autonomy

The theory of the stateless award is grounded on the notion that the will of the parties should be respected and that it is this, not a *lex arbitri*, which gives binding force to an award. It is worth reminding ourselves of the terms of the arbitration clauses in the cases referred to above. In *Götaverken* the arbitration clause provided that disputes were to be referred to arbitration and this was to take place in Paris under the I.C.C. Rules. These stated that the rules governing the procedure were to be those resulting from the I.C.C. Rules themselves, and, where they were silent, any rules which the parties (or failing them, the arbitrator) might settle, and whether or not reference was thereby made to a

---

[27] Judicial Code, Article 1717(4).

[28] It is an accepted principle that, while an enforcing court may refuse to recognise a foreign award, only the court of origin has power to annul it.

[29] See, e.g., William W. Park, "National Law and Commercial Justice: Safeguarding Procedural Integrity in International Arbitration" (1989) 63 Tulane L. Rev 647.

[30] Private International Law Act, Article 192(2).

[31] Arbitration Act 1999, section 51.

[32] Bruno Leurent, "Reflections on the International Effectiveness of Arbitration Awards" (1996) 12 Arb. Int. 269, 273.

municipal procedural law to be applied to the arbitration. So in this case the effect of the arbitration clause was neutral; the I.C.C. Rules contemplated that the parties or the arbitrator could, if they wished, resort to municipal law, but that they would not necessarily do so. In *Norsolor*[33] the position was the same except that the I.C.C. Court fixed Vienna as the place of arbitration. By contrast, in *Hilmarton*[34] the arbitration clause specifically provided that the arbitration "shall take place in Geneva under the law of the Canton of Geneva". If the theory of the stateless award is based on the overriding effects of party autonomy, how was the French Court of Cassation able to find that the *Hilmarton* award was not integrated into the Swiss legal system, to which the parties had expressly subjected the arbitral proceedings? In *Chromalloy*[35] the arbitration clause provided that "both parties have irrevocably agreed to apply Egypt [*sic*] Laws and to choose Cairo as the seat of the court of arbitration". We may note the use of the word "seat" rather than "place", emphasising the intention to choose Egypt as the place with which the arbitration was to have its juridical link. Again, one may ask, on what basis could the Court of Cassation disregard the express choice of the parties and instead determine that the award was not integrated into the Egyptian legal system? It seems that the principle of party autonomy is being used with a high degree of selectivity. The award derives its force from the agreement of the parties, but their decision to select a stated national law to govern the proceedings leading to the award is to be ignored![36]

The protection of legitimate expectations

A fundamental purpose of the conflict of laws, and the reason why national courts are ready in appropriate cases to apply a foreign law to a dispute and to recognise and enforce judgments of foreign courts, is to protect the legitimate expectations of the parties to the dispute, who would suffer injustice if their reasonable reliance on the applicability of the law having the closest connection to the matters in issue were to be frustrated.[37] Where the parties have, expressly or by implication, selected a curial law, then to deny legal effect to that selection is not only to undermine the very principle of party autonomy on which the theory of the stateless award is based but to frustrate their legitimate expectations. Of course, one of the tenets of the delocalisation concept is that in international arbitration we should seek to dispense with reliance on conflict of

---

[33] *Supra,* n. 18.
[34] *Supra,* n. 18.
[35] *Supra,* n. 19.
[36] It should be observed that we are here speaking not merely of a choice of venue, and the implications to be drawn from this, which are examined below, but explicit choice of the procedural law (in *Hilmarton*) or of the seat (*Chromalloy*).
[37] *Dicey & Morris on The Conflict of Laws,* 13th edn. (1993), para. 1–006.

laws rules altogether, since these are seen as merely perpetuating a national, rather than transnational, approach to the determination of disputes. Still, they have to face the question: what about party autonomy? Several answers have been propounded:

(1) The choice of seat is often a matter of mere convenience
This is a *canard* of long standing. It is doubtful whether it was ever true. Francis Mann, for example, wrote more than 30 years ago that choice of the seat "is usually far from fortuitous, but made for good and well-understood reasons and purposes".[38] More recently, it has been said[39] that:

> "The seat is typically fixed in a place where neither party has a place of business, e.g. the shores of Lake Leman. That location is not selected for its hotel facilities or charming setting, but essentially because of the parties' confidence in the neutrality of the forum, the quality of the Swiss Private International Law (FSPIL) and the competence of Swiss jurists, arbitrators and judges (the same applies to Paris, London, Stockholm and other places)."

(2) The choice of seat is often determined not by the parties but by the arbitral institution they have selected
This is true but not to the point. Parties choose an arbitral institution because of their confidence in its ability to administer the arbitration and to make a sensible decision on the selection of the seat in the light of relevant factors, including the adequacy of the legal regime governing international commercial arbitration.

(3) The choice of seat is often governed by the desire for neutrality
This is also true, but if anything reinforces the argument that the parties have given serious thought to the choice of seat. It is fanciful to suppose that they would be happy to select as the seat any place that happened to be convenient and neutral.

(4) The role of the arbitral tribunal is transitory and the seat has no necessary connection with the dispute
This may be true but proves too much, for it fails to explain why as a matter of principle or policy the law of an enforcing state should necessarily have any greater claim to recognition than the *lex loci arbitri*. There may be at least as much contact with the forum state as with the enforcement state, which may have no link with the parties or the transaction whatsoever and is involved merely because of the fortuitous existence of assets of the respondent within its jurisdiction. Consider the following:

---

[38] "Lex facit arbitrum" (*supra*, n. 6), 163.
[39] Leurent (1996) 12 Arb. Int. 269, 272.

"A German corporation and a French corporation enter into a contract under which the German corporation agrees to construct a plant in Milan for the French corporation. Any disputes are to be determined by an arbitral tribunal having its seat in Zurich and established in accordance with the arbitration rules of the Zurich Chamber of Commerce. The German corporation has its principal place of business in Berlin but other substantial places of business in Stockholm and Milan. It also has significant investments in New York but does not carry on any trading activity in the United States. The French corporation has its principal place of business in Paris but conducts substantial business activity in Milan and The Netherlands. It has no points of contact with the United States. The contract is made in Milan and is to be performed there. The French corporation, alleging that the plant did not comply with the contract specifications, invokes the aribtration clause. An award is made in favour of the French corporation but is set aside by the Swiss courts. The French corporation then applies to a US federal court in New York to enforce the award."

Of all the states connected to the dispute, the United States is the one whose link is the most tenuous. There are far more points of contact with the other states: France, Germany, Italy, Sweden and The Netherlands. For neutrality none of these is chosen; the parties consciously choose Switzerland, having confidence in the Swiss legal environment governing international commercial arbitration. On what basis can it be said that in terms of policy New York law has a stronger claim to consideration than Swiss law? But for the fact that the German company had assets in New York, there would be no ground whatsoever for New York courts even to entertain jurisdiction. The reason why it has to be given jurisdiction is, of course, that if it were not the successful claimant would have no way of reaching the assets. But that is simply a consequence of state sovereignty and power and has little to do with the question what law should be applied by the New York court.

The delocalisation theory undermines the concept of party autonomy in another sense. If, following annulment of the award, the parties engage in a fresh arbitration, appointing the same or a new panel of arbitrators, and pursue to the proceedings to a second award, why should not the consensual basis of the new arbitration proceedings, and the implicit acceptance of the nullity of the original award, be respected?[40] Why should the will of the parties be disregarded? And, if it is conceded that it should not be disregarded, we are left with the farcical position of two separate, and possibly conflicting, awards covering the same dispute, both of them having to be treated as valid under the theory of delocalisation.

Finality

Another fundamental purpose of the rules of conflict of laws is to help bring finality to disputes involving an international element. That is why English courts have traditionally declined to re-examine the judgment of a foreign court

---

[40] This fact situation also raises the question of estoppel, discussed below.

of competent jurisdiction in the absence of special reasons for so doing. *Interest reipublicae ut sit finis litium.*[41] The territorial approach, in insisting that the validity of an arbitral award is governed by the *lex arbitri*, has the great merit of subjecting the question of validity to a single decision at the court of origin. By contrast, denial of the function of a *lex arbitri* may involve litigation in every country in which the respondent has assets, and even within a single country may entail the case being taken up through a two-tier or even three-tier hierarchical chain and then, where the highest court acts as a court of cassation, being sent back again to a new lower court for a fresh determination. One has only to look at the history of the litigation in some of the cases referred to above to see the disastrous consequences of this. In *Hilmarton*[42] the Swiss award was taken through the hierarchy of courts in Switzerland and France, where the absurd position was reached that an award which had been set aside in Switzerland was granted *exequatur* by the Court of Appeal of Versailles, a second award resulting from fresh arbitration proceedings produced a different result but was in turn granted *exequatur* by the Versailles Court of Appeal, and the Court of Cassation, which had to do its best to resolve the muddle, made a decision which necessarily upheld one award (the first) and rejected the other. Ultimately the case ended up in English litigation, after which it was settled. In *Chromalloy*[43] the contract gave rise to proceedings in Egypt, France and the United States. So much for finality! As more than one commentator has pointed out, this is not delocalisation, it is multilocalisation.[44]

Avoidance of multiple jeopardy

Closely linked to the conflict of laws policy of promoting finality is its separate policy of avoiding double jeopardy. *Nemo debet vis vexari pro eadem causa.*[45] The effect of refusal to acknowledge any place for the *lex loci arbitri* is that the respondent against whom an award is made, having battled successfully through his own courts to have it set aside, is then faced with the prospect of having to relitigate the identical issues before the courts of every country in which he has assets. This can only be described as oppressive.

[41] *Dicey & Morris* (*supra*, n. 37), para. 14–110.
[42] *Supra*, n. 18.
[43] *Supra*, n. 19.
[44] See, e.g., Pierre Mayer, "The Trend Towards Delocalisation in the Last 100 Years", in Hunter, Marriott & Veeder (eds), *The Internationalisation of International Arbitration: The LCIA Centenary Conference* (Graham & Trotman/Martinus Nijhoff, London/Dordrecht/Boston, 1995), 46.
[45] *Dicey & Morris* (*supra*, n. 34), para. 14–110.

Economic efficiency

The exposure to a multiplicity of proceedings in a number of different countries also undermines what should be one of the purposes of international commercial arbitration, namely to promote economic efficiency in the handling of the dispute. A concept which provokes multiple lawsuits in different jurisdictions induces profligacy and the wasteful use of resources.

Estoppel

It is a general principle of law that a contracting party who pursues a particular course of conduct on which the other party reasonably relics cannot subsequently be allowed to follow a course which is inconsistent with the position he previously took. This principle of estoppel—reflected in civil law jurisdictions in the maxim *non concedit venire contra factum proprium*—has many manifestations. For example, in litigation an English court will take as its starting point the fact that a foreign judgment against a party by a court of competent jurisdiction creates an estoppel *per rem judicatem* precluding that party from relitigating the issue in England except where there are strong grounds to impeach the judgment, e.g. that it was obtained by fraud. In arbitration a similar principle prevails. Thus, it is widely accepted that a person who participates in arbitration proceedings and against whom an arbitral award is made cannot in general invoke a ground for attacking the validity of the arbitration agreement or the jurisdiction of the tribunal which he did not advance before the tribunal itself.[46]

One of the problems with the concept of the stateless award is that it fails to respect this well-established principle of estoppel. A party against whom an award is made decides to challenge it in the courts of the seat of the arbitration. If he is unsuccessful, why should he be allowed a second—or a third or fourth—bite at the cherry in proceedings before a court or courts elsewhere? Why, having embarked on a challenge under the *lex loci arbitri*, should he not be required to accept the outcome? Let us take the argument a step further. An arbitral award is set aside at the court of the seat. Thereupon the claimant institutes fresh arbitration proceedings in the same place. Why, having done this, should he be allowed simultaneously to enforce the first award in a foreign country? Why does not his institution of the second arbitral proceedings constitute an acceptance of the invalidity of the earlier award and an election to pursue his claim through the new proceedings?

---

[46] For a recent English decision to this effect see *Westacre Investments Inc.* v. *Jugoimport-S.D.R.P. Holdings Ltd.* [1999] Q.B. 740.

Inconsistency of judgments of foreign courts

A further consequence of the statelessness of an arbitral award is that it gives rise to the strong possibility of conflicting decisions of different foreign courts. This is surely a strange way of promoting the internationality of arbitration. Take the case where, after the annulment of an award, the claimant institutes fresh arbitration proceedings and is again successful but this time secures an amount only half of that given in the first award. What happens then? Is he to have the option to go back to the first, annulled, award. The present position would seem to be that the claimant can enforce the larger award in France and countries which follow the approach of French law but is restricted to the smaller award in countries which do not follow the French line. This hardly seems the best way of promoting predictability or uniformity in international arbitration.

There is another problem which is potentially even more acute. In the legal systems of some countries (which included Germany until it amended its arbitration law) the effect of annulment of an award is not to leave the way open for a fresh arbitration but to restore the ordinary competence of the courts, so that a fresh proceeding by way of action rather than arbitration becomes admissible. That proceeding may lead to a judgment which is required to be recognised and enforced elsewhere under bilateral or regional conventions, such as the Brussels Convention on Jurisdiction and the Enforcement of Judgments in Civil Matters. So, for example, the annulment of an award in one such state will have no effect in France, the courts of which would apply its own arbitration law to enforce the award, while those same courts would at the same time be duty bound to recognise and enforce the judgment upholding the claim in the post-annulment litigation. Of course, a solution would have to be found, and would be found—but why create the problem in the first place?

The privileged status of arbitration agreements

Another important factor overlooked by the protagonists of the stateless award is that a written arbitration agreement is not like an ordinary contract. Around the world it is given special, and highly prized, privileges. In the first place, a valid agreement to arbitrate invoked by a party against whom court proceedings are instituted effectively halts the proceedings. This is mandatory for the courts of states parties to the New York Convention[47] and is also specifically provided in the UNCITRAL Model Law.[48] Secondly, the parties and their arbitrator have much more freedom in the conduct of the arbitration than national judges. They need not follow rules of procedure or evidence prescribed for actions by the *lex fori*, nor are they required to apply the conflict rules of the *lex fori* in

---

[47] Article II(3).
[48] Article 8(1).

determining the applicable law in the absence of party choice. Thirdly, judicial review of an arbitral award is very much more restricted than an appeal against a judgment. Fourthly, an arbitral award can be enforced in the country of the award as if it were a judgment without the need for an action on the award. Finally, under the New York Convention and conventions with similar objectives[49] an award made in one state can be enforced in all other contracting states[50] where the conditions set by the convention and any implementing legislation are satisfied. This is a hugely important privilege, which is much more extensive in geographical scope than that accorded to judgments of courts.

These privileges derive from national laws and international conventions, not from contract. How can parties to an arbitration claim the benefit of such laws and conventions and simultaneously ascribe the binding force of the arbitral award exclusively to their mutual will? If it is the case that the agreement to arbitrate is the sole source of the binding nature of the award, then let the parties be bound by the consequences attaching to any normal contract, namely that the sole method of enforcement is by an action on the award and that the resulting judgment will not enjoy the finality of an arbitral award or the benefit of the New York Convention.

Comity and co-operation

If the courts of other countries followed the example of the French courts it is clear that Article V of the New York Convention would become a dead letter. No court would have any regard for the decisions of foreign courts setting aside an award; all courts would take refuge in their own arbitration law. Such an approach is subversive of the very internationality which the theory of statelessness is proclaimed to advance. Moreover, it is incompatible with the mutual courtesy and respect which each state and its courts are expected to show to other states and their courts as regards laws and decisions made by the latter within their respective jurisdictions. The principle of comity embodying such notions of mutual courtesy and respect has had varying impact at different stages in its history. At one time it was thought to be the basic principles upon which the conflict of laws rested. Later it was downgraded to a more subsidiary role as state courts came to the view that comity as such did not provide a reliable basis for deciding when to exercise self-restraint in the face of proceedings and judgments in foreign courts. Yet there are now indications that the concept of comity is regaining ground. In England, for example, one reason

---

[49] For example, the European (Geneva) Convention on International Commercial Arbitration 1961 and the Inter-American (Panama) Convention on Arbitration 1975.

[50] Assuming, in the case of the New York Convention, that the state of origin is a contracting state or that the state of enforcement has not made a declaration under Article I(3) limiting its obligation to the enforcement of awards made in another contracting state.

why it is invoked is to avoid jurisdictional conflicts. That is why English courts, in granting world-wide *Mareva* injunctions (now "freezing orders"), are careful to stipulate that enforcement abroad requires the approval of the requisite foreign court.

> "The jurisdiction to make such orders is now firmly established. It is exercised with caution and a sufficient case to justify its exercise must always be made out; but such orders are nowadays routinely made in cases of international fraud and the conditions necessary in order to preserve international comity and prevent conflicts of jurisdiction have become standardised."[51]

That is why also they have regard to considerations of comity in cross-border insolvency cases.[52] But the case can be put even more strongly. We have now moved beyond the concept of self-restraint and towards active international co-operation in civil procedure. This has come about through a variety of means: legislation, of which again insolvency law provides an example:[53] judicial activism, particularly in the field of cross-border insolvency, where independently of legislation judges of national courts sought ways to assist their counterparts in foreign countries; and the work of international organisations in promoting cross-border collaboration in specific fields, such as cross-border insolvency,[54] and in civil proceedings generally.[55] For the world of international arbitration to revert to a system in which each state paid regard only to its own laws, and each court only to judicial decisions within its own jurisdiction, would severely impede the cause of international co-operation in dispute resolution. The internationalisation of arbitration does not depend on, and is not promoted by, the concept of statelessness, which the courts of enforcing states adopting such a concept never see as applying to their own enforcement orders; on the contrary, all the concept achieves is a fragmentation of decision-making as each court focuses exclusively on its own powers and refuses to countenance a proper law for courts of the seat of the arbitration.

Disappearance of the *raison d'être* for disregard of the curial law

Finally, the main cause of the reluctance for concern of courts of enforcement states to defer to rulings of courts of origin, namely the hostility of local courts in a number of jurisdictions to the concept of arbitration and their assertion of

---

[51] *Credit Suisse Fides Trust S.A.* v. *Cuoghi* [1998] Q.B. 818, 824, *per* Millett, L.J.

[52] See, e.g., *Re Paramount Airways Ltd* [1993] Ch 223; *Jyske Bank (Gibraltar) Ltd.* v. *Spjeldnaes* [1999] 2 B.C.L.C. 101.

[53] Insolvency Act 1986, section 426.

[54] See e.g. the UNCITRAL Model Law on Cross-Border Insolvency 1997.

[55] E.g. the American Law Institute Project on Transnational Rules of Civil Procedure, in which international organisations such as UNIDROIT have been invited to participate.

excessive jurisdiction over arbitral proceedings and awards, has largely (though not entirely) disappeared as state after state has departed from its traditional arbitration rules and enacted legislation along the lines of the UNCITRAL Model Law. As one authority has rightly commented, if member states of the European Communities had sufficient confidence in each other's courts to ratify the Brussels and Lugano conventions providing for the mutual recognition and enforcement of judgments, why should they not have the same confidence in judgments of courts of other states setting aside arbitral awards?[56]

5 CONCLUSION

The objections to the concept of the stateless aware are overwhelming and should now be universally accepted. None of the arguments in favour of the stateless award has explained why, apart from *force majeure*, the courts of an enforcement state should be considered to have a prerogative denied to others. If, which is not suggested, there is to be a single court the judgments of which are in principle to have effect *erga omnes*, it should be the court of the seat. France is almost alone in its advocacy of the stateless award and is believed to be unique in not even allowing its courts to invoke the setting aside of an award in the court of origin as a ground for refusing recognition and enforcement in France. French scholars and French courts have over the years made an immense contribution to the liberalisation of international commercial arbi-tration. Faced with widespread opposition to the concept of the stateless award they could perform a further and signal service to international arbitration by gracefully withdrawing from their present approach, which is seen in most countries as a step too far. This change of direction would itself be an act of leadership, not of defeat, and would help to restore the transnational character of international commercial arbitration.

The most appropriate solution is that based on fulfilling the twin objectives of satisfying legitimate expectations and fostering international co-operation among courts. Article VII of the New York Convention is here a stumbling block in that it encourages states to bypass Article V and invoke their own laws. That is damaging to the process of internationalisation which the Convention itself has done so much to foster. A strong case can be made for amending Article VII of the Convention by restricting its scope to treaties entered into by

---

[56] J.-F. Poudret, "Quelle solution pour en finir avec l'affaire Hilmarton?—Réponse à Philippe Fouchard" [1998] Rev. Arb. 7, 14–15. See also Klaus Peter Berger, *International Economic Arbitration*: Studics in Transnational Economic Law, vol. 9 (Kluwer Law and Taxation, Deventer, Netherlands, 1993), 96–97. See also William W. Park, "Duty and Discretion in International Arbitration" (1999) 93 A.J.I.L. 805, 813.

the enforcing state—removing that part of Article VII which enables a party to invoke the more favourable provisions of the law of enforcement—and by leaving courts of enforcing states to rely on the discretion already available to them under Article V, a discretion which itself should be exercised with caution.[57] This should go hand in hand with a self-denying precept of legislatures and courts to the effect that, while the court of enforcement must inevitably have the last word to cater for exceptional cases, in principle judgments of courts of the seat enforcing, suspending or annulling an award should be respected, as should findings of fact by such courts. Obviously there will be such exceptional cases, e.g. fraud discovered only after the judgment. But adherence to the general principle is essential if we are to respect party choice, to avoid the cost, inconvenience and risk of inconsistent decisions resulting from a multiplicity of proceedings, and to foster rather than damage mutual respect and co-operation among courts of different states.

---

[57] Albert Jan van den Berg, "Residual Discretion and the Validity of the Arbitration Agreement in the Enforcement of Arbitral Awards under the New York Convention of 1958" in Chang *et al.*, *Current Legal Issues in International Commercial Arbitration* (University of Singapore, 1997), 335–336, noting that the discretion to allow enforcement despite a ground for refusal under Art. V was designed to cater for two situations, namely minor procedural irregularity and failure to raise before the arbitral tribunal the objection to the tribunal's jurisdiction advanced as a challenge to the award before the court of enforcement.

Appendix

Convention on the recognition and enforcement of foreign arbitral awards. Done at New York on 10 June 1958

Article V

1   Recognition and enforcement of the award may be refused, at the request of the party against whom it is invoked, only if that party furnishes to the competent authority where the recognition and enforcement is sought, proof that:

(a) The parties to the agreement referred to in article II were, under the law applicable to them, under some incapacity, or the said agreement is not valid under the law to which the parties have subjected it or, failing any indication thereon, under the law of the country where the award was made; or

(b) The party against whom the award is invoked was not given proper notice of the appointment of the arbitrator or of the arbitration proceedings or was otherwise unable to present his case; or

(c) The award deals with a difference not contemplated by or not falling within the terms of the submission to arbitration, or it contains decisions on matters beyond the scope of the submission to arbitration, provided that, if the decisions on matters submitted to arbitration can be separated from those not so submitted, that part of the award which contains decisions on matters submitted to arbitration may be recognised and enforced; or

(d) The composition of the arbitral authority or the arbitral procedure was not in accordance with the agreement of the parties, or, failing such agreement, was not in accordance with the law of the country where the arbitration took place; or

(e) The award has not yet become binding on the parties, or has been set aside or suspended by a competent authority of the country in which, or under the law of which, that award was made.

2   Recognition and enforcement of an arbitral award may also be refused if the competent authority in the country where recognition and enforcement is sought finds that:

(a) The subject matter of the difference is not capable of settlement by arbitration under the law of that country; or

(b) The recognition or enforcement of the award would be contrary to the public policy of that country.

Article VI

If an application for the setting aside or suspension of the award has been made to a competent authority referred to in article V(1)(e), the authority before which the award is sought to be relied upon may, if it considers it proper, adjourn the decision on the enforcement of the award and may also, on the application of the party claiming enforcement of the award, order the other party to give suitable security.

Article VII

1   The provisions of the present Convention shall not affect the validity of multilateral or bilateral agreements concerning the recognition and enforcement of arbitral awards entered into by the Contracting States nor deprive any interested party of any right he may have to avail himself of an arbitral award in the manner and to the extent allowed by the law or the treaties of the country where such award is sought to be relied upon.

2   The Geneva Protocol on Arbitration Clauses of 1923 and the Geneva Convention on the Execution of Foreign Arbitral Awards 1927 shall cease to have effect between Contracting States on their becoming bound and to the extent that they become bound, by this Convention.

Chapter 14

Pre-judgment Interest in the Conflict of Laws

Anthony Guest

Francis Reynolds has been my colleague, friend, and collaborator in both *Chitty on Contracts* and *Benjamin's Sale of Goods* for over forty years. Being more precise than I am, he would no doubt be able to put an exact figure on the period. During that time, however, he will not have noted any particular enthusiasm on my part to venture into the subject of the conflict of laws. But I do so on this occasion in order to pay tribute to his own interest and expertise in the subject.

The issue discussed in this paper is the relationship between the applicable law (*lex causae*) and English law as the *lex fori* in relation to pre-judgment interest.

1 CONTRACTUAL INTEREST

Where interest is payable on a loan or other debt by virtue of an express or implied contractual term, it was well established at common law that the liability to pay interest up to the date of judgment, and the rate of interest payable, were determined by the law applicable to the contract under which the debt was incurred.[1] The position is the same under the Rome Convention, which has been implemented in the United Kingdom by the Contracts (Applicable Law) Act 1990. There is no express mention of interest in Article 10(1) of the Convention, which deals with the scope of the law applicable to a contract by virtue of the Convention. But Article 10(1) provides that the applicable law is to

---

[1] *Bodily* v. *Bellamy* (1760) 2 Burr. 1094; *Dewar* v. *Span* (1789) 3 T.R. 425, 427; *Harvey* v. *Archbold* (1825) 3 B. & C. 626; *Anon* (1825) 3 Bing. 193 (H.L.); *Thompson* v. *Powles* (1828) 2 Sim. 194; *Mount Albert B.C.* v. *Australasian etc. Assurance Soc. Ltd.* [1938] A.C. 224. See also *Barcelo* v. *Electrolytic Zinc. Co. etc. Ltd.* (1932) 48 C.L.R. 39; *Wanganui etc. Board* v. *Australian Mutual Provident Soc.* (1934) 50 C.L.R. 581; *Associated Loan Co.* v. *Callaghan* (1957) 9 D.L.R. (2d) 559; *Rosencrantz* v. *Union Contractors Ltd.* (1960) 23 D.L.R. (2d) 473; *Montreal Trust Co.* v. *Stanrock Uranium Mines Ltd.* (1965) 53 D.L.R. (2d) 594.

govern in particular "(a) interpretation" and "(b) performance". The reference to "interpretation" means that the law which governs the contract will determine, for example, whether a term requiring the payment of interest can or cannot be implied even though not expressed,[2] whether an express term to pay interest up to the date of payment does or does not imply an agreement to pay interest beyond that date in the event of a default in payment,[3] whether by course of dealing or by trade custom there is a right to capitalise interest at periodic rests,[4] and what rate of interest (if any) is to be implied if no rate is expressly stated.[5] The reference to "performance" is, perhaps, less clear, since Article 10(1) submits "performance" to the law which governs the contract, but Article 10(2) provides that in relation to the "manner of performance" regard is to be had to the law of the country in which performance takes place. The editors of *Dicey and Morris on The Conflict of Laws*,[6] however, cogently point out that the liability to pay interest as provided for in the contract, and the rate of interest payable, relate to the content of the obligation to be performed, and not to the manner of performance. They are therefore governed by the law applicable to the contract under the Convention. Rule 196(1) in *Dicey & Morris* in consequence states:[7]

> "The liability to pay contractual interest and the rate of such interest payable in respect of a debt, e.g. in respect of a loan, are in general determined by the law applicable to the contract under which the debt is incurred, e.g. by the law applicable to the contract under which the loan is made."

It is the law which governs the contract which will therefore normally determine whether an express provision for the payment of interest is valid and effective or whether it is void on the ground of usury or otherwise.[8] That law will also determine whether the rate of interest is capped or controlled[9] and whether it is permissible to stipulate for compound interest, or interest upon interest, or only for simple interest.[10] It will also determine whether or not it is permissible to include a term which provides for a variable rate of interest and,

---

[2] *Great Western Insurance Co.* v. *Cunliffe* (1874) L.R. 9 Ch. 525; *Re Marquis of Anglesey* [1901] 2 Ch. 548; *Re Duncan & Co.* [1905] 1 Ch. 307.

[3] *Cook* v. *Fowler* (1874) L.R. 7 H.L. 27, 37.

[4] *National Bank of Greece S.A.* v. *Pinios Shipping Co. (No. 1)* [1990] 1 A.C. 637.

[5] *Re Commercial Bank of South Australia* (1887) 36 Ch.D. 522, 529. See also *Re Savage's Estate* (1908) 29 N.L.R. 397 (South Africa).

[6] 13th edn. (1999) (hereafter "*Dicey & Morris*"), §§ 32–191 to 32–197, 33–374.

[7] *Ibid.*, § 33R–371.

[8] *Harvey* v. *Archbold* (1825) 3 B. & C. 626; *Thompson* v. *Powles* (1828) 2 Sim. 194; *Shrichand* v. *Lacon* (1906) 22 T.L.R. 245; *Rosencrantz* v. *Union Contractors Ltd.* (1960) 23 D.L.R. (2d) 473.

[9] *Barcelo* v. *Electrolytic Zinc Co. etc. Ltd.* (1932) 48 C.L.R. 391; *Wanganui etc. Board* v. *Australian Mutual Provident Soc.* (1934) 50 C.L.R. 581; *Associated Loan Co.* v. *Callaghan* (1957) 9 D.L.R. (2d) 559.

[10] *Montreal Trust Co.* v. *Stanrock Uranium Mines Ltd.* (1965) 53 D.L.R. (2d) 594.

in particular, whether a term which enables the creditor to vary the rate of interest at his discretion[11] or which provides for a higher rate of interest after default[12] will be upheld. Controls imposed by English law as the *lex fori* or by the law of the place where the contract is to be performed are in principle irrelevant unless English law or the *lex loci solutionis* (as the case may be) is also the law applicable to the contract.

To this general rule, however, there are a number of exceptions:

(1) The wide freedom conferred on the parties by the Rome Convention to choose the applicable law is restricted by Article 3(3), which provides:

> "The fact that the parties have chosen a foreign law, whether or not accompanied by the choice of a foreign tribunal, shall not, where all the other elements relevant to the situation at the time of the choice are connected with one country only, prejudice the application of rules of law of that country which cannot be derogated from by contract, hereinafter called 'mandatory rules'."

An English court would therefore, for example, notwithstanding an express choice of English law as the law applicable to the contract, have to apply the mandatory rules of German law (which render void in certain circumstances a contractual term for the payment of interest upon interest, i.e. the compounding of interest)[13] where all the other elements relevant to the situation at the time of the choice were connected with Germany only. The purpose of this provision is to prevent the evasion of mandatory rules (as defined therein) by choosing a foreign law to govern a contract which has no real foreign connection but is essentially a domestic contract. The precise scope of the provision is not free from difficulty,[14] but, in practice, it is likely to be of very narrow application where an action is brought in an English court on a contract which is expressly governed by English law. The reference to *all* the other elements relevant to the situation being connected with *one* other country means that the court will have to apply foreign mandatory rules only in the unlikely event that parties in a foreign country have chosen English law to govern their contract although there is no connection with England or any other country but their own.[15]

(2) In the case of certain consumer contracts, Article 5 of the Rome Convention[16] places a restriction on the effect of a choice of law in contracts subject to the Article:

> "... a choice of law made by the parties shall not have the result of depriving the

---

[11] See *Lombard Tricity Finance Ltd.* v. *Paton* [1989] 1 All E.R. 918.

[12] *Lordsvale Finance Plc* v. *Bank of Zambia* [1996] Q.B. 752.

[13] BGB, § 248(1).

[14] See *Dicey & Morris* §§ 32–129 to 32–140; *Chitty on Contracts*, 28th edn. (1999) vol. I (hereafter "*Chitty*") §§ 31–057 to 31–063.

[15] *Chitty*, § 31–057. Lasok and Stone, *Conflict of Laws in the European Community* (1987), 377–378.

[16] See *Dicey & Morris*, §§ 33–001, 33–008 to 33–018; *Chitty*, §§ 31–086 to 31–093.

consumer of the protection afforded to him by the mandatory rules of the law of the country in which he has his habitual residence."

provided that any one of three specified conditions are satisfied. The first condition is if, in the country of the consumer's habitual residence, the conclusion of the contract was preceded by a specific invitation addressed to the consumer, or by advertising, and the consumer has taken in the country of his habitual residence all the steps necessary on his part for the conclusion of the contract.[17] The second condition is if the other party or his agent received the consumer's order in the country where the consumer was habitually resident.[18] The third condition is confined to contracts of sale of goods: if the consumer travelled from the country of his habitual residence to another country and there gave his order, provided that the consumer's journey was arranged by the seller for the purpose of inducing the consumer to buy.[19] An English court would therefore be bound to give effect to the mandatory rules of French law which protect the consumer by limiting the rate of interest payable under a consumer contract[20] if the consumer had his habitual residence in France and the other requirements of the Article were satisfied. The contracts falling within Article 5 are quite likely to include provisions requiring the consumer to pay interest, namely, any contract "the object of which is the supply of goods or services to . . . the consumer for a purpose which can be regarded as being outside his trade or profession, or a contract for the provision of credit for that object". However, not all agreements made with a consumer which provide for the payment of interest by him would be caught: for example, a contract for the provision of credit for the purchase of land would not fall within its provisions. Moreover, the conditions referred to above severely limit the application of the Article and, where English law has been chosen by the parties, it would be very rare for an English court to have to apply the mandatory rules of the country of a consumer's habitual residence by virtue of its provisions.

(3) The right of a creditor to claim contractual interest may be affected by the rule of common law laid down in *Ralli Brothers* v. *Compania Naviera Sota y Aznar*[21] that a contractual obligation in a contract governed by English law will be unenforceable if and in so far as it requires or necessarily involves performance which is unlawful by the place of performance. It will be recollected that, in that case, an English contract for the carriage of jute to Barcelona provided that freight was to be paid by the charterer to the shipowner at the rate of £50 per ton on delivery of the cargo at Barcelona. Subsequently, before arrival of the ship, the Spanish Government issued a decree fixing the

---

[17] *Dicey & Morris*, §§ 33–009 to 33–014.
[18] *Ibid.*, § 33–014.
[19] *Ibid.*, § 33–015.
[20] Consumer Code, L 313–3.
[21] [1920] 1 K.B. 614; affd [1920] 2 K.B. 287.

maximum rate of freight at £10 and making it illegal to pay more. The Court of Appeal held that the shipowner could not recover more than £10 per ton. If, therefore, a loan agreement governed by English law requires that payments of interest be made in Saudi Arabia, and the law of Saudi Arabia makes it illegal to pay interest, the creditor will be unable to enforce the obligation to pay interest in an English court. By the same token, a restriction placed by the law of the place where payments must be made making it illegal to pay interest in excess of a statutory maximum will similarly be upheld.[22] The precise extent of the rule in the *Ralli Brothers* case is nevertheless controversial. The editors of *Dicey & Morris* convincingly argue that, as here formulated, it is rule of English public policy applicable to English contracts and not a rule of the conflict of laws.[23] It is therefore not affected by the Rome Convention. There are, however, dicta which suggest that the rule would apply irrespective of the law which governs the contract, that is to say, it would apply even if, for example, the contract of loan were governed by French law.[24] The editors of *Dicey & Morris* do not accept this view, but, if it is correct, consider that it would be difficult to reconcile it with the Convention, which in principle requires the law which governs the contract to be applied.[25] The issue is, however, as they point out,[26] unlikely to arise for decision as the requisite combination of factors would be very rare. Indeed, in relation to contractual interest, it would predicate a case in the English courts to recover interest payable under a contract governed by the law of State X which provided for the payment of interest in State Y (where the payment of interest or the payment of interest over a certain maximum rate is illegal), the law of State X nevertheless still permitting enforcement of the term relating to interest. It is submitted that there is no convincing reason of policy why an English court in such a situation should step in and refuse to enforce the interest term when the law governing the contract permitted recovery.

(4) Under Article 16 of the Rome Convention, an English court is free to

[22] See *Montreal Trust Co.* v. *Stanrock Uranium Mines Ltd.* (1965) 53 D.L.R. (2d) 594, 615 (compound interest). *Cf. Mount Albert B.C.* v. *Australian etc. Assurance Soc. Ltd.* [1938] A.C. 224, 241 (not illegal).

[23] *Dicey & Morris*, § 32–144. See also *Kahler* v. *Midland Bank Ltd.* [1950] A.C. 24, 48; *Société Co-operative Suisse des Cereales* v. *La Plata Cereal Co. S.A.* (1949) 80 Ll.L.Rep. 530, 543–544; *Walton (Grain and Shipping) Ltd.* v. *British Italian Trading Co.* [1959] 1 Lloyds' Rep. 223, 236; *Bangladesh Export Import Co. Ltd.* v. *Sucden Kerry S.A.* [1995] 2 Lloyd's Rep. 1, 5; Cheshire and North, *Private International Law*, 12th edn. (1992) (hereafter "*Cheshire & North*"), 519; Mann (1937) 18 B.Y.I.L. 97, 107–113; Morris (1953) 6 Vand. L.Rev. 510; Reynolds (1992) 108 L.Q.R. 553.

[24] *Zivnostenska Banka* v. *Frankman* [1950] A.C. 57, 78; *Mackender* v. *Feldia A.G.* [1967] 2 Q.B. 590, 601. See also *R.* v. *International Trustee for the Protection of Bondholders A.G.* [1937] A.C. 500, 519; *Kleinwort Sons & Co.* v. *Ungarische Baumwolle Industrie A.G.* [1939] 2 K.B. 678, 697.

[25] *Dicey & Morris*, §§ 32–145 to 32–147; *Chitty*, § 31–115; Reynolds (1992) 108 L.Q.R. 553.

[26] *Dicey & Morris*, § 32–148.

refuse to apply the law chosen in the contract on the ground that the application of that law would be "manifestly incompatible with the public policy ("*ordre public*") of the forum".[27] It would not uphold a contractual provision for the payment of interest where this would be contrary to English public policy, for example, where the principal sum on which interest is payable is money expended in influencing public officials.[28] Nor would it give effect to a rule of the applicable law which, for example, deprived the creditor of interest by legislation which was penal and discriminatory.[29] But a general provision of the applicable law which invalidated any agreement for the payment of interest would not be contrary to English public policy.

(5) The "extortionate credit bargain" provisions contained in sections 137–140 of the Consumer Credit Act 1974[30] may, where an action is brought in an English court, override the obligation to pay interest under the law otherwise applicable to the contract. By section 137(1) of the Act, if the court finds a credit bargain extortionate, it may reopen the credit agreement so as to do justice between the parties. This power is not confined to credit agreements within the financial limits of the 1974 Act but extends to any credit agreement where the debtor is an "individual", i.e. not a body corporate. A credit bargain is extortionate if it:

(a) requires the debtor or a relative of his to make payments (whether unconditionally or on certain contingencies) which are grossly exorbitant, or

(b) otherwise contravenes ordinary principles of fair dealing.

In the vast majority of cases which have so far come before the courts, the court has been asked to re-open the agreement on the ground that the interest payable under it was grossly exorbitant. It is not open to the parties to contract out of these sections. Section 173(1) of the Act provides:

> "A term contained in a regulated agreement or linked transaction, or in any other agreement relating to an actual or prospective regulated agreement or linked transaction, is void if, and to the extent that, it is inconsistent with a provision for the protection of the debtor ... contained in this Act ..."

and section 140 extends the protection of sections 137–139 to agreements that are not regulated agreements. There is therefore no doubt that these provisions are "mandatory rules" of English law in the sense referred to in Article 3(3) of the Rome Convention; that is to say, they cannot be derogated from by contract.

---

[27] See *Dicey & Morris*, §§ 32–226 to 32–334; *Chitty*, §§ 31–160 to 31–162.

[28] *Lemenda Trading Co. Ltd.* v. *African Middle East Petroleum Co. Ltd.* [1988] Q.B. 448.

[29] *Re Friedrich Krupp A.G.* [1917] 2 Ch. 188; *The Playa Larga* [1983] 2 Lloyds' Rep. 171, 190.

[30] Guest and Lloyd, *Encyclopedia of Consumer Credit Law* (1974), §§ 2–194/2— 2–194/20; *Dicey & Morris*, §§ 33–031 to 33–037.

It follows that an English court would be bound to entertain an application to re-open a credit agreement on the ground that the interest payable was grossly exorbitant, even if that agreement was expressly governed by a foreign law which knew no such principle, in circumstances which fell within Article 3(3) or Article 5 of the Convention. However, it has been pointed out above that these two Articles are of very limited scope. It is very unlikely that circumstances would arise where an English court would be in a position to reopen such a credit agreement due to the existence of the circumstances envisaged by those Articles.

Of potentially greater impact is Article 7(2) of the Rome Convention.[31] This provides that nothing in the Convention is to restrict the application of the rules of the law of the forum in a situation where they are mandatory irrespective of the law otherwise applicable to the contract. In this provision, however, the concept of "mandatory rules" is narrower than that in Articles 3(3) and 5. Not only must those rules be mandatory in the sense that they cannot be derogated from by contract but they must also be mandatory irrespective of the law applicable to the contract. The Consumer Credit Act 1974 gives no indication whether sections 137–140 of the Act are mandatory in this sense. Suppose that an action is brought in an English court to recover interest due under a moneylending agreement which is expressly stated to be governed by (say) the law of Bermuda.[32] The creditor is a Bermudan company and the debtor is a citizen of the United Kingdom who, at the time of the loan, was working in Bermuda and who borrowed the money to consolidate and pay off debts contracted there. The debtor claims that the interest payable on the loan was grossly exorbitant and applies to have the loan agreement reopened. Do sections 137–140 of the 1974 Act have effect notwithstanding that the parties have chosen the law of Bermuda (which imposes no control over interest rates) as the law which governs their contract? On one view, on the true construction of section 137(1), an English court is required to intervene, to do justice between the parties irrespective of any choice of a foreign law. On this view, the rules in sections 137–140 are mandatory in the sense of Article 7(2) and the English court can therefore apply them as mandatory rules of the law of the forum even though Bermudan law is otherwise applicable to the contract. On another view, however, the purpose of the 1974 Act is to protect debtors in the United Kingdom market, and only in that market,[33] so that it is only in that situation will the court apply the extortionate credit bargain provisions irrespective of the applicable law. Since, in the example given, the debtor, in taking the loan, was

---

[31] *Dicey & Morris*, §§ 32–132 to 32–133; *Chitty*, § 31–064.

[32] By Article 1(1), 2 of the Convention, the rules of the Convention are to be applied even though they point to the law of a state which is not a contracting state nor a member of the EC.

[33] Guest and Lloyd, *Encyclopedia of Consumer Credit Law* (1974) §§ 2–194/8, 2–194/14.

not dealing in the United Kingdom market, the rules are to that extent not mandatory in the sense of Article 7(2). They could not therefore be applied by an English court as mandatory rules of the forum when the parties have chosen Bermudan law as the law which governs their contract. So far there has been no judicial consideration of this problem. It would also be open to the debtor to rely on Article 16 of the Convention, referred to above. But it is questionable whether sections 137–140 of the 1974 Act establish a principle of "public policy" in English law (in the sense intended by Article 16)[34] which is to be applied irrespective of the law applicable to the contract or the place of performance unless enforcement of the transaction would be contrary to the public interest or morality because of the presence of some further vitiating factor such as fraud, coercion or undue influence.

The better view, it is submitted, is therefore that the court is unlikely to allow a debtor under a contract governed by a foreign law to rely on sections 137–140 of the Consumer Credit Act 1974 to challenge the contractual rate of interest agreed unless (a) the very exacting requirements of Article 3(3) or Article 5 of the Convention are satisfied, or (b) the circumstances surrounding the credit bargain are so compelling as to require the court to intervene irrespective of the fact that the law applicable to the credit agreement is a foreign law.

(6) A term in a consumer contract relating to interest may, in an English court, be challenged as unfair under the Unfair Terms in Consumer Contracts Regulations 1999.[35] Those Regulations implement Council Directive 93/13/EEC on unfair terms in consumer contracts. There is little doubt that they are "mandatory rules" in the sense of Article 3(3) of the Convention, that is to say, rules of English law which cannot be derogated from by contract. They could therefore seemingly be applied by an English court in the circumstances set out in Article 3(3) or Article 5 of the Convention even though the contract in question was governed by a foreign law. But Regulation 9 contains a specific provision with respect to choice of law clauses:

> "These Regulations shall apply notwithstanding any contract term which applies or purports to apply the law of a non-Member State, if the contract has a close connection with the territory of the Member States."

"Member State" is defined[36] to mean a State which is a contracting party to the E.E.A. Agreement, i.e., the Agreement on the European Economic Area signed at Oporto as amended by the protocol signed at Brussels. The effect would

---

[34] See *Dicey & Morris*, §§ 32–237 to 32–334. *Cf.* Guest and Lloyd, *Encyclopedia of Consumer Credit Law* (1974), § 2–194/15.

[35] S.I. 1999 No. 2083, revoking and replacing S.I. 1994 No. 3159. Those Regulations implemented Council Directive 93/13/EEC on unfair terms in consumer contracts: O.J. No. L95, 21.4.93, p. 29.

[36] Regulation 3(1).

appear to be that an English court would, under this provision and Article 7(2) of the Convention, apply the Regulations irrespective of the choice of the law of a non-member State as the law applicable to the contract if the contract has a close connection with the territory of any member State but (by inference) could not displace that law, whether by virtue of Article 3(3), Article 5, Article 7(2) or Article 16, where the contract has no such close connection. Thus, in the example of the Bermudan contract referred to above, an English court could not invalidate the interest rate term as unfair under the Regulations as the contract would have no close connection with the territory of any member State. However, neither the Regulations nor the Directive from which they derive give any indication as to how "close" the connection must be for the Regulations to apply notwithstanding the choice of the law of a non-member State.

On a fair assessment, however, these six exceptions do not make any major inroad into the principle that the obligation to pay interest, and the rate of interest, are governed by the *lex causae*.

2 STATUTORY INTEREST ON COMMERCIAL DEBTS

The Late Payment of Commercial Debts (Interest) Act 1998 provides for the payment of interest on certain debts. The Act applies to a contract for the supply of goods or services where the purchaser and supplier are each acting in the course of a business, other than an "excepted contract".[37] Section 1(1) of the Act states:

> "It is an implied term in a contract to which this Act applies that any qualifying debt created by the contract carries simple interest."

subject to and in accordance with Part I of the Act. Interest carried under that implied term (in the Act referred to as "statutory interest") is to be treated, for the purposes of any rule of law or enactment (other than the Act), relating to interest on debts, in the same way as interest carried under an express contract term.[38] There is therefore no doubt that, in principle, the obligation to pay statutory interest arises if, but only if, the law of part of the United Kingdom governs the contract and does not arise where the law applicable to the contract is a foreign law.

However, section 12 of the Act contains specific provision on the conflict of laws. By subsection (1):

> "This Act does not have effect in relation to a contract governed by the law of a part of the United Kingdom by choice of the parties if—

---

[37] Section 2(1).
[38] Section 1(2).

(a)	there is no significant connection between the contract and that part of the United Kingdom; and
(b)	but for that choice the applicable law would be a foreign law."

A "foreign law" is defined to mean the law of a country outside the United Kingdom.[39] So, for example, in an English court, if the law chosen by the parties is English law, though but for this choice the law applicable to the contract under the Rome Convention would be the law of California, then, if there is no "significant connection" between the contract and England, the obligation to pay statutory interest will not be implied. There is no indication of what amounts to a "significant" connection, although it would appear to be something less than a "close" connection as mentioned in the Unfair Terms in Consumer Contracts Regulations 1999. The drafting of the subsection also produces the somewhat curious result in the above example that, if there is a significant connection between the contract and another part of the United Kingdom, e.g. Scotland, but no such connection with England, the Act will not have effect in relation to the contract. Moreover, it would seem that, where the subsection operates, a creditor who has no claim to interest under the Act (because it is excluded) would not have a claim under what would have been the applicable law had English law not been chosen, since that law would not be the applicable law.

Subsection (2) of section 12 further provides:

"This Act has effect in relation to a contract governed by a foreign law by choice of the parties if—
(a)	but for that choice, the applicable law would be the law of a part of the United Kingdom; and
(b)	there is no significant connection between the contract and any country other than that part of the United Kingdom."

The Act contains provisions which limit the ability of the parties to oust or vary the right to statutory interest. Thus, if the parties have chosen New York law to govern their contract, and apart from that choice the applicable law under the Rome Convention would be the law of England, an English court will hold the Act to have effect if there is no significant connection between the contract and any country other than England. The purpose of the subsection appears to be to prevent evasion of the obligation to pay statutory interest by the device of subjecting the contract to a foreign law. In this respect, it resembles Article 3(3) of the Convention, although it is slightly less rigorous in that it does not require all the elements relevant to the situation at the time of the choice to be connected with England alone before the choice is overruled. Again a "significant" connection is not defined but seems to be something less than a "close" connection: the subsection will not affect the parties' choice of law if there is a significant connection between the contract and any other country, for example,

---

[39]	Section 12(3).

New York, or France, or even another part of the United Kingdom (such as Scotland). Presumably the subsection is justifiable in terms of the Convention by Article 7(2), the English court being entitled to apply the "mandatory rules" of the Act as the law of the forum irrespective of the fact that a foreign law is otherwise applicable to the contract.

In a number of European countries the general rule is that, where no provision has been made for the payment of contractual interest, a creditor is entitled to claim interest at a rate prescribed by law.[40] The obligation to pay interest is usually triggered by a demand by the creditor for payment or at least by the non-payment of the debt on the date fixed by the parties for payment. Although the obligation is imposed by law and is not consensual, it arises out of and may be sufficiently connected with a contract, i.e. to pay the principal debt, to persuade an English court to give effect to it if it is imposed by the law applicable to the contract. But an examination of the foreign statutory provision may show, for example, that the right conferred on the creditor is one to recover interest by way of damages. In that case, the conflict rule may differ, as discussed below.

3 INTEREST BY WAY OF DAMAGES

a. Contract

In many legal systems the law makes provision for the recovery of interest by way of damages where, as a result of the non-payment of money, the creditor has been compelled to borrow replacement funds at interest or has been unable to use the money to earn interest.[41] The recovery of interest may depend upon proof by the creditor that such loss has actually occurred or it may be presumed by law to have been sustained at or up to a certain rate (say, 4 per cent).[42] However, it is well established in English law that, as a general rule, damages are not recoverable for the non-payment or late payment of money.[43] At common law a creditor cannot therefore normally recover interest by way of general damages for breach of contract in respect of the period between the date when a contractual debt becomes due and is unpaid and the date of payment or

---

[40] See the Law Commission, *Law of Contract: Report on Interest*; Law. Com. No. 88, Cmnd. 7229 (1978), paras 40–41.

[41] France: C.C., Arts. 1146–1149; Germany: BGB, §§ 246, 288; Switzerland, Code of Obligations, 104, 106; Mann (1985) 101 L.Q.R. 30.

[42] France, Germany and Switzerland all have statutory or usual rates, but additional interest may be recoverable in certain circumstances.

[43] *Page* v. *Newman* (1829) 9 B. & C. 378; *London, Chatham & Dover Ry Co.* v. *South Eastern Ry Co.* [1893] A.C. 429; *President of India* v. *La Pintada Compania Navegacion S.A.* [1985] A.C. 104. A limited power to award interest was conferred upon the courts by the Civil Procedure Act 1833 (Lord Tenterden's Act), s. 28 (now repealed).

judgment.[44] The reason appears to be that such damage is "generally presumed not to be within the contemplation of the parties".[45] To this general rule, however, there are exceptions.

First, where the debtor has promised to pay a debt by a certain day with interest up to that date, interest is recoverable by way of damages for late payment of the debt. This is not an implied or notional extension of the contractual right to interest, since damages will not necessarily be awarded at the contractual interest rate.[46]

Secondly, if, as the result of the late payment, the creditor has incurred interest charges in obtaining finance from an alternative source, such loss may be recoverable as special damage provided that it was in the reasonable contemplation of the parties at the time they made the contract that such charges would probably be incurred.[47]

Interest by way of damages differs from interest on a debt or damages which may be awarded under the Supreme Court Act 1981 (see below) in that it is an entitlement and not discretionary, compound interest may be awarded where this is necessary to compensate a claimant for his loss and not merely simple interest, and such damages are recoverable even though the principal sum has been paid before action brought.[48]

At common law, a distinction was drawn between rules relating to remoteness of damage, heads of damage and the duty to mitigate damage—which were governed by the law applicable to the contract—and rules relating to measure (in the sense of quantification) of damage—which were governed by the *lex fori*, as they were treated as matters of procedure.[49] Article 10(1)(c) of the Rome Convention[50] now provides that the law applicable to the contract by virtue of the Convention is to govern in particular

---

[44] See the Law Commission, *Law of Contract: Report on Interest*: Law Com. No. 88; Cmnd. 7229 (1978); Mann (1985) 101 L.Q.R. 30; F. D. Rose, "Interest", ch. 11 of Birks and Rose (eds), *Lessons of the Swaps Litigation* (2000).

[45] *Trans Trust S.P.R.L.* v. *Danubian Trading Co. Ltd.* [1952] 2 Q.B. 297, 306 (Denning, L.J.), citing Bullen & Leake, *Precedents of Pleadings in Personal Actions in The Superior Courts of Common Law*, 3rd edn. (1868), 51.

[46] *Cook* v. *Fowler* (1874) L.R. 7 H.L. 27, 32, 35; *Re Roberts* (1880) 14 Ch.D. 49.

[47] *Trans Trust S.P.R.L.* v. *Danubian Trading Co. Ltd.* [1952] 2 Q.B. 297, 306, 307; *Wadsworth* v. *Lydall* [1981] 1 W.L.R. 598. See also *Ozalid Group (Export) Ltd.* v. *African Continental Bank Ltd.* [1979] 2 Lloyd's Rep. 231; *Bacon* v. *Cooper (Metals) Ltd.* [1982] 1 All E.R. 397.

[48] Interest cannot be recovered under the Supreme Court Act 1981, section 35A on sums paid late but before any proceedings are begun: *I.M. Properties Plc* v. *Cape & Dalgleish (a firm)* [1999] Q.B. 297.

[49] *Livesley* v. *Clemens Horst Co.* [1925] 1 D.L.R. 159; *D'Almeida Araujo Lda* v. *Sir Frederick Becker & Co. Ltd.* [1953] 2 Q.B. 329, 388; *Boys* v. *Chaplin* [1971] A.C. 356, 378, 381–2, 383, 394; *Dicey & Morris*, §§7–034, 32–198; *Chitty*, § 31–138; Cheshire and North, 515–517.

[50] See *Dicey & Morris*, § 32–199; *Chitty*, § 31–137.

"within the limits of the powers conferred on the court by its procedural law, the consequences of breach, including the assessment of damages in so far as it is governed by rules of law."

There can be no doubt that the question whether interest is recoverable by way of damages for breach of contract is governed by the law applicable to the contract.[51] Thus, if an action is brought in an English court for failure to pay a debt due under a contract governed by Swiss law, it is the law of Switzerland which will determine whether or not interest is recoverable by way of damages for breach of the contract.[52] The fact that no such damages would be recoverable in English law is irrelevant. The editors of *Dicey & Morris*, however, take the view that it is probable, in the sphere of contractual obligations, that the common law distinction has survived the statutory implementation of the Rome Convention in the Contracts (Applicable Law) Act 1990.[53] The measure or quantification of damages would still be governed by the *lex fori*. Whether or not this is the case depends in particular on the meaning and scope of the words, "including the assessment of damages in so far as it is governed by rules of law".[54] It is arguable that Article 10(1)(c) has modified the common law position in that, whenever the assessment of damages (including the measure or quantification of damages) is, according to the applicable law, governed by rules of law, an English court would have to apply those rules to the exclusion of English law as the *lex fori*. Moreover, the reference in Article 10(1)(c) to "within the limits of the powers conferred on the court by its procedural law" should be construed narrowly and be understood to refer to procedural matters such as, for example, the limits imposed on the power of the court to award periodic (as opposed to lump-sum) payments,[55] but not to permit the court to avoid the application of foreign rules of law relating to the assessment of damages by classifying them as procedural and so subject to the *lex fori*. On the other hand, Article 1(2)(h) provides more generally that the rules of the Convention do not apply to procedure.

With specific reference to the matter of interest as damages, Rule 196(2) of *Dicey & Morris* states[56]

"The liability to pay interest as damages for non-payment of a debt is determined by

---

[51] *Manners* v. *Pearson* [1898] 1 Ch. 581, 588; *Société des Hotels Le Touquet Paris Plage* v. *Cummings* [1922] 1 K.B. 451, 460; *Miliangos* v. *George Frank (Textiles) Ltd. (No. 2)* [1977] Q.B. 489, 496–497; *Helmsing Schiffahrts GmbH & Co. K.G.* v. *Malta Drydocks Corpn.* [1977] 2 Lloyd's Rep. 444, 449–450.

[52] *Miliangos* v. *George Frank (Textiles) Ltd. (No. 2)* [1977] Q.B. 489; Swiss Code of Obligations, 104, 106.

[53] *Dicey & Morris*, §§ 32–199, 33–384. *Cf. Chitty*, § 31–138.

[54] See the Giuliano-Lagarde Report [1980] O.J.C. 282/1, p. 33. For reference to the Report, see the Contracts (Applicable Law) Act 1990, s.3(3)(a).

[55] Morse (1982) 2 Ybk.Eur.L., 107, 154.

[56] *Dicey & Morris*, § 33R–371.

the law applicable to the contract under which the debt is incurred, but (*semble*) the rate of such interest is determined by English law."

The submission in relation to the law which determines the rate of interest is admitted by the editors to be "controversial".[57] Two cases require consideration. Both were decided before the Contracts (Applicable Law) Act 1990 and references in them to the "proper law" should now be understood as referring to the applicable law.

In *Miliangos* v. *George Frank (Textiles) Ltd. (No. 2)*[58] an action was brought in the High Court by a Swiss seller against an English buyer to recover the price of goods sold and delivered. The contract of sale was governed by Swiss law. For the purpose of the proceedings it was agreed between the parties that

> "The law of Switzerland allows the award of interest by way of damages to compensate a plaintiff who has not been paid the price due under a contract for the sale of goods for the period between the time his cause of action accrued and judgment."

The plaintiff's entitlement to interest by way of damages was not therefore in issue, but only the rate of interest. Bristow, J. said:[59]

> "I therefore ... hold that, while you look to the proper law of the contract to see whether there is a right to recover interest by way of damages, you look to the *lex fori* to decide how much. Here it is agreed that the law of Switzerland gives a right to interest by way of damages. The *lex fori*, in the form of s.1 of the [Law Reform (Miscellaneous Provisions) Act 1934] empowers me to award interest at my discretion, apart, as I hold, from compound interest."

He held that interest should be awarded at a rate at which someone could reasonably have borrowed Swiss francs in Switzerland at simple interest and not at compound interest.

In *Helmsing Schiffahrts GmbH & Co. K.G.* v. *Malta Drydocks Corporation*[60] an action was brought in the High Court in respect of money which was repayable to the shipowner under a shipbuilding contract. An issue arose as to the rate of interest to be awarded at the discretion of the court under the Law Reform (Miscellaneous Provisions) Act 1934. The contract was governed by English law so that both the law applicable to the contract and the *lex fori* were English law. It was therefore unnecessary to consider any matter of the conflict of laws. In his judgment, however, Kerr, J.[61] took a different view from that of Bristow, J. in the *Miliangos* case:

> "The view ... expressed in [Dicey, *The Conflict of Laws*, 9th edition, and *Halsbury's Laws of England*, 3rd and 4th editions] is that both the right to interest and its amount should be determined by the proper law. I would respectfully suggest that this view is

---

[57] *Ibid.*, § 33–387.
[58] [1977] Q.B. 489.
[59] *Ibid.*, 497.
[60] [1977] 2 Lloyd's Rep. 444.
[61] *Ibid.*, 449–450.

more consonant with principle. The proper law results from the express or implied choice of both parties or from the nature of the transaction. The *lex fori*, if it differs, merely results from the choice of the plaintiff and may even be more or less fortuitous according to where it happens to be convenient to institute proceedings. For instance, if there were a statutory exclusion or limitation of interest under the proper law, there would be no reason for awarding interest to a plaintiff merely because he institutes proceedings in a jurisdiction which does not have such a provision. The inconvenience of it being occasionally necessary to adduce evidence on interest rates in another country appears to me to be of little weight and difficulty ..."

He nevertheless did not think it right to express a concluded view on the matter: the point would require further consideration at a higher level.

The difference between the two views remains unresolved.[62] Having regard to the conflict of authority and now also to Article 10(1)(c) of the Convention, it is difficult to say which of these two views would in fact be followed. But it is suggested that, if the applicable law fixes or limits the rate of interest to be awarded by way of damages, this would ordinarily be regarded as a matter of substance[63] and the applicable law would normally prevail. But the exercise involved in, for example, deciding whether the rate should be that appropriate to the currency in which the debt is expressed (the *prima facie* rule in English law)[64] or some other rate, e.g. that appropriate to the currency in which judgment is given, or to the currency of the creditor's country, or to the currency of the country where the debt is payable, would be treated as a matter of procedure, as would such other matters as the date from which and the date to which interest is to run and whether interest is simple or compound. These would be determined by English law as the *lex fori*.

b. Bills of exchange

Specific provision is also made for the recovery of interest by way of damages by section 57 of the Bill of Exchange Act 1882,[65] which states:

[62] Both decisions were considered by the Court of Appeal in *The Pacific Colocotronis* [1981] 2 Lloyd's Rep. 40, but the Court of Appeal did not have to refer to this point as both the *lex fori* and the applicable law were English. See also Law Com. No. 124, which report prefers the view of Bristow, J., and the Law Commissions, *Private International Law: Foreign Money Liabilities*: Law Com. W.P., No. 80 (1981), paras. 4–22 to 4–27, setting out arguments.

[63] *Dicey & Morris*, § 7–038 (unless the foreign law is such as to negative this view, i.e. where it is procedural).

[64] *Miliangos* v. *George Frank (Textiles) Ltd. (No. 2)* [1977] Q.B. 489; *The Pacific Colocotronis* [1981] 2 Lloyd's Rep. 40; *Empresa Cubana Importadora de Alimentos* v. *Octavia Shipping Co. S.A.* [1986] 1 Lloyd's Rep. 273, 292. *Cf. Helmsing Schiffahrts GmbH & Co. K.G.* v. *Malta Drydocks Corpn.* [1977] 2 Lloyd's Rep. 444. See *Dicey & Morris*, Rule 196(3), and §§ 33R–371, 33–391 to 33–392.

[65] See *Dicey & Morris*, § 33R–365; *Chalmers & Guest on Bills of Exchange, Cheques and Promissory Notes* 15th edn. (1998) (hereafter "*Chalmers & Guest*") §§ 1445, 1460–1467.

"Where a bill is dishonoured, the measure of damages which shall be deemed to be liquidated damages, shall be as follows:

  (1) The holder may recover from any party liable on the bill, and the drawer who has been compelled to pay the bill may recover from the acceptor, and an indorser who has been compelled to pay the bill may recover from the acceptor or from the drawer, or from a prior indorser—

  (a) the amount of the bill;

  (b) interest thereon from the time of presentment for payment if the bill is payable on demand, and from the maturity of the bill in any other case;

  (c) the expenses of noting, or, when protest is necessary, and the protest has been extended, the expenses of protest."

The rules of the Rome Convention do not apply to "obligations arising under bills of exchange, cheques, or promissory notes"[66] There is no provision in the 1882 Act which deals expressly with the measure of damages where laws conflict. At common law the measure of damages recoverable from a party to a bill or note was treated as a matter of substantive law and was therefore determined by the law which governed that party's contract on the instrument.[67] By section 72(2) of the 1882 Act the interpretation of the drawing, indorsement, acceptance, or acceptance *supra protest* of a bill, is determined by the law of the place where such contract is made. It is a matter of controversy[68] whether this subsection either directly or by inference subjects the issue of the measure of damages to the law of the place where each several party entered into his contract on the instrument (the *lex loci contractus*) or whether the applicable law is unaffected by this subsection and is that of the place where that party undertook that he would pay the instrument (the *lex loci solutionis*). Whichever view is adopted, if the law applicable to a party's obligation on the instrument is a foreign law, that law will determine the measure of damages payable by him on dishonour of the instrument, and not English law as the *lex fori*. It also follows in any event that the measure of damages recoverable from one party may therefore differ from that recoverable from another.[69]

More difficulty arises with respect to the rate of interest. Since the Rome Convention does not apply, it is arguable that the rate of interest is an aspect of the measure or quantification of damages which, at common law, is governed by English law as the *lex fori*. Thus, if an action is brought in an English court by the holder of a bill against the drawer and the law applicable to the drawer's obligation on the bill is the law of a country which adheres to the Geneva Uniform Law on Bill of Exchange (where the rate of interest on a dishonoured bill is fixed at 5 per cent), the holder could nevertheless claim and be awarded

---

[66] Article 1(2)(c).

[67] *Allen* v. *Kemble* (1848) 6 Moo.P.C. 314; *Gibbs* v. *Fremont* (1853) 9 Exch. 25; *Re Gillespie, ex p. Robarts* (1886) 18 Q.B.D. 286, 292; *Re Commercial Bank of South Australia* (1887) 36 Ch.D. 522, 525.

[68] *Chalmers & Guest*, §§ 1462–1464; *Dicey & Morris*, § 33–344.

[69] *Chalmers & Guest*, § 1466; *Dicey & Morris*, § 33–344.

interest at the rate ordinarily awarded in an English court, i.e. at the short term investment rate. The contrary argument is that, if the foreign law fixes or limits the interest rate, this is normally a substantive matter which ought to be determined in accordance with the law which governs the drawer's obligation and not a procedural question to be determined by the *lex fori*. This latter argument might well prevail. For the rest, the English court would be free to determine the rate of interest and the other procedural matters referred to above as in other situations where interest is claimed as damages for breach of contract.[70]

c. Tort

Section 11(1) of the Private International Law (Miscellaneous Provisions) Act 1995 provides:

> "The general rule is that the applicable law is the law of the country in which the events constituting the tort or delict in question occur."

Although exceptions to this general rule are provided for in the Act, it is submitted that it is for the applicable law to determine whether interest is recoverable by way of damages in tort.[71] In English law, interest is not recoverable in tort cases by way of damages. But, if an action is brought in an English court in respect, for example, of a motor accident in France (the applicable law being French law), the court should award interest by way of damages if an award of damages would in French law include interest.[72] An issue may, however, arise as to the rate at which such interest is payable. Again, it is submitted that a rule of the applicable law which fixed or limited the rate of interest would normally be regarded as substantive but the determination of the rate of interest would otherwise be treated as procedural and it would be for English law to decide what would be the appropriate rate in the particular case.[73]

d. Restitution

At common law, interest is not payable by way of damages for late payment of money due under a claim in restitution.[74] But a foreign legal system might provide for interest to be awarded by way of damages, or as compensation, for late payment of a restitutionary claim. Alternatively a legal system might award

---

[70] *Cf. Gibbs* v. *Fremont* (1853) 9 Exch. 25.

[71] The "double-actionability" rule has been abolished by the 1995 Act.

[72] C.C., 1153–1.

[73] Contrast *Elkins* v. *East India Co.* (1717) 1 P. Wms. 395.

[74] See F. D. Rose, "Interest": ch. 11 of Birks and Rose (eds), *Lessons of the Swaps Litigation* (2000). But interest may be awarded under s.35A of the Supreme Court Act 1981 (*B.P. Exploration Co. (Libya) Ltd.* v. *Hunt (No. 2)* [1983] 2 A.C. 352) or in equity. See *Westdeutsche Landesbank Girozentrale* v. *Islington L.B.C.* [1996] A.C. 669.

interest as part of that claim, the defendant being required to restore to the claimant the benefit enjoyed by having had the use of the money in the intervening period.[75] The Rome Convention does not, in England, apply to claims in restitution.[76] Rule 200(1) in *Dicey & Morris* states:[77]

> "The obligation to restore the benefit of an enrichment obtained at another person's expense is governed by the proper law of the obligation."

The editors then go on, in Rule 202(2), to set out how the proper law is arrived at.[78] It is submitted that an English court should apply the proper law of the obligation to determine whether interest should be awarded in respect of a claim in restitution, and should do so whether the proper law awards interest by way of damages or compensation or treats interest as part of the restitutionary claim. Again the rate of interest (except where this is fixed or limited by the proper law) should be regarded as a matter related to assessment or quantification and so governed by English law as the *lex fori*.

4 INTEREST ON A DEBT OR DAMAGES

This is, perhaps, the most controversial of the topics here discussed. It is submitted that a distinction should be drawn between interest by way of damages (considered above) and the power of a court or arbitrator to award interest on a debt or damages. The former is in principle determined by the law applicable to the obligation (contract, tort, or restitution, as the case may be). But the latter is, in English law, with one exception, the creature of statute. It is arguable that the conferment by statute of a power to award interest on a debt or damages is procedural in nature and is to be applied in an English court as the *lex fori*.

To take the exception first. At common law, interest was not awarded on damages in respect of the period before judgment. This was not the case in the Admiralty court, where a claimant who was entitled to damages in a collision or salvage action, and in certain other cases, might recover interest on those damages so as to compensate him for the period over which they had been withheld. As Sir Robert Phillimore explained in *The Northumbria*[79] "[T]he

---

[75] See Alison Jones, *Restitution and European Community Law* (2000).

[76] This may be inferred from the fact that the United Kingdom has taken advantage of the reservation allowed by Article 22(1) to Article 10(1)(e). See Contracts (Applicable Law) Act 1990, s.2(2). See also *Kleinwort Benson Ltd.* v. *Glasgow City Council* [1999] 1 A.C. 153 (Brussels Convention).

[77] *Dicey & Morris*, § 34R–001.

[78] *Ibid.*, §§ 34R–001, 34–019 to 34–041.

[79] (1869) L.R. 3 A. & E. 6, 10, cited with approval in *The Berwickshire* [1950] P. 204, 209; *The Norseman* [1957] P. 224, 231.

Admiralty, in the exercise of an equitable jurisdiction, has proceeded upon another and a different principle from that on which the common law authorities appear to be founded. This principle adopted by the Admiralty Court has been that of the civil law, that interest was always due to the obligee when payment was not made, *ex mora* of the obligor; and that, whether the obligation arose *ex contractu* or *ex delicto*". In an earlier case, however, Dr Lushington had made it clear that the court was awarding interest on damages and not by way of damages. In *The Amalia*[80] he said:

> "Upon what grounds, then, was interest given? Interest was not given by way of indemnification for the loss, for the loss was the damage which had accrued; but interest was given for this reason, namely, that the loss was not paid at the proper time. If a man is kept out of his money, it is a loss in the common sense of the word, but a loss of a totally different description, and clearly to be distinguished from a loss which has been done at the moment of collision."

The Admiralty rule has, however, largely if not entirely been replaced in practice by the discretionary power to award interest on damages given by the Supreme Court Act 1981.

It must nevertheless be admitted that the distinction between interest by way of damages and interest on damages is not an easy one to draw and may not have been universally accepted even in Admiralty.[81] Indeed the editors of *Dicey & Morris* draw no such distinction and treat both situations as governed by the same rule, namely that set out in Rule 196(2) referred to above.[82] This refers the liability to pay interest on damages to the applicable law. The problem is most acute where the applicable law makes no provision whatsoever for the recovery of interest. If the view set out in *Dicey & Morris* is correct, then, for example, where an action is brought in an English court claiming damages under a contract governed by a foreign law, the court could not exercise its statutory power to award interest on damages if interest was not recoverable under the foreign law. Likewise, in the case of a tort committed abroad, there would be no power in the English court to award interest if the law of the place where the tort was committed did not provide for interest.

Two statutory provisions require to be considered: section 35A of the Supreme Court Act 1981 and section 49 of the Arbitration Act 1996.

a. Supreme Court Act 1981, section 35A

At common law, the court had no power (except in Admiralty cases and cases in equity) to award interest on a debt or damages to compensate a claimant for

---

[80] (1864) 5 New Rep. 164n, following Lord Stowell in *The Dundee* (1827) 2 Hagg. Adm. 137, 143.

[81] *Liesbosch Dredger* v. *S.S. Edison* [1933] A.C. 449, 469 ("interest . . . as further damages").

[82] *Dicey & Morris*, § 33R–371.

being kept out of his money during the period prior to judgment.[83] However, the Law Reform (Miscellaneous Provisions) Act 1934, section 3, gave to the courts a power to include an award of interest in the sum for which judgment was given in any proceedings, tried in any court of record, for the recovery of any debt or damages. The power thus conferred was a discretionary power ("the court may, if it thinks fit …"). Between 1934 and 1969 interest was seldom asked for or awarded in respect of damages for death or personal injury. But the law was changed by the Administration of Justice Act 1969, section 22, which provided that, in every case of personal injury or wrongful death where the damages exceeded £200, the court was to exercise the power to make an award of interest under the 1934 Act unless it was satisfied that there were special reasons why no interest should be given.

These provisions are now re-enacted and extended in the Supreme Court Act 1981, section 35(A). Subsection (1) provides:

> "Subject to rules of court, in proceedings (whenever instituted) before the High Court for the recovery of a debt or damages there may be included in any sum for which judgment is given simple interest, at such rate as the court thinks fit or as rules of court may provide, on all or any part of the debt or damages in respect of which judgment is given, or payment is made before judgment, for all or any part of the period between the date when the cause of action arose and—
>
>   (a) in the case of any sum paid before judgment, the date of the payment; and
>   (b) in the case of the sum for which judgment is given the date of the judgment."

In relation to a judgment given for damages for personal injuries or death which exceed £200, then, under subsection (2), interest must be included "unless the court is satisfied that there are special reasons to the contrary". It does not seem sensible, from the point of view of the conflict of laws, to draw a distinction between the power of the court under subsection (1) and that under subsection (2). The question is whether, in exercising its power to award interest under either subsection, the court is giving effect to procedural or substantive rights. The editors of *Dicey & Morris* are firmly of the view that the power is substantive and so governed by the *lex causae*. Authority is divided, but such English authority as there is suggests the contrary, i.e. that it is procedural and so governed by the *lex fori*.

In *Midland International Trade Services* v. *Sudairy*[84] an action was brought in England by the plaintiff to recover a debt due under a judgment given in Saudi Arabia. The defendant contended that, since no interest was recoverable in Saudi law, no interest could be awarded under section 35A. Hobhouse, J. held that section 35A was procedural and could therefore always be invoked in English legal proceedings regardless of the *lex causae*. The reasons given by him were as follows: (1) a successful plaintiff had no right at common law to recover interest by way of general damages for the late payment of money; (2)

---

[83] *President of India* v. *Lips Maritime Corp.* [1988] A.C. 395, 425.
[84] No. 189-FO-197; *Financial Times*, 2nd May 1990.

the statutory power under the Act to award interest on a debt or damages was discretionary and could only be exercised in connection with legal proceedings; and (3) the statute did not confer on the plaintiff any right to interest independent of legal proceedings.

In *Brunei L.N.G. Sendirian Berhad* v. *Interbeton B.V.*[85] Fuad, J. in the Court of Appeal of Brunei declined to follow the decision of Hobhouse, J. In that case an application was made in the Brunei High Court for summary judgment under R.S.C. Order 14 to recover certain milestone payments due under a construction contract which was expressly stated to be governed by English law. There was no contractual provision for the payment of interest and the Brunei High Court rules did not sanction an award of pre-judgment interest. The Brunei Court of Appeal nevertheless upheld an award of such interest. Fuad, J. said:[86]

> "With very great respect to the views expressed in the *Midland* case, in my opinion the right given by section 35A to claim interest is a matter of substantive law even though it is subject to rules of court and is discretionary. A litigant seeking to recover a debt or damages has a statutory right to claim interest and to invite the court to exercise its discretion in his favour. If he follows the right procedure he can insist on the court considering his claim, as a matter of law, even though the court has a discretion to refuse an award, and the rate of interest is in the discretion of the court, unless rules of court otherwise provide for the rate ..."

The issue in the case, however, was whether the Brunei High Court was—by virtue of the fact that the contract was governed by English law—clothed with the powers given to an English court by the 1981 Act. Fuad, J. held that it was. He relied, in particular, on previous English cases[87] which were decided at a time when arbitrators had no statutory jurisdiction to award pre-judgment interest. These had held that there was an implied term in the submission to arbitration that the arbitrator should decide the dispute in accordance with the contract and that every right and discretionary remedy given to a court of law by statute could be exercised by him. It is, of course, open to a foreign court to decide whether or not it will exercise the powers conferred on the English High Court to award interest on a debt or damages in respect of a contract governed by English law. But it does not follow that an English court must relinquish those powers because the contract in question is governed by a foreign law.

The third case is *Kuwait Oil Tanker Company S.A.K.* v. *Al Bader*,[88] where an action was brought in England to recover damages in respect of a tort committed in Kuwait. It was argued that, since the *lex causae* was that of Kuwait and since the law of Kuwait did not permit the recovery of interest, no interest on damages was recoverable by the plaintiffs under section 35A or

---

[85] (1996) 14 Const.L.J. 117.

[86] *Ibid.*, 120.

[87] *Edwards* v. *G.W. Ry Co.* (1851) 11 C.B. 588; *Chandris* v. *Isbrandtsen Moller Co. Inc.* [1951] 1 K.B. 240.

[88] (17th December 1998) unreported (QB: Com. Ct).

otherwise. Moore-Bick, J. held that section 35A was procedural, and not substantive, in nature. He said

> "Mr Brodie [for the defendants] submitted that the effect of the statutory provisions relating to interest was not merely to introduce a procedural remedy where none existed at law but to modify the substantive rules themselves, but I cannot accept that. The grounds put forward by Hobhouse, J. for regarding the court's power to award interest under section 35A as procedural are in my judgment compelling and for that reason I would respectfully adopt his conclusion. It follows that I am satisfied that I have jurisdiction to award simple interest in this case under section 35A of the Supreme Court Act whatever may be the position under the law of Kuwait."

Nevertheless, in case he was wrong on this point and in order to exercise his discretion, he went on to consider whether interest was in fact recoverable under the law of Kuwait and came to the conclusion, on the basis of the expert evidence put forward, that in the particular circumstances of the case it was so recoverable.

It is suggested that the view of Hobhouse, J., endorsed by Moore-Bick, J., is to be preferred to that of *Dicey & Morris* and the Court of Appeal of Brunei. However, in *Dicey & Morris*,[89] it is argued that, in contract cases, the right to claim interest under section 35A belongs to the "consequences of breach", which under Article 10(1)(c) of the Rome Convention are stated to be governed by the applicable law. This quite formidable argument can be countered by saying (1) that the rules of the Convention do not apply to "procedure" (Article 1(2)(h)), (2) that the power conferred by section 35A falls within the words "within the limits of the powers conferred on the court by its procedural law", and (3) that in any event an award under section 35A is not a "consequence of breach" but, less directly, is compensation payable to the plaintiff for being kept out of his money of which the defendant has in the meantime had the use.

If it is accepted that section 35A is procedural and so governed exclusively by English law as the *lex fori*, this does not mean that the provisions of the applicable law relating to interest are to be disregarded. Those provisions still remain relevant when the court comes to exercise its discretion under the section. For example, where the applicable law is that of an Islamic country which does not permit the recovery of interest in certain circumstances, there is no reason why the court should not take this fact into account when exercising its discretion, especially in contract cases if the parties can be taken to have impliedly waived the recovery of interest. The same reasoning applies where the applicable law fixes or limits the interest recoverable. On the other hand, in a particular case, the refusal or limitation of interest under the applicable law might cause undue hardship to the claimant or unjustly enrich the defendant and there is no reason why the court should not, in appropriate circumstances, award

---

[89] *Dicey & Morris*, § 33–385.

interest under section 35A at variance with the provisions of the applicable law, though limited always to simple interest.

The applicable law relating to interest may also be relevant in another way. Subsection (4) of section 35A prohibits the court from awarding interest "in respect of a debt ... for a period during which, for whatever reason, interest under the debt already runs". Interest could not therefore be awarded under the section where, under the applicable law, contractual interest is payable or where the law confers a right to recover interest on an overdue debt. Subsection (4) does not apply to prevent the court from awarding interest in respect of damages (as opposed to a debt)[90] even though under the applicable law interest is recoverable as of right by way of damages. But the court is empowered only to award simple interest and therefore would be unlikely, when exercising its discretion, to award interest on interest.

It is submitted that the classification of section 35A as procedural is to be preferred, since it enables the court to take account of the provisions of the applicable law but nevertheless preserves the discretionary power of the court in appropriate cases to reach a solution which justice demands, both in deciding whether or not to award interest and in deciding at what rate and for what period interest should run, though limited always to simple interest.

The County Courts Act 1984, section 69, is in the same terms as section 35A of the 1981 Act and does not require separate consideration.

b. Arbitration Act 1996, section 49

The Arbitration Act 1996, section 49 provides as follows:

> "(1) The parties are free to agree on the powers of the tribunal as regards the award of interest.
> (2) Unless otherwise agreed by the parties the following provisions apply.
> (3) The tribunal may award simple or compound interest from such dates at such rates and with such rests as it considers meets the justice of the case—
>   (a) on the whole or part of any amount awarded by the tribunal, in respect of any period up to the date of the award;
>   (b) on the whole or part of any amount claimed in the arbitration and outstanding at the commencement of the arbitral proceedings but paid before the award was made, in respect of any period up to the date of payment.
> (4) ...
> (5) ...
> (6) The above provisions do not effect any other power of the tribunal to award interest."

It is to be noted that the arbitral tribunal has power to award compound interest

---

[90] *Dalmia Dairy Industries Ltd.* v. *National Bank of Pakistan* [1978] 2 Lloyd's Rep. 223, 274, 302.

even though this power is not given to the court under the Supreme Court Act 1981 or the County Courts Act 1984.

Section 49 is in Part I of the 1996 Act and section 2(1) of the Act states "The provisions of this Part apply where the seat of the arbitration is in England and Wales or Northern Ireland". The section therefore refers to the *lex arbitri* and not to the law applicable to the arbitration agreement or to the law applicable to the contract in which the arbitration agreement is contained. It is therefore submitted that the arbitral tribunal has, subject to the agreement of the parties, the power to award interest under this section even though the law applicable to the contract in respect of which the dispute has arisen or the law applicable to the arbitration agreement (if different) limits or imposes conditions on the availability of interest or does not recognise any right to interest. It is, of course, again open to the tribunal, in exercising its discretion under the section, to take into account any restrictions relating to interest contained in the applicable law. But it is submitted that the fact that the applicable law imposed such restrictions would not in itself justify the inference that the parties had impliedly agreed that the provisions of section 49(3)–(6) should not apply or should be varied.

Subsection (6) of the section makes it clear that the tribunal still has the power to award interest in a case where it is payable pursuant to an express or implied contractual term or where it is recoverable by way of damages. In such a case, as mentioned above, the tribunal would apply the law applicable to the contract. Although there is no specific provision similar to subsection (4) of section 35A of the Supreme Court Act 1981, it seems unlikely (despite the ability to award compound interest) that the tribunal would then go on to award interest under section 49 in respect of a debt where interest was payable as of right or in respect of interest payable by way of damages.

5 INTEREST IN EQUITY

Interest may be awarded in English law as ancillary relief in respect of equitable remedies such as specific performance, rescission or the taking of an account.

At common law, it would seem that the availability in an English court of equitable remedies such as injunction and specific performance was regarded as a matter for English law as the *lex fori*.[91] The award of interest as ancillary relief would also be so regarded. However, under the Rome Convention, the availability of the remedy of specific performance can be said to relate to "the consequences of breach", which, under Article 10(1)(c), is subject to the law applicable to the contract. The editors of *Dicey & Morris* take the view,[92]

---

[91] *Bascher* v. *London Illustrated Standard Co.* [1900] 1 Ch. 73 (injunction); *Boys* v. *Chaplin* [1971] A.C. 356, 394; *Dicey & Morris*, §§ 7–006, 32–200.
[92] *Dicey & Morris*, § 32–200. See also *Cheshire & North*, 516; *Chitty*, § 31–139.

tentatively, that this is the case. While it would still be possible to argue that the award of interest as ancillary relief is a procedural matter and still governed by the *lex fori*, it seems probable that the adoption of the *lex contractus* as suggested by *Dicey & Morris* would lead to the conclusion that it, too, was subject to the law applicable to the contract.

With the respect to an award of interest as ancillary relief to the equitable remedy of rescission, the question whether one party is entitled to rescind the contract, e.g. for misrepresentation, would seem to be determined by the applicable law, so that the matter of interest would be governed by that law and not by the *lex fori*. More doubt might surround an award of interest as part of the process of taking an account, as the taking of an account may be procedural in nature and so subject to the *lex fori*.

The payment of interest may be ordered by an English court where money has been obtained or retained by fraud, or where it has been withheld or misapplied by a person in a fiduciary position who is accountable for profits; and, in contrast with the common law, compound interest may be awarded.[93] The question whether the imposition of a constructive trust is a matter of procedure or substance has yet to be authoritatively determined.[94] But in *Kuwait Oil Tanker Company S.A.K.* v. *Al Bader*[95] Moore-Bick, J. held that, if the defendant incurred an obligation under the *lex causae* which required him to account for property received, that would provide a sufficient basis for holding him liable as constructive trustee in England, and that, insofar as property had been obtained in Kuwait, the substantive obligations which arose in consequence were to be determined by the law of Kuwait.[96] On the other hand he held that:

> "An award of compound interest in accordance with equitable principles is in the nature of a remedy designed to ensure that the wrongdoer makes full restitution. As such I think the jurisdiction to make such an award is to be regarded as part of the procedural law of the *lex fori*."

It is submitted that this view is correct and that it is appropriate to regard this equitable jurisdiction as a matter of enforcement or procedure governed by the *lex fori*.

---

[93] *Burdick* v. *Garrick* (1870) L.R. 5 Ch.App. 233; *Re Emmets' Estate* (1881) 17 Ch.D. 142; *Re Barclay* [1899] 1 Ch. 674; *Wallersteiner* v. *Moir (No. 2)* [1975] Q.B. 373. But see *O'Sullivan* v. *Management Agency and Music Ltd.* [1985] Q.B. 428; *Westdeutsche Landesbank Girozentrale* v. *Islington L.B.C.* [1996] A.C. 669.

[94] See *Dicey & Morris*, §§ 34–032, 34–033. *Cf. Re Polly Peck International Plc (No. 2)* [1998] 3 All E.R. 812.

[95] (17th December 1998) unreported (QB: Com. Ct).

[96] Following Chadwick, J. in *Arab Monetary Fund* v. *Hashim*, 15th June 1994, unreported.

6 CONCLUSION

There is no single satisfactory solution which would resolve the conflict between the *lex causae* and the *lex fori* with respect to pre-contract interest. In principle the *lex causae* will govern, but it is necessary to allow English law as the *lex fori* to override the applicable law in a limited number of situations where it is felt that protection is needed against abuse. There is also, more contentiously, in addition an argument for allowing the English court as the court of the *forum* to apply the rate of interest economically appropriate to the claim on which it is giving judgment and in certain circumstances to exercise a residuary discretion to award such interest as it thinks fit where it considers this to be necessary to do justice between the parties.

Chapter 15

The Enforceability of Agreements under E.C. and U.K. Competition Law[1]

Richard Whish[2]

1 INTRODUCTION

During the year that Francis Reynolds taught me the law of contract, the United Kingdom acceded to the European Economic Community, as it then was. Prior to that, competition law in the United Kingdom consisted mainly of the Restrictive Trade Practices Acts 1956 and 1968, the Resale Prices Act 1964 and the Fair Trading Act 1973. Not unreasonably, these somewhat arcane pieces of legislation were not taught to undergraduates, although Jeremy Lever was teaching them to postgraduates on the B.C.L. course. Within the syllabus for the law of contract, I came across the idea of a contract being unenforceable because of possible detriments to the competitive process only in the context of the restraint of trade doctrine, the House of Lords' judgment in *Esso Petroleum Co. Ltd.* v. *Harper's Garage (Stourport) Ltd.*[3] being relatively recent and undoubtedly problematic. My recollection is that the scope of the doctrine (and the direction in which doors were moving[4]) occupied most of our time, rather than a consideration of the industrial economics of competition policy. I also recall the distaste that had been expressed by Ungoed-Thomas, J. in *Texaco Ltd.*

---

[1] See generally on this issue Braakman, *The Application of Articles 81 and 82 of the EC Treaty by National Courts in the Member States* (European Commission, 1997); Kerse, *EC Antitrust Procedure*, 4th edn. (1998), ch. 10; Smith, in Freeman and Whish (eds.), *Butterworths Competition Law* (1991), Div. XI; Jones, *Private Enforcement of Antitrust Law in the EU, UK and USA* (1999).

[2] I would like to acknowledge the considerable help provided by Christopher Brown, my research assistant at the Centre for European Law, King's College London, in the preparation of this essay.

[3] [1968] A.C. 269.

[4] It will be recalled that their Lordships concluded that the restraint of trade doctrine was applicable, *inter alia*, where a contract "closed a door" (that is to say where it took away a legal freedom of one of the contracting parties) but not where it "opened a door"

v. *Mulberry Filling Station Ltd.*[5] at the prospect of judges being called upon to adjudicate upon what were obviously complex economic or even political issues. This same distaste had manifested itself during the passage of the Restrictive Trade Practices Bill through Parliament in 1955–56.[6]

How different the position looks as we enter the new millennium. Competition law is now a substantial subject in its own right, and is widely taught in universities at undergraduate and postgraduate level. Commercial law firms have substantial competition law practices. More than eighty countries in the world now have systems of competition law, and others are in the course of preparing new laws. This in turn means that there are large numbers of officials in regulatory agencies responsible for the enforcement of the competition rules. The operation of cartels (E.C. Treaty, Article 81) and the abuse of a dominant position (Article 82) which have an effect on the pattern of trade between member states can attract enormous fines under Community law;[7] the Competition Act 1998 introduced for the first time in the United Kingdom the possibility of fines for infringements of domestic law.[8] In the U.S., imprisonment and individual liability to fines for the responsible officers of a recalcitrant company is a real possibility.[9] Damages and/or injunctions may also be

---

(for example, by enabling someone to take a commercial tenancy of a property, albeit subject to a restriction only to sell petrol there that had been purchased from the landlord; since, prior to the tenancy, the tenant had no right to sell petrol at all from that property, the door in such a case had been opened, not closed).

[5] [1972] 1 W.L.R. 814.

[6] See Whish, *Competition Law*, 3rd edn. (1993), 123.

[7] For recent examples in the European Community, see *Pre-insulated Pipes* [1999] O.J. L24/1; [1999] 4 C.M.L.R. 402 (fines totalling ECU 92 million for infringements of Article 81) and *TACA*, [1999] O.J. L95/1; [1999] 4 C.M.L.R. 1415 (fines totalling ECU 273 million for infringements of Article 82). In the U.S., the largest fines ever in a cartel case were imposed in the case of *Vitamins* in 1999: Hoffmann-La Roche was fined $500 million for its part in a nine-year long vitamin cartel; BASF was fined $225 million; Takeda, $72 million; Eisai, $40 million; Daiichi, $25 million; and Lonza, $10.5 million: see U.S. Department of Justice Press Release of 20th May 1999.

[8] Competition Act 1998, section 36. See also O.F.T. draft guideline 423 on the appropriate amount of a penalty.

[9] See, e.g. U.S. Department of Justice Press Releases of 20th May and 19th August 1999: two former executives of Hoffmann-La Roche agreed to plead guilty, serve four- and five-month jail sentences and pay fines of $100,000 and $150,000 respectively for their roles in the vitamin cartel. See also U.S. Department of Justice Press Release of 29th September 1999: a former executive of U.C.A.R. International Inc. agreed to serve a 17 month jail term and individually to pay a $1.25 million fine for conspiring to fix the price and allocate the volume of graphite electrodes sold in the U.S. and elsewhere. As a deterrent, there is no question that being away from the family on Thanksgiving Day is going to have a greater effect than the imposition of a corporate fine, no matter how large that fine might be.

available to plaintiffs who can demonstrate that they have suffered harm as a result of infringements of the competition rules.

Many systems of competition law deploy an important additional sanction in order to persuade undertakings to obey the law: the sanction of voidness. Just as an agreement in restraint of trade could be unenforceable where it was unreasonable as between the parties and/or in the public interest,[10] so too, by virtue of Article 81(2) of the E.C. Treaty, an agreement that restricts competition in the sense of Article 81(1) and which is not exempted under Article 81(3) is stated to be void. The sanction of voidness may not always be a very real one: the members of a price-fixing cartel or a market-sharing scheme would not normally think of trying to enforce their agreements in a court. Their main concern would be to conceal the cartel from the European Commission, though it has considerable powers to unearth this type of practice[11] and to penalise the recalcitrant firms.[12] Similar powers are given to the Director-General of Fair Trading under the Competition Act 1998.[13] In other cases, however, the sanction of voidness may be much more significant. For example, if a patentee grants a licence of his patent, he will calculate carefully what rate of royalties the licensee should pay and protracted negotiations may take place to settle the other terms of the bargain, for example on the quantities to be produced, the areas in which they are to be sold and the treatment and ownership of any improvements made by the licensee. For his part, the licensee will often have been granted an exclusive territory in which to manufacture and sell. If it transpires that certain aspects of the licence are void and unenforceable, this undermines the deal struck between the parties. The same would be true of an exclusive purchasing term between a supplier and a distributor (as typically occurs in agreements for the sale and purchase of beer and petrol) or non-competition covenants imposed on the parents of a joint venture. In these cases, the threat that competition law poses is not that the European Commission or some other competition authority will impose a fine, but that a key term of a commercial contract will be unenforceable in commercial litigation.

Judges tend to be hostile by instinct to what may be seen as technical—even scurrilous—attempts to avoid contractual obligations by invoking points of competition law.[14] However the European Court of Justice's judgment in *Eco Swiss China Time Ltd.* v. *Benetton*[15] has confirmed how important the sanction of voidness is considered to be in the legal system of the Community: where an

---

[10] On the restraint of trade doctrine generally, see *Chitty on Contracts*, 28th edn. (1999), ch. 17.

[11] See Regulation 17/62, Articles 11 (information) and 14 (investigations).

[12] Regulation 17/62, Articles 15 (fines) and 16 (periodic penalties).

[13] Competition Act 1998, sections 25–44.

[14] See *infra*, 307–309.

[15] (*Case C–126/97*) 1st June 1999, unreported.

agreement truly does infringe Article 81(1), voidness must follow. At the risk of over-simplification, the E.C.J. was asked by the Dutch Supreme Court to determine whether the competition rules in the Treaty could be considered to be rules of public policy: on this question turned the possibility of an appeal being brought against an arbitral award.[16] The E.C.J. was quite clear:

> "36. However, according to Article 3(g) of the EC Treaty (now, after amendment, Article 3(1)(g) EC), Article 81 EC (ex Article 85) constitutes a fundamental provision which is essential for the accomplishment of the tasks entrusted to the Community and, in particular, for the functioning of the internal market. The importance of such a provision led the framers of the Treaty to provide expressly, in Article 81(2) EC (ex Article 85(2)), that any agreements or decisions prohibited pursuant to that article are to be automatically void.
>
> 37. It follows that where its domestic rules of procedure require a national court to grant an application for annulment of an arbitration award where such an application is founded on failure to observe national rules of public policy, it must also grant such an application where it is founded on failure to comply with the prohibition laid down in Article 81(1) EC (ex Article 85(1))".

In the U.K. the Competition Act 1998, which entered into force on 1st March 2000, prohibits an agreement that infringes the so-called "Chapter I prohibition" and which is not exempted by virtue of the provisions in sections 4–11. The Chapter I prohibition in large part imports Article 81(1) into domestic law, but without the requirement that there should be an effect on trade between member states; sections 4–11 effectively replicate Article 81(3) of the Treaty. In a case under the Competition Act, it is sufficient that the agreement affects trade "within the U.K.". Where an agreement infringes the Chapter I prohibition, section 2(4) provides that it shall be void. Thus the position under the U.K. Act follows that in the EC. In this essay I intend to examine the issue that voidness gives rise to *as between the parties to a contract* in the competition law of the E.C. and the U.K. As we shall see, these are complex, and they have not all been resolved. This will be a fruitful source of litigation for many years to come. The essay will not consider the separate question of whether damages are available to *third* parties who are harmed by anti-competitive behaviour, although it will consider whether one co-contractor may have a remedy in tort for damages against its other co-contractors.[17]

2 ARTICLE 81

Article 81(1) and Article 82 are directly applicable and produce direct effects: they give rise to rights and obligations on the part of individuals, and national courts have a duty to safeguard them.[18] It follows that it is open to one of the

---

[16] The case is discussed further *infra*, 316–317.
[17] See *infra*, 310–313.
[18] *B.R.T.* v. *S.A.B.A.M.* (*Case 127/73*) [1974] E.C.R. 51; [1974] 2 C.M.L.R. 238.

parties to an agreement to argue that a contractual obligation is unenforceable, and that a judge of a national court should rule accordingly where an infringement is demonstrated. The Commission has for a long time been eager that Articles 81 and 82 should be enforced more frequently in national courts, thereby relieving it of some of the burden of enforcement: "enforcement" for this purpose would include not only the awarding of injunctions and/or damages to third parties harmed by anti-competitive behaviour, but also declaring anti-competitive agreements to be void. Quite simply, the Commission lacks the resources to police the competition rules across a Community of 15 member states with well over 350 million inhabitants; the problem will intensify as at least ten new member states accede to the Community in the first decade of the new millennium. The Commission is strongly of the view that it should concentrate its efforts on prosecuting the really serious infringements of the law, while also developing competition policy and legislation and engaging in a dialogue at the international level in order to deal with the complex issues arising from an increasingly global economy.

The Commission has for several years devoted a section of its Annual Report on Competition Policy to the application of Community law by national courts,[19] and it has produced important guidance in its *Notice on Co-operation between National Courts and the Commission in Applying Articles 81 and 82 of the EC Treaty*[20] in which it indicated the circumstances in which, in its view, it would be appropriate for a national court to deal with a case, and the extent to which it (the Commission) might be able to assist with questions arising during the proceedings. In a companion *Notice on Co-operation between National Competition Authorities and the Commission in handling cases falling within the scope of Articles 81 or 82 of the EC Treaty*[21] the Commission has also encouraged national competition authorities to become more involved in the enforcement of the competition rules. Both Notices are part of a movement towards the decentralisation of the enforcement of the competition rules. While it is probably true to say that there has been less litigation of the competition rules in domestic courts than might have been anticipated (and hoped for on the part of the Commission), there can be no doubt that, in the future, the combination of the Commission's determination to achieve decentralisation, the proposals contained in its White Paper on modernising the enforcement of competition law[22] and the fact that society is more litigious anyway, means that there will be many more cases. Competition law litigation is here to stay.

---

[19] See, e.g. the *26th Report on Competition Policy*, 335–340, and the *27th Report on Competition Policy*, 343–351.
[20] [1993] O.J. C39/6; [1993] 4 C.M.L.R. 12.
[21] [1997] O.J. C313/3.
[22] See *infra*, 306–307.

a. The "problem" of Article 81(3) and the Commission's role in relation to exemptions: current position

One problem in relation to Article 81 needs to be explained at the outset, since it has a confusing effect on the possibilities available to a judge before whom the enforceability of an agreement is in issue. Agreements, decisions and concerted practices caught by Article 81(1) are declared by Article 81(2) to be automatically void; this provision is tempered, and is complicated, by the possibility of exemption under Article 81(3). The Commission shares with national courts the competence to apply Article 81(1); the same is true of Article 82. The Commission has adopted several "block exemptions", exempting entire categories of agreements defined on a generic basis, provided that they satisfy the quite formalistic conditions that they contain: national courts are able to apply the provisions of the block exemptions.[23] Thus, for example, Regulation 1983/83[24] provides block exemption for exclusive distribution agreements and Regulation 1984/83[25] for exclusive purchasing agreements. Regulation 1984/83 contains special rules for the beer and petrol sectors. However, the Commission has exclusive competence to grant individual exemptions under Article 81(3),[26] and this frequently causes problems for the national court.

The monopoly granted to the Commission to give individual exemptions was explicable in the circumstances of 1962: the criteria in Article 81(3) for exemption—for example that an agreement will confer on consumers "a fair share" of any improvement in "technical or economic progress"—were felt to be best administered by a Community institution in a position to make decisions in accordance with Community policy. At that time, competition law was little known or understood in Europe, and it seemed natural that the complex issues raised by Article 81(3) should be decided upon "at the Centre" rather than in the member states themselves. As we shall see, there are proposals now to decentralise determinations under Article 81(3) as well—to national competition authorities and national courts[27]—although the proposals are quite controversial. For the purpose of this essay, the point to note is that the "bifurcation" of functions—a national judge can apply Article 81(1), but only the Commission can grant an individual exemption—has stultified litigation in national courts. On many occasions where A has sued B claiming that an agreement is unenforceable, B has notified the agreement to the Commission in order to seek an individual exemption: at that point B can argue that the domestic case should be stayed pending the outcome of the Commission's

---

[23] *Delimitis* v. *Henninger Bräu* (*Case C–234/89*) [1991] I E.C.R. 935; [1992] 5 C.M.L.R. 210, at paras 45–46.
[24] [1983] O.J. L173/1.
[25] [1983] O.J. L173/5.
[26] Regulation 17/62, Article 9(3).
[27] See *infra*, 306–307.

investigation, since only the Commission can grant an exemption and since, as the E.C.J. held in *Delimitis* v. *Henninger Bräu*,[28] a national court must not reach a conclusion that would be inconsistent with the Commission's finding. At the very least, this will entail a substantial delay in the proceedings, and may have an impact on how the case is eventually settled. What should the domestic court do while a notification for individual exemption is still pending?

Generally speaking, an agreement can benefit from individual exemption only where it has been notified to the Commission; a very narrow range of agreements fall outside this proposition.[29] It follows that almost all unnotified agreements are automatically void if they are caught by Article 81(1) unless they benefit from block exemption;[30] Article 1 of Regulation 17/62 provides that the prohibition of Article 81 applies irrespective of whether a decision to that effect has been taken by the Commission. Where parties to an agreement do notify their agreement to the Commission in the hope of obtaining a negative clearance or individual exemption, the position is more complicated; the same is true where the agreement does not require notification to qualify for individual exemption as a result of the provisions in Article 4(2) of Regulation 17/62. The domestic court is not able to grant individual exemption to an agreement, this being solely within the competence of the Commission. If the national court were to strike down the agreement, this would be inconsistent with the eventual decision of the Commission if it were to grant an exemption; on the other hand the national court has an obligation to enforce Articles 81 and 82, and a refusal to apply them wherever a notification has been made to the Commission could amount to a dereliction of that duty. The position would be simpler if notified or non-notifiable agreements were valid until the Commission decides not to grant an exemption. However it is clear that "new" agreements[31] do not benefit from provisional validity.[32] That is to say, such agreements only become valid at the point when a favourable decision is taken

---

[28] (*Case C–234/89*) [1991] I E.C.R. 935; [1992] 5 C.M.L.R. 210.

[29] See Regulation 17, Article 4(2).

[30] National courts are permitted to consider whether an agreement falls within a block exemption: *De Bloos* v. *Bouyer* (*Case 59/77*) [1977] E.C.R. 2359; [1978] 1 C.M.L.R. 511; *Hydrotherm* v. *Compact* (*Case 170/83*) [1984] E.C.R. 2999; [1985] 3 C.M.L.R. 224.

[31] That is to say agreements entered into after Regulation 17/62 came into effect or, in the case of member states that have joined the common market since it was formed, agreements entered into after Accession; "old" agreements entered into prior to Regulation 17/62 do benefit from provisional validity: see, e.g. *Delimitis* v. *Henninger Bräu* (*Case C–234/89*) [1991] I E.C.R. 935; [1992] 5 C.M.L.R. 210, para. 49; the same is probably true of "accession" agreements, although the point has not been dealt with by the E.C.J.

[32] On provisional validity see *Kerse* (*supra* n. 1), paras 10.05–1012; *Smith* (*supra* n. 1), paras [63]–[67].

in respect of them, although that validity can be retrospective to the date of notification.[33]

The issue of parallel Commission investigations and domestic proceedings came before the Court of Appeal in *M.T.V. Europe* v. *B.M.G. Records*.[34] In this case, M.T.V. was a third party claiming damages against seven defendants for infringements of Article 81. A notification of the agreement in question had been made to the European Commission. Lord Bingham, M.R. (as he then was) said that as a general proposition the national court should stay proceedings pending a decision by the Commission in the interests of legal certainty, unless the answer to the complaint is clear. However, Lord Bingham went on to add that it did not follow from this that there should be a general stay of all steps in the action: it may, for example, be reasonable to allow the preparation of an action for trial, provided that this did not lead to a decision in advance of that made by the Commission. Litigants should be treated fairly, and this was a matter for the national court to assess. On the facts of this case, the Court of Appeal upheld the order of Evans-Lombe, J. at first instance, ordering a stay of the action over the summer months of 1994 while the matter was being argued in Brussels, but thereafter allowing preparation of the case for trial, subject to an agreement not to set the action down for trial. In *Williams* v. *Welsh Rugby Union*[35] Eady, J. ordered a stay of proceedings where a dispute had arisen between Cardiff R.F.C. and the Welsh Rugby Union. Cardiff had brought an action against the W.R.L.; the International Rugby Union sought to be joined in the action. The I.R.U.'s rules had been notified to the Commission, and the W.R.U. intended to notify. Eady, J. allowed the I.R.U.'s application to be joined, and agreed to its and the W.R.U.'s application for the action to be stayed. His view was that the issues at hand—professionalism in sport and the social and economic implications thereof—were topical and ripe for consideration by the Commission; this was demonstrated by its own document *Broadcasting of Sports Events and Competition Law*;[36] the fact that there could be a long delay while the Commission investigated was not, in itself, a reason for opposing a stay. In *Philips Electronics* v. *Ingman Ltd*.[37] Laddie, J. applied Lord Bingham's ruling in *M.T.V. Europe*, ordering a stay of proceedings pending the outcome of the defendants' complaint (that the plaintiff's commencement of a patent action entailed infringements of Community Competition rules) to the Commission.

[33] Regulation 17/62, Article 6(1).
[34] [1997] 1 C.M.L.R. 867; [1997] Eu. L.R. 100.
[35] [1999] Eu. L.R. 195.
[36] 2nd June 1998. See also *Application of EC competition law to sport*, Commission Press Release I.P. (99) 133.
[37] [1998] 2 C.M.L.R. 839.

b. Expansion of the range of non-notifiable agreements: the new regime for vertical restraints

As noted above, national courts are able to apply the provisions of a regulation conferring block exemption, so that the problem of the Commission's monopoly in relation to individual exemptions does not arise where an agreement satisfies the terms of one of these regulations. Literally thousands of agreements are drafted in such a way that block exemption can safely be claimed: these legal instruments provide a "safe haven" for many agreements, the enforceability of which might otherwise be in doubt. Without entering upon the important debate as to whether the Article 81(1) prohibition should attach in the first place to agreements providing for exclusive distribution or purchasing rights,[38] two important changes to the law in relation to so-called "vertical agreements" should be noted.

First, the Council has adopted a new Regulation which enables the Commission to adopt wider block exemptions for vertical agreements in the future than has been the case historically.[39] The Commission published a draft block exemption on vertical agreements in the *Official Journal* on 24th September 1999,[40] together with extensive draft guidelines. The new regulation was adopted on 22nd December 1999, and will be much wider in scope than its predecessors;[41] for example, it will apply to any vertical agreement for the supply of goods for resale or for processing and to services agreements; the existing block exemptions apply only to the supply of goods for resale. The new regulation will also be more flexible (less formalistic), and will adopt an overtly economic approach, in that it will apply only to agreements where the market share of the supplier or the purchaser exceeds 30 per cent.[42] The effect of the new block exemption should be that many more vertical agreements will be block exempted, with the hoped-for consequence that they will not need to be litigated in national courts; and that, by being block-exempted, the particular problem of an agreement requiring *individual* exemption, which is now in the

[38] If Article 81(1) were applied in a less formalistic manner to agreements which in truth are often pro- rather than anti-competitive, the need for exemption would not arise.

[39] *Council Regulation (EC) No. 1215/1999 amending Regulation No. 19/65/EEC on the application of Article 81(3) of the Treaty to certain categories of agreements and concerted practices* [1999] O.J. L148/1.

[40] Commission Regulation (EC) No. 2790/1999 [1999] O.J. L336/21; [1999] O.J. C270/7.

[41] The new regulation will replace Regulations 1983/83 and 1984/83, already referred to *supra*, fns 24 and 25, and Regulation 4087/88 ([1988] O.J. L359/46) on franchising agreements.

[42] On this point, see Article 3 of the new block exemption; in most cases, it is the market power of the supplier that matters (Article 3(1)); however, in the case of an exclusive distribution term, it is the purchaser's market share that is relevant (Article 3(2)).

gift only of the Commission, will not arise. The second change is an important innovation: vertical agreements no longer need to be notified *ex ante* in order to be capable of exemption.[43] A new Council Regulation[44] amends Article 4(2) of Regulation 17/62 by providing that any vertical agreement can be exempted, whether it has been notified or not. This does not overcome the problem of the national court in having to decide whether to stay domestic proceedings pending the outcome of the Commission's decision: as the law currently stands the Commission retains its monopoly to grant individual exemption.[45] However, it does deal with the current problem that an exemption can, as a general proposition, only be retrospective to the date of notification and not before. A national court could now stay its proceedings while the Commission makes a decision to exempt and then, assuming that exemption is forthcoming, declare the agreement always to have been legal. The requirement to notify for exemption was an inducement to undertakings to notify, something which the Commission now wishes to discourage and, eventually, to stop altogether.[46] Council Regulation 1216/99 entered into force on 18th June 1999.

c. The Commission's proposal to abolish the notification system

A radical proposal is contained in the *White Paper on Modernisation of the rules implementing Articles 85 and 86 of the EC Treaty*,[47] which the Commission published on 28th April 1999. In this document the Commission says that an entirely new approach to the enforcement of the competition rules is now called for. The circumstances of 1962, when the original implementing Regulation was adopted, were very different: competition law in Europe is now mature, well-known and all member states have their own systems. As a result, the Commission says that it no longer needs a monopoly over the grant of individual exemptions; national competition authorities and national courts, in its view, are now just as capable of applying Article 81(3) as the Commission itself. Furthermore, the Commission's view is that there is no longer a need for a system of notification. Instead of individual exemption entailing an "authoris-ation" on the part of an administrative body such as itself, the Commission intends that Article 81 should become directly applicable in its entirety.

The White Paper raises important issues for judges in national courts. Clearly, if they become able to apply the provisions of Article 81(3), the discussion above about the need to stay an action while the Commission's

---

[43] See *supra*, 303.
[44] *Council Regulation (EC) No. 1216/1999 amending Regulation No. 17: First regulation implementing Articles 81 and 82 of the Treaty* [1999] O.J. L148/5.
[45] See however, *infra*, Part 2(c).
[46] See *infra*, 306–307.
[47] Commission Programme 99/027.

decision is sought becomes otiose. On the other hand, the possibility of courts making judgments about the criteria in Article 81(3) calls into question whether those criteria are justiciable; and also raises the problem of consistent application of the competition rules throughout the Community. Without entering further into this debate here, suffice it to say that the White Paper seems likely to increase the number of cases in which the complex assessments called for by Article 81 fall to be decided by the courts rather than the competition authorities.

d. The classic "Euro-defence"

Moving from the procedural issues that result from the notification system, this essay turns to the success (or otherwise) of the enforcement of the competition rules in contractual disputes. As already suggested, there seems little doubt that the judicial mind is unsympathetic to the Article 81(2) defence, where one party to an agreement attempts to walk away from it on the ground that it is void under competition law. *Pacta sunt servanda* has a powerful influence where one person purports, on the basis of a "technicality" of competition law, to avoid a contractual obligation.

In the *George Michael* case[48] the singer sought to argue that his recording contract with Sony was in restraint of trade at common law and an infringement of Article 81, and was therefore void and unenforceable: on this occasion, the matter came before the court not as a Euro-defence, but in an action on George Michael's part for a declaration. The court rejected both claims. As to Article 81(1), Parker, J. was not satisfied that the recording contract was capable of producing an appreciable effect on trade between member states. More generally, the judge was clearly unimpressed at an attempt to avoid an agreement which had been entered into as a settlement of earlier litigation between the parties, the singer at the time of such settlement having received legal advice from leading lawyers in the U.K. and U.S. with specialisation in the law of publishing agreements. *Interest rei publicae ut finis litium sit* in conjunction with *pacta sunt servanda* were a powerful combination on this occasion.

The Euro-defence was invoked in two cases arising from the plight of Lloyds' names in *Society of Lloyd's* v. *Clementson*[49] and *Higgins* v. *Marchant & Eliot Underwriting Ltd.*[50] In *Clementson*, Lloyd's itself was suing Clementson; his defence was that the Central Fund Byelaw of the Society of Lloyd's itself infringed Article 81(1). The Court of Appeal had concluded that it was at least arguable that Mr Clementson would be able to run such a Euro-defence,

---

[48] *Panayiotou* v. *Sony Music Entertainment (U.K.) Ltd.* [1994] E.M.L.R. 229.
[49] [1997] L.R.C.R 175; [1995] 1 C.M.L.R. 693; [1995] C.L.C. 117.
[50] [1996] 3 C.M.L.R. 313 (Q.B.); [1996] 3 C.M.L.R. 349 (C.A.).

and therefore allowed an appeal against its having been struck out. Sub-sequently, the defence did indeed fail. In the *Marchant* case, two cash calls had been made on a Lloyd's name, Dr. Higgins, by Marchant & Elliott Underwriting Ltd. Dr. Higgins' case was that the agreement between him and Marchant & Elliott infringed Article 81 and was therefore unenforceable. Rix, J. considered that the *Clementson* case was distinguishable, as what was there in issue was whether the Central Fund Byelaw of Lloyd's itself infringed Article 81(1). Here, the agreement that Marchant sought to enforce was a separate agreement between it and Dr. Higgins. For Higgins, it was argued that this agreement was entered into pursuant to the Lloyd's regime, and amounted effectively to an attempt to enforce the rules of the overall system. Thus it was also tainted and was unenforceable. This was rejected by Rix, J.[51]

> "No case has been cited to me in which A has been unable to enforce his lawful rights under contract with B because A has been instigated to litigate against B by C in furtherance of C's unlawful agreement or decision. Such a doctrine would be immensely far-reaching and damaging to lawful rights."

Rix, J.'s judgment was upheld in the Court of Appeal. Judicial disfavour of Euro-defences shines through: "through the ingenuity of his lawyers [Dr. Higgins] relies upon the Article to evade payment of his debts. It is our task to see whether that ingenuity has been well directed and will avail him".[52]

Another failed Euro-defence can be seen in *Oakdale (Richmond) Ltd.* v. *National Westminster Bank Plc.*[53] Chadwick, J. dismissed an argument that the restrictive terms of an all-monies debenture arrangement, which provided for a lender to have control over the borrower company's book debts and which was necessary to protect the bank against the risks it had assumed, were anti-competitive. On the contrary, the judge was satisfied that these terms were necessary to such agreements and, as such, promoted competition. This judgment is of interest in that the judge did not "merely" reject the defence, but positively recognised that contractual restrictions can often be pro-competitive: as such it sits happily with judgments of the E.C.J. such as *Delimitis* v. *Henninger Bräu*[54] and *Gøttrup Klim* v. *D.L.G.*[55] in which that court has provided an important lead in showing that contractual restrictions are not necessarily restrictions of competition; indeed contractual restrictions often provide a positive contribution to the competitive process.

---

[51] *Ibid.* [1996] 3 C.M.L.R. 313, 331–332.
[52] [1996] 3 C.M.L.R. 349, 355–356, *per* Leggatt, L.J.
[53] [1997] Eu. L.R. 7, 40; affd. [1997] 3 C.M.L.R. 815.
[54] (*Case C–234/89*) [1991] I E.C.R. 935; [1992] 5 C.M.L.R. 210.
[55] (*Case C–250/92*) [1994] I E.C.R. 5641; [1996] 4 C.M.L.R. 19.

e. Severance

The proceeding section reveals that judges may view with distaste technical invocations of the competition rules in order to avoid contractual obligations. However, there will be occasions when voidness does follow from an obvious infringement of Article 81(1); the facts of *Eco Swiss China Time* v. *Benetton*[56] reveal how this might happen. Where Article 81(1) is successfully invoked in litigation, a problem can arise over the effect of the voidness upon the remainder of the agreement. The E.C.J. has held that, provided it is possible to sever the offending provisions of the contract from the rest of its terms, the latter remain valid and enforceable.[57] However the Court did not lay down a Community-wide principle of severance, so that the mechanism whereby this is to be effected is a matter to be decided according to the domestic law of each member state.[58] This in turn gives rise to issues under the Brussels[59] and Rome Conventions;[60] the former determines where litigation may take place in civil and commercial cases, while the latter determines the law that should be applied in contractual disputes. Assuming that severability is regarded as a matter of substance rather than procedure, the Brussels Convention ought not to affect the outcome of litigation, since in principle the Rome Convention should lead to the same finding of the applicable law, wherever the litigation takes place; however, the determination of the applicable law may be crucial to the outcome of the litigation, since different member states have different methods of severing unlawful restrictions from contracts. It seems unfortunate that such a matter as this should be left to national law, since the enforceability of a contract may vary according to the applicable law; it might be argued that the impact of Article 81(2) ought to have uniform effect throughout the Community.

As a matter of English contract law severance is possible in certain circumstances, although the rules on this subject are quite complex.[61] The Court of Appeal was called upon to examine severability in a Competition Law context in *Chemidus Wavin Ltd.* v. *Société pour la Transformation.*[62] A patentee was suing for royalties payable under an agreement that arguably infringed Article 81(1). The Court held that the minimum royalties provision was

---

[56] (*Case C–126/97*) 1st June 1999, unreported.

[57] *Société Technique Minière* v. *Maschinenbau Ulm (Case 56/65)* [1966] E.C.R. 235; [1966] C.M.L.R. 357; *Société de Vente de Ciments et Bétons de l'Est* v. *Kerpen and Kerpen GmbH (Case 319/82)* [1983] E.C.R. 4173; [1985] 1 C.M.L.R. 511.

[58] *Ciments et Bétons (Case 319/82) (ibid.); V.A.G. France S.A.* v. *Establissements Magne S.A. (Case 10/86)* [1986] E.C.R. 4071; [1988] 4 C.M.L.R. 98.

[59] *Brussels Convention on Jurisdiction and the Enforcement of Judgments in Civil and Commercial Matters, 1968.*

[60] *Rome Convention on the Law Applicable to Contractual Obligations 1980.*

[61] See *Chitty on Contracts*, 28th edn. (1999), ch. 17, §§185ff.

[62] [1978] 3 C.M.L.R. 514.

enforceable, irrespective of whether other parts of the agreement might infringe Article 81(1). Buckley, L.J. said:[63]

> "It seems to me that, in applying Article [81] to an English contract, one may well have to consider whether, after the excisions required by the Article of the Treaty have been made from the contract, the contract could be said to fail for lack of consideration or on any other ground, or whether the contract would be so changed in its character as not to be the sort of contract that the parties intended to enter into at all."

In *Inntrepreneur Estates Ltd.* v. *Mason*[64] Michael Barnes, Q.C., sitting as a Deputy Judge of the High Court, held that, where a beer tie infringed the competition rules, it did not follow that a covenant to pay rent would also be unenforceable. Applying the test in *Chemidus Wavin*, the judge had no difficulty in severing the tie, leaving the rest of the agreement intact. A similar result was reached by the Court of Appeal in *Inntrepreneur Estates (G.L.) Ltd.* v. *Boyes*.[65] It is unsurprising that the judges in these cases found the argument unappealing that the tenant of a public house could be relieved of the obligation to pay rent to the landlord as a collateral consequence of an (arguably) unlawful beer tie. A contrary finding would have devastating consequences to landlords of large portfolios of public houses.

f. Void or illegal?

Agreements which infringe Article 81(1) are stated by Article 81(2) to be void; however an important question is whether they are "merely" void or whether they are also illegal. On this classification turn the important issues of whether any money paid under the contract by one party to the other would be irrecoverable, applying the principle *in pari delicto potior est conditio defendentis*,[66] and whether one party to the agreement could bring an action against the other for damages for harm suffered as a result of the operation of the agreement. The question whether agreements contrary to Article 81(1) are illegal has been brought before the courts in numerous cases in recent years. Typically, the cases involve exclusive purchasing agreements between tenants of public houses and landlords of public houses, who may or not themselves be brewers. The tenants have raised numerous complaints against the landlords— about the exclusive purchasing tie itself, about the high rents that may be payable for the premises, about the price that they have to pay for the beer, and about the competitive disadvantage that they suffer compared with publicans in the "free" trade, who may be able to obtain beer more cheaply. Disgruntled tenants in these circumstances have deployed a range of arguments, intended to

---

[63] *Ibid.*, 520.
[64] [1993] 2 C.M.L.R. 293 (Q.B.).
[65] [1993] 2 E.G.L.R. 112.
[66] See Goff and Jones, *The Law of Restitution*, 5th edn. (1998), ch. 24.

remedy their situation by recourse to principles of the laws of contract, tort, set-off and restitution. It should be said straightaway that these claims have for the most part been unsuccessful, and a raft of recent decisions in the brewery sector, either clearing[67] or exempting[68] standard tenancy agreements in this sector should, in large part, bring an end to this particular round of litigation. Similar arguments have arisen in relation to exclusive purchasing agreements for the purchase of petrol, where the tenants' complaints resemble those of publicans.

It has now been settled by the Court of Appeal that the agreement is illegal rather than merely void. In *Gibbs Mew Plc* v. *Gemmell*[69] it held (admittedly *obiter*, as the Court was satisfied that the agreement in question did not offend Article 81(1)) that the parties to an agreement that infringes Article 81 cannot bring an action in tort or in restitution for compensation for any harm suffered, since they are themselves party to an illegal agreement: "the parties to a beer tie offending Article [81] are the cause, not the victims, of the distortion, restriction or prevention of competition".[70] Of the claim by a tenant that he had entered into an agreement with the landlord that had caused it economic loss, and that he should be able to sue the landlord for damages in tort for breach of statutory duty, the Court of Appeal was emphatic:[71]

> "It is a counterclaim based on the principle that in entering into the lease, the Plaintiffs were in breach of statutory duty. It passes all understanding how contracts freely entered into could give rise to a cause of action in one of the parties entering into it, on the ground that the other party was in breach of duty. If the argument for the Defendant is right, the contract is an illegal contract. The parties entering into it are *in pari delicto*".

The Court of Appeal therefore considers that, where two parties enter into an agreement that infringes Article 81(1), they are acting *in pari delicto*, with the inexorable consequence that neither can bring an action against the other that would have the effect of enforcing an illegal contract. It is interesting to speculate whether an argument could be made to the contrary: that the tenant in a case such as *Gibbs Mew* is not truly *in pari delicto*, but is rather the weaker of two parties and the victim of oppressive, and anti-competitive, conduct on the part of the more powerful landlord/brewer. A similar characterisation could be made of the relationship of an oil company and the tenant of a petrol station or a

---

[67] That is to say declaring the non-application of Article 81(1) on the ground that an agreement does not restrict competition to an appreciable effect, as in the case of Greene King's tenancy agreements: see *Roberts/Greene King* Commission Press Release IP (98) 967, on appeal *Roberts* v. *Commission* (*Case T–25/99*) (judgment pending).

[68] See e.g. *Whitbread* [1999] O.J. L88/26; [1999] 5 C.M.L.R. 118; *Bass* [1999] O.J. L186/1; [1999] 5 C.M.L.R. 782; *Scottish and Newcastle* [1999] O.J. L186/28; [1999] 5 C.M.L.R. 831.

[69] [1998] Eu. L.R. 588 (C.A.).

[70] *Ibid.*, 604.

[71] *Ibid.*

powerful patentee and a weak and oppressed licensee. There have been arguments to the effect that there should be at least a possibility of restitutionary recovery,[72] and that Community law should ensure that, in these relationships, the more powerful of the two parties should not be able to benefit from its oppressive behaviour by retaining money had and received. Backing for the idea that a weaker person should have a remedy could be found in the opinion of Advocate General van Gerven who said, in the *Delimitis* case,[73] that certain provisions of Regulation 1984/83 on exclusive purchasing agreements in the brewery sector seemed precisely to reflect such a policy:

> "[Article 8(2)(b) of Regulation 1984/83] reveals the intention of affording better protection to the competitive freedom of contracting parties in a weak economic position and of granting less readily exemption from the prohibition under Article [81(1)]".

It could be argued that provisions of the block exemption on car dealerships[74] and on technology transfer agreements[75] are similarly motivated. In the view of this author, these views are incorrect: the function of Article 81 is to prohibit agreements that are harmful to the competitive process, and all the parties to such agreements should be held equally accountable for the harm caused. Article 81 is not about achieving fairness *between the parties to an agreement*; there may be other doctrines—for example of duress, coercion, inequality of bargaining power—which may provide relief to disappointed parties to agreements, but the achievement of reasonable bargains is beyond the legitimate scope of Article 81. The position, however, is different where a contracting party complains that it is the victim of oppressive contractual terms and conditions imposed upon it *by a dominant firm*: the terms of Article 82 itself suggest that in such a case the victim should be entitled to relief.[76]

A multitude of issues came before the Court of Appeal in 1999, in what for ease of reference may be referred to as the *Crehan* case.[77] Among the issues was the scope of the judgment of the Court of Appeal in *Gibbs Mew* and what is referred to in the judgment of Morritt, L.J. in *Crehan* as the "co-contractor issue". He noted the arguments against enabling the tenant to bring an action in tort for damages, and the views of the Court of Appeal in *Gibbs*. He also noted that there are arguments to the contrary; for example in the U.S. case-law it had

---

[72] See Alison Jones, "Recovery of Benefits Conferred Under Contractual Obligations Prohibited by Article 81 or 82 of the Treaty of Rome" (1996) 112 L.Q.R. 606; Jones, *Restitution and European Community Law* (2000).

[73] *Supra*, n. 28, at para. 23.

[74] Regulation 1475/95.

[75] Regulation 240/96.

[76] See *infra*, 317–319.

[77] *Crehan* v. *Courage Ltd.*; *Byrne* v. *Inntrepreneur Beer Supply Co. Ltd.*; *Langton* v. *Inntrepreneur Beer Supply Co. Ltd.*; *Smith* v. *Greenalls Management Ltd.*; *McCaughey* v. *Walker Cain* [1999] Eur.L.Rep. 834.

been determined that a co-contractor can bring an action where it has suffered harm as a result of an agreement that infringes the U.S. antitrust legislation.[78] The Court of Appeal concluded that, on this point, a reference to the E.C.J. under Article 234 would be made:

> "We are minded to refer to the E.C.J. the question whether, assuming that a party to a prohibited agreement may be someone who is given rights against the other party by virtue of Article 81 which are protected under Community Law, and assuming that such a party has been damaged by actions taken under the agreement by the other party, the national court is obliged as a matter of Community Law to award damages to the injured party".

Clearly this is a reference of great importance: the average time for the E.C.J. to deliver an opinion is currently in the region of 21 months, so that an answer to this question is unlikely before 2001.

g. Transient voidness

A different issue to have come before the Court of Appeal is whether the statutory prohibition in Article 81(2) may be "turned on and off" depending on the surrounding facts. In *Passmore* v. *Morland Plc*[79] the Court of Appeal upheld the Chancery Division's judgment that an agreement could move from voidness to validity (and back again) according to the effect that it might be having on the market. Mr Passmore was the publican of a pub in Aldershot, under a tenancy granted by the Inntrepreneur Pub. Co. The tenancy contained an exclusive purchasing term that Passmore should purchase beer exclusively from I.P.C. Subsequently, the reversion of the lease was acquired by Morland Plc, a relatively small brewer. In a dispute between Morland and Passmore, the latter claimed that the beer tie was unenforceable as a result of the application of Article 81. Essentially, the question for the Court of Appeal was as follows.[80] Suppose that the exclusive purchasing term was unenforceable when entered into, since I.P.C. owned 4,500 pubs containing similar ties which, cumulatively, could foreclose access to the market by other brewers (this being the essential issue according to the judgment of the E.C.J. in *Delimitis*). If some of those pubs were subsequently to come into the hands of a small brewer such as Morland, might it follow that, because those agreements did not contribute to any foreclosure because of its much weaker position in the market, they would cease to be unenforceable? In other words, is the logic of the prohibition in Article 81(1) in conjunction with the declaration of voidness in Article 81(2) that

---

[78] *Perma Life Mufflers Inc.* v. *International Parts Corp.* (1968) 392 U.S. 134 (C.A., 7th Circ.).

[79] [1998] 4 All E.R. 468 (Ch.); [1999] 3 All E.R. 1005; [1999] 1 C.M.L.R. 1129 (C.A.).

[80] Note the claims for damages and restitution could not be pursued because of the Court of Appeal's ruling in *Gibbs Mew*.

agreements can, over a period of time, float into and out of voidness, depending on market conditions? The Court of Appeal, upholding the order of Laddie, J. below,[81] was clear that this was indeed the position. Three passages of the judgment of Chadwick, L.J. state the position clearly. First:[82]

> "[A]n agreement which is not within Article 81(1) at the time when it is entered into—because, in the circumstances prevailing in the relevant market at that time, it does not have the effect of preventing, restricting or distorting competition—may, subsequently and as the result of change in those circumstances, come within Article 81(1)—because, in the changed circumstances, it does have that effect".

Later:[83]

> "It must follow, also, by parity of reasoning, that an agreement which is within the prohibition of Article 81(1) at the time when it is entered into—because, in the circumstances prevailing in the relevant market at that time, it does have the effect of preventing, restricting or distorting competition—may, subsequently and as a result of a change in those circumstances, fall outside the prohibition contained in that Article—because, in the changed circumstances, it no longer has that effect".

Later again:[84]

> "The prohibition is temporaneous (or transient) rather than absolute; in the sense that it endures for a finite period—the period of time for which it is needed—rather than for all time".

Towards the end of his judgment, Chadwick, L.J. dealt with an argument on behalf of Passmore that the principle of legal certainty should have as its consequence that the tie was and remained unenforceable, consistently with the Court of Appeal's judgment in *Shell U.K. Ltd.* v. *Lostock Garage*:[85] the Court of Appeal (Lord Denning, M.R. dissenting) held there that a restrictive covenant that was valid when entered into should remain valid, even if subsequent circumstances made it unreasonable or unfair to enforce it. Ormrod, L.J. felt that the opposite conclusion "would introduce into the law an unprecedented discretion in the court to suspend for a time a term in a contract; the repercussions of this are quite unforeseeable and unmanageable".[86] On this, Chadwick, L.J. concluded in *Passmore*[87] that "it has to be recognised that what was seen, in *Shell U.K. Ltd.* v. *Lostock Garage Ltd.*, as a wholly novel doctrine is now enshrined in community competition law".

It will readily be appreciated that the combination of transient voidness (as in *Passmore*) and illegality that is consequent upon that voidness (as in *Gibbs*

---

[81] [1998] 4 All E.R. 468.
[82] [1999] 3 All E.R. 1005, 1014 g–h.
[83] *Ibid.*, 1015 c–d.
[84] *Ibid.*, 1015 e–f.
[85] [1976] 1 W.L.R. 1187.
[86] *Ibid.*, 1202.
[87] [1999] 3 All E.R. 1005, 1023 f–g.

Mew) may give rise to some exquisitely complex litigation in the future. For example, a restitutionary claim could be successful where money has been paid during the enforceable period of an agreement's lifetime, but not where made during its void period; evidence will be required that successfully pinpoints the moment when validity turned to voidness and vice versa. As mentioned above, the E.C.J. has been asked in the *Crehan* case to provide an opinion on the co-contractor issue; in the meantime, the House of Lords has refused leave to appeal in both *Gibbs Mew* v. *Gemmel* and in *Passmore* v. *Morland*.

h. The duties of a national court

An issue that has occupied the courts of some member states and the E.C.J. has been the extent to which a national court is obliged, of its own motion, to raise and consider points of Community law: should a domestic court simply adjudicate upon those matters that the parties have chosen to litigate, or should it adopt an active role in raising, for example, the possibility that a contract violates the competition rules? This issue came before the E.C.J. in *Van Schijndel* v. *Stichting Pensioensfonds voor Fysiotherapeuten*[88] and *Peterbroeck Van Campenhout & Cie* v. *Belgium*.[89] In *Van Schijndel* the appellants were sued for unpaid contributions to a compulsory professional pension scheme in the Netherlands. They had contested, unsuccessfully, in the Dutch court of first instance and in the first appellate court that they could not be obliged to join the scheme under Dutch law. Their appeal reached the Dutch Supreme Court, where the question was raised whether the first appellate court should have considered, of its own motion if necessary, whether the national law in issue was compatible with the competition rules in the Treaty. The Dutch Supreme Court referred the matter to the E.C.J. The E.C.J. dealt with two issues. First (and uncontroversially) it held that, if national law provided that domestic courts must raise of their own motion points of law based on binding domestic rules, they must also do so where binding Community rules are concerned: anything else would amount to a discriminatory treatment of Community law. The second issue was more complex. What should the position be where under domestic law a court may raise points of its own motion, but only within the subject-matter of the dispute and based on the facts before it: does Community law impose in such circumstances an obligation on the domestic courts to go beyond this "passive role"? The E.C.J.'s answer was that there was no such obligation. This ruling is consistent with the policy of "procedural autonomy", according to which the E.C.J. will abstain from dictating to the courts of the member states how litigation should be conducted and what remedies should be

[88] (*Cases C–430/93 and 431/93*) [1995] I E.C.R. 4705; [1996] 1 C.M.L.R. 801. On these two cases, see Heukels (1996) 33 C.M.L.R. Rev. 337.
[89] (*Case C–312/93*) [1995] I E.C.R. 4599; [1996] 1 C.M.L.R. 793.

available. The decision in *Van Schijndel* not to require judges pro-actively to investigate whether an agreement infringes the competition rules is a reasonable restraint on the part of the E.C.J.

In the *Peterbroeck* case the facts were rather different. Here the question was not whether judges had a positive duty to raise points of competition law, including going beyond the facts of the case as disputed between the parties. Rather, in *Peterbroeck* the E.C.J. was asked whether a domestic rule was void, where the rule prevented a national court from considering of its own motion after a fixed period whether a measure of domestic law is compatible with a provision of Community law when that provision had not been invoked by the litigant. On this point the Court held that such a rule could be void if it might prevent the effective application of Community law; there are occasions on which the principle of procedural autonomy may have to yield to the importance of *effet utile*.

i. The duties of an arbitrator

In *Eco Swiss China Time Ltd.* v. *Benetton International N.V.*[90] the E.C.J. was asked to consider the impact of the competition rules in the Treaty on arbitration proceedings. Benetton had granted a trade mark licence to Eco Swiss to market watches under the Benetton name. Benetton subsequently terminated the licence and Eco Swiss referred the matter to an arbitrator, under Dutch law, in accordance with the agreement. The arbitrator awarded Eco Swiss substantial damages. No competition law point was taken by the parties, and the arbitrator did not raise one. In fact the trade mark licence infringed Article 81(1) and was ineligible for block exemption under Regulation 240/96 on technology transfer agreements. Benetton decided to try to prevent the enforcement of the award of damages on the basis that to do so would amount to enforcing an agreement that was contrary to EC competition law. Under Dutch law, an arbitration award can be challenged before the courts, in the absence of agreement between the parties, only on grounds of public policy. The Dutch Supreme Court held that the enforcement of competition rules did not amount to public policy in Dutch law, so that if the matter were purely domestic Benetton would be unsuccessful. However, since Benetton's case rested on the Community competition rules, the matter was referred to the E.C.J. under Article 234.

As noted above, the E.C.J. stressed the fundamental importance of the competition rules in the Treaty, and the importance of the sanction of enforcement in ensuring compliance with them. A consequence of this was that, if domestic law allowed an appeal against an arbitration award on grounds of public policy, the possibility that there might be a breach of the Community competition rules should be investigated. On a separate point, the E.C.J.

[90] (*Case C–126/87*) 1st June 1999, unreported.

recognised that domestic procedural rules which prescribe time limits for the challenging of arbitral awards could have the effect of preventing an appeal based on the competition rules; provided that the time limits were not so fierce as to infringe the requirement of effective application of the competition rules, they would themselves be valid.

Without saying anything about the obligations of arbitrators themselves, the case is of obvious importance to their role. Arbitration is intended to enable parties to disputes to reach reasonably rapid and cheap settlement of disputes. If an arbitrator ignores points of competition law, but these can subsequently be raised on appeal—as, subject to the time limit point, in Dutch law in *Eco Swiss Time*—the speedy and cheap solution would be undermined. The arbitrator ought, therefore, to apply his or her mind to the issue; albeit that, according to *Van Schijndel*, there is no obligation pro-actively to root out infringements of the competition rules. It seems likely that the E.C.J. will be asked in due course to look further into the precise obligations of both judges and arbitrators in circumstances such as these.

3 ARTICLE 82

It may be that a contractual term infringes Article 82, because it amounts to an abuse of a dominant position, as well as infringing Article 81. For example, an agreement to purchase one's entire requirements of a particular product from a dominant firm is quite likely to infringe both Article 81 and Article 82,[91] because it might foreclose access to the market on the part of competitors; it is irrelevant for this purpose whether the undertaking that accepts the obligation is willing or unwilling to accept it.[92] Similarly a system of loyalty rebates, which falls short of a contractual requirement not to buy from competitors but which may have the same effect, may amount to an abuse.[93] In this case it has been assumed that the prohibition of Article 82 means that the offending provisions are void (although interestingly there is nothing on the face of Article 82, as there is in the case of Article 81, to say so). A customer tied by an exclusive purchasing commitment which infringes Article 82 could safely ignore it and purchase supplies elsewhere. The impact of any such invalidity on the remainder of the agreement would raise the same question of severability discussed above.[94] Of course, the judge will wish to be satisfied on the facts that there is indeed an infringement of Article 82, which requires *inter alia* a

---

[91] See for example *Hoffmann La Roche* v. *Commission (Case 85/76)* [1979] E.C.R. 461; [1979] 3 C.M.L.R. 211.

[92] *Ibid.*

[93] *Ibid.* For a recent finding of abuse in such a case, see *British Airways* 14th July 1999, unreported (Commission decision).

[94] *Supra*, 309–310.

demonstration of an appreciable effect on trade between member states; a Euro-defence based on Article 82, by a tenant of buildings used for the provision of flight catering services at Heathrow Airport, failed in *Heathrow Airport Ltd.* v. *Forte (U.K.) Ltd.*[95] When Article 82 is raised before a national court the task for the judge is not complicated by the problem of notification which was discussed above,[96] because it is not possible to apply for an exemption under Article 82 as it is under Article 81(3). A judge does have discretion to adjourn a case if the Commission is investigating the same matter, and he could if he wished refer an issue of legal uncertainty to the E.C.J. under Article 234.

An interesting question is whether an agreement that infringes Article 82 is simply void, or whether it is also illegal. It will be recalled that in *Gibbs Mew* the Court of Appeal held that an agreement that infringes Article 81(1) is illegal, so that no action in restitution, tort or contract can be brought by one party against the other. In the case of Article 82, there may be a good argument that the position is different, or at least more complex. Article 82(2)(a) on its face envisages, for example, that abuse might lie where a dominant firm imposes "unfair purchase or selling prices or other unfair trading conditions" on its customers. Thus, the party to an agreement who has been abused in this way ought, presumably, to be able to claim that it has been improperly treated. This would suggest that the same agreement, which would be regarded as illegal if the dominant firm sought to enforce it, and which is illegal for the purposes of Article 81, ought not to be so regarded where a claim is brought by the customer under Article 82. This was indeed argued in the *Gibbs Mew* case.

Authority that the customer ought to have a remedy under Article 82 can be found in *GT-Link A/S* v. *De Danske Statsbaner.*[97] Charges were imposed by the DDS, the Danish state-owned railway undertaking, on GT-Link, a ferry operator making use of DDS-owned ports. These charges were arguably in breach of Article 82. A Danish court asked the E.C.J. a series of questions concerning the compatibility of the charges with Community law, including whether GT-Link could recover then, assuming them to be unlawful. The E.C.J. held that charges levied by a member state in breach of Community law must be repaid (citing *Comates* v. *General des Douanes et Droits Indirects*);[98] it added that the same would be true of a public undertaking such as DDS which was responsible to the Danish Ministry of Transport and governed by the Budget Act. What is of interest about this judgment is whether the E.C.J. would have decided the same way had the defendant not been a public undertaking of the type specified in the judgment, but a "normal" private sector dominant firm. It is clearly arguable that, since Article 82 is directly effective and since national

---

[95] [1998] E.C.C. 357; [1998] Eu. L.R. 98.
[96] *Supra*, 302–305.
[97] (*Case C–242/95*) [1997] I E.C.R. 4449; [1997] 5 C.M.L.R. 601.
[98] (*Case C–122–218/95*) [1997] I E.C.R. 165.

courts must give practical effect to the rights that this entails, any victim of abusive behaviour should be able to recover. In other words, the *GT-Link* case should not be regarded, or regarded only, as a state liability case, but as a case on the obligations of dominant firms to compensate those whom they abuse.

4 U.K. LAW

The Competition Act 1998, section 2(4) provides that "Any agreement or decision which is prohibited by subsection (1) is void." This of course mirrors Article 81(2). Section 60 of the Act provides that its provisions must be interpreted consistently with the jurisprudence of the E.C.J. (and the Court of First Instance), and that regard must be had to the decisions of the European Commission. It follows that judgments of the E.C.J. such as *Société Technique Minière* v. *Maschinenbau Ulm*,[99] *Société de Vente de Ciments et Bétons de l'Est* v. *Kerpen and Kerpen GmbH*[100] and *Eco Swiss Time*[101] will all be relevant to the proper interpretation of section 2(4) and the consequences of infringing the Chapter I prohibition. It is to be expected that the issues discussed so far in this essay, and numerous others arising from the same point that anti-competitive agreements can be void and illegal, will be litigated in future not only under Community, but also under domestic competition law.

5 CONCLUSION

To return to the beginning: competition law is a vastly different subject today from what it was when I studied the law of contract for the first time. Interestingly, though not surprisingly, the judicial distaste at that time for avoiding contractual obligations through reliance on the restraint of trade doctrine seems to be replicated when Article 81(1) is invoked by a disappointed contracting party; Article 82, however, seems to give rise to different considerations. What is certain is that there will be more, rather than less, litigation under the competition rules in the future, and that the complexity of matters that come before the courts is likely to increase rather than to diminish.

[99] *Supra*, n. 57.
[100] *Ibid.*
[101] *Supra*, n. 15.

Chapter 16

Contract, Public Law and Accountability

Paul Craig

All public institutions have to make choices as to how public services are delivered. This essay will focus on the increasing use made of contracting-out as a method for service delivery. The discussion will begin by considering contracting-out in the U.K., with particular emphasis being placed on the problems of accountability and control. The main focus of the essay will however be on the European Community. It will be seen that the resignation of the European Commission in 1999 was due primarily to failures in relation to Community programmes where contracting-out was used. There will be an analysis of these problems and of the general lessons which can be learned about the use of contract for the attainment of policy objectives.

1 THE DOMESTIC CONTEXT: CONTRACTING-OUT

The government in the U.K. has always had to make contracts in order to purchase the goods and services which it requires. Recent years have, however, witnessed increased use of contractual language over a broader area.[1] Contractual ideas have influenced the relationship between Next Steps Agencies and their sponsoring departments, even though there is no real contract because the agency possesses no separate legal personality. Contracting-out has now become one preferred way of securing the provision of public services.

A number of *economic arguments* have been put in favour of contracting-out.[2] It is said that public sector "in-house" monopolies are inefficient; that there is "open-ended" financial commitment to public sector "in-house" units; that competition generates new ideas; and that contractors can be penalised for

---

[1] Freedland, "Government by Contract and Private Law" [1994] P.L. 86.
[2] Hartley and Huby, "Contracting-Out Policy: Theory and Evidence": Kay, Mayer and Thompson, *Privatization and Regulation—The UK Experience* (1986) 289.

defective performance and late delivery. The economic arguments are, however, not all one way. It has been argued that private contractors can be unreliable; that private contractors can use low bids to eliminate the in-house capacity; that competitive tendering entails monitoring costs; and that it can be difficult for the public body to maintain control over the bodies to whom service provision has been contracted-out.

It is moreover clear that contracting-out raises broader issues of *accountability* for the provision of public services. The fact that the activity has been contracted-out, rather than being privatised, means that the state retains responsibility for its provision. There is nonetheless always the danger that a contractor who was intended only to "execute" a chosen policy may come to have a real influence over the choice of policy itself. This may be particularly so where the subject-matter is technically complex, where the public officer responsible for overseeing the contract is hard-pressed with other work or where the very ascription of responsibility for the contract within the public body is unclear. Nor should it be forgotten that, when work is contracted-out to private firms, they will not normally have a "public service ethos", but will be principally concerned with the interests of their shareholders.[3]

Contracting-out should not however always be thought of negatively in terms of accountability. Contracts can help to sharpen accountability by defining goals, setting targets and monitoring performance, thereby structuring administrative discretion. As Harden states,[4] contract does "offer an opportunity to make real progress towards greater accountability by clearly identifying who is responsible for a policy, what it is, whether it is being carried out in practice and if not, why not". The Labour Government's documentation on contracting-out and the Private Finance Initiative goes into considerable detail in its specification of the performance conditions which have to be met by those who contract with the government and how risk is allocated between the government and the private supplier. These techniques of control are not, however, self-executing. They require positive input from the government side. In order that programmes can be made accountable, government must be as clear as possible in the terms of the contract as to what it requires of the contractor. Management within government must also be capable of assessing the completed work.

In addition to the economic arguments and those concerning accountability, contracting-out also requires us to think about the possible application of *public law principles* to contracted-out activities. The contract itself will provide the basis for the legal rights and duties of the respective parties. It may however be argued that the private party should also be bound by principles which have

---

[3] Faulkner, "Public Services, Citizenship, and the State—The British Experience 1967–97", in Freedland and Sciarra (eds), *Public Services and Citizenship in European Law, Public and Labour Law Perspectives* (1998) 42–44.
[4] *The Contracting State* (1992) 71.

traditionally been applied to public bodies. It is clear as a matter of principle that, if the public body is fulfilling a statutory function, then it will be subject to the normal public law principles. If it chooses to fulfil part of that statutory remit by contracting-out to a private undertaking, then it would be contrary to principle for the citizens' protection to be reduced as a result of this organisational choice. Thus, either the parent department maintains a residual public law responsibility for the tasks which have been contracted-out, or the private contracting party must itself be subject to the rigours of the public law controls where this is appropriate.

Governments in the U.K. have over the last two decades come to favour contracting-out for the provision of public services. The Conservative Governments under Margaret Thatcher and John Major required departments to review their activities in the light of five options. The activity could be abolished, privatised, contracted-out, given to a Next Steps Agency or the status quo could be maintained. The contracting-out option applied both to activities performed in-house and to those for which agencies were responsible. Market testing[5] was a key criterion for deciding between these options.[6]

The Labour Government of Tony Blair has sought to distance itself from some of the more extreme implications of the previous government's market-oriented strategy. It has nonetheless adopted much of the same general strategic thinking. Its approach towards service delivery at the central level is to be found in its document on *Better Quality Services: Guidance for Senior Managers*.[7] The objective is said to be "Better Government". Market testing and contracting-out will be used when these can be shown to offer better value for money, that is better quality services at optimal cost. Existing plans for market tests and contracting-out will therefore proceed, unless the Minister is satisfied that better value for money can be attained by other means. Ministers are to remain accountable for services contracted-out to the private sector. It is incumbent on each Department to review all of its activities within a five year period[8] in order to decide which of five options to pursue.[9] The service can be abolished if it is no longer needed; it can be restructured internally after benchmarking[10] has been used to diagnose problems; it can be strategically

[5] *The Citizen's Charter, First Report*, Cm. 2101 (1992) 60–64, contains a detailed breakdown of market testing being carried out by different government departments and agencies.

[6] *The Government's Guide to Market Testing* (1993).

[7] (1998). See also, *Better Quality Services: A Handbook on Creating Public/Private Partnerships through Market Testing and Contracting Out* (1998).

[8] *Ibid.*, para. 7.

[9] *Ibid.*, para. 9.

[10] Benchmarking is a form of self-assessment designed to help public bodies to improve their performance against the European Foundation for Quality Management (E.F.Q.M.) European Business Excellence Model, *Public Sector Benchmarking Project Phase Three* (October 1998).

contracted-out;[11] it can be market tested, with an in-house team bidding against external bidders; or it can be privatised.

2 THE EC: THE COMMITTEE OF INDEPENDENT EXPERTS, ITS ORIGIN AND CRITERIA OF OPERATION

There had been concern in the EC for some considerable time about fraud and mismanagement. Newspaper reports revealed instances of fraud in the Common Agricultural Policy, the Court of Auditors brought to light instances of mismanagement of certain Community policies, and U.C.L.A.F. (the Commission body co-ordinating the fight against fraud) investigations showed in greater detail the ways in which Community funds were being misused. The European Parliament repeatedly expressed its dissatisfaction with the management of the Community's financial resources. This culminated in a resolution of 14th January 1999 which called for a Committee of Independent Experts to be convened under the auspices of the European Parliament and the Commission with a mandate to detect and deal with fraud, mismanagement and nepotism. It was for the Committee to decide how far the Commission as a body, or individual Commissioners, had responsibility for such matters. The Committee was also to conduct a fundamental review of the Commission's practices in the award of all financial contracts. The Committee was to produce its report within two months, by 15th March 1999. In technical legal terms the Committee is not a Community institution, nor is it a Community agency. It has no formal investigative powers. It derived its authority solely from the agreement of the Parliament and the Commission, and saw itself as a temporary advisory committee operating by consent.

   The Committee began its report by defining its primary terms of reference. Fraud was taken to mean "intentional acts or omissions tending to harm the financial interests of the Communities", and included misappropriation of funds.[12] Mismanagement was said to be a broader concept and encompassed "serious or persistent infringements of the principles of sound administration, and, in particular, to acts or omissions allowing or encouraging fraud or irregularities to occur or persist".[13] It would normally be the result of negligence in the exercise of public management functions. Nepotism was "favouritism shown to relatives or friends, especially in appointments to desirable positions which are not based on merit or justice".[14]

---

[11] The service is bought from the private sector after competition in which only external bidders take part.

[12] Committee of Independent Experts, *First Report on Allegations regarding Fraud, Mismanagement and Nepotism in the European Commission* (15th March 1999), para. 1.4.2.

[13] *Ibid.*, para. 1.4.3.

[14] *Ibid.*, para. 1.4.4.

The Committee emphasised that these categories could well overlap, and emphasised also that they were but examples of a more fundamental idea that public servants should be held to proper standards of behaviour. The higher the office, the more demanding were those standards. The core of minimum standards was that public officials should act in the general interest of the Community, with complete independence. Decisions should be made solely in terms of the public interest on the basis of objective criteria. Such officials should also behave with integrity and discretion, and should be open and accountable in their dealings with the public.[15]

3 CRISIS, IMMEDIATE REACTION AND SOBER REFLECTION

Exigencies of time meant that the Committee could only investigate a limited number of Community policies. It nonetheless produced a 146 page Report by the stipulated date, and this had an immediate, dramatic effect: the Commission resigned *en bloc*.

The resulting crisis was the dominant headline in newspapers across Europe, being the focus of attention in quality papers and the tabloid press alike. For many Euro-sceptics it was proof of what they had always maintained, empirical vindication of the "rottenness at the heart of Europe". The tabloid press in the U.K., much of which had lost no opportunity in the past to berate the E.C. and its officers, vied to devise ever more cutting headlines. Individual sentences plucked from the Committee's Report lent themselves readily to the media sound-bite age. The concluding paragraph spoke in terms of its "becoming difficult to find anyone who has even the slightest sense of responsibility" within the Commission,[16] and there were earlier references to a mismatch between the objectives assigned to the Commission, and the way in which it had elected to fulfil them.[17]

Whether those who were so ready to dance on the grave of the outgoing Commission had actually read the Report may well be doubted. There is often an inverse correlation between the strength of one's feelings and the depth of one's knowledge. An executive summary is probably as far as most people got. Some may even have read the actual conclusion in the report itself.

It is however only by reading the entire Report that one can really begin to understand precisely what went wrong in the cases investigated by the Committee. And it is only by reading the Report that one is able to form any view about the conclusions reached by the Committee.

---

[15] *Ibid.*, para. 1.5.4.
[16] *Ibid.*, para. 9.4.25.
[17] *Ibid.*, para. 9.4.5.

This is not to deny the existence of matters of real concern which were brought to light by the Committee. Its Report performs an extremely valuable function in bringing together data on the problems encountered in the running of a number of important Community policies. It is moreover no bad thing in the long term for the Commission to have been publicly criticised in this manner, since there were doubtless those in the Commission who were arrogant, personally and "institutionally" to others in the Community.

It is nonetheless important to stand back now that the dust has settled and see what general lessons can be learned from the events which have occurred. It is equally important to place these events within the more general context of decision-making by public bodies. It becomes readily apparent when reading the material in this way that the difficulties encountered were those inherent in contracting-out by a public arm of government. We have already touched on some of these in the previous section: the blurring of the line between policy formation and policy implementation; the difficulty of ensuring proper financial accounting in relation to the activities undertaken by the private contractor; the importance of a proper line of management within the public body; and the fact that the private contractor will normally not be imbued with a public ethos in its decision-making, but will rather have the interests of its shareholders uppermost in its mind.

Lessons from the past must not be forgotten. We should use them in order to build a more effective and efficient pattern of Community decision-making for the future. This is recognised by the Committee of Independent Experts. Its Report contains interesting suggestions for the future. There are also passages which indicate that the problems revealed would not have occurred if decision-making had taken place in-house. The fact that contracting-out has generated problems in certain instances does not however mean that it should be rejected as a method for delivering Community public services. There is, in many instances, no viable alternative to contracting-out for the effective discharge of many Community policies. Where this is so we should concentrate our attention on developing techniques to ensure that contracting-out functions as an effective and efficient mechanism for the provision of Community public services. Relevant reforms will be considered below. Before considering such matters it is necessary to have a detailed look at the Community policies analysed in the Committee's Report.

4 THE COMMITTEE OF INDEPENDENT EXPERTS' DETAILED CRITIQUE

a. Tourism

The first case discussed in detail by the Committee of Experts was in many respects the worst. It concerned fraud and mismanagement in relation to tourism. Resolutions passed by the Council and European Parliament as early as 1983–1984 prompted the Commission to propose to the Council a programme to highlight the economic significance of tourism in the E.C., and to integrate tourism more closely with other Community policies than hitherto. In due course 1990 was designated as European Year of Tourism by the Council,[18] and this was followed in 1992 by the Council's adoption of a three year action plan to assist tourism.[19] The total sum involved in these projects was 39.3 million ECUs. The implementation of the action plan was entrusted to the Commission. DG XXIII took responsibility and a specific unit was set up within Directorate A to implement the Community tourism policy. There were two main problems with the administration of this policy.

The Head of the Tourism Unit engaged in *unauthorised activities* which gave rise to embezzlement, corruption and favouritism. The Committee of Experts felt that the Commission had been slow in checking whether the accusations levelled against the Head of the Unit were well founded, that the internal inquiries were incomplete, and that the penalty imposed was too lenient.[20]

There were *problems with the use of external consultants to whom work had been contracted-out*. The action plan for tourism entailed calls for tenders for specific projects, and also the payment of subsidies. In 1988 the Commission decided to use an outside consultant which would provide it with expert staff, premises and the requisite infrastructure to enable it to undertake some of these tasks more effectively. A firm called Euroconseil was chosen. The Committee of Experts criticised the fact that there was no adequate supervision of the consultants with the result that "those consultants performed managerial duties incumbent on officials and played an important role in the selection and monitoring of projects",[21] and there were unjustifed payments made to the firm. There were also conflicts of interest because Euroconseil on occasion proposed assistance, in return for payment, to an applicant for a Community subsidy when it was responsible for registering such applications and recommending projects to the Commission.[22]

Underlying these specific concerns was a more general problem which, as we shall see, was a factor in all of the programmes studied by the Committee of Experts: insufficient staff within the Commission. The tourism project was managed by eleven people subject to Staff Regulations, and an external consultancy. Most of the staff members were on one year contracts, renewable twice, unless they were appointed to a temporary post. The shortage of human

---

[18] Council Decision 89/46/EEC.
[19] Council Decision 92/421/EEC.
[20] *Supra*, n. 12, paras 2.8.1–2.8.3.
[21] *Ibid.*, para. 2.5.6.
[22] *Ibid.*, para. 2.5.11.

resources undoubtedly contributed to management weaknesses and administrative failures.[23] The Committee of Experts was critical of the College of
Commissioners for proposing the tourism initiative without having the
resources to do the job, more especially since the action plan involved the
management of a large number of undertakings.[24]

b. The M.E.D. programmes and co-operation with Southern Mediterranean Countries

The M.E.D. programmes for decentralised co-operation with non-member
countries of the southern Mediterranean began in 1992 after the Gulf war with
Iraq. The aim was to strengthen political and economic co-operation with these
countries in order to counterbalance the aid given to countries in Central and
Eastern Europe. There were five such programmes depending on which type of
partner institution was involved: M.E.D.-Urbs (regional authorities); M.E.D.-
Campus (universities); M.E.D.-Invest (enterprises); M.E.D.-Avicenne
(research centres); and M.E.D.-Media (media professionals). A central theme
of the programmes was that governmental structures should be avoided and that
funds should be channelled to non-governmental organisations, with the object
of being close to civil society. The total budget for 1992–1996 was 116.6
million ECUs.

The management structure for this programme was organised at four levels:
DGIB had authority within the Commission; A.R.T.M. (Agency for Trans-
Mediterranean Networks), had responsibility for the administration and
financial management of the five programmes; T.A.O.s (Technical Assistance
Offices), of which there was one for each programme, had responsibility for
technical supervision; and specific projects, of which there were 496 in total.

The principal criticism of the M.E.D. programmes was that the Commission
had illegally delegated its powers to a third party, A.R.T.M., rather than merely
sign a service contract. The terms of the contract entrusted A.R.T.M. with the
implementation of the financing of the programme and gave it broad powers to
manage the programme as a whole. The Commission's Legal Service, which
was consulted as to the legality of the draft contract between the Commission
and A.R.T.M., was unwilling to go on record and state that the contract was
legal. It did indeed express the orthodox view that discretionary powers must be
exercised by officials. The Legal Service of the Court of Auditors was even
more forthright in its opinion that the delegation by the Commission of its
management powers in respect of the M.E.D. programmes to A.R.T.M. was in
breach of the enabling regulation governing these programmes, and also more
generally that it violated Community law concerning the delegation of powers.

[23] *Ibid.*, para. 2.7.7.
[24] *Ibid.*, para. 2.9.1.

A Special Report of the Court of Auditors concluded that the Commission had in reality delegated its powers to a third party rather than merely concluded a service contract.

The Court of Auditors and the Committee of Experts were also critical of the fact that *the initial contract between A.R.T.M. and the Commission was by way of private treaty, without any competitive tendering*, as were the early contracts concluded between the Commission and T.A.O.s.

A further concern related to *conflicts of interest* between the Commission and A.R.T.M. and A.R.T.M. and T.A.O.s. Two of A.R.T.M.'s founding companies (F.E.R.E. and I.S.M.E.R.I.) were simultaneously acting as T.A.O.s for the M.E.D. programmes. Moreover, there were, in the early stages, two members of A.R.T.M.'s board who belonged to these T.A.O.s which gave rise to a "manifest conflict of interest".[25] F.E.R.E. and I.S.M.E.R.I. secured more than 60 per cent of the available technical assistance appropriations for the M.E.D. programmes, which meant that, because of their membership of the board of A.R.T.M., they "were able to participate in the process of negotiating contracts concluded with themselves".[26] Furthermore, it appears that Commission officials were present at A.R.T.M. when the choice of F.E.R.E. and I.S.M.E.R.I. was approved.

The Committee of Experts concluded that the Commissioner in charge when the M.E.D. programmes were established did bear some responsibility for not giving Commission officials clear instructions and an appropriate framework for the operation of this new Community policy. The Committee's Report acknowledged that the Commission did not have sufficient manpower to undertake the task in-house,[27] but felt that this did not excuse delegation to the private sector without a sufficient control structure. Nor did it serve to excuse the failure to comply with tendering rules and the conflicts of interest which occurred as a result of the nature of the relationship between the Commission and A.R.T.M. and between A.R.T.M. and the T.A.O.s.[28]

c. E.C.H.O. and humanitarian assistance

E.C.H.O., the European Community Humanitarian Assistance Office, was set up on 1st March 1992 to give the E.C. a more effective means for providing aid in emergency relief situations. Experience had taught the Commission that "its usual administrative mechanisms were too slow to provide assistance with the necessary speed, and, incidentally perhaps, they failed to give the Community contribution to disaster relief a visible dimension commensurate with its scale".[29] During its first six years it disbursed some 3,500 million ECUs in aid. It

[25] *Ibid.*, para. 3.5.6.
[26] *Ibid.*, para. 3.5.9.
[27] *Ibid.*, paras 3.4.1–3.4.3.
[28] *Ibid.*, paras 3.8.1–3.8.4.
[29] *Ibid.*, para. 4.1.1.

did so largely through partner organisations such as non-governmental organisations (N.G.O.s). E.C.H.O. itself was established as a new Directorate. The demands upon it grew exponentially in the years immediately following its establishment, but there was no corresponding increase in the staff available to it. Nor were there well recognised financial or organisational procedures in place to regulate its activities.[30]

The investigation of E.C.H.O. centred on four contracts awarded in 1993–1994 for the provision of humanitarian aid in the former Yugoslavia and in the Great Lakes region of Africa. The Committee of Experts focused on a number of issues arising from these contracts.

The first concerned *staffing and the irregular use of budgetary appropriations*. The contracts referred to in the previous paragraph were awarded to three companies, two of which were in fact controlled by the third. These contracts were fictitious in the sense that none of the activities to be financed thereunder existed in reality. The money was in fact used to finance a group of eleven staff working as a unit within the E.C.H.O. office in Brussels. These staff were legally employed by the contractors, but were often proposed to them by E.C.H.O. itself. Appropriations intended to be used for operations were therefore used to finance staffing and this constituted irregular expenditure. Many of those within E.C.H.O. regarded this as a mere administrative irregularity, in the sense that the money was being used to cover a shortfall in staffing, and that without such additional staff E.C.H.O. could not perform the tasks assigned to it. The Committee of Experts took a different view. It concluded that, if the "system" itself was inadequate, then it invited irregularity. Where, as in the case of E.C.H.O., this involved outright fabrication, then it led to a risk of fraud which was too high.[31] Such a method of making up for staff shortages was also felt to be open to possible favouritism.[32]

The Committee of Experts was critical of the *lateness of the Commission's response to the problems in E.C.H.O.* The first of the fictitious contracts began in August 1993. Commission intervention only took place four years later when a whistleblower intervened. For the Committee this meant that regular management and control mechanisms had failed for too long to identify any anomaly in the contracts which were not being used for their ostensible purpose.[33]

It was moreover clear that the *Commissioners themselves were aware of the nature of the problem*. The Commissioners responsible for E.C.H.O., Marin until 1994 and then Bonino, were aware of the difficult staffing situation in E.C.H.O., and of the existence of "submarine" staff within E.C.H.O. who were

---

[30] *Ibid.*, para. 4.2.2.
[31] *Ibid.*, para. 4.2.5.
[32] *Ibid.*, paras 4.2.33–4.2.38.
[33] *Ibid.*, para. 4.2.10.

financed from operating appropriations.[34] Repeated requests were made for more official staff. Commissioner Marin did give explicit instructions in February 1994 that the use of submarine staff should cease, but the Committee felt that he did not pursue the matter as he should have done.[35]

The *flow of information from the Commission to the Parliament was also criticised by the Committee*. The provision of such information was said not to have been spontaneous, but to have been driven by pressures, such as the leakage to the press of a U.C.L.A.F. report, and the persistence of the rapporteur for the Parliament's Committee on Budgetary Control.[36]

d. Leonardo and vocational training

In 1995 the Commission launched the Leonardo da Vinci programme. It had originally been formulated by DG XXII, which was responsible for matters concerning education, training and youth. The programme was authorised by a Council Decision.[37] The objective was the implementation of a vocational training policy in support of intitiatives conducted by the individual member states. The programme was to last for a maximum period of five years, from 1995–1999, and it had an appropriation of approximately ECU 620 million. The report of the Committee of Independent Experts began its analysis of this programme on the following assumption:[38]

> "Normally, such a programme would have been implemented by the Commission's services themselves. However, because of a lack of staff within DG XXII, and since it appeared impossible to redeploy the necessary staff from other services in the Commission, it was decided to outsource the implementation of the project to a 'technical assistance office' following a public call for tender."

An open tender process was held at the end of 1994 and a firm called Agenor S.A. was awarded the five-year service contract, which was renewable annually. Agenor therefore constituted the technical assistance office (T.A.O.) for the Leonardo programme. Its main function was to manage several thousand project proposals per year and involved "complex processing procedures through a chain of operations leading to the selection of some 750 projects per year by the Commission".[39] Agenor itself was a French company which had shareholders from different member states, but the controlling shareholding

---

[34] The Committee did however find that no Member of the Commission knew of the existence of the fictitious contracts until after the U.C.L.A.F. inquiry had been initiated: *ibid.*, para. 4.2.20.

[35] *Ibid.*, para. 4.2.18.

[36] *Ibid.*, para. 4.2.27.

[37] 94/819/EC.

[38] *Supra*, n. 12, para. 5.2.2.

[39] *Ibid.*, para. 5.2.3.

was held by the French group C.E.S.I. (Centre d'Etudes Superieures Indus-
trielles). C.E.S.I. itself was a non-profit making association whose aim was to
provide permanent training courses for senior management. Its own management board consisted of representatives from employers' organisations and
four major French firms.

The Committee's report focused on three deficiencies in the way in which
this programme was run.

The initial criticism related to the *performance by Agenor of its role as T.A.O.
in the Leonardo programme*. Two audits were conducted of Agenor, one by DG
XXII itself, another by DG XX in conjunction with U.C.L.A.F. They revealed a
number of matters of serious concern. Agenor was in receipt of detailed
information about the requirements of the future Leonardo programme prior to
publication of the tender. The company had committed a number of breaches of
its contract conditions. It was not in compliance with national tax laws, nor with
those relating to social security. There was a poor system of internal control,
combined with a highly centralised management style operated by the director
of the company. There was some evidence that funds had been misappropriated,
and evidence also of favouritism, as exemplified by the appointment of the
Director's wife to a senior management position.

The second criticism voiced by the Committee of Independent Experts
related to *the way in which the matter was dealt with by the Commission*. It is
clear that the primary wrongdoing was that of Agenor, the T.A.O. It is also clear
that the Commission itself had responsibility to oversee the discharge of the
Leonardo programme by Agenor. The Committee takes the Commission to task
for not properly discharging this responsibility. It questions whether it can be
"considered credible or probable that the overwhelming number of deficiencies
that have become apparent, and which had been predicted, ... could occur and
continue over several years without ... having become known, through
informal channels at the Commission ... at the highest level of DG XXII".[40]
Agenor's contract was finally terminated on 31st January 1999. The Committee
was equally critical of the response from DG XXII to the provisional final audit
report from DG XX which was submitted to it for observation and comment on
6th November 1998.[41]

> "Even if it has to be conceded that the TAO contract itself provided a high level of
> freedom of action for the Leonardo/Agenor TAO, DG XXII certainly allowed an
> extension of the scale of independence through tacit acceptance and/or indifference.
> In this Committee's opinion, the remarks of the Director-General of DG XXII,
> although concealing the real problems, did nevertheless disclose findings that should
> have alerted the Commissioner who, in turn, should have informed the Commission.
>   Responsibility for the facts assessed above, lies certainly with the Commissioner

---

[40] *Ibid.*, para. 5.4.9.
[41] *Ibid.*, paras 5.4.11–5.4.12.

concerned,[42] either because of non-intervention in a situation known to be highly unsatisfactory, or because of a failure to make inquiries about the true situation in a file which, from the outset ... should have been followed up with special care."

The final criticism made by the Committee was that the *European Parliament was kept in the dark about the problems with the Leonardo programme*. This was of particular importance given that in the summer of 1998 the Parliament was working on its report for a proposed Leonardo II programme which would follow on from the Leonardo I programme currently under discussion. It was clear that information regarding the implemenation of Leonardo I would have been of central importance when deciding on the possibility of a follow-up programme. Inquiries were made by the M.E.P. responsible for the E.P.'s report concerning rumours about problems with Leonardo I. The Commission's response came from President Santer. The Committee of Experts characterised this response as formally correct, but in substance misleading. A second letter from the same M.E.P. was left unanswered.[43]

e. Nuclear safety

The Commission has had some responsibility in relation to nuclear safety since 1975. The Chernobyl accident in 1986 revealed the dangers of nuclear plants in the Soviet Union which did not conform to state of the art safety requirements. The E.C. therefore decided to allocate in the order of 845 million ECUs for nuclear safety programmes. The money was to be used to support domestic safety upgrading programmes and the Community aid constituted approximately 1 per cent of the expenditure required on 65 nuclear stations. The Community resources were delivered under the T.A.C.I.S. and P.H.A.R.E. programmes, which were concerned respectively with aid for economic transition in Russia and other New Independent States, and with aid to countries in Central and Eastern Europe. DG IA within the Commission managed the programme. The Committee of Experts drew heavily on a Report of the Court of Auditors[44] which had been critical of the way in which Community resources had been delivered.

The Court of Auditors' Report expressed concern at the *excessive delegation and transfer of responsibilities to third parties*. The Committee of Experts put the matter in the following way.[45]

"The DG IA unit in charge of the programmes did not have the necessary manpower at its disposal, in terms of numbers and expertise, to draw up the nuclear safety

---

[42] This was Edith Cresson.
[43] *Supra*, n. 12, paras 5.6.8–5.6.10.
[44] Special Report No. 25/98, O.J. [1999] C35/1.
[45] *Supra*, n. 12, para. 7.4.1.

programmes, follow them up and monitor implementation. For this reason, the Commission delegated some of its responsibilities to the Twining Programme Engineering Group (T.P.E.G.) and to supply agencies to such an extent that the Court of Auditors termed these delegations excessive and likely to jeopardise the institution's independence."

It is however clear from reading the Committee of Experts' Report that it did not share all of the criticisms voiced by the Court of Auditors.[46] T.P.E.G. was a consortium of E.C. electricity generators who were responsible for pressurised-water reactors. While the Court of Auditors felt that the Commission had delegated too many of its planning responsibilities to T.P.E.G., the Committee of Experts was more neutral in this respect. It recognised the input of DG IA into planning, and acknowledged the value of the expert assistance provided by all the major electricity generators in the E.C. Nor did the Committee of Experts agree with the view taken by the Court of Auditors about the use of supply agencies. Such bodies were used for the implementation of complex, large-scale projects. They verified the neutrality of technical specifications, organised invitations to tender, verified technical reports, drew up contracts with the supplier appointed by the Commission, and ensured payment of invoices in line with the contract. The Court of Auditors had criticised the use of such agencies on the ground that they complicated programme implementation, contributed to delays and allowed excessive advances to be paid. The Committee of Experts took a different view. It felt that the use of such agencies was both inevitable and beneficial. It was inevitable because the Commission was not in a position to undertake detailed project management itself, since it did not have the necessary expertise. It was beneficial because the alternative to using agencies would have been to entrust the tasks to the electricity generators who were responsible for on-site assistance and this would have given too many powers to such firms. Supply agencies were therefore used by DG IA to assist it in administering the supply contracts.

The Committee of Experts while cognisant of the internal staffing problems within the Commission, was nonetheless concerned about the fact that there was little attempt to preserve through archives the expertise of national experts who were on short fixed-term contracts with the Commission. They also expressed doubts as to whether the efforts to co-ordinate the various directorates within the Commission which had an interest in nuclear safety would be successful.[47]

The other main concern mentioned in the Court of Auditors' Report was as to *the method by which contracts had been awarded*. The Commission had awarded many of the service contracts through private treaty, rather than competitive tendering. DG IA justified recourse to this procedure because of the

[46] *Ibid.*, paras 7.4.9, 7.7.2.
[47] *Ibid.*, paras 7.7.2–7.7.4.

exceptional nature of the activity in question, and because the Commission wished to use the E.C.'s power station operators for contracts concerning a large number of nuclear sites. The Commission also maintained that the Community purse had been protected, since it had not been shown that the costs charged pursuant to these contracts was too high. In those cases where competitive tendering had been used, there were question marks as to the Commission's ability to carry out the necessary cost analyses and its capacity to make provision in the contracts for the legal means for cost control.

The Committee of Experts concluded that there were no grounds for saying that the implementation of the nuclear safety programme gave rise to fraud or serious irregularities.

f. The Security Office

The Commission's Security Service provides for the internal and external security of the Commission's premises and of the staff working therein. It also provides security cover for Commission staff when they are on missions. The work was contracted-out to security companies and in the period between 1992–1997 the contract had a value of 79,500 million ECUs. The contract was awarded to I.M.S. Group 4/Securitas for the period between 1992 and 1997.

It became clear that there were a number of problems with the way in which security cover was provided. A newspaper report was the catalyst for an investigation by DG XX and U.C.L.A.F. The reports from these bodies revealed that there was evidence to suggest that Group 4's tender application had been manipulated after the submission of tenders and prior to the formal opening of the tender procedure in order to give it an advantage in the selection process; that the contract had been modified in favour of Group 4 through the inclusion of an annex and this was a serious violation of internal rules; that the Security Office had recruited a number of "ghost" employees paid for under the contract in a way which bypassed normal procedures; and that there were problems with individual senior personnel within the Security Office.

The Committee of Experts acknowledged that such internal Commission inquiries occurred quickly once the press allegations had appeared. It nonetheless felt that the inquiries did not go far enough and that the results of the audits should have been followed up sooner. The Commissioner responsible for the Security Office was President Santer. The Committee concluded that neither he nor his office took any meaningful interest in the functioning of the Security Office, and that this allowed a "state within a state"[48] to develop.

---

[48] *Ibid.*, para. 6.5.7.

g. Allegations of favouritism

The final substantive inquiry undertaken by the Committee was into allegations of favouritism against individual Commissioners. Many of these allegations were said by the Committee to be unfounded. The most serious allegation which the Committee upheld was against Commissioner Cresson, who appointed a close friend to a job for which he was not qualified, where the work performed by that person was deficient in terms of both quantity and quality.

5 THE COMMITTEE OF INDEPENDENT EXPERTS' CONCLUSIONS

The final section of the Report contains the Committee's conclusions from the detailed studies which it had undertaken. Three general points stand out in this respect.

The first is that, in the Committee's view, the Commissioners did not have sufficient control over their section of the administration. There were no cases found in which Commissioners were directly or personally involved in fraudulent activities, but protestations by the Commissioners that they were unaware of the problems later brought to light were "tantamount to an admission of a loss of control by the political authorities over the Administration that they are supposedly running".[49] There were moreover some instances found where the Commissioners or the Commission as a whole bore some responsibility for instances of fraud, irregularities or mismanagement in their services.[50]

The second point which is of note in the Committee's conclusions concerns the issue of staffing. We have already seen that one of the common themes in the programmes studied was the need to contract-out because of inadequacies in the staffing levels within the Commission. The Committee was not on the whole sympathetic with this rationale for the manner of carrying out Community policies.

It was of the view that the Commission should never have taken on policies when it lacked the proper resources to do so. Thus, speaking of the M.E.D. programmes, the Committee states that the "Commission as a whole deserves serious criticism (as in other cases under review) for launching a new, politically important and highly expensive programme without having the resources—especially staff—to do so".[51] Similar sentiments are expressed about the E.C.H.O. policy, where the Committee stated that the "Commission as a whole must be held accountable for the fact that a major policy initiative

---

[49] *Ibid.*, para. 9.2.2.
[50] *Ibid.*, para. 9.2.3.
[51] *Ibid.*, para. 9.2.5.

was launched without the service concerned, E.C.H.O., being given the means to implement the policy".[52] Speaking of the Leonardo programme, the Committee concluded by saying that "the Commission as a whole is again open to criticism for the under-resourcing phenomenon which is at the root of the need to delegate public sector responsibilities to outside consultants".[53]

The Committee also felt that the Commission should have made better use of the staff which it did possess. Thus, the Committee speaks of a failure by the Commission to set priorities, and the fact the Commissioners had a collective responsibility to adopt a joint stance on the human resources problem which had been noted by individual Commissioners.[54] The report notes the difficulties of redeploying existing staff from one DG to another, referring to the compart-mentalisation of the directorates-general and the "existence of as many fiefdoms as there are Commissioners".[55]

The third point which emerges from the Committee's conclusions is that the control and audit procedures within the Commission were not able to rectify the problems in good time. The Court of Auditors did produce reports on many of the cases studied, but these were only considered in depth by one arm of the budgetary authority, the European Parliament. Within the Commission itself control in terms of prior approval had not proved to be very effective, as exemplified by the fact that many of the irregularities brought to light had been approved by Financial Control. Internal audits were in reality conducted by a small unit within DG XX, and U.C.L.A.F., even though the latter was primarily responsible for fighting fraud. Both bodies worked hard, but the line which demarcated their respective responsibilities was not clear, and the Committee found that there seemed to be some competition between the two.[56]

6 THE DELIVERY OF PUBLIC SERVICES WITHIN THE E.C.: SOME REFLECTIONS

The Report by the Committee of Independent Experts is, as stated earlier, to be welcomed for bringing together and evaluating data on a number of programmes administered by the Commission. The Committee's conclusions should be taken seriously. There are however two issues on which there is something more to be said both about responsibility for what occurred in the past, and the lessons which can be learned for the future.

---

[52] *Ibid.*, para. 9.2.6.
[53] *Ibid.*, para. 9.2.7.
[54] *Ibid.*, paras 9.4.3–9.4.4.
[55] *Ibid.*, para. 9.4.6.
[56] *Ibid.*, para. 9.4.18.

a. The ascription of responsibility for taking on policies where there were staff shortages

We have already seen that shortage of staff in-house was one of the major reasons why the Commission contracted-out work connected with these programmes. We have seen also that the Committee was for the most part unsympathetic to the Commission in this respect for three reasons: the Commission should never have proposed and undertaken these programmes without the requisite staff; it should have calculated the aggregate calls on its resources and prioritised between such demands; and the Commission should have asked for budget increases to cover the extra staffing required. All three parts of this critique can be questioned.

The conception of policy formation in the E.C. which underlies the *first part of this critique* is overly simplistic. The picture of Community decision-making captured in the aphorism "the Commission proposes, the Council disposes" may well have characterised policy-making in the early years of the Community. It no longer captures the more complex reality whereby Community legislation is made now. The European Parliament has, since the Single European Act, had a real input into the content and timing of such legislation. Its power has been further expanded by the Treaty of European Union and the Treaty of Amsterdam. Nor is it meaningful to regard the Council as a mere passive receptor, awaiting legislative proposals which emanate from the Commission. Approximately 40 per cent of the proposals which come from the Commission originate in detailed suggestions made by the Council pursuant to Article 208 E.C. Even where the proposal does originate from within the Commission it will be thoroughly reviewed and digested by the Committee of Permanent Representatives (C.O.R.E.P.E.R.), which is the support mechanism for the Council.

The quotations mentioned in the previous section all lay the blame for proposing and undertaking policies with inadequate resources on the Commission. It is however clear that if blame is to be ascribed in this respect it should not be so readily laid solely at the door of the Commission. The programmes under examination did not emerge simply as a result of a Commission initiative. There were often resolutions and the like passed by the Council and European Parliament which were then developed by the Commission. This is in fact recognised at certain points in the Committee's Report, albeit not developed in any real detail. Thus, the Committee states that the "European Parliament and the Council have imposed on the Commission more and more tasks, while at the same time applying rigorous budgetary restrictions".[57] Later in its Report the Committee talks of the problems encountered in the programmes studied being based on a "mismatch between the objectives assigned to the Commission, in the context of the new policy laid

---

[57] *Ibid.*, para. 5.8.2.

down by the Council and the Parliament, on a proposal from the Commission, and the resources which the Commission has been able, or has chosen, to employ in the service of that new policy".[58]

To the extent that the Council and Parliament played a real part in the intitiation or modification of the proposals which led to these programmes, let alone the fact that they formally voted that the programmes should go ahead, they cannot evade all responsibility for ensuring that the resources were there to do the job. Legislative power within the E.C. is shared between the Council, European Parliament and Commission. So too should legislative responsibility. The Commission did of course bear a share of the blame for undertaking policies where it was ill-equipped to do so. The Council and European Parliament cannot however be considered blameless in this respect.

The *second part* of the Committee's critique was, as we have seen, that the Commission should have better calculated the overall demands on its resources and that the College of Commissioners should have drawn up a list of priorities. There is force in this point. There should and could have been more macro-level planning by the Commission. The difficulties of undertaking such exercises should not however be forgotten. This is particularly so in the context of a decision-making structure such as the E.C., where legislative power is shared between a number of important players. A consequence of this is that it might be difficult for the Commission to determine precisely when, or indeed whether, a new programme would come "on line". Proposals for a programme might well be included in the legislative agenda for a particular year, but whether they are actually enacted as legislation by the Council and Parliament might be affected by a whole range of factors which cannot easily be foreseen ahead of time. Accurate macro-level planning is obviously all the more difficult in such circumstances.

The *final element* of the Committee's critique concerning resourcing is that the Commission should have pressed for budget increases. The Committee's response to the use of contracting-out, auxiliary staff and the like because of the shortage of staff was that "the Commission can put forward whatever proposals it sees fit with regard to its Establishment Plan when it submits its preliminary draft budget to the budgetary authority".[59] It was for that reason that the Committee felt that the "excuses referring to the shortage of human resources were at odds with the decisions taken by the Commission itself to continue the policy of austerity budgets since 1995".[60] How much leeway the Commission really had to propose such budget increases may be doubted. The framing and passage of the budget is a complex process in which the Commission, Council and European Parliament all possess formal legal powers. These powers shape,

---

[58] *Ibid.*, para. 9.4.5.
[59] *Ibid.*, para. 9.4.2.
[60] *Ibid.*, para. 9.4.2.

but do not determine, the actual budget which is approved for any one year, since this will be dependent upon broader political and economic factors. The Committee itself recognised that the Council and Parliament were imposing on the Commission an increasing range of tasks, while at the same time maintaining rigorous budget restrictions.[61] In these circumstances the Commission would almost certainly have had to make a political calculation as to whether it was realistic to press for budget increases relating to staff. Any political institution will have to decide whether it is worth using up scarce "political capital" in furtherance of objectives which are unlikely to be fulfilled. The Commission is no exception in this respect. It could of course be argued that if the Commission did feel thus constrained it could simply have declined to take on new programmes. Yet this too oversimplifies the way in which political institutions operate. The Commission would have been loath to refuse to take on important new initiatives pressed by the Council and Parliament, since this would have looked like failure on its part whatever the reality was. It would have been difficult to do so, more especially when they took the form of the E.C.H.O. programme. The Commission could moreover have felt that it could cope by using contracting-out to cover the short fall in staffing. It is to the broader issues concerning contracting-out that we should now turn.

b. Contracting-out, lessons from the past and prospects for the future

The Committee's Report provides *valuable lessons* about contracting-out in the E.C. Many of the policies implemented in the past had been executed with the help of national bureaucracies. The programmes analysed in the Committee's Report were of a different nature. They were either designed consciously to by-pass national bureaucracies, as in the case of the M.E.D. programmes, or they entailed the direct evaluation of large numbers of project bids, as in the case of the Tourism and Leonardo initiatives, or the very nature of the programme necessitated working with a range of non-governmental organisations, as in the case of the E.C.H.O. The nature of these programmes therefore required more in the way of direct implementation of policy than had been the case hitherto. In the absence of sufficient staff in-house, it became necessary to contract-out much of the work.

The Reports of the Court of Auditors, and that of the Committee of Experts, show the need for proper supervision if contracting-out is to be acceptable. Indeed the costs of such supervision need to be borne in mind when undertaking the economic calculus about the pros and cons of this strategy. The

---

[61] *Ibid.*, para. 5.8.2.

Committee's more general words about contracting-out in the context of the Leonardo programme could be extended to all of the cases studied:[62]

> "The implementation of Community programmes by private contractors can only be accepted on the basis of a guarantee that the essence of the public function is not abandoned into the hands of the private contractor. Moreover, those private contractors must be subject to contractual provisions imposing strict obligations in the general interest, and the public authorities must effectively supervise this action. It is clear that such supervision has not been exercised with sufficient care in the present case *vis-à-vis* the Leonardo/Agenor T.A.O. It would seem that excessive confidence has been placed in the T.A.O. and thus excess reliance on outside consultants".

This quotation provides a suitable point for turning our attention from the past to consider the *prospects for the future*. Notwithstanding this extract, the impression created by some of the Committee's Report is that contracting-out was an unfortunate by-product of the internal Commission resourcing problem. If this problem had been properly addressed there would have been less need for recourse to contracting-out. There is no doubt that, if the Commission had possessed more resources in-house, there would have been no need for the subterfuges used to staff E.C.H.O., supervision of all the programmes would have been that much easier, and there would have been less likelihood that public sector policy responsibility would have been transferred to the private sector, as was the case in relation to some of the programmes.

It should nonetheless be recognised that contracting-out must and should remain an option for the delivery of public services by the E.C. in the future. Not only must it remain an option, it will in many instances still be the best option all things considered. The more programmes which are committed to the direct responsibility of the Commission, where implementation is to take place without direct input from national bureaucracies, the more the Commission will need to have recourse to contracting-out. In some cases this will be obvious. The best example from the Report is nuclear safety, where the Committee recognised the necessity to contract-out because of the highly complex, technical nature of the work. However, if one stands back and considers many of the other programmes analysed in the Committee's Report, it becomes readily apparent that some use of contracting-out would be desirable. Programmes such as Tourism and Leonardo involved the collection of data, the establishment of criteria by which to evaluate projects and the actual evaluation of particular proposals. Even if the staffing pressures within the Commission were to be alleviated it is by no means clear that it would be desirable, either in terms of efficiency or effectiveness, for this work to be done in-house. The staff would not have any expertise in the relevant areas. It would be desirable to have Commission staff who had the relevant expertise to be able to assess the quality

---

[62] *Ibid.*, para. 5.8.3.

of the work undertaken by the company to which the task had been contracted-out. Short-term appointments within the Commission are already made, and the more flexibility in this respect the better. Contracting-out in such areas, subject to effective oversight by the Commission, will therefore often be the optimal method of delivering Community programmes. The fact that problems have been revealed in certain areas should not lead to rejection of the very idea of contracting-out.

7 CONCLUSION: THE PRODI COMMISSION AND INSTITUTIONAL REFORM

Romano Prodi is the new President of the Commission, following the resignation of Jaques Santer and his team. Prodi has lost no time in introducing reforms designed to restore faith in the Commission. There is a paper on the *Formation of the New Commission.*[63] It has a new Code of Conduct for Commissioners which contains strict rules about the declaration of interests, and which outside activities Commissioners are allowed to pursue. The same paper also has detailed rules about the formation and role of the Commissioners' private offices. This is reflective of the fact that there has been concern in the past over the influence which they have wielded. A separate paper entitled the *Operation of the Commission*[64] deals with a number of matters. The Rules of Procedure have been revised. New working groups of Commissioners have been established to ensure the better preparation and co-ordination of the Commission's activities.[65] Increased emphasis has been placed on closer Internal Co-ordination within the Commission.[66] This is of particular importance. The broad range of activities for which the Commission is responsible, combined with increased decentralisation as exemplified by the fact that Commissioners will now be housed within their departments, has furthered the need for closer internal co-ordination to ensure the consistency and effectiveness of the Commission's actions. The setting of priorities, and the relationship between Commission activities and the resources necessary to fulfil them, are accorded particular prominence.[67] In his first major address to the European Parliament Romano Prodi emphasised these new initiatives.[68] He

[63] 12th July 1999.
[64] 12th July 1999.
[65] Such groups have been established to deal with the following areas: Growth, Competitiveness and Employment; Equal Opportunities; Reform; Interinstitutional Relations; and External Relations.
[66] *The Operation of the Commission* (12th July 1999) 18–22.
[67] *Ibid.*, 18, 20.
[68] *Speech by Romano Prodi, President-designate of the European Commission, to the European Parliament*, 21st July 1999.

also made it clear that, although it is not formally dealt with in the Treaty, he would not hesitate to ask for the resignation of an individual Commissioner should this prove to be necessary. All of his new team had accepted their portfolios on this understanding.

The Prodi reforms will clearly be of significance in restoring the Commission's public credibility, and in ensuring that the institution as a whole works more effectively in the future. It should also be recognised that the reforms do not, in and of themselves, address the particular problems which were revealed in the Committee of Independent Experts' Report. It may well be that the general reforms, such as those concerned with internal co-ordination and staff mobility, will have an effect in this respect. It may also be the case that the Prodi Commission will consider more specific such proposals in due course. Some such initiatives will be needed to ensure that contracting-out can continue to play a role in the delivery of Community services, without the problems revealed by the Committee's Report.[69]

---

[69] The Second Report of the Committee of Independent Experts, September 1999, came too late for inclusion within this essay.

Chapter 17

The Contracts (Rights of Third Parties) Act 1999 and the Law of Carriage of Goods by Sea

Sir Guenter Treitel

1 INTRODUCTION

The object of this paper is to discuss the impact of the Contracts (Rights of Third Parties) Act 1999 on a number of well-known problems relating to international carriage of goods. A full discussion of the Act will be found elsewhere;[1] but to set the scene for the present discussion a number of its salient principles must be set out here.

(a) The Act amends but does not abolish the common law doctrine of privity of contract. In the words of the Law Commission's Report on which the Act is based, the effect of the Act will be to create "a general and wide-ranging exception to the third party rule but it [will leave] that rule intact for cases not covered by the statute".[2]

(b) The principal provision of the Act is contained in section 1 by which a third party (C) will be entitled to enforce a term in a contract between the promisor (A) and the promisee (B) if the contract either "expressly provides that he may"[3] *or* "the term purports to confer a benefit on him"[4] unless (in the latter case) "it appears on a proper construction of the contract that the parties [i.e. A and B] did not intend the term to be enforceable by"[5] [C]. It is also necessary for C to be "expressly identified in the contract by name or as a member of a class or as answering a particular description"[6] and C will not have a right to enforce a

---

[1] Treitel, *The Law of Contract*, 10th edn. (1999) (hereafter "Treitel") 600–614. That discussion was written while the Bill which became the Act was nearing completion of its passage through Parliament.

[2] *Privity of Contract: Contracts for the Benefit of Third Parties*: Law Com. No. 242 (1996) (hereafter "Report") § 5.16; and see *ibid.*, § 13.2.

[3] Section 1(1)(a).

[4] Section 1(1)(b).

[5] Section 1(2).

[6] Section 1(3).

term "otherwise than subject to and in accordance with any other relevant term of the contract".[7] Where a contract term excludes or limits liability, references in the Act to C's "enforcing" the term are to be construed as references to his availing himself of the exclusion or limitation.[8]

(c) The common law doctrine of privity is generally thought to have two limbs or branches: that C cannot take the *benefit* of a term of a contract between A and B; and that C cannot be *bound* by a term in such a contract. The exception created by the Act will be to the first branch of the doctrine: it will not directly affect the second branch. In the context of the present discussion, C will be adversely affected by a term of a contract between A and B only where the right which C seeks to enforce against A is what may be called a derivative right, that is (for present purposes) a right under the contract between A and B. Suppose, for example, that A contracts with B to render services to C, and C seeks, in reliance on the Act, to enforce A's promise. In such an action, a term excluding or restricting A's liability for breach of the contract between A and B can be relied on by A against C.[9]

(d) Where C has a right under section 1 to enforce a term of a contract between A and B, then the right of A and B to rescind or vary the contract by agreement without the consent of C is limited but not altogether removed. The general principle, laid down in section 2, is that A and B lose the right to rescind or vary the contract by agreement if C has communicated his assent to the term to A, or if A knows that C has relied on the term, or if A can reasonably foresee that C would rely on the term and C has in fact relied on it;[10] but these conditions may be modified by the terms of the contract[11] and it is also open to the court to dispense with C's consent in specified conditions: e.g. where C's consent cannot be obtained because his whereabouts cannot reasonably be ascertained.[12]

(e) Section 3 of the Act contains an elaborate set of provisions designed to deal with the situation in which A seeks, in an action by C to enforce a term of the contract, to rely by way of defence or set-off on matters which would have been available to A if proceedings for the enforcement of the contract had been brought by B. The general principle is that A can so rely on such a matter against C if it "arises from or in connection with the contract [between A and B] and is relevant to the term".[13] Under this provision A could, for example, rely as

---

[7] Section 1(4).

[8] Section 1(6). See further *infra*, § 3.

[9] Section 3(2). The Act will not affect problems such as those which arose in *Lord Strathcona S.S.Co.* v. *Dominion Coal Co.* [1926] A.C.108 or *Port Line Ltd.* v. *Ben Line Steamers Ltd.* [1958] Q.B.146.

[10] Section 2(1).

[11] Section 2(3).

[12] Section 2(4); and see section 2(5).

[13] Section 3(2).

against C on a valid exemption clause or on B's repudiatory breach. The general principle applies also where "enforcement" by C takes the form of reliance[14] on an exemption clause in the contract between A and B: he cannot rely on the clause if it would not have protected him, had he been a party to that contract.[15] The general principle stated above can be modified by contrary agreement between A and B;[16] and provision is also made for A to be able to rely on defences and counterclaims against C which would not have been available to A against B but would have been available to A against C if he had been a party to the contract. [17]

(f) Section 6 of the Act lists a number of exceptions to the general principle of section 1 under which C can acquire the right to enforce against A a term of a contract between A and B. In some of the excepted cases the common law rules as to contracts for the benefit of third parties will continue to apply, so that as a general rule the third party will acquire no rights. This is, for example, the effect of the provision in the Act that "Section 1 confers no right on a third party to enforce (a) any term of a contract of employment against an employee . . ."[18] In another group of excepted cases, C has or can acquire rights under the contract under other rules of law established independently of the Act. This second group of exceptions includes one which is of particular significance for our present purpose: namely that contained in section 6(5) ("the section 6(5) exception"), which refers to certain contracts for the carriage of goods by sea and to certain contracts for the international carriage of goods by rail, road and air. Third parties can acquire rights under such contracts by virtue of other legislation, such as the Carriage of Goods by Sea Act 1992, in conditions there specified; and the carefully regulated schemes of this legislation could be disrupted if third parties (such as consignees of goods) could under the 1999 Act acquire rights to enforce terms of contracts of carriage to which they were not original parties in circumstances other than those specified in such other legislation. The precise relationship between the legislative schemes here referred to and the 1999 Act gives rise to many problems which are by no means easy to resolve; the present discussion of them will be restricted to contracts for or involving the carriage of goods by sea.

(g) The third party is not deprived by the Act of any rights which he may have apart from its provisions. This is the effect of section 7(1), by which "Section 1 does not affect any right or remedy of a third party that exists or is available apart from this Act." Although the reference here is only to "section 1", it follows that many other provisions of the Act will likewise not apply where C's

[14] Under section 1(6) (*supra*, at n. 8).
[15] Section 3(6): e.g. if the clause were invalid, or did not satisfy the requirement of reasonableness, under the Unfair Contract Terms Act 1977.
[16] Section 3(3).
[17] Section 3(4)
[18] Section 6(3).

rights or remedies arise apart from the Act. In particular, section 2 of the Act applies only "where a third party has a right *under section 1* to enforce a term of the contract" and section 3 applies only "where, *in reliance on section 1*, proceedings for the enforcement of a term of a contract are brought by a third party". The rules contained in section 2 as to rescission and variation by agreement between the contracting parties, and those contained in section 3 as to defences and related matters available to the promisor, will therefore not apply where the third party seeks to enforce a right or to rely on a defence available to him apart from the Act. This point is of considerable significance where the third party can assert rights both under the Act and apart from its provisions: in such a case the third party could, by bringing his claim apart from the Act, avoid the restrictions imposed by it on claims made under it.

(h) The common law doctrine of privity does not prevent the promisee from enforcing a contract made for the benefit of a third party; and this position is preserved by section 4 of the Act.[19] For our purpose, a point of particular importance is that the promisee may be able to recover damages in respect of the third party's loss. [20] Obviously, however, the promisor should not in such a case be made liable for the same loss both to the promisee and to the third party; and the Act therefore directs the court in such a case to "reduce any award to the third party to such extent as it thinks appropriate to take account of the sum recovered by the promisee".[21]

2 BUYER, SELLER AND CARRIER

The question to be discussed here is what effects, if any, the 1999 Act will have on the situation in which a contract of carriage is made between a carrier of goods by sea and one of the parties to a contract for the sale of the goods. Can the other party to that contract make a claim against the carrier under the 1999 Act?

a. C.i.f. sales

Where the sale is on c.i.f. terms, the contract of carriage will normally (though not invariably[22]) be made between the seller and the carrier on bill of lading terms; and rights under that contract will (again normally but not invariably) be transferred to the buyer on tender of shipping documents. At this stage, the buyer will become the lawful holder of the bill and rights under the contract of

---

[19] See *infra*, § 6. B could, for example, still claim specific performance in favour of C, as in *Beswick* v. *Beswick* [1968] A.C. 58.

[20] E.g., under the rule in *Dunlop* v. *Lambert* (1839) 6 Cl. & F. 600, discussed *infra*, in § 6.

[21] Section 5.

[22] See *infra*, after n. 30.

carriage will be vested in him by virtue of the Carriage of Goods by Sea Act 1992, section 2(1). Such a case falls squarely within the section 6(5) exception to the operation of the 1999 Act. This provides that "Section 1 confers no rights on a third party in the case of (a) a contract for the carriage of goods by sea . . ."[23] The last eight words refer in the first place to a contract which is "contained in or evidenced by a bill of lading"[24]—an expression which here has "the same meaning as in the Carriage of Goods by Sea Act 1992".[25] The same meaning applies (*mutatis mutandis*) where the contract of carriage is contained in or evidenced in a sea waybill which identifies the buyer as the person to whom delivery is to be made[26] and where the contract of carriage is one under or for the purposes of which a "ship's delivery order" is given: e.g. where the seller, for the purpose of performing his obligations under the contract of sale, procures such an order (as defined by the 1992 Act) identifying the buyer as the person to whom the carrier has undertaken to deliver the goods.[27] In all of these cases, the buyer will get rights of suit against the carrier under the contract of carriage if the requirements laid down in the 1992 Act for the acquisition of such rights are satisfied.[28] If these requirements are not satisfied, he will not get any such rights either under the 1992 Act or under section 1 of the 1999 Act. Equally, the extinction of the seller's rights as an original party to the contract of carriage, or their transfer to the buyer by virtue of section 2(5) of the 1992 Act, is not affected by section 4 of the 1999 Act:[29] the effect of this section is that "section 1" of the Act (i.e. the acquisition of rights by the third party *under that section*) will not affect the promisee's rights of enforcement. This provision therefore does not apply where "section 1" is excluded (by section 6(5)) and the third party has acquired rights under the contract of carriage by virtue of some *other* rules of law (i.e. those contained in the 1992 Act).

The foregoing discussion deals with the situation, usual in a c.i.f. contract, in which it is the seller who is the original party to the contract of carriage. It is also possible (if rare) for the bill of lading which is taken out for the purpose of the performance of such a contract to be issued in the name of the buyer as shipper.[30] If this is done, the buyer will be an original party to the contract of

[23] Section 6(5)(a).

[24] Section 6(6)(a) ("or a corresponding electronic transaction:" see Carriage of Goods by Sea Act 1992, section 1(5)).

[25] 1999 Act, section 6(7)(a). The Carriage of Goods by Sea Act 1992 does not actually *define* "bill of lading".

[26] 1999 Act, sections 6(5), 6(6)(a), 6(7)(a) and Carriage of Goods by Sea Act 1992, sections 1(3), 5(3). For "corresponding electronic transactions", see *supra*, n. 24.

[27] 1999 Act, sections 6(5), 6(6)(b), 6(7)(a) and the Carriage of Goods by Sea Act 1992, sections 1(4), 5(3). For "corresponding electronic transactions, see *supra*, n. 24.

[28] For a full discussion of these requirements, see *Benjamin's Sale of Goods*, 5th edn. (1997) (hereafter "*Benjamin*") § 18–059 *et seq.*

[29] See *supra*, § 1(h).

[30] E.g., *Hansson v. Hamel & Horley* [1922] 2 A.C. 36.

carriage and will not need to invoke any exception to the doctrine of privity for the purpose of asserting rights under that contract. It will be the seller who will be the potential "third party" and normally he will have no interest in enforcing it.[31] But in at least two situations he may acquire such an interest. The first is that in which the buyer has and exercises the right (arising in consequence of the seller's breach) to reject the shipping documents or the goods (and hence the documents) and in consequence of the rejection the seller becomes the lawful holder of the bill of lading. It follows from the section 6(5) exception to the 1999 Act that rights under the contract of carriage would be transferred to the seller by virtue of section 2(1) and (2)(b) of the 1992 Act and that he would have no claim under the 1999 Act. The second situation in which the seller may have an interest in enforcing the contract of carriage made (on the present supposition) between the buyer as shipper and the carrier is that in which the contract of sale is what has been called "a c.i.f. contract with variations"[32] because it makes the amount payable depend on the quantity of goods which arrive at the destination specified in the contract of sale or provides that this contract is to be void if the ship carrying the goods is lost. Such provisions in effect leave the risk of loss with the seller (contrary to the general rule that risk passes on or as from shipment[33]); and the seller may wish to hold the carrier liable for the loss that he has to bear. He will not be able to assert his claim in tort for negligence if property has passed to the buyer before the loss,[34] typically on payment against documents;[35] and a claim in bailment will be, to say the least, problematic since the bill of lading, in the case put, will be in the buyer's name and hence acknowledge receipt of the goods from the buyer, making him (rather than the seller) the bailor, even though the actual delivery of the goods to the carrier may have been made by the seller. The seller may therefore wish to make his claim in contract and he would have considerable difficulty in making good such a claim under the 1992 Act if only part of the goods had been lost, for in such a case the seller would never become the "lawful holder" of the bill within section 2(1) of that Act. But the contract of carriage would nevertheless be contained or evidenced in a bill of lading and so fall within the section 6(5) exception, so that the seller would have no claim under the 1999 Act even if he could satisfy the requirements of its section 1 by arguing that he was a member of a class expressly identified[36] in the bill of lading by virtue of the words, "or order" (or similar expressions). Two possibilities are open to the seller in such a case.

---

[31] Since risk will normally have passed to the buyer on or as from shipment: *Benjamin*, § 19–092.

[32] *Ibid.*, § 19–006 nn. 26, 29.

[33] See *supra*, n. 31.

[34] *Cf. Leigh & Sillivan Ltd.* v. *Aliakmon Shipping Co. Ltd. (The Aliakmon)* [1986] A.C. 78.

[35] *Benjamin*, §§ 19–080, 19–085.

[36] Within section 1(3) of the 1999 Act.

The first is to argue that the circumstances in which the goods were delivered by him to the carrier gave rise, before the issue of the bill of lading naming the buyer as shipper, to an antecedent contract between seller and carrier. Such a contract could be either implied, from the seller's presenting, and the carrier's accepting, the goods for carriage, or express, in the form of a booking (or "freight contract") made by the seller before the shipment and having contractual force.[37] The question would then arise whether such a contract gave the seller rights against the carrier in respect of the latter's failure properly to perform that (antecedent) contract: it would give such rights, if it contained a promise by the carrier to the seller to carry the goods to the intended destination, but not if the only promise made by the carrier to the seller was one to issue a bill of lading containing or evidencing a contract for the carriage of the goods between carrier and buyer. The question whether an antecedent contract in the latter terms conferred any rights on the *buyer* under the 1999 Act is one which is more likely to arise where the sale is on f.o.b. than where it is on c.i.f. terms and is therefore discussed later in this paper.[38]

The second possibility is for the seller to induce the buyer to make a claim against the carrier under section 2(4) of the 1992 Act, though it is an open question whether the seller would have an "interest or right in relation to goods" within that provision merely because they were at his risk.[39] If this question were answered in the negative, the seller would have no remedy either under the 1992 Act or under the 1999 Act. His position could be more favourable if the goods had been wholly destroyed. In such a case, the buyer would have no interest in retaining the bill of lading and might well be willing to transfer it to the seller making him its lawful holder and thus giving him rights of suit under section 2(1) of the 1992 Act. For reasons given elsewhere it is submitted that the bill would not be (at the time of the transfer) a "spent" bill so that the seller would have a right of action on the bill even though the case did not fall within either of the two exceptions stated in section 2(2) of that Act to the general rule that no such rights are transferred to the holder of a "spent" bill.[40] The result would be that the seller's rights would not be subject to the restrictions imposed by the 1999 Act on the rights of third parties arising under it.

The significance of the points so far made in this section of this paper is twofold. First, the conditions in which a third party can acquire rights under the 1992 Act differ from those in which a party will be able to acquire rights under the 1999 Act: for example, a person may become the "lawful holder" of a bill of lading for the purposes of section 2 of the 1992 Act without being "expressly identified" in the contract of carriage so as to satisfy the requirements of the

---

[37] As in *Hansson* v. *Hamel & Horley* [1922] 2 A.C. 36: see p. 43 of the report.
[38] See *infra*, after n. 50.
[39] *Benjamin*, § 18–064.
[40] *Ibid.*, § 18–077.

1999 Act.[41] Secondly, the contents of the rights acquired under the 1992 Act may differ from those which a third party would (but for the section 6(5) exception) acquire under the 1999 Act. The point may be illustrated by reference to cases such as *Leduc* v. *Ward*[42] and *The Ardennes*[43] in which the terms of the contract of carriage were varied by extrinsic agreement between shipper and carrier. In the former case, the bill of lading did not permit deviation but the shipper had acquiesced in the deviation which occurred, so that, against him, it was not a breach of contract. The transferee of the bill was nevertheless entitled to treat the deviation as a breach in respect of which he could recover damages. It seems that he would similarly be so entitled under the 1992 Act, at least so long as he did not know of the shipper's assent to the deviation.[44] If the case were not excepted from the 1999 Act, and the claim were made under it, the carrier would no doubt be able to rely on the extrinsic agreement against the transferee as a "matter that arises from or in connection with the contract and is relevant to the term"[45] (i.e. to the term specifying the route). No doubt this difference between the 1992 Act and the 1999 Act is explicable, at least in part, on the ground that the transferability of bills of lading would be unduly hampered if a "matter" such as an extrinsic agreement between shipper and carrier were available as a defence against a bona fide transferee. The question exactly which defences against the shipper are available to the carrier against a transferee making a claim under the 1992 Act is a difficult and complex one which cannot be re-examined here.[46] The point to be emphasised is that the 1999 Act in this respect treats the promisor more favourably than the 1992 Act does.

b. F.o.b. sales

A similar set of problems can arise where the sale is on f.o.b. terms; and these problems are usually discussed in the light of the well-known account given by Devlin, J. in *Pyrene Co. Ltd.* v. *Scindia Navigations Co. Ltd.*[47] of the relations between, on the one hand, the carrier and, on the other, the buyer and seller where goods are shipped in pursuance of such a contract. The following discussion is concerned with the impact on the situations described in that case of the 1999 Act. It will deal only with the *general* question of contractual relations between the buyer and/or seller on the one hand and the carrier on the other; the *particular* issue which arose in the *Pyrene* case, of the effect of

---

[41] Section 1(3); *supra*, at n. 6.
[42] (1885) 20 Q.B.D. 475.
[43] [1951] 1 K.B. 55.
[44] *Benjamin*, § 18–064.
[45] 1999 Act, section 3(2)(a).
[46] See *Benjamin*, §§ 18–065 to 18–074.
[47] [1954] 2 Q.B. 402, 424.

exemption clauses on a third party, will be considered later in this paper.[48] It will be recalled that in that case Devlin, J. distinguished between three situations.

The first is that of "the classic type" of f.o.b. contract, in which the buyer's duty is simply to nominate the ship on which the goods are to be loaded and the seller's duty is "to put the goods on board for the account of the buyer and procure a bill of lading in terms usual in the trade. In such a case, the seller is directly a party to the contract of carriage at least until he takes out a bill of lading in the buyer's name".[49] The last four words here seem to indicate that the bill names the buyer as shipper so that at this stage he becomes an original party to the contract of carriage which previously had been between seller and carrier; presumably the change of parties takes effect by way of either a variation or a novation of the original contract between seller and carrier. No doubt the new contract is that contained in or evidenced by the bill of lading, so that any question of the acquisition of third party rights under this contract will fall within the section 6(5) exception, so as to be governed by the 1992 Act and not by the 1999 Act. But the original contract between seller and carrier is *not* contained in or evidenced by a bill of lading, having not only come into existence before the bill of lading contract, but being also between different parties. Hence it does not fall within the definition of a "contract for the carriage of goods by sea" in the terms of the 1999 Act,[50] so that at first sight it is not within the section 6(5) exception, with the result that rights of enforcement under this contract can, under section 1(1) of the Act, be conferred on a third party (such as, typically, the buyer). That is, indeed, not entirely clear since, in Devlin, J.'s words, the seller has put the goods on board "for the account of the buyer" and this phrase could be interpreted to mean that he has done so as agent of the buyer. If so, the buyer would have been a party to the pre-bill of lading contract *ab initio* and in that event his rights of enforcement would not arise under section 1(1) of the 1999 Act, since this confers rights of enforcement only on "a person who is *not* a party to" the contract containing the term which he seeks to enforce. More probably, however, the words "for the account of the buyer" do not carry any implication of agency but merely provide the carrier with a good discharge if he delivers the goods to the buyer. The position, then, is that the original (pre-bill of lading) contract is between seller and carrier, while the new (bill of lading) contract is between buyer and carrier.

This analysis can give rise to difficulties under the 1999 Act if the terms of the new contract differ from those of the old: the difficulties arise from the general principle that, once a third party has acquired rights of enforcement under the 1999 Act, the contracting parties cannot, without the third party's consent,

---

[48] See *infra*, § 3(a).
[49] [1954] 1 Q.B. 402, 424. *Cf. Sunrise Maritime Inc.* v. *Uvisco Ltd. (The Hector)* [1988] 2 Lloyd's Rep. 287, 289.
[50] See section 6(6) and 6(7).

rescind or vary the contract by agreement so as to extinguish or alter those rights after one of the circumstances specified in section 2(1) of the Act has occurred.[51] The difficulties arise because the buyer may have acquired rights by virtue of the 1999 Act under the pre-bill of lading contract and because those rights may differ from those which he has under the later bill of lading contract. The general view hitherto has been that the relations between buyer and carrier are then governed by the terms of the latter contract alone; and there are, it is submitted, two ways of preserving this position under the 1999 Act. The first is to say that the buyer has consented (within section 2(1) of the 1999 Act) to the variation. He may not, indeed, have done so at the stage at which (in Devlin, J.'s words) the seller "takes out" the bill of lading, since at that stage the buyer is unlikely to be aware of its terms. But he can be said to have done so at the later stage at which the bill is tendered to, and accepted by, him against the payment; or it could be argued that, by contracting on f.o.b. terms and nominating the ship, the buyer has consented in advance to the seller's taking out the bill of lading in (to quote Devlin, J. again) "terms usual in the trade". The second line of argument is to rely on section 1(4) of the 1999 Act, by which "This section does not confer any rights on a third party to enforce a term of a contract otherwise than subject to and in accordance with any other relevant term of the contract." It can be argued that the pre-bill of lading contract is subject to an implied term that it is to be superseded by another contract when the bill of lading is taken out and that the contractual relations of all the relevant parties are then (so far as the carriage operation is concerned) to be governed by the terms of the bill of lading alone. Since the whole pre-bill of lading contract is (in the present situation) implied from conduct, there should be little difficulty in convincing the court that such a term is to be implied. The implication could be said to arise either in fact[52] (under the "officious bystander" or "business efficacy" tests) or in law because such a term was one of the "legal incidents" of the "kind of contractual relationship" here under discussion.[53]

The impact of the 1999 Act on the second of the three situations discussed by Devlin, J. in the *Pyrene* case is, by contrast, relatively simple to analyse. The situation in question is that in which "the seller is asked to make the necessary [shipping] arrangements; and the contract may then provide for his taking the bill of lading in his own name and obtaining payment against the transfer, as in a c.i.f. contract".[54] No reference is here made to any pre-bill of lading contract; and, even if there were such a contract, it would be between the same parties as the bill of lading contract itself. Nor would any rights be likely to be conferred by any such pre-bill of lading contract on the buyer so that the difficulties

---

[51] See *supra*, § 1(d).
[52] Treitel, 184.
[53] *Ibid.*, 188.
[54] [1954] 2 Q.B. 402, 424.

discussed above[55] as to the buyer's consent to the variation of the earlier by the later contract would not arise. The buyer's rights under the bill of lading contract would arise on his becoming the lawful holder of the bill. It would for this purpose make no difference whether the bill of lading, which is stated to be "in the seller's name" (i.e. to name him *as shipper*) were also to his *order* or to the order of the buyer. In either case, the acquisition of rights under the contract of carriage would be governed by section 2 of the 1992 Act and the case would be within the section 6(5) exception to the 1999 Act. The extinction of the seller's rights under the contract of carriage is likewise governed by section 2(5) of the 1992 Act; those rights will not be preserved by section 4 of the 1999 Act. The reasoning which supports these conclusions is the same as that (set out above[56]) which applies in the normal case of a c.i.f. seller's taking out a bill of lading in his own name and later transferring it to the buyer in performance of his duties under the c.i.f. sale.

A variant on Devlin, J.'s second situation is illustrated by *Hanjin Shipping Co. Ltd.* v. *Procter & Gamble (Philippines) Ltd.*,[57] where a cargo booking having contractual force was made by the f.o.b. seller's agent with the carrier's agent, naming the buyer's agent as the consignee to whom delivery was to be made. The seller having instructed the carrier to return the goods to the port of loading, no bill of lading was ever issued,[58] and it was held that the only contract which had come into being was the cargo-booking contract to which the buyer was not a party. Under the 1999 Act, such a case would therefore not fall within the section 6(5) exception; and whether the cargo-booking contract could confer rights on the buyer under section 1 of the Act would depend on factors analogous to those discussed below in section 5 of this paper.

The third of the situations discussed by Devlin, J. in the *Pyrene* case again gives rise to problems in relation to the 1999 Act; these are in kind similar to those (already discussed[59]) which arise from the first of those situations. The third situation is that in which the buyer books space in the carrying ship; the seller then performs his duty by putting the goods on board, obtaining a mate's receipt which he then hands to the buyer to enable the latter to obtain a bill of lading. In Devlin, J.'s discussion,[60] the buyer acts through a forwarding agent, but for our present purpose this complication may be ignored. As already noted,[61] the actual question in the *Pyrene* case was whether the seller was *bound* by terms of the bill of lading contract between buyer and carrier and this aspect

---

[55] Before n. 51.
[56] *Supra*, § 2(a).
[57] [1997] 2 Lloyd's Rep. 341.
[58] *Ibid.*, 345.
[59] After n. 51.
[60] [1954] 2 Q.B. 402, 424.
[61] *Supra*, n. 48.

of the case is, for reasons to be given below,[62] not affected by the 1999 Act. But it is clear that Devlin, J. also thought that the seller had acquired contractual *rights* against the carrier. In his view, if the ship "sail[ed] off without loading the goods", then the seller would be in breach of his contract with the buyer and so the seller must have some "redress against the ship".[63] The first limb of this argument may, with respect, be doubted, since it is at least arguable that in the case put it is the buyer (not the seller) who is in breach of the contract of sale in that he has failed to give shipping instructions which are "effective".[64] But that is not the point of direct concern here: that point lies in Devlin, J's conclusion that there was a "wider principle" than agency, by which "the third party takes those *benefits* of the contract which appertain to his interest therein".[65] This view has encountered a good deal of judicial hostility[66] but the question now arises whether on similar facts the seller will at least *prima facie* acquire rights by virtue of section 1 of the 1999 Act. The answer to this question is far from clear; it would depend on the seller's ability to show that he was "expressly identified"[67] in the cargo-booking contract and on the carrier's inability to show that he and the buyer did not intend the seller to have an enforceable right against the carrier requiring him to take the goods on board.[68] Even if the seller succeeded on these points, he would not necessarily acquire rights against the carrier *by virtue of the 1999 Act*. Section 1(1) of that Act confers rights only on a person who "is *not* a party to a contract"; and the now preferred explanation of the *Pyrene* case is that, in the situation here under discussion, the seller *is* a party to some contract, either because the buyer acted at least to a limited extent as his agent for the purpose of establishing a contractual relationship between him and the carrier,[69] or because an implied contract (to load the goods) arose when "by delivering the goods alongside the seller impliedly invited the shipowner to load them and the shipowner impliedly accepted that invitation".[70] The possibility of the seller's *prima facie* acquiring rights under the 1999 Act is therefore only one of a number of analyses; but it is at any rate one that cannot be ruled out.

Granted that, at the stage which has so far been reached, the seller may have *prima facie* rights under section 1 of the 1999 Act, the question arises as to the

---

[62] *Infra*, § 3(a).
[63] [1954] 1 Q.B. 402, 425.
[64] *Benjamin*, § 20–041.
[65] [1954] 2 Q.B. 402, 426.
[66] See especially *Scruttons Ltd.* v. *Midland Silicones Ltd.* [1962] A.C. 446, 471.
[67] 1999 Act, section 1(3).
[68] *Ibid.*, section 1(2).
[69] [1954] 2 Q.B. 402, 426, viewing this analysis with some scepticism.
[70] *Ibid.*, 426, approved in *Scruttons Ltd.* v. *Midland Silicones Ltd.* [1962] A.C. 446, 471.

effect of this position on the course of dealing that is likely to follow. Three possibilities call for discussion:

(1) At one extreme, no bill of lading is ever issued because the goods are never shipped. In such a case no "contract for the carriage of goods by sea" within section 6(5) of the 1999 Act comes into existence,[71] so that the rights (if any) of the seller will be determined in accordance with section 1 of the 1999 Act.

(2) At the other extreme, a bill of lading relating to the goods in question may be used in spite of the fact that those goods were never shipped. Such a bill may be a perfectly accurate and honest document: it may be a "received for shipment" (as opposed to a "shipped") bill, and a contract contained in or evidenced by a "received" bill would fall within the definition of a "contract for the carriage of goods by sea" in section 6(5) of the 1999 Act.[72] Hence the seller could not assert any rights under that contract by virtue of the 1999 Act; and it seems that any rights which he might have had under the 1999 Act as a third party to the pre-bill of lading contract would cease to exist for the reasons given above[73] in discussing the first of the types of cases described by Devlin, J. Alternatively, the bill of lading might be a "shipped" bill of lading and so contain a false statement as to the fact of shipment. The mere issue of a bill of lading containing such a false statement does not give rise to a contract of carriage,[74] though a carrier who issues such a bill may be liable to a lawful holder of the bill by virtue of section 4 of the 1992 Act (but probably not by virtue Article III.4 of the Hague-Visby Rules).[75] Such liability, however, would arise by virtue of a statutory estoppel: i.e. not because there is a contract of carriage, but because the carrier is estopped from denying the fact of shipment. In any event, the seller could not rely on section 4 of the 1992 Act in the situation here under discussion since the bill has not been transferred to him; since even if it had been so transferred he would not be a "lawful holder" within section 4 if he knew that the goods had not been shipped;[76] and since section 4 is intended to give rise to claims in respect of non-delivery or short delivery, as opposed to claims for damage caused by the carrier's failure to perform his contractual duty of care. If, then, there was *no* contract of carriage contained or evidenced in the bill of lading, because no goods had been shipped, then the case would not fall within the section 6(5) exception. Any claims which the seller might have under the 1999 Act as a third party to the pre-bill of lading

---

[71] This follows from section 6(6) and 6(7) of the 1999 Act.

[72] This follows from section 6(6) and 6(7) of the 1999 Act, read together with the Carriage of Goods by Sea Act 1992, section 1(2)(b).

[73] After n. 51.

[74] *Heskell* v. *Continental Express Ltd.* [1950] 1 All E.R. 1030.

[75] *Benjamin*, §§ 18–023–18–026.

[76] Carriage of Goods by Sea Act 1992, section 5(2).

contract between buyer and seller would survive; though, as we have seen,[77] it is far from clear that he actually would have such claims.

(3) Between the two extremes just discussed lies an intermediate situation which is illustrated by the facts of the *Pyrene* case itself. The subject matter of the litigation was a fire tender which had been sold by the seller to the buyer together with other goods; the whole consignment was presented by the seller to the carrier in pursuance of shipping arrangements made between buyer and carrier; and (as already noted[78]) Devlin, J. said that these arrangements conferred a contractual right on the seller to have the goods taken on board. The fire tender was dropped and damaged while being loaded; consequently it was not shipped; but the bill of lading covering the whole shipment "was issued to [the buyer's agent] … but with the fire tender deleted from it".[79] Devlin, J.'s view that the seller had acquired contractual rights as a third party beneficiary (under what he called the "wider principle") has probably not survived in the light of later judicial discussions of the *Pyrene* case,[80] but it is arguable that on similar facts the pre-bill of lading contract will be capable of conferring rights on the seller as a third party under section 1 of the 1999 Act. The question then is whether the subsequent issue of the bill of lading with the fire tender deleted will preclude the application of section 1 by virtue of the section 6(5) exception. There is on such facts "a contract for the carriage of goods by sea" within that subsection,[81] and the parties to that contract are the same as the parties to the pre-bill of lading contract under which (if no bill of lading had been issued) the third party might have acquired rights by virtue of section 1: both these contracts are between buyer and carrier. It is (with some hesitation) submitted that the applicability of the section 6(5) exception to facts such as those which actually occurred in the *Pyrene* case should depend on whether the subject matter of the bill of lading contract was substantially the same as that of the pre-bill of lading contract. If it was, the section 6(5) exception should apply; if it was not, the seller's rights (if any) should depend on section 1.

Nothing in the foregoing discussion affects any rights or remedies which the seller might have apart from the Act: e.g. rights arising by virtue of agency, implied contract or further exceptions to the common law doctrine of privity which might be created by judicial decision. Any such rights or remedies are expressly preserved by section 7(1) of the 1999 Act.[82]

---

[77] *Supra*, after n. 63.
[78] *Ibid.*
[79] [1954] 2 Q.B. 402, 413.
[80] *Supra* at n. 66.
[81] See the 1999 Act, section 6(6) and 6(7).
[82] See *supra*, § 1(g) of this paper.

3 CLAUSES EXCLUDING OR LIMITING LIABILITY

Section 1(6) of the 1999 Act provides that, "where a term of a contract excludes or limits liability in relation to any matter, references in this Act to the third party enforcing the term shall be construed as references to his availing himself of the exclusion or limitation". It follows from this that, where the requirements of enforceability by a third party stated elsewhere in the Act are satisfied in relation to such a clause (here to be called an exemption clause), the third party can avail himself of the clause. Thus the third party can avail himself of the clause if the contract expressly so provides[83] or if the term purports to confer a benefit on him[84] (so long as it does not appear on a proper construction of the contract that the parties did not intend the term to be enforceable by him[85]); he must also be "expressly identified"[86] in the contract by name, as a member of a class or as answering a particular description. The third party may not rely on the clause if he could not have done so, had he been a party to the contract:[87] e.g. if, on that supposition, the contract would have been ineffective under the Unfair Contract Terms Act 1977 or if the term had been subject to the requirement of reasonableness under that Act and that requirement had not been satisfied. In the present context, moreover, the section 6(5) exception (discussed above) does not apply since that exception is itself subject to an exception stated in its concluding words: "except that a third party may in reliance on . . . section [1] avail himself of an exclusion or limitation of liability in" (*inter alia*) "a contract for the carriage of goods by sea". It was not the purpose of the 1999 Act to alter the rules under which, prior to its coming into force, a third party could take the benefit of an exemption clause in a bill of lading (or in certain other transport documents[88]) or to inhibit the further developments of these rules.

The following discussion will deal the effect of the 1999 Act on exemption clauses in bills of lading. The exemptions and limitations of liability available to a carrier of goods by sea under the Hague-Visby Rules, no less than those available to him under the Hague Rules, will be assumed to be so available by virtue of a "term of a contract". This is not the place for entering into a debate on the question whether the fact that the Hague-Visby Rules "have the force of law"[89] deprives the carrier's exemptions and limitations under those Rules of their juridical character as terms of the contract.

---

[83] 1999 Act, section 1(1)(a).
[84] *Ibid.*, section 1(1)(b).
[85] *Ibid.*, section 1(2).
[86] *Ibid.*, section 1(3).
[87] *Ibid.*, section 3(6).
[88] Such as sea waybills and land and air carriage documents.
[89] Carriage of Goods by Sea Act 1971, section 1(2).

a. Binding third parties

The provisions of the 1999 Act referred to above specify the circumstances in which a third party (C) can take the *benefit* of a contract between A and B. They do not deal directly with the question whether a third party can be *bound* by such a contract. This was the actual question which arose in the *Pyrene* case,[90] where it was held that the seller was indeed bound by the limitation of liability available to the carrier under the Hague Rules which governed the bill of lading contract between the carrier and the buyer. The 1999 Act does not seek to alter the general common law rule that a person is not bound by a contract or by a term in a contract to which he is not a party;[91] but there are circumstances in which it might lead indirectly to the conclusion that the third party is, in a sense, so bound. In this context, a part of Devlin, J.'s reasoning in the *Pyrene* case remains relevant.

Having referred to the "wider principle" (sc. than agency) by which a third party can take the benefit of a contract, Devlin, J. said: "the third party takes those benefits of the contract which appertain to his interest therein, but takes them, of course, subject to whatever qualification with regard to them the contract imposes".[92] The "wider principle" may not have prevailed at common law;[93] but it is now enshrined in the 1999 Act, and a "qualification" similar to that stated by Devlin, J. continues to restrict its operation. That is, where C's only claim against A is one for the enforcement of a term in C's favour in the contract between A and B, then C's right of enforcement will in general be subject to any defences which A would have had against B.[94] But this is true only where C's right against A is what may be called a derivative right: i.e., where it is derived from the contract between A and B and has no other legal basis. The reasoning would not apply where C had a right against A which arose independently of the contract between A and B. There is no doubt that, in a situation resembling that in the *Pyrene* case, C (the seller) would now be regarded as having a cause of action against A (the carrier) in tort simply by virtue of A's "proximity" to C or to C's goods;[95] the contract between A and B (the buyer) would be simply part of the history leading to that proximity and not a legal basis of C's cause of action against A in tort for negligence. If C so formulated his claim, nothing in the 1999 Act would affect it. That, of course, is not to say that there might not be some other legal basis for holding C bound by the exemption clause in the contract between A and B. Agency, implied contract, bailment on terms and "transferred loss" are legal techniques that may,

[90]   [1954] 2 Q.B. 402.
[91]   Report, § 10.32, 7.6.
[92]   [1954] 2 Q.B. 402, 426.
[93]   *Supra*, at n. 66.
[94]   1999 Act, section 3(2).
[95]   *Cf. Hispanica de Petroleos S.A.* v. *Vencedora Oceanica Navegacion S.A. (The Kapetan Markos N.L.) (No. 2)* [1987] 2 Lloyd's Rep. 321, 340.

on appropriate facts, lead to C's being so bound.[96] The only point made here is that he will not be so bound by virtue of the 1999 Act.

There remains the possibility, illustrated by *The Aliakmon*,[97] that C may not have any claim in tort against A because, when the goods were damaged, C had no proprietary or possessory interest in them and that C has no contractual claim against A as a third party under the 1999 Act because the contract in question fell within the section 6(5) exception, being contained in or evidenced by a bill of lading. Lord Goff of Chieveley has said that a situation such as that which arose in *The Aliakmon* would now be governed by the Carriage of Goods by Sea Act 1992, so that C (the buyer) would have a right to sue A (the carrier) in contract if C had become the lawful holder of the bill of lading.[98] In such an action, C's right against A would be what has here been called a derivative right, so that it would be subject to any exceptions or limitations in the contract between A and B (the shipper). If C had not become the lawful holder of the bill (and no other document[99] capable of transferring contractual rights under the contract of carriage had come into existence), he would continue to have no rights either in tort or in contract. His only hope would be to persuade B to bring an action for his benefit under section 2(4) of the 1992 Act; and the outcome of such an action would depend on whether C would be regarded as having an "interest or right in or in relation to the goods" within that subsection merely by virtue of their being at his risk.[100] If such an action were *prima facie* available, B's claim would of course be subject to any terms in the contract between A and B, so that C would indirectly be adversely affected by such terms.

b. Benefiting third parties: Himalaya clauses

Himalaya clauses were, as is well known, devised to avoid the effects of the decision in the *Midland Silicones* case,[101] where a majority of the House of Lords had held (i) that a firm of stevedores engaged by the carriers to unload goods from their ship were not entitled, as against the consignee of goods which the stevedores had negligently damaged, to the benefit of the limitation of liability available to the carriers under the bill of lading by virtue of the incorporation in it of the Hague Rules; and (ii) that the consignee was not bound by a term in the contract between the carriers and the stevedores giving the stevedores the benefit of the same limitation. Neither of these points is affected

---

[96] See Treitel, 588 *et seq.*

[97] *Leigh & Sillivan Ltd.* v. *Aliakmon Shipping Co. Ltd. (The Aliakmon)* [1986] A.C. 785.

[98] *White* v. *Jones* [1995] 2 A.C. 207, 265.

[99] Such as a sea waybill or ship's delivery order: see the Carriage of Goods by Sea Act 1992, section 2(1)(b) and (c).

[100] *Benjamin*, § 18–084.

[101] *Scruttons Ltd.* v. *Midland Silicones Ltd.* [1962] A.C. 446.

by the 1999 Act. The second is not so affected for the reason given in the immediately preceding discussion[102] (the consignee's claim being a tort claim in negligence: and not what has just been described as a derivative claim based on the contract of carriage). The first is not so affected because the bill of lading contained no reference to the stevedores: thus their attempt to rely on the limitation provision would fail under the 1999 Act because they were not "expressly identified in the [bill of lading] contract",[103] if for no other reason.

The efficacy of Himalaya clauses as devices for conferring the benefit of bill of lading exemption and limitation clauses on third parties is now generally recognised, subject to qualifications (and possible qualifications) to be discussed below. The persons relying on such clauses are usually employees of the carrier or independent contractors employed by him, such as stevedores or subcontracting carriers;[104] and, while there is no universally accepted form of Himalaya clause, such a clause is likely to contain one or more of three elements. First, it may purport to exempt the carrier's servants, agents and independent contractors from liability for acts or defaults in the course of their employment for the carrier. At common law, this part of such a clause would not achieve the desired effect: the doctrine of privity of contract would preclude the servant, agent or independent contractor from relying on it,[105] nor (as English law now stands) could such a person invoke the doctrine of vicarious immunity.[106] Secondly, the clause may seek to secure the benefit of the exemptions or limitations for the third party by use of the exception to the doctrine of privity which is recognised in equity in cases of trusts or promises: i.e. by making the carrier trustee of the shipper's promise to give the benefit of these provisions to the carrier's servants, agents or independent contractors. The efficacy of this component of the clause remains in doubt since "the conception of a trust attaching to a benefit of an exclusion clause extends far beyond conventional limits".[107] Thirdly, the clause may seek to achieve the desired result by treating the carrier as having acted as agent of his servants, agents or independent contractors for the purpose of securing for them the benefit of the exemption clause. It is this aspect of Himalaya clauses which has been decisive in making the benefit of bill of lading exemptions and limitations available to such persons. Two aspects of this agency reasoning should be stressed before considering the impact on all this of the 1999 Act.

---

[102] *Supra*, after n. 95.

[103] 1999 Act, section 1(3).

[104] E.g. *New Zealand Shipping Co. Ltd. v. A. M. Satterthwaite & Co. Ltd. (The Eurymedon)* [1975] A.C. 154; *Salmond & Spraggon (Australia) (Pty) Ltd. v. Port Jackson Stevedoring (Pty) Ltd. (The New York Star)* [1981] 1 W.L.R. 138.

[105] *The Mahkutai* [1996] A.C. 650, 664.

[106] *Adler* v. *Dickson* [1955] 1 Q.B. 158; *Scrutton Ltd.* v. *Silicones Ltd.* [1962] A.C. 446 (*supra*, n. 101).

[107] *Southern Water Authority* v. *Carey* [1985] 2 All E.R. 1077, 1083.

First, the effect of such reasoning is to bring about a direct contractual relationship between the shipper (or a consignee to whom the shipper's rights have passed, e.g. by transfer of the bill of lading) and the servant, agent or independent contractor. Such a person is therefore at the same time a "third party" to the bill of lading contract and an immediate party to the contract that arises by virtue of the Himalaya clause. That contract has been described by Lord Wilberforce as "a bargain initially unilateral but capable of becoming mutual" and as becoming "a full contract" when the third party "performed services by discharging the goods".[108] More recently it has been said that the contract would be regarded as "nowadays bilateral"[109]—apparently as one concluded when the shipper accepted the bill of lading. This view would lead to the conclusion that the stevedore would be contractually liable to the shipper (or consignee) if he simply refused or failed to unload the goods; and it is respectfully submitted that it is, for this reason, less plausible than Lord Wilberforce's view of the nature of the contract. The difference of views on this point has, as we shall see,[110] some possible significance on the impact of the 1999 Act. Whatever its precise nature, the contract which arises between the shipper (or consignee) and the third party is a kind of collateral contract with certain parasitic qualities.[111]

Secondly, it appears from a much-quoted passage from the speech of Lord Reid in the *Midland Silicones* case that the agency reasoning will apply only if there is both a declaration of agency in the Himalaya clause and also (as a separate requirement) "authority from the stevedore ... or perhaps later ratification".[112] The latter requirement in principle depends on evidence extrinsic to the bill of lading. It has been a constant source of debate in cases concerning Himalaya clauses,[113] and has occasionally prevented the "third party" from being able to rely on the clause.[114] Its purpose is not altogether clear;[115] and in the case of a limitation or exemption clause the "third party" will usually[116] wish and be able to satisfy it by subsequent ratification; it is only in

---

[108] *The Eurymedon* (*supra*, n. 104) [1975] A.C. 154, 167–168.
[109] *The Mahkutai* [1996] A.C. 650, 664.
[110] See *infra*, at n. 132.
[111] See *infra*, at n. 124.
[112] [1962] A.C. 446, 474.
[113] See, e.g. *The New York Star* (*supra*, n. 104); *The Mahkutai* (*supra*, n. 105).
[114] *The Suleyman Stalskiy* [1976] 2 Lloyd's Rep. 609.
[115] One could see the force of the requirement if the clause in question could impose an *obligation* on the third party; but a clause exempting him from liability can scarcely have this effect.
[116] There might be an exception arising under the common law rule in *Kelner* v. *Baxter* (1866) L.R. 2 C.P. 174 if the third party was not in existence when the contract of carriage was made.

the case of clauses which may affect the third party adversely[117] (so that he may not wish to ratify) that the requirement is likely to have any practical effect.

It seems that the effect of the 1999 Act will be considerably to simplify the drafting of Himalaya clauses by in effect reversing the common law position with regard to the first component of such a clause, as described above.[118] If, for example, the Himalaya clause expressly provides that the "third party" is to be entitled in his own right to "enforce" the term (usually *another* term) of the contract which excludes or limits the liability of the carrier, then the third party will be entitled to avail himself of the exclusion or limitation by virtue of sections 1(1)(a) and 1(6) of the Act. For this purpose, it will, moreover, no longer be necessary for the clause to declare that the carrier was acting as agent for the third party; nor will Lord Reid's requirement of "authority from the [third party] . . . or perhaps later ratification"[119] continue to apply. The reason for this is that, in order to avail himself of the exclusions or limitations in the contract of carriage by virtue of what may become (after the Act has come into force) a "new style" Himalaya clause, the third party will no longer need to establish (as at common law he must) that a direct contractual relationship (or collateral contract) has arisen between him and the carrier. He merely has to show that he is the sort of "third party" who is capable of acquiring, and has acquired, rights of enforcement under the 1999 Act. For this reason, too, the third party need no longer provide consideration for the shipper's (or consignee's) promise to exempt him from, or to limit his, liability; for the third party's right of enforcement under the 1999 Act is not dependent on his having provided consideration.[120] In practice this last change will have little practical significance since consideration for the shipper's or consignee's promise to the third party was usually provided by the latter's performance of his contract with the carrier.[121]

These changes will result in a welcome simplification of the law; but for a number of reasons to be given in the discussion that follows the old law relating to Himalaya clauses will not altogether lose its practical significance.

The first reason for this position lies in the point already made above that the third party's right to avail himself of an exclusion or limitation under section 1(6) of the Act is (like any right of enforcement under it) subject to its provisions and in particular to those which specify the extent to which the third party's rights are subject to the rights of promisor and promisee to rescind or vary the contract by agreement[122] and to defences, set-offs and other matters which the promisor (i.e. in this context, the shipper or consignee) could have

---

[117] As, for example, in *The Mahkutai* [1996] A.C. 650: *cf. infra* at n. 139.
[118] *Supra*, at n. 105.
[119] *Supra*, at n. 112.
[120] Report, § 6.8, n. 8.
[121] The leading modern authority on the point is *The Eurymedon* [1975] A.C. 154.
[122] 1999 Act, section 2.

raised against the promisee (i.e. the carrier).[123] The right which a "third party" may have at common law to rely on an exemption clause in a bill of lading under the collateral contract between himself and the shipper or consignee which comes into being as a result of the operation of a Himalaya clause is not, of course, subject to these provisions; but his position under the Act and his position under a Himalaya clause at common law is likely to be less significant in practice than it is in theory.

The reason for this approximation of the two positions lies in the parasitic qualities of the collateral contract which comes in to existence as a result of the conduct of the relevant parties, where the bill of lading contains a Himalaya clause. Generally, a Himalaya clause will extend to the "third party" only the same protection as the contract gives to the carrier, so that the "third party" will not be protected from liability for damage done by him to the goods before performance of the contract of carriage has begun or after performance of that contract has been completed.[124] This position can be explained on the ground that a Himalaya clause typically protects the "third party" only while he is acting "in the course of or in connection with the course of his employment"[125] by the carrier. But this explanation will not serve to explain the further rule (or group of rules) which precludes the "third party" from relying on the main contract of carriage on account of certain defects in it. In a South African case in which the rights of the parties were governed by English law,[126] A had contracted to tow B's barge and had for this purpose hired a tug from C who sought to rely on a Himalaya clause in the contract between A and B. It was held that he was not entitled to do so since B had been induced to enter into the main contract with A by A's misrepresentation and had rescinded that contract on that ground. C was not protected by the exemption clauses in the main contract since "once those … exemptions … fall away on rescission of the [contract between A and B], nothing remains to exempt C".[127] This reasoning would not apply where C sought to rely as against B on an exemption or limitation in the contract between A and B, and B attempted to defeat such reliance on the ground of A's repudiatory breach. The general rule in such a case is that the exemptions do not retrospectively "fall away on rescission" of the contrast between A and B: they do so only with prospective effect.[128] Hence at common law B could not normally set up such a breach to prevent C from relying on the exclusion or limitation with respect to losses suffered by B before he had

---

[123] *Ibid.*, section 3.

[124] See *Raymond Byrke Motors Ltd.* v. *Mersey Docks & Harbour Co.* [1986] 1 Lloyd's Rep. 155; *The New York Star* [1981] 1 W.L.R. 138, where the point is implicit.

[125] Words taken from the Himalaya clause in *The Eurymedon* [1975] A.C. 154.

[126] *Bouygues Offshore* v. *Ultisol Transport Contractors* [1996] 2 Lloyd's Rep. 153n.

[127] *Ibid.*, 165.

[128] *Photo Production Ltd.* v. *Securicor Transport Ltd.* [1980] A.C. 827.

rescinded his contract with A, though there may be an exception to this general rule where the breach by a carrier takes the form of an unjustified deviation.[129]

Under section 3(6) of the 1999 Act, a third party cannot "enforce" (i.e. avail himself of) an exemption or limitation clause "if he could not have done so (whether by reason of particular circumstances relating to him or otherwise) had he been a party to the contract". This fiction is not always easy to apply to the case in which a subcontractor employed by the carrier seeks to rely on an exemption or limitation clause in the contract of carriage. Suppose, for example, that the carrier has committed a breach of his undertaking as to seaworthiness, and that this breach is so serious as to justify the shipper or consignee in rescinding the contract of carriage. The third party (e.g. a subcontracting carrier or a stevedore engaged to unload the goods) then does further damage to the goods. The carrier's breach would not preclude the third party from relying on an exemption or limitation clause (where the requirements of section 1 of the 1999 Act were satisfied) if the shipper or consignee had *not* yet rescinded before the damage caused by the third party's wrongful conduct had been done; but it is less clear what the position would be if, before then, the shipper or consignee *had* rescinded. Would the fiction that the third party had been a party to the contract suffice to impose on him an obligation with regard to the seaworthiness of the ship so as to justify the rescission against him? An affirmative answer to this position might be plausible where the third party was a subcontracting carrier. At first sight, it is much less plausible to say that an obligation of seaworthiness was imposed by the fiction on a subcontractor such as a stevedore who took no part in the operation of carrying the goods, or on an employee of the carrier. Yet such a conclusion might be supported on the ground that section 3(6) is intended to apply, in the context of exemption and limitation clauses, the general principle (embodied in section 3(2)) that the promisor should be able to rely as against the third party on any matter on which he could have relied as against the promisee that arises from or in connection with the contract and is relevant to the term which the third party seeks to "enforce".

A second situation in which the common law rules relating to Himalaya clauses may retain some practical significance is that in which the parties to the main contract in which the Himalaya clause is contained vary that contract by agreement in a way that could prejudice the third party: e.g. if the parties to a bill of lading agreed to raise the limit of the carrier's (and hence the third party's) liability. At common law, there would appear to be no restriction on their power to do so *before* the collateral contract arising by virtue of the Himalaya clause has come into existence. Once that contract has come into existence the effect of a variation of the main contract would appear to depend on the construction of

---

[129] *Ibid.*, 845, 850. Contrast *The Antares (No.2)* [1987] 1 Lloyd's Rep. 424, 428. It is not the purpose of this paper to give a full discussion of this controversy.

the collateral contract. It will be recalled that a Himalaya clause (as already noted) typically gives the third party the benefit of some *other* provision of the main contract. The collateral contract might, then, refer *either* to those other provisions as they stand when the collateral contract came into being *or* to those other provisions as they are agreed upon by the parties from time to time. On the first view, the variation would not affect the third party's right to avail himself of the original limitation clauses; on the second, it could affect that right. The 1999 Act does not fully take either of these positions. The general principle (stated in section 2(1)) is that the parties may not, without the third party's consent, vary the contract by agreement so as to extinguish or alter the third party's rights in a number of specified situations, of which the most likely to apply in the present context is that "the promisor can reasonably be expected to have foreseen that the third party would rely on the term and the third party has in fact relied on it".[130] It would follow from this that the contracting parties' power to vary the contract of carriage by agreement to the prejudice of the third party would be lost once the carrier's subcontractor had begun the performance of the subcontract, though only if he knew (or perhaps if he had reason to know) of the term limiting his liability. Since it is probably at the stage of commencement of performance by the subcontractor that the collateral contract arises at common law, the position under the 1999 Act will, thus far, normally resemble the common law position. But the two positions are not identical since under the 1999 Act the contracting parties can be deprived of their power of variation before such foreseeable action in reliance: e.g. by the third party's communication of his assent to the term to the promisor.[131] If the common law collateral contract is indeed a unilateral one,[132] the mere communication of the third party's assent to the promisor would not suffice to bring it into existence. There is also under the 1999 Act a judicial discretion to dispense with the third party's consent in specified circumstances and to impose terms on the exercise of this discretion;[133] and these rules have no counterpart at common law.

The third reason why the common law relating to Himalaya clauses may retain some practical importance is that section 1(6) of the 1999 Act applies only where the third party seeks to avail himself of a contract term which "excludes or limits" liability. It thus does not apply to, for example, arbitration, choice of forum or exclusive jurisdiction clauses; and the Law Commission Report on which the 1999 Act was based indicates that such clauses were not intended to fall within the scope of the proposed reform.[134] Although the express

---

[130] 1999 Act, section 2(1)(c).

[131] *Ibid.*, section 2(1)(a).

[132] For a submission that this is the better view of the nature of this contract, see *supra* after n. 108.

[133] 1999 Act, section 2(4)–(6).

[134] Report, § 14.15.

provisions to this effect in the Law Commission's Draft Bill[135] (appended to the Report) have no counterpart in the 1999 Act, the same restriction on its scope is inherent in the wording of its section 1(6) since clauses of the kind here in question[136] do not "exclude or limit liability". The reason why such clauses are outside the scope of the 1999 Act is that the purpose of the Act is to enable contracting parties to confer *rights* on a third party, while under clauses of the kind here under discussion he would not only acquire rights but also be subjected to duties.[137]

It was precisely for this reason that the Privy Council held in *The Mahkutai*[138] that a third party could not at common law take the benefit of an exclusive jurisdiction clause in a contract which also contained a Himalaya clause. This decision was, however, based on the construction of the Himalaya clause, which provided that the carrier's subcontractors were to have the benefit of "all exceptions, limitations, provisions and liberties" in the bill of lading. These words were construed so as to refer only to other terms in the bill which *benefited* one of the parties to it and not to the exclusive jurisdiction clause since this was a "mutual agreement" creating "mutual obligations".[139] Since this conclusion was based simply on the construction of the phrase (quoted above[140]) in the Himalaya clause, it leaves open the possibility that the parties could by the use of sufficiently clear words make the benefit of an exclusive jurisdiction clause available to a third party; and, since at common law it would so be available by virtue of a collateral contract, there would be no difficulty in principle in also imposing obligations on the third party.[141] The resulting situation would then be one in which the benefit of the exclusive jurisdiction clause would be available to the third party at common law but not under the 1999 Act; and it would be so available only if the common law requirements developed in the cases on Himalaya clauses were satisfied.

What may be called the old learning on Himalaya clauses will also retain its practical significance where a third party could rely on an exemption or limitation clause both under the 1999 Act and at common law. The 1999 Act expressly preserves any right of the third party which exists or is available apart from its provisions[142] so that if his common law right to rely on an exemption or limitation clause in the bill of lading is for some reason more favourable to him

---

[135] See that Draft Bill, section 6(2) (d) and (e).
[136] *Cf.* Unfair Contract Terms Act 1977, section 13(2).
[137] Report, § 14.18.
[138] [1996] A.C. 650.
[139] *Ibid.*, 666.
[140] *Supra*, in the preceding sentence but one.
[141] The contract could, on Lord Wilberforce's analysis quoted, *supra*, at n. 108, "become mutual".
[142] Section 7(1).

than his right under the 1999 Act, then he will still be able to rely on the former right.

A final point relating to Himalaya clauses arises from the fact that the 1999 Act will (in the words of section 1(1)) confer rights on "a person who is *not* a party to a contract." Where a Himalaya clauses operates at common law, it does so because the person who is a "third party" to the bill of lading *is* a party to a collateral contract (typically with the cargo-owner). It might therefore be argued that such a person is not a "third party" within the meaning of the 1999 Act since he *is* "a party to a contract" with the claimant against whom the "third party" sets up the exemption or limitation clause. Acceptance of this argument would lead to the strange conclusion that section 1(6) would apply only where a third party would *not* be protected at common law by virtue of a Himalaya clause. It is submitted that this undesirable conclusion is not supported by the words (quoted above)[143] of subsection 1(1). The words "not a party to a contract" must no doubt be interpreted in a somewhat restrictive sense, to mean "not a party to a *relevant* contract". But the bill of lading clearly is such a relevant contract so that a person who is not a party to *that* contract is a "third party" for the purposes of the 1999 Act even though he is also a party to another relevant contract, i.e. to the collateral contract arising by virtue of the Himalaya clause.

4 CHARTERPARTIES

A charterparty is not a "contract for the carriage of goods by sea" for the purpose of section 6(5) of the 1999 Act;[144] and this fact raises novel aspects of some familiar problems which arise where a carriage operation is the subject both of a charterparty and of a bill of lading. The problem is whether or to what extent what has in this paper been called "the section 6(5) exception" applies in cases of this kind. It will be recalled that under this exception "section 1 confers no rights on a third party in the case of—(a) a contract for the carriage of goods by sea ..." Two situations call for discussion.

The first is that in which goods are shipped by the shipper on a ship which the shipper has chartered from the shipowner. A bill of lading is then issued by the shipowner to the shipper. At this stage, the bill of lading is between shipper and shipowner a mere receipt and does not contain or evidence a contract for the carriage of the goods.[145] Hence the section 6(5) does not apply (there being no

---

[143] *Supra*, in the first sentence of this paragraph.
[144] This follows from the definitions of the phrase in section 6(6) and (7) of the Act.
[145] See e.g. *Rodocanachi, Sons & Co.* v. *Milburn Bros.* (1886) 18 Q.B.D. 67, 75, 78, 79; *Leduc* v. *Ward* (1888) 20 Q.B.D. 475, 479; *President of India* v. *Metcalfe Shipping Co. Ltd. (The Dunelmia)* [1970] 1 Q.B. 289, 305, 308.

"contract for the carriage of goods by sea" within the 1999 Act) so that a third party can acquire the right to enforce a term of the charterparty under section 1 of the 1999 Act. Such rights could, for example, be acquired by a broker to whom commission was to be paid under a term of the charterparty (but who was not a party to it)[146] or by a third party to whom under that contract the shipowner had promised to deliver the goods. But if the bill of lading is then transferred to another third party who becomes a lawful holder of it, rights of suit under the bill of lading can be acquired by that third party, as transferee of the bill, by virtue of the Carriage of Goods by Sea Act 1992, section 2(1): this was the position before the coming into force of that Act[147] and it was not the purpose of the Act to change the law on this point.[148] At this stage, therefore, there is a "contract for the carriage of goods by sea" within the 1999 Act so that the section 6(5) exception would seem to apply; and this point could be significant where the rights of the transferee were, under the bill of lading, less favourable to him than his rights as a third party under the charterparty. Could he then assert the latter rights by virtue of section 1 of the 1999 Act in preference to his rights as transferee under the 1992 Act? At first sight, it might appear that he could rely on section 2(1) of the 1999 Act, by which the contracting parties cannot vary his rights without his consent. But it is submitted that this argument would not prevail, for section 2(1) only applies to a variation "by agreement" between the parties; and in the case put the variation occurs not by such agreement, but by operation of law on the transfer of the bill of lading. This conclusion can also be supported by the further argument that, in the case put, the transfer of the bill of lading must be within the contemplation of the parties to the charterparty and therefore it should be an implied term of the charterparty that any rights conferred by it on the third party should be superseded by rights acquired by the third party on the transfer to him of the bill of lading. Any rights of the third party under the charterparty would be "subject to"[149] that term.

The second situation is that in which goods are shipped under a bill of lading which is later transferred to the charterer of the ship. Before the transfer of the bill of lading, there is clearly a "contract for the carriage of goods by sea" within the section 6(5) exception to the 1999 Act, so that no rights can be acquired under section 1 of the Act by the transferee. After the transfer of the bill of lading, a further distinction was drawn at common law (and continues to be drawn after the Carriage of Goods by Sea Act 1992[150]) between two types of case. The first was that in which the transferee had chartered the carrying ship

---

[146] E.g. *Les Affiéteurs Réunis S.A.* v. *Leopold Walford (London) Ltd.* [1919] A.C. 801.

[147] E.g. *Leduc* v. *Ward* (1888) 20 Q.B.D. 475, 479; *Compania Comercial y Naviera San Martin S.A.* v. *China National Foreign Trade Corp. (The Costanza M)* [1981] 2 Lloyd's Rep. 150.

[148] Law Com. No. 196, Scot Law Com. No. 130 (1991) § 2.54.

[149] 1999 Act, section 1(4).

[150] Law Com. No. 196, Scot. Law Com. No. 130 (1991) § 2.54

for the very purpose of taking delivery of the goods from the shipper: e.g. where the transferree was a buyer on f.o.b. terms and had chartered the ship in order to perform his duty to take delivery under that contract. In such a case, the bill of lading becomes in the transferee's hands a mere receipt and the contractual relations between him and the shipowner are governed by the charterparty.[151] Hence at this stage there is no longer a "contract for the carriage of goods by sea" within the section 6(5) exception, so that rights under the charterparty can be acquired by a "third party" under section 1 of the 1999 Act. No such rights can, however, be acquired by the transferree of the bill of lading since he is, *ex hypothesi*, a party to the contract contained in the charterparty and so not a "third party" to that contract within section 1 of the 1999 Act.[152] It is, however, conceivable that the *transferor* of the bill of lading might seek to assert rights *under the charterparty*: e.g., in respect of damage to goods which were still at his risk when damaged. If he could satisfy the requirements of section 1, then he would not be precluded (in the present type of case) from making such a claim under that section by the section 6(5) exception. The second type of case is that in which there is no connection between the charterparty and the transaction in pursuance of which the bill of lading was transferred: in a case of this kind, the bill of lading (in respect of the shipment in question) governs not only the relations between shipper and carrier but also those between carrier and transferee.[153] Thus there is for the purpose of the section 6(5) exception a "contract for the carriage of goods by sea" throughout and no third party could acquire rights under that contract under section 1 of the 1999 Act. This reasoning could, for example, apply where goods were sold afloat on c.i.f. terms to a buyer who happened to be the charterer of the carrying ship and to whom the bill of lading covering the goods sold was transferred by the seller.

For the avoidance of doubt, it should finally be repeated that the section 6(5) exception does not prevent any third party from availing himself of an exclusion or limitation clause in the contract of carriage,[154] so that nothing in the immediately foregoing discussion applies where a third party seeks to invoke such a clause.

5 REDIRECTING GOODS

Under the so-called rule in *Mitchell* v. *Ede*[155] a shipper of goods on bill of lading terms may, even though the bill makes the goods deliverable to a named

---

[151] *The Dunelmia* [1970] 1 Q.B. 289 (*supra*, n. 145).
[152] This follows from section 1(1) of the 1999 Act.
[153] *Calcutta S.S. Co. Ltd.* v. *Andrew Weir & Co.* [1910] 1 K.B. 759.
[154] See the concluding words of the subsection.
[155] (1840) 11 Ad. & E.L. 888; *Elder Dempster Lines* v. *Zatai Ishaz (The Lycaon)* [1983] 2 Lloyd's Rep. 548.

consignee, nevertheless be entitled to direct the carrier to deliver those goods to another person. Whether he is in fact so entitled depends on the construction of the bill, which may be a contract to deliver the goods *either* to the order of the named consignee (or his order) *or* (more usually) to the order of that named consignee or to *such other person as the shipper may direct*; and even if the bill on its true construction bears the latter meaning a point may come when the shipper can no longer redirect the goods.[156] Our concern here is not with the details of these rules but with the point that, for two reasons, they are not affected by the 1999 Act. First, where the contract is contained in or evidenced by a bill of lading, the case falls within the section 6(5) exception. And, even where that exception did not apply, e.g. because the contract of carriage was contained in a charterparty (and so not within the section 6(5) exception), the shipper would not be precluded from redirecting the goods by the provisions of section 2 of the Act which prevents the parties from extinguishing or altering the third party's rights by varying the contract by subsequent agreement. If the contract on its true construction is one to deliver to A or as the shipper may direct, it is not *varied* by the shipper's directing the carrier to deliver the goods to B: such delivery is merely performance of the contract in accordance with its terms. Moreover a contract of this kind probably does not confer any rights on A under section 1 of the 1999 Act, for the power to divert the goods to another person would indicate that the parties did not intend the term providing for delivery of the goods to be enforceable by A,[157] or that any right to delivery which he might at one time have had was "subject to"[158] the shipper's power to order delivery to be made to another person.

6 PROMISEE'S RIGHTS

Section 4 of the 1999 Act provides that "Section 1 does not affect any right of the promisee to enforce any term of the contract". Under this section the right of the promisee in certain exceptional cases to recover damages in respect of a third party's loss[159] is preserved;[160] and our present concern is with one of these exceptional cases, namely that which arises under the so-called rule in *Dunlop* v. *Lambert*,[161] as interpreted in *The Albazero*.[162] Under that rule, a shipper of goods can recover damages from the carrier in respect of loss of or damage to

---

[156] See *Benjamin*, § 18–012.
[157] 1999 Act, section 1(2).
[158] *Ibid.*, section 1(4).
[159] See generally Treitel, 550–555.
[160] For safeguards against the promisor's being made liable twice over, see *supra*, after n. 19.
[161] (1839) 6 Cl. & F. 600.
[162] *Albacruz (Cargo Owners)* v. *Albazero (Owners) (The Albazero)* [1977] A.C. 774.

the goods even though the resulting prejudice is suffered, not by the shipper, but by the consignee: e.g. because the risk had passed to the consignee when the loss or damage occurred. That rule was, however, restricted in *The Albazero*: it was there held not to apply where the consignee was brought into a direct contractual relationship with the carrier by the operation of the Bills of Lading Act 1855; nor would it now apply where such a relationship had come into being as a result of the operation of the Carriage of Goods by Sea Act 1992. The reason for this restriction was that the shipper's right to sue the carrier for loss suffered by the consignee was needed to avoid the injustice which would arise if the carrier had committed a breach of the contract of carriage but the shipper could not recover damages in respect of that breach because he had suffered no loss, while the consignee had no cause of action because he was not a party to the contract. If the consignee *had* become a party to the contract, this reasoning no longer applied and the shipper could not recover damages in respect of the consignee's loss.[163] Our concern is with the impact on this reasoning of the 1999 Act.

Where the contract between shipper and carrier is contained in or evidenced by a bill of lading, the case will fall within the section 6(5) exception so that no rights can be acquired by the consignee under section 1 of the 1999 Act. It follows that the scope of the rule in *Dunlop* v. *Lambert* will not, in such a case, be affected by that Act. The question whether the shipper can recover damages from the carrier in respect of the third party's loss will therefore depend primarily on whether the consignee has acquired rights under the contract of carriage by virtue of section 2(1) of the Carriage of Goods by Sea Act 1992. If for some reason rights have not been acquired by the consignee in this way (e.g. because the bill of lading was never delivered to him or because it lacked a requisite endorsement),[164] then the rule in *Dunlop* v. *Lambert* can still apply so as to entitle the shipper to recover damages in respect of the third party's loss. If rights under the contract of carriage have been acquired by the consignee by virtue of section 2(1) on the transfer to him of the bill of lading, then the rights of the shipper as an original party to the contract are extinguished.[165] There is thus no scope for the application of the rule in *Dunlop* v. *Lambert*;[166] and even if there were such scope the reasoning of *The Albazero* would preclude its operation in such a case.

The rule in *Dunlop* v. *Lambert* is not, however, restricted to cases in which the contract of carriage is contained in or evidenced by a bill of lading. It can apply also where that contract is contained in a charterparty between shipper

---

[163] *Ibid.*

[164] The consignee would in such case not be the "holder" of the bill (Carriage of Goods by Sea Act 1992, section 5(2)) so that he could not acquire rights under the contract of carriage by virtue of section 2(1) of the 1992 Act.

[165] *Ibid.*, section 2(5)

[166] *Supra*, at n. 163.

and carrier; and, since the charterparty is not a "contract for the carriage of goods by sea" within the 1999 Act,[167] a case of this kind would not be within the section 6(5) exception. This would be so even if the carrier had issued a bill of lading to the charterer, since between these parties the bill would operate as a mere receipt;[168] and, even if the shipper transferred the bill of lading to the consignee, the charterparty contract would not be transferred to the consignee by virtue of section 2(1) of the 1992 Act nor would the shipper's rights under it be extinguished under section 2(5) of that Act. These results follow from the fact that the charterparty contract is not a "contract of carriage" within the 1992 Act.[169] Hence the case would be governed by the rule in *Dunlop* v. *Lambert* as explained and limited in *The Albazero*.[170] It is at this stage of the argument, however, that the impact of the 1999 Act falls to be considered. It is possible for the consignee to acquire a right to enforce a term of the charterparty as a third party under section 1 of the 1999 Act; and, if he has acquired such rights, then the reasoning of *The Albazero*[171] would seem to preclude the operation of the rule in *Dunlop* v. *Lambert*. That reasoning admittedly is in terms concerned only with the case in which the consignee has acquired rights under the contract of carriage as transferee of the bill of lading. But the underlying rationale of *The Albazero* restriction on the scope of the rule in *Dunlop* v. *Lambert* is simply *that* the consignee has acquired rights against the carrier: *how* (i.e. by what legal mechanism) he has acquired them is not the decisive point. It is true that one recent extension of the rule in *Dunlop* v. *Lambert* to the field of building contracts has allowed a claim by the promisee in respect of the third party's loss in spite of the fact that the third party had its own contractual claim against the promisor.[172] But the case in question is open to criticism precisely because it is inconsistent with the very basis of the rule in *Dunlop* v. *Lambert*; and such an extension of the rule will no longer be necessary once the third party can acquire his own right of enforcement against the promisor under section 1 of the 1999 Act. It is, in any event, submitted that the extension would not be applied to contracts for the carriage of goods by sea, where the rationale, and the limitations on the scope, of the rule in *Dunlop* v. *Lambert* are well established, and where *The Alberzo* would directly bar such an extension.

The 1999 Act might also affect the converse situation in which a bill of lading containing or evidencing a contract of carriage was later transferred to the charterer of the carrying ship. This was the position in *The Sanix Ace*,[173] where

---

[167] This follows from section 6(6) and (7) of the 1999 Act.
[168] *Supra*, at n. 145.
[169] 1992 Act, section 5(1) (definition of "contract of carriage").
[170] *Supra* at nn. 161–163.
[171] See especially *supra* at n. 163.
[172] *Alfred McAlpine Construction Ltd.* v. *Panatown Ltd.* (1998) 58 Const. L.R. 58.
[173] *Obestain Inc.* v. *National Mineral Development Corp. (The Sanix Ace)* [1987] 1 Lloyd's Rep. 465.

the charterer, to whom the bill had been transferred, resold the goods to end-users to whom risk passed on shipment but to whom no bill of lading was ever transferred. It was held that the charterer could recover damages in respect of the loss suffered by the end-users when the goods were damaged in transit, in consequence of unseaworthiness amounting to a breach by the shipowner of the contract of carriage. One reason given for this result was that, if the carriers were not liable to the charterer for substantial damages, there would be "no-one who could recover substantial damages from the carriers".[174] It has been suggested above[175] that, under the 1999 Act, a case of this kind would not fall within the section 6(5) exception, so that there would be a possibility of the end-user's acquiring rights to enforce a term of the charterparty under section 1 of the 1999 Act. Whether the end-users could have satisfied the requirements of section 1 of the Act is, on facts such as those of *The Sanix Ace*, not at all clear;[176] but where they could have done so then the case would now appear to fall within the *Albazero* exception[177] to the rule in *Dunlop* v. *Lambert*.

It may be objected that all the foregoing discussion is inconsistent with section 5 of the 1999 Act since this section envisages that a claim by the promisee for damages in respect of the third party's loss can succeed even though the third party also has a claim under section 1 of the Act: indeed, the very purpose of section 5 is to protect the promisor in such cases from double liability. It is, however, submitted that such an objection to the suggested impact of the 1999 Act on the rule in *Dunlop* v. *Lambert* would not be decisive. The general rule that a promisee cannot recover damages in respect of the promisee's loss is subject to many exceptions[178] other than that contained in the rule in *Dunlop* v. *Lambert* and the *Albazero* exception to that rule does not in terms apply to these other exceptions or to all of them. Section 5 deals with the exceptions generally and therefore does not negative the argument that one of those exceptions (i.e. the rule in *Dunlop* v. *Lambert*) will no longer apply where the third party has acquired a right of enforcement under section 1 of the 1999 Act.

---

[174] *Ibid.*, 470. The end-users would have had no tort claim against the carriers as no property (or possessory interest) had passed to them when the damage was done: *The Aliakmon* [1986] A.C. 785.

[175] *Supra*, after n. 150. The charterer in *The Sanix Ace* was an f.o.b. buyer who had chartered the ship for the purpose of taking delivery from his supplier so that the bill of lading became in his hands a mere receipt: *supra*, at n. 151.

[176] It does not appear from the report whether the requirements stated *supra*, in § 1(b) were satisfied.

[177] *Supra*, after n. 162.

[178] Treitel, 550–551.

7 THIRD PARTY'S OTHER RIGHTS OR REMEDIES

Section 7(1) of the 1999 Act preserves "any right or remedy of a third party that exists or is available apart from this Act". One application of this subsection which is of particular interest in the present context relates to the so called "*Brandt* v. *Liverpool*" implied contract[179] which can arise between carrier and consignee, giving rise to reciprocal rights and duties between them, even though the consignee is not, and has not become, a party to the contract contained in or evidenced by the fill of lading. As is well known, this device originated to get over the difficulty that there was no privity of contract between these parties, and it continued to flourish even after the privity problem had been dealt with by the Bills of Lading Act 1855 because of the "property gap" in that legislation.[180] Now that this gap has been closed by the Carriage of Goods by Sea Act 1992, the practical importance of the *Brandt* v. *Liverpool* contract is much reduced; but it is not altogether eliminated since there may still be situations, even after this Act, in which there will be no contractual relationship by virtue of the Act between the carrier and the person to whom delivery of the goods was or should have been made: e.g. where delivery is taken under a bill of lading which lacks a requisite endorsement or under a delivery order not amounting to a "ship's delivery order" within the 1992 Act or under a letter of indemnity. This is not the place to go into detail on these points.[181] Our sole concern here is with the impact of the 1999 Act on such implied contracts.

Two points only need to be made. The first is that the *Brandt* v. *Liverpool* contract is not itself a "contract for the carriage of goods by sea" within the definition of that phrase in the 1999 Act. It follows that the implied contract does not (though the antecedent bill of lading contract does) fall within the section 6(5) exception. The second is that section 1 of the 1999 Act does not apply to the implied contract for the more fundamental reason that this contract is a direct contract between the carrier and the person receiving (or claiming) delivery. Hence neither of them is a "third party" within the 1999 Act, i.e. "a person who is not a party to a contract". It is true that the receiver is not a party to the bill of lading contract, but the term which he is seeking to enforce is a term, not of that contract, but of the implied contract; while the carrier is a party to both these contracts. The parties' rights under the implied contract therefore continue to be enforceable at common law and are not subject to the provisions of the 1999 Act.

---

[179] Named after *Brandt* v. *Liverpool Brazil and River Plate Steam Navigation Co. Ltd.* [1924] 1 K.B. 575.
[180] *Benjamin*, §§ 10–058–18–058A.
[181] See *Benjamin*, § 18–103.

8 DELIVERY ORDERS

The section 6(5) exception applies not only where a third party seeks to enforce a term of a contract contained in or evidenced by a bill of lading or a sea waybill,[182] but also where he bases his claim on a contract of carriage "under or for the purposes of which there is given an undertaking which is contained in a ship's delivery order".[183] The expression "ship's delivery order" here has the same meaning as in the Carriage of Goods by Sea Act 1992:[184] that is, it means a document which (not being a bill of lading or a sea waybill) "contains an undertaking which (a) is given under or for the purposes of a contract for the carriage by sea of goods to which the document relates …; and (b) is an undertaking by the carrier to a person identified in the document to deliver the goods to which the document relates to that person".[185] By virtue of section 2(1)(c) of the 1992 Act, rights of suit under the contract of carriage[186] will be vested in the person so identified. The point of excepting this situation from section 1 of the 1999 Act is to ensure that the acquisition of contractual rights by the "person identified" in the ship's delivery order is to be governed by the 1992 Act and not by the 1999 Act.

The typical situation in which delivery orders are used to secure delivery of goods to a person who is not a party to the contract of carriage is that in which goods are shipped in bulk on A's ship by B who then sells part of the bulk to C (and no doubt other parts of it to D, E, etc.). In such a case, there will or may be two contracts. The first is the contract between A and B, which will typically be one contained in or evidenced by a bill of lading though it could also be one contained in or evidenced by a sea waybill and it is arguable that the 1992 Act might apply even where that contract was one contained in a charterparty.[187] It is this contract which is excepted by section 6(5) from the scope of section 1 of the 1999 Act, the point of the exception being to preserve the legislative scheme by which the acquisition of rights by C under this contract is to be governed by the 1992 Act and not by the 1999 Act. The second contract which may arise is one between A and C by reason of A's having in the order given an "undertaking" to C to deliver the goods to C. If there is acceptance of this undertaking by, and consideration moving from, C, and contractual intention, this undertaking will amount to a direct contract between A and C. *This* contract is not in terms within

---

[182] 1999 Act, section 6(6)(a).

[183] *Ibid.*, section 6(6)(b).

[184] *Ibid.*, section 6(7)(a).

[185] 1992 Act, section 1(4); for a full discussion of this definition, see *Benjamin* §§ 18–129 to 18–136.

[186] I.e. in the present context, "the contract under or for the purposes of which the undertaking contained in the [ship's delivery] order was given", 1992 Act, section 5(1)(b) (definition of "contract of carriage").

[187] *Benjamin*, § 18–132.

the section 6(5) exception, which applies, in the case of a ship's delivery order, only to the contract "under or for the purposes of which"[188] the undertaking contained in the order was given and not to any contract which may be contained in , or arise by reason of, the undertaking contained in the order itself. But section 1 of the 1999 Act will not apply to the enforcement by C of the latter contract since in this contract C is not a "third party" within the 1999 Act: it must be stressed again that this expression refers to "a person who is *not* a party to a contract" (i.e. to the one, the enforcement of a term of which is sought);[189] and in the case put C *is* a party to that contract. Since the direct contract between A and C may by express or implied reference incorporate some of the terms of the contract between A and B, C may thus indirectly acquire rights originally conferred on B by that contract. This result will, however, follow as a matter of general common law and not by virtue of the 1999 Act.

The section 6(5) exception is, in cases where its operation depends on the giving of a delivery order, expressed to apply only where that order is a "ship's delivery order"[190] as defined by the 1992 Act. Where the order is one which does *not* fall within this definition, the contract "under or for the purposes of which" it was given may well itself be contained in or evidenced by a bill of lading, so that *that* contract will fall within the section 6(5) exception. But this will not be true of the contract which may arise from the subsequent conduct of the parties, e.g. from A's attornment to C.[191] The contractual effects of such an order other than a "ship's delivery order" within the 1992 Act will therefore not be affected by that Act; nor, in the case just put, will C's right to enforce such a contract be governed by section 1 of the 1999 Act since C would be a party to that contract and hence not a "third party" within section 1.

A further complication can, however, arise. An order may fail to qualify as a "ship's delivery order", not only where it "contains" no undertaking at all (as in the case just put), but also where it does contain an undertaking but this undertaking is addressed (so to speak) to the wrong person. An order which contained an undertaking by A (the carrier) addressed to B (the shipper) to deliver the goods to C (the consignee) would not be a "ship's delivery order" within the definition of this expression in section 1(4) of the 1992 Act, for that definition requires the person to whom the undertaking is given to be the *same* person as the person to whom the goods were to be delivered.[192] If such an order had contractual force between A and B, then that contract would not be within the section 6(5) exception since the only delivery orders to which that exception refers are ship's delivery orders and since in any event the exception applies only to the contract "under or for the purposes of which" the undertaking

---

[188] 1999 Act, section 6(6)(b).
[189] *Cf.* the final paragraph of § 3 of this paper.
[190] 1999 Act, section 6(6) and (7).
[191] *Benjamin*, § 18–126, 18–127.
[192] *Ibid.*, § 18–135.

contained in the order was given. The contract between A and B contained in, or arising under, the order itself could then fall within section 1 of the 1999 Act since it would be a contract between A and B which purported to confer a benefit on C. That contract could, moreover, incorporate by express or implied reference at least some of the terms of the contract of carriage between A and B. In this way terms of that contract would, notwithstanding the fact that the contract of carriage fell within the section 6(5) exception, become enforceable by a third party under section 1 of the 1999 Act.

The Publications of Francis Reynolds 1963–1999

BOOKS

1968   (Ed. with B. J. Davenport) *Bowstead on Agency*, 13th edn. (Sweet & Maxwell, London, 1968) (458 pp.).

1976   (Ed. with B. J. Davenport) *Bowstead on Agency*, 14th edn. (Sweet & Maxwell, London, 1976) (437 pp.).

1985   (Ed.) *Bowstead on Agency*, 15th edn. (Sweet & Maxwell, London, 1985) (533 pp.).

1992   *The Butterworths Lectures 1990–91: The Implementation of Private Law Conventions in English Law* (Butterworths, London, 1992) 1–53 [with P. B. H. Birks, "Civil Wrongs: A New World", pp. 55–112].

1996   *Bowstead & Reynolds on Agency*, 16th edn. (Sweet & Maxwell, London, 1996) (721 pp. and 13 pp. Appendix) (with the assistance of Dr Michele Graziadei).

CONTRIBUTIONS TO BOOKS

1968   (Ed.) Vol. II: Ch.1 "Agency" (pp. 1–76) of A. G. Guest (Gen. Ed.), *Chitty on Contracts*, 23rd edn. (Sweet & Maxwell, London, 1968) (with 6 Supplements 1970–1975).

1974   Part Four "Defective Goods" (pp. 321–456) and Part Five "Consumer Protection" (pp. 457–476) of A. G. Guest (Gen. Ed.). *Benjamin's Sale of Goods* (Sweet & Maxwell, London, 1974).

1977   (Ed) Vol. I: Ch.19 "Assignment" (pp. 537–568); Vol. II: Ch.1 "Agency" (pp. 1–79) and (with D. R. Harris and A. G. Guest) Ch. 11

"Sale of Goods" (pp. 856–1013) of A. G. Guest (Gen. Ed.), *Chitty on Contracts*, 24th edn. (Sweet & Maxwell, London, 1977), (with Supplement 1979).

1981   Part Four "Defective Goods" (pp. 341–506) and Part Five "Consumer Protection" (pp. 507–548) of A. G. Guest (Gen. Ed.). *Benjamin's Sale of Goods*, 2nd edn. (Sweet & Maxwell, London, 1981).

1982   "The Applicability of General Rules to Private Law", Ch. 5 of S. Anderman et al. (eds), *Law and the Weaker Party* (Professional Books, London), vol. II: *The English Experience* (1982) 91–110 [reprinted as ch. 1 of R. Cranston (ed.), *Commercial Law* (Dartmouth Publishing Co. Ltd, Aldershot, 1992), 3–21].

1983   (Ed.) Vol. II: Ch.1 "Agency" (pp. 1–88) and (with D. R. Harris and A. G. Guest) Ch. 11 "Sale of Goods" (pp. 1007–1190) of A. G. Guest (Gen. Ed.), *Chitty on Contracts*, 25th edn. (Sweet & Maxwell, London, 1983) (with Supplement 1986).

1987   "Discharge by Breach as a Remedy", Ch. 7 of P. D. Finn (ed.), *Essays on Contract* (Law Book Company, 1987), 183–199.

        Part Four "Defective Goods" (pp. 407–605) and Part Five "Consumer Protection" (pp. 607–656) of A. G. Guest (Gen Ed.). *Benjamin's Sale of Goods*, 3rd edn. (Sweet & Maxwell, London, 1987).

1989   "Protection of Small Businesses in English Law", Ch. 7 of S. Anderman et al. (eds), *Law and the Weaker Party* (Professional Books, London), vol. II: *The Comparison I* (1989), 210–213.

        (Ed.) Vol. II: Ch.1 "Agency" (pp. 1–99) and (with A. G. Guest and D. R. Harris) Ch.11 "Sale of Goods" (pp. 1131–1340) of A. G. Guest (Gen. Ed.), *Chitty on Contracts*, 26th edn. (Sweet & Maxwell, London, 1989).

1992   Part Four "Defective Goods" (pp. 425–683) of A. G. Guest (ed.). *Benjamin's Sale of Goods*, 4th edn. (Sweet & Maxwell, London, 1992).

1994   Vol. II: Ch.1 "Agency" (pp. 1–98) of A. G. Guest (Gen. Ed.), *Chitty on Contracts*, 27th edn. (Sweet & Maxwell, London, 1994) (with Supplements 1996 and 1997).

        Ch. 2 "A Note of Caution" (pp. 18–28) (in Part I: The Vienna Convention on the Sale of Goods) and Ch.12 "Drawing the Strings

Together" (pp. 156–161) (in Part III: Innovations in Contract) of P. Birks (ed.), *The Frontiers of Liability: Volume 1* (Oxford University Press, Oxford, 1994).

1996   "Some Agency Problems in Insurance Law", Ch. 4 of F. D. Rose (ed.), *Consensus Ad Idem: Essays on the Law of Contract in Honour of Guenter Treitel* (Sweet & Maxwell, London, 1996), 77–95.

    "The Agent as a Fiduciary in English Law", Ch. 23 of P. Wetterstein and A. Beijers (eds), *Essays in Honour of Hugo* Tiberg (Juristförlaget, 1996), 525–539.

1997   "When is an Agent's Authority Irrevocable?", Ch. 10 of R. Cranston (ed.), *Making Commercial Law: Essays in Honour of Roy Goode* (Clarendon Press, Oxford, 1997), 259–175.

    "The Factor's and Auctioneer's Contracts", ch. 10 of E. Z. Lomnicka and C. G. J. Morse (eds), *Contemporary Issues in Commercial Law: Essays in Honour of Professor A. G. Guest* (Sweet & Maxwell, London, 1997), 161–173.

    Part Four "Defective Goods" (pp. 459–668) of A. G. Guest (ed.). *Benjamin's Sale of Goods*, 5th edn. (Sweet & Maxwell, London, 1997).

1999   Vol. II: Ch.1 "Agency" (pp. 1–95) of H. G. Beale (Gen. Ed.), *Chitty on Contracts*, 28th edn. (Sweet & Maxwell, London, 1999).

PERIODICALS

1978–   *Journal of Business Law*. Departmental Editor ("Agency").

1981–87   *Oxford Journal of Legal Studies*. Editorial Committee.

1983–   *Lloyd's Maritime and Commercial Law Quarterly*. General Editor 1983–87; Consultant Editor.

1986–90   *Malaya Law Review*. Member, Editorial Advisory Board.

1987–   *Law Quarterly Review*. Editor.

1991–   *Singapore Journal of Legal Studies*. Member, Editorial Advisory Board.

1995   *Journal of Contract Law*, Volume 9, Issue 1 (1995): Special Issue: *Essays for Brian Coote* edited with J. W. Carter, with Editorial, 1–2.

ARTICLES AND NOTES

1963   "Warranty, Condition and Fundamental Term" (1963) 79 *Law Quarterly Review* 534–555.

1965   (with G. H. Treitel) "Consideration for the Modification of Contracts" (1965) 7 Malaya L.R. 1–23.

1967   "Warranty of Authority" (1967) 83 *Law Quarterly Review* 189–196.

1969   "Personal Liability of an Agent" (1969) 85 *Law Quarterly Review* 92–103.

1970   "Election Distributed" (1970) *Law Quarterly Review* 318–347.

1972   "Himalaya Clause" (1972) 88 *Law Quarterly Review* 179–184.

        "Estate Agents and Deposits Again" (1972) 88 *Law Quarterly Review* 184–189.

        "Insurance Company's Agent as Agent for Proposer" (1972) 88 *Law Quarterly Review* 462–464.

        "Himalayan Clause" (1972) 88 *Law Quarterly Review* 464.

1974   "Himalaya Clause Resurgent" (1974) 90 *Law Quarterly Review* 301–306.

1976   "Discharge of Contract by Breach" (1976) 92 *Law Quarterly Review* 17–20.

        "Affirmation after Fundamental Breach" (1976) 92 *Law Quarterly Review* 172–174.

        "Prospective Vendor's Liability to Repay Deposit" (1976) 92 *Law Quarterly Review* 484–487.

1978   "The Unfair Contract Terms Act 1977" [1978] *Lloyd's Maritime and Commercial Law Quarterly* 201–210.

        "Agency: Theory and Practice" (1978) 94 *Law Quarterly Review* 224–238.

        "Liability of Agents" [1978] *Journal of Business Law* 161–163.

        "Forwarding Agents" [1978] *Journal of Business Law* 163.

        "Liability of Auctioneers" [1978] *Journal of Business Law* 163–164.

        "Proposed EEC Directive on Commercial Agents" [1978] *Journal of Business Law* 164–165.

"Bribery of Agent" [1978] *Journal of Business Law* 165–167.

(with J. Beatson) "Bribery of an Agent" (1978) 94 *Law Quarterly Review* 344–347.

"Fiduciary Duties in Agency in the Absence of Prior Existence of Agency Relationship" [1978] *Journal of Business Law* 250–251.

1979   "Again the Negligent Stevedore" (1979) 95 *Law Quarterly Review* 183–187.

"Liability of Agent; Election" [1979] *Journal of Business Law* 150–151.

1980   "Estate Agents Act 1979" [1980] *Journal of Business Law* 39–42.

"The Negligent Stevedore Yet Again" (1980) 96 *Law Quarterly Review* 506–508.

1981   "Personal Liability of Agent" [1981] *Journal of Business Law* 32–33.

"Duties of Agent" [1981] *Journal of Business Law* 33.

"Agency in Chartering" [1981] *Journal of Business Law* 33–34.

"Agent's Commission" [1981] *Journal of Business Law* 34–35.

"Miscellaneous" [1981] *Journal of Business Law* 35.

"Duties of Agent" and "Agent's Commission" [1981] *Journal of Business Law* 285.

"Discharge of Contract by Breach" (1981) 97 *Law Quarterly Review* 541–549.

1982   "Liability of Agent on Ratification by Principal" [1982] *Journal of Business Law* 38–39.

"Fraud of Agent" [1982] *Journal of Business Law* 40.

"Agency in Chartering" [1982] *Journal of Business Law* 41.

"Contract for Unformed Company" [1982] *Journal of Business Law* 41–42.

"Agency of Necessity" [1982] *Journal of Business Law* 114–116.

"Demise Clause in Bills of Lading" [1982] *Journal of Business Law* 116–117.

"Apparent Authority of Agent of Company" [1982] *Journal of Business Law* 496–497.

"Apparent Authority of Solicitor" [1982] *Journal of Business Law* 497.

"Apparent Ownership; Factors Act 1889" [1982] *Journal of Business Law* 497–498.

"Constructive Notice in Commercial Transactions" [1982] *Journal of Business Law* 498–499.

"Personal Liability of an Agent" [1982] *Journal of Business Law* 499–500.

"Demise Clause in Bills of Lading" [1982] *Journal of Business Law* 500.

1983   "Practical Problems of the Undisclosed Principal Doctrine" (1983) 36 *Current Legal Problems* 119–140.

"Authority to Make Representations as to Authority of Other Agents" [1983] *Journal of Business Law* 409–410.

"Agent's Liability for Misrepresentation Inducing Contract" [1983] *Journal of Business Law* 410–411.

1984   "Apparent Authority; Bribery of Agent" [1984] *Journal of Business Law* 145–147.

"Constructive Notice in Commercial Transactions" [1984] *Journal of Business Law* 147–148.

"Constructive Trust" [1984] *Journal of Business Law* 148.

"Whether Agent Holds Remittance on Trust" [1984] *Journal of Business Law* 148–149.

"Agent Who is His Own Principal" [1984] *Journal of Business Law* 149.

"Agent's Liability in Tort to Third Parties" [1984] *Journal of Business Law* 149–151.

"Attornment to Agent of Undisclosed Principal" [1984] *Journal of Business Law* 151–152.

"Anticipatory Breach of Condition (*The Afovos*)" [1984] *Lloyd's Maritime and Commercial Law Quarterly* 189–190.

"Rejection of Documents (*Gill & Duffus* v. *Berger & Co. Inc.*)" [1984] *Lloyd's Maritime and Commercial Law Quarterly* 191–193.

"Signature by Agent of Company Qualifying as a Fraudulent Misrepresentation or a Misrepresentation Actionable Under Misrepresentation Act 1967" [1984] *Journal of Business Law* 248–249.

"Liability of Unauthorised Sub-Agent to Principal" [1984] *Journal of Business Law* 249–251.

"Limitation of Shipowner's Liability (*The Marion*)" [1984] *Lloyd's Maritime and Commercial Law Quarterly* 363–364.

"Assumpsit Duties (*The Zephyr*)" [1984] *Lloyd's Maritime and Commercial Law Quarterly* 376–377.

"Agent's Duty to Disclose His Own Breaches of Duty" [1984] *Journal of Business Law* 334–335.

"Supposed Doctrine of Watteau v. Fenwick" [1984] *Journal of Business Law* 410–411.

"Time for Ratification" [1984] *Journal of Business Law* 411–412.

"Foreign Tonnage Limitation Not a Ground for Refusing Stay of Action (*The Benarty*)" [1984] *Lloyd's Maritime and Commercial Law Quarterly* 545–546.

"Attornment to Agent of Undisclosed Principal" (1984) 4 *Oxford Journal of Legal Studies* 434–437.

1985   "Apparent Authority; Vicarious Liability; Bribes" [1985] *Journal of Business Law* 140–143.

"Agent Who is His Own Principal" [1985] *Journal of Business Law* 143–146.

"Attornment to Agent of Undisclosed Principal" [1985] *Journal of Business Law* 144.

"Fiduciary Duties of Exclusive Distributor" [1985] *Journal of Business Law* 145–146.

"Tort Actions in Contractual Situations" (1985) 11 *New Zealand Universities Law Review* 215–232.

"Proper Law of a Brandt v. Liverpool Contract (*The Elli*)" [1985] *Lloyd's Maritime and Commercial Law Quarterly* 188–190.

"Undisclosed Principal Doctrine" [1985] *Journal of Business Law* 462–463.

"Effect of Quotation of Freight Rate (*Aotearoa International Ltd* v.

Scancarriers A/S)" [1985] *Lloyd's Maritime and Commercial Law Quarterly* 412–413.

"Assumpsit Duties (*The Zephyr*)" [1985] *Lloyd's Maritime and Commercial Law Quarterly* 414.

"Singapore and the Visby Rules" (1985) 6 *Singapore Law Review* 163–170.

1986   "The Significance of Tort in Claims in Respect of Carriage by Sea" [1986] *Lloyd's Maritime and Commercial Law Quarterly* 97–111.

"Authority to Sign Bill of Lading" [1986] *Journal of Business Law* 220–221.

"Personal Liability of Signer of Cheque" [1986] *Journal of Business Law* 221.

"Authority of Agent of Foreign Corporation" [1986] *Journal of Business Law* 221–223.

"Apparent Authority; Principal's Liability for Fraud of Agent; Bribery of Agent" [1986] *Journal of Business Law* 396–397.

1987   (with L. T. East) "Extension of Time, Deck Stowage and the Time Bar (*Kenya Railways* v. *Antares Pte. Ltd (The Antares)*" [1987] *Lloyd's Maritime and Commercial Law Quarterly* 146–147.

(with A. T. Scotford) "Third Party Rights on Insurance Contracts (*Trident General Insurance Co. Ltd* v. *McNeice Bros Pty Ltd*)" [1987] *Lloyd's Maritime and Commercial Law Quarterly* 258–259.

"The Demise Clause and the Hague Rules (*Kaleej International Pty Ltd* v. *Gulf Shipping Lines Ltd*; *Carling O'Keefe Breweries of Canada Ltd* v. *C.N. Marine Inc. (The Newfoundland Coast)*" [1987] *Lloyd's Maritime and Commercial Law Quarterly* 259–261.

"Ratification" [1987] *Journal of Business Law* 378–380.

"Authority of Agent of Foreign Corporation" [1987] *Journal of Business Law* 380.

"Orders Under Charterparties (*The Kanchenjunga*; *The Epaphus*)" [1987] *Lloyd's Maritime and Commercial Law Quarterly* 408–410.

1988   "Loss of Right to Reject" (1988) 104 *Law Quarterly Review* 16–18.

"The Demise Clause (*The Jalamohan*)" [1988] *Lloyd's Maritime and Commercial Law Quarterly* 285–286.

"Uncertainty in Contract" (1988) 104 *Law Quarterly Review* 352–355.

1989   "Privity of Contract, the Boundaries of Categories and the Limits of the Judicial Function" (1989) 105 *Law Quarterly Review* 1–4.

"Forum Non Conveniens in Australia" (1989) 105 *Law Quarterly Review* 40–43.

"Bribery of Agent" [1989] *Journal of Business Law* 61.

"Gratuitous Agents" [1989] *Journal of Business Law* 62.

"Personal Liability of Agent" [1989] *Journal of Business Law* 62.

"Apparent Authority of Solicitor Giving Undertaking on Behalf of a Client" [1989] *Journal of Business Law* 63.

"Orders Under Charterparties (*The Kanchenjunga*)" [1989] *Lloyd's Maritime and Commercial Law Quarterly* 415–416.

1990   "Reform of the Bills of Lading Act" (1990) 106 *Law Quarterly Review* 1–2.

"Contract: Recent Developments" (Ninth Commonwealth Law Conference April 1990) [1990] *New Zealand Law Journal* 395, 398–401 (also 402–403, 403, 405).

"The Notions of Waiver (*The Kanchenjunga*)" [1990] *Lloyd's Maritime and Commercial Law Quarterly* 453–455.

"The Demise Clause Again (*Carling O'Keefe Breweries of Canada Ltd* v. *C.N. Marine Inc. (The Newfoundland Coast)*" [1990] *Lloyd's Maritime and Commercial Law Quarterly* 494.

"Agency of Necessity" [1990] *Journal of Business Law* 505–508.

"Tort Actions in Contractual Situations: Recent Developments" (1990) 2 *Singapore Academy of Law Journal* 251–273.

1991   "Legitimate Last Voyage (*The Peonia*)" [1991] *Lloyd's Maritime and Commercial Law Quarterly* 173–176.

"The Bills of Lading Act: Reform Nearer?" (1991) 107 *Law Quarterly Review* 355–357.

"The Law Commission 25 Years On" (1991) 107 *Law Quarterly Review* 517–519.

"Solicitors and Conflict of Duties" (1991) 107 *Law Quarterly Review* 536–540.

1992   "*Vita Food* Resurgent" (1992) 108 *Law Quarterly Review* 395–398.

          "Illegality by *Lex Loci Solutionis*" (1992) 108 *Law Quarterly Review* 553–555.

          "Carriage of Goods by Sea Act 1992" (1992) 108 *Law Quarterly Review* 569.

          "Time Charterparties: Is the Owner the Carrier?" (1992) 94 Il Diritto Maritimo 1083–1103.

1993   "The Carriage of Goods by Sea Act 1992" [1993] *Lloyd's Maritime and Commercial Law Quarterly* 436–444.

1994   "Unfair Contract Terms" (1994) 110 *Law Quarterly Review* 1–3.

          "The Ultimate Apparent Authority" (1994) 110 *Law Quarterly Review* 21–25.

          "Apparent Authority" [1994] *Journal of Business Law* 144–147.

          "Fiduciary Duties of Estate Agents" [1994] *Journal of Business Law* 147–149.

          "Election and Merger" [1994] *Journal of Business Law* 149–152.

          "When the Undisclosed Principal Cannot Intervene" [1994] *Journal of Business Law* 260–263.

          "Insurance Policies for the Benefit of Others With An Interest" [1994] *Journal of Business Law* 263–265.

          "Commercial Agents Directive" [1994] *Journal of Business Law* 265–270.

1995   "Contract: Codification, Legislation and Judicial Development" (1995) 9 *Journal of Contract Law* 11–28.

          "Bailment on Terms" (1995) 111 *Law Quarterly Review* 8–10.

          "Abolition of Market Overt" (1995) 111 *Law Quarterly Review* 76.

1997   "Privity of Contract" (1997) 113 *Law Quarterly Review* 53–54.

          "Overriding Policy of the Forum (*Akai* v. *People's Insurance*)" [1997] *Lloyd's Maritime and Commercial Law Quarterly* 177–182.

          "The Enforcement of Contracts Involving Corruption or Illegality in Other Countries" [1997] *Singapore Journal of Legal Studies* 371–395.

1998   "Overriding Policy of the Forum: The Other Side of the Coin (*Akai* v. *People's Insurance*)" [1998] *Lloyd's Maritime and Commercial Law Quarterly* 1–3.

"Breach of Warranty of Authority; A Point Elucidated" [1998] *Journal of Business Law* 151–153.

1999   "The Carriage of Goods by Sea Act 1992 Put to the Test (*The Berge Sisar*)" [1999] *Lloyd's Maritime and Commercial Law Quarterly* 161–164.

BOOK REVIEWS

1975   S. M. Waddams, *Products Liability* (1974): (1975) 91 *Law Quarterly Review* 565–566.

1978   F. Staubach, "The German Law of Agency and Distributorship Agreements"; G. La Villa and M. Cartella, "Lawyers at the Court of Milan": [1978] *Journal of Business Law* 307–308.

1986   H. G. Collins, *The Law of Contract* (1986): (1986) 102 *Law Quarterly Review* 628–634.

1988   K. T. Schiels, *Tramp Agency Practice* (1987): [1988] *Lloyd's Maritime and Commercial Law Quarterly* 410–411.

        M. Dockray, *Cases and Materials on the Carriage of Goods by Sea* (1987): (1988) 104 *Law Quarterly Review* 486–487.

1989   D. W. Greig and J. R. L. Davis, *The Law of Contract*; K. E. Lindgren, J. W. Carter and D. J. Harland, *Contract Law in Australia* (1986); D. E. Allan and M. E. Hiscock, *Law of Contract in Australia* (1987); *Journal of Contract Law*, vol. 1, no.1 (1988): (1989) 105 *Law Quarterly Review* 155–160.

1990   J. F. Wilson, *Carriage of Goods by Sea* (1988): (1990) 106 *Law Quarterly Review* 166–169.

1991   R. A. Addrusse, *Conduct Unbecoming* (1990): (1991) 107 *Law Quarterly Review* 170–171.

        C. Debattista, *Sale of Goods Carried by Sea* (1990): (1991) 107 *Law Quarterly Review* 171–173.

1994   L. Collins (Gen. Ed.), *Dicey and Morris on the Conflict of Laws*, 12th edn. (1993): (1994) 110 *Law Quarterly Review* 681–683.

1995   J. Murdoch, *Law of Estate Agency and Auctions* (1995) 111 *Law Quarterly Review* 175–176.

D. Yates (Gen. Ed.), "*Contracts for the Carriage of Goods by Land, Sea and Air*" [1995] *Lloyd's Maritime and Commercial Law Quarterly* 155–156.

J. Cooke, J. D. Kimball, T. Young, D. Martowski, A. Taylor and L. Lambert, *Voyage Charters* (1993): (1995) 111 *Law Quarterly Review* 355–356.

1997   S. C. Boyd, A. S. Burrows and D. Foxton, *Scrutton on Charterparties and Bills of Lading* (1997) 113 *Law Quarterly Review* 350–354.

1998   K. C. T. Sutton, *Sales and Consumer Law*, 4th edn. (1995): (1998) 13 *Journal of Contract Law* 87–88.

PERSONALIA

1999   "The Rt Hon. Lord Denning of Whitchurch" (1999) 115 *Law Quarterly Review* 1.

Index

393